P9-DIA-586

PRACTICAL
Operations Management

Natalie C. Simpson

University at Buffalo (SUNY)

Philip G. Hancock

Glenochil Associates, LLC

HERCHER Publishing Incorporated

Naperville, Illinois

ABOUT THE AUTHORS

Natalie Simpson is an Associate Professor of Operations Management and Strategy at the University at Buffalo (SUNY) School of Management. Natalie received a BFA from the University of North Carolina School of the Arts and both an MBA and PhD from the University of Florida. She has earned numerous distinctions including the SUNY Chancellor's Award for Teaching Excellence.

Philip Hancock is co-owner of Glenochil Associates, LLC, a consultant and trainer, and a Certified Professional in Supply Management (CPSM) and Supplier Diversity (CPSD). Philip received an MBA and PhD from Napier University in Scotland, and has substantial experience in both commercial banking and government procurement.

Philip and Natalie served as the original tutors in the NoteShaper™ video tutorials accompanying the practice problems in this book.

HERCHER Publishing Incorporated
Naperville, Illinois 60564

Richard T. Hercher Jr., *Publisher*
Elizabeth Hercher, *Editorial Assistant*
Carol Rose, *Managing Editor*
Laurie Entringer, *Designer*
Precision Graphics, *Composition*
Tributary Sales Resources, *Marketing*
Courier Companies, Inc., *Printing*

Cover photo, Getty Images

Printed in the United States of America

ISBN: 978-1-939297-00-6

PHOTO CREDITS

Chapter 1
Productivity in Road Construction, Fotolia. Energy as Input, Fotolia. Landfills as Processes, Fotolia. Recycling as Transformation, Fang Song. Mining as Transformation, Fotolia. Physical Therapy as Pure Service, Fotolia. Containerized Freight and Global Supply Chains, Fotolia. Military Operations, Fotolia. Temp Facilities in Project, Event, and Incident Management, Fang Song. Incident Management in Health Care, Fang Song. Studio cameraman, Fotolia.

Chapter 2
Enterprise Resource Planning (ERP) in Retail Chains, Fotolia. Labor-Intensive Processes in Modern Manufacturing, Fotolia. The Complexity of Flexibility, Fotolia. Quality and Perception in Service Systems, Fotolia. Modern Make-to-Order Goods Production, Fotolia. Automobiles as Maturing Products, Fotolia. Process Selection in Agriculture, Fotolia. Electricity generating facility, Fotolia.

Chapter 3
Modern-Day Apprenticeships, Fotolia. Customer Perception in Visitor Reception Areas, Fotolia. Some Requirements of Brainstorming, Fotolia. The Distinction between Natural and Assignable Variation, Catherine Chen Kuan Yu, King Zhi Quan, and New Wei Sian. End of Life Cycle Problems from Changing Technology, Fotolia. Mass Customization of Emergency Vehicles, Fotolia. Solar Panel Installation and Process Safety, Fotolia. Construction site, webcam, June 7, 2012, Germany.

Chapter 4
Demand Forecasting for Time-Sensitive Products, Fang Song. Supermarket Forecasting Error, Patrick Tasner. Forecasting Construction Activity, Daniel Divirgilio. Copy center, Matthew Raffel.

Chapter 5
Design vs Effective Capacity of Parking, Matthew Raffel. Capacity Cushion at a Commuter Train Station, Mardiani Tri. Two Queues for Two Bank Machines, Wu Xiaoling. Maintaining Queue Discipline with Take-a-Number System, Fang Song. Loss of Queue Discipline on a Serpentine Line, Ahn Byung Hyun. Toll plaza, webcam, May 28, 2012, eastern USA.

Chapter 6
Custom Kitchen Cabinetry as ATO operation, Fang Song. Wine racks, Fotolia.

Chapter 7
Precedence Relationships Between Tasks, Cai Jinxuan. The Risks in an Unusual Project, webcam, June 6, 2012, New York. Construction site, webcam, June 7, 2012, Germany.

Chapter 8
Locating the Global Population, webcam, June 10, 2012, Tokyo. Measuring Distance in Urban Landscapes, Sagarika Das. Link between Maritime and Ground-based Logistical Systems, webcam, June 7, 2012, Lyttelton, New Zealand. Hub-and-Spoke Passenger Networks, Jiang Luwei. Government Influence on Ground-based Logistics, Fotolia. Maritime Freight Containers at Dockside, Fotolia. People on street corner and outside vendors, webcam, June 10, 2012, Times Square, New York.

Chapter 9
Upstream Inventory in the Restaurant Supply Chain, Jen Hartung. Information Technology as Strategic Security, Daniel Divirgilio. Handling Inventory as a Third Party, Fotolia. Border Delays in Global Sourcing, webcam, June 14, 2012, Vancouver, British Columbia. Contract Monitoring and Compliance in Construction, Daniel Divirgilio. Child playing soccer, Fotolia.

Chapter 10
Retail SKUs, Eunice Lim. Raw Materials as Finished Goods, Fang Song. Pipeline Stock, webcam, June 4, 2012, Panama Canal. Inconvenient Direct Storage Costs, Fang Song. Retail Stock Out, Wu Xiaoling. The C Items from an ABC Policy, Fotolia. Animal hospital, Fotolia.

Chapter 11
Chasing Demand by Renting Temporary Locations, Daniel Divirgilio. Leveling the Demand for Roadways with Pricing, Lee Wei Bin. Dependent Demand Items within an External Hard Drive, Jeffrey Szczepaniak. Wine racks, Fotolia.

Chapter 12
The Presence of High Fixed Costs, Fotolia. Bakery Bin-based Signaling Systems, Jiang Luwei. Wireless Devices for Inventory Tracking, Fotolia. Railcars moving coal, Fotolia.

Chapter 13
Assignable Variation in Fresh Eggs, Steven Cervino. Toll plaza, webcam, May 28, 2012, eastern USA.

Chapter 14
Four Work Centers in an Industrial Job Shop, Fotolia. The Challenge of FCFS, Fotolia. Bottleneck Problems with Real-Time Traffic, King Zhi Quan and Khiew Zhi Qiang. Making Work Center Assignments Obvious in Dynamic Systems, Fotolia. Telecommunications in Event Management, Fotolia. Copy center, Matthew Raffel.

Chapter 15
Planning Volunteer Operations, Jiang Luwei. Disruptive Innovation in Steel Making, Fotolia. Cognitive Bias Against Black Swans, Fotolia. Strategic Risks in Airline Schedules, Fotolia. Structure Fires as Emergencies, Fotolia. Urban Flooding Crisis, Fotolia. Risk Management in Maritime Shipping, Fotolia. Redundancy from Green Technology, Fotolia. Trade Show Single-Period Inventory Planning, Justin Maggio. One Temporary Organization from Three Available Groups, Fotolia. Bricolage with Cargo Containers, Fotolia. Airport Towers for Situational Awareness, Fotolia. Effeciency versus Effectiveness in Donkey Transport, Fotolia. The Last-Mile Problem after an Earthquake, Fotolia. Studio cameraman, Fotolia.

TO THE INSTRUCTOR

This book differs from other OM textbooks. First, we were determined to tell the whole story of operations management, including an entire chapter on incident and disruption management, recognizing that operations don't always proceed as planned. Second, we wanted to provide this balanced story of OM at a reasonable price to students. We felt both objectives were worthy and both could be achieved, provided that we rebooted the format for this kind of text by framing concepts and analytics with a practical bent. Our aim is to provide a learning tool students will use more of---and more affordably too. In our fifteen concise chapters, we hope to convince students that operations management is action itself, meaning that they should pick up a pencil and try it. To pursue all these ambitions simultaneously, we developed several features you'll see throughout the manuscript:

- **Threaded scenarios.** Every time an analytical methodology is introduced, it is demonstrated in the context of a case study that unfolds throughout the chapter. These demonstration scenarios "thread" through the general discussion of each chapter, presenting conceptual material in action. One major objective of the threaded scenarios is to clarify how operations management is an active process, by viewing it through the eyes of one who is putting the tools to work.
- **Tiered end-of-chapter content.** To support self-guided learning, end-of-chapter content is divided into tiers of resources, each suited to a different purpose. After each summary, key word review, and discussion questions, chapter exercises begin with a set of *Minute Answer* problems, or qualitative quiz questions most appropriately answered with one or two words. Minute Answer serves as a warm-up conceptual review to the subsequent *Quick Start* problems, which are quantitative questions that require the application of a single formula or numerical principle. Quick Start is followed by *Ramp Up* questions, which are also single-answer quantitative queries, but many are quite challenging. Ramp Up questions require additional confidence in the material, because some aspect of each problem is hidden. Chapter practice problems conclude with full-scale, multipart *Scenarios*, many of which are similar to threaded scenarios earlier in the chapter. Finally, each chapter concludes with a two-paged case study, requiring a methodology from within the chapter but also requiring some creative adaptation to address the issues posed there. Short answers to all practice problems are available in the back of the text, but case notes are available only to instructors.
- **Online support.** To keep the overall size of this book under control, we placed some problems in the book, but more problems—with answers—online at NoteShaper.com. To help with those moments when students get stuck, the NoteShaper™ site also houses a library of video tutorials providing step-by-step instruction on how to solve each of the problems in the book, accessible for a small fee.

We also controlled the size of the book by being really picky about the photographs. Honestly, this book has fewer pictures than some OM textbooks, but each of ours had to earn its space by telling some part of the OM story. We tried to use good page composition to make the book easier to use, nice to look at, and relatively lean, considering the size of that story.

SOME ROADS NOT TAKEN

No matter how we economized through page design, everything OM would not fit in this book. While we take no joy in not writing about something valuable, we had to make some hard choices about what to leave out. Here is our thinking about about three of these choices in particular:

- **History of operations management.** Operations management can be traced back thousands of years. While OM's deepest roots are rarely acknowledged, some textbooks do examine history from the Industrial Revolution through to the present day, chronicling the names of famous contributors to the field. Instead, we wove the mention of important names into the book's content throughout, forgoing a specific historical section.

- **Linear programming.** Linear programming and related algorithms such as the transportation and assignment methods are powerful techniques in optimization. It grieved us to exclude discussion of them from the text, especially when you can see the results of their use in certain sections, such as the optimal aggregate plan for Main House Gaming in Chapter 14. But we structured this text with the principle of never introducing a technique without explaining exactly how you could put that technique to work. We hope to complete a small companion volume for this book soon, dedicated to linear programming, optimization, and other supporting topics from decision science.
- **Forecasting techniques.** Almost every OM textbook has a chapter on forecasting, including this one. We can imagine that most OM textbook authors aren't completely happy with their forecasting chapter (like us), because there is so much more that could be included. Techniques such as centered moving averages, nonlinear regression analysis, and trend-adjusted exponential smoothing are just a few of the many intriguing tools that we don't cover, simply because we couldn't find space.

ACKNOWLEDGMENTS

Like many complex creative endeavors, this book did not appear instantly, nor is it the result of a few people. What we wrote first appeared as bulky, black-and-white spiral-bound prototypes of today's book, hauled around by over 1,200 undergraduate students at the University at Buffalo (UB) and the Singapore Institute of Management (SIM). We are forever grateful to this first wave of patient contributors, as their sharp eyes corrected and refined the manuscript each semester for two years before we then submitted it for publication. Thank you also to David Wagner of Great Lakes Graphics and Printing at UB, who would marshal these rough-cut, ever-changing, course-pack versions into production on short notice, without missing a single deadline or misplacing a single page.

UB and SIM students shaped this textbook's illustrations as well, because many of the images you see now were originally captured by them. We would like to thank Fang Song in particular, for providing no less than eight of the images of important conceptual content. In addition we thank these student photographers:

Byung Hyun Ahn	Eunice Lim
Patrick Tasner	Lee Wei Bin
Jiang Luwei	Mardiani Tri
Steven Cervino	Justin Maggio
Wu Xiaoling	Catherine Chen
Khiew Zhi Qiang	Sagarika Das
King Zhi Quan	Daniel Divigilio
Matthew Raffel	Jennifer Hartung
New Wei Sian	Cai Jinxuan
Jeffrey Szczepaniak	

Several colleague reviewers provided useful suggestions that we did our best to incorporate into the final version. As in any other operation, we faced conflicting requests and suggestions, which we tried to balance with our overall goals of a practical and affordable text. We are especially grateful to the following colleagues for their thoughtful investment of time and personal expertise:

Arash Azadegan—*Rutgers University*
Gregory Bier—*University of Missouri*
Susan Cholette—*San Francisco State University*
Chen H. Chung —*University of Kentucky*
Lori Cook—*DePaul University*
Matthew Drake—*Dusquesne University*
Derrick D'Souza—*University of North Texas*
Harold Frazer—*California State University, Fullerton*
Hector Guerrero—*College of William and Mary*
Apurva Jain—*University of Washington*
Gordon Johnson—*California State University, Northridge*
Casey Kleindienst—*California State University, Fullerton*
Taeho Park—*San Jose State University*
Cynthia Wallin—*Brigham Young University*
Theresa Wells—*University of Wisconsin, Eau Claire*

We hope all will be happy with the published result.

Copy editor Carol Rose trained the manuscript to speak out both confidently and correctly. Carol combed through each page of what you see today, although those adolescent pages didn't flow or even look nearly as nice as they do now. Our grateful thanks to Carol for her exceptional skill, and to Laurie Entringer, Kirsten Dennison, and Jan Troutt for their transformative design work.

Finally, like anything new, this book needed a champion. Thank you, Dick Hercher, for stepping into that role and bringing all of us together.

Natalie C. Simpson
Philip G. Hancock

TO THE STUDENT

Begin, be bold and venture to be wise.
—Horace

Operations management is ultimately about human endeavor, so it applies to any industry and any organization, be it a global supply chain for consumer goods, a local nonprofit agency, or an individual entrepreneur's latest project. While you may have been unaware of its formal terminology, you've been observing and participating in operations for years before you opened this book. Perhaps you felt a distinct frustration when you couldn't locate the back of a long waiting line, so you weren't sure where you should stand. In that case, the phrase "queue discipline" probably wasn't floating through your thoughts, but you were annoyed with this concept nonetheless. You may have once considered packing two of something because it was especially important to have at least one, such as bringing two calculators to an exam. You aren't likely to have thought explicitly of the role of redundancy in strengthening reliability, but that is the principle you were considering. Thus, the purpose of this introductory book is really to reintroduce you to a topic you began many years ago, this time empowering your senses with new language and analytics.

This book differs from other OM textbooks. First, we were determined to tell you the whole story of OM, including an entire chapter on incident and disruption management, recognizing that your endeavors won't always proceed smoothly, but that is no reason to be either fearful or unprepared. And yet, we wanted to create an affordable textbook, plus we hoped to convince you that operations management is action itself, meaning that you should pick up a pencil and try it for yourself, to make it your own. To pursue all these ambitions simultaneously, we developed several features you will see throughout the upcoming pages:

- **Threaded scenarios.** Operational analysis is an active process, one that you can—and in the future, probably will—participate in. We want you to see operations management as both an exciting and a hands-on undertaking that you can be involved in. To start you in that direction, each chapter features threaded scenarios in which each technique discussed in general is then put to work immediately in the setting of a certain organization. Within the scenario, you see the problem through the analyst's eyes, unfolding in the analyst's own handwriting. In this first phase of learning, you are looking over someone else's shoulder, watching this person tackle the situation, and seeing what insight they draw from it.
- **Tiered chapter problems.** When you arrive at the end of a chapter, you naturally look for similar problems to practice. To support your learning, practice problems here are divided into four distinct tiers, each with a different suggested purpose. To begin, *Minute Answer* questions are short, qualitative queries that can be answered with a word or two, quizzing you on conceptual terms and relationships. Minute Answer questions are suggested as a warm-up to computational practice. To start working with numbers, try *Quick Start* problems: these are always single-answer queries, requiring the direct application of a single equation or method from the chapter. Once your confidence begins to build, try that chapter's *Ramp Up* problems next, although please don't discourage too quickly. Like Quick Start, *Ramp Up* problems are short, single-answer questions, but unlike Quick Start many of these questions are rather difficult. *Ramp Up* problems are puzzles, where something is missing or disguised, requiring use of the same material as from Quick Start, but more creative thinking. Finally, the problem sets end in *Scenarios*, inviting you to work as the analyst. These are the more comprehensive problems, providing an extended description of some situation and multipart questions to solve. Here you won't be using a single equation, but you will be working through many of the same analytical steps you first saw unfolding in the threaded scenarios earlier.
- **Online support.** Analysis takes practice, and sometimes you get stuck. To help with practice but keep the size of this book under control, we placed some problems in the book, but more problems—with

answers—online at NoteShaper.com. To help with those moments in which you sometimes get stuck, the NoteShaper™ site also houses a library of video tutorials providing step-by-step instruction on how to solve each of the problems in the book, accessible for a small fee.

While we don't know if you are considering a supply chain major or if you consider yourself an artist (or both), what we do know is that there's something, somewhere in the story of OM that is of value to you. Keeping this in mind, we've set out to weave this story from as many different endeavors as possible, including agile manufacturing, health care, disaster relief, airline logistics, and event management. We hope you'll see something in that rich landscape that fits your ambitions.

Thank you for your interest in operations management. We wish you the best of luck, wherever you may venture.

Natalie C. Simpson
Philip G. Hancock

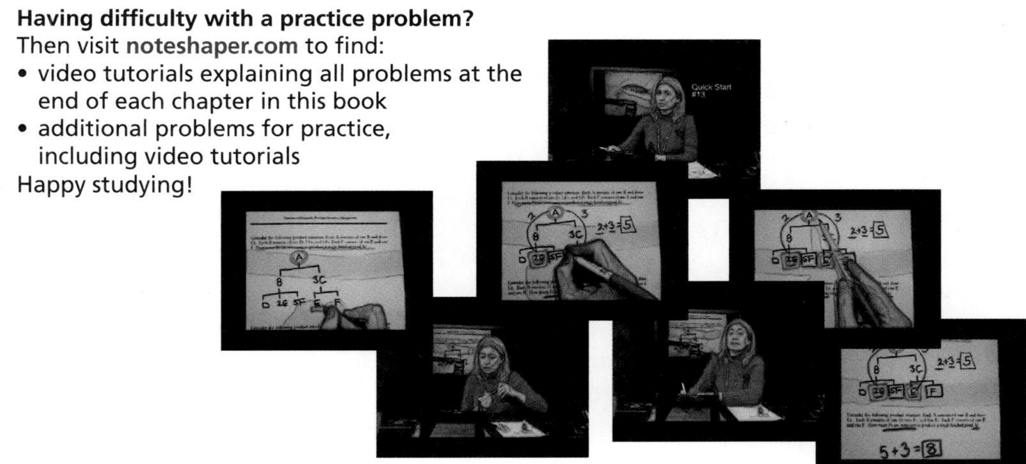

Having difficulty with a practice problem?
Then visit **noteshaper.com** to find:
• video tutorials explaining all problems at the end of each chapter in this book
• additional problems for practice, including video tutorials
Happy studying!

BRIEF CONTENTS

CONTENTS

PART 2

PLANNING OPERATIONS

PART 4

ACTION AND ADAPTION

PART 1 ESSENTIALS

CHAPTER 1

Introduction to Operations Management

Before I speak, I have something important to say.
—Groucho Marx

MAJOR SECTIONS

IN THIS CHAPTER, LOOK FOR...

- Operations management as the creation of value, making it the heart of any organization.
- The balance of productivity, sustainability, and responsibility in successful operation.
- Types of decision making and product, and degree of uncertainty and control.
- Operations within an organization, as well as supporting professional and academic societies.

INTRODUCTION

At the heart of any organization are its operations—the activities that define it. This description holds true whether the organization is a global brand manufacturer such as Apple or Toyota, a major retailer like Home Depot, a nonprofit organization such as the International Red Cross, or a local gas station or health care clinic. Purchasing, assembly, shipping, settling accounts, stocking, and even communicating are but a few examples of many different actions unfolding within these organizations, united by a single purpose: to create value for a customer.

Operations management may be the oldest of all the business disciplines. Some of the earliest examples of written language are 5,000 year-old Egyptian and Sumerian inventory records, a vital tool of operations still in action today. In fact, one of the oldest known textbooks of any type, *De Re Metallica*, teaches operations in the context of mining and metallurgy. Written by Georgius Agricola in 1556, this textbook described organized, high-volume manufacturing some 350 years before Henry Ford is credited with introducing the world to modern manufacturing practices.

Simultaneously, operations management is one of the youngest of all business disciplines, based on formal recognition. Subjects such as marketing and finance were formally taught in business curricula decades before operations first appeared as "production management" or "factory management" in the 1950s. As a subject, operations has evolved rapidly since the days of factory management, recognizing the need to create value in individual projects, service settings, nonprofit organizations, and multiorganizational global supply chains. Operations management also includes valuable action in disorganized settings, its modern-day frontier of agility, incident management, and creative activity.

Operations management is present in some form anywhere a person or a group moves forward toward a goal. Regardless of what name it is given at that moment, the widespread nature of operations makes it both exciting and perhaps a bit puzzling at first. So we begin our study of operations management by examining several frameworks to organize and clarify its wonderful diversity.

ESSENTIAL OPERATIONS MANAGEMENT

operations
A set of activities dedicated to the transformation of inputs into outputs of greater value.

One of the simplest and most enduring descriptions of operations is *transformation*. Any undertaking transforming some set of resources into some result can be thought of as an operation. Figure 1.1 illustrates this as the classic input/output model of operations management. While simplified, this model helps clarify what operations such as manufacturing, health care, agriculture, and education have in common. Like all other operations,

FIGURE 1.1 **A Model of Any Operation**

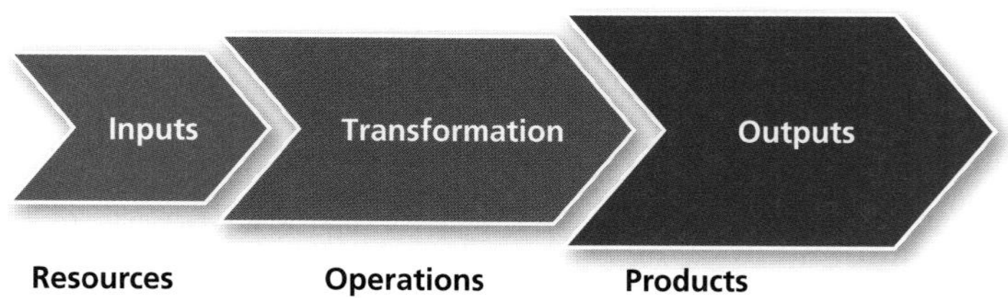

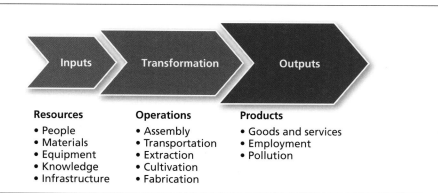

Resources
- People
- Materials
- Equipment
- Knowledge
- Infrastructure

Operations
- Assembly
- Transportation
- Extraction
- Cultivation
- Fabrication

Products
- Goods and services
- Employment
- Pollution

each is an example of a particular set of inputs being transformed into a particular set of outputs, with most but not necessarily all of those outputs being intentional or beneficial. The transformation sector in the center of Figure 1.1 most closely represents the operation itself. While the inputs and outputs of any given operation are identifiable entities such as people, knowledge, and goods, the associated operation consists of processes, or actions taken to create the outputs. Thus, *operations management* is the planning and facilitating of those actions.

processes
Activities that transform inputs into outputs.

Describing operations management as transformation focuses on the actions themselves, but another way to understand operations is to consider the purpose of those activities, or what they achieve. Returning to Figure 1.1, the fundamental purpose of any operation is to produce outputs more valuable than inputs consumed. Thus, the purpose of operations management is to create value, and the literal difference in value between outputs and inputs is a performance measure known as value-added or value creation. Successful value creation ultimately depends on a balance of related achievements, some of which are easy to evaluate and others less so. Figure 1.2 introduces these three interdependent elements: productivity, sustainability, and responsibility.

value-added
The difference between the total value of the outputs and the total value of the inputs associated with an operation.

value creation
Achieving positive value-added.

Productivity

Productivity measures the success of the operation by comparing its inputs to its outputs, and is generally the most visible and measurable of the three issues linked in Figure 1.2. While value-added refers to the difference between the value of inputs and outputs, productivity compares the same values as a ratio, such as cars per shift or miles per gallon. Historically, technological innovation increases the productivity of most, although not all, transformation processes. Inappropriately low productivity indicates lost opportunity to create additional value from the same set of inputs, a wastefulness that highlights the fused area between productivity, sustainability, and responsibility.

productivity
A measurement of value creation, calculated as a ratio of the values of output to input.

Sustainability

While productivity is a familiar measure of performance, high productivity does not necessarily indicate a well-managed operation. As Figure 1.2 suggests, successful value

Elements of Value Creation | **FIGURE 1.2**

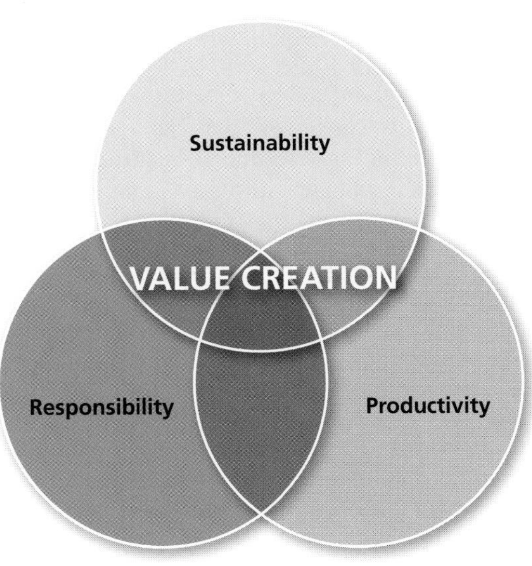

Productivity in Road Construction

Paving roads illustrates both the input/output transformation model and the concept of productivity. Grouped together on the right of this picture are three major inputs of road construction: raw materials, specialized equipment, and skilled labor. Visible to the left is their combined output, the new road. Modern road construction illustrates how technology usually advances productivity; this operation requires less labor than would have been needed several decades ago. This increase in productivity is achieved through the use of more sophisticated equipment, the increased expense of which must be fairly reflected in any productivity study when comparing this operation to older paving practices.

sustainability
The degree to which activity with immediate benefit does not incur greater costs in the long term.

creation also depends on the sustainability of that operation, the extent to which operating at a particular time does not create greater costs to be paid in the future. Lack of attention to sustainability can occur at any of the three stages in Figure 1.1, although problems with inputs are particularly familiar throughout history. Consider these examples:

- Archeological findings suggest many early cities suffered a pattern of overshoot-and-collapse in the use of nearby resources, including those of the Mesopotamians, the Mayans, and the Anasazi. Each of these groups used available technology to concentrate population, build increasingly sophisticated structures, and advance knowledge in areas such as astronomy, mathematics, and management. However, little remains of these achievements because each community exhausted a necessary resource, often available forest, triggering extinction of the city and often loss of its innovative advances.
- Sixty million buffalo roamed North America prior to the 1870s, when buffalo hunters began killing the animals for their hides, which were transformed into clothing, machinery drive belts, rugs, and other products. As buffalo were harvested at a much higher rate than their population could regenerate, these herds were destroyed within 20 years, and the buffalo hide industry died with them.
- Concern for the unsustainable consumption of resources such as fossil fuels, forest, and fresh water continue to present day. More recently, rare earth minerals used in the creation of high-performance electric motors, LEDs, and computer tablets have been added to this list of concerns. This dilemma in sustainability brings with it an irony that dependence on these resources is currently necessary to lessen dependency on other nonrenewable resources, as rare earth minerals are vital to the production of wind turbines, energy-efficient lighting, and electric vehicles.

Although human history supplies many sad examples of failure to focus on the sustainability of inputs, an operation can fail just as readily if the practices used in transformation do not likewise conform to the principles of sustainability. From history, two particular patterns of bad practice have nicknames of their own:

- *Boomtowns.* Boomtowns are communities that grow rapidly around the development of a single resource. Some boomtowns like the Australian gold-rush center of Ballarat do survive to become broader economies long after the original resource is depleted. Most, however, become ghost towns, abandoned when their original operations fail. The resulting loss and wasted infrastructure of a ghost town echoes the overshoot-and-collapse cycle of ancient communities.

Energy as an Input

Electrical energy is an input of almost any modern operation. However, this input often raises troubling questions of sustainability. Pictured here are the cooling towers of a nuclear power plant, releasing harmless water vapor into the atmosphere. While this plant generates electricity without air pollution, it also creates highly radioactive waste as an output, which must then be stored for hundreds of years. Note the railroad tracks and hopper cars visible at the bottom of this picture, indicating that this electrical generation facility does not rely exclusively on nuclear power. These rail cars are evidence of nearby use of large amounts of a dry commodity such as coal. Coal supplies half of all electrical generation in the United States and is responsible for much of its air pollution. While coal-fired generation does not possess the higher construction costs or the risk of catastrophic failure associated with nuclear power, it is a nonrenewable resource, raising further questions about its sustainability.

- *Bubbles.* Bubbles are the economic equivalent of boomtowns, in which investors and organizations trace an overshoot-and-collapse pattern through unsustainable activity, drawn in by some immediate benefit and disregarding longer-term reality. This often takes the form of investing in an operation far beyond its intrinsic value, leading to a meltdown at some future time. As an example, the global financial crisis of 2007–10 was triggered largely by the collapse of housing prices around the world, a bubble formed from historically low interest rates and the unsustainable activity of housing buyers, banks, and construction companies alike.

Finally, but by no means less important, sustainability concerns the outputs of an operation as well. Sustainability addresses the intended products of an operation as well as any other consequences, creating two major areas of output concern:

- *Pollution.* Polluting of air, soil, and water brings long-term consequences potentially greater than the short-term value creation releasing the pollution. Although societies have struggled with control of pollution for centuries, the recent accumulation of carbon emissions in the atmosphere has raised new alarm. Linked to global climate change, these emissions result from fossil-fuel-burning operations that power much of the world's transportation and energy infrastructure.
- *Disposal.* Disposal of intended products after use can be problematic if this last phase of their life cycle is not carried out in a manner consistent with long-term sustainability. Unfortunately, ample evidence of neglect for this issue exists, apparent in the example of used clothing, the fastest-growing source of trash in American landfills today. In the United States, 12.8 million tons of textiles were disposed of in 2008, up from 1.8 million tons in 1960, or an increase of over 600% during a time in which the population discarding that clothing grew by only 73%. This not only suggests a distinct waste of value, it also stresses the finite resource of safe landfill area.

Sometimes fixing unsustainable practices in disposal can simultaneously solve problems with input availability. This type of problem solving is inspired by biomimicry, or the imitation of natural systems. Natural systems form continuous cycles of consumption, production, reclamation, and regeneration, whereas the traditional view of an operation in Figure 1.1 is linear, starting and stopping at discrete points. Newer approaches

biomimicry
The imitation of natural processes and systems.

Landfills as Processes

A landfill accepts and buries discarded waste, and many landfills are complex logistical operations. A well-managed landfill builds barriers to protect its surrounding environment, monitors incoming materials to prevent burial of hazardous substances, and covers allowable garbage daily to further minimize exposure. Landfills also attempt to use as little space as possible, by crushing and compacting waste before burial. Modern landfill operations do not stop there, recognizing that reducing the amount of waste is far more effective than simply compacting it for burial. As a result, modern facilities feature preprocessing areas like the one pictured here, where reusable materials such as metal are recovered from the arriving discards, for removal and recycling elsewhere.

green
Assures sustainability.

to production are said to be green if they are sustainable, and these approaches are also better described as cycles that loop the straight-line system of Figure 1.1 back upon itself. In many cases, green practices avoiding the wasteful disposal of some product or by-product do not create an input for that same green process, but do create a valuable input for some other process, such as the recycling of discarded tires into durable landscaping material.

lean
Operating without waste.

We can think of sustainability as broken into three general levels. Achieving the first level means "getting the basics right" with the system as it is, such as recycling whenever possible and turning off lights when not needed. The second level is "learning to think sustainably," and it is at this level that operations management is often the most active and effective. This thinking requires assessing the impact of decisions across both an operation and its broader supply chain partners, with a view to incorporating new lean (reducing waste in all forms) and sustainable practices wherever possible. As an example, a sawmill producing lumber might achieve the first level of sustainability by optimizing its cutting patterns to extract the maximum lumber product from incoming trees, and minimizing use of electricity and fossil fuels by careful selection and maintenance of its equipment. To climb to the second level, however, the same mill may seek useful

Recycling as Transformation

The internationally recognized symbol for recycling consists of three block arrows folded into a Mobius loop, as shown on this collection bin. Created by a college student in the early 1970s, this symbol suggests an unending use of outputs as inputs, which is a circular reformatting of the traditional model of operations in Figure 1.1. This is also a good example of biomimicry, because recycling is an effort to mirror nature's theme of repeating cycles of transformation.

applications for its current waste products, such as preparing its wood bark and scrap for use in paper products, and/or resolve to purchase inputs exclusively from sustainable sources (timber companies that replant trees after harvest). The third and top level of sustainability involves benchmarking, auditing, and governance to bring clarity to the environmental impact of the organization's practices, which may require the sawmill to reorganize its habitual operation completely.

Assessing sustainability is more tricky than calculating productivity because it requires calculating the future cost of a present action, and some degree of uncertainty concerning the future always exists. Here, management is key in determining whether all foreseeable future consequences have been acknowledged and explored to the best of the organization's ability.

Responsibility

Responsibility has multiple dimensions. Corporate social responsibility concerns the quality of interaction between a business and surrounding society, whereas employees of a corporation also have direct responsibilities to perform for their employer. Corporate social responsibility is at its most visible when a business publicly assumes responsibility for damage inflicted by its operation, such as accident response and voluntary recalls. However, corporate social responsibility is defined largely by an obligation to pursue sustainability. Some corporations such as Campbell Soup and Dow Chemical have vice presidents of social responsibility and sustainability, but these issues are not limited to job titles for particular managers. Some argue that decision making in any organization is driven by the incentives offered to the decision makers, and little progress toward long-term sustainability will be made if performance measurement and rewards emphasize short-term results. Not surprisingly, many companies recognized for corporate social responsibility have invested considerable effort in developing "green" scorecards and other new managerial tools to naturally motivate responsible decision making, seeking that highest level of achievement in sustainability.

responsibility
An obligation to perform.

Responsible decision making guides ethical behavior. Ethics are simply rules that identify good versus bad behavior, and these rules vary between cultures and even between large organizations. Ethics are not tangible and specific like legal code. And, as Thomas Paine so aptly stated, "A long habit of not thinking a thing is wrong gives it a superficial appearance of being right." Technology and rapid innovation can create operational practices that do not appear wrong only because they have yet to offend during their relatively brief history, but that does not necessarily mean these new practices are appropriate or advisable. Blindly accepting an operation as ethical until such time

ethics
Principles governing conduct, delineating good from bad.

Mining as Transformation

Virtually every product begins with the processes of mining, logging, and/or farming. Each of these processes transforms the natural landscape, but none more dramatically than surface mining, pictured here. Surface mining requires removal of large amounts of earth to expose the substance of value to the operation, such as coal, metal ore, or limestone. In a few cases, the resulting tiered pit is large enough to be seen from outer space. Responsible surface mining includes a reclamation phase, in which the pit is rehabilitated into a stable ecological landscape as the last stage of activity at that mining site. However, this responsibility is not always met. Active mining has ended in this picture, evident from the flooded pit floor and lack of logistical activity, yet efforts to reclaim this site are likewise missing.

as it violates some standard of sustainability often comes at great cost. As an example, deep-water oil extraction had been a generally acceptable practice despite the fact that little was known about how to fight ruptures at those depths. A lack of accidents at such depths created little concern for this issue until April 20, 2010, when an explosion aboard the oil platform DeepWater Horizon resulted in an oil leak 1 mile below the ocean's surface. British Petroleum then struggled for 3 months to stop this leak, which produced the largest oil spill in history.

CLASSIFYING OPERATIONS

Because operations management is embedded in all organized activity, we categorize different operations according to common traits, to clarify similarities among organizations. Figure 1.3 illustrates four common frameworks for organizing various operations into useful groupings, each one providing insight into some aspect of successful management within the groups.

Tangibility

tangibility
The degree of perceivable, physical essence of a product.

goods
Tangible products.

services
Intangible products.

Operations management is often internally organized into goods versus services, classifying each operation according to the tangibility of its product. Declaring something tangible generally indicates that it is solid and can be perceived by sense of touch. However, whether a product is perceivable by touch does not completely explain its tangibility; most products are some mix of tangible and intangible elements. Nonetheless, products recognized by the customer as physical objects, including grocery items, personal electronics, and clothing, are broadly referred to as goods. In contrast, services provide valuable actions but little or no tangible content, describing products from Internet access to education to medical care.

Surprisingly, this seemingly simple issue can have powerful consequences in operations management. Figure 1.4 illustrates a few distinctions between goods and services in operations, although this categorization most accurately represents the two extreme ends of a continuum. While the tangibility of a product is not generally as simple as a yes or

FIGURE 1.3 Classifying an Operation with Four Different Frameworks

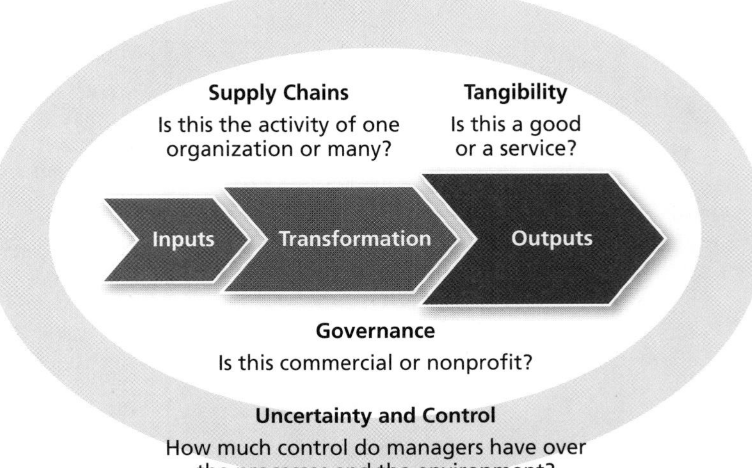

Comparing Goods and Services **FIGURE 1.4**

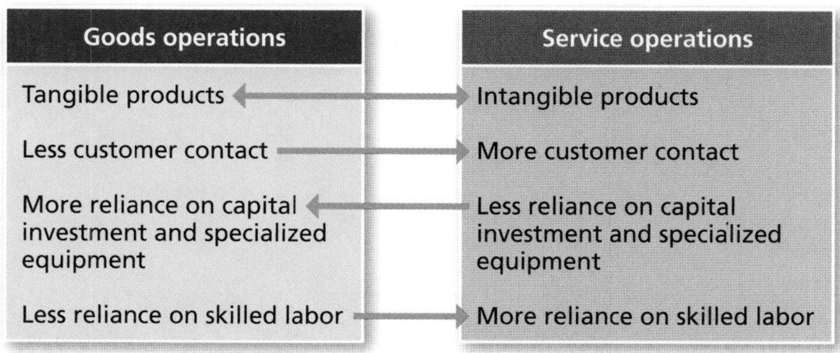

no answer to a question about touch, it is helpful to look at the two extremes first to better understand the blending of goods and services.

Goods operations
Service operations
Tangible products
Intangible products
Less customer contact
More customer contact
More reliance on capital investment and specialized equipment
Less reliance on capital investment and specialized equipment
Less reliance on skilled labor
More reliance on skilled labor

Goods Operations Manufacturing is the production of goods, although not all goods are manufactured. The term *manufacturing* implies mass production, whereas goods might be custom-made or grown or extracted from the ground. One positive result of producing something physical such as an automobile is that this output is likewise storable as inventory, at least for some short period of time. This single condition of storage capability provides multiple benefits:

inventory Tangible items awaiting sale or use.

- The operation can be located where it is most beneficial for production, and the product shipped elsewhere.
- Less customer contact is required of the operation because goods need not be produced where they are consumed.
- The operation can respond to surges in demand by stockpiling goods early, instead of increasing production capacity.

stockpiling Producing or securing goods in advance of demand.

Furthermore, goods production tends to involve a lower variability of both inputs and outputs than service operations. This allows easier prediction, planning, and evaluation on behalf of the system. Successful manufacturing operations, then, put this relative wealth of reliable information to use in developing the most efficient processes possible, requiring higher levels of capital investment in specialized equipment.

Service Operations Manufacturing presents challenges, but the provision of services may be more challenging. Because services are intangible, they cannot be stored for future use. In general, service operations suffer these restrictions:

- Most services must locate where the customer has access to the operation, not where the operation can function best. This issue of location can become so competitive that a large retailer may purchase strategically located property even though this organization has no intention of building a new store. Rather, the purchase prevents competing retailers from building at that beneficial location.
- Many services require the customer as an input to the process, so customer contact is higher overall. Further, this visibility of the operation itself can potentially bias the customer's perception of product quality.
- Services cannot be stockpiled for future use, so service operations have fewer options to handle fluctuating demand. These operations are often obligated to maintain idle capacity to absorb unexpected demand.

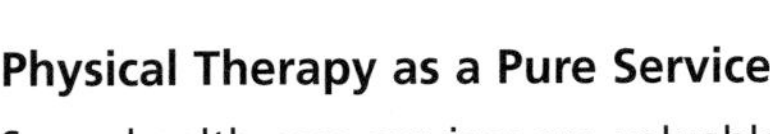

Physical Therapy as a Pure Service

Some health care services are valuable products that include little or no tangible content. In this picture, value is created through the interaction of the physical therapist on the right and her client on the left. One distraction in this pure service example is the presence of specialized tangibles such as the parallel bars the client is using for support, but these are inputs to the physical therapy process, not outputs.

Services usually cope with higher variability of inputs and outputs, making prediction and planning more difficult. Where manufacturers often raise substantial capital to create a competitive factory, service operations are more likely to rely on finding skilled labor for success. Even simple measurements and comparisons can be problematic in a service setting, due to difficulties in capturing input and output information.

Blending of Goods and Services In reality, most products result from a blend of tangible and intangible elements, placing them somewhere along the spectrum first suggested by Figure 1.4. For this reason it is difficult to identify an example of a pure good or pure service. Even something as tangible as a car or clothing usually requires shipping to a convenient retail location, and this intangible but valuable element of the product is bundled into its purchase price. Any example of a theoretically pure service would require valuable action without a trace of physical evidence, not even a paper invoice or billing statement.

With examples from the extremities of Figure 1.4 relatively rare, it is more common to find operations balancing goods production and service provision in the creation of their products. In fact, any tangible good that is highly perishable usually represents a successful balance of goods and service, in that half of the organization's efforts are invested in the creation of the good and the other half in its quick distribution and resupply. Perishable goods can refer to products that literally spoil, such as fresh food and restaurant meals. However, the term *perishable* simply indicates a short shelf life. Many products perish not by physically deteriorating but by becoming obsolete rather quickly. Examples of this type of perishability include newspapers, magazines, fashion apparel, and other time-sensitive merchandise.

Supply Chains

Any operation is a system—a web of related parts cooperating toward some common purpose. Sometimes this system is a set of parts within a single organization, while other operations involve the interactions of multiple organizations as a single system. Figure 1.5 provides a common example from the internal perspective, a so-called bill of materials that describes the assembly of some electronic product. This core concept from inventory planning describes the relationships among production requirements within a particular product, and is crucial to coordinating the larger plans supporting its production.

bill of materials
A description of all raw materials and intermediate assemblies required to create a finished product.

A Bill of Materials

FIGURE 1.5

An example of an internal system in operations management

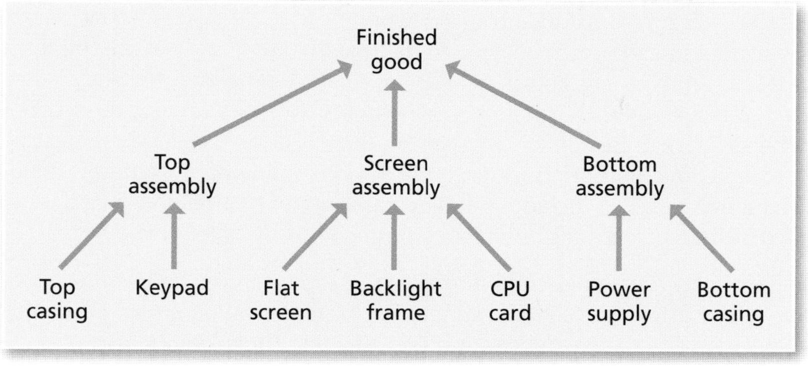

Finished good
Top assembly
Screen assembly
Bottom assembly
Top casing
Keypad
Flat screen
Backlight frame
CPU card
Power supply
Bottom casing

Operations management addresses these internal issues:

- Facility design, identifying the best layout to support the operation.
- Scheduling of facilities, personnel, and equipment.
- Statistical quality control, monitoring various points in ongoing production for inappropriate deviations from the firm's standards.
- Waiting lines, modeling, and improving any wait time created by the operation.

Coordinating these issues internally is challenging in and of itself but successful management of multiorganizational networks requires more sophisticated efforts. When the scope of a system is wide enough to include every organization participating in the ultimate delivery of a particular product to an end customer, a complete supply chain for that product must be coordinated. Almost all consumer products are provided through supply chain networks like the one pictured in Figure 1.6. Each organization within this

supply chain
A system consisting of all organizations that play some role in supplying a particular product to a customer.

A Supply Chain System

FIGURE 1.6

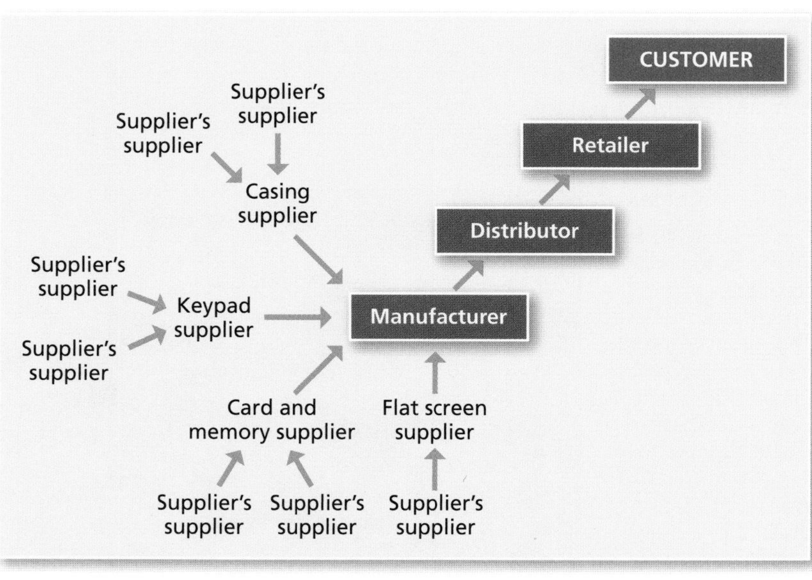

network might only communicate with one other organization, although the customer's experience with the product is ultimately dependent on all of them. Furthermore, modern supply chains often link up organizations and customers throughout the world, and include additional logistical organizations working in the linkages between those businesses appearing in Figure 1.6, devoted to the transportation of goods along the arrows.

Figures 1.5 and 1.6 are not unrelated; both depict dependencies between parts of a system that progressively add value to some product. Not surprisingly, the processes associated with Figure 1.5 are sometimes referred to as a value chain, signifying an internal network of functions that bring value to the product being produced there. The broader supply chain in Figure 1.6 includes all the complexity of internal value chains while also requiring that these conditions be satisfied throughout the supply chain:

value chain
A system consisting of all functions within an organization that play some role in adding value to the organization's product.

- The flow of both material and information must be coordinated among organizations, which may be located anywhere. For example, cotton grown in North America is often shipped to sites in Asia for processing into thread and fabric, and that fabric is shipped elsewhere for cutting, the result of which is shipped still elsewhere for sewing. It is not uncommon for this product to circle the world twice before arriving in a retail store as finished cotton clothing.
- Vital information must be shared rapidly among different organizations. While modern technology supports these relationships, sharing of information can be complicated by the fact that organizations may be participating together in a supply chain serving customers in one market, but competing against each other in some other market, and thus reluctant to share sensitive information.
- All organizations must cooperate to optimize delivery as a single system. Often the best answer from the organization's isolated perspective is not part of the best answer for the larger system, and supply chain management requires individual firms to support what is best for the chain as a whole. If the more complex supply chain solution is not found and implemented successfully, the broader system falls victim to local optimization, in which each supply chain partner behaves according to their individual internal perspective, dragging down the coordinated performance of the whole.

local optimization
Localized problem solving that ignores any larger problem of which the local decision is a component.

Rapid advances in communication and information technology have elevated some traditionally firm-level functions such as purchasing and quality management to more strategic levels of planning. Although both the term and the practice of supply chain management originated with the manufacturer Hewlett-Packard, this concept is not limited to the delivery of manufactured goods. The opportunities and the challenge of supply chains occur anywhere multiple organizations must interact to provide customer value, which includes many important service industries, including health care.

Containerized Freight and Global Supply Chains

A freight container is a steel box approximately 40 feet long, often seen traveling roads as the box trailer in a truck-and-trailer combination. The advantage of freight containers is that they are easily transferred among roads, railways, and ocean vessels without unpacking the goods within, allowing organizations to move products through global supply chain networks. Pictured here is a typical container yard, where several thousand cargo boxes await loading at a busy port. These boxes likely contain a wide variety of goods, ranging from electronic components, lumber, and food flavorings to finished clothing, microwave ovens, and toothpaste.

Governance

When comparing operations, successful networks pay attention to the different forms of governance, or ownership of the operations. Grouping by governance often brings together operations with common perspectives in decision making.

Commercial Enterprise Generally, commercial enterprise is the most familiar form of governance in the study of business and management. A commercial operation is managed to ultimately yield a profit, distributing some of its value creation back to its ownership. Such an operation may be privately owned or publicly traded, where the payment of dividends to shareholders represents partial distribution of value. This type of operation must account for the interests and income of its ownership when making decisions, and is also most likely to feel the pressures of competition. Not surprisingly, it is a commercial enterprise that often invests considerable effort in branding its output to distinguish itself from its competitors, giving rise to well-known global entities such as Google, McDonald's, and Exxon Mobil.

Nonprofit Operations A nonprofit operation does not distribute surplus value back to its ownership and is often excused from income taxes paid by commercial organizations. A nonprofit operation has governing ownership nonetheless, and is not necessarily immune to the issue of competition. In fact, in some industries commercial, for-profit operations compete with nonprofit counterparts, such as hospitals, package delivery, and education. Nonprofit operations are generally service operations, providing value to some constituency and reinvesting any surplus back into the funding of the operation. A nonprofit organization not owned by a government is known as an NGO, or nongovernmental organization. Who precisely does own and manage an NGO can vary widely, with examples including religious organizations, social clubs, charitable foundations, and individuals. Global disaster relief is an example of one industry dominated by nonprofit organizations in general and NGOs in particular, with the International Red Cross being one well-known participant.

NGO
A nongovernmental organization, understood to be a nonprofit organization as well.

Government Activities Any government is essentially a nonprofit operation, engaged in the provision of government services. Furthermore, some national governments own all or part of manufacturing organizations involved in the production of goods ranging from automobiles to cigarettes. This is a relatively rare condition in the market economy of the

Military Operations

Government and nonprofit organizations often face the most challenging problems in operations management, compared to commercial corporations. As an example, the aircraft carrier here is essentially a mobile airport, and the complexity of managing this operation compared to a land-based airport does not stop with the fact that it changes location. This aircraft carrier requires at least 5,000 employees to operate, planning and serving at least 15,000 meals daily from an internal warehouse storing up to 70 days of groceries. In addition to the complexities of aviation and global travel, the carrier operates a nuclear power plant, a desalinization plant for fresh water, and employs at least six doctors in its own 50-plus bed hospital. While the vessel itself is nuclear and only refuels every 15 to 20 years, it must also store and manage several million gallons of aviation fuel onboard, to supply arriving planes.

FIGURE 1.7 Varying Levels of Uncertainty and Control in Operations

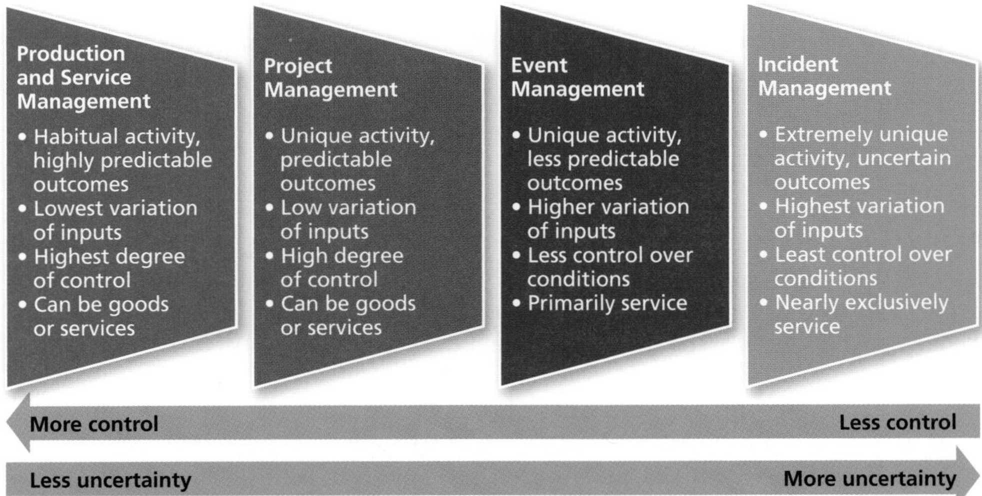

United States, but governmental service operations do make up a significant portion of overall activity within the US nonetheless, accounting for a substantial amount of its gross national product. This aggregated spending represents the provision of services ranging from education to the global logistics of military operations.

Uncertainty and Control

Operations management has historically focused on control. Good control of an operation includes efficient implementation of decisions, accurate prediction of outcomes, and prevention of external interference. These are all reasonable assumptions in some industrial settings, but many modern operations do not enjoy high levels of control, due to the nature of their business.

When control shifts away from a decision maker, uncertainty takes its place, although this person or group must still decide how best to proceed. Operations that are literally exposed to the environment, such as building construction and outdoor events, naturally suffer higher degrees of uncertainty and lower degrees of control. Uncertainty decreases with practice, so managing a unique event presents more uncertainties than the daily management of a long-running operation. When operations management is considered under all possible conditions, it is often loosely subdivided along this range of uncertainty versus control, as illustrated in Figure 1.7.

Production and Service Management Production implies deliberate creation of value over time, such as in the manufacturing of a good or the provision of electricity. While operations management can be argued to be as old as organized human activity, production management was the first form of operations management to be recognized as a teachable business discipline. Mass production minimizes uncertainty because it transforms a narrow range of carefully selected inputs within a facility designed to reliably create only certain outcomes. Ongoing operation of this permanent facility allows for the accumulation of data and experience to use in further improving the efficiency of the system—a methodology known as scientific management.

scientific management A methodology stressing the use of data collection and analysis to redesign processes and improve efficiency.

While high volume production emerged during the Industrial Revolution of the 1770s, production management owes many of its principles to the emergence of scientific management in the early twentieth century, initially championed by the engineer Fredrick W. Taylor. Early production management focused on the manufacturing of goods, but now is equally applicable to services. The routine operation of a multiscreen movie theater is a good example of production management in a service setting, where it can be referred to specifically as service management. Figure 1.6 illustrates this group of goods or service providers as one of four equal-sized categories, although it is important to remember that this left-hand category is the origin and the stronghold of operations management. Most of modern commercial enterprise still falls in this category.

Project Management A project differs from the traditional understanding of production in that a project is completed once, resulting in some unique form of value creation. Projects may create something tangible, such as the construction of a building or the painting of a portrait, or something intangible, such as providing legal service to a particular client concerning a particular case. Some industries are project-based: while the routine operation of a movie theater is as an example of production management, the creation of the movies exhibited in that theater is project-based. The product is unique, but the creation process being governed by project management is still quite predictable; management can make detailed plans and implement these plans with a high degree of efficiency. This uniqueness does, however, usually increase the variability of the inputs required when compared to repetitive production management, increasing uncertainty somewhat and generally increasing the importance of coordination and communication within the system.

project
A unique collection of activities creating a particular outcome.

Project management is arguably older than sustained production management. The Industrial Revolution refers to mass manufacturing taking over from older, more project-based crafting to provide goods. Interestingly, some argue that a revolution in information technology has enabled project management to reclaim much of that territory, as growing sectors of many national economies are dependent on the agile and technology-enabled activities of project-based firms such as software and Web developers. Other firms are under increasing pressure to practice more effective project management within ongoing operations, to respond to the changing conditions of the modern marketplace. Both strategic improvements to existing operations and rapid development of exciting new products rely on teams of employees skilled at project management.

Event and Incident Management The term *event* has several meanings, but the type of operation best known as an event is in fact a particular type of project. The activities associated with the completion of a successful event are undertaken within a known and planned time interval, and thus event planning and management are examples of project management. However, event management is a more challenging form of

Temporary Facilities in Project, Event, and Incident Management

Temporary structures are common to many projects, particularly those subject to higher degrees of uncertainty in the environment. The personnel in this picture are waiting to provide medical assistance during a simulated disaster, working from a series of tents that will serve as a temporary medical center. Similar to these temporary physical facilities, project management often requires use of temporary organizational structures, just as the personnel here are temporarily assigned to this undertaking, leaving their roles in nearby permanent hospitals.

project management because events are highly permeable projects, meaning that they are strongly influenced by their environments. As an example, an event such as an outdoor festival is heavily influenced by issues such as weather and crowd attendance, neither of which managers can plan for precisely or control directly. Although projects in general can provide goods or services, events are usually some form of service involving some issue of performance, and are sometimes described as "softer," meaning more vulnerable, than the "hard" projects discussed under project management, due to their highly dependent and less predictable natures. While filming a movie in a studio requires more traditional project management, staging a concert or play requires event management. Other examples of event management include conference and banquet planning, sports management, scheduled surgery, and time-sensitive logistics.

incident
An unscheduled event requiring immediate resolution.

An incident presents a manager with the maximum challenge of uncertainty, as incidents are essentially unscheduled events that abruptly require completion. Thus, incidents are usually unexpected exceptions or disruptions to other types of planning, creating a need for a specialized form of project management. Incident management includes product recalls, such as the rapid removal of 228 million eggs from US supermarkets in 2010, and large-scale emergencies, such as stopping the high-speed flow of oil from a leaking pipe 1 mile underwater in the Gulf of Mexico. Unlike traditional production management, event and especially incident managers often rely on iterative planning for success. In iterative planning the manager launches and continuously revises plans despite controlling very little of the project and its circumstances. Because the manager is not likely to have all the information needed to create a complete plan before implementation must begin, incidents are the "softest" projects of all.

iterative planning
Deliberately adjusting plans at short intervals, to reflect new information.

While grouping operations in Figure 1.7 clarifies when particular approaches such as scientific management or iterative planning are more or less relevant to certain situations, these four categories do not function separately. It is not uncommon to find two or more in practice within a given operation. Consider for example, managing a large resort hotel. The hotel's efficient daily operation (housekeeping, laundry, and grounds maintenance) is an example of *production management*. Installation and changeover of hotel-wide holiday-themed decorations requires good *project management* to avoid disrupting ongoing operations. Generating revenue from booking, hosting and catering events for guests requires skilled *event management*. Finally, assuring the safety and satisfaction of guests requires careful attention to *incident management*, such as resolving complaints or providing emergency response within the resort.

In Scenario 1a we classify operations for an emergency response provider.

Incident Management in Health Care

The health care industry provides examples of operations subject to higher levels of uncertainty and less direct control than other types of businesses. Emergency medicine requires skillful incident management, because little or no patient information is available to the providers in advance of treatment and current conditions can change rapidly. These issues are made even more challenging when this intervention must be accomplished outside of a permanent facility, such as in the temporary field hospital in this picture. This scene also highlights incident management's dependence on the rapid formation of temporary teams, as the exact skill sets of personnel cannot be matched to the exact needs of an incident in advance.

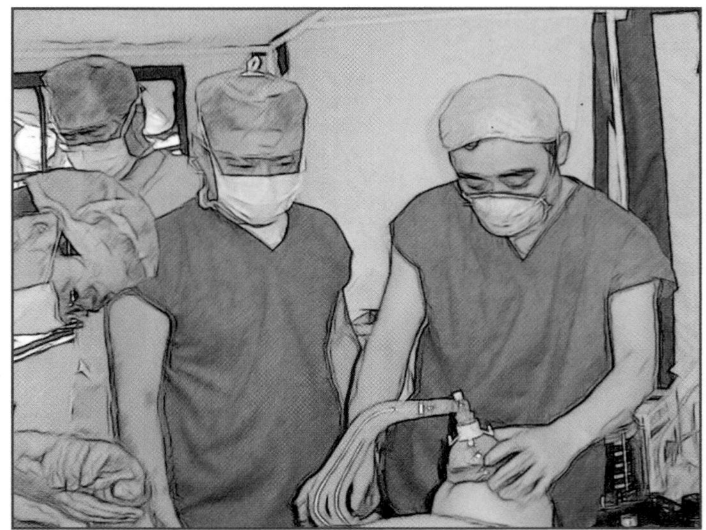

Classifying Operations

Scenario 1a

Regional Disaster Relief Services (RDRS) provides emergency assistance to the victims of large-scale natural disasters. RDRS relies on fund-raising to support its permanent network of 15 warehouses, housing its inventory of tents, trailers, tools, portable lighting, water-filtration equipment, and electrical generators. Upon news of a disaster within its logistical reach, RDRS activates both its permanent staff and groups of volunteers to deploy from one or more of the warehouse headquarters and provide assistance in the field until permanent services are restored to the citizens of the disaster area.

What kind of operation is RDRS?

Analysis

Even with only a brief paragraph of information about RDRS, we know several distinct features of RDRS's operation:

BRIEF ASSESSMENT OF RDRS

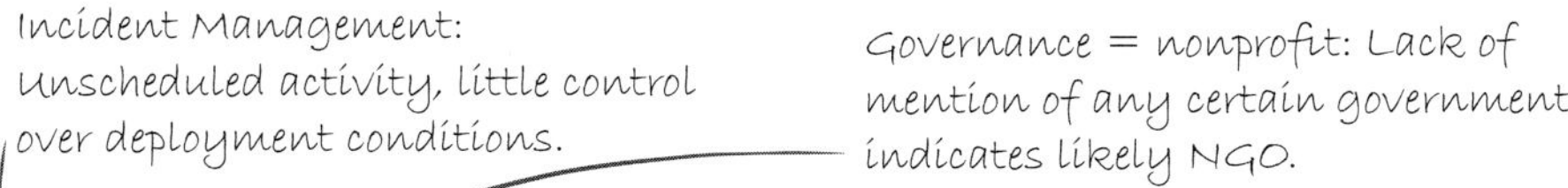

Incident Management:
Unscheduled activity, little control over deployment conditions.
Governance = nonprofit: Lack of mention of any certain government indicates likely NGO.

Repeating and highlighting the paragraph here, "Regional Disaster Relief Services (RDRS) provides emergency assistance to the victims of large-scale natural disasters. RDRS relies on fund-raising to support its permanent network of 15 warehouses, housing its inventory of tents, trailers, tools, portable lighting, water-filtration equipment and electrical generators. Upon news of a disaster within its logistical reach, RDRS activates both its permanent staff and groups of volunteers to deploy from one or more of the warehouse headquarters and provide assistance in the field until permanent services are restored to the citizens of the disaster area."

INPUT/OUTPUT MODEL

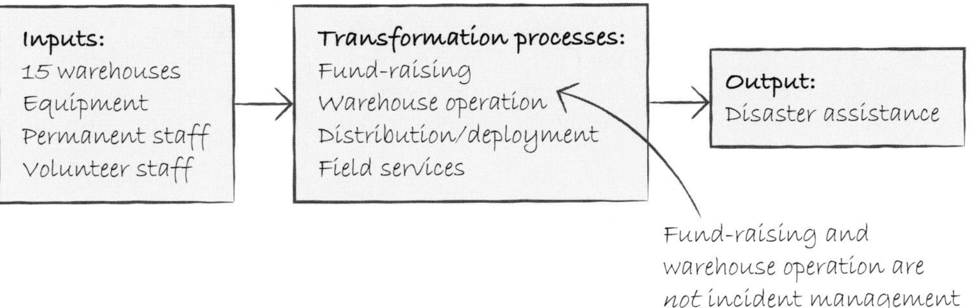

Insight Regional Disaster Relief Services (RDRS), as its name implies, is a service provider, highly reliant on labor and the deployment of stocks of staged equipment. The reference to fund-raising indicates RDRS is a nonprofit organization, and likely an NGO. RDRS provides an interesting example of an operation with both a controlled production management side (its warehouse headquarters and fund-raising operations) and a dynamic, on-demand incident management side (its response and field service operations). ■

OPERATIONS MANAGERS

Since operations management represents the creation of value, just about every purposeful endeavor is practicing (although not necessarily successfully) some aspect of operations management. Operations management is ultimately about decision making, to guide the activities of an organization ever closer to its goals.

Decision Making

All managers are decision makers, selecting alternatives from sets of choices. In the context of organizations, this selection process can be viewed as three layers of an interrelated hierarchy, illustrated in Figure 1.8.

strategy A methodology and resulting plan that identifies the long-term goals of an organization.

planning horizon The farthest point in the future considered in decision making.

business analytics Continuous investigation of business performance using large volumes of data.

Strategic Decisions In the managerial hierarchy of decision making, strategy is depicted at the top-most level because it occurs first. Strategic decision making focuses on selecting the goals and overall direction of an organization, and can also be described as broadscale, long-term planning. If the consequences of a decision, good or bad, will be felt for more than 1 year, it is usually fair to declare it strategic. This issue of how much of the future is considered in and/or influenced by a decision is known as a planning horizon. Traditionally, long planning horizons have implied infrequent decision making, as each decision itself affects one or more of the years ahead. Modern operations, however, are taking increasing advantage of their access to large volumes of current data to guide decision analysis through business analytics, the continuous investigation of incoming data for strategic insights.

Examples of areas within operations management that fit the description of strategic decision making are product design, capacity planning and location planning. While good decisions at the strategic level are critical, note that the hierarchy of decision making does not mean strategic decisions are necessarily more powerful or significant than decisions made elsewhere in the hierarchy. This hierarchy refers only to chronological sequence: strategic decisions are the first and decisive steps in an ongoing process that continues with tactics.

tactics Means to pursue strategic goals with available resources.

Tactical Decisions Much of the management in operations management is devoted to tactics, the ongoing process of determining how to pursue goals. Tactical decision making combines the goal-related input from the strategic level with the reality of resources available, identifying solutions ready for implementation. Tactical decisions also differ

FIGURE 1.8 The Hierarchy of Decision-Making

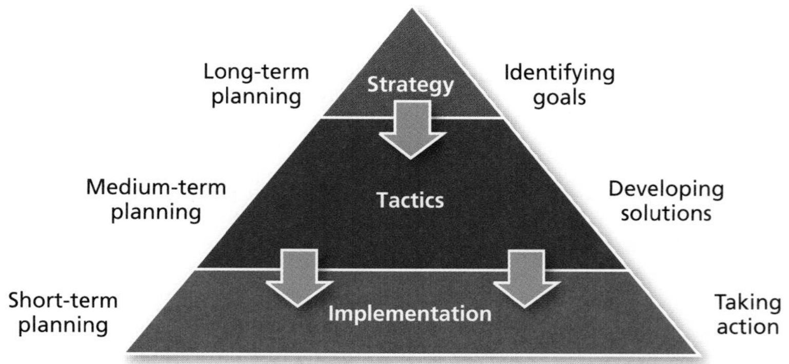

from strategic decisions in that tactics rarely address planning horizons longer than a single year, and may propose solutions only a few weeks in length. Often the focus at the tactical level is optimization, or the development of the best possible solution given the combinination of strategic objective and resource availability. As examples, developing inventory control policies or analyzing waiting lines in a service system often focuses on identifying the least costly alternative. However, the greater the complexity or uncertainty in the planning environment, the more likely tactical decision makers will shift focus to finding good feasible solutions to support strategic goals, as pursuit of one absolute best answer is not practical. Furthermore, at extremely high levels of uncertainty in fast-moving environments, the line between tactical planning and actual implementation becomes quite fuzzy.

Implementation Implementation is the bottom level of the hierarchy of decision making, but no less important. Implementation accepts the solutions identified at the tactical level and puts them into action. Because implementation is guiding action, it is also sometimes referred to as the operational level of the hierarchy, but that label is somewhat of a misnomer because operations management spans the entire area illustrated in Figure 1.8, not simply the base of the pyramid. Implementation involves short-term decisions and may involve very little decision making if the operation enjoys high degrees of control and certainty. As an example, operation of an assembly line at this level consists of assuring that the appropriate personnel and materials required by the tactical design of the assembly line are actually in place for its daily operation. This can involve many small decisions, such as which employee should staff which workstation along the line. In contrast, implementation may require substantial decision making and creativity in situations such as disaster relief, where the overall strategic goal is fairly obvious and implementation must begin before there is time to create a complete and detailed plan at the tactical level.

We explore the hierarchy of decision making further in Scenario 1b.

Classifying Operational Decisions

Scenario 1b

Regional Disaster Relief Services (RDRS) owns a fleet of 500 all-terrain vehicles (ATVs), stationed among its 15 warehouse locations when not in use. Normally, RDRS relies on other agencies for air transport in disaster areas, but recently it proposed the purchase of six helicopters during a joint meeting of its warehouse managers. The RDRS managers were not excited by the opportunity, arguing that ground operations had always been the core competency of RDRS and that it was more important to resolve disputes over the proper allocation of ATVs than to acquire aviation at great expense. These disputes refer to several warehouses located close to large wilderness areas having no idle ATVs available since last spring, keeping their ATVs deployed in support of relief operations throughout the wildfire season instead. These warehouse managers would prefer that idle ATVs from urban-area RDRS warehouses be transferred to their warehouses, but urban RDRS managers argue against this. Urban managers point out that the wilderness area managers are without ATVs because they leave their ATVs in remote areas for long periods, speculating that an additional emergency might occur even after the initial rescue or evacuation is completed. The urban warehouse managers suggest that, if the wilderness area managers want more ATVs sitting in their warehouses, then they should put more effort into promptly retrieving the ones already assigned to them.

How many different decisions have been discussed at this joint meeting of the warehouse managers? At what level in the hierarchy of decision making are these decisions?

Continues

Analysis

This discussion at the RDRS warehouse manager's meeting included three distinct decision points, at three different levels in the hierarchy. We can highlight the first decision like this:

HELICOPTER PURCHASING DECISION

To buy or not to buy?

Acquisition of helicopters would significantly broaden the scope of RDRS

Repeating and highlighting the paragraph here, "The RDRS managers were not excited about the opportunity, arguing that ground operations had always been the core competency of RDRS and that it was more important to resolve the dispute over the proper allocation of ATVs than to acquire aviation at great expense."

*Long-term consequences and risk = **strategic***

The second decision frames the dispute between the warehouse managers, while the third decision is the pushback proposal from the urban warehouse managers:

ATV FLEET ALLOCATION DECISION

Where should the ATVs be assigned?

*Resource Allocation = **tactical***

Again, we repeat the key sentences: "it was more important to resolve disputes over the proper allocation of ATVs than to acquire aviation at great expense. These disputes refer to several warehouses located close to large wilderness areas having no idle ATVs available since last spring, keeping their ATVs deployed in support of relief operations throughout the wildfire season instead. These warehouse managers would prefer that idle ATVs from urban-area RDRS warehouses be transferred to their warehouses."

ATV RETRIEVAL DECISION

How soon after a remote assignment should an ATV be returned to its warehouse?

Key sentences: "Wilderness area managers are without ATVs because they leave their ATVs in remote areas for long periods, speculating that an additional emergency might occur even after the initial rescue or evacuation is completed. The urban warehouse managers suggest that, if the wilderness area managers want more ATVs sitting in their warehouses, then they should put more effort into promptly retrieving the ones already assigned to them.

*Leaving their ATVs on speculation versus retrieving ATVs promptly concern actions = **implementation***

Insight The RDRS warehouse managers discussed three decisions at three different levels of decision making. The opportunity to acquire helicopters is an issue of strategy; it calls for a significant change to the scope of RDRS's operations, with the considerable risk that comes with a large investment outside of its past experience. The dispute over the ATVs is tactical decision making; it is a proposal to reconfigure the distribution of an existing set of resources. Urban warehouse managers are resisting that change by proposing that wilderness area managers change how they currently deploy ATVs. Resolving this suggestion directly guides future actions and is easily reversed if it proves unsuccessful, both strong indications of implementation-level decision making. ■

Operations Management within an Organization

Operations management is a distinct discipline with a membership of people who spend the majority of their time directly involved with operational issues. Locating operations management in an organization begins with considering how it relates to other business disciplines within that particular organization. Operations is considered one of the three central functions of any business organization, sharing this distinction with the disciplines of marketing and finance, while other disciplines such as information technology and human resources support this combined endeavor. Although active in any organization, operations is not necessarily of equal significance relative to other business functions, given the nature of the organization. Figure 1.9 gives four illustrations of the relative mix of these three functions in four different organizations.

In retailing organizations such as car dealerships or supermarkets, marketing naturally plays a central role in the success of the enterprise. However, a supermarket can be considered a somewhat more operations-intensive endeavor than a car dealership, as the nature of its inventory is more complex (multiple suppliers, thousands of items) and not as readily storable for long periods. Similarly, operations management is a concern in both banking and health care, but the lower half of Figure 1.9 emphasizes the hospital

Relative Mix of the Three Business Functions in Various Firms | **FIGURE 1.9**

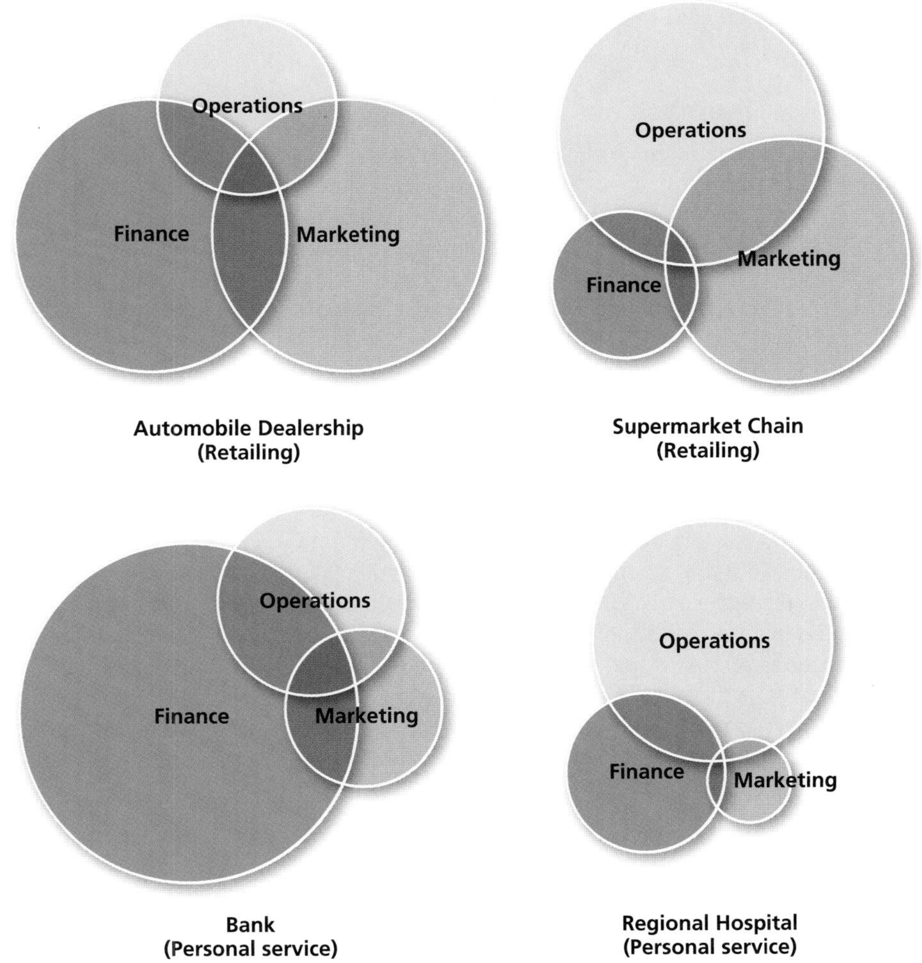

as extremely operations-intensive, requiring the simultaneous coordination of many different patients and professionals, rapid scheduling of a wide variety of resources, and management of a diversity of inventory and information.

Jobs and Job Titles in Operations

Successful entrepreneurs have a solid understanding of operations, fully aware that marketing and finance alone will not keep them afloat. You've probably seen an establishment boasting an "owner operated" plaque. Within larger organizations, people who specialize in operations may be called operations managers, but can also be found working under other job titles:

- Anyone called a manager or a planner in combination with another term is usually dedicated to that aspect of operations management. Examples include production planners, supply chain managers, project managers, and event planners.
- Any job title that indicates responsibility for a mission-critical asset usually focuses on the operation of that asset. Examples here include store manager, branch manager, plant manager, fleet manager, and location manager.
- Other operations-intensive job titles indicate a particular subject area within the discipline of operations that the holder of the title specializes in, such as scheduler, inventory planner, or quality coordinator.

Finally, many consultants work intensively in operations management, particularly when providing assistance with information systems development, business process mapping, and quality improvements.

Professional Organizations and Certifications

Organizations for operations professionals serve a variety of purposes, including social networking and recruiting, developing and distributing new knowledge in the discipline, and recognizing those who have achieved particular levels of knowledge through exams and certifications. Some organizations consist largely of practitioners, while others represent gatherings of practitioners, consultants, and academics. Regardless of their particular emphasis, these groups generally welcome the participation of interested students.

Professional Societies Professional societies are dedicated to supporting the knowledge base of the profession and supporting the careers of those who pursue it. Thus, these societies focus on practitioners and often offer education and certification specific to the profession. Here are some of the most widely recognized professional societies for operations management:

- APICS, The Association for Operations Management (www.apics.org). APICS offers one of the oldest and most widely recognized credentialing programs in operation management, the five-exam CPIM (Certified in Production and Inventory Management).
- ISM, The Institute for Supply Management (www.ism.ws). ISM offers a variety of certifications in purchasing, procurement, and supply chain management, including the CPSM (Certified Professional in Supply Management).
- PMI, Project Management Institute (www.pmi.org). PMI offers a variety of certifications in project management and scheduling, including the PMP, or Project Management Professional.

Professional societies are generally organized into local chapters that meet periodically for educational and networking opportunities, and host larger annual conferences to do the same across regions. These societies often welcome student membership with discounted fees, to support their early pursuit of professional credentials and to provide students with wider access to job networking opportunities.

Academic Societies Other societies consist largely of researchers, professors, and students of subjects related to operations management:

- POMS, The Production and Operations Management Society (www.poms.org).
- DSI, The Decision Sciences Institute (www.decisionsciences.org).
- INFORMS, The Institute for Operations Research and the Management Sciences (www.informs.org).
- The OR Society or Operational Research Society (www.orsoc.org.uk).

Academic societies emphasize the publication and distribution of new research findings, as well as the further development of instructional curriculum. Similar to professional societies, academic societies host regional and international conferences for the exchange of ideas and often welcome student membership at discounted prices.

About this Book

In a certain sense, this book is an operation, whose inputs include paper stock, ink, specialized publishing software, and readers. Hopefully, its outputs are not limited to a somewhat more used version of its physical self once read. To achieve positive value-added, this book must assist in the creation of knowledge, and maybe even enthusiasm, for its subject. It relies heavily on a blended process of written narrative, conceptual graphics, anecdotal illustrations, and practice problems. In the spirit of productivity (every reader has a limited budget of time), the book uses these processes in a consistent fashion within each of its 15 chapters, allowing you to anticipate the road ahead and steer according to your own preferences.

Operations management is a broad topic, and each of the 15 chapters also belongs to one of four smaller focus groups:

- **Chapters 1–4: Essentials.** The first four chapters are devoted to getting started in some sense. This chapter lays out the domain of operations management, a theme that Chapter 2 continues with its discussion of business and operations strategy, including an expanded discussion of productivity. Chapter 3 examines the end product—specifically, how it is chosen and improved. Chapter 4 then supplies the last puzzle pieces needed to get started, some estimate of the future ahead.
- **Chapters 5–8: Planning Operations.** These four chapters borrow mostly from the strategic top of the decision-making pyramid in Figure 1.8, discussing capacity planning and waiting, process and facility selection, project management, and location planning and logistics. These are all complex decisions to be weighed carefully in advance, the essence of good planning.
- **Chapters 9–12: Managing Operations.** These chapters begin travel toward the base of the pyramid in Figure 1.8, beginning with Chapter 9, where we explore vital distinctions between strategic and tactical choices. The remaining three chapters discuss contrasting applications of tactical decision making as inventory management, aggregate and material requirements planning, and lean operations.
- **Chapters 13–15: Action and Adaptation.** The final three chapters of this book are "in the moment," where choices have been made and set in motion, but operations management is far from finished. Chapter 13 describes how ongoing processes can be monitored and managed even as they operate. Chapter 14 explores planning that can't be done in advance and yet may have to be done repeatedly. Chapter 15 concludes with the reality that plans rarely unfold precisely as anticipated, the ultimate challenge in operations management.

Although the chapters follow a logical progression, reading and working through them in numerical order is not mandatory. Each chapter strives to be its own argument for its corner of the larger domain.

SUMMARY

Operations management is a paradox. It is both the oldest and one of the youngest business disciplines, evident when a single entrepreneur opens a small business, a nonprofit organization musters volunteers to fill sandbags against flooding, and a large corporation carefully coordinates shipments across a global supply chain. Each of these settings contains the creation of value, the singular mission of a successful operation.

Operations management bundles together all actions required to create value. These actions transform inputs into a more valuable set of outputs, including but not limited to finished products for the customer. The relative success of this process is expressed by its productivity, although long-term success of the operation should hinge upon sustainable and responsible management practices as well. Virtually any organized undertaking can be thought of as an operation, and thus it is useful to categorize similar operations according to important shared features such as tangibility of the product or level of uncertainty in the operating environment. Operations managers can likewise be found in most organizations, working under a variety of related job titles.

Key Terms

bill of materials
biomimicry
business analytics
ethics
goods
green
incident
inventory
iterative planning
lean
local optimization
NGO
operations
planning horizon
processes
productivity
project
responsibility
scientific management
services
stockpiling
strategy
supply chain
sustainability
tactics
tangibility
value-added
value chain
value creation

Discussion Questions

1. Which is more important, strategic or tactical decision making?
2. How does the hierarchy of decision making relate to these four categories of operations: production, project, event, and incident management?
3. Why is the measurement of productivity more challenging in the provision of services, when compared to measuring the productivity of a goods-producing operation?
4. What are the advantages that can be gained if a product does not necessarily need to be consumed at the place it is produced, and how does this relate to supply chain management?
5. Does a pure good exist? If so, what would be an example? Can a pure service exist?
6. Why would sustainability alone not necessarily guarantee the survival of an organization?
7. Identify several situations in which more than one of the following would be practiced simultaneously: production management, project management, event management, and incident management.

PROBLEMS

Minute Answer

Short answers appear in Appendix A. Go to **NoteShaper.com** for full video tutorials on each question.

1. Consider a shipping company that carries freight by truck. Name three inputs to this operation.
2. Value-added refers to the difference in the overall value of what and what?
3. In the hierarchy of decision making, what level is below strategic decision making?
4. Does a service operation usually experience higher or lower variability in its inputs and outputs, when compared to goods production?
5. Ethics are principles that define what?
6. What is the farthest point in the future considered in decision making called?
7. Optimization refers to the identification of what?
8. What are tangible goods awaiting sale or use called?
9. Which involves the greatest degree of uncertainty, an event or an incident?
10. What does NGO stand for?
11. Does a service operation often require higher or lower capital investment at start-up, when compared to goods production?
12. Is the objective of efficiency likely to be more central to planning in production or incident management?

Quick Start

13. A bank must decide which branch office to assign the account of a particularly important and high-maintenance client. Is this an example of a strategic, tactical, or implementation level of decision?
14. A bank must decide if a particular branch office should be closed and its current location sold to another bank. Is this an example of a strategic, tactical, or implementation level of decision?
15. A bank has just received an electronic signal that one of its ATMs is out of service due to a lack of cash to distribute. The bank must decide whether to send a courier to restock the ATM immediately (after business hours) or to allow it to remain out of service until the main banking operation opens the following business day. Is this an example of a strategic, tactical, or implementation level of decision?
16. An organization must decide whether a particular shipment should be sent by air freight or surface (ground) trucking. Is this an example of a strategic, tactical, or implementation level of decision?
17. An organization must decide between Singapore, London, or Buffalo as the location for the construction of a new manufacturing facility. Is this an example of a strategic, tactical, or implementation level of decision?

Ramp Up

18. Consider the following four situations: negotiating a lease for drilling oil, drilling for oil, refining fuel from oil, and transporting fuel orders to retail locations by tanker trucks. Now consider the following grid, which indicates four positions marked A,

B, C, and D. Each of these positions indicates differing levels of tangibility and control over an operation's external environment:

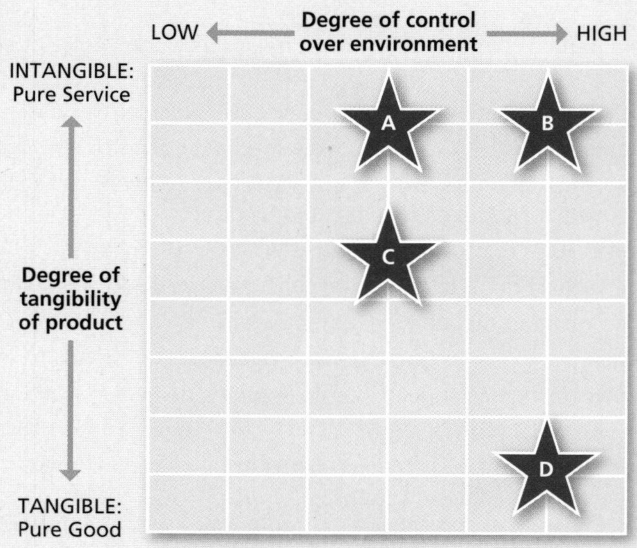

Match each of the four points on the grid to each of the four operations proposed, assuming each grid location can be used only once.

19. Consider the following five situations: maintenance of a network of ATMs, production and packaging of cake mix, a barn raising in which an entire fast-food restaurant is torn down and completely replaced in 48 hours, hosting and promotion of the performance of a touring musical group, and repair of an electrical grid to restore electricity to homes after a storm. Now consider the following grid, which indicates five positions marked A, B, C, D, and E. Each of these positions indicates differing levels of tangibility and operation types:

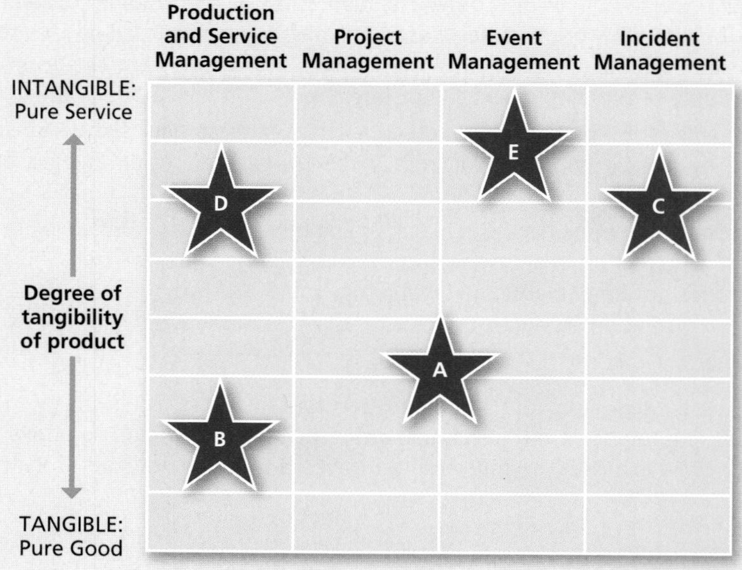

Match each of the five points on the grid to each of the four operations proposed, assuming each grid location can be used only once.

CASE STUDY: CONVEX PRODUCTIONS

Convex Productions produces full-length motion pictures for distribution worldwide. Convex has just purchased the rights to a movie script entitled *Native Sun*, which it intends to develop as its next project. *Native Sun* is the story of an orphaned human raised by an alien race, visiting Earth on business and becoming entangled in intrigue there. Its simultaneous classification as science fiction/fantasy and action/adventure is expected to draw a broad audience, and Convex hopes to minimize production costs by recruiting the best business partners early.

Convex cannot start until it raises the funding necessary to film *Native Sun*. At this point, Convex is confident it can finance most of *Native Sun* through a combination of its own cash and a substantial outside investment from executive production company and long-time partner Malomar Pictures. Bringing in Malomar Pictures as a silent partner also secures its subsidary Malomar Worldwide as the distributor of *Native Sun* to theaters upon its release. Other early agreements, providing smaller amounts of initial cash, are listed in the Tentative Licensees table below.

Tentative Licensees in Addition to Malomar Worldwide

Licensee	Subject of License
Stratospheric LLC	Nontheatrical distribution, primarily airlines. Does not include home distribution.
Manta Distribution	All home distribution rights, including the sale of physical formats, video-on-demand, and eventual syndication to television.
Main House Gaming	Permission to create and sell *Native Sun* module for existing *Solar Twilight* multiplayer computer game.
JAZ Events	Production and distribution of all nonelectronic merchandise, including *Native Sun*–themed toys and apparel.

With this combined funding, Convex Productions can launch the preproduction phase of *Native Sun*. Convex intends to run the *Native Sun* production office out of its own organization, so it must begin its search for a director, assistant director, casting director, and production designer immediately. Convex will also contribute a unit production manager, legal services, and storyboard artists from its own staff. Convex hopes this combined group will then complete all preproduction work in no more than 6 months, recruiting the cast and crew and creating the detailed plans to follow during filming. Although Convex is a producer of major motion pictures, it does not itself own any of the infrastructure required for filming. Before the preproduction work of *Native Sun* is finished, Convex must finalize negotiations with several key contractors listed in the Tentative Contracts table, below, to move forward.

Tentative Contractors for *Native Sun*

Contractor	Services Provided
Lamplight Studios	Three sound stages for filming and all associated equipment. Also provides filming equipment and support on location.
Epic Scenery Studios	Scenery and costume construction.
Visual Effects Factory	Special effects, computer-generated imagery, and postproduction filming editing.
Rayburn Logistics	All ground transportation and fleet management, including shipment of scenery pieces from Epic to Lamplight Studios and diesel generators for electricity on location.
Great Plains Catering	All food service, all locations. Includes catering of promotional events and edibles used in the film.

Ideally, all filming and postproduction would be completed within a year of the conclusion of preproduction, although the exact finish time is difficult to estimate this early in the preproduction process. Because investors in *Native Sun* won't receive any return until the finished film starts selling tickets at Palomar Worldwide's theater outlets, Convex Production must use part of its own cash now to purchase a completion insurance policy. This policy covers part of the risk of Convex's business partners should *Native Sun* not finish as planned, which is vital to winning their confidence and investment at this stage in the process.

Questions

1. Write a paragraph describing Convex Production as an operation. Does Convex produce goods or services? What type of operation is it? What does it control and what are its uncertainties?
2. Use the input/output model to diagram *Native Sun* as an operation, organizing the information provided here beneath the three stages suggested by the model.
3. Now use the input/output model to diagram Convex Productions as an operation, organizing the information provided here beneath the three stages suggested by the model.
4. What do your two diagrams reveal about the relationship between *Native Sun* and Convex Productions? (Why are they not identical diagrams?)

BIBLIOGRAPHY

Austin, R., and L. Devin. 2003. *Artful Making: What Managers Need to Know About How Artists Work.* Upper Saddle River, NJ: FT Prentice Hall.

Binkley, C. 2010. "On Style: How Green is My Sneaker?" *The Wall Street Journal*, July 22, p. D1.

Crawford, L., and J. Pollack. 2004. "Hard and Soft Projects: A Framework for Analysis." *International Journal of Project Management* 22: 645–53.

Gore, A., and D. Blood. 2010. "Toward Sustainable Capitalism." *The Wall Street Journal*, July 24, p. A21.

Gowdy, J. 2007. "Avoiding Self-Organized Extinction: Toward a Co-evolutionary Economics of Sustainability." *International Journal of Sustainable Development & World Ecology* 14: 27–36

Hayes, R. 2002. "Challenges Posed to Operations Management by the 'New Economy.'" *Production and Operations Management* 11(1): 21–32.

Lubin, D., and D. Esty. 2010. "The Sustainable Imperative." *Harvard Business Review* (May): 43–50.

Meredith, J. 2001. "Hopes for the Future of Operations Management." *Journal of Operations Management* 19: 397–402.

Paine, T. 1776/1986. *Common Sense*. New York: Penguin Books.

Senge, P., G. Carstedt, and P. Porter. 2010. "Innovating our Way to the Next Industrial Revolution." *MIT Sloan Management Review* 42(2): 24–38.

Sprague, L. 2007. "Evolution of the Field of Operations Management." *Journal of Operations Management* 25: 219–38.

Voss, C. 2007. "Learning from the First Operations Management Textbook." *Journal of Operations Management* 25: 239–47.

PART 1 ESSENTIALS

CHAPTER 2

Providing Goods and Services

I stayed in a really old hotel last night. They sent me a wakeup letter.

—Steven Wright

MAJOR SECTIONS

IN THIS CHAPTER, LOOK FOR...

- The distinction between and blending of business strategy and operations strategy.
- Ongoing trends such as enterprise resource planning, business analytics, and globalization.
- Sources of competitive advantage.
- Broad options in processing, and their ties back to competitive strategy.
- Product life cycle.
- Productivity as a numerical measure of process performance.

INTRODUCTION

Any organization, large or small, must first choose its purpose for existence, and then pursue that purpose through its operations. Once the initial choices are made, an organization identifies strategies and develops plans to bring its operations into action. For successful organizations, strategic decision making is never truly finished, but rather evolves throughout the lifespan of the organization. We begin by looking at the planning process available to best guide this evolution.

BUSINESS STRATEGY

strategy
A methodology and resulting plan that identifies the long-term goals of an organization.

In general, a strategy is a long-term plan, committing a person or organization to a particular path toward certain goals. In business strategy, this planning process is expected to flow through a series of stages, pictured in Figure 2.1. Decisions made at each stage are then carefully expressed in a series of public statements.

Vision, Mission, and Values

vision
An organization's defining statement about the future.

The vision, mission, and values of an organization are the highest statements of why the organization exists, what is to be achieved through its activities, and how the organization will pursue these goals. An organization's vision statement provides the why and where, describing the future that represents the organization's overarching reason for

FIGURE 2.1 **Individual Elements of the Strategic Planning Process**

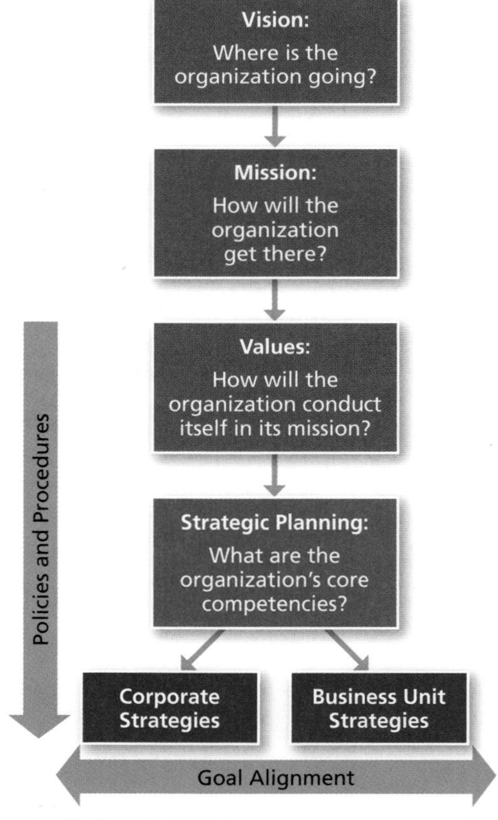

existence. Vision statements usually dedicate the business to some broad picture of the future, such as the industrial equipment manufacturer Caterpillar's vision:

> "Be a global leader in customer value."

A mission statement establishes how an organization is going to create its vision of the future. The vision statement of the Scottish Prison Service, a governmental organization, is similar to Caterpillar's in that it expresses the desire for recognition of leadership. Its mission statement, however, provides a detailed list of actions to pursue that particular future:

mission
An organization's statement about what it's doing to meet its vision.

> "To keep in custody those committed by the courts, to care for prisoners with humanity, to play a full role in the integration of offender management services..."

The mission statement of soft-drink manufacturer Coca-Cola provides a similar pattern of broad activity toward a vision:

> "To refresh the world, to inspire moments of optimism and happiness, to create value and make a difference..."

As Figure 2.1 illustrates, a vision statement declares a direction and a mission statement chooses a path forward in that direction, so it is expected that a mission statement might change over time, as changing conditions might change the best path, but the corporate vision should remain fairly constant.

Although vision and mission are two distinct concepts, not all organizations develop two distinct statements, often focusing on mission instead. While service company Google lacks a single definitive vision statement, its mission statement is itself a powerful vision of the future:

> "To organize the world's information and make it universally accessible and useful."

Other companies fuse the vision and mission into a single combined statement, such as this vision followed by mission statement for Internet retailer Amazon:

> "To be earth's most customer centric company; to build a place where people can come to find and discover anything they might want to buy online."

An organization should state its core values alongside its vision and mission. A value statement specifies the principles that will determine how the organization behaves in achieving its mission and vision. As an example, Coca-Cola states its guiding values as:

> "Leadership, Collaboration, Passion, Diversity, and Integrity."

The emphasis of a value statement is on behaviors and ethics, as it is these values that shape decision making as the mission statement flows into detailed policies and practices. Once the highest-level vision, mission, and value statements are formulated, the strategic planning process can begin.

Strategic Business Plans

Business plans flow from the vision, mission, and value statements of an organization. Here decision making begins to combine internal conditions (such as available resources) with the external environment (such as interactions with customers, competitors, and government regulations). Large organizations often establish both corporate and business unit strategies from the earlier phases of strategic planning, creating the branches visible at the bottom of Figure 2.1. Corporate strategies further define the area of business in which the organization will compete overall, and allocate its internal resources to support that strategy. Large organizations are often divided into smaller business units, and it is not uncommon for each of these units to then develop a vision, mission, and business unit strategy, all adapted from the broader organizational decisions made earlier. However, at the point that different divisions, business units, or departments all express individualized versions of some larger plan, the problem of goal alignment becomes critical. Goal alignment is achieved if all the separate plans suggested across the bottom of Figure 2.1 are compatible with each other and support the planning indicated higher on the diagram. One common example of weak goal alignment is two business units separately deciding to compete in the same market, placing them in direct competition with one another. Another example is each of two business units deciding upon a major capital investment such as factory expansion, when they could coordinate or share the investment to the benefit of the larger organization. Good goal alignment cannot be achieved without good communication across the entire structure of an organization, a requirement that presents greater challenges as organizations become larger and internally more complex.

business unit
A segment of a larger organization, usually managed as a profit-and-loss center.

goal alignment
Developing goals compatible among business units and consistent with higher-level goals of that organization.

Supporting Strategic Plans through Operations

Historically, competitive advantage often derived from the ownership of tangible assets, such as the massive manufacturing complexes of Ford Motor Company or Bethlehem Steel. Changes in technology in the 1980s marked a turning point in this history, when companies such as Walmart, owning relatively little physical infrastructure, emerged to dominate their markets. These companies leveraged largely intangible abilities such as supply chain partnering to enhance their own operations while making use of the capabilities of other organizations, an approach to competitiveness largely unheard of at that time. Such breakthroughs with operations have evolved into now familiar strategies for many industries, supported in part by several interrelated trends: enterprise resource planning, data mining and business analytics, e-commerce, globalization, and sustainability.

Enterprise Resource Planning Computer applications in business began as isolated programs assisting in certain tasks or functions, such as inventory control, machine scheduling, or payroll. As the supporting technology improved, so did these programs, and one critical improvement was the integration of different applications and the sharing of databases across an organization. The resulting enterprise resource planning (ERP) system provides one electronic platform across which all users within an organization share the same data and information, updating all corners of the system as they make decisions in real-time. For example, consider a customer service representative who must cancel an online order that has not yet shipped. In an ERP system, that representative enters this decision once, but that single entry alerts the packing department to the cancellation, automatically updates the current inventory available, refunds the charge to the customer's credit card, and records the unusual incident for follow-up by a quality improvement team.

enterprise resource planning (ERP)
A strategic information system that integrates all functional areas of an organization.

Installation of an ERP system was itself a popular business strategy in the 1990s, fueled in part by its emergence at a time when many businesses feared their older, isolated applications might fall prey to the so-called Y2K bug in the year 2000. While potentially

Enterprise Resource Planning (ERP) in Retail Chains

Retailers operating chain stores must stock multiple locations with goods from a single inventory system. These retailers often depend heavily on their ERP systems to provide holistic views of inventory transactions that are otherwise scattered across a wide area. The pharmacist pictured here accesses an ERP system as she discusses the availability of a product with a customer. The computer screen reports both the amount available in the local stock behind her, the corresponding amounts available at nearby stores in the same retail chain, and any inbound orders for new stock.

costly to implement, the benefits of ERP include automation of once cumbersome transactions, better utilization of resources through real-time visibility of assets, better goal alignment in decision making across otherwise separate units, and lower inventory levels from better control. An ERP system also enables integration of an organization's internal information system with those of its partner organizations such as suppliers, allowing this organization to work seamlessly with and benefit from outside capabilities. Finally, ERP systems offer the ability to accumulate large quantities of data in an orderly fashion, creating the necessary foundation for business analytics.

Data Mining and Business Analytics Mathematical analysis seeks patterns and relationships in data, to glean useful information. Operations management embodies this process, employing mathematics to explore and improve ongoing activity. As the volume of available business data increased with the growth of information technology, the concept of a data warehouse emerged. A data warehouse is a database into which current data from operational systems are steadily uploaded for later analysis and reporting. A data warehouse at the heart of an active ERP system stores large amounts of organized data uploaded from different areas of the organization, which can then be analyzed for new patterns through a process known as data mining. When the data warehouse and analytical processes such as data mining are used in support of business strategy, this powerful combination of technology, process, and goal is known as business analytics. This newer source of potential competitive advantage differs from earlier applications of mathematical analysis to business in three key ways:

data warehouse Database of an organization's ongoing operations archived for analysis and decision support.

data mining Analysis of data in search of new patterns and relationships.

business analytics Continuous investigation of business performance using large volumes of data.

- **Business analytics is an ongoing, iterative process.** Historically, decision makers in an organization might pause, collect data, and conduct a particular investigation through the use of quantitative analytical techniques. Business analytics proposes continuous use of those techniques, as strategy is constantly guided through back-and-forth iterations of investigation. This reconceiving of the activity called data analysis is similar to the iterative planning habits of operations adapted to rapidly changing environments.
- **Business analytics focuses on the discovery of new insight within data.** Data crunching is not a new process, but this ability is traditionally used to monitor known issues through established performance metrics. While this provides valuable information, it does not take full advantage of the data or the analytical techniques.
- **Business analytics integrates data across products, departments, or other natural divisions within the organization.** Without the benefit of a data warehouse

iterative planning Deliberately adjusting plans at short intervals to reflect new information.

compiling data feeds from different areas such as sales, accounts, and production simultaneously, analysts would often work with the data of each area separately, to investigate issues of that area specifically. Working from the strengths of an ERP system, business analytics can investigate issues across these boundaries, to better inform strategic decision making for the entire organization.

While business analytics adds new power to strategic planning, its success depends first on the ready availability of quality data. Given that the data warehouse is in place, business analytics strengthens the feedback loop from operational activity to the strategy level of the firm.

e-commerce
Buying and selling product through electronic transactions.

business-to-business (B2B)
Commercial transactions between organizations.

business-to-consumer (B2C)
Commercial transactions between an organization and individual consumers.

E-Commerce Although businesses began interacting electronically many years earlier, the full potential of so-called e-commerce did not become apparent until the growth of Internet usage in the 1990s. To date, the earlier business-to-business activity remains a significant part of e-commerce, as firms still seek greater efficiencies through seamless electronic ordering and payment of their suppliers. This integration advanced further with the opportunity to link ERP systems, fostering coordination between supply chain partners. However, it is the Internet that enabled this same process to support business-to-consumer transactions, creating much of the e-tailing market of today. The advent of e-commerce transformed some firms like banks and travel agencies completely, and reshaped almost every other industry with the new opportunities and threats posed by an Internet-empowered customer.

The seamless flexibility of e-commerce is now the norm, an expectation of the modern business environment. However, while e-commerce speeds transactions and facilitates the flow of information, it rarely provides a product by itself. Thus, e-commerce often brings operations to the center of business strategy, as organizations then strive to successfully serve the complex, fluid, and time-sensitive market it creates.

third-party logistics (3PL)
Outsourcing logistics activities to a provider.

Globalization Globalization refers to the formation of international networks and systems. While globalization includes concepts such as social networking and holistic views of the human experience, it is the globalization of trade networks that has particular relevance to business strategy and operations management. In the 1990s, advances in information technology combined with a series of historical trade agreements to create new conditions such that even smaller companies could explore sourcing opportunities virtually anywhere in the world. Within another decade, much of that sourcing had been won by manufacturers in Asia, creating many of the global supply chain networks familiar today. The concept of third-party logistics (3PL) emerged from this shift, as some companies specialized in moving goods between distant supply chain partners, an information-intensive industry unto itself. Responding to the trend of globalization, goods and service providers broadened their strategies to recognize both new opportunities in sourcing and potential new markets in a global strategy.

Globalization continues to evolve, and business strategy with it. Although complex supply chain networks can tap into efficiencies and talent across the world, these vast logistical networks are sensitive to fuel prices and widely exposed to naturally occurring disruptions. Volcanic eruptions in Iceland or floods in Thailand no longer inflict damage on those locations alone, but disrupt and even paralyze commercial activity in seemingly unrelated locations through their supply chain links. The next phase of globalization may see organizations developing multiple sourcing options worldwide, creating global networks of regional centers from which to respond and adapt to ever-changing conditions.

Sustainability Sustainability is a requirement for any operation to survive in the long run, an imperative independent of technological innovation or changing trade patterns. However, some argue that sustainability is taking over from globalization as the next megatrend in business strategy, noting that increasing numbers of companies recognize

Labor-Intensive Processes in Modern Manufacturing

Although technology has transformed manufacturing, not all modern mass manufacturing relies on sophisticated equipment instead of people. For example, denim jeans are assembled through largely manual processes such as the rivet setting in this picture. Following the trend of globalization, much of this processing has shifted and concentrated in countries offering the lowest cost of the labor critical to this type of production. Furthermore, much of this work has shifted as subcontracting, in which the original organization hires a local organization to produce on its behalf. In some cases, this has put the corporate value statement at the center of a new controversy: if the quality of life of a subcontractor's employees is not consistent with the values that an organization dedicates itself to on behalf of its own employees, is that organization upholding its own values? If not, then does this responsibility stop with the first subcontractor, or does it extend farther along the supply chain? If so, how is the original organization to know what values are practiced by the subcontractor's suppliers, with whom it has no direct contact?

renewable energy and sustainable resource practices as new areas for profitability and market growth. The continued evolution of globalization to increase the resilience of supply chain networks is consistent with the mission of sustainability, blurring the distinction between these two megatrends.

OPERATIONS STRATEGY

Once vision, mission, and values are declared, operations moves an organization toward its envisioned future, following the path defined by the mission and value statements. Many strategic decisions remain at this point, translating earlier strategy statements into actionable plans for the organization. During this translation, operations strategy must identify and clarify the products to be offered and how these products will compete for customers. Choices made here then inform strategic selection of processes to create these products, to best use existing resources in pursuit of vision and mission. This use of resources must then be measured and monitored, as it represents the vital issue of productivity.

Core Competencies and Competitive Strategy

Large corporations often organize and evaluate themselves according to their output, creating internal divisions dedicated to certain markets, certain product lines, or both. While this is a sensible and functional framework, it can hide an issue critical to the long-run success of that company, its core competency. A core competency is a distinct set of abilities unique to that company, the theoretical source of its competitive advantage. By definition, a core competency does not necessarily reside inside a single division of a large organizational structure. Consider Honda Motor Company: Its worldwide production includes competitive offerings in automobiles, motor cycles, electrical generators, outboard motors, off-road vehicles, and lawn equipment. However, its core competency does not concern any of these products in particular. Honda is recognized globally for "engines and powertrains," which lie at the heart of each of the products mentioned.

core competency Specific ability that distinguishes a business from its competitors.

By definition, competitive strategies should follow from core competencies, and core competencies themselves are usually found in operations, because they reflect the capabilities of a system. Furthermore, identifying a core competency within a complex system is vital for reasons beyond simply identifying the source of the system's current success. Core competencies are believed to power the development of new products, as reflected in Honda's innovative expansion into a diversity of uses for internal combustion engines. A core competency, if unrecognized, can also be eroded by the outsourcing of processes critical to the competency, a decision that might appear sensible if those processes are considered only in isolation. Once an organization has declared its core competency, it typically chooses one or more specific dimensions on which to develop its competitive strategy further.

Cost Minimizing the cost of a product would seem a logical strategy for competitive advantage, either to pass the savings to the customer and win market share, or to increase profitability on the same base of sales revenue. However, intense competition for customers based on cost is most closely associated with mature products, as we discuss later in this chapter. Although any business would be foolish to completely disregard the issues of productivity and cost savings during operation, pursuing a lowest-cost goal alone is not usually enough to remain competitive.

Speed Some organizations distinguish themselves with the speed of their operations, and these organizations may or may not compete through cost as well. Customers expect both low cost and high speed when choosing a fast-food restaurant, whereas they expect to pay more for fast delivery when choosing a shipping company. Speed and cost are often linked, and speedier performance may even lower an organization's costs by lowering inventory levels or increasing production from the same infrastructure base. Interestingly, a reputation for speed and a reputation for ontime delivery are not always the same issue, as an organization can choose a reputation for ontime reliability, always delivering according to schedule, but not necessarily provide the product quickly. As an example, cable companies providing in-home installation sometimes advertise their ability to conduct that installation within a narrow window of time, allowing the homeowner to better coordinate with that visit. The stated window of time, however, may be weeks after the homeowner orders the service.

Responsiveness and Flexibility A fast provider is also not necessarily a responsive organization, as responsiveness measures the overall effectiveness of the organization in meeting the customer's particular needs, not simply its promptness. The greater the complexity of individual requirements and/or volatility in customer demand, the greater the challenge of successful response. Organizations that choose to compete through

The Complexity of Flexibility

This industrial machine shop combines basic materials and processes with skilled human judgment to create highly customized products for specific clients. One challenge of this flexible production system is to organize, track, and update each of its unique internal projects. Some of this daily complexity is visible here in the use of multiple paper notes spread across the pallets of materials by these machinists.

responsiveness must cultivate flexibility within their operations, because they cannot know in advance precisely what will be required of them.

Quality and Reliability Many organizations compete through product quality. Luxury goods are an obvious example. Customers expect these products to contain premium ingredients and to conform to exacting specifications. Quality, however, is more complex than premium-priced goods and first-class service. Competing on quality may overlap heavily with responsiveness, as an organization strives to serve an individual's exact tastes. However, competitive product quality doesn't necessarily require a customized product as demonstrated by McDonald's, which launched the fast-food industry by demonstrating the competitiveness of a narrow, inflexible menu of low-cost food items delivered with unfailing reliability. This reliability is itself a powerful form of quality, in that quality is ultimately measured by the customer's satisfaction with the product. Consistency and reliability allow a customer to plan around a product, confident of exactly what will be received, a feature that may prove critical to high satisfaction and loyalty to a particular provider. Product quality is also far more difficult to assess than speed or cost, because it is ultimately determined by human perception. As a result, customer perception of a product's quality may be influenced by factors not directly related to that product, such as cleanliness of the lobby where the customer waited before entering a facility or the greeting from a receptionist there.

Even though an organization chooses one strategy or perhaps a combination of cost, speed, responsiveness, and quality to distinguish itself from its competitors, this does not mean that the other dimensions can be ignored. Logically, the fastest and highest-quality product in the world will not succeed if the customer cannot afford it, nor will the lowest-cost product succeed if it does not meet the customer's needs. This raises the distinction between order qualifiers versus order winners, a useful model of the inner workings of competitive advantage.

Order qualifiers are the minimum standards that an organization must achieve to simply be considered by the customer. For any given product, every dimension discussed here suggests an order qualifier, such as "priced no higher than $10," "delivered sometime that day," or "available online." Order winners, however, are further requirements that provide competitive advantage over other businesses that qualify, such as "lowest price" or "includes choice of colors." Order winners, as the name suggests, are the dimensions that an organization prioritizes to win the customer's business.

order qualifiers
Minimum competitive characteristics necessary to be considered for a customer's order.

order winners
Those characteristics that give a product competitive advantage.

Order qualifiers are theoretically mandatory for all organizations in the market, but these requirements have been known to change over time. Previously successful organizations can suddenly lose market share if they fail to notice that some competitor's order

Quality and Perception in Service Systems

Customers are the ultimate judges of product quality, although this evaluation is not necessarily based on the product directly. Customer perception of quality—versus direct measurement of the product—is a particular concern for services. For example, the customers in this picture are purchasing food, and will logically judge its quality by weighing factors such as appearance, taste, temperature, and price. However, the customers' ultimate perception of this restaurant meal will likely also include reactions, positive or negative, to the environment around the food, particularly their interactions with the restaurant staff member in the foreground. The employees of a service system can have a powerful influence over that business's reputation for product quality, more so than employees preparing goods for distribution to customers elsewhere.

winner, such as the option of electronic payment, has evolved into an order qualifier in the mind of the customer. Even the organization that first introduced that order winner with great success can lose its competitive advantage if it fails to notice this change; its previously successful strategy is no longer distinctive.

Process Selection

Organizations are often defined by their products in the minds of the public, such as Dominos' being a pizza franchise or the Red Cross' being disaster relief. However, the successes of such organizations are often determined more by how they provide product than by the goods being delivered. Core competency and competitive strategy should dictate an organization's product, but this alone does not decide what processes will be needed; product selection and process selection are distinct strategic decisions.

processes Activities that transform inputs into outputs.

The product choices of an organization are usually quite visible, as these are the outputs it offers to its customers. Products can be anything deliberately created from inputs, from printed circuit boards to petroleum to financial consulting. Consumer products fill the shelves of retail stores, yet these are usually the products of distant manufacturers, not the retailer offering the goods for sale. The retailer's product is the convenient availability of the manufacturer's product, a service to the customer. Note that the retailer selects a process through which to make the product available, deciding how to transform its resources into successful sales. Retailers like Walmart build multiple stores and focus on sales through in-person shopping, while retailers such as Amazon focus on making the same goods available through online shopping and parcel shipments. Other industries provide more examples of multiple processes supporting the same product, such as the choice between satellite uplink versus land-based cable networks for data transmission and home entertainment, or the choice between microwave energy versus convection heating for rapid food preparation.

One highly strategic choice is the degree to which a product will be customized. A customized product places added demands on a process because each product is unique, meeting the specific requirements of a particular customer. Creation of products in this fashion is known as make-to-order, which often requires that the customer waits while the product is created. Emergency surgery, tailored clothing, most building construction, and courier jet services are all examples of customized production processes.

make-to-order A system that produces low volumes of customized product.

When goods are produced through a highly customized process, they are often recognized as hand-crafted, requiring skilled workers. The left-hand side of Figure 2.2 lists more characteristics associated with such products, such as slow, low-volume, one-by-one

FIGURE 2.2 Customized versus Standardized Production Processes

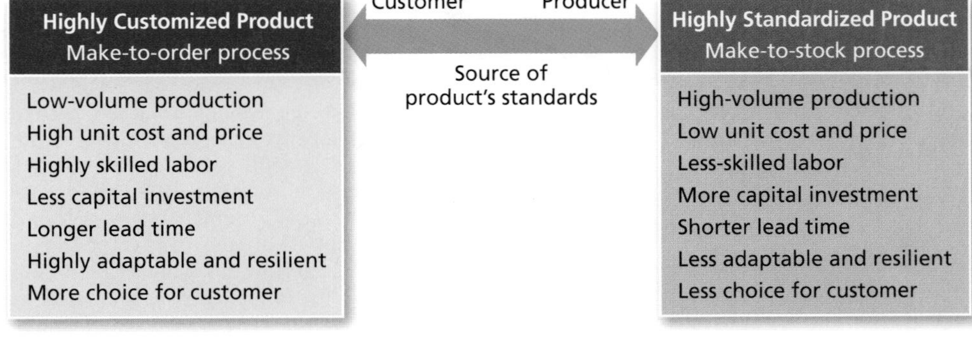

Highly Customized Product
Make-to-order process
Low-volume production
High unit cost and price
Highly skilled labor
Less capital investment
Longer lead time
Highly adaptable and resilient
More choice for customer
Customer
Producer
Source of
product's standards
Highly Standardized Product
Make-to-stock process
High-volume production
Low unit cost and price
Less-skilled labor
More capital investment
Shorter lead time
Less adaptable and resilient
Less choice for customer

Modern Make-to-Order Goods Production

Almost all goods production was essentially make-to-order until a few centuries ago. Today make-to-order is an optional process, and many skilled people still provide individualized goods for clients around the world. In this picture, a craftsman builds electric guitars, even though this same product is mass-manufactured elsewhere. Consumers who purchase guitars here expect to pay more than if they purchased from standardized retail stock, but also expect their more expensive purchases to conform more closely to their individual tastes. This is an essential trade-off between make-to-order and make-to-stock production, true for almost any consumer good.

production and relatively high costs. Selecting a make-to-order process strategy implies that responsiveness will be a particularly powerful order winner in the customer's eyes, because this type of process cannot compete strongly based on speed or low cost.

Most modern consumer products are not individually customized to the consumer's preferences. Most providers of everyday items have adopted a high degree of standardization into their processes, removing the flexibility to create specific features for individual customers. This allows mass production of similar items which, in the case of goods, tend to accumulate before sale. It is this potential accumulation of high volumes of output for later consumption that is the origin of the term make-to-stock, the opposite of a make-to-order process. As an example, modern beverage bottling facilities often measure their product output rates in hundreds or even thousands of bottles per minute, and thus are capable of filling vast warehouses with finished stock daily.

make-to-stock
A system that produces high volumes of standardized product.

The make-to-stock approach may apply to services as well, although the term in this context is a bit confusing, because services cannot literally store their output as inventory. Nonetheless, one example of this approach in services is a specialized automotive service shop, such as the Jiffy Lube franchise. These garages compete by offering a narrow range of stock maintenance services such as oil changes, investing in specialized equipment to provide these few service products quickly. In contrast, full-service garages are often stocked with more generic equipment for automotive repair, but the skilled mechanic in residence provides a wider variety of repair services, customized to the particular needs of each vehicle.

Product Life Cycle

The preferred choice of process may also be influenced by the age of a product. This observation is motivated by the product life cycle, a marketing model that divides the sales history of any product to phases similar to that of a biological organism. When the historical sales of a product are aggregated across all producers and brands, this volume often describes a curve across time, as illustrated in Figure 2.3.

product life cycle
Generalized pattern of phases in product demand over time, from incubation to decline.

Although the product life cycle model does not dictate that every product will experience the same pattern of sales volume, it does clarify the fact that many consumer products have evolved through these four distinct phases:

- **Incubation.** All products begin in an introductory phase, in which a small number of innovators and entrepreneurs bring the new product to market. Here the product is produced and sold in small volumes and prices are relatively high. As an example, the personal computer (PC) was largely unknown to the world in the early 1970s, when hobbyists were building and marketing early versions of this product.

FIGURE 2.3 Product Life Cycle Model

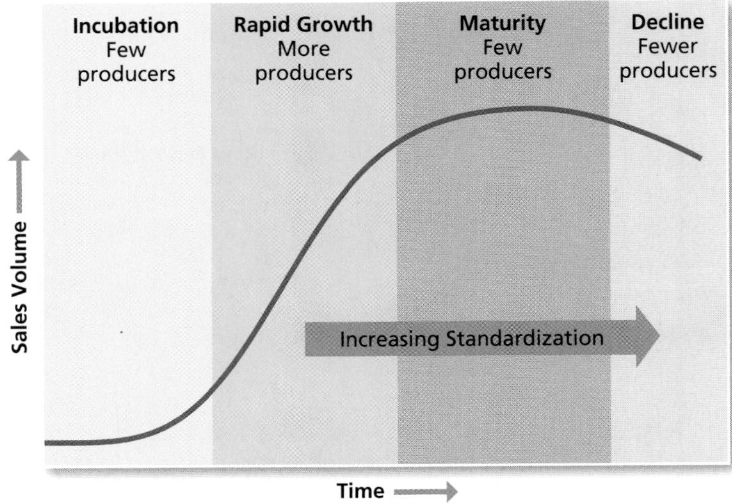

- **Rapid growth.** A product may not necessarily survive its incubation phase, but if it does, it generally enters on a distinct period of rapid growth. Now the product becomes known to its intended market, and more organizations enter the market to meet the new demand. For example, three companies, Apple, Tandy, and Commodore, introduced the three brands of PC that are credited with launching this market in 1977. Sales of personal computers then grew rapidly throughout the 1980s, with manufacturers including IBM, Atari, Compaq, Dell, Hewlett-Packard, Apricot, Digital (DEC), and Sequa all adding their own offerings to this mix.
- **Maturity.** At some point in a product's history, its providers are likely to saturate its market and demand levels off. The product is now said to be mature, and this maturity often prompts the exit of some of the businesses that joined during the rapid growth phase, while the remaining providers produce in higher volumes and compete on price. Continuing with the example of the PC, note that only a few of the companies mentioned above continue to manufacture PCs today. Several of the missing companies closed down their PC product lines during the 1990s, when slowing of the rapid growth phase first became evident.
- **Decline.** The product life cycle model theorizes that any mature product will eventually move into decline, replaced by the rapid growth of some new offering. However, if and when this decline takes place varies with the nature of the product in question, and even how the product is defined for the purpose of drawing the curve. For example, if personal computers are defined as the desktop hardware they began their life cycle as, then this product began its decline in the mid-2000s, as the wireless mobility of smaller laptop and notebook computers fueled their popularity as a substitute. However, if "personal computer" is defined as any personal device running complex applications, including desktops, laptops, notebooks, tablets, and smartphones, then product life cycle analysis would indicate that demand for this product is still growing.

Although the product life cycle is a marketing model, these phases have implications for process choice in operations. Note that a product usually begins as the customized output of some innovator, being scarce and somewhat costly in its early years. As Figure

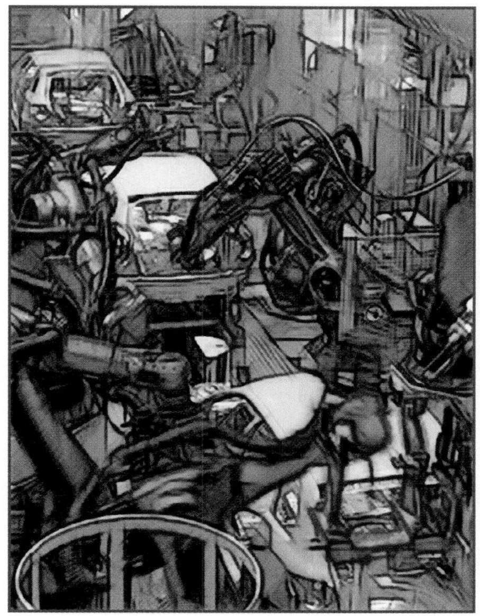

Automobiles as Maturing Products

While customers do have many choices when purchasing automobiles, they usually buy this product from existing stock. Most automobiles are mass manufactured by relatively few producers when compared to a century ago, when over 75 companies built automobiles in the United States alone. Highly efficient automation processes have brought production costs down when compared to early automobile production, but this picture hints at the high level of capital investment that becomes necessary to establish high-volume, standardized production.

2.3 indicates, successful production of this product often requires increasing standardization as the product grows older, when higher demand fuels the need for higher production volume and increasing competition forces down its price. While new products tend to be more customized and are offered in many changing formats, one trademark of mature products is a high degree of standardization that pressures its few large providers to spend heavily on advertising to differentiate their otherwise similar offerings.

Productivity

One simple measure of success in operations strategy is the degree of value-added in the resulting operation, or the difference between the value of its inputs and the value of the outputs created from those inputs. Value-added is easily recognized when examining consumer goods, a gallon of gasoline being more valuable to a motorist than a gallon of crude oil, or a sweater more valuable to a holiday shopper than the woolen fibers used as its inputs. However, value-added is not always a simple issue when evaluating processes for strategic insight. Consider the case of a city fire department, an emergency operation that is often measured by the dollars of damage from building fires within its service area. A better measure of value-added would estimate the dollars not damaged at each of those same fires, as this is the desired result from the fire department's operation. Unfortunately, estimating dollars protected from damage during a fire requires estimating dollars of damage if the fire department had not responded to that same fire, a theoretical event, and the seemingly simple issue of measuring value-added is revealed to be quite complex.

value-added
The difference between the total value of the outputs and the total value of the inputs associated with an operation.

Productivity is another common measure used in the evaluation of processes and systems. Productivity differs from value-added in two ways, the first being that productivity is stated as a ratio of output to input, where value-added is simply the difference in those same values. Second, unlike value-added, productivity is not always a comparison of the overall input and output values. When productivity is based on such estimates, it is referred to specifically as a total productivity measure. More common than total measures, however, are partial measures, which focus on the relationship between a particular output and input, or broader multifactor measures that consider a particular output compared to the value of a set of inputs.

productivity
A measurement of value creation, calculated as a ratio of the values of output to input.

total productivity measure
A ratio of the combined value of all outputs to the combined value of all inputs of an operation.

partial productivity measure
A ratio of a particular output to a particular input of an operation.

Partial Productivity Measures Partial productivity measures monitor the use or yield of one particular input of interest. Many partial measures of productivity are familiar from daily life. Consider these:

- MPG, or miles per gallon, evaluating a combustion engine's use of gasoline.
- Mbps, or megabits per second, evaluating a network connection's productivity against time.
- Words per minute, evaluating a keyboard operator's productivity against time.

To calculate a partial measure, the output is divided by the input, as we see in Scenario 1.

Scenario 1

Partial Productivity Measures

Lanark Farms sells fresh strawberries, growing the fruit both in open fields and within long clear plastic hoop tents, known as its tunnel operation. Last year, Lanark's 50 acres of open fields produced 25 tons of fresh strawberries, while the longer growing season under its 10-acre tunnel operation produced 20 tons. How productive is Lanark's open-field operation? Is it more productive than Lanark's tunnel operation?

Analysis

We will do a partial productivity calculation because we have data for only one input (acres of land) and one output (fresh strawberries). We must consider two different operations, however (open fields versus tunnel), so it is helpful to organize this information in table form:

PARTIAL PRODUCTIVITY MEASURES FOR LANARK

Operation	Output: Tons of Strawberries	Input: Acres of Land	Measure
Open fields	25	50	25/50 = 0.5 tons per acre
Tunnel	20	10	20/10 = 2.0 tons per acre

Insight The productivity of Lanark's open fields could be expressed as a half ton of strawberries per acre while its tunnel operation yields 2 tons of strawberries per acre. A larger result indicates higher productivity, so Lanark's open-field operation is *not* more productive than its tunnel operation, even though open fields produced the majority of its overall output last year. Rather, it would be fair to say that Lanark's tunnel operation appears to be four times as productive per acre as its open fields. ■

Process Selection in Agriculture

Technology provides a choice of agricultural processes, each with costs and benefits. The vegetables in this picture are growing in a high-tunnel operation, in which the plants are farmed beneath long, unheated plastic tents. This process is recognized for its high productivity relative to its physical inputs, as these inexpensive structures can often extend the growing season of farmland to nearly year-round. However, this same process requires more intensive monitoring and expert management, when compared to the older process of open-air farming.

Multifactor Productivity Measures Multifactor productivity measures monitor the use of a collection of inputs supporting the production of an output. Common inputs involved in a multifactor comparison include labor, materials, and/or overhead expense, and thus calculating a multifactor measure reflecting these issues requires this comparison:

multifactor productivity measure
A ratio of a particular output to the combined value of a set of inputs of an operation.

$$\text{Multifactor productivity} = \frac{\text{output}}{\text{labor} + \text{materials} + \text{overhead, etc.}}$$

Arguably, a multifactor measure is a closer approximation to the true productivity of a complex system. However, calculating such a measure requires the combining of dissimilar items in the denominator of the ratio. To rationally sum together items such as hours of labor and yards of material, we must first convert them into their monetary value, as we do in Scenario 2a.

Multifactor Productivity Measures

Scenario 2a

Consider the case of Lanark Farms, first introduced in Scenario 1. One key to the productivity of Lanark's tunnel operation is the higher air temperatures under the plastic tents, extending the length of the growing season but making the plants more vulnerable to the spread of disease. As a result, Lanark spends $225 per acre for preventative chemical treatments in its tunnel operation, whereas it spends only $20 per acre for similar treatment of its open fields. Furthermore, the tunnels themselves cost $250 per acre to construct and maintain throughout the year. Regardless of whether Lanark's strawberries are grown by its tunnel operation or in open fields, this product requires $125 per acre to plant and $600 per ton to harvest and pack. Now how productive is Lanark's open-field operation? Is it more productive than its tunnel operation?

Analysis

We must consider four factors associated with producing strawberries, two of which differ between the open field and tunnel operations. To create a multifactor measure, we group all relevant costs into the denominator of the productivity ratio, while the numerator remains tons of strawberries. We first calculate the four cost components on an annual basis:

ANNUAL COSTS FOR LANARK

Operation	Chemical Treatment ($/acres)	Tunnel Expenses ($/acres)	Planting ($/acres)	Harvesting and Packing ($/tons)
Open-air fields	50 × 20 = $ 1,000	50 × 0 = $ 0	50 × 125 = $ 6,250	25 × 600 = $ 15,000
Tunnel	10 × 225 = $ 2,250	10 × 250 = $ 2,500	10 × 125 = $ 1,250	20 × 600 = $ 12,000

Remember: all calculations must be compared on the same basis. In Lanark's case, this requires recognizing that the chemical, tunnel, and planting expenses are all calculated per acre, while the harvesting and packing expenses are calculated per ton of strawberries

Continues

produced. Once these calculations are complete, we can group them into multifactor productivity measures:

MULTIFACTOR MEASURES FOR LANARK

Operation	Tons of Strawberries	Total Expenses	Multifactor Measure
Open-air fields	25	1,000 + 0 + 6,250 + 15,000 = $22,250	25/22,250 = 0.00112
Tunnel	20	2,250 + 2,500 + 1,250 + 12,000 = $18,000	20/18,000 =0.00111

Insight Now the productivity of Lanark's open-air fields is expressed as 0.00112 tons of strawberries per dollar of expense. (Assuming a ton is 2,000 pounds, this translates into 2,000 × 0.00112 = 2.24 pounds of fresh strawberries per dollar of expense.) As a higher ratio indicates higher productivity, these calculations indicate that open-air fields are the more productive operation, but by a very narrow margin. ■

The literal value of a multifactor measure such as the productivity of open-air fields in Scenario 2a is usually not easy to visualize or interpret. Multifactor measures become meaningful mostly through comparison with other multifactor measures, such as the comparison between the values 0.00112 versus 0.00111 when comparing the open-air fields to the tunnel operation in Scenario 2a. In this context, it is not uncommon to translate the comparison into percent difference, for better insight into the significance of the difference. To calculate the percent difference between some operation *B* and some operation *A*, we can use the following formula:

$$(B - A)/A = \text{Percent difference in } B \text{ compared to } A$$

Productivity measures are often monitored over time, requiring comparison of the same system in different time periods to detect any changes in its operation. Productivity can likewise be compared between different operations in the same time period, as we do in Scenario 2b.

Scenario 2b

Calculating and Interpreting Percent Difference

Consider the continuing case of Lanark Farms' strawberry production. Scenario 2a indicated that the productivity of open fields was greater than that of Lanark's tunnel operation, with a calculated multifactor productivity ratio of 0.00112 compared to the tunnel operation's ratio value of 0.00111. What is the percent difference in the productivity of open fields when compared to the tunnel operation?

Analysis

The two ratios calculated for Scenario 2a are certainly close in value, even though the actual annual cost of the open fields ($22,250) is considerably more than that of the tunnel operation ($18,000). To express the percent difference between the two operations:

PERCENT DIFFERENCE IN PRODUCTIVITY BETWEEN THE TWO LANARK OPERATIONS

$$(0.00112 - 0.00111)/0.00111 = 0.9\%$$

Insight This analysis indicates that Lanark's open fields are about 1% more productive than its fresh strawberry tunnel operation. However, this does not mean that growing strawberries in open fields is strictly better than growing strawberries in tunnels, even in the context of Lanark Farms specifically. Practically speaking, these two approaches appear similar in terms of productivity, which would be consistent with Lanark's maintaining both operations. Furthermore, one or both of the operations may have additional features and advantages not addressed here but relevant to Lanark Farms' business strategy, such as the tunnel operation's ability to provide fresh strawberries late in the year. ■

Calculating productivity lends transparency to the inner workings of an operation, allowing its "health" to be measured in terms of value creation from the resources at hand. However, like any performance measure, a productivity ratio is only as meaningful as its assumptions, and care should be taken to avoid overinterpretation of this convenient calculation. If an operation's ratio drops over time, declaring that operation's productivity in decline implies that its actual performance is eroding or malfunctioning. In reality, it is possible that the operation is functioning perfectly, while the drop in the ratio value is the result of an increase in the corporate overhead expense assigned to the operation and included in the ratio denominator. Furthermore, this change could be entirely unrelated to the operation, such as the sale of another division increasing its share of the overall overhead burden of the company.

Finally, productivity does not exist in isolation. High productivity is not desirable at the expense of sustainability, as an operation can appear highly productive in the short-term, when in fact it is stripping away some resource faster than the resource can regenerate, dooming itself to collapse. Because sustainability addresses the complete, long-term costs of any operation, it might be thought of as the only true total productivity measure.

SUMMARY

An organization begins by stating its vision, mission, and values. These statements define its overarching goal and chosen path into the future, which its strategic business plans then translate into tangible actions. These plans define the goods and/or services that the organization will provide to fulfill its mission, as well as broadly sketch how these products will be created. Choices made here should be consistent with any core competencies of the firm, the source of its competitive advantage against other organizations, and will likely also be shaped by powerful ongoing trends in technology and globalization.

Any organization completes its mission through its operations. The borders between corporate business strategy and operations strategy are fuzzy, if they exist at all. Once a product is identified in a business strategy, operations strategy selects processes to support its production. Processes transform inputs into outputs, providing goods and services, and often many options exist in processing, such as the degree of standardization in the chosen process. Extreme standardization lowers production costs but reduces customer choice, which links back to earlier choices in competitive strategy, such as a decision to prioritize affordability over responsiveness. Choices in operations strategy are often consistent with the product life cycle model, which suggests that products begin as higher-priced custom offerings and then grow more standardized as their sales volume increases over time. Processes of all types must then be monitored for their performance in their chosen roles, by comparing their actual outputs to their actual inputs in some measure of productivity.

Key Terms

business analytics
business-to-business (B2B)
business-to-consumer (B2C)
business unit
core competency
data mining
data warehouse
e-commerce
enterprise resource planning (ERP)
goal alignment
iterative planning
make-to-order
make-to-stock
mission
multifactor productivity measure
order qualifiers
order winners
partial productivity measure
processes
product life cycle
productivity
strategy
third-party logistics (3PL)
total productivity measure
value-added
vision

Discussion Questions

1. Where are the boundaries of an organization's value statement? Should it look for these values in itself, its immediate business partners, and/or the partners of its partners?
2. Should the value statement of an organization always match the values of its customers?
3. Why is the measurement of productivity more challenging in the provision of services, when compared to measuring the productivity of a goods-producing operation?
4. Why would high productivity not necessarily guarantee competitiveness?
5. What is the relationship between planning and decision making? Do these two activities always occur simultaneously? Does one depend upon the other?

PROBLEMS

Short answers appear in Appendix A. Go to **NoteShaper.com** for full video tutorials on each question.

Minute Answer

1. In a vision statement, an organization carefully describes its desires concerning what?
2. Is a highly standardized product usually produced through a make-to-order or a make-to-stock processing strategy?
3. Does providing customized products generally involve less capital investment or less skilled labor, when compared to more standardized products?
4. If a product is produced in high volume by a few large organizations, what phase of the product life cycle is it most likely in?
5. The product life cycle suggests that what will happen to the price of a product as it ages?
6. At what phase of the product life cycle are the most organizations offering the product to the customer?
7. When calculating productivity measures, do higher or lower results indicate improvement?
8. If two different departments in the same organization each develop strategies that bring them into competition for the same customer, that organization is suffering from a problem with what?

9. At what stage of the product life cycle is price competition likely to be the greatest?
10. Is a core competency believed to be a source of competitive advantage or corporate vision?
11. If a customer considers a feature a necessity but is not impressed by it, is this feature an order qualifier or an order winner?
12. In theory, if the total combined value of every output of a system could be compared to the total combined value of every input to that same system, the resulting ratio would be called what?

Quick Start

13. If the multifactor productivity measure of one electrical generation plant is 12.934, while the same measure when calculated for a second plant is 12.023, which plant is more productive?
14. In a machine shop, six employees repaired 45 engines during a 5-day workweek. How would the productivity of the machine shop best be described?
15. Five Customs and Immigration officers worked 7 hours each to check visas and stamp the passports of 673 arriving visitors at an airport terminal. What is the labor productivity of this group of five officers?
16. Eight part-time workers at an airline catering facility prepared 2,010 meals in 6 hours. What is the labor productivity of the part-time workers at this facility?
17. A road-paving crew required 8 hours to repave a 3-mile stretch of road, using $5,000 in materials. The crew consisted of three workers who each earn $25 an hour. Calculate a multifactor estimate of productivity for this crew.

Ramp Up

Reminder: Short answers appear in Appendix A. Go to **NoteShaper.com** for full video tutorials on each question.

18. An automobile assembly plant produced 600 cars during a 5-day workweek. It then produced 500 cars the following week, although it only operated 4 days due to a national holiday. During which week was the plant more productive?
19. One road-paving crew of six people worked 8 hours to pave 25 miles of two-lane road, while a smaller crew of four people worked 12 hours to pave 15 miles of four-lane road. Which crew was more productive, and by how much?
20. Two projects of equal value have been evaluated using a multifactor productivity measure that combined labor-hours at $30 per hour and overhead expense calculated as 20% of labor expense. The two projects were judged to have been equally productive, although the first project used twice as many labor-hours. At what rate was overhead expense being charged to the second project?

Scenarios

21. Link's Lumber creates pressure-treated utility poles from pine logs bought from several surrounding pine plantations. At the Link's Lumber operation, a batch of 100 pine logs yields 85 utility poles with 5 labor-hours required to process the entire batch. Link's Lumber is owned by Artemis Link, whose brother Devious Link is planning to marry Betty Davis, owner of Northlands Pine Plantation. Artemis expects that his future sister-in-law will sell him pine logs for the same price he is paying to purchase them from other growers right now. The difference in Northlands Pine Plantation logs, however, is that they are considerably higher-quality wood than the logs he purchases from his current suppliers. If Betty agrees to sell him Northlands Pine Plantation pine logs, each batch of 100 logs can be expected to yield 100 utility

poles, although it will take an additional 4 labor-hours per batch to process the higher-quality wood.

a. What is the current labor productivity at Link's Lumber?

b. What will happen to labor productivity at Link's Lumber if indeed Artemis Link is able to purchase Northlands Pine Plantation lumber from Betty?

c. Suppose that Link's Lumber currently buys batches of 100 pine logs for $40, but Betty will want $60 for a batch of 100 Northlands Pine Plantation logs. Assuming labor at $30 an hour, what are the appropriate multifactor productivity measures for production from the current logs and production from Northlands Pine Plantation logs?

22. Archer Contracting repaved 50 miles of two-lane county roadway with a crew of six employees. This crew worked 8 days and used $7,000 worth of paving material. Nearby, Bronson Construction repaved 30 miles of four-lane interstate roadway working 10 days with a crew of five people using $9,000 of paving material. Both Archer Contracting and Bronson Construction rented the same paving equipment to complete their respective assignments, costing each $1,500 a day.

a. Calculate the labor productivity of both Archer Contracting and Bronson Construction. Who is the most productive according to this measure?

b. Assume that both Archer Contracting and Bronson Construction pay their employees $15 an hour and each employee works 8 hours per day. Calculate the multifactor productivity of each firm. Now who is the most productive and by how much?

c. Now assume that both Archer Contracting and Bronson Construction pay their employees $35 an hour and each employee works 8 hours per day. Calculate the multifactor productivity of each firm. Now who is the most productive and by how much?

d. Why does the conclusion concerning who is the most productive differ when employees receive $15 an hour (part b) versus $35 an hour (part c)?

CASE STUDY: ROTHERA POINT UTILITIES

Rothera Point Utilities (RPU) provides customers with 7 million megawatt-hours (MWh) of electricity each year. RPU operates three different generation facilities to meet this demand: the Rothera Point Power Plant, the Deer Hammock Generation Station, and the newer M.R. Smith Solar Array. Both Rothera Point and Deer Hammock have capacities of 800 megawatts (MW) each, although their daily operation is much different. RPU's Rothera Point Power Plant is a conventional coal-burning power station that operates at a steady pace throughout the year. In contrast, Deer Hammock houses two combined-cycle gas turbine generators, which start up and shut down as customer demand for electricity rises and falls throughout the day. RPU's third facility, the M.R. Smith Solar Array, is a commerical photovoltaic solar farm, covering 50 acres with panels that combine for a peak output of 75 MW, given the sun is shining. These facts and the costs common across each of these facilities are summarized in the Data from Previous Year table.

Data from Previous Year

	Rothera Point Power Plant	Deer Hammock Generation Station	M.R. Smith Solar Array
Installed capacity	800 MW	800 MW	75 MW
Technology	Coal-fired	Gas turbine	Solar (photovoltaic)
Last year's total output	6,132,000 MWh	714,700 MWh	153,300 MWh
Annual operations and maintenance cost	$5,600,000	$5,600,000	$2,614,250
Annual levelized capital expense	$32,000,000	$19,200,000	$13,500,000

Annual operations and maintenance reported in the table are the direct costs of running the facility, not including fuel. Levelized capital expense reflects RPU's annual payment on the original investment required to construct the facility, prorated over its expected lifespan. What does not appear in the table is the issue of fuel for each facility, because this issue differs among them. Rothera Point Power Plant burns half a ton of coal for every megawatt-hour it operates, meaning that it requires 350 tons of coal to run for 1 hour at its preferred operating level of 700 MW. Last year this coal cost RPU an average of $190 per ton, including delivery to the plant. Natural gas is sold by volume, not weight, and last year RPU purchased natural gas for Deer Hammock at an average rate of $12 per 1,000 cubic feet. When operating, Deer Hammock consumes 10,000 cubic feet of natural gas per megawatt-hour of electricity provided. In contrast, the M.R. Smith Solar Array has no fuel costs, only availability issues. The M.R. Smith installation does not include any system for storing electricity, and thus can only contribute to RPU's generation during daylight hours, contributing less when the weather is not favorable.

Generally, only coal-burning Rothera Point operates overnight, because its preferred operating level matches this baseline demand nicely. RPU then adds full use of the solar farm's output as the sun rises and customer demand for electricity increases, firing up the gas turbines at Deer Hammock to fill in as demand spikes above the combined capability of the first two facilities. RPU is concerned by recent rumors that a tax may be placed on CO_2 emissions from power plants, which has particular implications for RPU because of its heavy reliance on Rothera Point. Rothera Point's coal-burning generators release 2,000 pounds of CO_2 for every megawatt-hour of electricity generated compared to only 1,100 pounds of CO_2 per megawatt-hour from Deer Hammock and no emissions from M.R. Smith.

Questions

1. Calculate the multifactory productivity of each RPU generation facility, based on last year's data. Are your findings consistent with RPU's current use of these facilities?
2. Suppose that a tax is imposed on CO_2 emissions at a rate of $0.10 per pound of CO_2. What would be the total annual tax payable at Rothera Point and Deer Hammock, assuming last year's operating levels? What are their updated productivity measures?
3. If a tax rate of $0.10 per pound of CO_2 emission were imposed next year, would you advise RPU to change its operating strategy for its current three plant system? Explain your reasoning.
4. Given the rumors of a tax on CO_2 and potential changes to fuel prices in the future, should RPU change its installed technology mix in the long run? Within these technologies, how would you recommend RPU distribute the 7 million MWh of electrical output among the three generation processes in the future system, given it can invest further in any of them?

BIBLIOGRAPHY

Blackstone, J., ed. 2010. *APICS Dictionary,* 13 ed. Chicago: APICS, The Association for Operations Management.

Davenport, T. 2006. "Competing on Analytics." *Harvard Business Review* (January): 99–107.

Dhalla, N., and S. Yuspeh. 1976. "Forget the Product Life Cycle!" *Harvard Business Review* (January/February): 102–12.

Gottfredson, M., R. Puryear, and S. Phillips. 2005. "Strategic Sourcing: From Periphery to the Core." *Harvard Business Review* (February): 132–39.

Hamel, G., and C. K. Prahalad. 1990. "The Core competence of the Corporation." *Harvard Business Review* (May): 79–91.

Hayes, R., and S. Wheelwright. 1979. "Link Manufacturing with Process and Product Life Cycles." *Harvard Business Review* (January/February): 133–40.

Hill, T. 2000. *Manufacturing Strategy*. Chicago: McGraw-Hill.

Lubin, D., and D. Esty. 2010. "The Sustainable Imperative." *Harvard Business Review* (May): 43–50.

Simchi-Levi, D., J. Peruvankal, N. Mulani, B. Read, and J. Ferreira. 2012. "Is It Time to Rethink Your Manufacturing Strategy?" *MIT Sloan Management Review* 53(2): 20–22.

PART 1 ESSENTIALS

CHAPTER 3

Product Quality and Development

Don't pay any attention to the critics—don't even ignore them.
—Samuel Goldwyn

MAJOR SECTIONS

IN THIS CHAPTER, LOOK FOR...

- The origins of and differences among three differing definitions of product quality.
- Total quality management (TQM) versus traditional quality control.
- Problem-solving tools vital to ongoing improvement efforts.
- Certifications and awards that guide improvement efforts.
- The product development process.

INTRODUCTION

Quality has many definitions. For example, quality can mean a defining characteristic, as in "that particular dye adds a metallic quality to the appearance of the fabric." Quality in casual conversation usually signals a particularly positive characteristic, "that is quality fabric," indicating the fabric is superior to at least some other fabrics. To add to this complexity, operations management simultaneously embraces both viewpoints, quality as achievement measured versus quality as achievement that measures up well.

Understanding the elusive nature of quality is critical to delighting a customer. This requires both understanding and upholding the quality of a current product and using this knowledge to develop even better offerings. The line between product quality management and product development is fuzzy at best, so we begin with the exploration of quality itself.

MULTIPLE DIMENSIONS OF PRODUCT QUALITY

Modern quality management recognizes that product quality exists on at least three levels simultaneously. While each of these levels is equally important to the long-term success of an operation, we first consider the layers separately, beginning with the oldest viewpoint.

Quality as Conformance

quality of conformance The degree to which the output of an operation meets the producer's expectations.

Products are described by design specifications, such as those of the two-pin audio adapter pictured in Figure 3.1. When this particular adapter is measured and is found to match the specifications, it is said to have satisfactory quality of conformance. Any failure to meet the specifications in Figure 3.1 would not only represent poor quality of conformance, it would imply that this particular two-pin adapter has a defect and may be unfit for customer use.

Modern-Day Apprenticeships

Some complex and premium products are produced through hands-on processes largely unchanged for hundreds of years. Pictured here are a master craftsman and an apprentice, a team not uncommon to carpentry, masonry, electrical work, and many other highly skilled manual processes. Apprenticeships require new craft workers to acquire specialized knowledge through direct interaction with both the production process and more experienced craft workers. In a certain sense, the apprenticeship is the medieval ancestor of the modern internship, in which a student learns by direct participation in the ongoing activities of an organization.

An Example of Product Specifications

FIGURE 3.1

Audio cable adapter

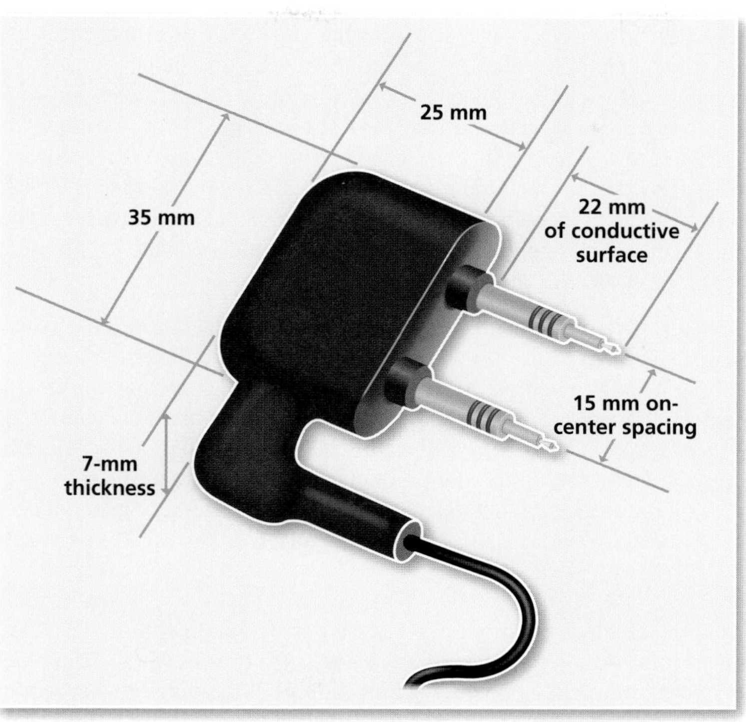

Viewing quality as an issue of adhering to standards is at least as old as the early craft guilds present in many cultures throughout the world. Ancient craft guilds were groups of craftsman who defined their trades and trained apprentices to create products such as woven cloth, weapons, and masonry buildings, each according to that guild's standard practices. Although quality of conformance dates back to ancient history, it is still relevant today. Most modern organizations could not function without recognizing product standards and verifying that ongoing production is consistent with those specifications and specified practices. What is different between medieval guilds and modern organizations is the fact that guilds defined quality entirely by their own internal standards. In contrast, modern organizations must recognize that a complete definition of quality is far more complex, with meeting the customer's expectations at the top of the list.

Quality as Perception and Expectations

Quality of conformance requires a product to conform to the producer's specifications, but this conformance does not guarantee that the product will be a success. The success of a commercial product requires that customers actually purchase it. Furthermore, the broader issue of value creation for any kind of product cannot be confirmed if, in fact, that product is never consumed. While this disconnect between satisfactory quality of conformance and actual value creation has always existed, it did not gain widespread attention until the 1980s, when a series of complex commercial products conforming to manufacturers' expectations failed to remain competitive. This clarified the idea of quality of design—or measuring quality in terms of the degree to which a product meets the customer's expectations. If a product meets or exceeds a customer's expectations, it has

quality of design
The degree to which the output of an operation meets the customer's expectations.

satisfactory or excellent quality of design. If the product disappoints the customer, it is of poor quality, regardless of its degree of conformance to the original specifications.

Quality of design also clarifies why it is often more challenging to manage quality for a service operation than for a manufacturing process. Customers form expectations of a product from their perception of that product, and this perception is usually fairly accurate in the case of tangible goods such as the audio adapter pictured in Figure 3.1. Services are intangible, however, and how they are perceived by a customer can be influenced by forces external to the product itself. To recognize this, recall that a customer who examines the two-pin audio adapter in Figure 3.1 is not likely to mistake any of its major attributes, such as its color, size, weight, or functionality. However, that same customer might perceive a competent service as distinctly unsatisfactory if any of the following influences interferes with the customer's perception:

- *Someone is rude to the customer.* The service product itself may be flawlessly accurate, but the insulted customer will not perceive it as so. Note that a customer is not likely to have any contact, rude or otherwise, with someone working within the manufacturing operation of a tangible product the customer is consuming.
- *The service facility is messy or unappealing.* Customers purchasing tangible products rarely see the facility in which the products are produced, so this seldom influences their perception of the product. Service facilities, however, are generally within view of the customer purchasing the service, and thus the facility itself can shape perception.
- *The service is completely intangible.* The greater the lack of physical evidence that value is being created, the more likely the customer's perception, based largely on the senses, may stray from an accurate assessment of that value. Thus, highly intangible services often take deliberate action to force some tangible element into their product's presentation, such as an extended service warranty (a promise of support in the future) being sold in a physical box complete with brightly branded label and barcode. The customer who agrees to pay for the promise of service can then take possession of the physical representation of that promise, and this helps the customers to perceive that the purchase price was appropriate.

Even when customer perception is not an issue, customer expectation may well be. Quality of design also recognizes those situations that adversely influence the customer's expectations. For example, new products are more prone to fail the test of customer expectation simply because they are new, and the customer does not have any previous

Customer Perception in Visitor Reception Areas

Service systems must pay careful attention to the customer's perception of their products. Pictured here is a credit card transaction, but the customer's impression of this service and the entire organization behind it may be heavily influenced by her interaction with this desk attendant and the design of the desk area. Note that this lobby features a view of outside greenery to increase the visitor's sense of space, while the desk area consists of warm wood tones and patterns in natural stone. These choices in material appear informal and yet encourage a perception of calm and permanence, and thus are common to reception areas.

experience on which to base expectations. Customers can also base their expectations on the price of the product; expectations may become unrealistic when the product is priced too high or too low. Finally, a customer can be expected to form expectations of a product from its marketing, and even a valuable product can fail to meet those expectations if it is overhyped.

Quality as Improvement

The most abstract and yet profound view on quality and quality management emphasizes improvement. Note that quality of conformance represents a steady-state to be carefully maintained, and even quality of design can be treated as meeting the customers' expectations consistently without moving beyond that threshold. Following close behind the emergence of quality of design, however, was a fundamental shift in thinking that suggested quality should not be framed as something to be maintained, but rather something to be forever pursued and improved. This shift became one of the defining characteristics of a comprehensive quality methodology now known broadly as total quality management, or TQM.

TOTAL QUALITY MANAGEMENT

The word *total* in the phrase total quality management emphasizes that the three different dimensions of quality discussed at the opening of this chapter are pursued simultaneously in an integrated effort. The 1980s are often cited as the period in which the concept of TQM first gained widespread recognition and adoption, particularly in the United States, although many components of TQM have a much longer history. In fact, TQM programs often feature the age-old tools and concepts of quality of conformance, but expand and improve them by integrating additional tools and concepts that address the vulnerabilities of the older viewpoint.

total quality management (TQM) Simultaneous and continuous pursuit of improvement in both the quality of design and conformance through the involvement of the entire organization.

Distinguishing Features

Three features distinguish modern product quality management:

- **Voice of the customer.** The customer ultimately defines product quality.
- **Employee involvement.** The entire organization routinely participates in some aspect of product quality.
- **Continuous improvement.** All quality management processes view improved quality as a perpetual opportunity, not a periodic endeavor.

Voice of the Customer Quality of conformance requires a product to conform to the producer's standards, and traditional quality control is dedicated to monitoring conformance. TQM, however, recognizes that the consumer of the product ultimately decides its quality, and thus achieving quality of conformance does not guarantee success without equal attention to quality of design. Logically, the specifications of the producer should reflect the expectations of the customer, but recognizing the voice of the customer in product design introduces a complicating factor, that of the customer's perception of the product. Technical specifications that matter little to the producer may have a profound influence over the customer's perception, particularly when the product itself is intangible. Consider these examples:

- Failure to maintain the first-come, first-served rule in a service situation can lead to dramatic changes in the customer's perception of waiting time and of the service itself.

- Personnel dressed in dark colors appear authoritative, while those dressed in light-colored clothing often give the impression of approachability.
- Professionals with messy desks seem inept. Those with books lining their office appear smarter. Finally, the presence of cutting-edge technology in the room implies that the professional is tech-savvy.

While achieving quality of design is largely an issue of determining what the customer would value in a product, understanding the relationships between certain technical specifications such as uniform shirt color and the customer's overall perception of the product may prove critical to its successful development.

Employee Involvement Unlike traditional quality management, TQM does not place quality in the hands of specialists by organizing full-time inspectors into their own department within the organization. TQM seeks instead to embed quality management throughout the organization and all its processes, shifting this responsibility to all employees. Inspection serves as a tool to assure quality during production, although a TQM program often assigns inspection to those employees closest to the product, the production workers. However, this shift of responsibility cannot be successful if those employees responsible for inspection do not have the authority to act upon any problems they might find. Thus, employee empowerment wherein employees can take independent action such as stopping production or rejecting a shipment of material is an important concept in the implementation of a TQM program.

employee empowerment Granting an employee the authority to take independent action on behalf of the overall operation.

Continuous Improvement Perhaps the most powerful feature of a successful TQM program is its devotion to continuous improvement. Traditional programs treat the issue of quality as a state to be maintained, through pursuit of some ideal amount of inspection. TQM not only shifts the responsibility for quality from a group of inspectors to every employee, but it also simultaneously shifts the perception of quality improvement from that of a project to an everyday activity. This integration of improvement into normal operation, also known as kaizen, creates a need for investigative, problem-solving tools made available to everyone in the organization.

kaizen Japanese term for a focus on continuous improvement.

Problem-Solving Tools

TQM's emphasis on both employee involvement and continuous improvement creates a need for tools beyond those of sampling and inspection. One effective tool enabling an entire organization to work continuously toward ever-increasing product quality is the quality circle, a group of employees partially dedicated to identifying opportunities for improvement and developing potential solutions. Quality circles are trained in the use of a variety of problem-solving tools that are otherwise not common to more traditional quality control programs.

quality circle A group of employees that meets regularly to discuss and develop opportunities for continuous improvement of an operation.

Pareto Analysis The restless nature of continuous improvement creates a need for investigative analysis within an organization, to identify opportunities for improvement. Pareto analysis offers a structured method of prioritizing these potential opportunities. Named in honor of the nineteenth-century Italian economist Vilfredo Pareto, this style of analysis on behalf of TQM begins by gathering data on the frequency of occurrences believed to contribute to some issue targeted for improvement. These observations can first be organized into a histogram, like the one in Figure 3.2, which suggests the frequency of various causes in delayed treatment by a hospital emergency room.

Pareto analysis The use of statistics to identify the factors most influential in a particular outcome of interest.

histogram A bar chart illustrating the relative frequency of occurrences in different categories.

Pareto analysis requires that these factors then be sorted by frequency and restated as a percent of total occurrences, as in Figure 3.3.

An Example of a Histogram

FIGURE 3.2

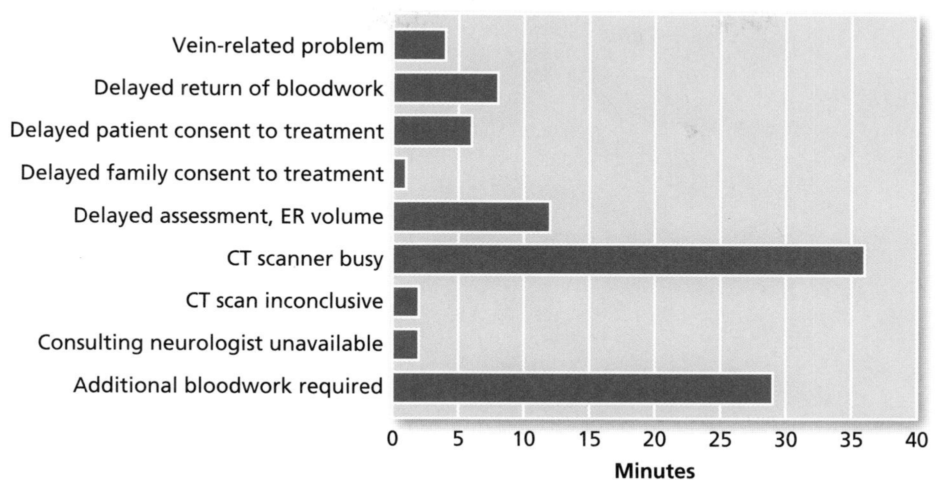

An Example of a Pareto Chart

FIGURE 3.3

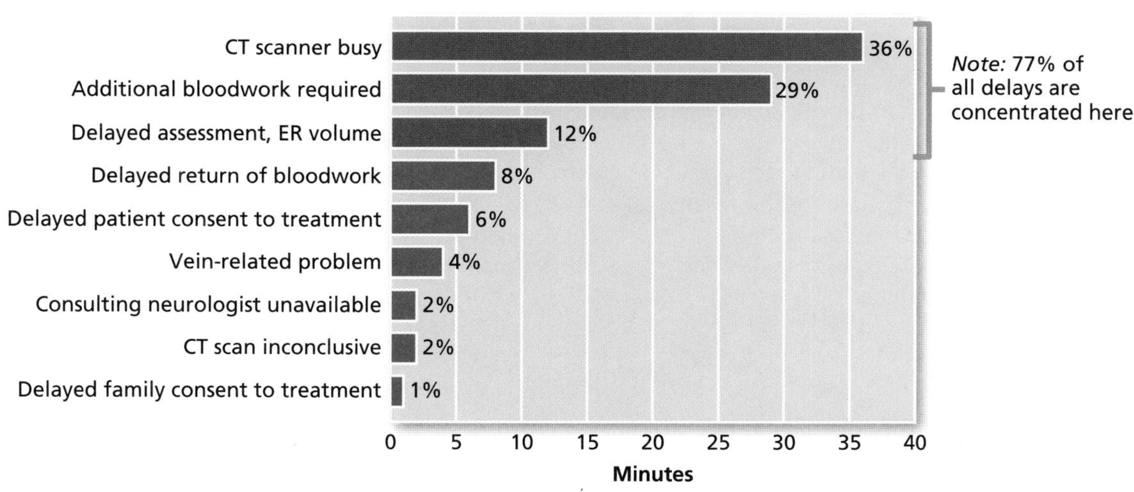

The purpose of the Pareto analysis is to highlight any pattern of "a critical few and a trivial many" that Vifredo Pareto first observed centuries ago. While a quality circle working on the project illustrated in Figures 3.2 and 3.3 identified nine different causes of delay in drug treatment, Pareto analysis reveals that three of those causes account for 77% of all delays, and one particular cause, a busy CT scanner, is responsible for over a third of those delays alone. The quality circle can now tighten its focus, perhaps recommending rental or purchase of an additional CT scanner or additional staff to draw and test blood, another major area of delay.

FIGURE 3.4 An Example of a Scatter Diagram and Correlation Coefficient

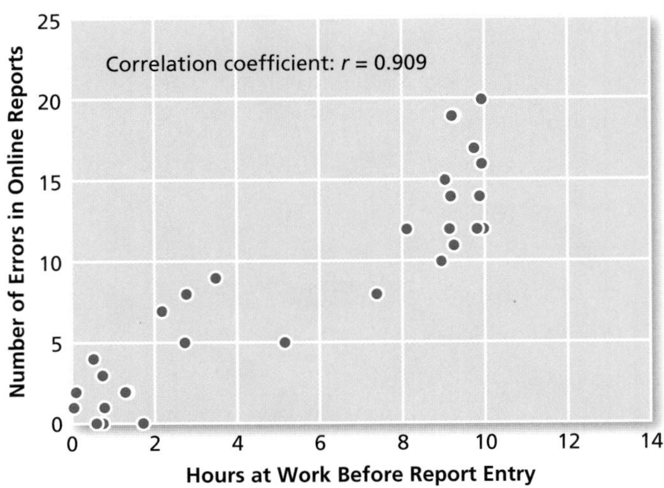

causal modeling Predicting an outcome by identifying its relationship with one or more other factors.

scatter diagram A graph of paired observations plotted as coordinate points to highight their relationship.

correlation coefficient A measure of the strength of any linear relationship between two sets of observations.

Causal Modeling TQM's emphasis on the pursuit of improvement requires identification of root causes. Causal modeling focuses on apparent relationships among elements of a system or situation, often by reviewing data for patterns that might predict some issue of interest. If such data is available, a scatter diagram can highlight possible relationships between two issues. In Figure 3.4, for example, we see a greater number of errors in online reports strongly associated with higher numbers of hours at work before report entry.

Although the clustering of data points in Figure 3.4 suggests that online reports entered later in the work shift are less accurate, this relationship can be clarified further by calculating the correlation coefficient for the underlying data. Correlation coefficients are broadly useful in any situation in which a linear relationship is suspected between any two issues under investigation. For any set of paired readings X and Y, where n is the number of paired observations, the correlation coefficient r can be calculated with this formula:

$$r = \frac{n(\Sigma XY) - (\Sigma X)(\Sigma Y)}{\sqrt{[n(\Sigma X^2) - (\Sigma X)^2] \times [n(\Sigma Y^2) - (\Sigma Y)^2]}}$$

The resulting value r will range between 1 and −1, and a value close to either limit indicates a strong linear relationship in the data. In contrast, a value near 0, the center of the range, indicates no linear relationship within the data. Figure 3.4 includes the correlation coefficient of the data plotted in that diagram, confirming a strong positive correlation of $r = 0.909$. While this does not prove that one issue is causing the other issue, it does suggests that anyone interested in improving the accuracy of online reporting should begin by exploring options to move this activity as early as possible in a work shift and/or investigate conditions at the end of the shift for more detailed understanding of the root causes of inaccuracy, such as employee fatigue.

Calculating a correlation coefficient requires finding the values of the various summary statistics in the correlation equations, as we demonstrate in Scenario 1.

Calculating Correlation Coefficients

Scenario 1

Lancaster Fleet Systems produces on-board information systems for law enforcement, fire/rescue, and delivery vehicles. Lancaster Fleet is particularly competitive in the law enforcement sector, counting some of the largest police departments in the world as its customers. Lancaster Fleet provides integrated packages of dashboard hardware and its own software, installed in patrol vehicles to provide services such as navigation, remote theft detection, database searches, and video imaging. Despite success, the marketing director at Lancaster Fleet is concerned that its product may be losing its competitive edge in this sector, based on the feedback from a survey of police departments. In this survey, departments were asked to rate the four best-known patrol car onboard information systems, based on four features that patrol officers identified as critical to their opinion of such a system:

- Good visibility—the degree to which officers could see information displays under all conditions.
- Speed—the time required to complete common queries, such as registration details.
- Helpfulness—the degree to which the officers perceived the system actually assisted in their daily work.
- Bulkiness—the degree to which the hardware infringed on the personal space and peripheral vision of the patrol car driver.

Disturbingly, survey results did not indicate a clear advantage for Lancaster Fleet over its competitors:

	Average Score on Survey (scale of 1 to 10)			
Brand	**Good Visibility**	**Speed**	**Helpfulness**	**Bulkiness**
Lancaster Fleet	5	5	5	10
Skye Systems	3	10	1	5
Integrated Patrol	1	3	10	1
Overland Information Channels	10	1	5	6

This survey indicates that Lancaster Fleet is the middle of the pack in terms of customer value, and its one dominant score for bulkiness represents a negative feature in the customer's eyes. The chief engineer assured the marketing director that this was not problematic, because "all onboard patrol car information systems are the same. It is the brand name Lancaster that sells our product, not anything special about its design." In a previous study, the engineering department identified only five technical design specifications that did vary among brands, including the size of the display screen and the size of the dashboard desktop area. The three other features were various choices in software design: differing degrees of the use of color, relying on click-throughs among small windows of information versus one larger, integrated window, and differing emphasis on autofilling the user's input activities. Engineering rated the top four onboard systems, including its own, according to these choices, and shared this report:

	Average Score from Engineering Department (scale of 1 to 10)				
Brand	**Size of Screen**	**Size of Desktop Area**	**Use of Color**	**Count of Click-Throughs**	**Autofill Activity**
Lancaster Fleet	6	10	5	5	4
Skye Systems	5	5	1	3	10
Integrated Patrol	2	6	10	8	1
Overland Information Channels	10	5	1	5	5

Continues

The marketing director wonders if there is any link between Lancaster's few design choices and its customer survey scores. Is there any significant correlation between the feedback from the engineering department and the feedback on the customer survey?

Analysis

The search for any significant correlation begins with calculating the correlation coefficient associated with every pairing of customer value feature and technical design specification. There are 4 × 5 = 20 pairs in total, so we will create an empty table to organize the work ahead:

LANCASTER FLEET CORRELATION STUDY

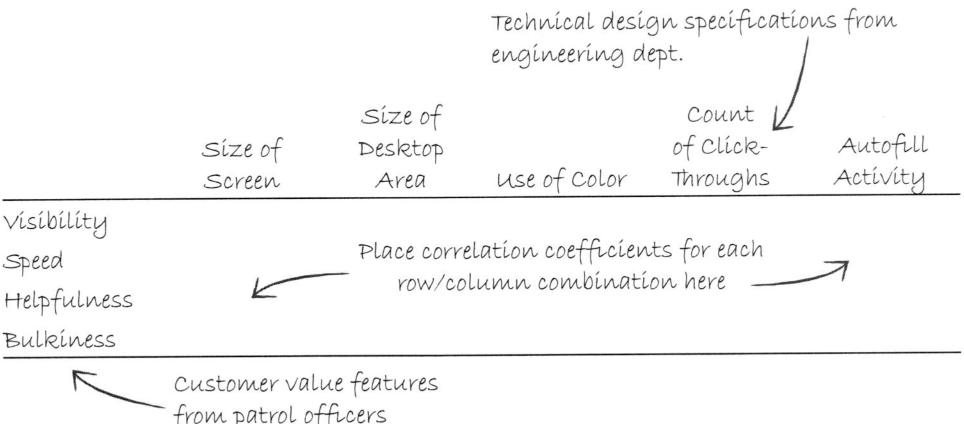

To calculate the first correlation coefficient that fits into the upper-left-hand corner of the empty table, we retrieve the data for the four brands' ratings on visibility (the row) and size of screen (the column), and we calculate the summary statistics necessary for the coefficient formula. If visibility data is *X* and size of screen is *Y*, then these calculations would look like this:

LANCASTER FLEET VISIBILITY (X) AND SIZE OF SCREEN (Y) SUMMARY STATS

Visibility (X)	X^2	Size of Screen (Y)	Y^2	XY
5	25	6	36	30
3	9	5	25	15
1	1	2	4	2
10	100	10	100	100
$\sum X = 19$	$\sum X^2 = 135$	$\sum Y = 23$	$\sum Y^2 = 165$	$\sum XY = 147$

Now we can calculate the coefficient of correlation, keeping in mind that there are four pairs of data for four brands, $n = 4$:

LANCASTER FLEET COEFFICIENT OF CORRELATION (VISIBILITY AND SIZE OF FLEET)

$$r = \frac{n(\sum XY) - (\sum X)(\sum Y)}{\sqrt{[n(\sum X^2) - (\sum X)^2] \times [n(\sum Y^2) - (\sum Y)^2]}}$$

$$= \frac{4 \times 147 - (19 \times 23)}{\sqrt{[4 \times 135 - (19 \times 19)] \times [4 \times 165 - (23 \times 23)]}}$$

$$= 151/153.13 = \mathbf{0.986\ (correlation\ coefficient)}$$

The result, 0.986, is very close to the coefficient's upper limit of 1.0, indicating an extremely strong positive correlation between high scores for visibility and larger screens, a logical relationship in product design. To finish the analysis, these calculations must be repeated for 19 other pairs of data, to complete the original table:

LANCASTER FLEET CORRELATION STUDY

	Size of Screen	Size of Desktop Area	Use of Color	Count of Click-Throughs	Autofill Activity
Visibility	0.986	-0.091	-0.662	-0.324	0.138
Speed	-0.349	-0.018	-0.298	-0.659	0.761
Helpfulness	-0.431	0.133	0.884	0.998	-0.967
Bulkiness	0.559	0.682	-0.475	-0.547	0.265

Correlation coefficients greater than 0.60 or less than -0.60 are highlighted to indicate significant correlation.

The value of a correlation coefficient deemed significant depends on the context of the study, but regardless of this exact breakpoint, the study here does suggest several interesting relationships between customer feedback and technical design specifications.

Insight The three strongest correlations in this study are between visibility and the size of the screen (calculated first), between helpfulness and the intensive use of click-throughs among windows of information, and between helpfulness and autofill functionality. However, helpfulness and autofill activity are strongly negatively correlated, suggesting that more automatic entry completion and correction by the software reduces a user's sense of its helpfulness. This further suggests that the industry may not yet understand fully what is helpful to the user in this context; autofill is intended to increase helpfulness, not decrease it. ■

One difficulty in causal modeling as discussed so far is that it requires the investigator to suspect a particular cause-and-effect relationship and to possess numerical data describing that relationship. In reality, casual modeling can be complicated by a lack of convenient data, and one issue under study may in fact result from many different causes, and not all those causes may be known to any single investigator. Causes themselves can even have causes, and may interact with other causes when contributing to an outcome, further obscuring the true issue of the root of the problem. Quality circles and employee involvement can be particularly helpful in such cases, in that a group of people directly involved with a complex process are more likely to succeed in its investigation by drawing on their combined individual experiences. Because TQM often relies on groups of people, brainstorming techniques are common to quality circles when working on such issues. One TQM tool particularly helpful to brainstorming a complex causal model is the fishbone diagram, like the one pictured in Figure 3.5.

brainstorming Collecting and discussing various ideas from group members to develop a solution to a target problem.

fishbone diagram Visual model to clarify cause-and-effect relationships.

Fishbone diagrams are also called cause-and-effect diagrams, or Ishikawa diagrams, named for their original author. The process begins by first identifying the undesired effect, such as the errors in online incident reports suggested in Figure 3.5. This becomes the head of the fish, and group members are then free to add ribs as they discuss the causes believed to contribute to that effect. Ideally, major categories of causes emerge from the discussion, such as the overarching problem of software bugs in Figure 3.5, under which specific causes in this category can be organized, such as the problem of pull-down menus reverting to default settings. Causes contributing to causes can even be clarified, such as the issue of humidity contributing to touchpad malfunction, which is itself a hardware problem in Figure 3.5. When finished, a fishbone diagram provides one

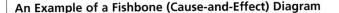

FIGURE 3.5 An Example of a Fishbone (Cause-and-Effect) Diagram

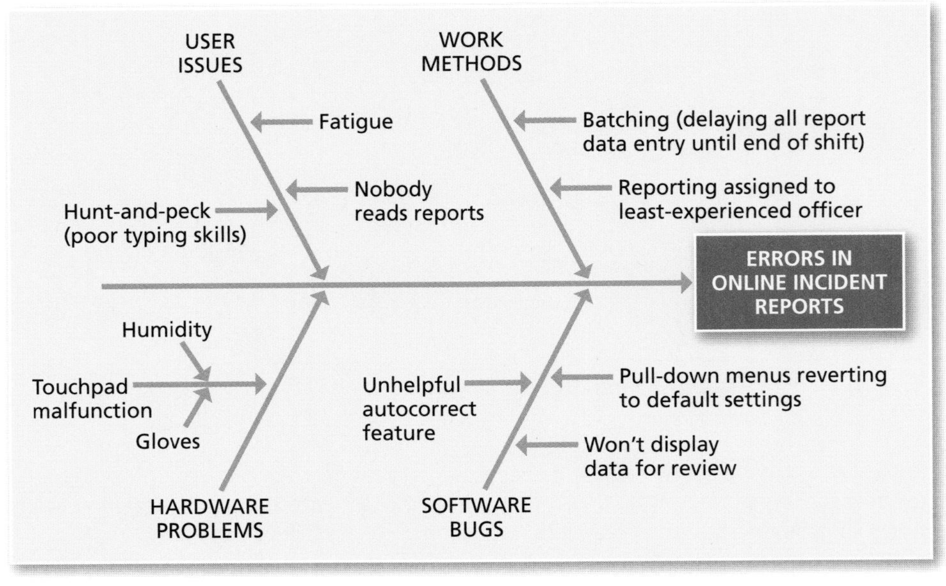

visual map of multiple perspectives and possible reasons for the outcome, useful in navigating toward future improvement of that effect.

control chart
Graph illustrating observed values in relationship to the allowable limits on those values.

statistical process control (SPC)
The monitoring of overall conformance through the ongoing evaluation of samples.

Control Charting Control charts of observed values relative to their allowable limits are commonly used in TQM programs and are examples of tools that originate from TQM's older foundation of statistical process control. While control charts are associated with monitoring processes for conformance to desired specifications, their highly visual nature and potentially proactive use are consistent with the spirit of TQM. Sample measurements taken at regular time intervals are graphed to scale on a control chart, where they can be compared to the control limits determined by the program. Figure 3.6 provides an example control chart, set against an illustration of the natural variation in the process that the sample data would reflect under normal conditions.

Some Requirements of Brainstorming

Brainstorming among employees is a powerful process that requires more than great ideas for success. Visible in this picture of a quality circle is the open meeting space needed to share documents and ideas, so all participants may view all contributions easily. Not visible but even more vital is the requirement that each of these quality circle members be released from their usual duties to participate in this meeting. This implies that elsewhere the organization is compensating for their absence, a potentially costly commitment.

An Example of a Control Chart

FIGURE 3.6

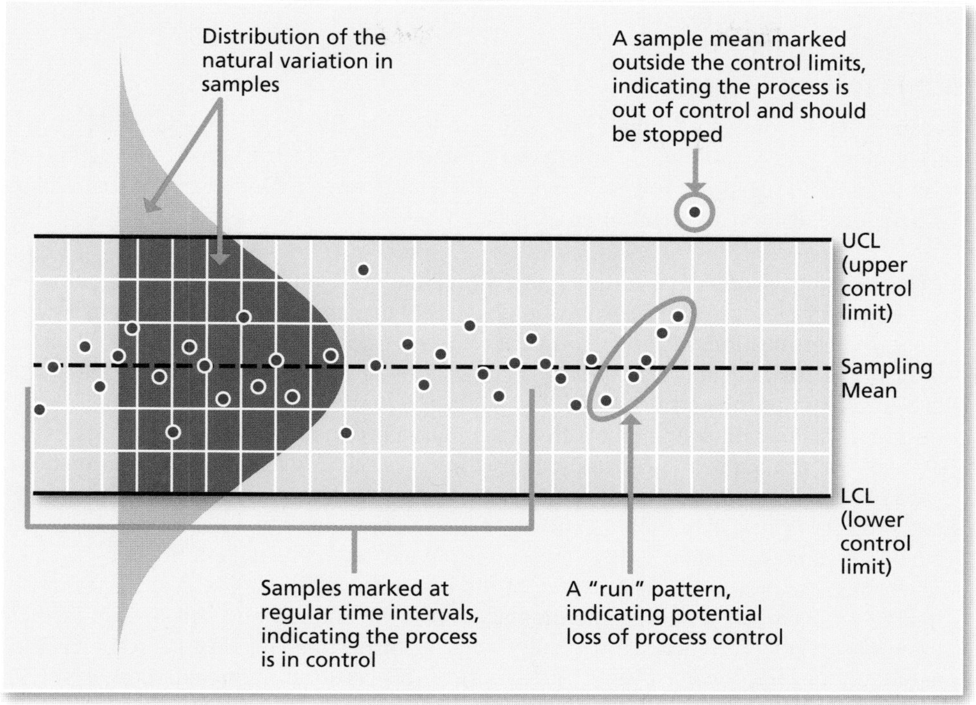

If a sample observation falls outside the control limits, such as the far right-hand sample in Figure 3.6, it signals nonconformance and strongly suggests halting production until the source of the problem is found. However, control charts can also assist in the prevention of defects by revealing unusual patterns within the acceptable limits, such as the run of steadily increasing sample observations indicated in Figure 3.6. This linear pattern is not consistent with the natural variation expected from the samples, indicating that another cause created those particular outcomes. Thus, the purpose of a control

natural variation The randomness inherent in a process; also known as random variation.

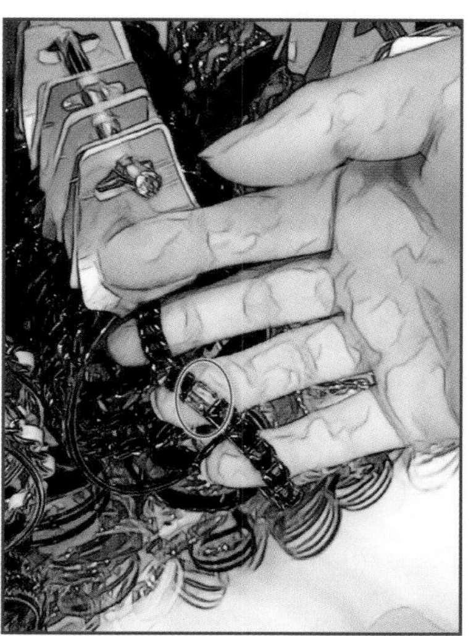

The Distinction between Natural and Assignable Variation

Inexpensive consumer products often provide visual examples of natural variation, such as the small differences in the sizes of glass beads used in this costume jewelry. However, this particular image includes assignable variation as well, marked with a red circle near the middle of the picture. Here, one glass bead is missing from its metal carrier in a linked bracelet, a distinct defect in this unit of sale. As the name *assignable* suggests, this feature was likely caused by some discoverable problem, such as the force of assembly occasionally breaking some beads, which then fall away from their carriers in smaller pieces during shipment. Tracing back the origin of defects such as this, to fix the cause and strengthen the production system, is a central principle of modern quality management.

assignable variation Deviations with a specific cause or source.

chart is not simply detection of nonconformance, but rather detection of assignable variation in the product being produced. Assignable variation is any variation with a specific cause. Its presence signals a halt to production and triggers the need to employ TQM tools to identify its cause.

Standards and Best Practices

Because TQM requires an organization to improve continuously, outside guidance and recognition prove inspirational. An organization may pursue certification, conduct benchmarking studies, or aspire to win a high-profile award, any of which can assist and motivate the organization's pursuit of excellence.

Six Sigma A quality management program emphasizing the application of analytical tools and widespread involvement of employees across the organization.

DMAIC Define, measure, analyze, improve, and control: emphasizes the various phases of the Six Sigma methodology.

ISO 9000 A certification of compliance with an internationally recognized set of quality management standards.

Certifications Both organizations and individuals can pursue public recognition for their efforts by earning formal certification in quality management. One of the most widely recognized certifications is Six Sigma, a data-intensive approach first developed by Motorola in the 1980s and now operational in thousands of organizations around the world. Six Sigma features the certification of individuals in particular, providing a formal regime of training in problem-solving tools that earn these employees the status of Green Belt or Black Belt in Six Sigma. These individuals then serve as the leaders of cross-functional teams of fellow employees pursuing continuous improvement through a series of projects. Each project is completed with careful attention to Six Sigma's signature DMAIC cycle of activity, an abbreviation for define, measure, analyze, improve, and control.

For organizations, ISO 9000 is one of the best-known international certifications for quality management, requiring the organization to be audited and certified as meeting minimum acceptable practices in quality control, inspection, managerial responsibility, and continuous improvement. Earlier versions of this certification process had been criticized for a heavy emphasis on the traditional concepts of inspection, documentation, and conformance, but a major revision reduced ISO 9000s documentation requirements and integrated more attention to the customer's viewpoint, creating a broader quality framework consistent with the principles of TQM.

benchmarking Measuring performance relative to some peer's performance, generally identified as best in class.

Benchmarking Benchmarking is an important element in any quality management program, particularly in the quest for continuous improvement. Benchmarking requires an organization to identify companies that represent either the standards the organization wishes to maintain or the kind of operation that the organization aspires to become. This organization then evaluates itself by comparing its own practices and resulting performance directly to the benchmark companies. Through this process, an organization should not only gain insight into where its own performance is weakest, but also ideally recognize what aspects of the benchmark organizations enable them to perform to a higher standard.

Quality Awards Quality award programs validate superior quality management, but unlike certification programs, the award is generally granted as a one-time-only recognition. The following three awards are highly recognized:

- **The Deming Prize.** Named after W. Edwards Deming, a foremost expert in quality control, this prize is administered by the Japanese Union of Scientists and Engineers (JUSE). The Deming Prize can be awarded both to companies in recognition for their superior practices and to individuals in recognition for their advancement of the field of quality management.
- **The Baldrige Award.** Named after the late Secretary of Commerce Malcom Baldrige, this award is administered by the National Institute of Standards and Technology (NIST) in conjunction with the American Society for Quality (ASQ). The Baldrige

Award encourages all organizations by recognizing annual winners across categories that include manufacturing, education, small business, and health care. Motorola, mentioned earlier as the developer of Six Sigma methodology, earned the Baldrige Award in 1988 for its initial Six Sigma efforts.

- **The EFQM Excellence Award.** This award is administered by the European Foundation for Quality Management (EFQM). Formally known as the European Quality Award, the EFQM Excellence Award annually recognizes the best TQM program in Europe from among its applicants, placing particular emphasis on sustainable results.

Since each award is a significant but one-time achievement, award programs do not usually monitor awardees for ongoing compliance to the program's standards. However, major award programs can provide more than just publicity to the award winners. Often the published guidelines used for judging are helpful to organizations seeking guidance on how to better their own product quality. Likewise, past award-winning organizations become natural candidates for benchmarking studies in other TQM programs.

In addition, the quality of consumer goods and services are continuously rated and ranked in a wide variety of public forums, according to varying definitions of quality. Electronic goods, automobiles, health care, and college education are all examples of products often reviewed in widely read studies conducted by organizations such as JD Powers and Associates, BusinessWeek, and Consumer Reports.

Vulnerabilities

An organization that takes a more traditional view of quality management is vulnerable to a possible disconnect between its own expectations and the customer's expectations of the product, as well as potential stagnation from viewing quality as a standard to maintain and not a mission to improve. Theoretically, an organization practicing TQM is shielded from these dangers through careful attention to the voice of the customer and the pursuit of continuous improvement. However, all TQM programs are not equally successful, and some fail outright due to TQM's own particular vulnerabilities. Note that TQM builds on the foundation of traditional quality of conformance, and thus requires additional time, resources, and funding when compared to an existing traditional system. These TQM-related expenses are not likely to be balanced immediately by increased revenue, if indeed the TQM efforts succeed in increasing revenue at all. Thus, TQM requires a long-term commitment from the organization that must be reflected in its leadership.

TQM also relies on the involvement of an entire organization in quality management, which may require a distinct change in organizational culture if it had previously considered quality to be the domain of specialists. Organizational culture is a powerful and yet unwritten set of rules governing the activities and attitudes of all the organization's members, an intangible force notoriously difficult to influence. While the changes in culture needed to support TQM may be difficult, they are not impossible, but this brings the focus back to TQM's vulnerable reliance on strong leadership within the organization.

PRODUCT DEVELOPMENT

It is difficult to separate exploration of product quality from the process of product development. TQM's central principle of continuous improvement is, in fact, a commitment to continuous product development, forever seeking new ways to delight the customer. Product development is a project-based endeavor, whether to improve an existing product design or to develop a completely new offering. Groups engaged in product development in organizations that otherwise operate large, ongoing processes are likely to operate very differently from their parent company. When the parent organization fails to recognize this, product development often suffers, as the parent attempts to steer this process with well-meaning misconceptions such as "Get it correct the first time," "Efficiency always improves a process," or "More is always better." Although each of these statements might make sense in an industrial setting, they are not consistent with successful creative activity, the foundation of good product design.

Designing for the Customer

A product exists for its customer, so the quality of a product's design is ultimately determined by that customer. That design began as an idea at an earlier point in time, brought through the process of product development to eventually emerge for the customer's ultimate consideration.

Idea Generation Ideas in product development come from virtually anywhere, and innovative companies cultivate multiple sources. In addition to the imagination of the product designer, ideas can stem from the following activities:

- **Studying the existing product.** The trouble-shooting nature of a TQM program inspires further development of existing offerings. As an example, the utility company Florida Power and Light undertook an in-depth study of its own operation, making a series of modifications from its findings. The resulting enhancements to the quality of its services were dramatic enough to win the Deming Prize.
- **Studying a competitor.** Benchmarking a product against its competition may naturally suggest further development. In some cases, organizations explore new product ideas by obtaining and dismantling another company's product, a process known as reverse engineering. Use of reverse engineering ranges from educational studies to the creation of clones or knock-off products that may infringe on intellectual property rights. As an example, Honda Motors struggles against clones of its own small engines, produced by competitors who have copied its designs so closely that most parts are interchangeable.
- **Asking a customer.** Just as customer feedback fuels product improvement, customer ideas are often the initial source of new product ideas. Large consumer product manufacturers such as Procter & Gamble conduct extensive market research to guide new product development, continuously listening to customer focus groups for new ideas and opportunities. Leveraging this viewpoint further, some companies credit success in product development to encouraging their own employees to use the current product on an ongoing basis.

reverse engineering Disassembling and evaluating a competitor's product.

Regardless of where an idea originated, the next phase of product development is exploration of that idea, and here is where short-sighted principles such as "get it correct the first time" may damage product development. Some portion of product ideas will naturally fail during a well-managed product development cycle, the perpetual by-product of creative activity. More relevant than the failures themselves is the assurance that they occur early enough in the cycle and that they inform other developmental ideas, a condition enhanced through rapid prototyping. Rapid prototyping emphasizes producing physical examples or mock-ups of an evolving design as quickly as possible. Rapid prototyping emphasizes speed so that one design project can be duplicated multiple times during the developmental process, a practice that may appear inefficient but has shown itself critical to innovation. Software beta versions often represent intermediate prototypes in this type of process.

rapid prototyping Creating physical examples of a design as quickly as possible, to allow further assessment and improvement.

Quality Function Deployment One common mistake in product development is to assume that more design features create a more competitive product. Successful companies such as Apple have repeatedly demonstrated the power of "less is more" in product design, but this principle is not as simple as it sounds. Its difficulty lies in discovering precisely how a product's potential technical features and the customer's perception of that product relate. To overcome this difficulty a company must bridge the gap between the two differing perspectives on product quality—quality as conformance and quality as customer perception and expectation.

Quality Function Deployment, or QFD analysis, provides a structured format for bridging this gap, mapping key relationships between the customer's and the product developer's viewpoint. The signature shape of a finished QFD model gives it its nickname, "house of quality," as shown in Figure 3.7.

quality function deployment (QFD) analysis
Modeling the mathematical correlations between customers' perception of a product and its technical design specifications.

First, QFD analysis requires the voice of the customer to be captured in consumer surveys and focus groups, outlining what the customer does consider valuable in a product. These customer attributes are listed in the left-hand side of the QFD diagram, and are expected to be in the customer's own words, such as a desire for "brightness" or "friendliness." In some cases, not all attributes are equally valuable to the customer, such as "it is more important to be accurate than to be quick," and such preferences can be documented on a weighted scale directly to the right of the attributes. Next, product developers must identify what aspects of the product's design are, in fact, flexible and thus open to new design choices. These technical specifications are listed across the top of the diagram, and the roof of the house of quality is formed by a table in which to mark any links or synergies between specifications.

Once this house-shaped framework of the QFD analysis is established, further mapping of customer attributes to technical specifications requires the collection of two sets

Format of House of Quality—QFD Analysis FIGURE 3.7

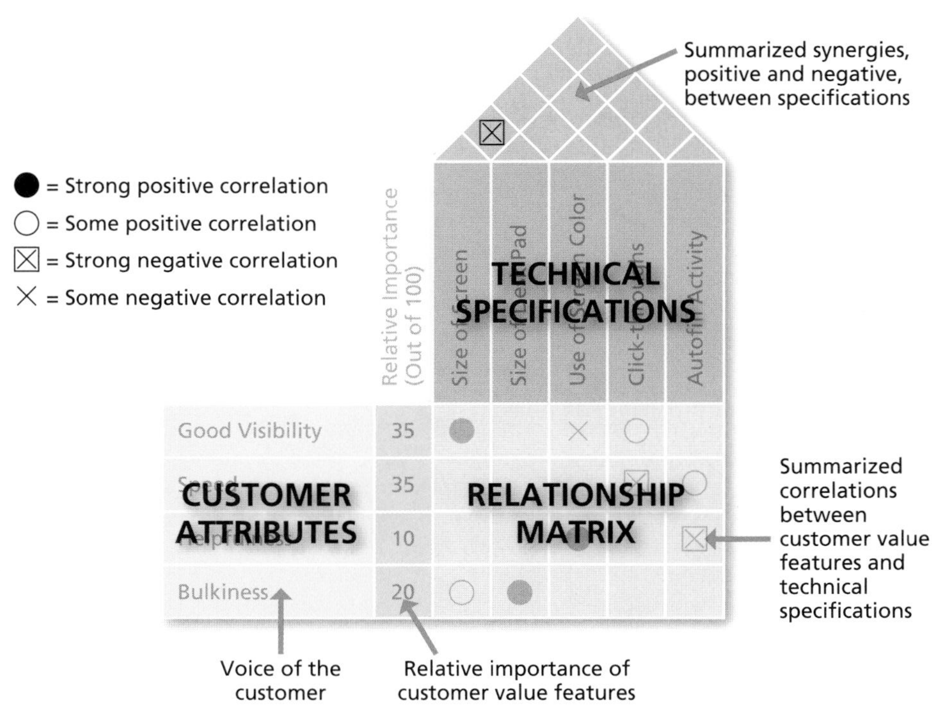

of data from two different groups of experts. One data set is the result of presenting a group of customers with several different examples of the product, asking them to rate each brand according to the customer attributes. The second data set results from evaluating the technical specifications of those same example products, as measured by product design experts. Neither of these data sets appears in Figure 3.7, but the relationship matrix in the diagram summarizes the correlations between each attribute's data and the data for each technical specification.

In Scenario 2a we construct a house of quality for Lancaster Fleet, first introduced in Scenario 1.

Scenario 2a

Building a Quality Function Deployment (QFD) Diagram

The marketing director at Lancaster Fleet realizes that correlation coefficients found earlier in Scenario 1 could be used in a QFD diagram to assist further design of patrol car onboard information systems. Each coefficient expressed the linear relationship between an average survey score for a particular customer value feature and the engineering department's rating of a particular technical specification:

LANCASTER FLEET CORRELATION STUDY

	Size of Screen	Size of Desktop Area	Use of Color	Count of Click-Throughs	Autofill Activity
Visibility	0.986	-0.091	-0.662	-0.324	0.138
Speed	-0.349	-0.018	-0.298	-0.659	0.761
Helpfulness	-0.431	0.133	0.884	0.998	-0.967
Bulkiness	0.559	0.682	-0.475	-0.547	0.265

Lancaster's chief engineer warned the marketing director that these coefficients are based on a limited amount of data. While engineering would consider coefficients as high as 0.6 or as low as –0.6 to be of some interest, these values would have to be at least 0.85 or –0.85 to be considered strong by that group. In addition, the chief engineer mentioned that not all the technical specifications are independent of one another. In particular, the chief engineer pointed to the relationship between the size of the screen and the size of the desktop area, because the limited space in the front of a patrol car creates a trade-off between the size of one versus the other, so that they both might fit in that space.

The marketing director remembered that a QFD study also includes some statement of the relative importance of customer attributes, but reviewing the records of the earlier focus groups of patrol officers doesn't reveal any statements concerning whether visibility, speed, helpfulness, or bulkiness, is any more or less important when compared to each other.

Given this information, create a finished QFD house of quality model for patrol car onboard information systems.

Analysis

As the marketing director noticed earlier, much of the information needed for the QFD model is already available. So let's draw the frame of the house and outline what little work remains to be done.

LANCASTER FLEET QFD MODEL FOR PATROL CAR ONBOARD INFO SYSTEMS

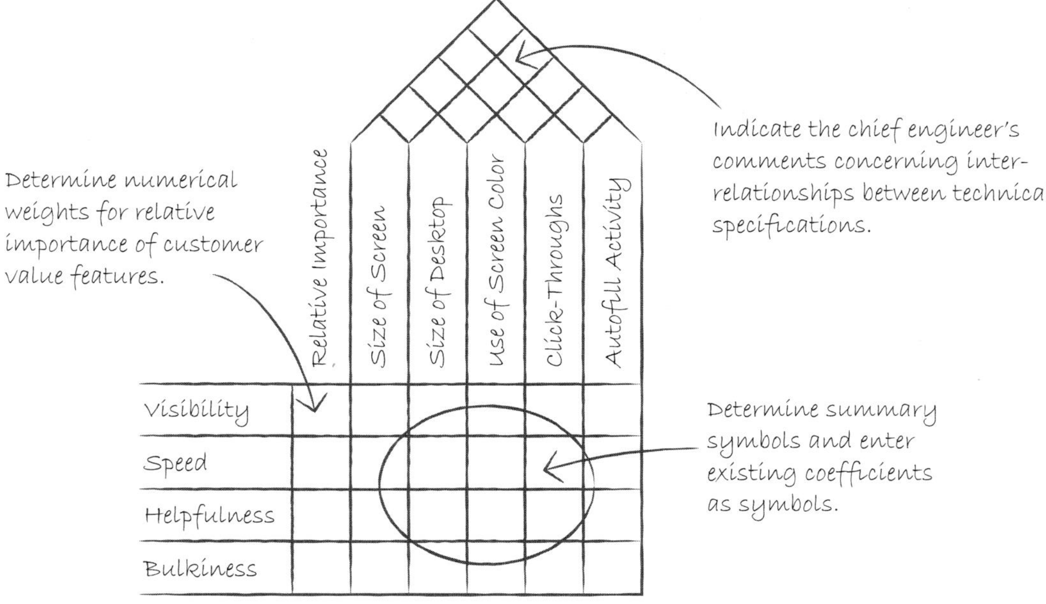

To begin with the roof of the house, let's review the chief engineer's comments for any important synergies, positive or negative, that might exist between the technical specifications:

LANCASTER FLEET QFD MODEL, FINDINGS FOR ROOF SECTION

FINDING: Size of screen and size of desktop area have negative synergy, as both must squeeze into same limited space. Use symbol for strong negative correlation to mark this box in the roof, based on the chief engineer's comments.

To act on this finding and to translate the earlier coefficient data into the finished QFD matrix, we must create a coding scheme to reflect significant correlations. Based on the other comments from the chief engineer, a logical set of symbols and ranges would be:

LANCASTER FLEET CORRELATION KEY

- ● = Strong positive correlation ($r \geq 0.85$)
- ○ = Some positive correlation ($r \geq 0.60$ but $r < 0.85$)
- ☒ = Strong negative correlation ($r \leq -0.85$)
- X = Some negative correlation ($r \leq -0.60$ but $r > -0.85$)

Continues

Using this key, we can populate both the main matrix and the roof of the QFD house of quality:

LANCASTER FLEET QFD MODEL FOR PATROL CAR ONBOARD INFO SYSTEMS

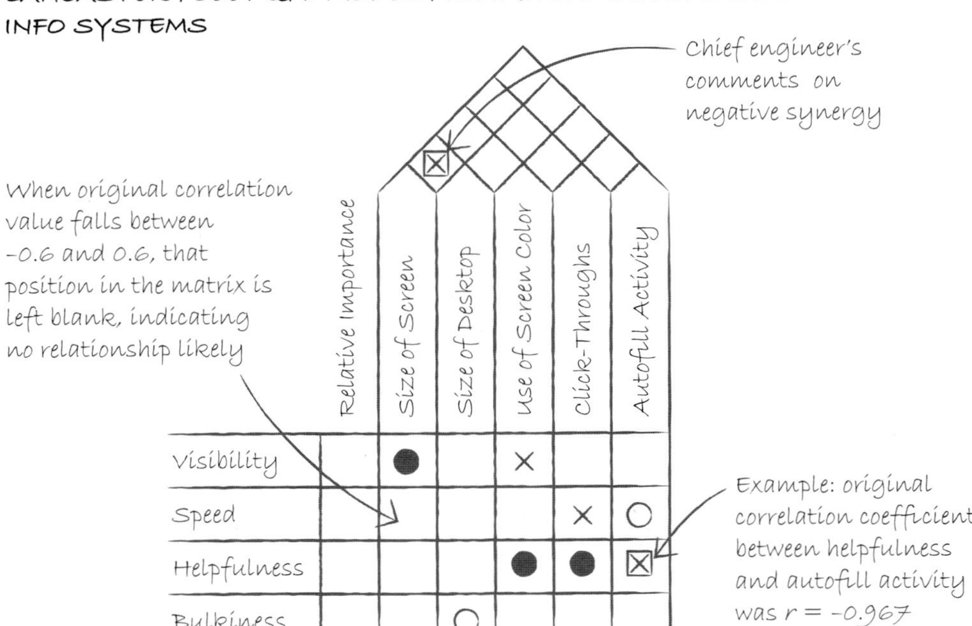

To finish the QFD diagram, we need to add the weights indicating any customer preference for one value feature over another. The marketing director could not find evidence of customers weighting one of the features more heavily when assessing the quality of an onboard information system, so these weights should be the same. Since there are four value features and 100-point scales are common, a logical weight for each of the features here would be 100/4 = 25 points each. With this, the diagram is complete:

LANCASTER FLEET QFD MODEL FOR PATROL CAR ONBOARD INFO SYSTEMS

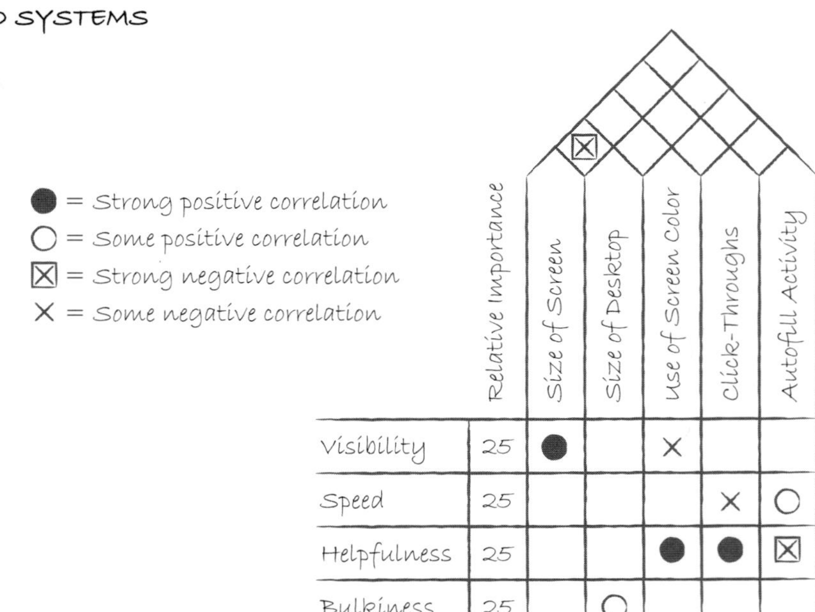

Insight The QFD house of quality for onboard information systems owes its size to the four attributes valued by patrol officers, versus the five technical specifications that Lancaster Fleet controls. Its largely empty attic communicates how the technical specifications, with the exception of size of screen and size of desktop, can be manipulated independent of one another. In contrast, its detailed interior signals the presence of several powerful relationships among these same specifications and the four attributes valued by the customer. ■

Highly correlated pairs of attributes and technical specifications, highlighted in the center of a QFD diagram, suggest how to improve the customer's perception through manipulation of those specifications in the product's design. This allows the customer's perspective to drive product development through technical specifications that the customer may not even be aware of. However, QFD analysis may not always indicate some obvious change, but it can reveal the presence of trade-offs, or difficult choices, between improvements on different customer attributes. This issue of trade-offs is obvious in the QFD diagram for Lancaster Fleet, which we discuss further in Scenario 2b.

Interpreting a Quality Function Deployment (QFD) Diagram

Scenario 2b

The chief engineer at Lancaster Fleet has requested recommendations for any changes to Lancaster Fleet's current design for patrol car onboard information systems.

Given the original data in Scenario 1 and the finished QFD model from Scenario 2a, what should the marketing director recommend?

Analysis

Further developing Lancaster Fleet's product begins with reviewing the Scenario 1 data to determine the current position of that product's design. Most of these scores suggested that the product was in the middle of the pack compared to competitors, but a few scores stand out:

LANCASTER FLEET QFD PATROL CAR ONBOARD INFO SYSTEMS, CURRENT RATINGS

Brand	Average Score on Survey (scale of 1 to 10)			
	Good Visibility	Speed	Helpfulness	Bulkiness
Lancaster Fleet	5	5	5	(10)

Customers consider Lancaster Fleet to be the bulkiest product, not a good attribute.

Brand	Average Score from Engineering Department (scale of 1 to 10)				
	Size of Screen	Size of Desktop Area	Use of Color	Count of Click-Throughs	Autofill Activity
Lancaster Fleet	6	(10)	5	5	4

Lancaster Fleet's design includes largest desktop area on the market.

These observations are of particular interest when reviewing the findings of Scenario 2a.

Continues

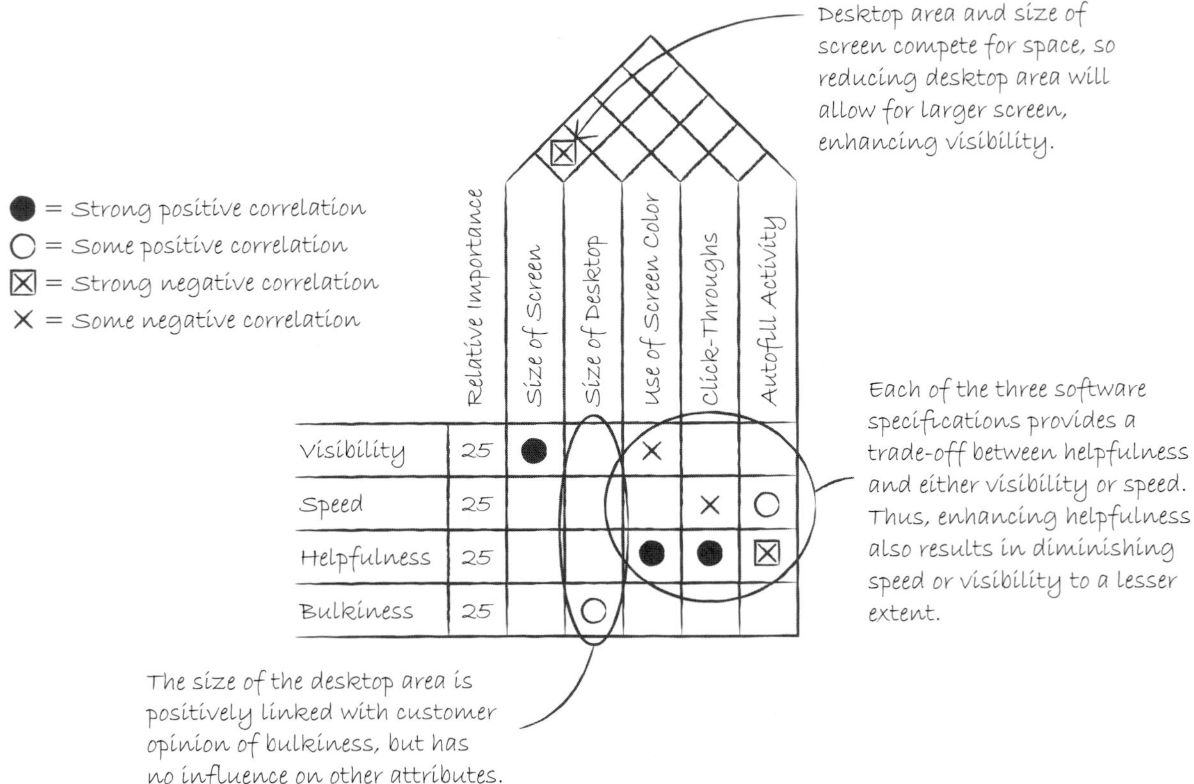
LANCASTER FLEET QFD MODEL FOR PATROL CAR ONBOARD INFO SYSTEMS
Desktop area and size of screen compete for space, so reducing desktop area will allow for larger screen, enhancing visibility.
● = Strong positive correlation
○ = Some positive correlation
⊠ = Strong negative correlation
× = Some negative correlation
Relative Importance
Size of Screen
Size of Desktop
Use of Screen Color
Click-Throughs
Autofill Activity
Visibility
Speed
Helpfulness
Bulkiness
25
25
25
25
Each of the three software specifications provides a trade-off between helpfulness and either visibility or speed. Thus, enhancing helpfulness also results in diminishing speed or visibility to a lesser extent.
The size of the desktop area is positively linked with customer opinion of bulkiness, but has no influence on other attributes.

Insight Lancaster Fleet should reduce the size of the desktop area in its patrol car on-board information systems. It currently has the largest desktop area in the market, and QFD analysis indicates that this feature does little except give the customer an impression of bulkiness. Furthermore, reducing the desktop area will allow room to increase in the size of the screen, which will enhance visibility from the customer's perspective. Lancaster Fleet could use some of these gains in visibility to cushion any potentially negative impact of increasing the use of screen color, allowing it to increase its ratings for helpfulness without losing ground on the visibility dimension. ■

Safety and Sustainability Ideally, the spirit of product development and the ethics of an organization would assure a customer's safety in using a product, but this is never guaranteed in reality. Failure to design for safety may not be completely the fault of product developers. New products bring unknowns whose unsafe nature may stay hidden for several years. As a result, governments are often active in specifying minimum safety standards, banning knowingly unsafe products, and monitoring for unforeseen consequences from current offerings. In the United States, the Consumer Product Safety Commission (CPSC) provides much of this service, although certain common products are assigned to other agencies, such as automobiles being governed by the National Highway Traffic Safety Administration and legal drugs by the Food and Drug Administration.

Sustainability of future production and minimization of environmental impact both begin with product development, although this has not always been the case. Even when

End of Life Cycle Problems from Changing Technology

When flat-screen technology took over from cathode-ray-based screens, televisions across the world experienced a wave of replacement. In this image, these old televisions are sitting at a dump site, although it is illegal to simply throw out an old television in a growing number of areas. Unfortunately, little thought was given to the full cradle-to-grave problem for older cathode-ray technology, which can introduce dangerous pollutants into landfills. As a result, tens of millions of old TVs are currently being held in storage in people's homes, because they do not have a convenient option for this product's safe disposal.

practicing conservation of raw materials such as oil and fresh water, organizations have traditionally used the cradle-to-gate planning approach, focusing on sustainability from the procurement of a resource up until its transformation into a product. Environmental problems and rapid changes in some technology have motivated a more modern cradle-to-grave approach, requiring developers to begin with the end in mind and design for the eventual disposal of products as well as their use. Cradle-to-grave thinking does not necessarily include recycling, in that the "grave" for a consumer product could be a landfill, although a cradle-to-grave designer would then specify biodegradable materials for the product, so that it might break down faster and make better use of landfill space.

cradle-to-gate Planning sustainability from the procurement of raw materials through the production of the product.

cradle-to-grave Planning sustainability from the procurement of raw materials through the final disposal of the product.

cradle-to-cradle Planning sustainability as a perpetual cycle of transformation, in which the disposal of one product provides the materials for another.

The ideal in product development is a cradle-to-cradle design, which plans explicitly for how a discarded product will be transformed back into something of value. This includes designing such that valuable materials are easily recovered for recycling, organic matter is free from chemicals that would prevent its repurposing into fertilizer or animal food, and entire subassemblies or finished products can be easily decommissioned at the end of their life cycle and adapted to alternative uses.

Despite the evolution of product development to embrace sustainability, many companies still struggle to define and measure this objective in the complex context of a modern supply chain. One heartening development in recent years has been the emerging power of social media to lend greater transparency to the practices of all organizations and to empower consumers to express their concerns and disapproval of unwise practices in a global forum. While sustainability has always been an ethical requirement, it is increasingly seen as a competitive imperative as well. Companies wisely listen to the voice of the customer, and hear growing demand for green products.

green Assures sustainability.

Designing for Production

Traditionally, a product would be designed first and then production processes would be specified next, to bring the product into production. This progression seems logical, but modern product design often gains new efficiencies by merging at least part of product development with its own production design phase, in pursuit of manufacturability.

manufacturability The degree to which a product can be created easily and reliably according to specifications.

concurrent engineering Integration of a product's design and process development phases, to enhance manufacturability.

Manufacturability The manufacturability of a product refers to the relative difficulty of providing it, a measure of both its design and the design of the processes used to produce it. Manufacturability of a design can be enhanced through teamwork known as concurrent engineering, in which developers and associated experts work on both the product and the production process design simultaneously. Improvements in the manufacturability of existing designs often focus on simplification, such as reduction in the number of components required to assemble a finished unit. This reduction is expected to improve efficiency, lower costs, and potentially improve quality, by eliminating the opportunity for mistakes.

Although the term *manufacturability* suggests the production of goods, the concept applies equally to services. As an example, introduction of web-based ordering of delivery food not only provides additional convenience for the customer, it significantly enhances the manufacturability of the delivery service. Web-based ordering simplifies the production process by enabling the customer to input requirements straight into the delivery kitchen's ordering system, eliminating both the need for an employee to document that order from a phone call and the opportunity for a mistake to be introduced into the recorded order from the phone conversation.

assemble-to-order (ATO) A system that produces standard modules to be modified and/or combined into a customizable product.

delayed differentiation An ATO strategy for stocking highly standardized components for later customization into finished goods, once a customer's requirements are known.

Mass Customization Mass customization is a goal of many goods and some service providers, implying the flexibility to meet individual customer needs with the efficiency of high-volume production processes. This flexibility from mass production is often achieved by designing the product around an assemble-to-order (ATO) processing scheme, in which seemingly customized finished goods are created from differing combinations of stock items. Many modern customized goods are in fact mass customized through an ATO design, such as laptops and even some building construction. Other organizations seek mass customization through delayed differentiation, enhancing the manufacturability of an item by identifying what components of the design all customers will share, versus what features will vary according to the individual customer's tastes or needs. Both the product and the process are then carefully designed such that the common elements are produced first in high volume, after which the custom elements can be easily added according to the customer's preference.

risk The possibility of loss or the source of such a possibility.

Safety and Sustainability The issues of safety and sustainability for the consumer are reflected in production as well. Many processes are naturally dangerous, and dangerous processes introduce risk, the possibility of unacceptable loss during operation. The greatest sources of risk, however, may surprise you:

- *Nature.* Farming, mining, logging, and fishing consistently top the list of the most dangerous processes around the world. These vital activities provide the materials from which all other tangible products are manufactured, but each shares a

Mass Customization of Emergency Vehicles

Fire trucks are custom-ordered by fire/rescue organizations, and individual orders for these costly items are often complex. However, the newly finished inventory of the fire truck manufacturer in this picture reveals that these vehicles all share standard features, and their customization is the result of differing combinations of stock items, such as the gray roll-up cabinet doors visible on most of these vehicles. This assemble-to-order approach is central to achieving mass customization.

profound source of risk: working with natural systems. Natural systems such as weather and existing rock faces are seldom controllable in any managerial sense, and may change rapidly without warning.

- *Heights.* Airplane pilots, structural metal workers, and roofers usually suffer more deaths per capita than most other occupations, due to the extreme consequences of even small mishaps in their work environments, combined with their exposure to the uncontrollable forces of weather.
- *Roads.* Delivery workers suffer all the usual hazards of driving, but their degree of exposure is far greater than any nonprofessional driver, due to the longer hours spent behind the wheel.
- *Heavy machinery.* Manufacturing, construction, and sanitation services all expose people to large pieces of moving machinery, usually under noisy conditions.

Product development includes responsibility for addressing risks in production. Maximizing safety and sustainability in production begins with identifying risk and then designing a means to prevent it, a practice known as proaction. Much of this overlaps with the search for root causes in product quality discussed earlier, as it is often difficult to divide a product from its production process in an analytical sense. As an example, a trucking company concerned with the safety of its drivers might examine past accident data and identify driver fatigue and angle of the sun as two root causes. To then design avoidance into its delivery service, the company might shorten its routes and eliminate the use of certain roads during certain hours, when the sun is lowest on the horizon in the direction of travel.

proaction
Avoidance of preventable risk, the first and most basic stage of risk management.

Governments are often active in workplace safety, developing and enforcing regulation of risky processes and practices. In the United States, the Occupational Safety and Health Administration (OSHA) is responsible for these regulations, although states and other authorities often have the option of requiring more restrictive regulation within their own borders. Globally, little agreement exists in regulations, so production in one country may be riskier than the same activity in another country. As an example, truck drivers in Australia, the United States, and Canada are required by law to operate in similar cycles of no more than 14 hours followed by 8 to 10 hours of rest, to prevent driver fatigue. However, the European Union limits this driving activity to 9 in every 24 hours for the same purpose, while some countries have no regulation over truck operation. Historically, such differences were not naturally apparent to consumers. Now, the power of social networking and information technology appear to be changing this dynamic for the better, providing new visibility to these differences as consumers take increasing interest in the origins of their purchases.

Solar Panel Installation and Process Safety

The growth of green technology has increased demand for retrofitting solar panels to existing rooftops, as pictured here. Like construction in general, this particular service can present serious safety concerns. The tiled slope, the nearby roof edge, and the skylight are all distinct threats to this pair of technicians, as is the possibility of accidental electrocution from the hardware. Mitigation of these risks begins with design of the product, such as limiting the size of individual panels, and continues with the process, such as working in teams. Potentially dangerous practices are governed by workplace safety regulations, but these rules can vary between governments. Climbing harnesses, for example, are sometimes required for this type of work, although not at the location pictured here.

Whether designing from the customer's or the producer's perspective, product development ultimately determines the future of an organization. Just as it is difficult to separate product development from quality management, it is challenging to find any boundary between it and business strategy, sustainability, and process management. In modern organizations an exact boundary is unlikely to exist at all, as the best of these operations seamlessly integrate creativity with productivity in ongoing efforts to better serve their markets.

SUMMARY

Quality management can be traced back over a thousand years, as early craftsmen developed the standards of their trades and taught those standards to others. It evolved further into the concepts of inspection for conformance, sampling, and statistical process control. Conformance to standards and specifications continues to this day as an intuitive and relevant definition of quality.

Where a more traditional approach to quality would focus on inspection and conformance, a modern quality management program integrates these issues with additional concerns. Principally, total quality management recognizes that the standards and specifications being used to judge conformance must reflect the customer's expectations, not simply the good judgment of the producer. Recognizing the voice of the customer introduces greater complexity, in that the customer brings both the issues of expectation and perception into the discussion of a product's quality, and customer's perceptions of intangible products can be particularly surprising to the unwary provider. TQM also frames quality as a quest for continual improvement, as opposed to the more static traditional view of quality as simply a desirable steady-state. Because a TQM program is never finished investigating itself for new opportunities to increase product quality, employees supporting this program use a variety of diagnostic and problem-solving tools such as Pareto analysis, fishbone diagrams and benchmarking. Ultimately, TQM requires the involvement of everyone in an organization to keep it developing in a positive direction, and leadership support is critical to maintaining this momentum.

It is difficult to separate the exploration of product quality from the process of product development. A product cannot be designed without the customer's voice, and TQM's devotion to continuous improvement encourages constant work toward improvement of that design. Companies may get design ideas from a wide variety of sources, but nonetheless need to develop them into designs with some mapping of their technical abilities back to the customer's desires, using tools such as quality function deployment. Ideally, the processes to be used in the future production of the design are developed concurrently with product design activity, for better efficiency, flexibility, sustainability, and safety.

Key Terms

assemble-to-order (ATO)
assignable variation
benchmarking
brainstorming
causal modeling
concurrent engineering
control chart
correlation coefficient
cradle-to-cradle
cradle-to-gate
cradle-to-grave
delayed differentiation
DMAIC
employee empowerment
fishbone diagram
green
histogram
ISO 9000

Key Terms (continued)

kaizen
manufacturability
natural variation
Pareto analysis
proaction
quality circle
quality function deployment (QFD) analysis
quality of conformance
quality of design
rapid prototyping
reverse engineering
risk
scatter diagram
Six Sigma
statistical process control (SPC)
total quality management (TQM)

Discussion Questions

1. How are quality of conformance and quality of design related to one another? Can a product achieve quality of design but not quality of conformance? Can the converse be true?
2. How does the concept of quality of design help explain why a product can be very successful in one country, but the same product can fail in another country's market?
3. Does a product's price influence the customer's perception or expectation of a product, or both? In any of these cases, is it a positive or negative influence?
4. What purpose do quality awards serve, beyond their role as a prize to the winning organization? What value can an award program provide organizations that have yet to even compete for that award?

PROBLEMS

Minute Answer

Short answers appear in Appendix A. Go to **NoteShaper.com** for full video tutorials on each question.

1. Which is the older concept, the idea of quality as conformance or quality as improvement?
2. Do control charts assist in monitoring quality as conformance or quality as improvement?
3. Which typically poses a greater challenge in designing and monitoring product quality, the production of a good or provision of a service?
4. A correlation coefficient of –0.95 indicates what?
5. Does a correlation coefficient indicate the strength of a curvilinear, linear, or inverse relationship?
6. Which tool is most useful in Pareto analysis, a scatter plot or a histogram?
7. Is a fishbone diagram or a control chart more likely to result from a brainstorming session?
8. Which is a better example of employee empowerment, a quality circle or a causal model?
9. Does remanufacturing of a product indicate a cradle-to-cradle or a cradle-to-grave design model?

10. If a component is deliberately left out of the main assembly of some product, is this the DMAIC cycle or delayed differentiation at work?
11. Does one broken egg within a carton of one dozen eggs represent natural or assignable variation among those eggs?
12. Identifying the correlations between customer perception and design specifications is the core of what analytical tool?

Quick Start

Quick Start QFD Matrix

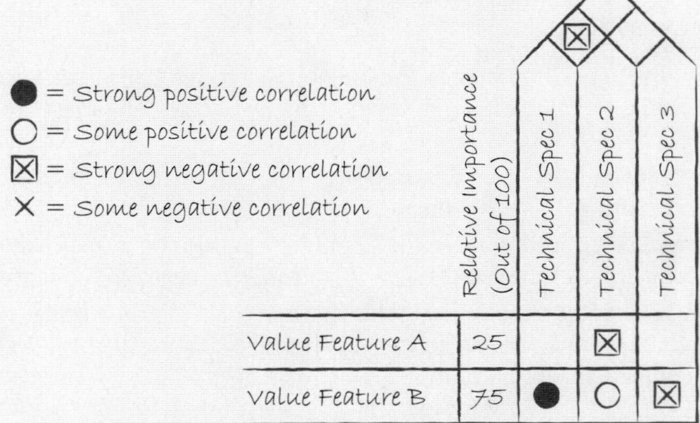

13. Consider the Quick Start QFD Matrix above. Of the two value features, which do customers consider three times more important?
14. If a change were made to Technical Spec 2 in the product's design, this would likely change the customer's opinion of which value feature the most?
15. Which technical spec can be most easily modified without changing current choices for the other two technical specs?

Ramp Up

16. In a recent survey, a 21-year-old gave a movie a score of 10, while a 73-year-old gave it a score of 5, a 45-year-old gave it a score of 7, and a 36-year-old gave it a score of 5. Based on these four responses, what is the correlation between age of moviegoer and score for the movie?

Reminder: Short answers appear in Appendix A. Go to **NoteShaper.com** for full video tutorials on each question.

Scenarios

17. AdventureLand theme park recently received a large number of complaints from customers who had endured delays while waiting to ride on AdventureLand's largest roller coaster, Monster Train. As newly appointed operations manager, you are considering the problem of delayed rides on Monster Train. By observing 100 delayed Monster Train rides over a 10-week period, you find that a variety of factors are contributing to the Monster Train delay problem. You summarize the results of your study in a diagram:

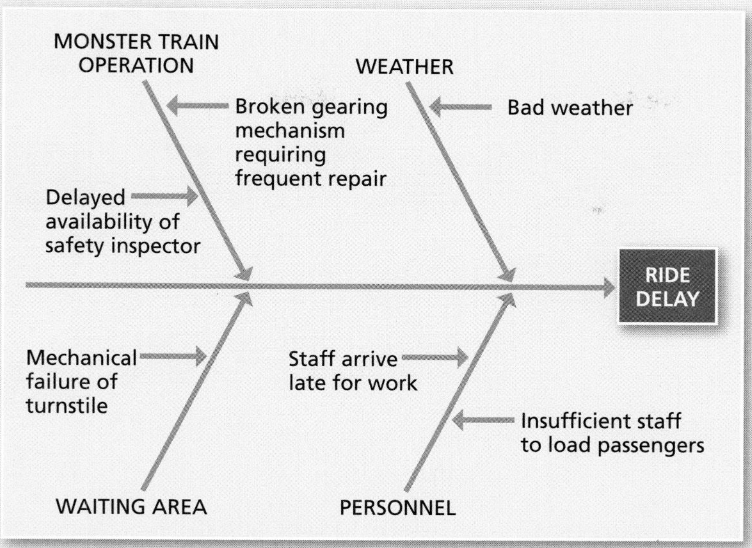

You also create this table to tally the frequency with which you observed various causes of delay:

Problem Areas	Number of Occurrences
Delayed availability of safety inspector	6
Mechanical failure of turnstile	30
Broken gearing mechanism requiring frequent repair	50
Staff arrive late for work	5
Bad weather	5
Insufficient staff to load passengers	4

a. Pareto analysis would suggest that AdventureLand theme park focus on which Monster Train problem areas?

b. The first diagram is often called a what?

c. Consider the following potential improvements that AdventureLand theme park is considering to address the Monster Train Delays:

- Improvement 1: Hire additional staff, both to load passengers and to serve as safety inspectors.
- Improvement 2: Replace the faulty gearing mechanism requiring frequent repair. The company selected to perform the Monster Train gearing replacement work has also agreed to fix the failing turnstile in the waiting area for free.
- Improvement 3: Fire the staff arriving late for work and hire replacements.
- Improvement 4: Invest in research and development to invent a weather-control device to prevent bad weather.

Since each of these potential improvements involves money, AdventureLand theme park can only undertake one improvement at a time and can only afford to complete two of the improvements listed above. Which improvement do you recommend first, and which should follow second, to reduce the frequency of customer complaints as quickly as possible?

18. You are a quality management consultant for the Beserk Tennis Ball Company. Beserk is redesigning its current model of tennis ball, and you are asked to use QFD analysis to make suggestions about tennis ball specifications. You survey customers, gather data, crunch numbers, and produce the following correlation matrix:

Technical Specifications	Easy to See	Doesn't Bounce Funny	Stays Bouncy	Stays Clean
Thickness of shell	–0.35635	0.991189	0.994933	–0.17159
Depth of nap	–0.98473	0.391293	0.292968	–0.9747
Density of nap	0.188562	0.724196	0.771694	0.272394
% Nylon in nap	0.208248	0.386664	0.623205	0.262111
% Latex in shell	0.236801	–0.97232	–0.98992	0.042232

The nap is the fuzzy covering on a tennis ball.

a. Which of the following is apparently true, looking at your correlation matrix?
   i. Customers indicate that tennis balls with thick shells stay bouncy longer.
   ii. Customers indicate that tennis balls with thin shells stay bouncy longer.
   iii. Customers indicate that tennis balls with thin shells stay clean.

b. Which of the following is apparently true, looking at your correlation matrix?
   i. How easy a tennis ball is to see is related to how much latex is used in creating its shell.
   ii. How easy a tennis ball is to see is related to the depth of its nap.
   iii. Customers think the current model of Beserk tennis ball bounces funny.

c. Beserk is considering changing the nap on its tennis balls. What suggestions do you have, based on your correlation analysis?
   i. If Beserk makes the nap deeper (fuzzier), customers will probably complain that the new model of Beserk tennis ball doesn't stay clean as long.
   ii. If Beserk increases the amount of nylon used in the nap, customers will probably complain that the new model of Beserk tennis ball doesn't stay clean as long.
   iii. If Beserk makes the nap deeper (fuzzier), customers will probably complain that the new model of Beserk tennis ball is more difficult to see.

d. Assume that customers considered the first three attributes to be equally important, and consider each one to be three times as important as the last attribute, Stays Clean. Furthermore, no known synergies exist among any of the technical specifications. Sketch a complete QFD house of quality diagram, organizing all of Beserk's product design information.

CASE STUDY: SUMMERLINE CONTRACTING

Summerline Contracting specializes in large urban construction projects, particularly transportation infrastructure such as tunnels and new rail lines. Summerline's projects require that roads and other areas within a city center be taken out of daily use to serve as a job site, which Summerline may occupy for a year or longer. To win these high-value contracts, Summerline Contracting must maintain a reputation for both high-quality work and good citizenship in the neighborhoods that it temporarily occupies, as its activities are naturally disruptive to ongoing activity there. However, Summerline's management has always found the reputation for good citizenship is much more elusive than the reputation for high-quality work. While Summerline can proudly point to its finished products for quality inspection, its management can't always explain why some job sites are well received by surrounding residents and other job sites are costly to Summerline's reputation. Focus group discussions with residents nearby current job sites suggest that this reputation does rest on four different attributes:

- *Appearance.* Sometimes residents actively complain about the ugliness of the nearby job site, whereas other times they have no opinion of it.
- *Quiet.* Nearly everyone interviewed expressed appreciation for a construction job site "keeping the noise down," but not everyone felt that Summerline Contracting attempted this.
- *Road safety.* Although Summerline works hard to keep its job sites safe, its activities often cause unavoidable congestion in city traffic. In turn, this congestion sometimes causes a sharp increase in automobile accidents in the area. Summerline discovered that its reputation was being credited with both causing these accidents when they happen and preventing accidents when few occurred.
- *Company behavior.* While residents spoke of "good behavior," Summerline management relabeled these comments "public relations," because resident opinion of company behavior appeared to be driven by what, if anything, they had read or heard about the job site in local media outlets. Although each focus group participant had an opinion of the company's behavior, almost no one had had any direct contact with Summerline personnel or knowledge of its broader business activities.

Summerline job site managers have not shown much interest in this citizenship project, because they claim there is very little that can be done at a job site to influence these four issues in the minds of nearby residents. To provide a high-quality product on time, efficiently, and with maximum safety for its own employees, all practices at all Summerline job sites are nearly identical. At a recent meeting, job site managers acknowledged only three variables among Summerline's sites:

- *Nocturnal activity.* Job site managers do make different choices concerning how much work to conduct at night. Activity scheduled outside regular business hours can be scheduled in overnight shifts, or during daylight hours on weekends and holidays.
- *Barrier fencing.* All job sites are surrounded by barrier fencing to keep them secure, but the degree of investment in that fencing varies. At one extreme, some job sites work behind 12-foot solid walls that have been painted by a local artist on the public side, while at the other extreme a few have only 8-foot chain link barriers that block neither the view nor the dust from the site itself.
- *Fleet washing and painting policies.* All job sites operate a small fleet of vehicles and construction equipment. This fleet is washed regularly and even painted to repair natural wear marks at some locations, although less regularly at others. Opinion is divided among job site managers over how valuable this activity is.

As a follow-up to the earlier focus groups, Summerline Contracting identified five similar past projects with which to explore these issues further. Management collected what data they could on each of the five job sites, as measures of each of four valuable aspects of citizenship discussed by the residents:

Summerline Contracting Job Site Citizenship Data

Valuable Aspect	Thomson Reservoir Road	Marymount Parkway Lines	Bodmin Overpass	Serangoon North Upgrade	Rivervale Plaza
Appearance— Number of complaints to Summerline office or local authorities	0	4	0	0	10
Noise—Number of complaints to Summerline office or local authorities	0	3	0	14	0
Road safety— Number of auto accidents around job site (PDO = property damage only, no injuries)	0	2 PDOs	3 PDOs & 1 injury accident	9 PDOs & 5 injury accidents	4 PDOs
Good company behavior—Media hits, good and bad, naming job site in local TV and text reporting	1 brief TV report on small fine to Summerline for garbage bins	3 unfavorable TV and newspaper reports citing Summerline's activities	1 TV report on Summerline workers rescuing dog fallen into nearby drains	7 unfavorable TV and newspaper reports citing Summerline's activities	3 unfavorable TV and newspaper reports citing Summerline's activities

Summerline management then audited the records of each of the same five job sites, to determine what decisions were made concerning the three job site design variables:

Summerline Contracting Job Site Design Data

Variables	Thomson Reservoir Road	Marymount Parkway Lines	Bodmin Overpass	Serangoon North Upgrade	Rivervale Plaza
Nocturnal activity—Number of payroll hours clocked outside of daylight at job site	16,014 labor hours	7,440 labor hours	15,840 labor hours	0	15,624 labor hours
Barrier fencing— Composition and treatment of site fence, from photos on file	12-ft. solid barrier, decorated by local artist	8-ft. solid barrier, undecorated	8-ft. solid barrier, undecorated	8-ft.solid barrier, undecorated	8-ft. chain link barrier
Fleet washing and painting policies— Determined from phone interviews with job site managers and other personnel	Washed & damage repainted every other Monday	Washed monthly & damage repainted at end of project	Washed daily & damage repainted every Saturday	Washed monthly & damage repainted at end of project	Washed monthly & damage repainted at end of project

Questions

1. Based on this data, develop a QFD-style matrix for Summerline Contracting, relating the four job site citizenship ratings to the three job site design variables. Document your steps in translating the information provided into workable forms for the calculation of correlation coefficients. State any important assumptions you made.
2. Based on your QFD analysis, if Summerline Contracting can invest in only one of the job site design variables for its next project, which do you recommend, and why? Which, if any, do you recommend that it avoid?
3. QFD analysis is limited to the assumptions of the correlation coefficients from which it is constructed. As a result, this style of analysis relies on simple pairings of possible cause-and-effect relationships, and won't reveal if more complicated interactions exist, such as two design features each having a benefit, but the presence of both features canceling some benefit. Logically, could there exist more complex interrelationships among two or more of the job site design variables and one or more of the job site quality ratings, being missed by your matrix? If so, describe an example.

BIBLIOGRAPHY

Austin, R., and L. Devin. 2003. *Artful Making: What Managers Need to Know About How Artists Work.* Upper Saddle River, NJ: FT Prentice Hall.

Evans, J., and W. Lindsay. 2002. *The Management and Control of Quality,* 5th ed. Cincinnati, OH: South-Western/Thomson Learning.

Gass, S., and A. Assad. 2005. *An Annotated Timeline of Operations Research: An Informal History.* New York: Kluwer Academic Publishers.

Flaherty, E. 2009. "Safety First: The Consumer Product Safety Improvement Act of 2008." *Loyola Consumer Law Review* 21(3): 372–91.

Hauser, J. R., and D. Clausing. 1988. "The House of Quality." *Harvard Business Review.* (May/June): 63–73.

Hoyle, D. 2009. *ISO 9000 Quality Systems Handbook*, 6th ed. Oxford, UK: Elsevier.

Jablonski, C. 2011. "From End to End: Guiding New Product Development with Life Cycle Assessments." *APICS Magazine* 21(6).

Kaplan, R., and A. Mikes. 2012. "Managing Risks: A New Framework." *Harvard Business Review* (June): 48–60.

Kemp, S. 2006. *Quality Management Demystified.* New York: McGraw-Hill.

Kiron, D., N. Kruschwitz, K. Haanaes, and I. Streng Velken. 2012. "Sustainability Nears a Tipping Point." *MIT Sloan Management Review* 53(2).

Tague, N. 2005. *The Quality Toolbox,* 2nd ed. Milwaukee, WI: ASQ Quality Press.

Thomke, S., and D. Reinertsen. 2012. "Six Myths of Product Development," *Harvard Business Review* (May): 84–94.

PART 1 ESSENTIALS

CHAPTER

4

Forecasting

The future isn't what it used to be.

—Paul Valéry

MAJOR SECTIONS

IN THIS CHAPTER, LOOK FOR...

- Contrasting approaches to forecasting, including the choice between utilizing human intuition versus mathematical modeling.
- Different measures of accuracy: ME, MAD, MSE, MAPE, and tracking signal.
- Forecasting tools, including linear regression, moving averages, and exponential smoothing.
- Use of forecasting tools for data analysis, as opposed to prediction.

INTRODUCTION

The word *forecasting* describes almost any attempt to anticipate the future. You have probably heard it used for such diverse activities as economic forecasting, weather forecasting, and personal fortune-telling. In operations management, forecasting is more specialized, usually focusing on one particular outcome—future demand on a given operation. The effective operations manager must, therefore, consider all relevant conditions and related outcomes to accurately plan for that demand. Imagine, for example, needing to anticipate customer visits or estimate materials needed. We will look at several different forecasting approaches available to meet such challenges.

FORECASTING APPROACHES

forecasting
Predicting future events.

Figure 4.1 summarizes several broad categories of forecasting methodologies that a manager might choose when attempting to predict demand on an operation. Each of these approaches suggests specific techniques, and each of the techniques has differing advantages and disadvantages. As Figure 4.1 suggests, the first and most strategic choice when selecting a forecasting technique is whether to use a qualitative or a quantitative approach.

Qualitative Forecasting

A qualitative forecasting approach attempts to capture human intuition, such as an expert's insight, when developing a prediction. Pictured as the left-hand-side branch of

FIGURE 4.1 Forecasting Methodologies

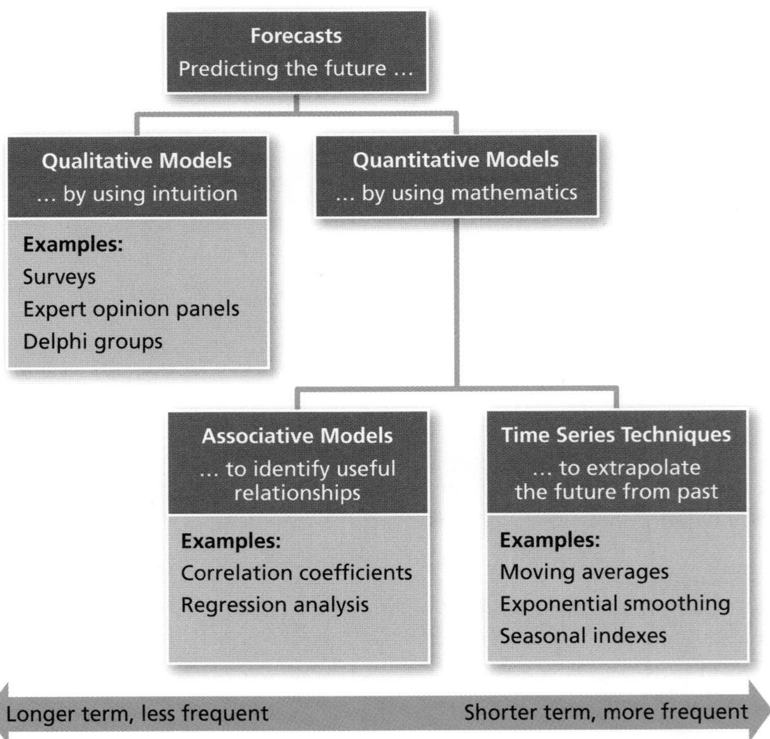

the forecasting map in Figure 4.1, qualitative techniques are structured methods for gathering the insight of forecast participants. How this insight is gathered and who exactly provides this insight varies among the techniques mentioned in the figure.

Surveys One method of gathering insight into the future is survey research, including consumer surveys and market research. This method poses questions to large numbers of people believed to have some knowledge of the outcome of interest, such as potential consumers of a product. These questions may be posed through web-based forms, paper-based questionnaires, or in personal interviews, with the resulting answers compiled and interpreted to create a forecast. Web-based technology in particular can support the process of crowdsourcing as a potential forecasting tool, allowing for the rapid generation of forecasts by averaging large numbers of independent responses to a single question.

crowdsourcing
Crowd outsourcing; combining independent efforts of many people to accomplish a task.

Expert Opinion Panels While surveys and crowdsourcing rely on the collection of insight from large numbers of people, expert opinion panels rely on a much smaller group believed to have superior knowledge of the future outcome. When these experts are also leaders and managers, the group may then be referred to as an executive opinion panel or a jury of executive opinion. An expert opinion panel brings its participants together to discuss the outcome of interest and then develops a prediction from the panel's consensus view.

expert opinion panel
A small group of highly knowledgeable people who develop prediction through discussion and consensus.

jury of executive opinion
An expert panel composed of managers.

Delphi Groups Like expert opinion panels, Delphi groups rely on a small number of experts to create a forecast. However, unlike expert opinion panels, Delphi groups never discuss their opinions, and may remain anonymous to one another even after the forecast is completed. This method, therefore, theoretically removes bias; stronger personalities or more influential members of the group do not have the opportunity to sway the opinions of fellow group members.

The Delphi method requires a facilitator to send each participant the forecasting question, gather the participants' responses, create an anonymous report of those responses, and distribute this report back to the participants. After the participants have read this report, the facilitator asks the question again, gathers a second set of responses, creates a second report, and distributes that report back to the Delphi group members. Because participants are encouraged to revise their answers after reading each report, this process repeats until a consensus is acheived.

Delphi method
A qualitative forecasting technique in which experts achieve consensus through a blind process via a facilitator.

Quantitative Forecasting

Quantitative forecasting relies on mathematics to develop predictions. Specifically, this approach relies on identification of useful relationships between a future outcome of interest and any other known factor or factors. Figure 4.1 illustrates two important branches within this type of analysis, associative models and time series analysis.

Associative Models In general, associative or causal models identify relationships between an outcome of interest and one or more factors that might be used to predict an outcome. Associative models are therefore based on two types of variable. The dependent variable is the outcome that depends on, or is influenced by, outside factors. Those external influential factors are in turn referred to as the independent variables.

Forecast managers often begin to investigate associations by visualizing the data as scatter plot diagrams, such as the one in Figure 4.2. Here the dependent variable is the delay between a drug's injection and relief of the patient's symptoms, or the needle-to-symptom-relief time. Figure 4.2 suggests a distinct association between this variable and the delay of the same injection from the onset of the patient's symptoms, or the symptom-to-needle time, for 30 patients.

causal modeling
Predicting an outcome by identifying its relationship with one or more other factors.

dependent variable
An outcome of interest influenced by one or more factors.

independent variable
A factor used to predict an outcome of interest.

FIGURE 4.2 Scatterplot Diagram

This plot suggests a potential association between promptness of drug treatment and effectiveness of treatment for 30 patients.

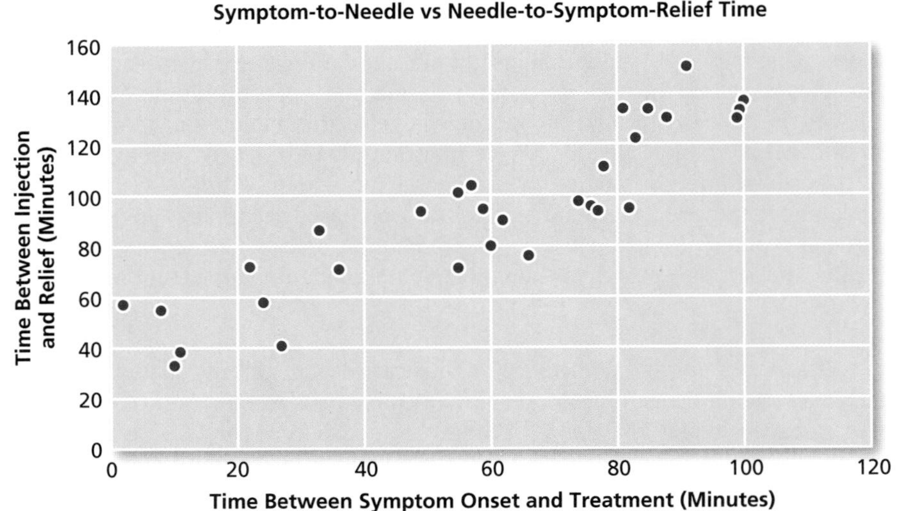

Specifically, the upward direction of the cloud of points describing the past 30 patients suggests that the longer the delay until the injection, the longer the actual time until relief after the injection. Knowledge of this relationship helps optimize the care of future patients. While visual examination of such graphs suggests many such relationships, mathematical techniques clarify and quantify the links, as we will see later in this chapter.

extrapolation Projecting existing data into the future.

time series Values observed in chronological order.

Time Series Analysis Where associative modeling attempts to predict a future outcome by identifying important links between the outcome and other factors in its environment, time series analysis assumes the future outcome is simply a function of that outcome's historical behavior. Thus, this approach focuses on past data in an attempt to project this behavior into the future, a methodology also known as extrapolation.

A time series is a set of observations of a particular outcome at regular intervals in time, creating a history that can be illustrated as a line graph. In the example in Figure 4.3, the outcome of interest is the total number of new housing construction projects, or housing starts in the US, as observed every month from January 1959 to June 2010.

Figure 4.3 suggests that monthly US housing starts may be the result of several distinct influences, such as the rhythmic peaks that mark summer as the busiest months for construction, or the broader rise and fall of those peaks in longer economic cycles. In general, time series analysis includes a process for clarifying these influences, known as time series decomposition. We discuss this "taking apart" of existing historical data to expose its component influences later in this chapter.

time series decomposition Modeling observed values based on identifiable component influences.

Selecting a Qualitative versus a Quantitative Approach

Generally, the logistics of qualitative approaches are more complex than the mathematical analysis of existing data, which translates into higher costs. However, while a quantitative analysis is usually less expensive, this approach is not always the most effective. In some cases relevant historical data is not available, such as when attempting to predict the sales of a new product. In other cases, historical data may be available, but the forecast required is so far forward in the future that the current data is likely to be of little relevance. In such cases, qualitative approaches are the better option. For this reason, qualitative approaches are often associated with forecasts having longer planning

planning horizon The farthest point in the future considered in decision making.

A Typical Time Series **FIGURE 4.3**

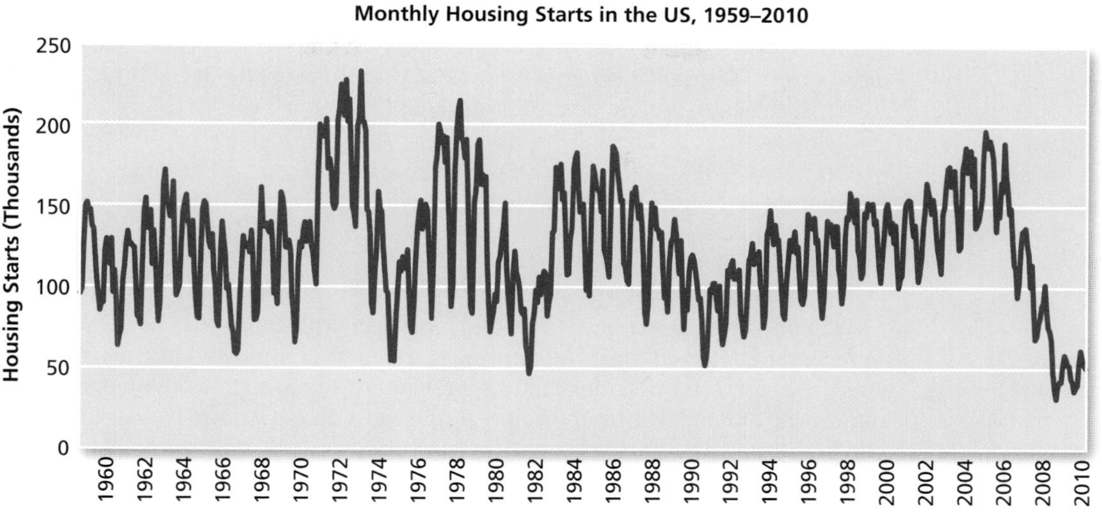

horizons, such as anticipating sales several years in the future. In contrast, highly convenient yet data-dependent quantitative techniques may be used for long-term forecasts, but are particularly helpful in generating frequent short-term forecasts, such as anticipating seasonal, weekly, or even daily sales. Selection of qualitative, quantitative, or a blending of these approaches is driven by the needs and the environment of the forecaster.

EVALUATING FORECASTS

Because so many forecasting techniques are available, it makes good sense to evaluate them, to determine which particular technique is most desirable for a given situation. Successful forecasts may lead to competitive advantage, so it is no surprise that we base our evaluations on accuracy, responsiveness, and cost. Though none of these measures should be considered in the absence of the others, accuracy is the natural focus of forecast evaluation.

Demand Forecasting for Time-Sensitive Products

Fresh Christmas trees are an excellent example of not only a seasonal but also a time-sensitive product, because their sales are limited to one holiday annually and their shelf life is quite short. The size of the shipment here is the result of a retailer's careful forecast of near-future demand. Interestingly, causal modeling has also shown correlation between fresh Christmas tree sales and demand for emergency services (house fires) and for landfill space. As a result, communities often work to defeat these links with holiday education campaigns on the safe keeping of these trees and postholiday collection programs to convert discarded trees into other useful products such as mulch.

Accuracy

Accuracy is the central measure of success in forecasting. Once we create a forecast, we must wait to see the actual outcome to determine the quality of that forecast. Accuracy can be expressed in several ways, including the common performance measures of error, mean error (ME), mean squared error (MSE), mean absolute deviation (MAD), tracking signal, and mean absolute percent error (MAPE).

error
The difference between an observed value and a predicted value.

Mean Error (ME) Error is the simplest measure of forecast accuracy. Once an actual outcome (A_t) in some period t becomes known, the error (E_t) in that period's forecast (F_t) is calculated as:

$$E_t = A_t - F_t$$

naïve forecast
Assuming a future value equals the most recent actual value available.

Figure 4.4 shows a portion of a spreadsheet with the actual data from Figure 4.3, compared to a naïve forecast of housing starts in each of those same months. In a naïve forecast a forecaster assumes that the next future value, such as the number of housing starts next month, will be the same as the most recent known value, in this case the number of housing starts observed in the current month. This forecasting technique is simulated for 618 months in the Figure 4.4 spreadsheet model, and the forecast error associated with each of those months appears in column E of the spreadsheet.

mean error (ME)
An average of forecast errors; useful for indicating forecast bias.

forecast bias
A tendency to create errors that are predominantly positive or negative.

Averaging forecast errors over time results in the performance measure known as ME, or mean error. Figure 4.4 displays the ME that results from averaging all values in column E, most of which are not visible in this sample view. While an error of zero indicates a perfectly accurate forecast, an *average* error of near or exactly zero, such as ME = –0.07 in Figure 4.4, does not necessarily signal accuracy. As you can see in column E in Figure 4.4 substantial forecasting errors occurred within the first year of the time series for US housing starts between 1959 and 2010. Therefore, we would be premature to declare these naïve forecasting values accurate based solely on a near-zero ME; the positive and negative error values canceled each other in the calculation. Ironically, while this renders ME an unreliable measure of accuracy in this case, it also makes ME an excellent measure of forecast bias.

Forecast bias is any tendency to make forecast errors of a certain type, such as consistently predicting too high or too low. Forecast bias is central to forecast evaluation because we can control for any error made consistently and thereby make more accurate forecasts in the future. While it appears that naïve forecasting is generating a wide range of errors in column E of Figure 4.4, the ME of –0.07 suggests it is not favoring any particular direction in those errors, or is free from forecast bias.

FIGURE 4.4 A Sample View of a Spreadsheet Model of Error Measures

Data from US housing starts, February 1959–July 2010 (618 months)

	A	B	C	D	E	F	G	H	I	J	K	L
1			Housing	Naïve	Forecast	Percent	Squared	Absolute	Absolute			
2	Month	Year	Starts (000s)	Forecast	Error	Error	Error	Error	Percent Error			
3	Jan	1959	96.2									
4	Feb	1959	99	96.2	2.8	2.8%	7.84	2.8	2.8%		ME:	-0.07
5	Mar	1959	127.7	99	28.7	22.5%	823.69	28.7	22.5%		MSE:	324.8
6	Apr	1959	150.8	127.7	23.1	15.3%	533.61	23.1	15.3%		MAD:	13.6
7	May	1959	152.5	150.8	1.7	1.1%	2.89	1.7	1.1%		MAPE:	11.6%
8	Jun	1959	147.8	152.5	-4.7	-3.2%	22.09	4.7	3.2%		Tracking signal:	-3.3
9	Jul	1959	148.1	147.8	0.3	0.2%	0.09	0.3	0.2%			
10	Aug	1959	138.2	148.1	-9.9	-7.2%	98.01	9.9	7.2%			
11	Sep	1959	136.4	138.2	-1.8	-1.3%	3.24	1.8	1.3%			
12	Oct	1959	120	136.4	-16.4	-13.7%	268.96	16.4	13.7%			
13	Nov	1959	104.7	120	-15.3	-14.6%	234.09	15.3	14.6%			
14	Dec	1959	95.6	104.7	-9.1	-9.5%	82.81	9.1	9.5%			
15	Jan	1960	86	95.6	-9.6	-11.2%	92.16	9.6	11.2%			
16	Feb	1960	90.7	86	4.7	5.2%	22.09	4.7	5.2%			

Supermarket Forecasting Error

Demand forecast errors often cause excess or shortage in reality. Here, an input error generated unintentionally low forecasts for a particular class of dried pasta at this supermarket. The telltale result is this conspicuous gap in shelf space within the pasta section, as the stock requested based on the inaccurate forecast numbers has been depleted unnaturally early.

Mean Squared Error (MSE) Because we cannot rely on the accuracy of data based on ME, we need another approach. One approach that prevents obscuring of errors is to square each forecast error, producing a nonnegative value. When all squared errors are averaged across a set of forecasts, the result is a performance measure called mean squared error, or MSE. If the set included n forecast errors, MSE can be stated as

mean squared error (MSE)
An average of the squared values of a set of forecast errors.

$$\text{MSE} = \Sigma E_t^2/n$$

Figure 4.4 indicates a MSE of 324.8 for the naïve forecast of housing starts between 1959 and 2010, although interpretation of this number is limited without the MSE of another method for comparison. MSE falls short in other areas as well. In summarizing accuracy as a single number, MSE penalizes large forecast errors by squaring them. As a result, an otherwise highly accurate forecasting method could suffer a few large errors, resulting in extremely large squared errors that average together with numerous small squared errors to produce an unimpressive MSE. This reading is then not a helpful statement of the true performance of that forecasting method. Supermarket sales that are interrupted by an unexpected event such as a blizzard or a hurricane are good examples of circumstances that can create a few large errors in an otherwise reliable stream of forecasts.

Mean Absolute Deviation (MAD) and Mean Absolute Percent Error (MAPE)
Another measure of forecast accuracy is to consider absolute errors only, dropping the issue of positive or negative deviation in the forecast. Averaging such observations into the single value known as mean absolute deviation (MAD) provides the same benefits as MSE, but without the exaggeration of larger errors. Generally, calculation of MAD for n forecasts of period t can be described as

mean absolute deviation (MAD)
An average of the absolute values of a set of forecast errors.

$$\text{MAD} = \Sigma |E_t|/n$$

Figure 4.4 indicates that the MAD earned by naïve forecasting of 1959–2010 US housing starts is 13.6. However, no simple rule determines whether the value 13.6 is "good" or "bad" as a MAD; that depends on what is being forecast. For example, if a forecaster maintained a MAD of 13.6 over many periods of predicting outcomes with actual values ranging in the thousands, this accomplishment would be much more impressive than the forecasting data set visible in Figure 4.4. Since US housing starts were stated in thousands, the naïve forecaster actually missed the actual by an average of 13,600 individual housing starts, or was off by an average of 13.6 when predicting numbers that ranged from 86 to 152.5 in the first 14 months of data visible in Figure 4.4. To get a better sense of the quality of a forecast, relative to the actual values being forecast, forecast error is often translated into percent error:

percent error
Forecast error divided by the corresponding actual value.

$$\text{Percent error in forecast for period } t = E_t/A_t$$

From the percent error in each forecast, as shown in column F of Figure 4.4, we can calculate an alternative measure known as mean absolute percent error (MAPE). In the case of the US housing start example, the MAPE visible in Figure 4.4 gives greater insight into the quality of the forecasts: the naïve forecast of housing starts each month is off by an average of 11.6% compared to the actual data.

mean absolute percent error (MAPE)
Average of the absolute values of a set of percent errors.

Tracking Signal Finally, a forecaster concerned with monitoring potential bias over time could consider calculating a tracking signal periodically. A tracking signal is a ratio of the sum of forecast errors divided by the MAD of the forecast over the same time period, or

tracking signal
Ratio of the sum of a set of forecast errors over the MAD of that forecast.

$$\text{Tracking signal} = \Sigma\, E_t/\text{MAD}$$

Returning once more to Figure 4.4, summing the values in column E and dividing that sum by the MAD of 13.6 yields a tracking signal of –3.3 for 618 months of naïve forecasting. In practice, firms recalculate their tracking signal at much shorter intervals than 618 months, monitoring for insufficient forecast performance in the form of a value that falls outside a set of predetermined limits. While these limits can be specific to particular situations, the tracking signal is expected to be centered on zero, with very small values indicating a lack of bias, but not necessarily high accuracy.

Because each forecasting technique suffers limitations, effective forecasters consider more than one measure, as demonstrated in Scenario 1.

Scenario 1

Error Measures

Livingston Medical Services provides nonemergency medical transportation, such as patient transfers between hospitals. Livingston has contracts in 60 metropolitan areas across North America and must staff its fleet of transportation vehicles according to projected demand for its services. Each month, Livingston used both a mathematical model and a jury of top managers to estimate overall demand for nonemergency medical transports within its combined service area:

Month	Math Model Forecast	Jury of Executive Opinion Forecast	Actual Number of Transports
January	13,128	12,500	12,480
February	12,009	13,000	11,568
March	12,649	13,500	13,244
April	16,387	16,000	15,560
May	16,190	16,000	16,034
June	23,002	24,000	23,400

How does Livingston Medical Service's mathematical forecasting model compare with the forecasts created by its jury of top managers? Which was more accurate during these past 6 months?

Analysis

To compare these two methods, we calculate error measures for each.

MATH MODEL FORECASTS

Month	Math Model Forecast Error (Actual – Forecast)		Squared Error	Absolute Error	Percent Absolute Error (Abs Error/Actual)
January	12,480 – 13,128 =	–648	419,904	648	5.19%
February	11,568 – 12,009 =	–441	194,481	441	3.81
March	13,244 – 12,649 =	595	354,025	595	4.49
April	15,560 – 16,387 =	–827	683,929	827	5.31
May	16,034 – 16,190 =	–156	24,336	156	0.97
June	23,400 – 23,002 =	398	158,404	398	1.70
		ME: –179.8	MSE: 305,846.5	MAD: 510.8	MAPE: 3.58%

Math Model Tracking Signal: (–648 – 441 + 595 – 827 – 156 + 398)/510.8 = –2.1

JURY OF EXECUTIVE OPINION FORECASTS

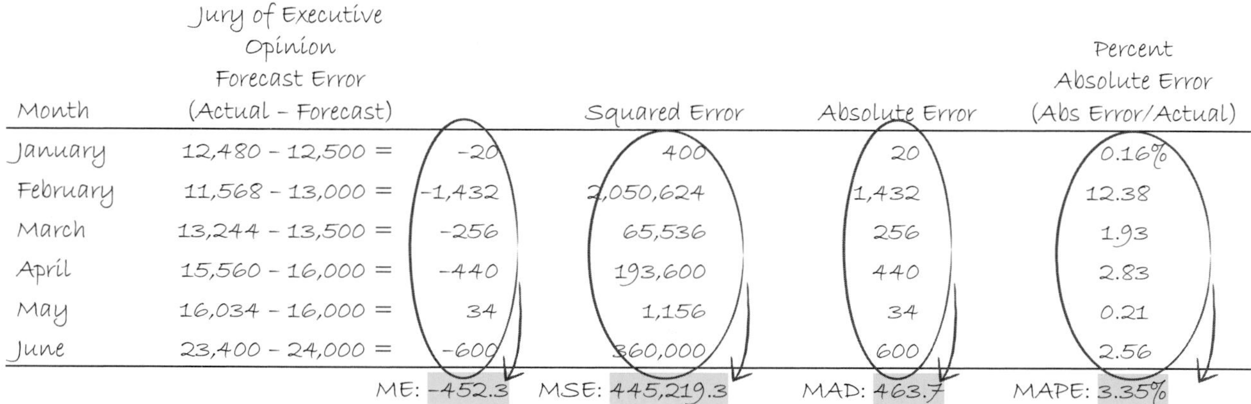

Month	Jury of Executive Opinion Forecast Error (Actual – Forecast)		Squared Error	Absolute Error	Percent Absolute Error (Abs Error/Actual)
January	12,480 – 12,500 =	–20	400	20	0.16%
February	11,568 – 13,000 =	–1,432	2,050,624	1,432	12.38
March	13,244 – 13,500 =	–256	65,536	256	1.93
April	15,560 – 16,000 =	–440	193,600	440	2.83
May	16,034 – 16,000 =	34	1,156	34	0.21
June	23,400 – 24,000 =	–600	360,000	600	2.56
		ME: –452.3	MSE: 445,219.3	MAD: 463.7	MAPE: 3.35%

Jury of Opinion Tracking Signal: (–20 – 1,432 – 256 – 440 + 34 – 600)/463.7 = –5.9

Insight Comparing the measures ME, MSE, MAD, MAPE, and tracking signal for each of the two sets of forecasts, we see that both forecasting methods appear similar in accuracy over these past 6 months, at least in terms of absolute error. While the jury of executive opinion has a slightly better MAD and MAPE, we cannot ignore its distinctly poorer MSE. Looking closer, the jury's February forecast was particularly inaccurate, causing a large squared error and inflating its MSE. The jury of executive opinion also earned a poorer ME and tracking signal when compared to the math model, revealing a possible bias toward higher forecasts that should be monitored further. ■

Responsiveness

responsiveness
The degree to which a technique modifies forecasts to reflect recent changes in past data.

A forecasting technique is called *responsive* if a distinct change in recent outcomes, such as a sharp rise in last month's sales, results in a similar change to future forecasts, such as a sharp increase in next month's sales forecast. While responsiveness sounds positive, it is important to understand that responsiveness and accuracy are two different features, and it is possible for a forecast to be both responsive and inaccurate. Naïve forecasting is considered a benchmark for responsiveness, because a forecaster cannot react more strongly to recent data than to assume that the most recent actual is also the best forecast for the next period. However, Figure 4.4 illustrates that the naïve approach, when applied to 618 months of US housing start data, is not particularly accurate.

Whether responsiveness is or is not a desired feature of a forecasting technique depends on the environment. If, in fact, the forecaster believes that recent changes in actual outcomes signal similar changes in the future, then responsiveness is desirable. However, if the outcome is subject to a great deal of random noise, responsiveness is less helpful because the change made to the forecast in response to the past is less likely to be a meaningful match to the future. Furthermore, if the outcome of interest is subject to a predictable pattern of changes through time, responsiveness alone never anticipates such patterns and always lags behind in mimicking the changes.

Cost

Finally, we cannot fully evaluate a forecasting technique for future use without considering its cost. In some instances, the cost of one technique compared to another is quite dramatic; as you would expect, the cost of recruiting experts to participate in a Delphi group is often far higher than simply plugging numbers into a formula in a spreadsheet. But don't be fooled: the cost of gathering the data needed to plug into those formulas might be high as well. Simpler techniques are often preferred for short-term forecasts that must be created repeatedly over time. Of course, an inexpensive forecasting technique that does not produce useful results is never a good option, which brings us back to the issue of accuracy.

ASSOCIATIVE TECHNIQUES

Associative techniques identify useful relationships between different sets of data, so that one set of data might be predicted by knowledge of the other set of data. Generally, the values within one set of data appear to at least partially depend on the second set of data, and if this association can be expressed quantitatively, it can then be used to project future values. Here are some examples of potential associations:

- *Demand for certain construction materials to housing starts.* The more housing projects underway, the greater the consumption of the required materials.
- *Demand for electricity and natural gas to outside air temperature.* Extremes in temperature cause spikes in household demand as people operate air-conditioners and furnaces in their homes.
- *Demand for college education to the unemployment rate.* The lower the unemployment rate, the somewhat less the demand for college education, as some people opt to take a job instead of attending college.

In these examples, demand for construction materials, electricity, and college education are the dependent variables; their behavior appears to depend on housing starts, outside air temperature, and the unemployment rate, respectively—the independent variables. The most popular tool for quantifying these relationships is regression analysis.

Regression Analysis

Regression analysis clarifies observed relationships between a dependent variable and one or more independent variables. Linear regression focuses specifically on the paired relationship of a dependent variable and one independent variable. This type of influence was suggested earlier by Figure 4.2, in which the amount of time that lapses between the onset of a patient's symptoms and the injection of a drug (symptom-to-needle time) appears strongly related to the amount of time the patient must wait for relief from the symptoms (needle-to-symptom-relief time). These two delays, when plotted as coordinate points for 30 patients, suggest an upward-sloping line, indicating that the longer a patient waits for an injection, the more time the drug then requires to bring relief. Figure 4.5 shows the same data as Figure 4.2, but includes a straight line that best describes this relationship. Restated, Figure 4.5 displays the one straight line that minimizes the squared errors between itself and the actual data points. Thus, the process of identifying such a line is also known as *least-squares regression*.

regression analysis Using mathematical relationships between two or more variables to predict future values.

Any line or linear relationship can be stated as an equation, displayed here in slope-intercept format:

$$Y = a + bX$$

where a is the Y-intercept of the line and b is its slope on the graph. In the case of Figure 4.5, this equation is $Y = 36.623 + 0.9661X$, implying that needle-to-symptom-relief time for a patient might be estimated by multiplying that patient's symptom-to-needle time by 0.9661 and adding 36.623 minutes to the result. The slope alone ($b = 0.9661$) implies that for each additional minute the injection is delayed, slightly less than 1 minute (0.9661) *more* of delay until relief after the injection occurs.

Note that a regression equation alone does not comment on whether a linear relationship is significant in any sense; it is always possible to draw a straight line across any cloud of points, regardless of what the points represent. The strength of the relationship in Figure 4.5 is visible both in the distinct shape of the cloud and in the values of r and r^2 displayed there, as we will discuss later in this section.

A Linear Regression Model of Highly Correlated Data (n = 30) **FIGURE 4.5**

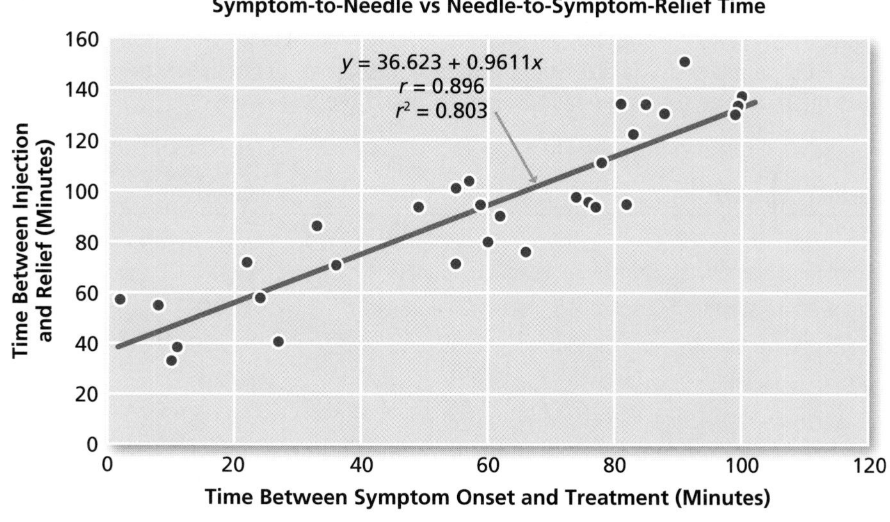

Calculating a Linear Regression Equation

Linear regression is a popular tool in business analysis. Calculating a regression equation for a given set of data identifies the specific values of the slope (b) and intercept (a) of a straight line that best fits that data.

Slope and Intercept The slope (b) and the intercept (a) of a linear regression equation can be determined with these two formulas:

$$b = \frac{\Sigma XY - n\overline{X}\overline{Y}}{\Sigma X^2 - n\overline{X}^2} \qquad a = \overline{Y} - b\overline{X}$$

Here X represents the independent variable data and Y represents the dependent variable data. The input value n refers to the total number of observations in the paired data set, such as $n = 30$ patients in the case of Figure 4.5.

Because of the popularity of this type of analysis, slope and intercept formulas are often preprogrammed functions on business calculators and within spreadsheet software. Without benefit of these technological short-cuts, most of the work required by the formulas is the calculation of component summary statistics such as ΣXY, which requires that each pair of independent (X) and dependent (Y) data values be multiplied together, and then the set of n resulting values be summed together. All these summary statistics can be calculated by creating a convenient work table from any set of data, as demonstrated in Scenario 2a.

Scenario 2a

Calculating a Linear Regression Equation

Livingston Medical Services provides different types of medical transportation, ranging from fully staffed mobile intensive care units to courtesy vans for transporting clients from their homes to medical appointments. Livingston also works with different types of organizations, negotiating contracts with governments, medical facilities, and assisted-living communities. While predicting the mix of transportation that an organization will require is important to Livingston's success as a provider, it was previously thought that these organizations were not similar enough to find any common factor associated with their demands. Recently, however, one director began to suspect differently, at least in the case of predicting demand for courtesy van transportation. While Livingston does provide this service to a variety of organizations, contracts with these organizations can all be described by a common measure: the total number of clients, or people who could potentially summon a courtesy van as per the contract. Comparing client data to actual annual courtesy van demand for seven contracts suggests there may be a strong relationship between these two issues:

Contracting Organization	Total Annual Clients	Actual Annual Courtesy Van Transports
Marion County Government, FL	10,558	1,042
Westwood Retirement Villas, Durham and Orange Counties, NC	22,010	2,560
Brookstone Hospital and Affiliated Clinics, Port Washington, NY	2,455	149
Outer Banks Senior Services, Wilmington, NC	1,405	186
Sumter County Health Services, Bushnell, FL	12,400	292
Greater Bay Dialysis Services, Baltimore, MD	5,410	1,128
Duval County Health Services, FL	20,200	2,203

What is the linear regression equation that best expresses this relationship? What does this equation suggest the annual demand for courtesy van transports would be for a potential contract with a new assisted-living facility that accommodates 2,100 clients?

Analysis

The first step in conducting a regression analysis is to clarify which set of data is the *X*, or independent variable, and which is the *Y*, or dependent variable. In this case, the annual number of courtesy van transports is the *Y*, in that the director suspects it depends on the total number of clients eligible through the contract, or *X*. At this point, we can develop the regression equation by first finding the summary statistics needed in the slope-intercept formula:

LINEAR REGRESSION SUMMARY STATS

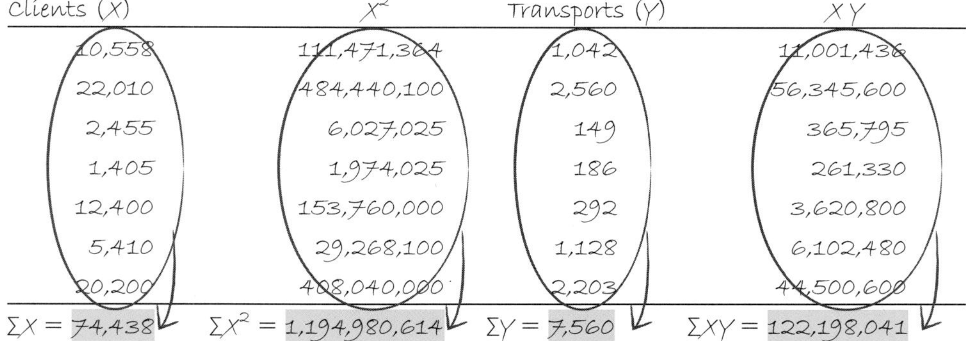

Clients (X)	X^2	Transports (Y)	XY
10,558	111,471,364	1,042	11,001,436
22,010	484,440,100	2,560	56,345,600
2,455	6,027,025	149	365,795
1,405	1,974,025	186	261,330
12,400	153,760,000	292	3,620,800
5,410	29,268,100	1,128	6,102,480
20,200	408,040,000	2,203	44,500,600
$\Sigma X = 74{,}438$	$\Sigma X^2 = 1{,}194{,}980{,}614$	$\Sigma Y = 7{,}560$	$\Sigma XY = 122{,}198{,}041$

We also include the average values of each set of observations:

$$n = 7 \qquad \bar{X} = \Sigma X/n = 74{,}438/7 = 10{,}634 \qquad \bar{Y} = \Sigma Y/n = 7{,}560/7 = 1{,}080$$

Once we calculate the summary statistics, we can complete the formulas for the slope and intercept of the linear regression equation:

LINEAR REGRESSION SLOPE AND INTERCEPT

$$b = \frac{\Sigma XY - n\bar{X}\bar{Y}}{\Sigma X^2 - n\bar{X}^2} = \frac{122{,}198{,}041 - 7 \times (10{,}634 \times 1{,}080)}{1{,}194{,}980{,}614 - 7 \times (10{,}634 \times 10{,}634)} = 0.10363$$

Now we determine that the equation that best expresses the linear relationship between the number of clients and the number of courtesy van transports is

$$a = \bar{Y} - b\bar{X} = 1{,}080 - 0.10363 \times 10{,}634 = -22$$

Finished Regression Equation

$$Y(\text{transports}) = a + bX\ (\text{clients}) \rightarrow Y = -22 + 0.10363X$$

To use this expression to estimate the demand for van transports for a potential contract with 2,100 clients, we substitute 2,100 for *X*:

ESTIMATE FOR CONTRACT WITH 2,100 CLIENTS

$$Y = -22 + 0.10363X$$
$$= -22 + (0.10363 \times 2{,}100) = 195.62\text{, rounded to 196 transports}$$

Insight This regression model suggests that if Livingston enters into a new contract with an assisted-living community with 2,100 clients, the contract will create demand for about 196 courtesy van transports annually. However, Livingston is strongly cautioned against making any further decisions based on this estimate until the strength of this linear relationship is investigated. Furthermore, Livingston should gather more historical data if possible, since this model is only based on seven observations of past client/courtesy van transport relationships. ■

correlation coefficient A measure of the strength of any linear relationship between two sets of observations.

Coefficient of Correlation (*r*) A correlation coefficient (*r*) is a value that expresses both the strength and the direction of a linear relationship. We can calculate this statistic for any two sets of observations *X* and *Y* by completing this formula:

$$r = \frac{n(\Sigma XY) - (\Sigma X)(\Sigma Y)}{\sqrt{[n(\Sigma X^2) - (\Sigma X)^2] \times [n(\Sigma Y^2) - (\Sigma Y)^2]}}$$

Regardless of the size of the original data set or its contents, the result of this formula is always between 1.0 and −1.0. A correlation coefficient near 1.0 indicates a strong positive correlation between the two factors in the data set, meaning that higher values of *X* were consistently associated with higher values of *Y*, and lower values of *X* with lower values of *Y*. This strong positive correlation is visible in Figure 4.5, where $r = 0.896$ is displayed as the correlation coefficient between symptom-to-needle time and needle-to-symptom-relief time for 30 patients treated with an injection. If *r* has a value near its lower limit of −1.0, this likewise indicates a strong relationship between the observations of *X* and *Y*, although this is a negative correlation or inverse relationship. In this case, when a value for *X* is observed as high, its associated *Y* observation is generally low, and vice versa. The observed relationship between gasoline prices and motel demand in the United States, for example, is a negative correlation: when gasoline prices increase, the number of motel room rentals tends to decrease, as customers decide against traveling by car and thus do not need a motel.

While a correlation coefficient can be calculated for any two sets of observations, a linear relationship does not necessarily exist between them. A correlation coefficient with a value near zero, the center of its range, indicates no distinct linear relationship exists between *X* and *Y*. To create a visual example of distinctly poor correlation, the US housing starts time series first introduced in Figure 4.3 can be reformatted as a scatter plot diagram in which each month's housing start value is plotted over that month's calendar year, as in Figure 4.6.

A linear regression equation fitted to this cloud of monthly housing starts indicates that the one linear relationship that best fits this data is

$$Y \text{ (monthly housing starts)} = 510.85 - 0.1943 \times X \text{ (the year)}$$

FIGURE 4.6 A Scatterplot of Poorly Correlated Data

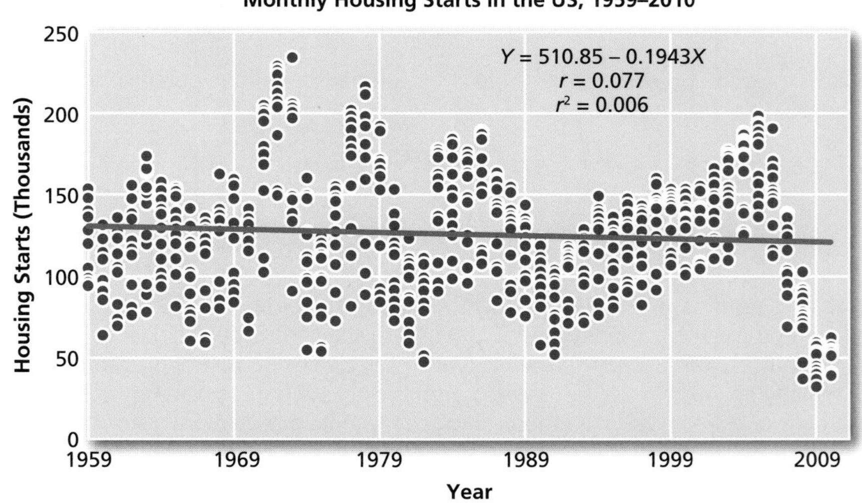

However, the corresponding correlation coefficient of $r = 0.077$ cautions that this isn't a very useful equation for predicting future housing starts, because the strength of the linear relationship is poor and may indeed be nonexistent in reality.

Coefficient of Determination (r^2) Another measure of the strength of a linear relationship is its coefficient of determination, or r^2. As the symbol r^2 implies, the coefficient of determination is the square of the correlation coefficient r. For example, the earlier high correlation between symptom-to-needle time and needle-to-symptom-relief time of $r = 0.896$ in Figure 4.5 corresponds to an r^2 of $(0.896)^2$, or 0.803. r^2 is always a value between 0 and 1, and this value provides an interesting commentary on the quality of the linear relationship between two variables, in that the r^2 of a regression model can be interpreted as the proportion of actual variation in Y that is explained by the regression equation. In the context of Figure 4.5, 80% of the actual variation in needle-to-symptom-relief time among 30 patients is explained by the equation displayed there. In contrast, Figure 4.6 indicates that the equation Y (monthly housing starts) $= 510.86 - 0.1943 \times X$ (the year) has an associated $r^2 = 0.006$. In other words, less than 1% of the actual variation in monthly housing starts is explained by that equation, which uses the numerical value of the year to predict those housing starts. In any associative model, the strength of relationships should be evaluated to determine if the model itself is likely to yield valid predictions in the future, as we see in Scenario 2b.

coefficient of determination Proportion of variation in a dependent variable that is explained by a regression model.

Evaluating the Strength of a Linear Relationship

Scenario 2b

Despite the low number of observations, the director of Courtesy Van Transportation for Livingston Medical Services is enthusiastic about the potential of the Scenario 2b regression equation to forecast future demand for courtesy van transports.

Consider the original data in Scenario 2a. What are the coefficient of correlation and the coefficient of determination for the linear relationship between number of clients and annual number of courtesy van transports? What does this imply about the strength of the linear relationship expressed by the equation $Y = -22 + 0.10363X$, first identified in Scenario 2a?

Analysis

The coefficient of correlation may be determined first, by retrieving many of the summary statistics calculated in Scenario 2a. We need to calculate one additional summary statistic for completion of the correlation coefficient formula, the sum of Y^2:

LINEAR REGRESSION SUMMARY STATS

Clients (X)	X^2	Transports (Y)	XY	Y^2
10,558	111,471,364	1,042	11,001,436	1,085,764
22,010	484,440,100	2,560	56,345,600	6,553,600
2,455	6,027,025	149	365,795	22,201
1,405	1,974,025	186	261,330	34,596
12,400	153,760,000	292	3,620,800	85,264
5,410	29,268,100	1,128	6,102,480	1,272,384
20,200	408,040,000	2,203	44,500,600	4,853,209
$\Sigma X = 74{,}438$	$\Sigma X^2 = 1{,}194{,}980{,}614$	$\Sigma Y = 7{,}560$	$\Sigma XY = 122{,}198{,}041$	$\Sigma Y^2 = 13{,}907{,}018$

Continues

This provides all the inputs needed to calculate both the coefficients of correlation and determination:

COEFFICIENT OF CORRELATION

$$r = \frac{n(\Sigma XY) - (\Sigma X)(\Sigma Y)}{\sqrt{[n(\Sigma X^2) - (\Sigma X)^2] \times [n(\Sigma Y^2) - (\Sigma Y)^2]}}$$

$$= \frac{7 \times 122{,}198{,}041 - (74{,}438 \times 7{,}560)}{\sqrt{[7 \times 1{,}194{,}980{,}614 - (74{,}438 \times 74{,}438)] \times [7 \times 13{,}907{,}018 - (7{,}560 \times 7{,}560)]}}$$

$$= 292{,}635{,}007/336{,}906{,}625 = 0.869$$

COEFFICIENT OF DETERMINATION

$$r^2 = (r)^2 = (0.869)^2 = 0.755$$

Insight The coefficient of correlation, 0.869, indicates a strong positive correlation between the number of clients eligible in a contract and the number of resulting courtesy van transports annually. The coefficient of determination, also known as the r^2 of this relationship, is 0.755. This indicates that about 76% of the variation in courtesy van transports (Y) across the seven contracts in the historical data is explained by the regression model $Y = -22 + 0.10363X$, where X is the client numbers associated with each of those contracts. Overall, this model shows promise as a tool for estimating courtesy van demand, although Livingston Medical Services is still advised to secure additional historical data. ■

Relevant Range and Nonlinear Relationships

A correlation coefficient and a coefficient of determination both provide convenient readings on the strength of a linear relationship, but an overview of associative modeling would not be complete without mention of a few other issues that should be considered before relying on such an equation to create forecasts. The first issue is that of the *relevant range* of the regression equation. Relevant range refers to the range of actual values within the historical data used to calculate the regression equation. In the case of courtesy van transport data first introduced in Scenario 2a, this is the equivalent of the range of contracts for as few as 1,405 clients (Outer Banks Senior Services) up to as many as 22,010 clients (Westwood Retirement Villas).

Note that the resulting Scenario 2a regression equation, $Y = -22 + 0.10363X$, might be used to forecast the annual number of courtesy van transports for a contract with only 20 clients, although the resulting forecast would be $-22 + 0.10363 \times 20 = -20$ transports annually. A negative number of courtesy van transports has no meaning in reality, and this abrupt loss of meaning, despite the equation's high r and r^2, is likely due to the fact that the past data did not contain any actual observations that small. In other words, the proposed value of $X = 20$ clients is substantially outside the relevant range of the regression model developed in Scenario 2a. If this equation were used in the future, it should be applied only for contracts of sizes similar to the existing range of 1,405 to 22,010 clients in the past data.

In addition, we must be careful not to overinterpret the meaning of r and r^2, particularly when these values are low. When r and r^2 are low, these values indicate a lack of linear relationship between the X and Y data, but we should not then conclude that no relationship exists at all. Consider again our earlier example of the relationship between air temperature and household demand for electricity, which can be distinctly nonlinear. Household demand for electricity is usually high when outside air temperature is uncomfortably low, then decreases as air temperature increases and electric heaters are no longer required for comfort. However, as outside air temperature continues to increase, demand for electricity starts climbing again as households activate air-conditioning units. If the r and r^2 were calculated for observed levels of electrical demand over this full range of air temperatures, the resulting values would be near zero, because this demand is not a linear function of air temperature. This does not mean that air temperature cannot be used to help predict electrical demand; there is a powerful relationship between the two factors. But we need to apply a nonlinear modeling technique to clarify this kind of relationship.

TIME SERIES TECHNIQUES

Time series techniques focus on the historical behavior of some outcome of interest, to predict its future behavior. This perspective, introduced earlier as extrapolation, frames forecasting largely as anticipating what will happen next, based on what has already happened. Time series techniques are favored approaches for shorter-term forecasting, although they are not strictly limited to short planning horizons.

Time Series Decomposition

One helpful process in time series analysis is time series decomposition, or the disassembly of historical data into a group of component influences that hypothetically combine to create the actual values observed. Theoretically, any time series can be "taken apart" to examine its components, and knowledge of the components and their relative importance can then be used to anticipate future behavior of the series. For example, the lowest graph in Figure 4.7 displays a portion of the historical time series first introduced as

Time Series Components FIGURE **4.7**

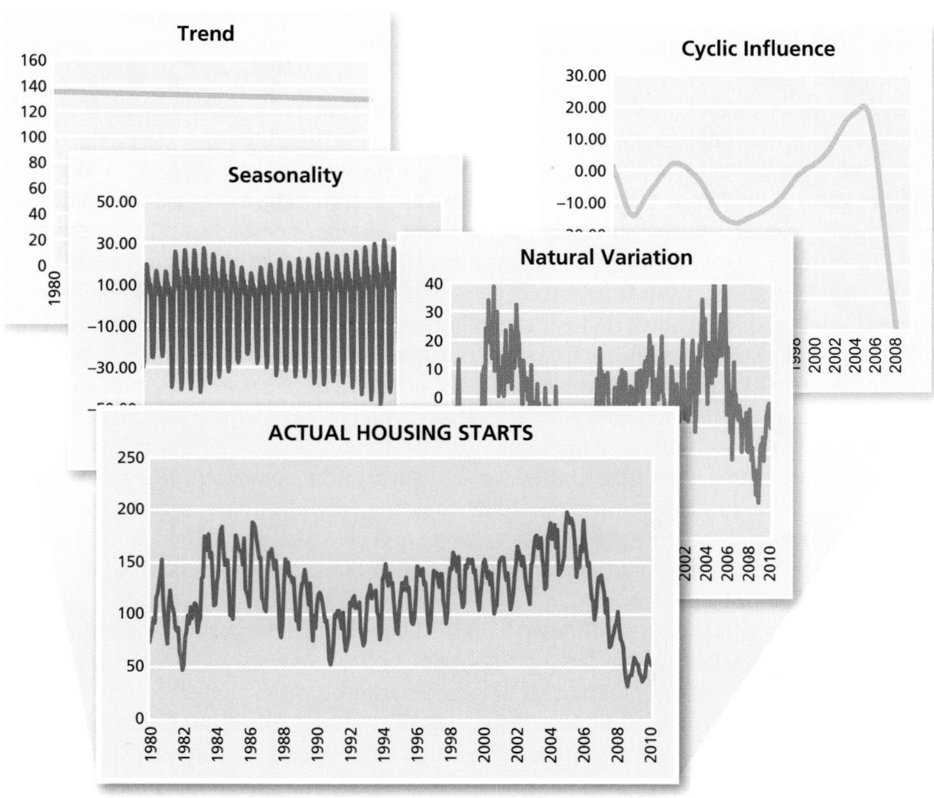

Figure 4.3, set against the time series components whose combined influences are likely causing the behavior visible in the actual data.

natural variation The randomness inherent in a process, also known as *random variation.*

known unknown A source of uncertainty known to a decision maker, usually evident in past experience or data.

assignable variation Deviations with a specific cause or source.

exogenous variation A nonrepeating deviation in a time series created by a distinct, identifiable external influence.

Black Swan An incident of extreme consequence, unexpected or considered highly improbable.

unknown unknown Uncertainty omitted from planning because the decision maker is unaware of its presence.

trend A sustained period of growth or decline.

seasonality A repeating pattern in a time series.

cyclic variation Seasonality with a cycle time longer than 1 year; generally associated with economic influences on time series data.

Natural and Assignable Variation One component of any time series is its natural variation, or random noise associated with the outcome of interest. Some time series are subject to significant randomness, while others are inherently more predictable. As complex as the US housing time series in Figures 4.3 and 4.7 appears, the natural variation between the months as time passes is not the dominant influence. While this uncertainty cannot be predicted perfectly, its influence is consistent and apparent in past data, making it a known unknown.

Any variation not inherent in a process can be referred to as assignable variation. One challenge of a time series analyst is to sift through a complex pattern of actual data to determine how much of the variation is natural and how much is assignable. Assignable variation indicates a specific cause for the variation, identification of which might assist in anticipating future behavior of the time series. One-time shocks to a time series from a distinctly external influence, such a sudden dip in consumer sales after a disruptive event, are called exogenous variations. Since exogenous variation is not, by definition, expected to repeat in the future, it is important to identify it in past data to carefully block or control its influence over forecasts developed for the future. A Black Swan refers to a particularly high-impact incident that can cause massive exogenous variation in an otherwise stable time series, but is not recognized as such until the moment of impact. Unlike the random noise of natural variation, Black Swans represent the unknown unknown, those exogenous factors that may shape future outcomes but are not represented in the behavior of past data.

Trend and Seasonality Trend is any sustained linear growth or decline across a time series, although every data point within the series does not necessarily grow or decline when compared to its neighbors. Trend analysis is a specific application of linear regression that hypothesizes that Y, the dependent variable, can be predicted through its linear relationship with X, the passage of time, where the passage of time is expressed as values on a number line.

If a time series does not appear to have a significant trend component, it may be referred to as a stationary series, whereas a series that is trending upward or downward across its history is said to be nonstationary. A stationary series, however, is not necessarily flat or easy to predict in the future. The US housing starts time series is fairly stationary across the history first visible in Figure 4.3, yet its behavior is quite complex. While a linear trend is not a significant influence across this history, much of the intricacies in actual monthly housing starts result from strong seasonality within this series. Seasonality is any pattern of high and low values that consistently repeats within a time series. Seasonality is also understood to repeat within a fixed amount of time, such as within a week, a month, or a year. The seasonality in Figures 4.3 and 4.7 is apparent because May, June, and July are consistently the peak months for housing starts within a year, while December, January, and February are consistently low months.

Seasonality in this particular time series is related to the seasons of the year, because housing construction must be at least partially coordinated with the weather. Seasonality in general, however, can be unrelated to the seasons of a calendar year, such as the seasonal pattern of passengers on a rapid-transit system, which consistently peaks and falls at certain times within a 24-hour day.

Cyclic variation is a pattern of growth and decline that is recognized as separate from seasonality, distinguished by the fact that the pattern may take several years to complete, and the length of this long pattern will not necessarily be the same each time it cycles. Figure 4.7 suggests a strong cyclic variation at work, because this type of variation represents the growth and recessions associated with economic cycles. Clearly visible within the pattern of actual monthly housing starts in Figure 4.7 are the influences of US economic recessions in the early 1980s and in 1990, as well as the impact of the recession of 2008–9.

Forecasting Construction Activity

Construction activity follows annual cycles in many regions, due to its unavoidable exposure to the environment. This infrastructure project is a good example, as the concrete necessary to complete these drains will only set reliably within a certain range of air temperature, and personnel working below ground must be wary of the potential for heavy rain in the area. Furthermore, this particular industry is of interest to forecasters elsewhere, in that the overall rise and fall of construction activity often reveals the broader cyclic variation of a local and national economy.

Seasonal Relatives While trends can be quantified and projected forward with linear regression, the nonlinear nature of seasonality requires a different approach. Once seasonality is recognized, a set of seasonal relatives can be calculated to express the pattern. We can use several methods to create seasonal relatives from past data, one being to calculate the average value of each season in the past data and then divide each of those values by the overall average of the season averages. We use this particular technique in Scenario 3a.

seasonal relatives
A set of numerical values that describe a seasonal pattern.

Calculating Seasonal Relatives

Scenario 3a

The director of courtesy van transportation for Livingston Medical Service suspects that demand for courtesy van transportation is highly seasonal, particularly for certain contracts in certain areas. For example, van drivers report that demand for courtesy van transportation is generally less during the month of December, because clients make fewer medical appointments during the holidays. Clients also make somewhat fewer medical appointments and require fewer transports during any bad weather season. To explore this, the director has gathered 4 years of monthly data on courtesy van transports made under Livingston's contract with Marion County in central Florida, a region known for extremely hot summer weather:

Month	2006	2007	2008	2009
January	151	141	191	163
February	75	76	95	117
March	92	67	103	78
April	81	70	87	59
May	48	34	34	52
June	37	34	39	48
July	35	43	35	48
August	39	51	49	46
September	102	88	92	102
October	181	197	162	145
November	145	98	109	120
December	35	33	37	64
Total:	1,021	932	1,033	1,042

What seasonal relatives would express the consistent monthly fluctuation in courtesy van transports in Marion County, Florida?

Continues

Analysis

Here, the seasons suggested by the past data are the months of the year. To calculate a set of seasonal relatives from the data, we must calculate averages for each month and then calculate an average of those averages.

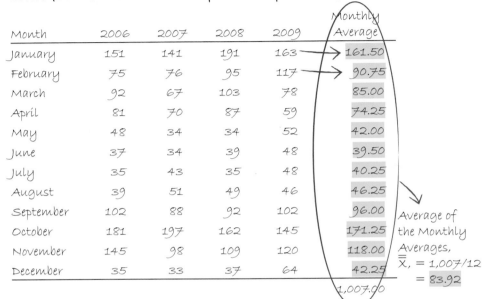

LIVINGSTON/MARION COUNTY MONTHLY AVERAGES

Month	2006	2007	2008	2009	Monthly Average
January	151	141	191	163	161.50
February	75	76	95	117	90.75
March	92	67	103	78	85.00
April	81	70	87	59	74.25
May	48	34	34	52	42.00
June	37	34	39	48	39.50
July	35	43	35	48	40.25
August	39	51	49	46	46.25
September	102	88	92	102	96.00
October	181	197	162	145	171.25
November	145	98	109	120	118.00
December	35	33	37	64	42.25
					1,007.00

Average of the Monthly Averages, $\bar{\bar{X}}$, = 1,007/12 = 83.92

Next, we divide each monthly average by the average of the averages. The resulting numbers are the set of seasonal relatives:

LIVINGSTON/MARION COUNTY SEASONAL RELATIVES

Month	Monthly Ave./$\bar{\bar{X}}$	Seasonal Relative
January	161.50/83.92 =	1.92
February	90.75/83.92 =	1.08
March	85.00/83.92 =	1.01
April	74.25/83.92 =	0.88
May	42.00/89.92 =	0.50
June	39.50/83.92 =	0.47
July	40.25/83.92 =	0.48
August	46.25/83.92 =	0.55
September	96.00/83.92 =	1.14
October	171.25/83.92 =	2.04
November	118.00/83.92 =	1.41
December	42.25/83.92 =	0.50
	TOTAL	12.0

This is a good check of the calculations, because a correct set of seasonal relatives should add up to the total number of seasons in the pattern—in this case, 12.

Insight This set of seasonal relatives appears to confirm the feedback of the courtesy van drivers: The low seasonal relative values for December and May through August indicate that these are low-demand months for courtesy van transportation, while the seasonal relative value of 1.92 for January and 2.04 for October indicate that these are busy months. ■

Any set of seasonal relatives has certain features, regardless of its origin. First, the values of a set of seasonal relatives should sum to the total number of seasons in the repeating pattern, such as 12 in the case of Scenario 3a. Individual seasonal relatives with values above 1.0 indicate busy periods in the pattern, in which demand is above average, and the largest seasonal relative is indicating the peak period within the seasonal pattern. Seasonal relative values below 1.0 indicate quiet, low, or below-average periods within the seasonal cycle.

Seasonal relatives can be used for two different purposes:

- **Seasonalizing data.** To introduce a seasonal influence into an existing data value, simply multiply the value by the seasonal relative of the desired season.
- **Deseasonalizing data.** To theoretically remove the seasonal influence from an existing data value, divide that value by its seasonal relative.

Seasonalizing data is associated with forecasting; it is not uncommon to forecast at an aggregate level first, and then break that larger forecast down into smaller, more detailed forecasts reflecting seasonality. For example, an annual sales forecast could be broken down into forecasts for the individual financial quarters by simply dividing the annual prediction by four, but the resulting quarterly forecasts assume that sales are identical for each quarter. If sales during each quarter are known to fluctuate according to some pattern, then this fluctuation can be incorporated into the four quarterly forecasts by multiplying the original, flat quarterly estimate by each of the four seasonal relatives. We demonstrate this process in Scenario 3b.

Using Seasonal Relatives to Seasonalize Forecasts

Scenario 3b

Marion County in central Florida has just renewed its contract for nonemergency medical transportation with Livingston Medical Services. During the renewal process, the director of courtesy van transportation learned that Marion County expects the total number of clients, or citizens eligible to summon Livingston's services, to increase to 14,500 by the start of next year. Using the regression equation first developed in Scenario 2a, the director forecasts that this increased number of clients will result in a total of −22 + 0.10363(14,500) = 1,481 (rounded) requests for courtesy van transportation next year. Approximately how many requests for courtesy van transportation can the Marion County drivers expect during each month next year?

Analysis

First we divide the director's annual forecast for courtesy van transportation by the number of seasons:

2012 SEASONAL FORECAST

1,481 (annual forecast for 2012)/12 (number of seasons) = 123.4

This number (123.4) represents the average number of courtesy van transports expected each month next year. However, this number is not likely to be useful to the van drivers, because it is already known that some months are much busier months for courtesy van transports than other months. Thus, the monthly estimate of 123.4 is said to be a deseasonalized value, because it does not recognize the seasonality in this situation. Seasonality can be easily introduced by our multiplying this number by the seasonal relatives of the various months:

Continues

2012 MONTHLY FORECASTS (rounded to nearest integer)

MONTH	MONTHLY FORECAST
January	123.4 × 1.92 = 237
February	123.4 × 1.08 = 133
March	123.4 × 1.01 = 125
April	123.4 × 0.88 = 109
May	123.4 × 0.50 = 62
June	123.4 × 0.47 = 58
July	123.4 × 0.48 = 59
August	123.4 × 0.55 = 68
September	123.4 × 1.14 = 141
October	123.4 × 2.04 = 252
November	123.4 × 1.41 = 174
December	123.4 × 0.50 = 62

Insight These monthly forecasts now better advise the Marion County drivers how many requests they may be handling each month next year. ■

While seasonalizing data is usually associated with producing detailed forecasts of the future, deseasonalizing data is often required to look back on the past. Specifically, deseasonalizing data is useful to compare an outcome across differing past seasons. This is common in the case of US housing starts, first introduced in Figure 4.3. Since the number of houses starting construction in a given month does appear to be influenced by the cyclic variation of the underlying US economy, this activity is closely watched to gauge the direction of the economy at any given time. However, housing starts rise and fall between months simply due to the seasonal component, so that any actual change between months might be unrelated to the underlying economic cycle. To address this, movements in deseasonalized housing starts, or seasonally adjusted housing starts, are monitored closely in business news for evidence of the economy's behavior. These values are actual housing starts with seasonal fluctuation removed, theoretically exposing the cyclic pattern underneath. That is, the actual values are deseasonalized by dividing the actual observation with the seasonal relative of the season of that observation, as demonstrated in Scenario 3c.

Scenario 3c

Using Seasonal Relatives to Deseasonalize Actual Data

During the analysis of the seasonality of monthly courtesy van transports in Scenario 3c, the director of courtesy van transportation did have monthly data for 2005, but the Marion County courtesy van drivers warned the director, "not to look at 2005, because 2005 was a very weird year, when we just didn't get the slow-down in transports you usually see between January and May." The director focused instead on 2006–9 to develop the season relatives, but now wonders if that was necessary, because the actual data from 2005 does suggest a slowing pattern of transports from January to May, despite the comments of the drivers:

Month	2005
January	168
February	122
March	120
April	108
May	70

Were the drivers wrong to suggest that something "weird" was happening with the transport demand pattern during the early months of that particular year?

Analysis

The director doubts the drivers because the slowing pattern of demand does appear in January through May of 2005, although the drivers maintain it was not the usual seasonal pattern. To examine this claim, we can deseasonalize these numbers by dividing each observation by each month's seasonal relative:

JANUARY–MAY 2005 SEASONAL ANALYSIS

Month	2005	Seasonal Relative	Deseasonalized Actual (Actual/Seasonal Relative)
January	168	1.92	168/1.92 = 87.50
February	122	1.08	122/1.08 = 112.96
March	120	1.01	120/1.01 = 118.81
April	108	0.88	108/0.88 = 122.73
May	70	0.50	70/0.50 = 140.00

Insight If the drop in transports between January and May had been expected with respect to the usual seasonal pattern, the deseasonalized actuals would emerge as similar numbers. However, when we review the deseasonalized values we see the opposite: the deseasonalized values have a broad range and actually trend *upward* toward May. This suggests that the Marion County drivers were not wrong in stating that these earlier months of 2005 were unusual. Although the actual numbers do drop from January through May, they apparently do not drop as fast as usual, just as the drivers described. ■

Deseasonalized values provide insight when compared to each other, such as the comparison of January through May in Scenario 3c. By (theoretically) removing the expected decline in courtesy van transport demand during this part of the year, the director has exposed something unusual in the demand pattern in 2005. However, precisely what has been exposed is not apparent. If the director remains concerned about the unusual pattern of demand in the first half of 2005, he must investigate the circumstances of this particular contract in that particular year more closely.

Simple Time Series Techniques

If a time series is stationary and free from distinct seasonal or cyclic influences, a forecaster has a choice of convenient techniques to create quick predictions of the near future of that series. One of the simplest such techniques is naïve forecasting, or assuming that what will happen next will be exactly what has just happened. If F_t is the forecast for a future period t and A_{t-1} is the actual outcome of the previous period, naïve forecasting can be stated formally as

$$F_t = A_{t-1}$$

Other time series techniques are slightly more sophisticated than naïve forecasting, two of the most common being moving averages and simple exponential smoothing.

Moving Averages One intuitive method for forecasting a future data point is to average a portion of its previous history. For example, a store could forecast Wednesday's sales for a particular item by averaging together the actual sales of that item on the previous Monday and Tuesday. This approach would be called a 2-day moving average, where "2-day" refers to the span of the moving average. The word "moving" refers to an assumption that once Wednesday has passed and the store needs a quick estimate of Thursday's upcoming sales, the store's forecaster will then average together the actual sales on Tuesday and Wednesday.

If the span of any moving average is symbolized by n, this technique for creating a forecast for any period t can be stated as

$$F_t = \frac{A_{t-1} + A_{t-2} + \cdots + A_{t-n}}{n}$$

simple moving average Predicts a value by averaging a fixed number of most-recent actual values.

weighted moving average Predicts a value by calculating a weighted average of a fixed number of most-recent actual values.

This approach is also called a simple moving average, because it gives each period within the span of past data the same weight in creating a forecast. If each past period does not deserve the same weight, usually because the most recent period is considered somewhat more important than the older periods, then the forecaster would prefer a weighted moving average. This technique first requires that any preferences be expressed as a set of weights across the periods, assigning greater values to the favored periods, with the sum of all weights resulting in a value of 1.0. If w_t represents the weight assigned to some period t, then the calculation of a weighted moving average can be expressed as

$$F_t = \frac{w_{t-1}A_{t-1} + w_{t-2}A_{t-2} + \cdots + w_{t-n}A_{t-n}}{n}$$

We demonstrate these techniques in Scenario 4a.

Scenario 4a

Simple Moving Averages and Weighted Moving Averages

Livingston Medical Services is considering how best to forecast total demand for future nonemergency medical transportation. Livingston has supplemented the past data introduced earlier in Scenario 1 with 3 earlier months in the same time series of actual number of transports required across all its contracts:

Month	Actual Number of Transports
October	10,230
November	12,004
December	10,990
January	12,480
February	11,568
March	13,244
April	15,560
May	16,034
June	23,400

Livingston is considering using either a simple 3-month moving average in the future, or perhaps a weighted 3-month moving average in which the more recent past month would receive a weight of 0.8, while the other 2 months would be weighted at 0.1 each. How would either of these two techniques have performed if they had been in use during these past months?

Analysis

To assess the performance of these two techniques, we simulate them with the past data. Since both suggested techniques require 3 months of actual past data, the earliest month that we can forecast in this simulation is January, drawing on the actual values from October, November, and December. In the case of the simple 3-month moving average, we average the actual number of transports for these 3 months (10,990, 12,004, and 10,230 transports) together, creating a forecast of 11,075. To simulate the forecast for February, we would repeat this process with the actual data from November, December, and January, and so on:

SIMPLE 3-MONTH MOVING AVERAGE
(Transport forecast rounded to the nearest integer)

Month	Actual	3-Month Moving Average	Error	Squared Error	Absolute Error	Percent Absolute Error (%)
October	10,230					
November	12,004					
December	10,990					
January	12,480	11,075	1,405	1,974,962	1,405	11.3%
February	11,568	11,825	-257	65,878	257	2.2
March	13,244	11,679	1,565	2,448,182	1,565	11.8
April	15,560	12,431	3,129	9,792,727	3,129	20.1
May	16,034	13,457	2,577	6,639,211	2,577	16.1
June	23,400	14,946	8,454	71,470,116	8,454	36.1
			ME: 2,812	MSE: 15,398,513	MAD: 2,898	MAPE: 16.3%

Forecasts are average of previous 3 months.

Simulating the use of a simple 3-month moving average allows us to calculate error measures, to use to compare techniques later. First, we repeat this simulation for the weighted moving average also proposed, in which the most recent month is multiplied by 0.8 and the 2 months prior to that are each multiplied by 0.1 before we sum the results into a forecast.

SIMPLE 3-MONTH WEIGHTED MOVING AVERAGE
(Transport forecast rounded to the nearest integer)

Month	Actual	3-Month Moving Average	Error	Squared Error	Absolute Error	Percent Absolute Error (%)
October	10,230					
November	12,004					
December	10,990					
January	12,480	11,015	1,465	2,145,053	1,465	11.7%
February	11,568	12,283	-715	511,797	715	6.2
March	13,244	11,601	1,643	2,698,135	1,643	12.4
April	15,560	13,000	2,560	6,553,600	2,560	16.5
May	16,034	14,929	1,105	1,220,583	1,105	6.9
June	23,400	15,708	7,692	59,173,018	7,692	32.9
			ME: 2,292	MSE: 12,050,364	MAD: 2,530	MAPE: 14.4%

January's forecast = (0.8 × 10,990) + (0.1 × 12,004) + (0.1 × 10,230)

Continues

Insight Comparing the two, the 3-month weighted moving average appears to have performed slightly better than the simple moving average in this simulation, but neither performance was impressive. For example, the simple moving average's MAPE of 16.3% and the weighted moving average's MAPE of 14.4% are similar in that both are substantially larger than the MAPEs of 3.58% and 3.35% earned by the two other forecasts we evaluated over the same time period in the earlier analysis of Scenario 1. While computationally simple and highly convenient, neither of these two techniques appears better suited to the task of forecasting nonemergency medical transports in the future. ■

Figure 4.8 graphs the actual number of transports in Scenario 4a, as compared to the two sets of forecasts generated. We see in this illustration why these simple techniques are preferred for only certain situations: their forecasts always lag behind any consistent trend or repeating pattern in the data. In the case of Scenario 4a, the actual number of nonemergency transports trends upward between October and June, and both techniques fail to keep pace with this consistent movement. The weighted moving average earned slightly better performance measures than the simple moving average because its increased weight on the most recent month increased its responsiveness to the ongoing change in monthly transports, a potentially valuable tendency discussed earlier.

simple exponential smoothing
Predicting a future value by combining the previous prediction and some portion of the error in that prediction.

Simple Exponential Smoothing One other popular time series technique is simple exponential smoothing, which produces forecasts for a future period t by combining the forecast from the previous period $t - 1$ with some portion of the error in that old forecast. Use of simple exponential smoothing requires the selection of an alpha value, α, that determines the portion of the old forecast's error used in updating the new forecast, as described by the simple exponential smoothing formula:

$$F_t = F_{t-1} + \alpha(A_{t-1} - F_{t-1})$$

FIGURE 4.8 Simple versus Weighted Moving Average Forecasts

Data from the Livingston Medical Services example

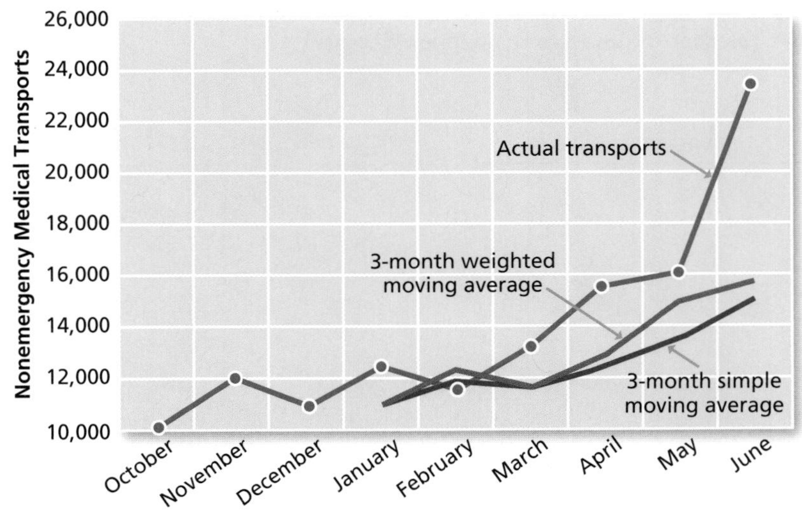

By definition, $0 < \alpha \leq 1.0$. Selecting the best alpha value to use is often determined by experimenting with different values on previous data, as we now demonstrate in Scenario 4b.

Simple Exponential Smoothing — Scenario 4b

Given that moving averages did not appear promising for future forecasting of nonemergency transports, Livingston Medical Services is now considering simple exponential smoothing for the same purpose. In particular, Livingston wishes to test alpha values of $\alpha = 0.05$ and $\alpha = 0.65$, to determine if either a low or a high alpha value would be particularly suited to this application.

Using the same past data listed in Scenario 4a and assuming in the case of both alpha values that the first month (October) begins with a perfectly accurate forecast, how does either of these two applications of simple exponential smoothing perform?

Analysis

We evaluate each alpha value separately, because each creates its own forecasts.

SIMPLE EXPONENTIAL SMOOTHING, $\alpha = 0.05$
(Transport forecast rounded to the nearest integer)

First forecast is assumed to be the same as the actual, for the convenience of the simulation.

All other forecasts are the result of the simple exponential smoothing formula, such as for December: 10,230 + 0.05 × (12,004 − 10,230) = 10,319

Month	Actual	Simple Exponential Smoothing	Error*	Squared Error*	Absolute Error*	Percent Absolute Error* %
October	10,230	10,230				
November	12,004	10,230				
December	10,990	10,319				
January	12,480	10,352	2,128	4,527,256	2,128	17.0%
February	11,568	10,459	1,109	1,230,654	1,109	9.6
March	13,244	10,514	2,730	7,452,249	2,730	20.6
April	15,560	10,651	4,909	2,4102,079	4,909	31.6
May	16,034	10,896	5,138	26,398,196	5,138	32.0
June	23,400	11,153	12,247	149,989,538	12,247	52.3
			ME: 4,710	MSE: 35,616,662	MAD: 4,710	MAPE: 27.2%

*Error measures calculated for January through June only, for easier comparison to the error measures of Scenario 4a.

Simple exponential smoothing with $\alpha = 0.05$ performs poorly, even in comparison to the unimpressive performance measures associated with the moving averages earlier in Scenario 4a. However, a different alpha value might produce better forecasts, so we evaluate the second proposed alpha value of 0.65 as well.

Continues

SIMPLE EXPONENTIAL SMOOTHING, α = 0.65
(Transport forecast rounded to the nearest integer)

Month	Actual	Simple Exponential Smoothing	Error*	Squared Error*	Absolute Error*	Percent Absolute Error* %
October	10,230	10,230				
November	12,004	10,230				
December	10,990	11,383				
January	12,480	11,128	1,352	1,829,026	1,352	10.8%
February	11,568	12,007	-439	192,418	439	3.8
March	13,244	11,722	1,522	2,317,917	1,522	11.5
April	15,560	12,711	2,849	8,116,031	2,849	18.3
May	16,034	14,563	1,471	2,164,143	1,471	9.2
June	23,400	15,519	7,881	62,108,363	7,881	33.7
			ME: 2,440	MSE: 12,787,983	MAD: 2,586	MAPE: 14.5%

*Error measures calculated for January through June only, for easier comparison to the error measures of Scenario 4a.

Insight Comparing the two performance measures, we see that simple exponential smoothing with the higher alpha value of 0.65 does appear to have performed better than the lower alpha value in this simulated forecasting, in that its ME, MSE, MAD, and MAPE are all more favorable values. However, these values are not particularly impressive and appear similar to the earlier unimpressive performance of the 3-month weighted moving average in Scenario 4a. Regardless of the alpha value, it would not be advisable to choose simple exponential smoothing as the forecasting technique preferred over the two existing techniques first discussed in Scenario 1. ■

The alpha value (α) in the exponential smoothing formula is also known as the *smoothing constant*, and graphing the two sets of forecasts from Scenario 4b in Figure 4.9 gives some insight into this name. We see that Figure 4.9 confirms that simple exponential smoothing suffers the same tendency to lag behind upward-trending data as do moving averages. However, the forecasts created with the higher alpha, α = 0.65, earned better accuracy measures in Scenario 4b because these forecasts appear in Figure 4.9 as somewhat more responsive to the trending actuals. In contrast, the lower α = 0.05 forecasts are said to be smoother and this link between the alpha value and the behavior of the resulting forecasts is what earns α the name of smoothing constant. In general, when selecting a time series technique, effective forecasters consider these factors:

- These techniques are best adapted to stationary time series largely influenced by natural variation.
- A particular technique or a particular parameter such as α is often selected for future use based on the quality of its performance during simulated use with past data, such as in the analysis of Scenarios 4a and 4b.
- When using simple exponential smoothing, a higher α yields a more responsive forecast. The highest possible value is α = 1.0, at which point simple exponential smoothing becomes naïve forecasting.
- When using weighted moving averages, the greater the weight given to the most recent past period, the more responsive the forecast. The greatest possible weight

Simple Exponential Smoothing Forecasts

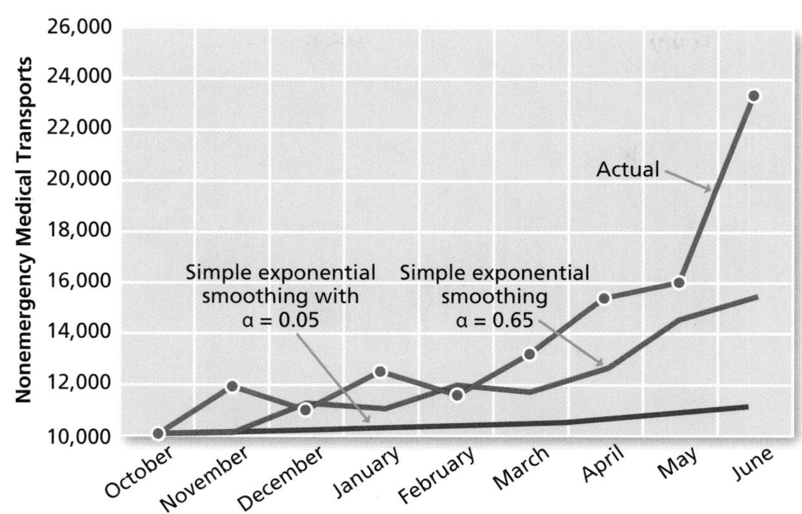

FIGURE 4.9

Data from the Livingston Medical Services example

that can be assigned is 1.0, at which point the weighted moving average becomes naïve forecasting.

- When using simple moving averages, the shorter the span of the moving average, the more responsive the forecast. The shortest span possible is one period, at which point the simple moving average becomes naïve forecasting.

While these simple time series techniques are not effective in the presence of distinct trends or seasonality patterns, there are more elaborate techniques better adapted to those circumstances, such as trend-adjusted exponential smoothing. Furthermore, these simpler techniques have useful applications beyond forecasting, as discussed next.

Prediction versus Historical Analysis

Ironically, forecasting techniques are not always used for forecasting the future. While a less responsive forecasting method might be poor at predicting the behavior of a certain outcome over time, that same technique could prove valuable in analyzing the history of that outcome. Figure 4.10 illustrates this, returning to the 1959–2010 US housing start data originally introduced in Figure 4.3. In Figure 4.10, exponential smoothing forecasts calculated with a very low alpha value, $\alpha = 0.02$, are superimposed across the actual housing start data.

Simple exponential smoothing with $\alpha = 0.02$ performs quite poorly as a forecasting tool during 1959–2010, earning accuracy measures even worse than naïve forecasting. However, the smoothness associated with the low alpha value flattens out both the random variation and the seasonality of the original time series, exposing the broader cyclic influence of the US economy. Any smoothing technique can be useful in detecting underlying shifts in data over time, such as analyzing a long noisy history of daily stock share prices. The very lack of responsiveness that sometimes renders a smoothing technique impractical for forecasting is what can make it helpful in investigating other influences at work in the past behavior of data.

Baseball player Yogi Berra once cautioned, "It is tough to make predictions, especially about the future." Forecasting can be one of the most frustrating tasks in operations

FIGURE 4.10 Actual versus Exponentially Smoothed Data, α = 0.02

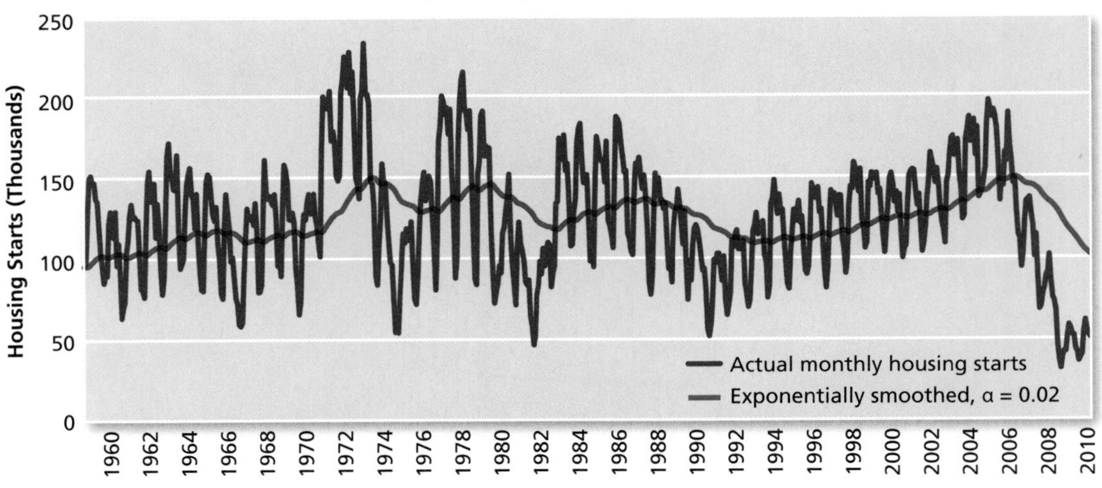

management, as most predictions are "wrong" at some level of detail. Fitting forecasting methods to past data does reveal useful patterns and relationships, but low error measures and a high r^2 guarantee nothing about what will actually happen next. When judging the work of a forecaster, we should always remember that "right" and "wrong" forecasts only exist in hindsight. Plans cannot be made without forecasts, and operations cannot be effective without plans, so it falls on the forecaster's shoulders to ably set that system in motion well before the actual future emerges as the present.

SUMMARY

Forecasting refers to most any attempt to predict an outcome, although forecasting in operations management usually focuses on anticipating some form of future demand on the operation. Forecasting approaches can be either qualitative or quantitative, relying on either human insight or mathematical models, or maybe some blend of both. Qualitative techniques tend to be more expensive, but quantitative techniques must be supported by a supply of relevant historical data, which may not be available in some situations. Nonetheless, quantitative techniques are more common in operations management, in that an ongoing operation usually generates the past data needed for this approach.

Forecast accuracy can be measured in a variety of ways, although accuracy is not always the sole issue of concern when using a particular technique. The issues of responsiveness and even the direct cost of the technique may be important as well.

Popular quantitative techniques can be divided into associative models and time series analysis. Associative modeling such as regression analysis identifies significant relationships between an outcome of interest and some factor or factors that are hypothesized as influencing its behavior. Once these relationships are expressed mathematically, the resulting regression equation can then be used to estimate future values of the outcome, based on known values of the other factors. In contrast, time series analysis focuses on the behavior of the outcome over time, in an attempt to project that behavior into the future. Time series analysis relies on the idea that the actual behavior observed in past data is created by a combination of component influences such as natural variation, exogenous variation, trend, seasonality, and cyclic influences. Attempts to identify and quantify these components are then attempts to "take apart" the past data, a process known as time series decomposition. Time series techniques such as moving averages and exponential smoothing are fairly simple, although better adapted to forecasting outside the influence of trends and seasonality. Smoothing techniques may even prove useful to historical analysis because of their unresponsive tendencies under certain conditions.

Key Terms

assignable variation
Black Swan
causal modeling
coefficient of determination
correlation coefficient
crowdsourcing
cyclic variation
Delphi method
dependent variable
error
exogenous variation
expert opinion panel
extrapolation
forecasting
forecast bias
independent variable
jury of executive opinion
known unknown
mean absolute deviation (MAD)
mean absolute percent error (MAPE)
mean error (ME)
mean squared error (MSE)
naïve forecast
natural variation
percent error
planning horizon
regression analysis
responsiveness
seasonal relatives
seasonality
simple exponential smoothing
simple moving average
time series
time series decomposition
tracking signal
trend
unknown unknown
weighted moving average

Discussion Questions

1. If one forecasting technique were more accurate than another technique when applied to past data, why would the first technique not necessarily be preferred for use in the future?
2. Some argue that a crowd of amateurs is often smarter than a group of industry experts when predicting future changes in technology. Why might this be true?
3. Does a high correlation between an independent and a dependent variable prove the independent variable has any influence over the dependent variable? Why or why not?
4. Quantitative forecasting focuses on past data to project future conditions. Even if this focus produces accurate forecasts, what might be dangerous about this approach?

PROBLEMS

Minute Answer

Short answers appear in Appendix A. Go to **NoteShaper.com** for full video tutorials on each question.

1. Does a moving average forecast become more or less responsive to changes in a data series when more data points are included in the average?
2. Does an exponential smoothing forecast become more or less responsive to changes in a data series when its alpha is increased?
3. If a forecast is too high when compared to an actual outcome, will that forecast error be positive or negative?
4. Are quantitative forecasting models generally used for shorter-term or longer-term decision making when compared to qualitative approaches?

5. What do quantitative forecasting techniques require, the absence of which makes them ineffective tools for predicting the future?
6. In time series analysis, any pattern that regularly repeats itself and is constant in length is referred to as what?
7. The use of which alpha would result in a smoother forecast, $\alpha = 0.2$ or $\alpha = 0.5$?
8. A forecasting technique that takes the previous forecast and adds some percentage of the previous forecast's error is called what?
9. Which forecasting technique is more qualitative, the Delphi method or linear regression?
10. Which calculation would reveal the bias in a forecasting technique, the mean error or mean absolute deviation?
11. To calculate a forecast's percent error, the forecast error is divided by what?
12. Assuming the same set of data is used in their calculation, which will always be the smaller (or perhaps equal) value, the correlation coefficient or the coefficient of determination?

Quick Start

13. Given forecast errors of 5, 10, −10, 0, 10, what is the ME?
14. Given forecast errors of 4, 8, and −3, what is the MAD? What is the MSE?
15. Given forecast errors of 4, 8, and −3, what is the tracking signal?
16. Given forecast errors of 3, 2, −2, and 9, what is the tracking signal?
17. Given forecast errors of 10, −2, 25, and 0 when actual values were 120, 145, 275, and 124, what is the mean absolute percent error?
18. Given an actual demand of 34 this period, a predicted value of 45 this period, and an alpha of 0.2, what would be the simple exponential smoothing forecast for the next period?
19. Given a forecast of 1,405 and an actual outcome of 1,670, what is the error in the forecast? What is the percent error?
20. Given a forecast of 2,105 and an actual outcome of 1,980, what is the error in the forecast? What is the percent error?

Ramp Up

21. You are observing the sales department staff using exponential smoothing to forecast monthly sales. Their forecast for January's sales was 12,000 units. January's actual sales figure became available yesterday: 10,000 units. Today, the sales department announced their sales forecast of 11,300 units for February. What alpha are they using to forecast sales?
22. The marketing department has just forecast that 10,000 units of item 778 will be ordered in the next fiscal year. Based on the marketing department's forecast and noting that the seasonal relative associated with the second fiscal quarter is 1.25, how many units of item 778 will be ordered during the second fiscal quarter?
23. Here are the errors associated with a particular forecast over the past 5 months, in chronological order: 5, 10, −15, 0, 8. In which month was the forecast perfectly accurate? In which month was the forecast the least accurate? In which month or months was the forecast too high?
24. A media company is investigating the relationship between movie ticket sales and book sales. The company has gathered information on 30 movies that were based on published books, with total movie ticket sales of \$7,058 million. Three-year sales of each movie's corresponding book totaled \$3,136 million. When each movie's

ticket sales is squared and these numbers summed together, the resulting value is $1,885,412 million, while squaring and summing together the corresponding 3-year book sales results in $551,300 million. Multiplying each movie's ticket sales by its 3-year book sales and summing these values equals $872,486 million. What are the correlation coefficient and the coefficient of determination for this hypothesized relationship between movie ticket sales and book sales?

Scenarios

Reminder: Short answers appear in Appendix A. Go to **NoteShaper.com** for full video tutorials on each question.

25. Tutoring Center needs to allocate tutors this week for office appointments, so it needs to forecast the number of students who will seek appointments. The director has gathered the following time series data recently:

Period	Student Appointments
4 weeks ago	95
3 weeks ago	80
2 weeks ago	65
Last week	50

a. What would naïve forecasting suggest as the number of student appointments that can be expected this week?

b. What is this week's forecast for student appointments using a 3-week moving average? What would the same forecast be using a 2-week moving average?

c. What would be this week's forecast for student appointments using exponential smoothing with alpha of 0.2, if the forecast for 2 weeks ago was 90?

d. If the director used these 4 weeks of data to create a linear regression, what does that linear regression formula suggest for this week's forecast of student appointments? What does the regression analysis suggest in general about student appointments at the Tutoring Center?

26. Below are the seasonal relatives that describe the weekly fluctuation in the number of distinct users logging into a website daily, also known as the number of unique appearances per day:

Day of the Week	Seasonal Relative
Monday	1.25
Tuesday	1.01
Wednesday	1.03
Thursday	1.09
Friday	0.94
Saturday	0.66
Sunday	1.01

a. Generally, what is the busiest day of the week for unique appearances on this website? Which is the least busy day of the week?

b. Last week, 750 unique appearances were observed on Monday, followed by 650 on Tuesday. Deseasonalize these numbers for comparison to each other. What does this suggest about Monday and Tuesday of last week?

c. A manager has forecast for the first full week of next month: an overall number of 3,500 unique appearances will be recorded throughout the 7 days of that week. Based on this estimate, which of the following is the most logical estimate of the number of unique appearances during the Thursday of that week? What is the most logical estimate of number of unique appearances during the Friday of that week?

27. The South Florida Water Management District (SFWMD) must develop a linear regression model that can be used to estimate the fresh water needs of various communities. SFWMD has collected data on 50 communities, noting each community's population and total annual fresh water consumption. Using this data, you have calculated the following regression equation:

$$Y = 200.12 + 24.9X$$

where X is the population of the community and Y is the total annual fresh water consumption, in acre-feet. (An acre-foot is enough water to cover 1 acre, 1 foot deep.)

a. Using this regression model for estimation, how much fresh water would a community of 1,500 people consume each year? A community of 45,000?

b. According to this regression model, each new person who moves to a community increases its annual fresh water consumption by how much?

c. According to this regression model, if a town were abandoned, such that no one was living there for the entire year, what would the town's fresh water consumption be? Is this possible?

28. The manager of a building supply center suspects that the monthly sale of rolled insulation for installation in attics depends on the average air temperature during the month. The manager has a spreadsheet with 42 months of past data on this subject, in which the overall average monthly temperature was 49 degrees Fahrenheit and the overall average sales of rolled insulation was 428 rolls a month. On that spreadsheet, the manager has created a column in which each month's average air temperature is multiplied by each month's sales of rolled insulation, and then these 42 numbers are summed together to create the value 873,931. In another column of the spreadsheet, the manager has squared each month's average air temperature, and then summed the 42 squared temperatures to obtain a value of 105,080.

a. Next month, the average air temperature is expected to be 35 degrees Fahrenheit. Use linear regression to predict next month's sales of rolled insulation.

b. The sum of the 42 months of average air temperature readings is 2,058 and the total sales of rolled insulation over that same time period was 17,976 rolls. The sum of the squared monthly sales of rolled insulation was 7,710,080. What percent of the variation in the sale of rolled insulation is explained by its linear relationship to average temperature during these past 42 months?

c. What is the value of the correlation coefficient between average air temperature and the sale of rolled insulation? What does this value suggest about the relationship between average air temperature and the sale of rolled insulation?

29. A manager has been using a certain technique to forecast demand for project management software at her store. Actual demand and her corresponding predictions are shown below:

Month	Actual Demand	Manager's Forecast
March	45	45
April	42	50
May	34	45
June	48	40
July	38	45

a. What was the manager's forecast error for April?

b. What was the manager's forecast percent error for July?

c. What are the mean error, the mean squared error, the mean absolute deviation, the mean absolute percent error, and the tracking signal for these 5 months of forecasting?

d. If the manager had used a 3-month moving average instead of her technique, what would have been her forecast for June? What would have been her percent error?

e. If the manager had used simple exponential smoothing with $\alpha = 0.2$ instead of her technique, what would the forecast for August be, assuming that simple exponential smoothing had produced a perfectly accurate forecast in March?

30. The service center at a large automobile dealership is trying to boost revenue by providing no-appointment-necessary oil changes to any type of vehicle that stops by the service center. To quickly estimate the number of these oil changes that the service center can be expected to complete in the upcoming week, the service manager has been using simple exponential smoothing with an alpha value of 0.1. The number of no-appointment-necessary oil changes that the service center completed over the past 4 weeks is listed here:

- 4 weeks ago: 25
- 3 weeks ago: 36
- 2 weeks ago: 33
- Last week: 28

Last week, the service manager's forecast for the number of no-appointment-necessary oil changes was 32.20.

a. What would be the service manager's forecast for this next week?

b. What was the error in the service manager's forecast last week?

c. Suppose the service manager decided to instead use a 3-week moving average. Now what would be the service manager's forecast for this next week?

31. Block Commodities has gathered the following information concerning rock salt deliveries to its clients, which it believes are highly seasonal:

	Rock Salt Deliveries (tons)				
Month	**Year 1**	**Year 2**	**Year 3**	**Year 4**	**Average Monthly**
January	75	76	95	117	90.6
February	48	34	34	52	42.0
March	35	48	12	56	37.8
April	22	34	35	25	29.0
May	2	6	12	1	5.3
June	3	5	2	10	5.0
July	28	33	35	28	31.0
August	145	98	109	120	118.2
September	181	197	162	145	171.1
October	190	201	220	180	197.8
November	100	101	110	98	102.3
December	81	70	87	88	81.6
Total	910	904	913	920	

a. Suppose Block Commodities calculated a set of seasonal relatives to express this monthly variation in rock salt deliveries, using this set of data. What would be the value of the seasonal relative for the month of July? What would be the value of the seasonal relative for the month of December?

b. Block Commodities believes that this year will be a busy year for rock salt deliveries, forecasting a total of 1,200 tons to be delivered during the year. Using this annual forecast and Block's set of seasonal relatives, what would be a logical forecast for May of next year? What would be a logical forecast for October of next year?

32. Dunkirk Consulting wishes to predict the amount of overhead expense that will be incurred by a consulting contract, to develop more accurate bids for future contracts. Dunkirk has the following data on 11 completed contracts, detailing how long the project took to complete and what the exact overhead expense was:

Project Code Name	Project Duration (days)	Overhead Expense, $
A11	72	$5,900
A12	158	10,303
A14	124	9,054
A18	96	6,644
A22	152	10,718
B2	174	10,332
B33	124	8,804
B23	105	8,884
B10	63	7,916
B14	58	8,267
B7	83	8,503

a. Using linear regression, develop a regression formula for predicting overhead expense, based on the duration of the project.

b. What is the R^2 of this linear regression model? What does that mean?

c. What does linear regression suggest about the overhead expense of a future project that is expected to be 110 days long?

d. A manager at Dunkirk Consulting feels that the overhead expenses of supply chain consulting projects are generally different from the overhead expenses of marketing consulting projects, because supply chain projects generally require more travel, while marketing projects generally require more spending on external media services. (In the table above, codes for supply chain projects begin with an "A" while marketing projects begin with a "B.") Considering this observation by the manager, develop a better way to use linear regression to forecast overhead expense. Using this method, how much overhead expense would be predicted for a 110-day project if it were a supply chain project? How much overhead expense for a 110-day marketing project?

CASE STUDY: TIGER STRIPE COPY CENTER

Tiger Stripe Copy Center is a small business located near a large university campus. Tiger Stripe Copy offers a range of services to walk-in customers, including passport photos, self-service copy machines, packaging and shipping, and the sale of course packs. Course packs are bound documents manufactured by Tiger Stripe Copy for purchase by students enrolled in particular classes at the nearby university. A university instructor usually delivers the original documents or files to Tiger Stripe Copy a few weeks before a semester begins, with students arriving after the start of classes to purchase their copies of that course pack. After delivery of the original materials, the dayshift manager for Tiger Stripe must determine how many copies will sell, to arrange production of those copies during the busy few weeks before each semester. Historically, Tiger Stripe has used the rule of thumb that a course pack production batch size should be two-thirds the size of the reported enrollment. However, the dayshift manager suspects that a better method of forecasting exists, and began collecting more detailed data on course packs and their sales last semester to investigate, shown here in the Course Pack Data table.

Course Pack Data from Previous Semester

Course	Reported Enrollment	Actual Sales	Purchase Optional?	Course	Reported Enrollment	Actual Sales	Purchase Optional?
AC 220	220	101	yes	MA 110	360	300	no
AC 222	210	95	yes	MA 112	340	281	–
AC 225	200	176	no	MA 220	300	251	no
AC 401	100	81	no	MA 222	280	231	no
AC 402	38	36	no	MA 310	250	145	–
AC 405	40	38	no	MA 350	250	101	yes
BA 100	450	195	yes	MA 355	250	91	yes
BA 200	400	159	yes	MA 420	40	37	no
BA 330	120	96	no	MB 101	250	201	no
BA 440	42	40	no	MB 102	220	180	no
EC 101	310	244	no	MB 444	35	33	no
EC 201	280	238	no	MB 561	35	34	no
EC 330	50	46	no	RE 335	150	77	yes
EC 331	50	50	no	WA 100	300	243	no
EC 335	100	88	no	WA 330	120	62	yes
ES 330	350	190	yes	WA 335	120	49	yes
ES 560	50	48	–	WA 560	50	48	no
ES 630	25	25	no	WA 610	20	20	no

The reported enrollment of each course was reported by the instructor, who completed a paper order form at the time of original manuscript drop-off. Thus, these enrollment numbers usually represent estimates by the instructor (as the class has not yet started), while actual sales data are exact values recorded by Tiger Stripe Copy. If, in fact, too few copies were made initially, Tiger Stripe was then forced to produce additional copies while customers waited, a process that is both more expensive and hurts Tiger Stripe's reputation for convenience.

This past semester, the dayshift manager added two more questions to the bottom of the instructor's order form:

- "Is this course pack required or optional for your students?"
- "Is this material available through any source other than Tiger Stripe Copy, such as downloadable from the Internet?"

If the instructor answered "optional" for the first question and/or answered yes to the second question, the course pack was marked as yes for Purchase Optional in the data table. Unfortunately, three instructors did not answer the questions at the bottom of their forms, so three courses in the table have no answer for Purchase Optional.

Questions

1. Use linear regression to investigate the dayshift manager's data and propose an improved methodology to determine course pack production batch sizes. According to your method, how many copies should be produced for a course with an estimated enrollment of 35 when the course pack is required? How many should be produced for a course with an estimated enrollment of 275 when the course pack materials are available through an alternate source?
2. Compare your methodology to Tiger Stripe Copy's historical rule of thumb, using the past data provided here. How much better is your method? Explain.
3. Identify the three courses whose instructors did not answer the Purchase Optional questions. Based on your previous analysis, what do you think their answers would have been for each of these courses?

BIBLIOGRAPHY

Chambers, J., S. Mullick, and D. Smith. 1971. "How to Choose the Right Forecasting Technique." *Harvard Business Review* (July/August): 45–70.

Makridakis, S., S. Wheelwright, and R. Hyndman. 1998. *Forecasting: Methods and Applications*. Hoboken, NJ: John Wiley & Sons.

McClave, J. E., P. G. Benson, and T. Sincich. 2009. *Statistics for Business and Economics*. Upper Saddle River, NJ: Prentice Hall.

Taleb, N. N. 2010. *The Black Swan: The Impact of the Highly Improbable.* New York: Random House.

Vollman, T. E., W. L. Berry, D. C. Whybark, and F. B. Jacobs. 2005. *Manufacturing Planning & Control Systems for Supply Chain Management.* Chicago: McGraw-Hill.

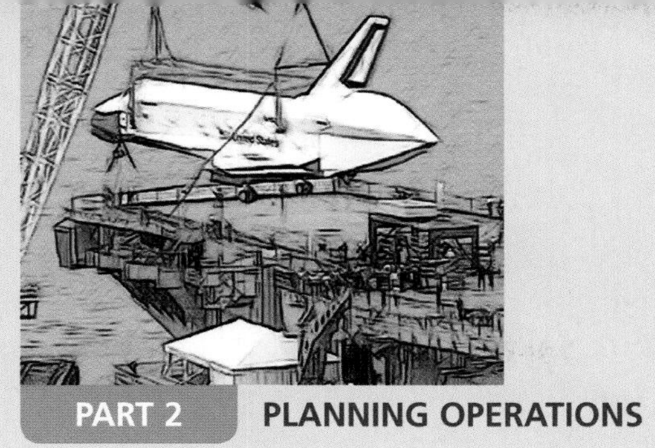

PART 2 PLANNING OPERATIONS

CHAPTER 5

Capacity and Waiting

Nobody goes there anymore. It's too crowded.

—Yogi Berra

MAJOR SECTIONS

IN THIS CHAPTER, LOOK FOR...

- Various forms of capacity, and how to assess them.
- Capacity strategies.
- The cost of waiting for available capacity.
- Factors that shape the formation of any line, and how to recognize them.
- One mathematical model mimicking a common type of waiting line.
- An alternate nonmathematical model of wait times that distinguishes between actual and perceived passage of time.

INTRODUCTION

Capacity measures an organization's ability to provide value. Ideally, an organization would have the ability to provide value to any customer at the moment of that customer's request, but this does not always occur in reality. When capacity is not adequate to meet all customer needs, some customers must wait. Investigating why an organization's capacity is not adequate or why its customers are waiting often reveals a complex trade-off between the cost of ability to serve and the cost of inability to serve immediately. To understand this balance we will examine how capacity is measured and manipulated in many different environments.

CAPACITY PLANNING

capacity
The productive capability of a system.

The term capacity can refer to a single machine or to an entire supply chain network; it represents the maximum value that can be provided by an operation. The issue of capacity planning is not nearly as simple as it might first appear, because capacity is rarely a single concept or issue for any given system.

Measuring Capacity

Capacity planning begins with intelligent selection of a unit of measurement. Some unit measures are well known for some facilities. Consider these:

- The capacity of classrooms, dining areas, passenger airplanes, and city buses can all be stated in seats.
- The capacity of a hospital is usually stated in beds.
- The capacity of an electrical generation plant can be stated in megawatts.

In these cases, capacity represents capability, or the essential size of the facility. In other situations, capacity might be better stated as a rate of productivity, such as pages per hour. However, any standardized expression of capacity can be misleading if proper attention is not paid to the reality of the facility under evaluation. For example, a 500-bed hospital can be expected to contain 500 beds for patients, but that same hospital could be suffering from a shortage of nursing staff, and thus cannot care for 500 patients. Even a 200-seat classroom does not necessarily have the capacity to serve 200 students, particularly if that classroom is to be used for exams that require every other seat to be left empty. While these exceptions are specific to the facility being discussed, this pattern of issues is common, giving rise to the identification of two different types of capacity.

Design versus Effective Capacity of Parking

While the design capacity of a parking area is clearly marked by painted spaces, many factors may lower its effective capacity. Pictured here is a predictable loss of capacity when snow covers the painted lines and drivers must guess at the location of spaces. This irregular spacing of cars results in a loss of parking, lowering effective capacity.

Design Capacity The design capacity of a facility is its theoretical maximum potential. To operate at this level assumes that nothing interferes with the design of the system, a distinctly optimistic assumption. Nonetheless, systems are often presented according to their design capacity, such as, "Lanark Regional Hospital is a 110-bed facility." Lanark Regional Hospital may have 110 patient beds fully supported by adequate equipment and staff, yet there may still be reasons why precisely 110 patients cannot be treated at any given moment in time; one or more rooms may be undergoing maintenance, for example. As another example, the design capacity of a parking garage is confirmed by counting its marked spaces, although it is reasonable to assume that a few spaces may be lost each day to the parking of oversized vehicles or the presence of broken glass awaiting cleanup.

design capacity
The theoretical maximum output of a system, assuming ideal operating conditions.

Effective Capacity The effective capacity of a system is expected to be less than its design capacity, in that it reflects the system's potential under normal operating conditions. Ideally no one would leave broken glass in a parking space, but that does happen occasionally within a large parking deck, and thus the effective capacity of the parking facility is somewhat less than its literal design. In this example, broken glass left in a space is a factor contributing to effective capacity, and such factors can be investigated for any system. The gap between the designed potential and the effective capacity of a facility often results from factors such as these:

effective capacity
The practical maximum output of a system, assuming normal operating conditions.

- Routine maintenance.
- Work breaks and mealtimes for the employees.
- Bad weather.

Another critical distinction between design and effective capacity is the degree to which a manager can influence either. Design capacity is notoriously fixed. Adjusting it to a higher number usually requires the physical expansion of a facility. Effective capacity, however, might be influenced to some degree if a manager can influence the factors that contribute to the gap. Often effective capacity can be increased by devoting more resources to certain factors, such as adding staff to decrease maintenance downtime.

Performance Measures Two performance measures to evaluate these contrasting types of capacity are utilization and efficiency. Utilization and efficiency are ratios comparing actual usage to the design and effective capacities, respectively:

utilization
Percent of design capacity in use.

efficiency
Percent of a resource in productive use.

$$\text{Utilization} = \frac{\text{actual output}}{\text{design capacity}} \qquad \text{Efficiency} = \frac{\text{actual output}}{\text{effective capacity}}$$

Efficiency is the more operational of the two measures. It states how much of a resource is being used, given its reasonable availability. Thus, by its definition, we might expect that efficiency could range as high as 100% for a certain facility, though its utilization would not likely reach that benchmark. Nonetheless, utilization better reflects the use of the total investment in the facility, as the entire design capacity had to be funded and constructed for use. Scenario 1 demonstrates these measurements.

Capacity Measures **Scenario 1**

Global Freightways would never load a Boeing 747-400 airplane with more than 124 tons of freight, although this aircraft is theoretically capable of carrying as much 140 tons, assuming that the weather is ideal for flying. The danger of loading a Boeing 747-400 airplane with greater than 124 tons of freight is the possibility that weather becomes quite poor at its

Continues

destination, forcing the pilot to land at a much faster speed than usual. This increased speed of landing puts increased stress on the landing gear of the airplane, and if the 747-400 is loaded with more than 124 tons of freight, there exists a very small possibility that this landing gear might suddenly fail during landing, leading to catastrophic loss of the airplane. Even though the possibility of such an event is very small, Global Freightways does not load more than 124 tons of freight on any Boeing 747-400.

What terminology best describes this issue of 124 tons versus 140 tons with respect to loading a Boeing 747-400? How are the issues of poor weather and increased landing speed best described? Suppose Global Freightways loads a Boeing 747-400 with exactly 120 tons of freight. What is Global Freightways' utilization of the airplane during a 4,400 mile trip?

Analysis

One hundred twenty-four tons is best described as the effective capacity of a Boeing 747-400 for Global Freightway's purposes, because that is the limit the company can reasonably rely on, given the realities of its daily operations. One hundred forty tons is best described as the design capacity of the same airplane, in that this is a theoretical upper limit on its capacity, referring only to ideal conditions. Thus the issues of poor weather and increased landing speed are good examples of factors dictating effective capacity, creating the gap between the capacity Global can plan on (effective) and what capacity the airplane is technically capable of (design). Calculating a measure such as utilization is a matter of identifying the data needed for the relevant ratio.

CALCULATING UTILIZATION OF 747-400

Design Capacity: 140 tons
Effective Capacity: 124 tons
Output (over 4,400 mile trip): 120 tons
Utilization: 120/140 = .8571 = 85.71%
Efficiency: 120/124 = .9677 = 96.77%

Insight Thus, Global Freightway's utilization of the Boeing 747-400 is nearly 86% on this particular trip. Efficiency, (which was not asked above) is nearly 97%. ■

Although Scenario 1 demonstrates the calculations associated with evaluating capacity, be cautious when interpreting these numbers. As noted earlier, we can expect efficiency to range as high as 100% in theory, and certainly the 97% efficiency in Scenario 1 appears quite good. However, while efficiency can range up to 100%, that does not necessarily mean it is desirable to operate at that level or near it. In capacity planning, desirability is largely determined by cost, and the operating level of a facility that minimizes the average cost of output produced is not necessarily the highest possible output level at which the facility can operate. Figure 5.1 illustrates a common pattern of average cost changes over increasing volume of system output. At low levels of output volume, average cost is often quite high, because the fixed cost associated with the facility is spread across very few units of output. For output volume, any increase to output level decreases average cost by spreading the fixed cost further, an important phenomenon known as economies of scale. Nonetheless, this benefit of increasing volume can be expected to end at some point, and any further increase in volume then increases average cost per unit produced, entering the realm of diseconomies of scale. At the turning point between the two ranges of volume in Figure 5.1 is the theoretically desirable optimal operating level, which might be well below the effective capacity of the system.

fixed cost Cost incurred regardless of the volume of associated activity.

economies of scale Decreasing average unit cost by increasing volume.

diseconomies of scale Increasing average unit cost by increasing volume.

Optimal Operating Level

FIGURE 5.1

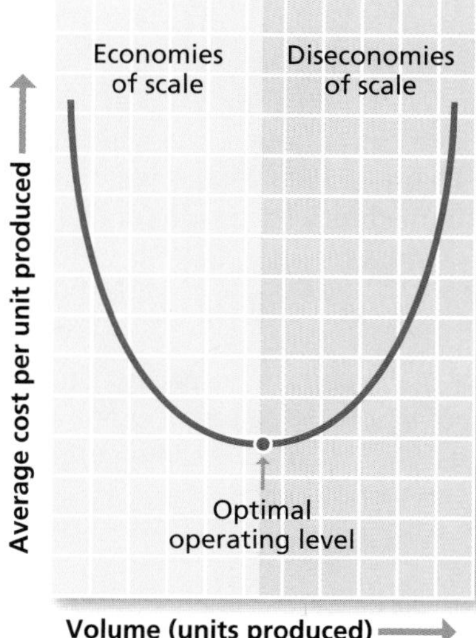

While economies of scale are generally driven by the spreading of fixed costs, what drives diseconomies of scale is more specific to the reality of a particular facility. Common causes of rising costs with rising volume include:

- *Traffic and congestion.* Once operating activity increases beyond a certain desirable level, the facility may have to work harder and spend more to simply stay organized and avoid confusion.
- *Maintenance.* Extremely high levels of activity can create need for additional maintenance and repair, while simultaneously robbing the schedule of time to conduct the additional work. If allowed to continue, this can invite even more costly breakdowns as the system wears down.
- *Overtime and burnout.* Extreme levels of activity often require employees to work overtime, increasing the cost of labor. People fatique as well, and sustained levels of extended work hours can lead to mistakes, employee burnout, and potentially higher employee turnover rates.

Finally, even though it is not possible theoretically, some facilities can operate *beyond* their design capacity. Instances of this represent extreme diseconomies of scale and are generally short exceptions to the facility's usual volume. As an example, large events can overwhelm the design capacity of parking facilities adjacent to the event. Here design is often temporarily ignored in favor of parking additional vehicles where they would not normally be tolerated, such as on the grass. This is not only costly to the landscaping, but also requires that the event employ parking staff to implement the overflow scheme.

variable cost
Cost that varies with volume of associated activity.

break-even point
A level of activity at which the revenue collected matches the costs incurred by that activity.

Break-even Points Break-even analysis is a well-known business tool useful in a variety of contexts, one of which is capacity planning. The commonly used expression "to break-even" indicates "just enough revenue to cover costs." If the fixed cost of the operation is designated FC, the variable cost per unit produced is VC, and the revenue collected per unit is R, the break-even point (Q_{BE}) is the level of production at which total revenue and cost are balanced:

$$FC + (VC \times Q_{BE}) = (R \times Q_{BE})$$

Solving the expression above for Q_{BE} creates the break-even formula:

$$Q_{BE} = \frac{FC}{R - VC}$$

Break-even analysis is commonly used in capacity planning because different options for design capacity expansion may have differing fixed and variable costs, so determining their break-even points may give better insight into which is most desirable. If a capacity option is available for a fixed cost of $50,000 and will produce at a cost of $2 products that can be sold for $10 a unit, the break-even point of that option is

$$Q_{BE} = \frac{FC}{R - VC} = \frac{50,000}{10 - 2} = 6,250 \text{ units}$$

If this firm produces precisely 6,250 units the capacity option theoretically pays for itself, although it must produce more that 6,250 to earn a profit and any amount less results in a loss on the operation. While this is a useful reading, interpreting break-even points in reality can be more complex, as we see in Scenario 2.

Scenario 2

Break-even Points

Global Freightways is considering the purchase of a new airplane to fly between Tokyo's Narita Airport (NRT) and Singapore's Changi Airport (SIN), a distance of 2,869 nautical miles. Global Freightways is evaluating two different models of Boeing aircraft: the Boeing 747-400, which can safely carry 124 tons of freight and the slightly smaller but more fuel efficient Boeing 777, which has an effective capacity of 104 tons. Costs associated with each model are summarized in the following table:

Aircraft Model	Monthly Fixed Debt Payment	Other Monthly Fixed Expenses	Operating Cost per Ton/Mile
Boeing 747-400	$1,367,000	$50,000	$1.45
Boeing 777	1,517,000	50,000	1.38

The operating cost per ton/mile is the cost to carry 1 ton of freight for 1 nautical mile. Global Freightways can earn $2 revenue per ton/mile on this route, and expects to fly this plane loaded in both directions between SIN and NRT. Thus, Global collects 2 × 2,869 = $5,738 per ton for freight flown between SIN and NRT, regardless of which airport is the point of departure. What does a break-even analysis indicate about the two choices of aircraft?

Analysis

Initially, the break-even formula is applied to the case of each aircraft:

BREAK-EVEN ANALYSIS FOR GLOBAL FREIGHTWAYS

Aircraft Model	Total Monthly Fixed Cost	Break-even Point
Boeing 747-400	$1,367,000 + 50,000 = $1,417,000	$1,417,000/(2 – 1.45) = 2,576,364 ton/miles per month
Boeing 777	$1,517,000 + 50,000 = $1,567,000	$1,567,000/(2 – 1.38) = 2,527,419 ton/miles per month

Break-even points are highlighted, but these values can be deceiving. First, it is tempting to say, that the Boeing 777 has a lower break-even point, but that is a dangerous statement considering that the Boeing 777 is a smaller aircraft and thus can move fewer tons each mile of a trip. Assuming Global would load each aircraft to its effective capacity, it is helpful to adjust the break-even points to reflect the reality of the differing capacities of the two aircraft:

BREAK-EVEN POINTS, ADJUSTED FOR AIRCRAFT SIZE

Boeing 747-400 2,576,364/124 = 20,777 fully loaded miles per month
Boeing 777 2,527,419/104 = 24,302 fully loaded miles per month

Now the Boeing 777 requires more usage to break even on its purchase, clarified by further converting these numbers to trips between the airports NRT and SIN.

BREAK-EVEN POINTS, ADJUSTED FOR SIZE AND ROUTE

Boeing 747-400 20,777/2,869 = 7.24 fully loaded NRT/SIN trips per month
Boeing 777 24,302/2,869 = 8.47 fully loaded NRT/SIN trips per month

Insight Thus, the Boeing 747-400 would need to fly 7.24 fully loaded trips each month, while the Boeing 777 would need to complete 8.47 fully loaded trips each month to earn back their associated costs. Since an aircraft cannot, in reality, make a partial trip, this means that the Boeing 747-400 must make a minimum of 8 trips and the Boeing 777 a minimum of 9 trips per month to breakeven. ■

Note that Scenario 2 does not identify which aircraft should be purchased. To make that recommendation, Global Freightways must first provide some estimate of how many trips are expected between NRT and SIN on a monthly basis. Given that Global does plan to make at least 9 trips per month, either the Boeing 747-400 or the Boeing 777 will break even, although they will earn different levels of profit.

Break-even analysis also helps clarify the strategic issue of subcontracting or outsourcing some portion of an organization's production. Reviewing the break-even formula reveals that the relative risk of not breaking even is driven by the fixed cost associated with the capacity option. Subcontracting or outsourcing production to another organization usually avoids fixed costs, because the external capacity is provided at some per unit rate of compensation. This per unit rate may be higher than the organization's own internal variable costs, but the opportunity to avoid the risk of a high fixed investment nonetheless makes outsourcing attractive. However, any organization should resist outsourcing a core competency of its business, because the business may lose its competitive advantage within its own market.

subcontract
To engage a third party in the provision of value to a customer.

outsource
To subcontract an internal process to an external provider.

core competency
Specific ability that distinguishes a business from its competitors.

Capacity Strategies

An organization often adopts a particular strategy to guide its capacity decisions over time. Studying the history of that organization can bring these strategies to light. Recall that to adjust the design capacity of an operation an organization must effect a bricks-and-mortar action such as the construction of a new facility or the shut-down of an existing one. When such an adjustment is made, the overall design capacity of the system essentially jumps upward or downward at the moment of implementation, adding or removing what some refer to as "capacity chunks." When these decisions are graphed over time, these chunks create a distinct step pattern like the one in Figure 5.2. The timing of these steps, relative to the demand on the operation, suggests the capacity strategy of the organization.

FIGURE **5.2** Conservative Capacity Strategy

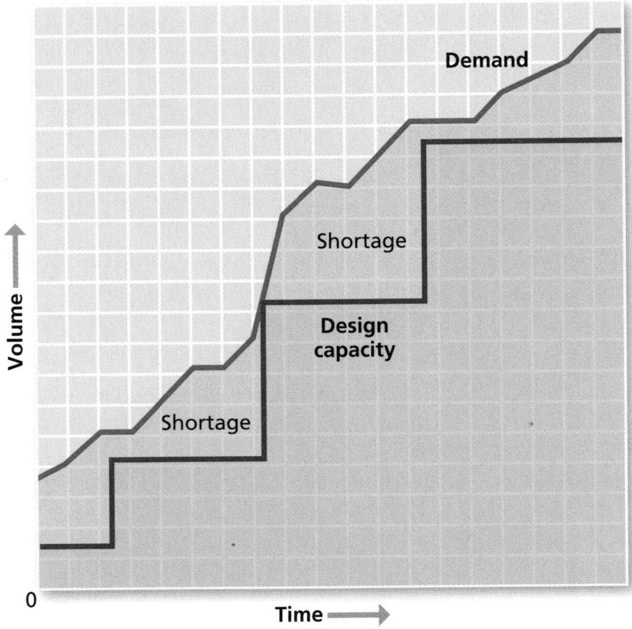

Conservative Strategies Figure 5.2 illustrates the capacity decisions of an organization pursuing a very conservative expansion strategy. That design capacity is adjusted upward only after demand on the system has increased to levels well beyond current capacity. This wait-and-see strategy provides the following advantages:

- High utilization rates throughout the organization's history can translate into high values for return on assets and other financial measures.
- Shortages created by delaying expansion might not necessarily translate into lost customers. The organization might be subcontracting this excess demand to another firm working on its behalf.

Although this strategy uses the design capacity to its fullest advantage, it suffers these disadvantages:

- Customer service is likely to suffer throughout the firm's timeline.
- Competitors may maximize opportunities to enter the market and establish themselves by claiming unmet demand.
- System overload may result in higher average costs than necessary.

In certain cases, some firms deliberately create and maintain shortages, enhancing the prestige of the product. Any organization that is a monopoly and/or maintains a perpetual wait list for its good or service is likely pursuing this strategy.

capacity cushion Largely idle capacity maintained beyond the expected load level of a system to absorb unexpected demand.

Aggressive Strategies An organization pursuing an aggressive capacity strategy expands in anticipation of growing demand, as pictured in Figure 5.3. Here the design capacity of the system is never allowed to fall below demand, resulting in adequate supply of its output throughout the organization's timeline. While no periods of shortage are present, Figure 5.3 reveals another strategic feature absent from Figure 5.2: capacity cushions. Because the organization is expanding in advance of demand, it maintains varying

Aggressive Capacity Strategy **FIGURE 5.3**

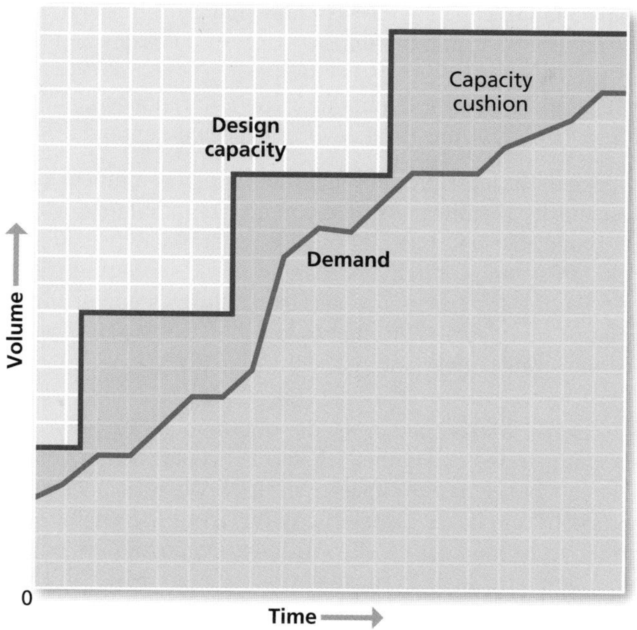

degrees of idle capacity (capacity above demand) throughout its history. These largely idle portions of its overall system are often referred to as capacity cushions to highlight their ability to absorb the shock of any abrupt and unexpected spike in demand.

Because this extreme capacity strategy is essentially the opposite of the conservative capacity strategy discussed eariler, the advantages of this strategy are a reflection of the disadvantages of its counterpart:

- Customer service is maximized throughout the firm's time line.
- Competitors have less incentive and opportunity to enter this marketplace.

Capacity Cushion at a Commuter Train Station

Commuter trains and other forms of public transport often suffer rapid increases and decreases in demand during the day and on certain days of the week. These operations must expand to meet the peaks in this demand, often leaving large parts of their systems idle during nonpeak periods. Here management shuts down the electrical power to its capacity cushion—an additional escalator—during nonpeak hours.

Likewise, the disadvantages of this strategy reflect the advantages of the conservative strategy in Figure 5.2:

- Aggressive expansion of capacity lowers utilization rates throughout the organization's history, possibly translating into lower return on assets and other financial measures.
- Increased costs associated with maintaining the idle capacity cushion often provide little or no direct benefit in the absence of unexpected demand.

Any system that appears at least partially idle at any given moment is likely aggressive in its approach to capacity planning. As an example, an ambulance would appear underutilized when compared to a city bus, although both are heavily utilized components in personal transportation systems. Often ambulances spend more time idle than city buses, because capacity planning for emergency services follows a somewhat more aggressive strategy than sizing of bus fleets. Why this would be true points to why any particular firm would prefer one strategy over another, which we discuss next.

Selecting a Strategy Most operations do not manipulate their capacity in such extreme fashions as illustrated in Figures 5.2 and 5.3. Instead they follow some balance of the conservative versus aggressive capacity strategy. What balance an operation would pursue is determined by the costs associated with Figure 5.2 versus 5.3, or the cost of unmet demand relative to the cost of idle capacity. Organizations enjoying a relatively small cost of unmet demand, such as those with customers who can't go elsewhere, can be expected to focus on efficient use of resources and follow more conservative strategies. As an example, expansion of parking capacity on a college campus can be expected to follow a somewhat more conservative strategy than practiced by a retail shopping center. This is because those seeking parking on campus cannot switch to a competitor on a daily basis, whereas those at the shopping center can. In contrast, organizations for whom the cost of unmet demand is unthinkably high, suggesting harm and possible loss of human life, maintain the greatest capacity cushions. This is typical of emergency response, the assets of which can stand idle most of the time. Here the cost of maintaining a mostly idle system becomes attractive when compared to risking a smaller system.

THE FORMATION OF WAITING LINES

Waiting is both a familiar and a costly activity. Lines form and customers wait when a system does not have adequate capacity to serve all customers at the precise times those customers place demands on the system. While greater capacity implies shorter waiting lines, greater capacity also implies greater costs to maintain that capacity. However, waiting usually does not add value, and can penalize an operation with a variety of costs, including lost sales and lowered customer perception of product quality. Thus, organizations choosing a capacity strategy often seek the most economic trade-off between the cost of the waiting incurred at a certain capacity level and the cost of the system capacity itself, as illustrated in Figure 5.4.

Figure 5.4 offers a visual explanation for why organizations tolerate a certain amount of customer waiting, despite the cost of such delays. The resulting lines, known more formally as queues, become a particular concern for the operations manager.

queue
A waiting line.

Queues come in many different forms, and do not always involve people standing in a line. Nonetheless, queues all share a common anatomy of factors that create the wait for some service process, and good waiting line management begins with understanding these components as they apply to a particular situation. Queuing theory offers mathematical tools to analyze the waiting in that situation, given a particular type of queue. Other models of waiting stress psychology, recognizing that most queues are, in fact, people being delayed. Better understanding of the psychology of waiting offers managers

queuing theory
The mathematical modeling of waiting lines.

Economics of Waiting

FIGURE 5.4

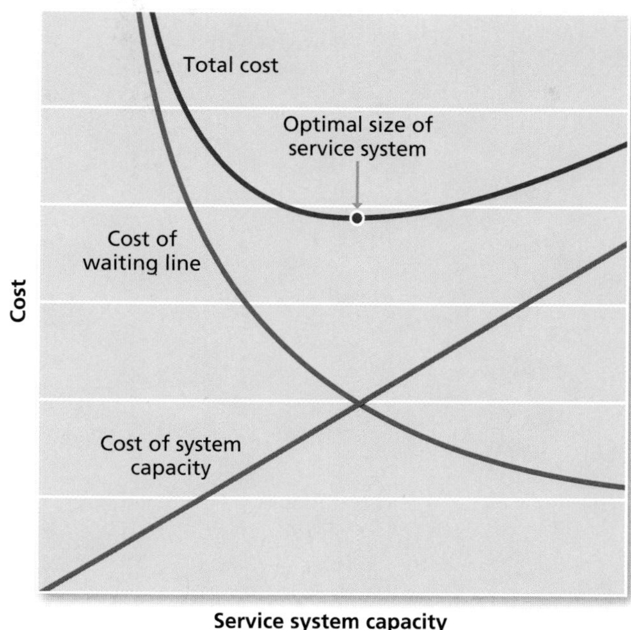

better insight into the true cost of waiting, and might prove just as vital as mathematical calculations when minimizing this cost in many service situations.

Modeling an existing or proposed waiting line begins with an audit of the combined factors that create it. These factors define the line and are often used to match a waiting situation under study with an existing mathematical model that best mimics its internal workings. Any queue forming in any situation can be modeled as the combined interaction of three basic components: customer arrivals, the queue itself, and the service system, illustrated in Figure 5.5. The differing details concerning these three parts describe situations as varied as a queue of customers waiting to use a cash machine versus a queue of accident victims waiting for emergency surgery or a queue of cars waiting to pass a construction zone.

Customer Arrivals

The first major component of any waiting line is the source of its customer arrivals. This component supplies a waiting line with its membership, and thus influences the overall waiting situation. To understand a particular waiting line's customer arrivals, we look at key arrival characteristics.

Nature of Arrivals One question to ask when studying a waiting line concerns the population size of potential arrivals: is this population distinctly limited in size? A finite calling population implies that the overall number of potential customers is small enough that customer arrival rate and the number of customers in the system are not independent events. For example, if three of only four potential customers have already arrived and are either being served or waiting for service, the chance that the fourth and last customer will arrive is different from the chance that any one of the four will arrive when the same system is standing idle. While this is a special case of arrivals, it often

finite calling population An environment in which the maximum number of potential arrivals to a waiting line is distinctly restricted.

FIGURE **5.5** The Basic Anatomy of a Line

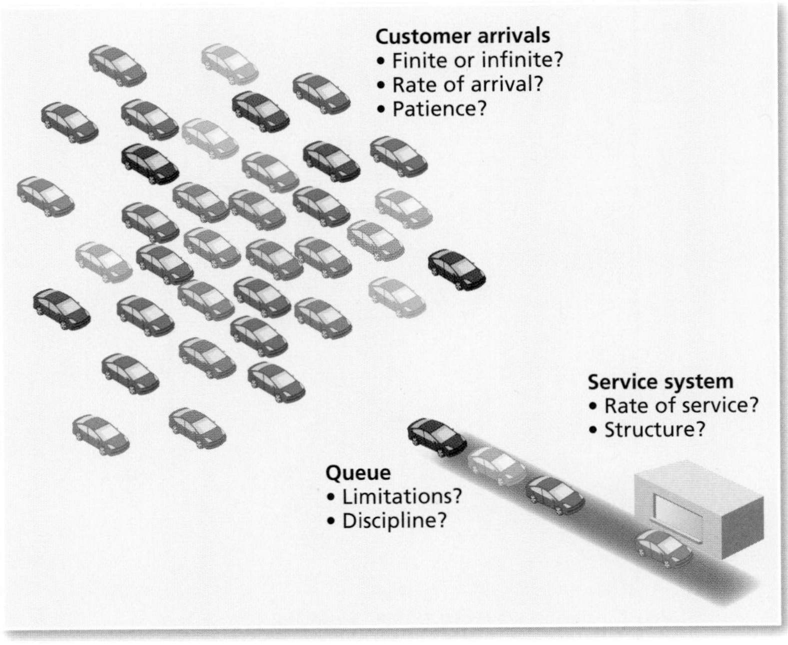

occurs within workgroups, such as when four people share a color laser printer or other peripheral device.

infinite calling population
An environment in which the number of potential arrivals to a waiting line is unrestricted.

Most lines are supplied by a so-called infinite calling population, although the number of potential customers is not likely to be truly infinite in any situation. An infinite calling population contains enough customers that the customer arrival rate and the number of customers in the system function independently: the arrival of one customer does not reduce the overall size of the population enough to change the probability that another customer arrival will follow. Most on-demand services, from arrivals at a restaurant to calls for ambulance service, can be characterized as supplied by infinite calling populations.

Distribution of Arrivals How customer arrivals are distributed across time is another important characteristic shaping a waiting line. One obvious example of this is whether arrivals are scheduled or unscheduled. If a system can schedule arrivals into appointments, we expect less waiting than a system that must serve random arrivals. However, many systems must serve random or at least semirandom arrivals, and here is where study of the distribution of those arrivals becomes critical. If an average of 5 customers appear every hour, does this average represent 3 to 6 customers an hour, or does this average include hours in which no customers arrive and other hours in which 10 or more arrive? To model the resulting line of customers, we must identify a probability distribution that best mimics the chances of these various conditions occurring. Traditionally, the Poisson distribution has been a good fit when describing random customer arrival. In the Poisson distribution, the probability of x customers arriving in a certain time interval, or $P(x)$, is determined by

Poisson distribution
A discrete probability distribution describing the likelihood of a particular number of independent events within a particular interval.

$$P(x) = (\lambda^x e^{-\lambda})/x!$$

FIGURE 5.6 **Probabilities of Various Arrivals, Poisson Distributed with Mean of 5**

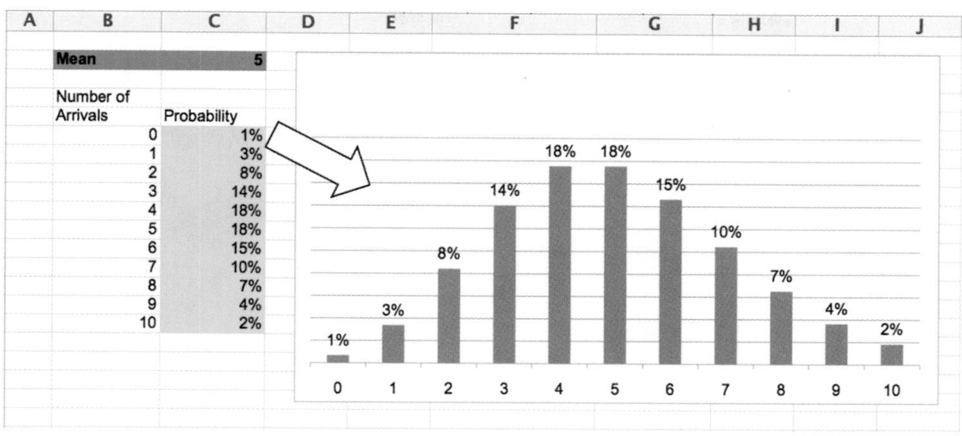

where λ is the mean number of customers that arrive in that time interval and e is 2.71828. Figure 5.6 displays a spreadsheet model employing this expression to calculate and display the probability of various numbers of customers arriving when the average number of customers that arrive in that time interval is five, or $\lambda = 5$.

In a situation with an average of 5 customers arriving every hour, the distribution in Figure 5.6 would be a good fit to the randomness around that average if 4 or 5 do arrive approximately a third of the time, between 3 and 6 approximately two-thirds of the time, and rarely more than 10 arrive in an hour.

Patience of Arrivals Another important characteristic of customer arrivals is their degree of patience. If every arriving customer joins the line and all customers wait until they are served, customer arrivals are said to be perfectly patient. This is important because mathematical models often assume arrivals are perfectly patient. When studying an existing line, remain alert to instances of impatience, as these must be addressed later in any numerical analysis. Two common forms of impatience may be observed among customers, each with a different impact on the waiting line itself:

- **Balking.** Balking occurs when a customer arrives and leaves immediately without joining the line. Balking generally occurs when a line is perceived as too long relative to the value of the service.
- **Reneging.** Reneging occurs when a customer arrives, joins the line, but leaves at some point without receiving the service. Similar to balking, reneging usually occurs if the waiting customer decides the remaining wait is too long relative to the value of the service.

balking
When an arriving customer decides against joining a line.

reneging
When an arriving customer joins a line, but then abandons it before being served.

Both balking and reneging are generally associated with longer lines and crowded systems, and both imply that the arriving customer has other choices. Other examples of impatient behavior include cycling, in which a customer rejoins the line immediately after being served, and switching, in which a customer changes queues within a multi-queue system.

The Queue

The second major component of a waiting line is the queue itself. When observing a line, there are two queue characteristics to watch for: any issue of limitation on the length of

Two Queues for Two Bank Machines

We can assume that these two queues represent two different populations of arrivals, the customers of the two banks offering cash withdrawal at this location. In either case, it is safe to describe the arrival population and the length of the line as technically unlimited and queue discipline as first-come, first-served for each population. Customers appear reasonably patient, although it is not known if some arriving customers are balking and looking for cash withdrawal elsewhere.

the queue and what rule is governing the order in which waiting customers are being served.

Limitations More often than not, no technical limitations exist on the length of a queue. While it may not be likely that the queue for a service such as an ATM would grow infinitely long, nonetheless no factor would prevent this, as the line could technically stretch throughout the mall, corridor, walkway, or around the building. Thus, most service queues are classified as *unlimited queues* simply because no such strict limitation governs them.

Limitations do occur in some situations, and it is important to note them in the analysis of a line. Limitations are sometimes physical restrictions of the system, like a phone system with a limited buffer space to store a flood of incoming calls. Another potential queue limitation might be organizational policy, such as no more than three customers may wait due to security concerns. Here a customer arriving when three customers are already waiting is required to leave immediately. Any customer arriving after a limited queue has reached its capacity is said to be blocked from the system.

blocking
Preventing customer arrivals from entering a system due to limitations on the allowable length of a queue.

Queue Discipline Queue discipline is a policy of the system specifying the order in which waiting arrivals are served. One of the most familiar rules for queue discipline is FCFS, a standard abbreviation for the agreement of first-come, first-served. However, this is not the only rule that might be in use:

queue discipline
Rules determining the order in which waiting individuals are served.

FCFS
First-come, first-served sequencing rule.

- Arrivals may be prioritized by their expected processing time, such as shortest processing time first or longest processing time first.
- Arrivals may be prioritized according to some degree of urgency, such as emergencies first at a walk-in clinic. If the arrivals were promised service by a certain deadline, they can be prioritized based on the urgency of that deadline. This is known as earliest due date first.
- Arrivals may be organized into special classes of priority, such as seating reservations first at a restaurant. Some large entertainment complexes such as theme parks sell premium-priced tickets that entitle those customers to higher priority when waiting to enter an attraction.

Finally, it is not uncommon for queue discipline to involve multiple rules. As examples, a restaurant may seat reservations first and a dentist's office may serve emergencies first, but the restaurant can be expected to return to FCFS after reservations have been seated, while a dentist's office will return to scheduled appointments if there are no other emergencies.

Capacity of the System

The third and final component shared by all waiting lines is the service system itself, or what the customer is waiting for. Important variations among systems concern the speed at which they can serve each customer, and their internal structure.

Distribution of Service Times Some systems can serve customers in a fixed, predictable amount of time that does not vary from one customer to the next. Examples of such systems are relatively rare, and usually involve automation, such as obtaining a parking ticket when entering an airport parking lot. Otherwise, the time to successfully serve customers can be expected to vary whether customers are in line to purchase varying amounts of items at a supermarket or have all arrived at an emergency medical center with various ailments. Service systems that require appointments must predict the time required in each case and fix the timing of service in advance of the customer's arrival.

Most waiting lines are associated with some amount of randomness concerning service times; even the best manager cannot control precisely how much time each customer requires to be served successfully. Management should, however, be able to report the average service time of an existing system, and inspection of past data may help determine how best to model the distribution of actual service times around that average. One popular assumption for service time distribution is exponential; the probability of a single service being completed within t minutes, or $P(\text{service time} \leq t)$, would be calculated as

$$P(\text{service time} \leq t) = 1 - e^{-\mu t}$$

where μ is the mean number of customers that can be served in a minute and e is 2.71828. If an average of one customer can be served per minute, Figure 5.7 shows how the distribution of 500 actual service times from that system might appear when service time is exponentially distributed. The use of an exponential distribution to model random service times is a common assumption in queuing theory, because it is a good fit for situations in which a random element is usually observed at a certain value, but is occasionally observed at a much higher value. As Figure 5.7 illustrates, over half of 500 randomly generated customers were served within 1 minute and almost all of them were served within 1.5 minutes. However, occasionally a customer within the crowd of 500 required several minutes for service, a concern that often arises among individuals using an on-demand service.

Randomly Generated Service Times **FIGURE 5.7**

Five hundred service times exponentially distributed with a mean length of service of 1 minute

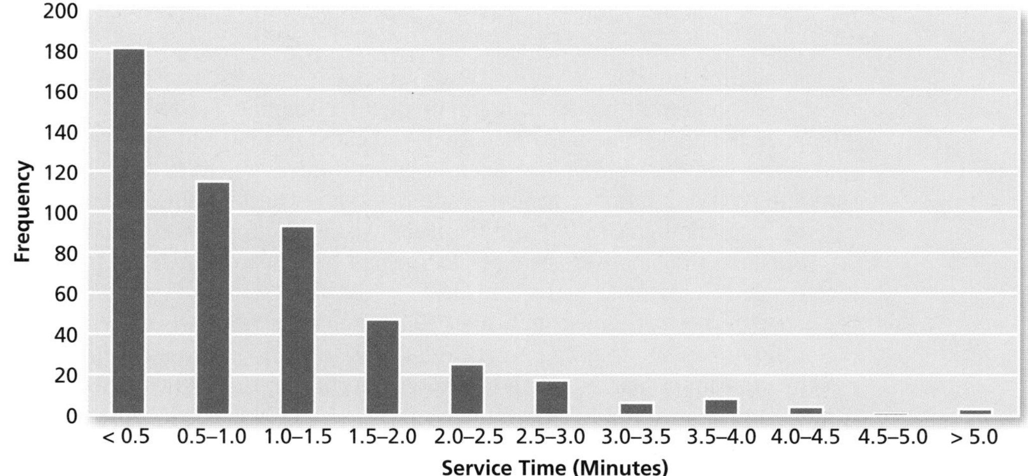

FIGURE 5.8 Single-Queue, Multiple-Channel System Structure

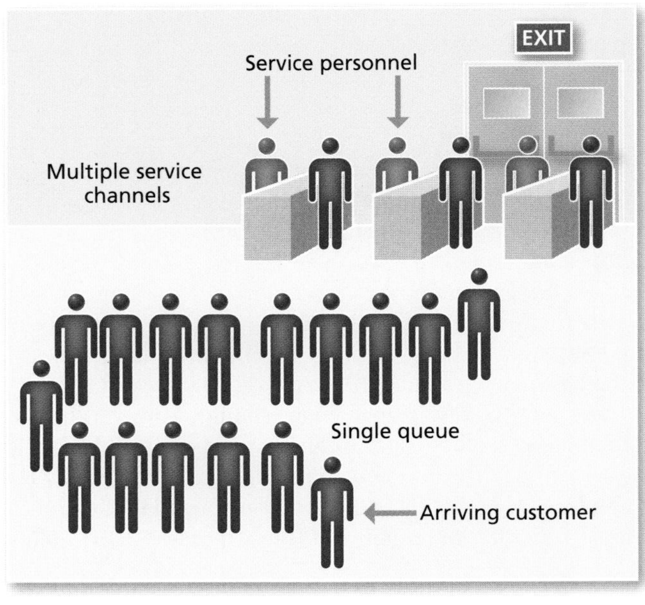

serpentine line
A single queue of customers waiting in a line that must bend one or more times to fit within the service facility.

System Structure If a system offers only one channel for service, then only one server can assist waiting customers and only one queue can form. This logical formation is known more formally as a single-queue, single-channel system. However, this structure offers options that must be chosen carefully. For example, Figure 5.8 shows a diagram of a system in which a single queue is formed to await service in a multiple channel system. This queue is also referred to as a serpentine line, familiar to customers at airports, amusement parks, post offices, and many other settings.

Serpentine lines are more efficient than another option in system structure, the formation of multiple queues to match multiple channels, as illustrated in Figure 5.9. Customers in a multiple queue system such as the checkout lanes of a supermarket can suffer greater delay due to being in a queue behind a customer who requires an unusually long amount of service time, such as a shopper in a dispute with the cashier. In contrast, a serpentine system would provide the same extended service to that particular shopper, but the single queue behind that shopper would keep moving, as other channels become available to assist other customers.

Serpentine queuing structure, however, does bring its own concerns. Management must work somewhat harder to maintain queue discipline. For example, the formation of a long, serpentine queue must usually be indicated by placing posts, gates, ropes, and/or ribbons around the waiting area to clarify to customers where to stand to maintain FCFS. Operating a take-a-number system is another answer to this same challenge of queue discipline, maintaining FCFS without requiring customers to remain standing in a long line.

Oftentimes the more efficient serpentine line system structure is not in use, because one long queue literally looks bad to the arriving customer. Systems that utilize serpentine lines are generally not concerned with the balking behavior discussed earlier: customers arriving at airports or at amusement park rides have already purchased their admission to the system and cannot readily switch to a competitor if they dislike the appearance of the line. A retail store, however, has reason to be concerned with this quick impression of its service, as the arriving customer may simply leave and shop elsewhere. Nonetheless, the technical superiority of the single line supported by multiple servers is attractive enough to motivate some retailers to innovate with hybrid systems such as the one pictured in Figure 5.10. This

Multiple-Queue, Multiple-Channel System Structure FIGURE **5.9**

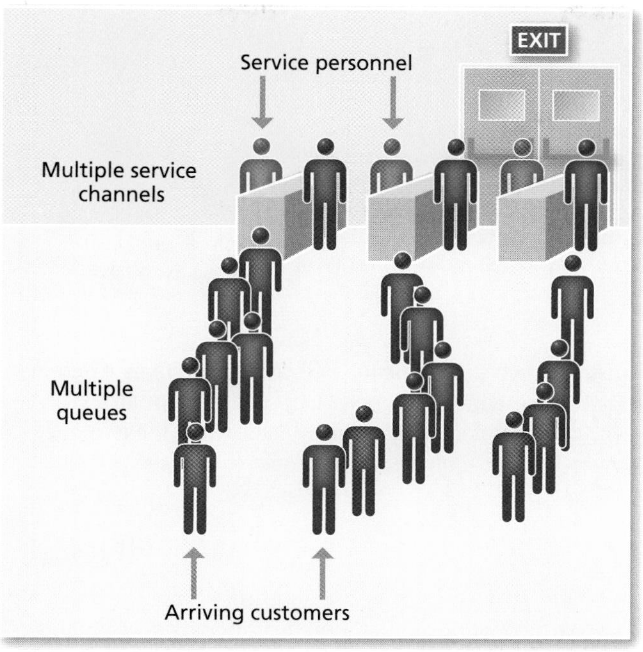

Hybrid Multiple-Channel System Structure FIGURE **5.10**

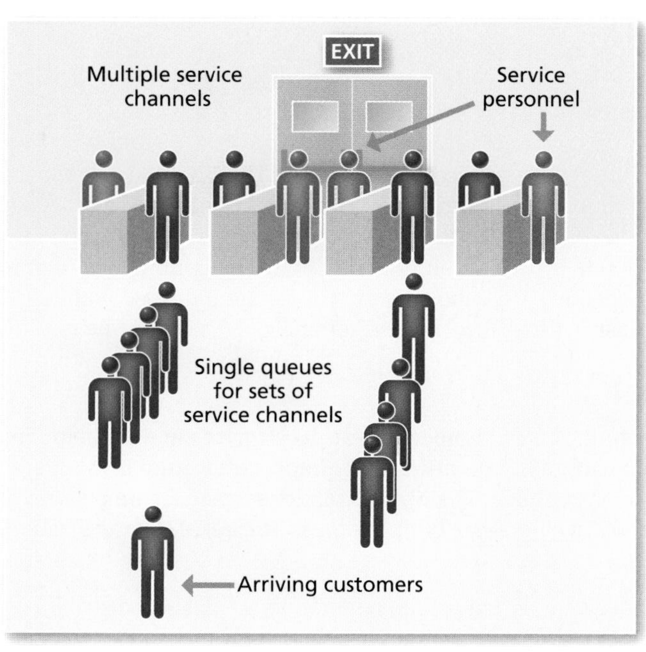

Maintaining Queue Discipline with a Take-a-Number System

Serpentine lines do not necessarily require waiting arrivals to stand in a single snakelike formation. To maintain FCFS queue discipline while allowing waiting customers to move about or sit down, some businesses operate a take-a-number system. The electronic sign board pictured here signals both who is next for service (in the left-hand column) and which server this customer should approach (in the right-hand column). While operating this system is more complex than requiring customers to stand in the order they arrived, such arrangements are popular when the wait may be lengthy, such as in government offices, and/or when the customer can interact with other parts of the system while waiting, such as browsing merchandise in retail settings.

illustration demonstrates two single-queue, dual-channel systems working in parallel. Ideally the pair of servers working with each queue here will prevent an individual customer from delaying others with unusual demands of the system, while the two queues will appear reasonably short compared to an equivalent single-queue, four-server system.

MATHEMATICAL MODELS OF WAITING

Although the most familiar examples of queuing from daily life are people standing in a line for service, the earliest work on mathematical modeling of queues concerned emerging telecommunication networks, starting with a 1909 publication by A. K. Erlang, an engineer for the Copenhagen Telephone Exchange. This modeling portrays a queue as the result of its interacting arrival and service distributions, and derives its expected performance mathematically, given a set of known characteristics. Thus, for any combination of assumptions discussed earlier as the anatomy of the line, there may already exist a mathematical model that conveniently predicts issues such as the average wait time, percent idle time, and average number of customers in that particular system.

Kendall notation
A labeling system for classifying waiting line models according to their initial assumptions.

Since there are many different potential combinations of waiting line assumptions, Kendall notation was established in the 1950s to organize and standardize the naming of all the resulting mathematical models. In Kendall notation, a particular queuing model is designated X/Y/Z if customer arrivals are described by the X distribution, service times are Y distributed, and the system consists of Z channels. Thus, a set of formulas for G/D/2 model a system with customer arrivals that are random but *G*eneral (no particular other probability distribution), service times that are *D*eterministic (known, unvarying), and consisting of two service channels. In Kendall notation, both the assumptions of Poisson distributed arrivals and exponentially distributed service time are indicated with an M, and thus one of the most popular mathematical models for analyzing a single line is known as M/M/1.

M/M/1 Model

tractable
Easy to use; yields insight with a limited number of calculations.

One obvious feature of a good model is that its structure and assumptions closely mimic the system it is meant to represent. Another important feature is that the model is considered tractable, or easy to use. The M/M/1 model is one of the most well known in queuing theory because it possesses both features. The M/M/1 model makes the following assumptions:

- Arrivals from an unlimited calling population are Poisson distributed with a mean of λ.
- Arrivals form a single queue of unlimited length using FCFS.
- Each arrival is perfectly patient, waiting for a single server whose service rate is exponentially distributed with a mean of μ.

These assumptions mimic many single lines for on-demand service reasonably well, and they are the basis for a series of formulas that can quickly estimate the operating characteristics of any such line. These formulas, pictured in Figure 5.11, provide a convenient method to predict the following:

- Overall system utilization. The portion of time the server will be busy serving a customer. This also represents the chance that any arriving customer will have to wait for service.
- The probability, P_n, of any certain number of customers in the system. P_0 is often of interest, in that the probability of no customers in the system is also the probability that any arriving customer could be served immediately.
- The average number of customers in the system (L_S) and the average length of line for service (L_q).
- The average wait in the line (W_q), as well as the average overall amount of time spent in the system (W_S), which includes waiting and being served.

To use the M/M/1 expressions in Figure 5.11, we must first identify the input parameters λ and μ. As with any formula, these values must be appropriate, or any resulting calculations are not likely to be correct. λ is always the average number of customers to arrive in some time interval, such as per minute or per hour. μ is always the average number of services that can be completed in that same time interval. Thus, if we know that an average of 12 customers arrives every hour ($\lambda = 12$), μ must be the average number of services performed in an hour. Since service times are more easily observed in terms of length, it is not uncommon to derive μ from a related observation such as "the average service time is 4 minutes." To adjust this statement of 4-minute service time, $\mu = 60/4 \times 15$ services per hour.

Provided that λ and μ are stated correctly, using the M/M/1 model is a matter of completing the formulas in Figure 5.11. Note that whatever time interval λ and μ do refer to, the waiting formulas W_q and W_S produce answers stated in that same time unit. Thus, if $\lambda = 12$ per hour and $\mu = 15$ per hour, the resulting W_q is 0.2667, meaning the average wait in the queue is 0.2667 hours. While this is the correct answer, it is often desirable to then adjust this to some more intuitive time unit, such as $0.2667 \times 60 = 16$ minutes. We apply the M/M/1 model in Scenario 3.

Operating Characteristics of the M/M/1 Queuing Model | **FIGURE 5.11**

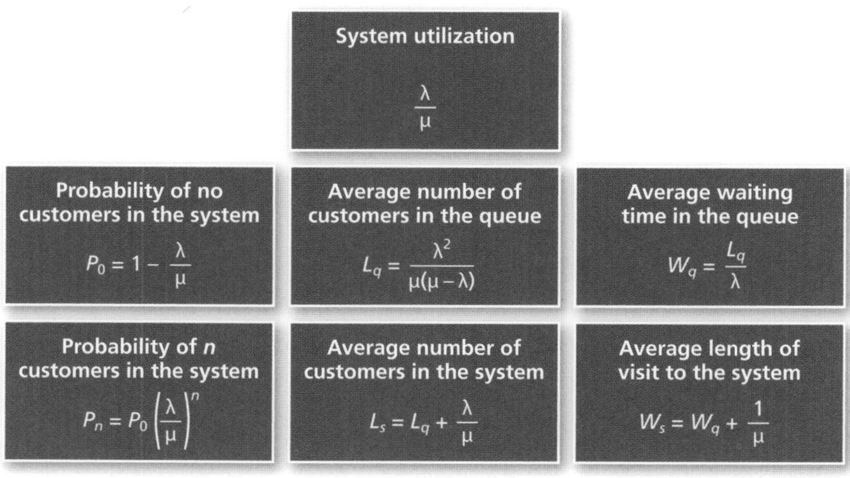

Scenario 3

An Application of the M/M/1 Model

Global Freightways offers discounts for clients willing to deliver air freight cargo directly to its depots for shipping. In large cities, Global Freightways depots are open to drop-off air cargo 24 hours a day, although only one agent is available to serve an arriving client during nonbusiness hours. A single agent requires an average of 20 minutes to complete the client's data entry, check the cargo, and process the payment for the shipment. At Global Freightways' Hong Kong depot, an average of one client arrives each hour during weeknight nonbusiness hours.

Ideally, a drop-off client would not be required to wait for service. Assuming this scenario meets all the assumptions of the M/M/1 model, what is the chance that a client arriving at the Hong Kong depot on a weeknight might have to wait for the agent for service? What is the average amount of time any client who drops off freight at that depot during a weeknight has to wait? What is the average total amount of time a client must spend at the Hong Kong depot, to successfully drop off a shipment during a weeknight?

Analysis

To answer any of the questions, we must first identify λ and μ, the means of the Poisson and exponential distributions of the M/M/1 model. Noting that λ is the average number of arrivals in a certain time interval and μ is the average number of services that could be completed in that same time interval:

WEEKNIGHT DROP-OFFS

$\lambda = 1$ per hour (drop-off clients)
20 minutes to serve each client
$\mu = 60/20 = 3$ per hour (clients served)
utilization $= \lambda/\mu = 1/3 = 33.33\%$

Insight Because the utilization of the M/M/1 system is also the probability that an arriving customer will have to wait for service, a client dropping off a shipment at the Hong Kong depot on a weeknight has a 33.33% chance (or one chance in three) of waiting for the agent to finish serving another client. Two-thirds of the Hong Kong depot's overnight clients can talk to the agent immediately, while one-third of them must wait until the agent finishes serving another client.

Now, to calculate the average wait for that agent, first calculate L_q, the average number of clients waiting, and then adjust to W_q, the average wait for the agent.

HONG KONG DEPOT WEEKNIGHT DROP-OFFS
(AVERAGE WAIT FOR AGENT)

$$L_q = \frac{\lambda^2}{\mu(\mu - \lambda)} = 1^2/(3 \times (3 - 1)) = 1/6, \text{ or } 0.16667 \text{ clients}$$

$$W_q = L_q/\lambda = 0.16667/1 = 0.16667 \text{ hours, or } 0.16667 \times 60 = 10 \text{ minutes}$$

Insight While only a third of clients experience a wait, the average wait for an agent across all weeknight clients at the Hong Kong depot is 10 minutes.

Finally, to calculate the average total amount of time a client must spend at the Hong Kong depot, or W_s:

AVERAGE TOTAL DELAY ON WEEKNIGHT DROP-OFFS

$$W_s = W_q + 1/\mu = 0.16667 + 1/3 = 0.5 \text{ hours, or } 0.5 \times 60 = 30 \text{ minutes}$$

Insight The average total amount of time a drop-off client spends at the Hong Kong depot on a weeknight is 30 minutes. This includes an average of 10 minutes waiting for the agent, and another 20 minutes being served by that agent. ■

Other Models

Many published waiting line models can be used as alternatives to the popular M/M/1 model. These other models have been developed to fit characteristics different from the assumptions of the M/M/1, such as its close cousin, the M/M/k model. The M/M/k model represents a single line with all the same assumptions as the M/M/1 model except that *k* number of servers are available to help the next person in line. Another close variation on the M/M/1 model is the M/D/1 model, with all the same assumptions of the M/M/1 model except the service time is not random, but rather a fixed, precise length of time, such as people queuing up for a highly automated service. Other models can represent finite calling populations, differing arrival rate distributions, and limited lines. In each case, analysis begins with an assessment of the particular line's defining characteristics, and then determination of an appropriate published model or building of a simulation that best mimics those characteristics.

PSYCHOLOGICAL MODELS OF WAITING

An alternative to modeling queues with probability distributions is to explore the human psychology that may be at work instead. Psychological modeling is somewhat younger than mathematical modeling, and assumes that the queue does consist of people. Most queues in service systems fit this description exactly, introducing the issue of the absolute versus the perceived time these people will be kept waiting.

Absolute versus Perceived Time

Mathematical models treat time as absolute, meaning that a particular delay such as 5 minutes is the same length of time regardless of the setting in which that 5-minute delay occurred. Thus, absolute time can also be thought of as time measured by the clock, and it is only logical to then conclude that an average wait of 5 minutes is better than an average wait of some longer amount of time, such as 15 minutes.

absolute time
The passage of time as measured by a clock.

perceived time
The passage of time as measured by a person, usually without the use of a clock.

Psychological models of waiting, however, focus on perceived time, or time as measured in the mind of the customer who is waiting. One customer may be delayed 5 minutes and yet perceive the delay as significantly more than 5 minutes, while another customer may be delayed 15 minutes but perceive that longer delay as almost no time at all. One of the central principles of psychological models of waiting is that the longer 15-minute delay in the previous example is *better* than the 5-minute delay, even though it represents three times the amount of absolute time. However, improving future wait times depends on determining precisely why a customer waiting 5 minutes perceived more time had passed, while a customer who waited longer perceived almost no delay. These factors influencing the perception of time are then the keys to reducing a future customer's wait without necessarily reducing the absolute time the customer is delayed.

Factors Influencing Perceived Time

A variety of environmental factors influence a customer's perception of time, although not all these factors are relevant in every situation. Some factors such as distraction, fairness, and interrupted waits are more likely to be within the control of a concerned manager, and thus can be used to manipulate perceived waiting time. Other factors like fear and the value of the service may be system characteristics over which a manager has little or no control, but nonetheless are active in determining the customer's perceived wait.

Distraction One powerful and familiar factor that influences a person's perception of time is distraction. Most any delay is perceived as a lesser amount of time if the person waiting is occupied in some sense. Thus, waiting areas for many services are supplied with magazines and video screens to distract customers from the passage of time. Waiting areas for extremely long queues at popular tourist attractions are often elaborately equipped for this, offering an informative presentation and/or entertainment specifically for members of the queue. However, the use of distraction is not confined to long delays; it is unwise to leave a customer completely unoccupied for even a short but unavoidable time before service. Thus, telephone call handling systems often provide music when a caller is put on hold, and websites provide some type of distracting clock animation when processing a request. Mirrors and mirrored surfaces have long been effective in distracting customers for a few seconds, which is why they are often found at strategic points along fast-moving queues in building lobbies.

Fear The principle that fear makes any wait longer may seem obvious, but the various sources of fear among customers can be surprising. People obviously fear pain and harm befalling either themselves or their loved ones, and thus callers to emergency numbers often overestimate the passage of the time that follows, due to the natural anxiety associated with emergency incidents. Here are some less obvious but common sources of fear:

- Customers fear loss of personal control. Often, when customers perceive that they have no control over their destinies, at least in the short term, this anxiety increases the perceived time they wait for a resolution. Waiting areas for medical and dental services are natural settings for this type of anxiety.
- Customers fear being forgotten. Once this anxiety sets in, customers lose confidence that they will actually be served and their perception of time expands. For example, customers might believe that their food order has somehow been lost by a restaurant kitchen, and that the staff is unaware that they are still waiting to be served.
- Customers fear that there will not be enough and they will not be served despite waiting. This fear may be unavoidable in the case of those who are waiting at the back of a queue for some popular but distinctly limited service, such as the purchase of concert tickets.

Using this principle to shorten perceived waiting time requires addressing these fears, if possible. In the case of genuine fear of pain or harm, there may be little that anyone can do to prevent these anxieties. In other cases, any potential fears—if unfounded—could and should be prevented through better communication with the customer. This might be as simple as a thoughtful yet precisely timed comment like "I haven't forgotten about you. Let me finish with this group and I'll be right back." Customers are also less likely to perceive delays substantially longer than actual if they know why they are waiting, and/or for how long they can expect to wait, both of which are issues of better communication to fight anxiety over the unknown.

Fairness Fairness is an issue of justice in the mind of the waiting customer. Any wait perceived as fair is usually also perceived as shorter than the same absolute time waiting when the delay was unfair. Reasonable delays can abruptly become unacceptable if the customer is given reason to think injustice has occurred. One potential source of perceived injustice is queue discipline. First-come, first-served (FCFS) is a common rule for queue discipline not because it is particularly efficient for prioritizing work, but simply because it is perceived as fair in many cultures around the world. If a waiting customer observes a violation of FCFS, such as another customer joining the front of a line, it is likely the waiting customer will become upset and impatient. To maintain fairness, then, the manager of an FCFS system must

- Enforce FCFS on behalf of the customers who are honoring the rule.
- Carefully design an unavoidably complicated queuing system to help prevent emotional reactions to the loss of FCFS. When queues grow long, confusion can

occur as to where an arriving customer should join those already waiting. Merging several queues into one queue is difficult without occasionally violating FCFS. Lane reductions leading into congested road construction sites are vivid examples of how FCFS can fail as some cars wait in the open lane while others travel ahead to merge somewhat later.

- In the case of a system employing a rule in addition to FCFS, communicate the use of this rule to others who are waiting. Explanations such as, "Sorry about that, but he was an emergency patient" or "Those folks had a reservation ... your table should be ready in a few minutes" usually restore a sense of justice when the delayed customer better understands what he or she has just witnessed.

Value of Service One unavoidable principle of waiting concerns the value of the service: the more valuable a customer perceives the service, the more willing that customer is to wait. This is illustrated by the spectacularly long lines that can form to purchase tickets to a one-time event such as a concert or movie premiere, with customers waiting a day or more at the ticket vendor's location. In contrast, if a customer does not perceive a service valuable, then the customer is much less willing to wait and generally overestimates the actual length of any delay.

Interrupted Waits One fascinating feature of the psychology of waiting is that people often perceive the sum of several short waits as shorter than one continuous delay of the same length. Thus, systems that cannot avoid long waiting times can work instead to break up those delays and shorten the perceived time spent waiting. Long queues for amusement park attractions partially achieve this by guiding a single serpentine queue through more than one waiting area. In this arrangement, when the customer moves to the front of a room and through a doorway, the customer generally perceives the wait in the first room as completed and the wait in the new area beyond the doorway as beginning.

Interrupted wait times can be broken down further into preprocess and inprocess waits. A preprocess wait occurs upon the customer's arrival at a busy system, and is generally perceived as longer than any equal amount of absolute time waiting at some stage after the service to the customer has started. Thus, any effort to change preprocess waiting into in-process waiting in the mind of the customer can help shorten perceived waiting time. Converting preprocess into in-process requires that meaningful contact be made with the waiting customer, initiating some aspect of the service. As an example, an unusually busy restaurant may distribute menus among the people waiting for seating. This practice not only helps distract the waiting customer and potentially speeds up ordering later, but it also gives the impression that the restaurant has already begun its service, even though the customer may be standing on the sidewalk outside the building.

preprocess wait
A delay occurring before any service begins.

inprocess wait
A delay occurring during the provision of a service.

Loss of Queue Discipline in a Serpentine Line

A single line forms from the arrivals at a ski lift in this picture, but the rapid arrival of many ski lift users has caused this process to break down, creating a situation in which new arrivals are unsure where to join the line. This loss of queue discipline can create dissatisfaction among the lift users, stemming from the system's inability to honor FCFS and keep the wait for the ski lift fair.

Capacity is ability to provide; thus capacity planning limits what an organization can provide. If an organization cannot provide enough, its customers may wait, but never indefinitely. While the question of size is simple, a great deal is at stake in its answer. Good capacity planning in the present is a necessary ingredient or successful operation in the future, so successful managers never lose sight of that question.

SUMMARY

Selecting the best capacity for a new facility begins with how best to measure it, and ultimately requires an organization to weigh the costs of too much versus too little ability to meet its customers' needs. Waiting lines form at the interaction between the customers' demands and the capacity chosen by the organization. Queuing theory offers mathematical models of waiting, allowing issues such as average time spent in the system and average number of customers in the line to be quickly estimated and evaluated. Queuing theory also treats time as absolute, or reliably measured by a clock, a rational assumption that can sometimes fail if the queue being modeled consists of people. Psychological models of waiting concentrate on time as perceived by people waiting and suggest factors in the environment that can influence that perception. Mathematical and psychological models are not mutually exclusive approaches to waiting line analysis, and any organization concerned with customer wait times is wise to consider both.

Key Terms

absolute time
balking
blocking
break-even point
capacity
capacity cushion
core competency
design capacity
diseconomies of scale
economies of scale
effective capacity
efficiency
FCFS
finite calling population
fixed cost
infinite calling population
in-process wait
Kendall notation
outsource
perceived time
Poisson distribution
preprocess wait
queue
queue discipline
queuing theory
reneging
serpentine line
subcontract
tractable
utilization
variable cost

Discussion Questions

1. Why aren't the effective capacity and the optimal operating level of any operation necessarily the same amount of activity?
2. Do capacity cushions represent waste?
3. In an economic model discussed in this chapter, the cost of waiting was a cost to whom? Is this necessarily the entire cost of waiting?
4. Is there any situation in which the cost of waiting is strictly linear? What would such a situation look like? How does the so-called cost of waiting vary between certain situations, such as waiting at the airport or waiting for medical treatment?
5. What is an example of a situation in which the cost of capacity is substantially more than the cost of waiting? What would the waiting line look like in that situation?
6. On what do the mathematical and the psychological modelers of waiting disagree?
7. Think of a particular single-queue, single-server waiting line situation. Which of the M/M/1 model assumptions is least likely to fit that actual situation?

PROBLEMS

Minute Answer

Short answers appear in Appendix A. Go to **NoteShaper.com** for full video tutorials on each question.

1. A certain facility has a design capacity of 2,500 units a day and an effective capacity of 2,225 units. Name one potential determinant of its effective capacity.
2. What is the volume of output that results in the lowest average unit cost of production at a facility known as?
3. If increasing the volume of production is likewise increasing the average cost per unit produced, the system is suffering from what?
4. Mirrors are sometimes placed in busy lobbies, waiting areas, and on elevator doors. Their purpose is often to make the time pass faster for people waiting in front of them. Which psychological principle of waiting best describes this?
5. What is the body of knowledge concerning mathematical modeling of waiting lines called?
6. You are observing a line of people at the ordering counter of a campus coffee house. This line has at least 15 people waiting to order. Suddenly you notice two people walk through the front door of the coffee house, stop when they see the other 15 people waiting to order, shake their heads, turn around, and exit the coffee house immediately. What you have just witnessed is an instance of customer impatience best known as what?
7. What does queue discipline determine?
8. The economic model of waiting lines minimizes the combined cost of waiting and what other cost?
9. In an M/M/1 system, if the customer arrival rate increases while service times remain the same, what happens to the waiting line for that service? What happens to the service system's utilization rate?
10. When an arriving customer leaves after joining an existing line for service but before being served, this behavior is called what?
11. What type of capacity assumes ideal operating conditions?
12. What type of capacity assumes normal operating conditions, including breaks for maintenance, etc.?
13. What is idle capacity maintained to absorb unexpected demand called?

Quick Start

14. A classroom has a design capacity of 60 seats and an effective capacity of 55 seats. If 45 students attend a class held at that location, calculate the utilization of that classroom during that class.
15. A classroom has a design capacity of 60 seats and an effective capacity of 55 seats. If 45 students attend a class held at that location, calculate the efficiency of that classroom during that class.
16. Branton Electric is considering the purchase of an entire cargo container filled with upgraded utility meters for $15,000. Branton can charge $50 for the installation of each upgraded meter, while the actual cost of the installation would be only $5. How many utility meter upgrades are necessary for Branton Electric to break even on this purchase?
17. A particular parking garage is designed with 1,000 spaces in which to park 1,000 individual cars. Assume, however, that every Mercedes car needs two such spaces. What then is the design capacity of the parking garage if it were dedicated to storing only Mercedes cars?

18. Customers arrive an average of 10 per hour and an average of 16 customers can be served in an hour. Assuming this is an M/M/1 model, what is the system utilization?
19. Customers arrive an average of 10 per hour and an average of 16 customers can be served in an hour. Assuming this is an M/M/1 model, what is the average length of the line?
20. Customers arrive an average of 10 per hour and an average of 16 customers can be served in an hour. Assuming this is an M/M/1 model, what is the average number of customers in the system?
21. Customers arrive an average of 10 per hour and an average of 16 customers can be served in an hour. Assuming this is an M/M/1 model, what is the average amount of time spent waiting in the line?
22. Customers arrive an average of 10 per hour and an average of 16 customers can be served in an hour. Assuming this is an M/M/1 model, what is the average amount of time a customer spends in the system?
23. Customers arrive an average of 10 per hour and an average of 16 customers can be served in an hour. Assuming this is an M/M/1 model, what is the probability of no customers in the system?

Ramp Up

24. The Kitti Kreme Donut production facility consists of three identical donut fry vats, each of which operated at 75% efficiency last month. If this facility produced a total of 150,000 donuts last week, what is the apparent effective capacity of one of Kitti Kreme's donut fry vats?
25. The effective capacity of a system is only 60% of its design capacity and its actual output is 80 units a day. If the system's design capacity is 300 units a day, how efficient is the use of this system?
26. Happy Pets Vet Clinic is considering renting a self-contained blood analysis machine for $500 a month, which would also require it to purchase the cartridges required for blood testing at $45 each. Happy Pets Vet Clinic treats an average of 20 dogs or cats a month requiring blood tests. (Happy Pets is currently sending these blood samples away for testing.) What is the minimum that Happy Pets Vet Clinic can charge its customers for blood tests to break even on the rental of the self-contained blood analysis machine?
27. Gallant Carpet Cleaning cannot meet demand with its current equipment. Gallant Carpet Cleaning is considering two new carpet cleaning machines. Machine A cleans carpets to residential standards, while machine B cleans and sanitizes carpets to hospital standards. Machine A costs $20,000 and machine B costs $50,000. The company estimates its cost per cleaning (including all chemicals) for machine A will be $8 and machine B will be $7. The revenue per carpet cleaned for A would be $40, while B could bring in $45 per carpet, due to the higher degree of sanitation provided. Machine B needs to clean how many more carpets than machine A to break even?
28. Cars arrive on average 10 minutes apart at a single toll booth with a Poisson arrival rate and an exponential service time averaging 1 minute. How often is this toll booth idle?
29. A system that is idle 50% of the time serves customers arriving at a rate of 10 an hour. Assuming this system fits the description of M/M/1, what is the average length of this service?

Scenarios

Reminder: Short answers appear in Appendix A. Go to **NoteShaper.com** for full video tutorials on each question.

30. Almance Technology sells the Solar Cat Eye System, which generates electrical power from solar cells built into the bright reflective lenses embedded in the surface of roadways to mark the travel lanes. (These lenses are referred to as cat eyes because they reflect headlights brightly at night, allowing the driver to see the borders of a lane when it is too dark to see painted stripes clearly.) When the Solar Cat Eye System is installed in the surface of a road, it allows the owner of the road to generate power that can charge batteries for nearby road signs, emergency phones, or signal lights, saving the cost of the electricity that would otherwise have to be purchased to operate these systems. A solar cat eye installation costs $100,000 to set up the operating system, plus $2,000 per mile of solar cat eyes installed directly into the road. Each mile of solar cat eyes creates the equivalent of $200 a year in revenue through its electrical generation, with no variable cost of generation.

a. Maricopa County is considering purchasing a solar cat eye installation for 100 miles of road it will repave this summer. How much would this system cost?

b. If Maricopa County does purchase the Solar Cat Eye System for its summer repaving project, how many years of electrical generation must it provide before it breaks even?

c. Some officials in Maricopa County have argued that this summer's repaving project is too small to support a technology upgrade such as the Solar Cat Eye System. However, the state highway Department might be convinced to share the $100,000 fixed cost with Maricopa County if it can share the same operating system. It will then purchase solar cat eyes and install them in a nearby state highway. If the two organizations can reach an agreement to share the fixed cost equally, how will this change Maricopa County's break-even point?

31. Tube Country rents circular rubber rafts that its customers use to float down the Ichituckni River. Tube Country owns a fleet of 200 rafts, each of which is returned on the same day it is rented, and each raft can only be rented once during a business day. Rough water along the Ichituckni River often causes rafts to become scratched and leak air, so the staff at Tube Country is constantly repairing rafts before their next rental. As a result, Tube Country estimates that 5% of its rental fleet is unavailable for rent at any given time. Tube Country rents rafts for $5 each, and incurs $1.00 in variable costs with each raft rental. Tube Country must also pay $20,000 in fixed business costs annually.

a. What is the daily effective capacity of Tube Country's fleet?

b. The issue of rough water creating the need for continual repairs can best be described as what?

c. Suppose Tube Country rents 100 rafts on a certain day. What is the utilization of Tube Country's raft fleet?

d. How many rentals does Tube Country need to break even each year?

e. How many rentals does Tube Country need to make in a year to earn $5,000 in profit?

f. Last year, the owner of Tube Country, Mr. Robert "Bobber" Gowdy, had the opportunity to acquire an additional 200 rafts for his rental fleet, when a competing raft rental company went out of business. Instead, Bobber Gowdy decided to keep his fleet at its original size of 200. "Even though we often rent all 200 rafts on a busy day," he said, "it wouldn't have been worth it, increasing the fleet size to 400. If you have any more than 200 rafts rented, you can't fit all of your rafts on the truck when you are collecting them back from the Ichituckni River. That means you then have to make multiple trips to the river. This costs more and takes more time, and the folks who run Ichituckni River State Park also charge you penalties for leaving your rafts around. Basically, if you get greedy and rent more than 200 rafts, you'll actually wind up making a lot less money." What Bobber Gowdy has just explained can best be described as what?

g. This year, Ichituckni River State Park has become concerned that too many people are floating down the river, scaring the wildlife. Bobber Gowdy has heard a rumor that Tube Country may be restricted to no more than 2,500 raft rentals annually. What is the minimum that Tube Country can charge for a raft rental and still break even if Tube Country rents exactly 2,500 rafts each year?

32. You have purchased a smart phone that has a battery system advertised as allowing 22 hours of talk time before it requires recharging. A friend of yours advises you that it is a good phone, but the 22 hours of talk time is a highly theoretical number, based on ideal conditions concerning the placement of the phone towers around you as you talk, the exact number of calls you initiated while talking, and the state of the battery when you last charged the phone. As a result of these issues, your friend warns you that you can generally only expect 20 hours of talk time from the battery system.

a. The issue of 22 hours of talk time is best described as what?

b. The issue concerning the actual placement of the phone towers around you as you talk is best described by what concept?

c. You only talk 10 hours a day on your phone, and you always recharge it overnight. If you just consider talk time, how efficient is your use of this phone's battery system?

33. Auto Shoppe is considering the purchase of a new engine computer code reader for $65,000. Auto Shoppe can charge $75 for the service of reading the codes from a single car engine, while the actual cost of the reading would be only $10 per car engine.

a. For how many cars would Auto Shoppe need to read the engine computer codes to break even on this purchase?

b. Suppose that the manager of Auto Shoppe is concerned about this purchase and has stated that if Auto Shoppe were to buy the new engine computer code reader, "the machine needs to pay for itself by the time we use it to read the codes of 200 car engines." The manager says this is because "those sorts of engine computer code readers go out of date very quickly, so if we don't get our money back soon, we will probably just wind up replacing the machine before it ever breaks even." What would Auto Shoppe need to charge for the service of reading each car engine, to break even when it reads the codes from 200 car engines?

34. Customers arrive at a ferry ticket office at the rate of 14 per hour on Monday mornings. This can be described by a Poisson distribution. Selling the tickets and providing general information takes an average of 3 minutes per customer and varies exponentially. One ticket agent is on duty on Mondays.

a. What is the average length of the line on Monday mornings?

b. On average, how long does a customer wait to buy a ticket on Monday mornings (in minutes)?

c. How long does it take to successfully buy a ticket on Monday mornings (in minutes)? (This includes time waiting in line and purchasing from the agent.)

d. What is the probability that an arriving customer has to wait to buy a ferry ticket on Monday morning?

e. What is the probability of exactly four customers in the ferry ticket office? This includes both customers waiting in line and those being served.

35. All trucks traveling on I-75 south of Ocala, Florida, must stop at a weigh station. This station has one set of scales, which can weigh an average of 18 trucks an hour, exponentially distributed. Trucks arrive at the weigh station at an average of 15 an hour, Poisson distributed.

a. What is the average delay a truck suffers at the I-75 weigh station? That is, what is the average total time the truck spends waiting and being weighed?

b. What is the probability that an arriving truck has to wait?

c. On average, how many trucks are waiting in line at the I-75 weigh station?

d. On average, how many trucks are at the I-75 weigh station?

e. What is the probability of no more than three trucks at the weigh station?

36. A single ATM is located on the ground floor of a shopping center. Service time at this machine is exponentially distributed. On average, the ATM machine can serve a customer in 2 minutes. Customer arrivals at the machine are Poisson distributed, with an average of 25 customers an hour.

a. What is the average amount of time required to get money from this ATM (in minutes)?

b. On average, how many people are waiting to use this ATM?

c. On average, how many customers could use this ATM in an hour?

d. What is the probability that the ATM machine is idle?

e. By how much would the wait for the ATM improve if new technology could reduce the average customer service time by 30 seconds?

37. Cars traveling from Canada to the United States through the Thousand Islands Border Crossing must stop for US Customs and Immigration. During the stop, each passenger in the car must present a passport for inspection by a US Customs Officer, answer questions, and declare certain valuables that may be in the car. On average, it takes a Customs Officer about 8 minutes to inspect passports and release a car for entry into the United States. Since the Thousand Islands Border Crossing is not heavily traveled at night, US Customs and Immigration keeps only one lane open at the checkpoint plaza and one officer on duty to process arriving cars. Between midnight and 6:00 a.m., a car arrives at the Border Crossing plaza at an average rate of five an hour.

a. Assuming this scenario meets the assumptions of the M/M/1 model, how busy is this customs officer during that time period?

b. What is the average wait to speak to that officer? What is the probability that someone is able to speak to the officer immediately upon arrival?

c. On average, how many cars are present at the Thousand Islands Border Crossing plaza during that time period?

38. The US Transportation Security Administration (TSA) operates six checkpoints for screening departing passengers at the Buffalo/Niagara International Airport. Each checkpoint consists of a baggage conveyor belt, CTX scanning/imaging machine, and a walk-through metal detector for passengers, although all six checkpoints are not necessarily operating all the time. This is because each checkpoint requires a team of three TSA employees to staff it, and there is not always a need to have six checkpoints running simultaneously. Passengers arriving at the airport are first met by a greeter who directs each passenger to one particular checkpoint that is in operation at that moment. Once greeted, each passenger then joins his assigned checkpoint's single line to be screened, and it takes an average of 1 minute to actually screen each passenger through the checkpoint. The greeter's job is to divide the arriving passengers evenly between the checkpoints in operation, although the rate at which passengers arrive at the airport and approach the greeter does vary with the time of day:

Time Period	Average Number of Passengers Arriving per Hour
5:01 a.m. to 6:00 a.m.	100
6:01 a.m. to 8:00 a.m.	290
8:01 a.m. to 4:00 p.m.	180
4:01 p.m. to 7:00 p.m.	290
7:01 p.m. to 10:00 p.m.	50

TSA must maintain enough checkpoints such that the average delay experienced at checkpoint screening is less than 10 minutes. This delay includes both the time the passenger might wait to be screened and the time being screened.

a. Recommend the number of checkpoints that TSA should operate during the various time intervals of the day described in the table above, keeping in mind that TSA would prefer to minimize the staffing required.
b. Based on your recommendations, what is the average length of the line in front of each checkpoint throughout the day? During what time of day is a passenger least likely to have to wait to be screened after talking to the greeter?

CASE STUDY: WMA EXIT 53 TOLL PLAZA

Western Motorway Authority (WMA) operates a network of toll roads connecting three urbanized areas. Each of its toll collection plazas offers a choice of payment methods to approaching drivers, including WMA FAST, a subscription service that allows drivers to pay wirelessly as they pass through a special toll lane without stopping. Exit 53 Toll Plaza is a typical WMA facility, equipped with five toll lanes, including one dedicated to WMA FAST subscribers only. The remaining four lanes are equipped with booths from which WMA attendants collect tolls manually, known as cash lanes even though attendants can process credit and debit card payments for an additional fee. Since exit 53 is the end point of a long commuter route into a city center, toll prices are too high at this plaza to make automated coin collection a practical choice, although WMA does use this technology elsewhere.

While exit 53 is equipped with five toll lanes, WMA only operates all five lanes during special events. The fully automated WMA FAST lane is always open to arriving subscribers and can process an average of one vehicle every 3 seconds. Attendants in the cash lanes generally average one vehicle every 15 seconds when busy, and WMA usually varies the number of open cash lanes between one and three, depending on traffic conditions. During the 24 hours of a typical weekday, exit 53 cycles between three levels of traffic conditions, described in the Weekly Data for Exit 53 table.

Weekday Data for Exit 53

	Traffic Conditions		
	Commuter Hours	Other Business Hours	Overnight
Relevant time periods	6 a.m. to 9 a.m.; 4 p.m. to 7 p.m.	5 a.m. to 6 a.m.; 9 a.m. to 4 p.m.; 7 p.m. to 8 p.m.	12 a.m. to 5 a.m.; 8 p.m. to 12 a.m.
Proportion of WMA FAST subscribers	75%	50%	25%
Average number of cars per hour	1,500	500	100

Approaching drivers who subscribe to WMA FAST follow brightly colored markers toward their dedicated lane, while the remaining drivers sort themselves evenly into short queues before the open cash lanes. Since frequent users of the tool plaza are more likely to subscribe to WMA FAST, the proportion of subscribers is highest during commute times and lowest overnight.

One serious concern for WMA is tailback, or the length of the queue of vehicles that forms in front of a busy cash lane tollbooth. If WMA has too few cash lanes open and the resulting tailback grows long, this creates unsafe congestion in the approach area where drivers slow their vehicles and choose a lane. To maintain a safe approach area, WMA has determined that this fluctuating tailback should not average more than four waiting vehicles per lane. To open a cash lane, WMA must schedule an attendant, who will work a 4-hour shift in that lane. On weekdays, attendants can be scheduled to start work at midnight, 4 a.m., 8 a.m., noon, 4 p.m., or 8 p.m..

Questions

1. Use the M/M/1 model to analyze a typical cash lane at the exit 53 toll plaza. On a weekday, what is the minimum number of cash lanes that need to open during each of the three traffic conditions, to keep average tailback down to four vehicles or less?
2. Now consider the start times and 4-hour shift length of the cash lane attendants. Combine your analysis from the first question with knowledge of these scheduling restrictions to recommend a work schedule for these attendants. How many attendants should start work at each of the 4-hour intervals described, to provide at least the minimum number of cash lanes?
3. Consider the probability that an arriving vehicle will find an idle cash lane open at exit 53, and can drive up and pay without waiting. Using your recommended weekday staffing schedule, when is this probability at its highest? When is it at its lowest?
4. Some people in WMA management are concerned over the high cost of WMA FAST lane installations. What is the utilization of the WMA FAST lane installation at exit 53?

BIBLIOGRAPHY

Anderson, D., D. Sweeney, and T. Williams. 2005. *An Introduction to Management Science: Quantitative Approaches to Decision Making*, 11th ed. Mason, OH: South-Western/ Thomson Learning.

Chao, Xiuli. 2000. *Design and Evaluation of Toll Plaza Systems.* National Center for Transportation and Industrial Productivity, New Jersey Institute of Technology, Newark, NJ.

Law, A. M and W. D. Kelton. 1991. *Simulation Modeling and Analysis,* 2nd Edition. Chicago: McGraw-Hill/Irwin.

Maister, D. 1985. "The Psychology of Waiting Lines." In *The Service Encounter*, edited by J. Czepiel, M. Solomon, and C. Suprenant. Lexington, MA: Lexington Books, pp. 113–24.

Norman, D. 2009. "Designing Waits That Work." *MIT Sloan Management Review* 50(4): 23–28.

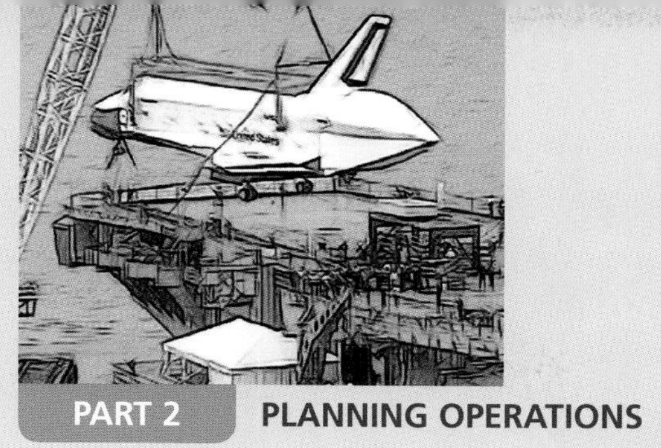

PART 2 PLANNING OPERATIONS

CHAPTER

Process and Facility Selection

I used to work in a fire hydrant factory. You couldn't park anywhere near the place.

—Steven Wright

MAJOR SECTIONS

IN THIS CHAPTER, LOOK FOR...

- Make-to-stock, make-to-order, and assemble-to-order processing strategies.
- Product, process, hybrid, and fixed-position layouts—and the relative abilities of each to support certain processing strategies.
- Three techniques for facility layout design—line-balancing, load-distance, and closeness ratings.

INTRODUCTION

Selection of a process strategy is a fundamental decision that then influences issues as diverse as the speed of production, the cost to the customer, and the likelihood that employees will grow bored by their work. The layout of a facility usually reflects a choice of process strategy, as certain layouts support some strategies better than others. In this chapter we will discuss three major process strategies, four types of facility layout supporting those strategies, and three techniques for designing such facilities.

PROCESS STRATEGIES

processes
Activities that transform inputs into outputs.

Processes are the actions that transform inputs into outputs. Thus, process strategies are differing approaches toward that transformation. The three basic strategies for processing inputs into finished products are make-to-stock, make-to-order, and assemble-to-order.

Make-to-Stock

make-to-stock
A system that produces high volumes of standardized product.

raw materials
Inventory brought in from outside the system.

finished goods
Inventory awaiting sale to consumers.

lead time
Delay between requesting a product and receiving it.

continuous processing
A make-to-stock strategy emphasizing uninterrupted production.

A make-to-stock operation transforms inputs into highly standardized products. As Figure 6.1 illustrates, this process strategy consumes raw materials and works uninterrupted to create a stock of finished goods. The assembly line is a familiar form of make-to-stock production, producing goods that can be stored for later consumption by a customer.

Make-to-stock systems emphasize the efficiency and high-volume production associated with mass manufacturing. A high degree of standardization of the product also implies a high degree of standardization of the processes, providing opportunities for specialized equipment and automation.

Although a make-to-stock system does not produce instantaneously, lead time as perceived by the customer is generally instantaneous, because the finished good is available off the shelf at some retail location. Thus, consumer goods are often produced by make-to-stock operations. The extreme version of this approach is continuous processing, where a single product is produced in great quantities by uninterrupted flow of inputs through an operation, such as the refining of gasoline from crude oil.

Service systems can pursue the equivalent of a make-to-stock strategy, although these systems cannot accumulate their output as true stock, or finished goods inventory. In this context, a service organization standardizes its value to the customer, removing variation to enable high-volume, inexpensive provision of the service. As an example, neither city bus systems nor commercial airlines transport customers to destinations at times according to each customer's choosing; few people need to visit a particular bus stop or airport terminal at exactly the moments that happen to be specified on the bus or flight timetable. Rather, these personal transport systems focus on operating an efficient, high-volume network of standardized times and destinations that customers use on-demand

FIGURE 6.1 A Make-to-Stock Operation

This system benefits from standardized production and offers customers shorter lead times.

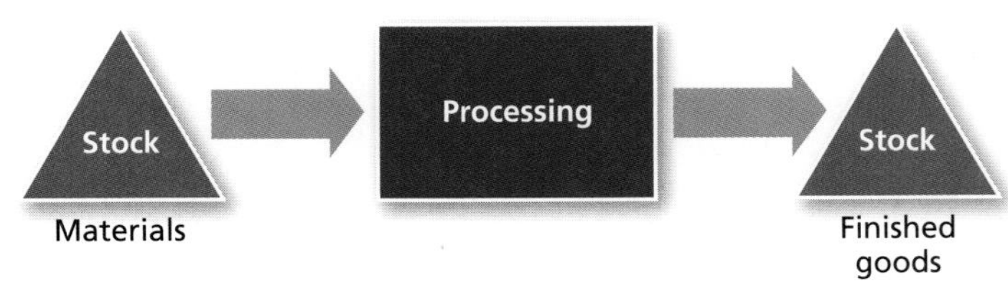

to suit their own purposes. If a customer desired transport to a more exact address at a particular time, that customer would consider hiring a taxi or chartering a private aircraft, a service provided by a considerably more expensive make-to-order system.

Make-to-Order

In a make-to-order processing strategy, transformation does not begin until specific customer demand is known. This delay implies longer lead times for customers, who must then wait while product is created according to their specifications. Figure 6.2 shows the pattern typical of a make-to-order approach to goods production, in which the system begins with a stock of materials—similar to Figure 6.1—but does not accumulate substantial stocks of inventory elsewhere. Each unit of finished product is assumed sold to and removed by the customer who triggered its production.

make-to-order
A system that produces low volumes of customized product.

The purpose of a make-to-order system is to provide a customizable product. Any custom-made good is created through this lower-volume process, and most services resemble make-to-order more closely than make-to-stock. In either case, the lower volume of production generally results in higher unit costs. This translates into more expense to the consumer, such as the higher fares paid for taxi versus bus service.

Assemble-to-Order

Assemble-to-order, or ATO systems, attempt to combine the benefits of make-to-order and make-to-stock. Also known as *make-to-assemble, options-oriented*, or *modular*, an assemble-to-order strategy uses a make-to-stock approach to generate standard subassemblies, also known as work-in-process, which it then uses to meet specific customer requirements in a make-to-order fashion. The purpose of this combination, illustrated in Figure 6.3, is to offer variety to the customer, while reducing customer lead time and gaining some of the efficiencies of make-to-stock production. Conceptually, fast-food restaurants provide visible examples of assemble-to-order. These organizations generally divide their operations when busy, with some personnel focusing on the production of a constant stock of work-in-process such as cooked meat patties and unpackaged fries,

assemble-to-order (ATO)
A system that produces standard modules to be modified and/or combined into a customizable product.

work-in-process (WIP)
Inventory resulting from transformation of raw materials, but not yet ready for sale to consumers.

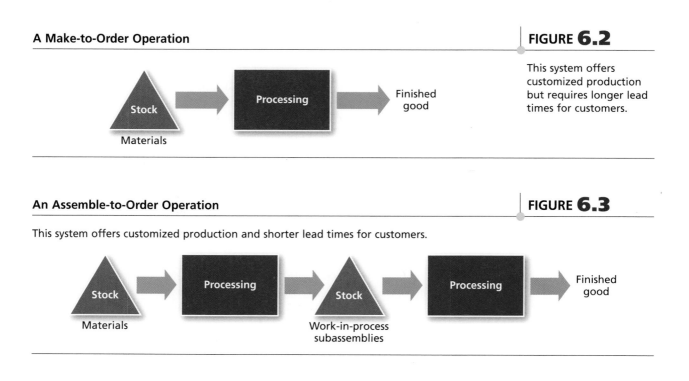

A Make-to-Order Operation

FIGURE 6.2

This system offers customized production but requires longer lead times for customers.

Stock
Materials
Processing
Finished good

An Assemble-to-Order Operation

FIGURE 6.3

This system offers customized production and shorter lead times for customers.

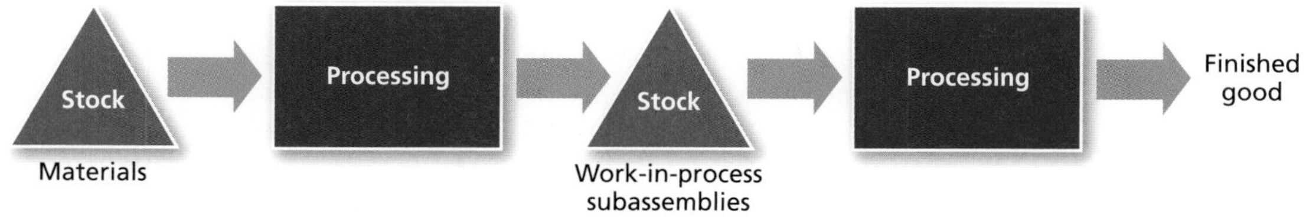

Custom Kitchen Cabinetry as an Assemble-to-Order Operation

The custom kitchen purchased by this couple is in fact a blend of stock components and a broad choice of finishing options, which the customers select in this planning session with a production representative. This gives the customers the impression of a product that was made to their order and yet available rather quickly, while the producer enjoys the lower costs of a make-to-stock operation.

while others focus on assembling specific meal requests as the customers arrive. However, assemble-to-order systems do not always delay completion of the product until the customer places a request. The wide variety of choices available at a car dealership is created largely by mixing stock subassemblies such as differing trim packages and technology options at the manufacturing plant, and even a so-called custom-ordered automobile is usually created with that same process.

business process reengineering Evaluation and improvement of an existing process design.

Many successful examples of assemble-to-order result from organizations rethinking older make-to-order or make-to-stock strategies, an undertaking known as business process reengineering. Hewlett-Packard reconfigured its own printer production so that installation of features that vary between global markets due to language and electrical voltage are delayed until the last stages of production. This redesign allows Hewlett-Packard to focus on the high-efficiency make-to-stock production of a mostly finished printer that can be quickly and accurately customized for sale anywhere in the world, a distinct assemble-to-order approach now recognized as delayed differentiation. Another innovation in assemble-to-order processing is remanufacturing, in which firms develop processes that can reuse subassemblies from older finished products, such as in the production of disposable cameras. While business process reengineering often focuses on improving the productivity of an operation, remanufacturing represents improvements that support both productivity and sustainability.

delayed differentiation An ATO strategy for stocking highly standardized components for later customization into finished goods.

remanufacturing Production of finished goods from the recycled components of returned goods.

A physical facility houses an operation's processes and must support its process strategy. Selecting a particular process strategy does not necessarily dictate what type of facility should be created to support it; additional factors should be considered before selecting an appropriate layout for the system. Nonetheless, process strategies and facility layouts are very closely linked. Four major types of facilities—product, process, hybrid, and fixed position layouts—support the process strategies discussed so far.

PRODUCT LAYOUTS

product layouts A configuration in which transformation proceeds along a single, unchanging pattern through a facility.

A product layout is defined by a single unchanging traffic pattern through the facility, as illustrated in Figure 6.4. This unchanging pattern marks the flow of transformation creating a highly standardized product, the logical choice of layout for make-to-stock production. One familiar example of a product layout is an assembly line, although not all product layouts fit that description. As the name suggests, what all product layouts do share is a devotion to the efficient production of a single standardized product.

Traffic Pattern of a Product Layout FIGURE **6.4**

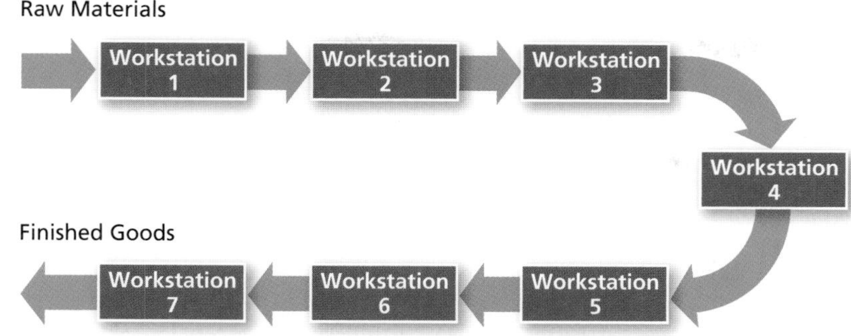

Advantages and Disadvantages

The fundamental advantage of a product layout is high efficiency. This efficiency results from an unchanging pattern of processing, designed to transform high volumes of standardized inputs into high volumes of standardized output. Other advantages often associated with product layouts include

efficiency
Percent of a resource in productive use.

- Relatively high utilization of resources.
- Relatively low reliance on skilled labor.
- Relatively low per-unit cost of production.
- Relatively less complex managerial planning and control required.

"Relatively" here means "relative to other types of facility layouts." Conversely, because this layout relies on an unchanging pattern to create large amounts of a single product, it suffers from these disadvantages:

- Little flexibility for the customer. The product is highly standardized.
- Relatively prone to disruption. A loss of any one workstation stops flow through the system. An unchanging flow also implies a steady rate of production, so it can be relatively difficult to adjust production volume to reflect rapidly changing demand.
- Relatively higher level of capital investment. Specialized infrastructure and equipment must be purchased for the transformation line.
- Relatively lower levels of job satisfaction. In a poorly managed layout, workers may become bored with repetitive, specialized tasks.

Some of the disadvantages of a product layout may be controlled through good management. As an example, cross-training workers in a variety of tasks may decrease boredom and increase general job satisfaction, while simultaneously helping protect the system from disruption when one worker is absent. Mixed model assembly may also be possible, in which different versions of a product such as an automobile are created by a single assembly line, offering the customer some variety. Regardless of how the product layout is managed, the initial design of the facility focuses on the design of its single path of transformation.

mixed model assembly
Production of a range of products with a single assembly line, primarily by varying features on an otherwise standardized product.

Designing a Product Layout

Because a product layout consists of a single path of transformation through a facility, the designer of that layout must assign all transformation processes to distinct locations along that path. Think of this as dividing the production work along the path, and the

line balancing
A product layout design technique which assigns the tasks to be performed at consecutive workstations, seeking to balance the workload among them.

algorithm
A procedure described by a series of steps.

cycle time
The 'pace' of a product layout, being the total amount of time each workstation has to complete its assigned tasks once during ongoing operation of the system.

more equitable the division of this work, the smoother the operation. This design technique is called line balancing, because its goal is to divide transformation as evenly as possible, balancing the workload along the path. Line balancing is an algorithm, producing a design through a series of steps, and the first of these steps concerns the cycle time of the line.

Cycle Time In a product layout, the unchanging path or line is typically organized into a series of distinct locations, or workstations. Since each workstation passes product along the path to the next workstation, each should be assigned the same amount of time to complete its assigned work. This allows a smooth, balanced flow of work among the workstations, and this equal budget of time given to each workstation to repeat its assigned work is known as the cycle time of the operation. This single length of time is extremely important to product layouts, because cycle time determines

- The amount of time a single workstation is given to complete its work on a single unit of product.
- The total number of workstations required in the layout. The shorter the cycle time, the less work can be accomplished at each workstation on each unit of product, and thus the more workstations needed to complete all the work required.
- The speed at which the layout produces finished product. A shorter cycle time means faster production.

A product layout cannot be designed without first selecting its cycle time. Figure 6.5 illustrates the range of choices in cycle time available to the layout designer.

At one extreme in Figure 6.5, a product layout cannot operate with a cycle time any shorter than the length of the longest task to be performed, or that task would never be performed successfully. At the other extreme, the longest cycle time that makes any sense equals the sum of all the tasks to be performed, although this implies an assembly line with only one workstation completing all tasks. In reality, the cycle time is likely somewhere in between, based on the desired capacity of the system being designed. We discuss how to derive a target cycle time from the desired total output of the system next, as the first step of the line-balancing technique.

heuristic
A procedure to develop a good, though not necessarily optimal, solution.

Line Balancing Line balancing distributes work evenly along the path of a product layout, enabling smooth, rapid flow of production. Line balancing is also a heuristic technique that can produce multiple solutions but cannot guarantee that any solution is necessarily the best answer to the scenario. As an algorithm, line balancing is best described as a set of steps:

1. Determine the cycle time for the layout.
2. Draw a precedence diagram, illustrating the tasks requiring assignment along the path of the layout. (optional)
3. Assign those tasks to workstations according to a predetermined decision rule.
4. Evaluate the efficiency of the resulting layout.

FIGURE 6.5 Potential Cycle Times for a Product Layout

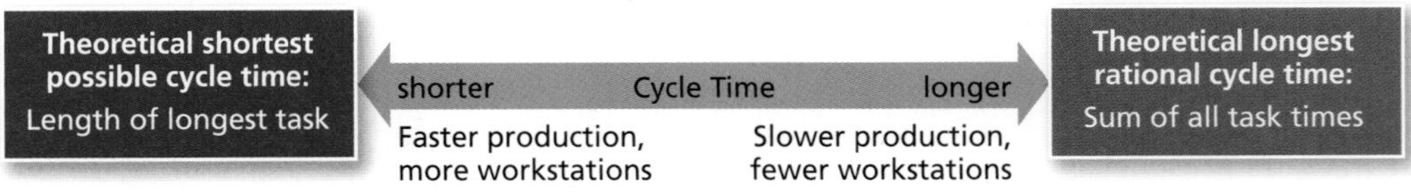

The design of a product layout is essentially complete at the end of step 3, but since the procedure cannot guarantee this design is best, it is wise to evaluate it for comparison with other designs.

Since cycle time is essentially the speed of production, the cycle time of a product layout must reflect the production capacity desired of that layout. To determine cycle time for line balancing, we must first know two pieces of information:

- **Operating time (OT)**—how long the line will operate. This interval can be expressed as how long each day it will operate, or how long each month, or how long throughout its entire lifetime.
- **Demand on the line (D)**—how many finished products the line must complete within its stated operating time.

With these two readings, we determine an appropriate cycle time for line operation with the following formula:

$$\text{Cycle time} = \text{OT/D}$$

The unit of measurement in which the operating time is stated becomes the unit that the cycle time is initially stated in, as we demonstrate in Scenario 1a.

Line Balancing, Cycle Time

Scenario 1a

Regional Disaster Relief Services (RDRS) has just learned of 400 people who must be relocated for an overnight stay in a nearby school gymnasium, due to widespread flooding of homes in a low-lying area. RDRS will use the supplies at its warehouse headquarters to assemble 400 overnight kits for each of the arrivals at the gymnasium shelter. Each kit consists of a pillow, a blanket, assorted toiletries, a water bottle, and a pair of socks. The 400 evacuees will arrive via buses at the gymnasium shelter in 12 hours, and RDRS estimates about 30 minutes will be required to set up for overnight kit assembly and another 90 minutes required to transport the finished kits to the shelter. What cycle time should be assigned to an overnight kit assembly line at the warehouse, so that the kits are in place when the evacuees arrive?

Analysis

We determine the cycle time by dividing the operating time (OT) by the output required during that time (D).

RDRS OVERNIGHT KIT ASSEMBLY CYCLE TIME

D = 400 kits
OT = 12 hours – 30 minutes setting up – 90 minutes delivery time = 10 hours
Cycle time = OT/D = 10/400 = 0.025 hours

Insight The cycle time that Regional Disaster Relief Services should use is 0.025 *hours*, or $0.025 \times 60 = 1.5$ minutes, or $1.5 \times 60 = 90$ seconds. Thus RDRS must set up the assembly line to complete a kit every 0.025 hours, or every 90 seconds. ■

Once we determine the cycle time, we can begin the design process. At this point, data must be collected on each of the tasks required to successfully create one unit of finished good. This data should specify both how much time is required to complete each task and whether any tasks must be performed in any certain order, a restriction known as a precedence relationship. Precedence relationships can be described in a variety of ways, but one common method for communicating dependency between tasks

precedence relationship A dependency between two tasks, usually requiring that one task be completed before the other task is started.

immediate predecessor A task that must be completed before another task can start.

is by specifying immediate predecessors, or tasks that must be finished directly before another task is started.

Once this data on finished product construction is gathered, the next step in line balancing is to illustrate the information as a precedence diagram. This step is not strictly necessary but highly recommended. It is generally easier to work with precedence data when diagrammed. Scenario 1b introduces a set of such data and demonstrates this step.

Scenario 1b

Line Balancing, Precedence Diagram

The tasks required to assemble Regional Disaster Relief Service's overnight kits must now be divided among the volunteers at the RDRS warehouse. Most of these kits are for adults, but some are for children. A child's overnight kit includes different toothpaste and smaller spare socks. The tasks required to assemble a single kit of either type are outlined in the following table:

Task	Description	Duration (sec.)	Immediate Predecessor(s)
A	Separate pillow from bulk shipment	30 sec.	none
B	Separate blanket and pillowcase from bulk shipment	60	none
C	Place pillow in pillowcase	45	A, B
D	Fold blanket and place in pillowcase	60	C
E	Separate water bottle from bulk and place on pillow	20	C
F	Assemble toothbrush, comb, and toothpaste in clear plastic toiletry bag; place on top of pillow	30	C
G	Affix "adult" or "child" sticker to toiletry bag, based on toothpaste type	10	F
H	Read sticker and place appropriately sized spare socks in pillowcase	10	G
I	Wrap entire kit in clear plastic with "adult" or "child" sticker visible on top	60	D, E, H

How should this data be arranged as a precedence diagram, to facilitate the design of an assembly line to complete the work?

Analysis

To create a precedence diagram of the kit assembly process, note which tasks do not have immediate predecessors, and draw these tasks with notes concerning their durations:

RDRS PRECEDENCE DIAGRAM

30 sec.

60 sec.

Next, add any tasks that depend on these tasks as immediate predecessors. In this case, the only such task is C, which requires both A and B to be completed before it can begin.

RDRS PRECEDENCE DIAGRAM

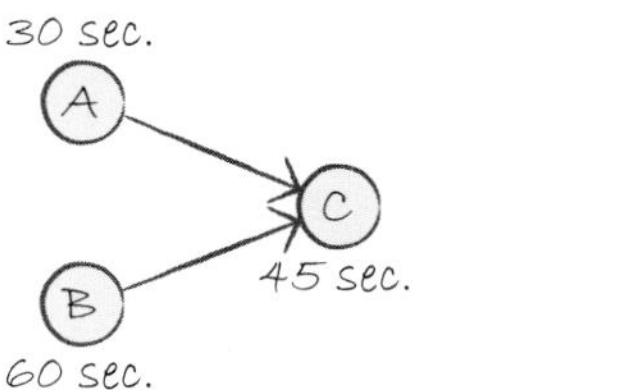

Three tasks require task C as an immediate predecessor, so these can be added next:

RDRS PRECEDENCE DIAGRAM

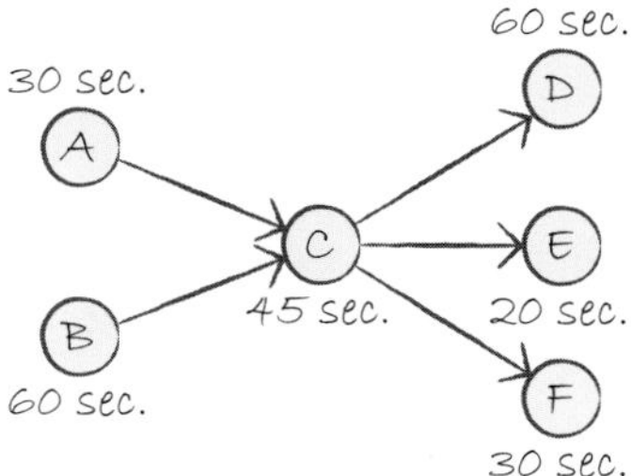

Repeat this process until all tasks are represented in the diagram:

RDRS PRECEDENCE DIAGRAM

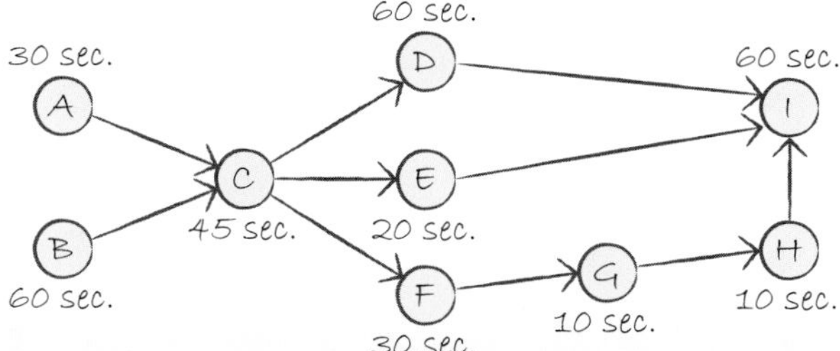

Insight The RDRS precedence diagram illustrates how the nine distinct tasks required to assemble an overnight kit must be sequenced, starting with the separation of individual soft goods from larger shipments (tasks A and B), and concluding with its final wrapping in clear plastic (task I). ■

Line balancing designs a product layout beginning with its first workstation. Eligible tasks are assigned to this workstation until its cycle time does not permit any further tasks. In the case of RDRS, these initial eligible tasks are A and B: separating the pillow, blanket, and pillowcase from the bulk shipments. Those tasks have no immediate predecessors and thus can be done without any preceding work. The line-balancing algorithm can be summarized in five columns across a worksheet, describing the data that must be updated each time a task is assigned to a workstation, such as pictured in Figure 6.6.

Column 1 of the worksheet indicates which workstation is receiving an assignment, while column 2 displays how much time that workstation has remaining to accommodate a new task. When a new workstation is added to the design and nothing has been assigned yet, its time remaining is the cycle time of the design. Column 3 refers to which tasks are eligible for assignment to the workstation, based on precedence relationships.

FIGURE 6.6 Line-Balancing Worksheet for RDRS

1 Station	2 Time Remaining	3 Eligible Task(s)	4 Eligible Task(s) That Fit	5 Assigned
First	90 sec.	A, B	A, B	?

Remember, only tasks A and B are eligible as initial tasks for the first workstation, but once both these tasks are assigned, task C becomes eligible, and so on. Column 4 is a reality check on column 3, screening out any eligible tasks that do not fit within the time remaining at that workstation. Thus, column 4 contains the finalized set of candidates for possible assignment to the workstation in column 1. Selection of one of these candidates is then recorded in column 5, although Figure 6.6 displays a question mark because this decision cannot be made without a decision rule. Here are some common decision rules used for line balancing:

- **Longest processing time (LPT).** Assuming that A and B in Figure 6.6 refer to RDRS, this rule would select task B first, the longer of the two tasks.
- **Shortest processing time (SPT).** This rule would select task A first for assignment, the shorter of the two tasks.
- **Greatest number of following tasks.** In the precedence diagram, both A and B have seven tasks following them, so this rule creates a tie. If, for example, the choice were between D and F, task F would be selected by this rule because it has three following tasks where D has only one.

Once a decision rule is specified, tasks can be assigned to workstations, as we see in Scenario 1c.

Scenario 1c

Line Balancing, Task Assignments

Given that Regional Disaster Relief Services (RDRS) must complete one overnight kit every 90 seconds to have the kits ready in time for delivery, the nine assembly tasks pictured below must be divided among the volunteers who work along one long table in the middle of the warehouse.

OVERNIGHT KIT ASSEMBLY DIAGRAM

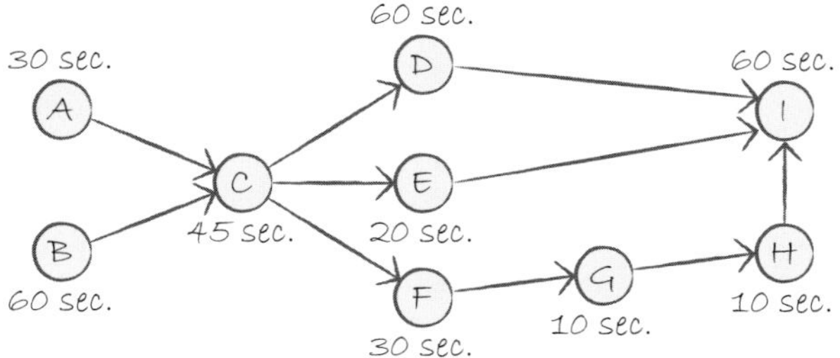

RDRS will use the LPT rule to balance its assembly line.

Analysis

An assembly line design begins with the first workstation, and proceeds to other workstations as the work is assigned. To begin, only tasks with no immediate predecessors are eligible for assignment, and the LPT rule decides which of those two tasks is assigned to the first workstation:

OVERNIGHT KIT STATION ASSIGNMENTS

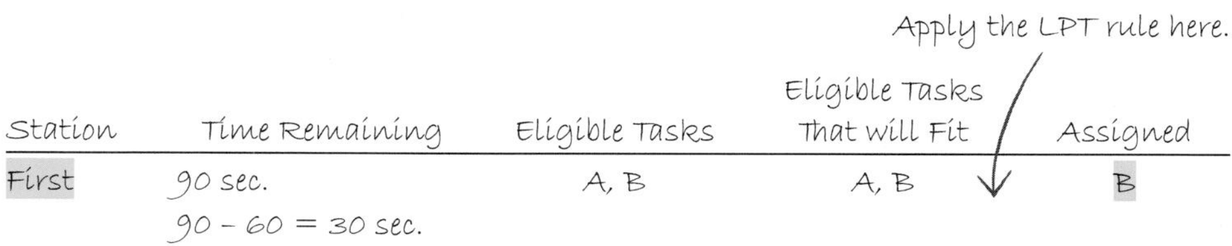
Apply the LPT rule here.

Station	Time Remaining	Eligible Tasks	Eligible Tasks That will Fit	Assigned
First	90 sec.	A, B	A, B	B
	90 − 60 = 30 sec.			

Note that when task B is assigned to the first workstation, 60 of the 90 seconds of cycle time are taken up by this task, but 30 seconds remain for use if another appropriate task can be identified. Task A remains eligible for completion, but work cannot proceed to task C until both A and B are completed.

OVERNIGHT KIT STATION ASSIGNMENTS

Station	Time Remaining	Eligible Tasks	Eligible Tasks That will Fit	Assigned
First	90 sec.	A, B	A, B	B
	90 − 60 = 30 sec.	A	A	A
	30 − 30 = 0 sec.			

With no time remaining for any further work to be done at the first workstation, its design is completed and we add a new workstation to the worksheet.

OVERNIGHT KIT STATION ASSIGNMENTS

Station	Time Remaining	Eligible Tasks	Eligible Tasks That will Fit	Assigned
First	90 sec.	A, B	A, B	B
	90 − 60 = 30 sec.	A	A	A
	30 − 30 = 0 sec.			
Second	90 sec.	C	C	C
	90 − 45 = 45 sec.			

With the assignment of C to the second workstation, three other tasks then become eligible for the next assignment. You might find it helpful to mark off tasks from the precedence diagram once you have created workstation assignments, to make newly eligible tasks more apparent.

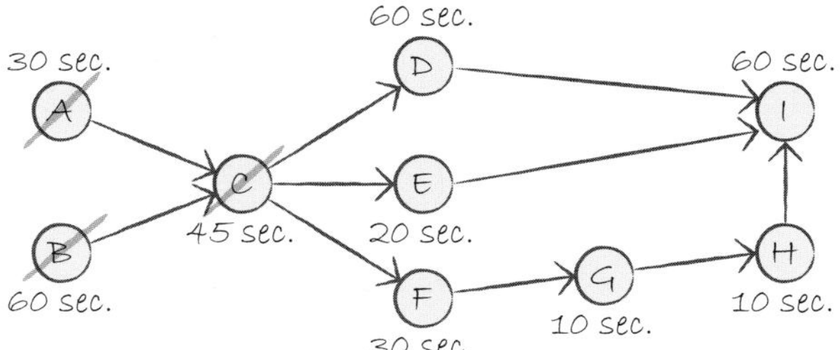

Continues

Task D becomes eligible, but with only 45 seconds remaining for work at the second station, task D will not fit:

OVERNIGHT KIT STATION ASSIGNMENTS

Station	Time Remaining	Eligible Tasks	Eligible Tasks That will Fit	Assigned
First	90 sec.	A, B	A, B	B
	90 − 60 = 30 sec.	A	A	A
	30 − 30 = 0 sec.			
Second	90 sec.	C	C	C
	90 − 45 = 45 sec.	D, E, F	E, F	F
	45 − 30 = 15 sec.			

We select task F over task E for assignment because it has the longer processing time. Assigning task F to the second station then makes task G eligible for assignment:

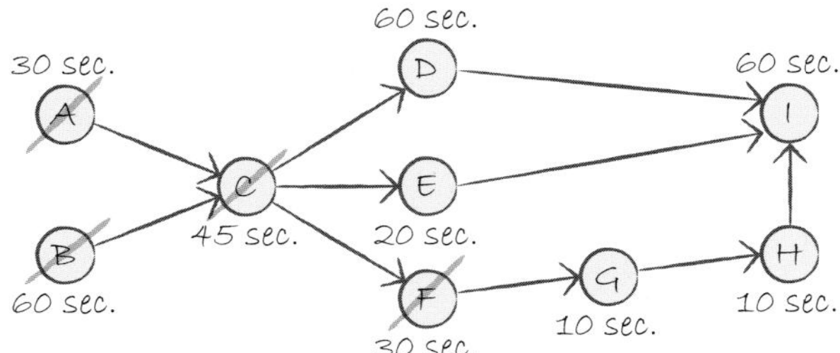

OVERNIGHT KIT STATION ASSIGNMENTS

Station	Time Remaining	Eligible Tasks	Eligible Tasks That will Fit	Assigned
First	90 sec.	A, B	A, B	B
	90 − 60 = 30 sec.	A	A	A
	30 − 30 = 0 sec.			
Second	90 sec.	C	C	C
	90 − 45 = 45 sec.	D, E, F	E, F	F
	45 − 30 = 15 sec.	D, E, G	G	G
	15 − 10 = 5 sec.	D, E, H	—	

At this point in the design process, there are 5 seconds of time available at the second workstation, and three tasks (D, E, H) eligible for assignment, but none of these tasks can be completed in the 5 remaining seconds. Thus, assignments to the second workstation are declared finished and a third workstation is added. We continue this process until all tasks are assigned, resulting in the finished design for the overnight kit assembly line.

OVERNIGHT KIT STATION ASSIGNMENTS

Station	Time Remaining	Eligible Tasks	Eligible Tasks That will Fit	Assigned
First	90 sec.	A, B	A, B	B
	90 − 60 = 30 sec.	A	A	A
	30 − 30 = 0 sec.			
Second	90 sec.	C	C	C
	90 − 45 = 45 sec.	D, E, F	E, F	F
	45 − 30 = 15 sec.	D, E, G	G	G
	15 − 10 = 5 sec.	D, E, H	-	
Third	90 sec.	D, E, H	D, E, H	D
	90 − 60 = 30 sec.	E, H	E, H	E
	30 − 20 = 10 sec.	H	H	H
	10 − 10= 0 sec.			
Fourth	90 sec.	I	I	I
	90 − 60 = 30 sec.			

Insight Thus, RDRS should organize the warehouse volunteers into four workstations. The first workstation should complete tasks A and B, separating pillow, pillowcase, and blanket from the bulk shipments. The second workstation receives these items and performs tasks C, F, and G, placing the pillow in the pillowcase, assembling the bag of toiletries, and affixing the appropriate adult/child sticker to that bag. The third workstation completes tasks D, E, and H with these materials, folding the blanket and placing it in the pillowcase, separating a water bottle from bulk, and adding it to the bundle with an appropriately sized pair of spare socks. The fourth and last workstation wraps the overnight kit in clear plastic for shipping, being careful to keep the adult/child sticker visible in the bundle. ■

The design described at the conclusion of Scenario 1c results from the decision rule used, longest processing time. Repeating the line-balancing algorithm with other rules yields alternate designs. As an example, repeating Scenario 1c using the shortest processing time rule results in an assembly line with five workstations, while the greatest number of following tasks rule produces another four-station design. Since line balancing is a heuristic, there is no guarantee that any of these solutions is best, but it creates a need to evaluate each potential solution for fair comparison with others.

Evaluating Solutions The primary goal of any product layout is highly efficient use of its workstations, and thus any layout produced by line balancing should be evaluated for its efficiency. This evaluation begins by reviewing the individual workstations in the design for idle time, such as the 5 seconds left over after the assignments to the second workstation were finished in Scenario 1c. However, the overall percent of workstation use can be calculated rapidly with only three pieces of information: the sum of the task times (ST), the cycle time (CT), and the total number of workstations required by the design (N). With these three values, efficiency of a product layout is expressed as:

$$\text{Efficiency} = \frac{\text{ST}}{\text{CT} \times \text{N}}$$

We can then calculate the balance delay, or percent idle time in a design, by subtracting its efficiency from 1.0. However, even if efficiency is high and balance delay is low for some layout, there is still no guarantee that these are the best values that can be achieved in that scenario. To explore this, we can calculate the theoretical minimum number of

balance delay
Percent of a workstation time not in productive use during the operation of a product layout.

workstations for comparison. The theoretical minimum number of workstations is quickly calculated from the same data:

$$\text{Theoretical minimum number of workstations} = \frac{ST}{CT}$$

As you can see, the theoretical minimum number of workstations is simply the ratio of the sum of the task times—also known as the theoretical maximum cycle time—to the value of cycle time used in the design. The result of this ratio is always rounded up to the nearest integer, so that if the sum of the tasks is 100 seconds and the cycle time is 40 seconds in some scenario, the theoretical minimum number of workstations is 100/40—three workstations. This does not guarantee that the scenario can be solved with a design using as few as three workstations, but it does guarantee that the scenario cannot be solved with two or fewer workstations. Thus, the actual number of workstations in an existing design can be compared to this value, and if the number of actual workstations is at or close to the theoretical minimum, the designer can be more confident in the desirability of the design. We demonstrate all these comparisons for Regional Disaster Relief Services in Scenario 1d.

Scenario 1d

Line Balancing, Evaluating Solutions

Within the solution developed in Scenario 1c, how much idle time does each workstation experience along the overnight kit assembly line? How efficient is the design? What is the balance delay in this design? Is this a good design?

Analysis

The idle time at each workstation along the Regional Disaster Relief Services (RDRS) kit assembly line is visible in the finished line-balancing worksheet. It appears as the cycle time remaining when a workstation is declared finished. Here is the current design and its distribution of work:

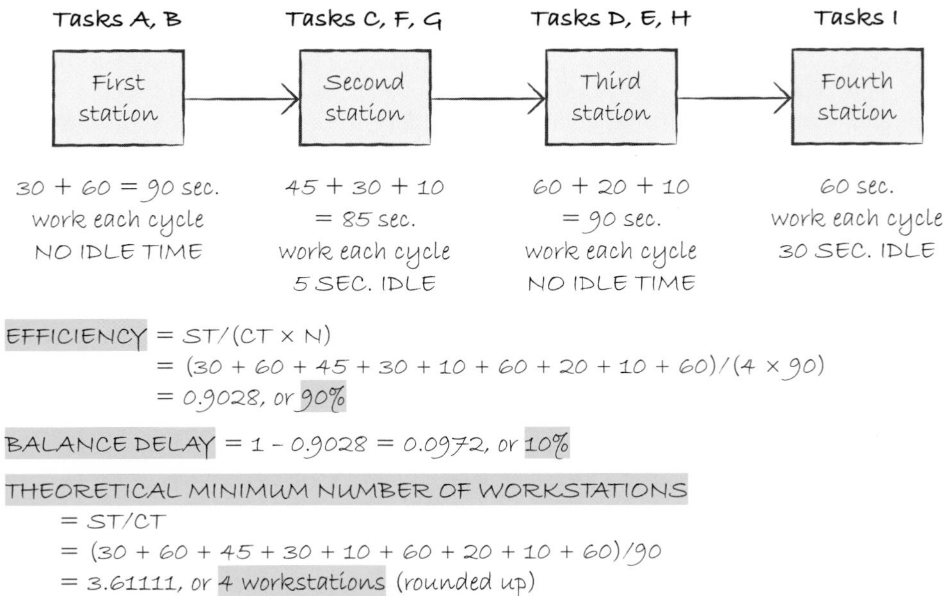

Insight RDRS's overnight kit assembly line is 90% efficient, with a 10% balance delay in the design. Since the number of workstations required by the design matches the theoretical minimum number of workstations, there are no alternate designs with fewer workstations or greater efficiency. In this design, the fourth workstation, which wraps the assembled kits for delivery, experiences the greatest amount of idle time. ■

Creative Applications

Line-balancing produces a set of assignments for a series of workstations to operate at a steady, predetermined rate of production. In reality, line balancing is sometimes combined with managerial creativity to loosen some of its limitations. For example, there is usually no reason that a product layout's unchanging path must be a straight line. While linear assembly lines are common historically, modern assembly line designers have found more benefit in curving these paths, particularly into the u-shaped format first suggested in Figure 6.4. Breaking from the convention of a straight assembly line allows for the creation of a central workspace for line personnel, giving them better visibility of each other, enhancing their ability to assist between workstations if needed, and consolidating any supply storage into a single area. Other creative adaptations can enable a line to operate at cycle times shorter than the theoretical minimum or to operate with a choice of cycle times.

Bottlenecks and Bottleneck Breaking Theoretically, a production line cannot operate at a cycle time any shorter than the length of the longest task, the theoretical minimum cycle time. In the case of Regional Disaster Relief Services (RDRS), this limitation is 60 seconds, meaning that overnight kits cannot be assembled any faster than 60 an hour or 600 in 10 hours. Because RDRS only needs 400 kits assembled in 10 hours, or a pace of 1 every 90 seconds, this limitation is not problematic.

Suppose, however, that RDRS expected twice as many evacuees, and thus needed 800 overnight kits assembled in 10 hours. To meet this requirement, the overnight kit assembly line would need to operate with a cycle time of 45 seconds, which is theoretically impossible because tasks B, D, and I would then not fit at any workstation. Tasks B, D, and I are the bottlenecks in this setting, ultimately governing the maximum pace at which the entire system can produce. While it is theoretically impossible for any line RDRS sets up to produce faster than one kit every 60 seconds, in reality there exist options that may be used to break this bottleneck limitation. Figure 6.7 illustrates one layout that would operate at a cycle time of 45 seconds for RDRS, employing double stations for each bottleneck operation. Each of these double workstations still requires 60 seconds to complete its task, but the combined efforts of each pair of workstations means each partner supplies the line every other cycle, or every 45 + 45 = 90 seconds. Coordinating this double workstation pattern does add a new layer of complexity to the operation of the kit assembly line, and the system pictured in Figure 6.7, although twice as fast as the original line developed in Scenario 1c, requires 11 workstations, making it only $325/(11 \times 45) = 65.6\%$ efficient.

bottleneck The most heavily utilized resource within a system.

Generally, doubling workstations is a good solution for breaking up the limitation imposed by the largest task in a production process. However, if twice as many kits were needed than originally planned in Scenario 1c, the warehouse crew should consider another adaptation: organize two identical assembly lines according to the original Scenario 1c design. In the case of twinning the slower design, each line would be 90% efficient and their combined output would provide 800 kits in 10 hours.

Varying Rates of Production Another theoretical restriction in line balancing is the fixed pace of production enforced by the choice of cycle time. While a balanced line is highly efficient, it is also intended to produce at a single steady rate, which does not always match the demand for its products. We saw one means of achieving variable production with a fixed rate layout in the context of RDRS: build multiple lines. While the overnight kit assembly line of RDRS is an example of a short-lived, temporary layout, organizations that wish to efficiently manufacture products at varying rates on an on-going basis can build duplicate lines, and activate or idle one or more of the lines to increase or decrease production as needed.

Multiple identical lines do allow the speed of production to be varied as demand rises and falls, but this creative application of line balancing obligates the organization to

FIGURE 6.7 **Product Layout**

RDRS overnight kit assembly line with cycle time of 45 seconds

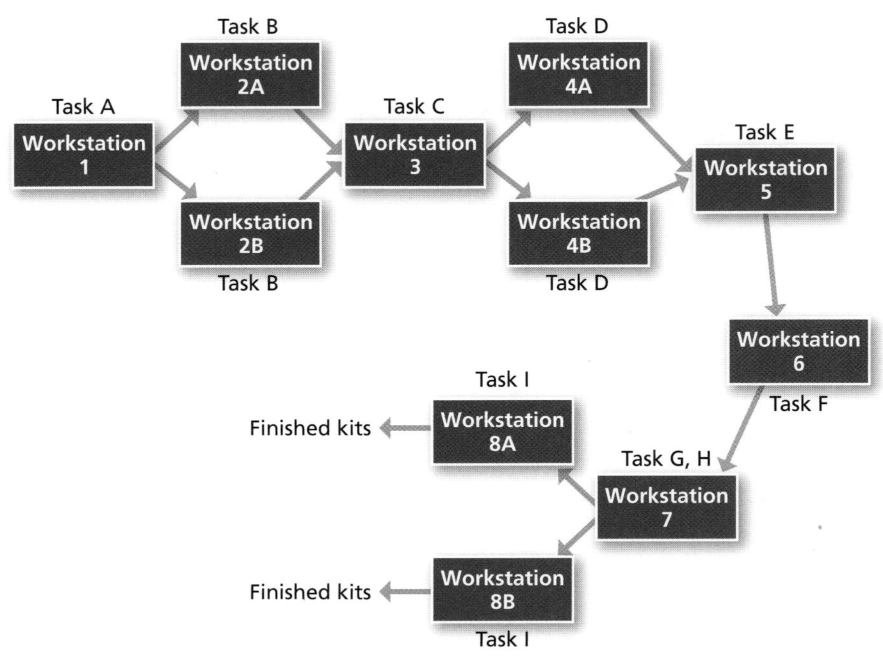

invest in redundant equipment. Service systems can be particularly troubled by a fixed production rate, because these systems do not have the option of using this pace to build up a stock of goods for sale during later, high-demand periods. Not surprisingly then, service systems offer some of the best examples of innovating with dynamic workstation assignments, where tasks can be shifted easily among workstations to rebalance the line and change its pace. A common example of this is the fast-food restaurant drive-through with two drive-through windows installed to serve customers, as pictured in Figure 6.8.

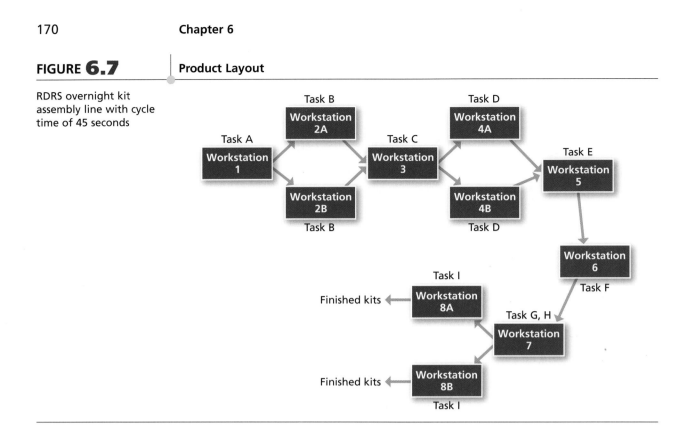

dynamic
Actively and continuously changing.

In general, drive-through service at a restaurant is a good example of the product layout concept, because this quick provision of a meal is created by routing all arriving cars along a single path past the menu board and the drive-through windows. In particular, the two-window system in Figure 6.8 enables the drive-through to operate at two different paces, allowing it to adapt to changing demand for drive-through service. During busy mealtime periods, this system can operate with three workstations, splitting most of the work between staff at the two different windows and allowing cars to move through at a pace of 30 an hour in the case of the Figure 6.8 data. However, during off-peak times, the restaurant has the option of closing one of the windows, reassigning its tasks and rebalancing the line to operate slower with fewer personnel, cutting the rate to 15 cars an hour, as in Figure 6.8.

PROCESS LAYOUTS

process layout
A configuration in which transformation proceeds along multiple, shifting patterns through a facility.

job shop
A process layout.

The opposite of a product layout is a process layout, organized around processes instead of a certain product. As Figure 6.9 suggests, there is no single, standard traffic pattern within a process layout. Each unit of product moves between processes according to its unique requirements. Thus, process layouts best support make-to-order strategies, creating customized output on demand from the client. For this reason, process layouts are commonly referred to as job shops when producing goods, such as custom printing,

FIGURE 6.8

Fast-food restaurant drive-through, allowing two different paces of service

Dynamic Workstation Assignments

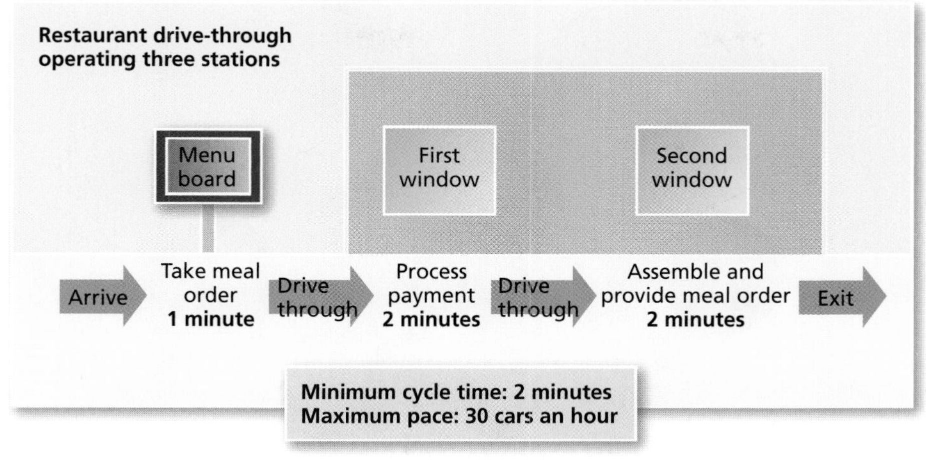

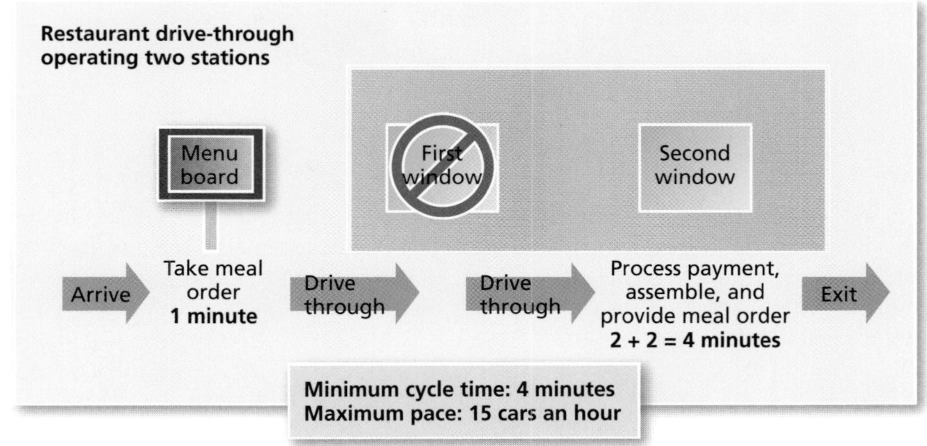

cabinetry, and tailored clothing. However, this style of facility is just as common in service settings, where the multiple traffic paths illustrated in Figure 6.9 represent the travel of people through the system, as in hospitals, retail stores, airports, military bases, and college campuses.

Advantages and Disadvantages

The major advantage of a process layout is flexibility, enabling it to support customized production. In general, the advantages and disadvantages of a process layout are the reverse of a product layout. In the case of advantages, the process layout is stronger where the product layout is weaker. In addition to offering more flexibility for the customer, process layouts offer other advantages:

- They are less prone to disruption. They can absorb fluctuations in demand more readily, so loss of any one process does not necessarily paralyze the system.
- They require a relatively lower level of capital investment, often relying on generic equipment.
- They effect a relatively higher level of job satisfaction in that the work environment is not as monotonous as it can potentially be in a more specialized layout.

FIGURE 6.9 Traffic Patterns of a Process Layout

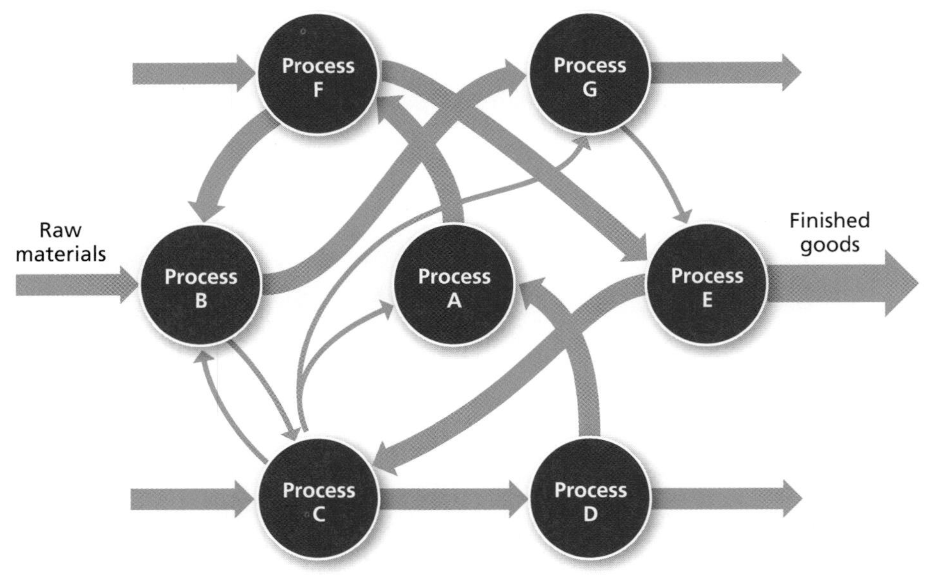

Since process layouts usually do not require large amounts of capital to purchase high-volume, specialized equipment and are better able to cope with changing and uncertain demand, start-up companies favor them. However, a process layout produces a low volume of customized product, creating some inefficiencies. Specifically, process layouts suffer these limitations:

- Relatively low utilization of resources.
- Relatively high reliance on skilled labor.
- Relatively high per-unit cost of production.
- Relatively more complex managerial planning and control required.

Designing process layouts requires determining the best arrangement of the processes, given complex, changing, and even unknown traffic patterns that connect these processes during use.

Designing a Process Layout

Designing a process layout can be a surprisingly complex undertaking, since n individual processes implies $n!$ possible layouts. If a facility houses eight distinct process areas, there are $8 \times 7 \times 6 \times 5 \times 4 \times 3 \times 2 \times 1 = 40{,}320$ potential layouts of those eight areas. The objective in designing the layout determines precisely which of those 40,320 layout plans is best. One common objective is to minimize overall traffic within the facility, achieved by calculating load distance.

load distance
A quantity multiplied by the distance that the quantity will travel, to create an overall expression of the work required by that action.

Load Distance Using a load-distance methodology to develop a process layout assumes that traffic between processes is the most important issue. This traffic may be goods that must travel between areas for processing, creating the loads that must be moved over certain distances in the layout. However, this same traffic might be people who must move between areas, and these people could be customers or employees. If d_{ij} represents the distance between processing areas i and j and v_{ij} represents the volume of traffic (tons of material, customer trips, etc.) between the same two areas, the total load distance of a layout with J processing areas can be expressed as

$$\text{Total load distance} = \sum_{i=1}^{J} \sum_{j=1}^{J} v_{ij} d_{ij}$$

Since a lower load-distance score is more desirable, layouts that score well will place areas that exchange high volumes of traffic (v_{ij}) in close proximity to one another to minimize distances traveled (d_{ij}). In some cases, it may be more important to minimize travel between certain departments versus others, such as the difference in the need to minimize travel distances between surgery and the recovery room versus between the gift shop and the cafeteria within a hospital floor. In these cases, a specific cost c_{ij} can be assigned for moving one unit of volume over one unit of distance between each pair of areas i and j. These costs are then incorporated into the original scoring system:

$$\text{Total load distance} = \sum_{i=1}^{J} \sum_{j=1}^{J} c_{ij} v_{ij} d_{ij}$$

Usually, however, it is enough to simply capture volume over distance in developing a layout, as we demonstrated in Scenario 2a.

Load Distance

Scenario 2a

RDRS is planning a new warehouse. This warehouse will consist of eight equally sized areas to be housed anywhere within the 10,000-square-foot floor plan pictured here:

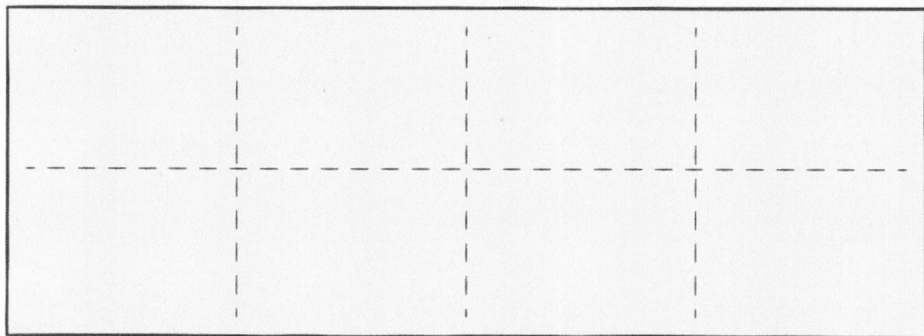

RDRS believes a good warehouse layout will minimize the load distance of relief supplies traveling through the warehouse, although many of the areas would not actually exchange relief supplies. RDRS has listed all eight areas and noted the estimated weight of supplies that would travel among them:

Warehouse Area (abbrev.)	Monthly Relief Supplies Exchanged with Other Areas (tons)
High rack storage 1 (HR1)	10 each with HR2 and HR3; 30 with SA
High rack storage 2 (HR2)	10 each with HR1 and HR3; 30 with SA
High rack storage 3 (HR3)	10 each with HR1 and HR2; 30 with SA
Staging area (SA)	30 each with HR1, HR2, and HR3; 50 with TN and SG
Tent storage (TN)	50 with SA
Soft goods storage (SG)	50 with SA
Administrative office (AO)	none
Tool crib (TC)	none

Analysis

The staging area appears to be central in the travel of supplies within the warehouse, as it is involved in exchange with all five of the various storage areas. This suggests that the

Continues

staging area should be located first, and its two busiest partnerships located as immediate neighbors:

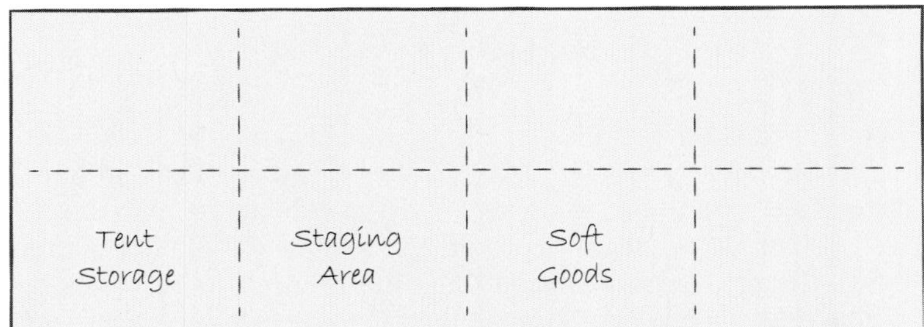

The three high rack storage areas would ideally be neighbors of the staging area, but this is physically impossible without moving tent storage and soft goods storage farther away. Doing so would be unwise because tent storage and soft goods storage involve more traffic with the staging area than high rack storage. So one possible compromise is

High Rack 1	High Rack 2	High Rack 3	Admin. Office
Tent Storage	Staging Area	Soft Goods	Tool Crib

Now we need to evaluate this layout in terms of total load distance. We begin by noting each load and the rectilinear distance each load is required to travel.

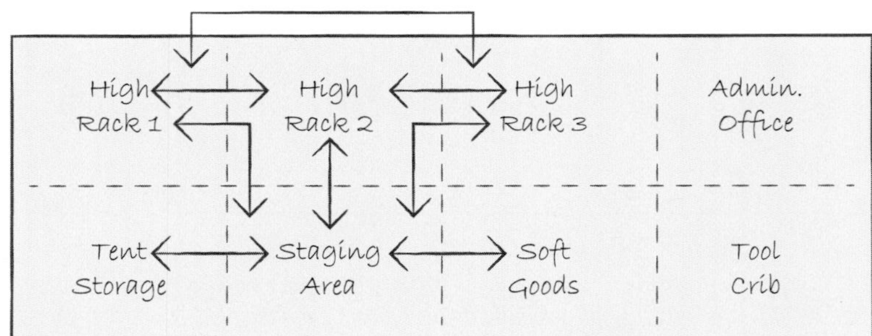

Trip	Load	Distance	Load × Distance
High Rack 1/High Rack 2	10	1	10 × 1 = 10
High Rack 2/High Rack 3	10	1	10 × 1 = 10
High Rack 1/High Rack 3	10	2	10 × 2 = 20
High Rack 1/Staging Area	30	2	30 × 2 = 60
High Rack 2/Staging Area	30	1	30 × 1 = 30
High Rack 3/Staging Area	30	2	30 × 2 = 60
Tent Storage/Staging Area	50	1	50 × 1 = 50
Soft Goods/Staging Area	50	1	50 × 1 = 50

Total load distance: 290

Insight Other arrangements exist, but this is the lowest load-distance score possible for RDRS's warehouse problem. ■

Note that we used the trial-and-error method to develop the finished layout in Scenario 2a. While the scenario demonstrated some helpful heuristic rules such as locating the heaviest traffic areas first, it did not demonstrate any particular technique to solve for the best layout. This is because no such procedure exists, just as in the case of line-balancing discussed earlier. Typically, a process layout is designed many times, with the load-distance score of each new design compared against others until the designer is satisfied with the best of the known designs. Computer-aided design is particularly helpful in this case, automating the calculations in Scenario 2a and allowing the comparison of hundreds or even thousands of potential layout patterns.

Closeness Ratings Minimizing traffic is not the only potential objective when designing a process layout. Some process layouts are designed to deliberately *maximize* traffic; longer traffic patterns for shoppers, for example, are sometimes associated with higher sales. Thus, frequently purchased items such as dairy products in a supermarket are often located at the back of the store, which also features long unbroken aisles, requiring the shopper to walk the entire length of the aisle before navigating elsewhere.

Traffic and traffic patterns may not even explain why one particular layout is more desirable and an alternate layout worse. In fact, the issue of traffic between process areas can only model why two areas should be located near each other, but cannot model a situation in which two areas should *not* be neighbors, such as keeping dusty sanding machines far away from a painting area. To this end, we can employ closeness ratings, a technique that incorporates both the desirability and undesirability of neighbors within a layout. This technique draws its name from the requirement that each potential pair of process areas be rated with a letter grade from a scale of importance of closeness:

closeness ratings Standard scoring system for the desirability of proximity within a facility.

A: Absolutely necessary

E: Especially important

I: Important

O: Ordinary importance

U: Unimportant

X: Undesirable

This scale gives the decision maker three degrees of distinct importance when expressing the relationship of desirable neighbors: A, E, and I. Often the importance of closeness is strongly influenced by the issue of traffic, first introduced in the load-distance model. For example, due to the extremely high amount of traffic between tent storage and the staging area in Scenario 2a, this pair of areas would likely be awarded a closeness rating of A, if this technique were employed to design the RDRS warehouse. Closeness ratings of O and U are essentially expressions of indifference by the decision maker, where O indicates that two areas being neighbors is positive, but of no particular priority, while U is reserved for complete indifference to the issue. Finally, a rating of X is assigned if two areas should be separated in the layout, the condition not recognized in load-distance. Once closeness ratings are assigned to all possible pairs of areas, this information is often organized into a table known as an REL diagram, pictured in Figure 6.10.

The ratings displayed in Figure 6.10 also indicate issues other than traffic patterns within the RDRS warehouse problem. In Scenario 2b we explore the quality of the layout developed with load-distance modeling.

FIGURE 6.10 REL Diagram

Closeness ratings for RDRS warehouse areas

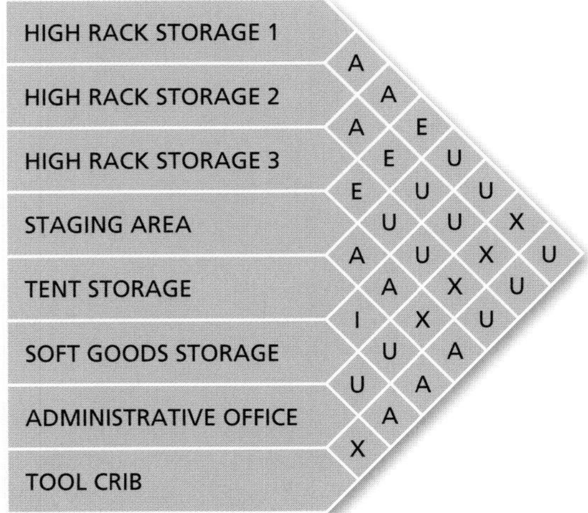

Scenario 2b

Closeness Ratings

RDRS is concerned with use of load distance to develop its warehouse plan. Interviews with warehouse employees reveal important issues of area location unrelated to the movement of supplies within the warehouse. As an example, employees were very critical of the layout developed in Scenario 2a because tent storage and the tool crib were located at opposite ends of the building. Tents are returned to the warehouse after use and require repair with tools stored in the tool crib, thus the employees preferred these two areas share a common border. Furthermore, the Scenario 2a layout locates the administrative office next to a high rack storage area, and RDRS employees indicated such a relationship was extremely undesirable, because that would require the administrative employees to wear protective hard hats around the tall racking. Taking all these factors into account, the warehouse employees have assigned an importance of closeness to each of any two areas, displayed earlier in Figure 6.10. To determine the desirability of the Scenario 2a layout, RDRS has chosen the following point values to each rating earned by the layout:

Rating	Points Earned
A	100
E	50
I	25
O	5
U	0
X	–100

According to this scale and the ratings specified in Figure 6.10, how desirable is the layout developed in Scenario 2a?

Analysis

To determine the desirability of the Scenario 2a layout we must calculate of the overall score earned by the closeness ratings designated for that design. First let's retrieve that layout and identify all the letter ratings that are present within the design:

RDRS WAREHOUSE DESIGN

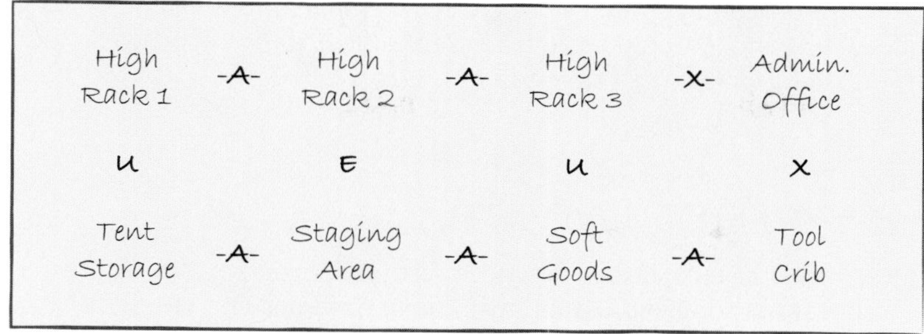

Number of A's: 5 Number of E's: 1
Number of I's: 0 Number of O's: 0
Number of U's: 2 Number of X's: 2

TOTAL LAYOUT SCORE:

(5 × 100) + (1 × 50) + (0 × 25) + (0 × 5) + (2 × 0) + (2 × −100) = 350

Insight The layout suggested in Scenario 2a scores a total of 350 according to RDRS's point scale. ■

Assigning a numerical value to each closeness rating for the layout allows its desirability to be summarized as a single score, but this score has little meaning without another score for comparison. Similar to load-distance analysis, closeness ratings is primarily a trial-and-error technique that encourages the layout designer to generate several alternatives in an attempt to improve scores. In the case of the warehouse for RDRS, this search for improvement could begin by speculating how to separate the administrative office from its undesirable neighbors in the current layout, because the resulting two X's create a 200-point penalty to the layout's score.

Like load-distance analysis, computer models can assist greatly in automating the calculations associated with each revision to the layout. In the case of RDRS's warehouse, Figure 6.11 shows a spreadsheet model using table lookup functions to calculate any

RDRS Warehouse Spreadsheet Model **FIGURE 6.11**

Sample views

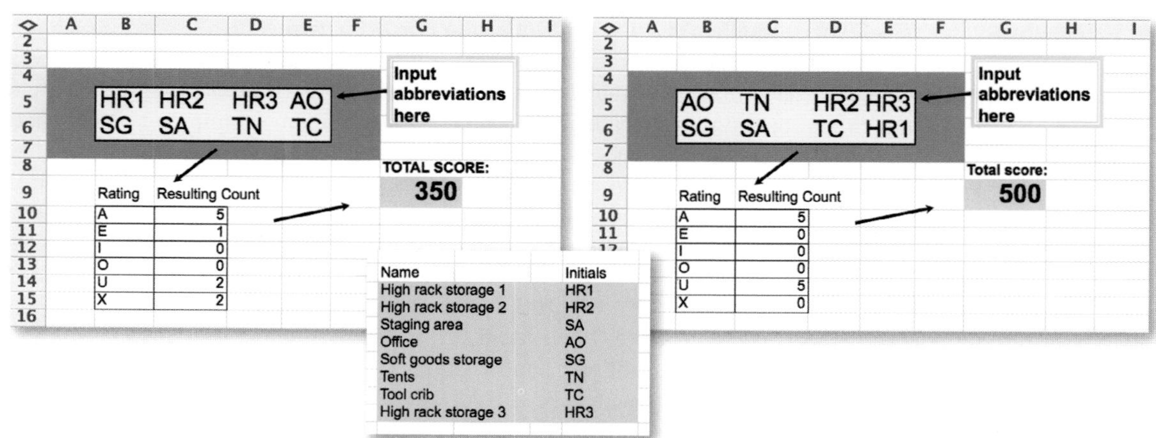

given arrangement of the areas discussed in Scenario 2b. As Figure 6.11 demonstrates, a considerably higher scoring layout can be created by grouping all high rack storage to one end of the building and locating the administrative office at the opposite end, buffered by soft goods and tent storage.

OTHER TYPES OF LAYOUTS

Product and process layouts loosely describe most production facilities but two other layout types also warrant some discussion: hybrid and fixed-position layouts.

Hybrid Layouts

hybrid layout
Any mix of elements from a product layout and a process layout, to gain the advantages of both.

cellular manufacturing
A complex production facility subdivided into smaller product layouts.

group technology
The organization of diverse products into families of similar production requirements.

A hybrid layout represents a mix of product and process layout, in an attempt to gain the advantages of both. If an assemble-to-order processing strategy is being pursued, its layout would likely contain both the unchanging, high-efficiency traffic patterns of the product layout (to produce the stock subassemblies) and some form of the less efficient, more flexible traffic of the process layout (to finish customer orders). Another form of hybridization seeks the same high-efficiency production of multiple products, but uses a different tactic. Cellular manufacturing, pictured in Figure 6.12, refers to a facility organized into multiple small product layouts, referred to as production cells. The combined output of these cells represents the variety of finished goods that would normally be associated with a job shop, yet the cells themselves achieve the internal efficiency of product layouts. This type of hybrid layout relies on the strategy of group technology, where all potential products must first be grouped into families, with all family members requiring similar processes. A production cell is then designed and dedicated to the production of each family, containing only those processes particular to that family.

Cellular manufacturing is a somewhat newer concept when compared to the traditional job shop or assembly line, originating in the machine-part industry. There large job shops producing hundreds or even thousands of different machined parts were reorganized into cellular layouts, producing groups of similar parts in areas dedicated to those part families. The concept is not limited to goods manufacturing, however; service systems can pursue this hybridization by identifying customers with similar needs and creating specialized areas to serve each group of similar customers.

functional organizational structure
An organization of specialists grouped into distinct departments.

matrix organizational structure
An organization that groups differing functions together according to requirements of the work.

While many organizations have successfully employed a cellular approach, this layout is not without disadvantages. One potential disadvantage of cellular manufacturing is that a large group of diverse products or customers may not necessarily split up neatly into distinct families. Figure 6.12 suggests this with two thin blue arrows illustrating occasional traffic between the cells, where one particular family member is not similar enough to be contained completely within its family. Another potential drawback when implementing a cellular layout is the purchase of redundant equipment. Note that processes A, B, C, and G appear in more than one cell in Figure 6.12, indicating they are all required by more than one family. A process layout such as the one pictured earlier in Figure 6.9 would only invest in machinery for processes A, B, C, and G once. Finally, creating a cellular layout may require redesign of the organization itself, in addition to rearranging the facility. Both product and process layouts are usually staffed with functional organizational structures, grouping personnel into departments according to their specialties. A cellular layout, however, distributes these functions across the production cells, suggesting a less traditional matrix organizational structure featuring work groups of differing specialists for each cell.

Traffic Patterns of a Hybrid Layout

FIGURE 6.12

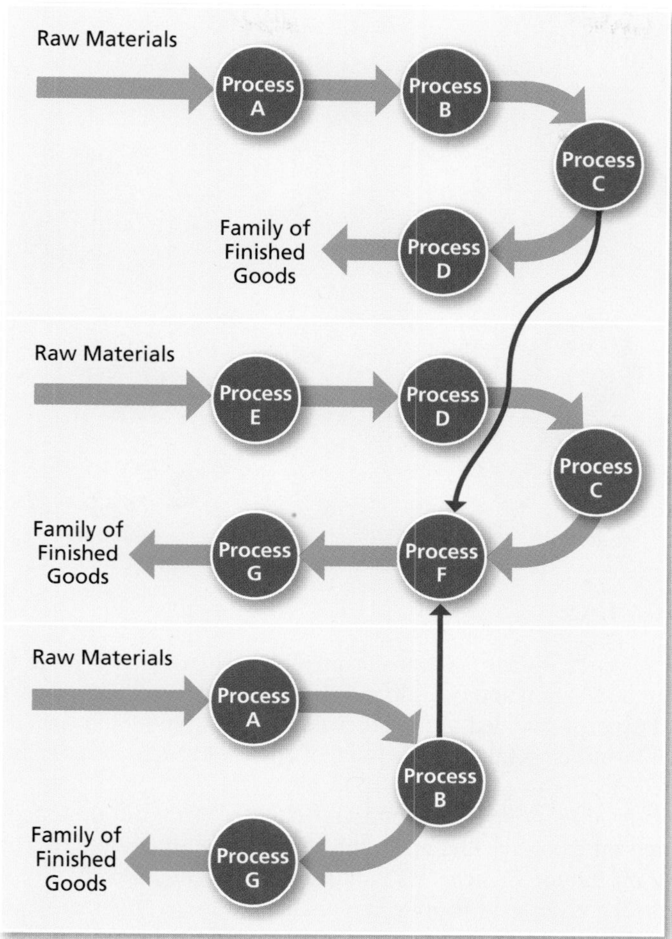

Fixed-Position Layouts

When transformation must take place at a certain location, the organization providing that transformation must implement a fixed-position layout. This might be a tangible manufactured product, such as the airplane pictured in Figure 6.13, which is too large to move along pathways through a facility and thus must be assembled in one place. However, any site-based service is also an example of fixed-position layout. Shipbuilding, carpet cleaning, building construction, and emergency medical response all share the same challenge of a fixed position: all processes required to create value must travel to that location and coordinate there.

fixed-position layout
A configuration in which transformation cannot move, requiring all supporting resources and processes to travel to that location.

Because the nature of a fixed-position layout often means there is no single facility to house all processes on a permanent basis, this layout is often more closely associated with project management than with sustained production. In addition to the expense

project
A unique collection of activities creating a particular outcome.

FIGURE 6.13 Traffic Patterns of a Fixed-Position Layout

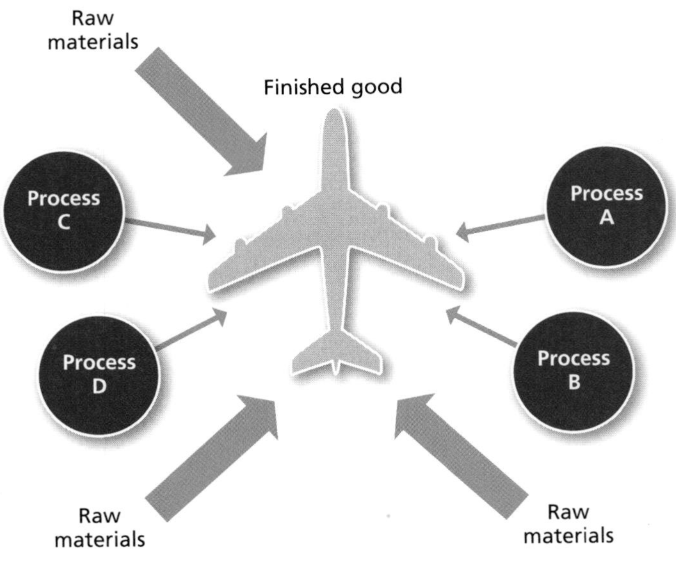

of moving resources to the site of transformation, fixed-position layouts require careful attention to communication and coordination among those resources. This adds a layer of complexity and expense avoided in the other three layout types, and thus the selection of a fixed-position layout is usually not an issue of choice, but rather of necessity.

A facility is a home to an operation. Poor choices made during process and facility selection become burdens that the operation must live with every day. Thoughtless layouts create wasted motion or needless confusion. Yet a good facility, like a home, often fades into the background as it enables its inhabitants to act, interact, and achieve their objectives. Facilities should never be taken for granted; thoughtful facility design does not happen automatically, nor can a facility take care of itself. Energy and creativity invested in the layout and care of any facility is usually money well spent.

SUMMARY

Processes are actions that create products, so selecting a particular process strategy ultimately shapes the activities involved in production. Selecting a make-to-order strategy implies that production begins when a customer's particular requirements are known, allowing the production of a single unit of product that fits those requirements exactly. A make-to-stock strategy builds greater volumes of a standardized product, lowering its costs to entice the customer who is deprived of the flexibility of make-to-order. Many firms have innovated with hybrid schemes such as assemble-to-order and delayed differentiation, attempting to gain the efficiency of building standard stock while nonetheless offering customers some flexibility and choice in the product.

As process strategies shape production activity, they likewise influence the design of the facilities dedicated to that activity. A make-to-stock strategy is often implemented as a product layout, recognizable by the single, unchanging pattern of traffic between the processes housed within the production facility. Product layouts produce standardized products with great efficiency, although they are relatively vulnerable to disruption due to their highly specialized nature. Distributing process activities to areas along the path of transformation through the facility is a design challenge known as line balancing. More robust but less efficient than a product layout is its rival the process layout, recognizable by complex and changing internal traffic patterns. Better suited to support make-to-order, process layouts allow customization of the product. The challenge of designing a process layout is determining the best location for the internal processes, which might simply be an issue of minimizing the expected traffic, such as in load-distance analysis. However, the best locations for processes may involve issues of desirable and undesirable proximity having little or nothing to do with traffic, so an alternative methodology such as closeness ratings may be more appropriate to guide the design. Hybrid layouts often group similar products into families to be produced in mini product layouts known as cells within the facility. These cellular layouts seek the best of product and process layouts, gaining efficiency while offering a variety of products. Finally, a fixed-position layout is easily recognized by the fact that the product never moves during its production and is generally implemented simply because this is the only way to create that particular product.

Key Terms

algorithm
assemble-to-order (ATO)
balance delay
bottleneck
business process reengineering
cellular manufacturing
closeness ratings
continuous processing
cycle time
delayed differentiation
dynamic
efficiency
finished goods
fixed-position layout
functional organizational structure
group technology
heuristic
hybrid layout
immediate predecessor
job shop
lead time
line balancing
load distance
make-to-order
make-to-stock
matrix organizational structure
mixed model assembly
precedence relationship
processes
process layout
product layouts
project
raw materials
remanufacturing
work-in-process (WIP)

Discussion Questions

1. When might it be desirable to have some amount of idle time at a workstation?
2. Of the four types of layouts discussed, hybrid layouts are historically the youngest. Which of the other three layout types is the oldest? Why?
3. The theoretical maximum cycle time of a product layout is the sum of the task times. How might it be argued that this would then no longer be a product layout?
4. Product layouts are vulnerable to disruption. What can a manager do to protect a highly efficient product layout from disruption?
5. Is a fixed-position layout actually a facility? Could it ever support a strategy other than make-to-order?

PROBLEMS

Minute Answer

Short answers appear in Appendix A. Go to **NoteShaper.com** for full video tutorials on each question.

1. An 80,000 seat stadium was created with what kind of facility layout?
2. Designing a process layout focuses on determining what?
3. Name two disadvantages of a product layout.

4. The grouping of processes needed to perform the similar work for families of products is known as what type of layout?
5. What closeness rating reflects indifference to the nearness or lack of nearness of two particular departments within a facility layout?
6. Two assembly lines build the exact same product. One assembly line has 15 workstations and the other has 20 workstations. Which assembly line builds that product faster?
7. Two assembly lines build the exact same product. One assembly line has a cycle time of 30 seconds and the other a cycle time of 90 seconds. Which assembly line has more workstations?
8. Which would be expected to be less expensive to the customer, a product that resulted from a make-to-stock process or the same product from an assemble-to-order process?
9. Which would be expected to offer greater variety to the customer, a product that resulted from a make-to-stock process or the same product from an assemble-to-order process?
10. Would reducing the cycle time of a product layout speed up its production or slow it down?
11. Project management is most likely to be associated with production within which of the four layout types?
12. Process layouts are often designed according to what objective?

Quick Start

13. A production line is to be designed to assemble a product. The assembly of this product requires three tasks, one of which requires 0.3 minutes to complete, one of which requires 1.4 minutes to complete, and one of which requires 0.7 minutes to complete. What is the minimum possible cycle time of this assembly line?
14. A production line is to be designed to assemble a product. The assembly of this product requires three tasks, one of which requires 0.3 minutes to complete, one of which requires 1.4 minutes to complete, and one of which requires 0.7 minutes to complete. If this production line has three workstations and a cycle time of 1.5 minutes, what is its efficiency?
15. A production line must produce 1,500 units every 4 hours of operating time. What is its cycle time in seconds?
16. A production line must produce 900 units every 10 hours of operating time. What is its cycle time in minutes?
17. If a production line has a cycle time of 90 seconds, how much can it produce in 8 hours?
18. An assembly line must create one finished product every 90 seconds. The sum of the task times required to create a product is 295 seconds. What is the theoretical minimum number of workstations for this assembly line?
19. An assembly line must create one finished product every 90 seconds. The sum of the task times required to create a product is 295 seconds. If one design for this assembly line uses four workstations, what is its efficiency?
20. What is the balance delay of an assembly line that is 65% efficient?

Ramp Up

21. A food court has a row of four locations available for food vendors. The food court manager must decide which of four food vendors should be assigned which

locations. Technically, any food vendor could be assigned any one of the four locations. The four food vendors who wish to rent locations are: Pops Are Us, Taco Madness, Ice Cream Scream, and Mega Pretzel. Theoretically, how many different possible layouts does the developer have available to consider?

22. You are standing outside Thompkin Bus Manufacturing Company, watching one finished school bus roll off their assembly line every 15 minutes. An employee, taking a break nearby, proudly states: "We build 40 of those buses every day, Monday through Friday." Based on what you see and have been told, how many hours a day does the Tompkin Bus Manufacturing Company operate?

23. An average of 50 customers travel between departments A and B each day. Unfortunately, department C is located between departments A and B, and no customers travel between department C and departments A and B. What is the load-distance score of this three-department layout?

24. An assembly line must create one finished product every 2 minutes. The sum of the task times required to create a product is 200 seconds. What is the theoretical minimum number of workstations for this assembly line?

Scenarios

Reminder: Short answers appear in Appendix A. Go to **NoteShaper.com** for full video tutorials on each question.

25. Two different companies produce and sell a certain product to customers. Each of the two companies starts with the same raw materials and creates the product through three stages of processing. But each of the two companies uses a different strategy to create the product, shown in the process flow diagrams of each company's operations below. In each diagram, the triangles represent inventory stocks, while the squares represent processing.

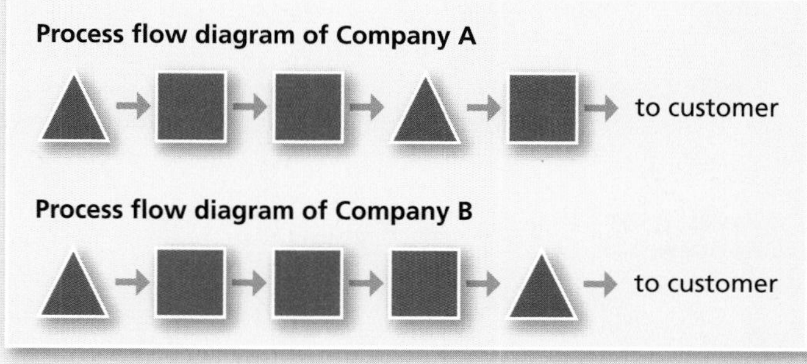

   a. From which company is purchasing the product likely to be less expensive?
   b. From which company is the customer likely to wait longer before receiving the product?
   c. Which company appears to be practicing delayed differentiation?
   d. Which company has adopted a make-to-stock process for production?

26. It takes a total of 400 seconds for one technician, working alone, to assemble one AirRules smartphone. However, AirRules manufactures its smartphones with 20 technicians staffing a 20-station assembly line, producing one smartphone every 30 seconds. Based on this information,
   a. How many hours must AirRules operate its assembly line to create 1,200 smartphones daily?
   b. What is the theoretical minimum number of workstations for an assembly line supporting the AirRules smartphone production described here?
   c. How efficient is the AirRules smartphone assembly line?

27. Digital Eye must design an assembly line to produce a new line of slim digital cameras. Assembling a single camera requires the completion of nine distinct tasks, and information about each of these tasks is provided below:

Task	Immediate Predecessors	Task Duration (sec.)
A	none	10 sec.
B	A	30
C	A	25
D	B	18
E	B	5
F	B	17
G	D, E	37
H	C, F	30
I	H	12

This assembly line operates 8 hours a day to produce 576 digital cameras daily. Digital Eye uses the LPT rule to create the design.

a. What is the cycle time of Digital Eye's assembly line, in seconds?

b. How many workstations are required by this design and what tasks are done at which workstation?

c. Which workstation enjoys the maximum idle time? How efficient is this design? What is the balance delay?

d. How does the actual number of workstations required by this design compare to its theoretical minimum number of workstations?

28. An industrial food processor needs to design a product layout for a new product, mint chocolate chip sandwiches. The company plans to use this new production line 8 hours a day to meet projected demand of 1,440 cases per day. The following table describes the tasks involved in the production of a mint chocolate chip sandwich.

Task	Immediate Predecessors	Task Duration (sec.)
A	none	4 sec.
B	A	14
C	B	20
D	B	12
E	C, D	6
F	E	8

a. Design this layout using the LPT decision rule and then repeat the design process using the SPT rule. What are the differences between the two designs? Which design is more efficient?

b. Suppose the food processor decides to implement the design created with the LPT rule. You have been hired to manage the production of mint chocolate chip sandwiches and you have just learned there may be two errors in the data originally used during the design process. In particular, you discover that both task A and task C will probably require 3 seconds more to complete than originally planned. Which of these two mistakes in the duration data is the most troubling to you, and why?

29. Consider the following diagram of a fast-food restaurant drive-through with three stops for each car following the path described by arrows in the diagram below. The time required to complete the work at each of these workstations is also listed here:

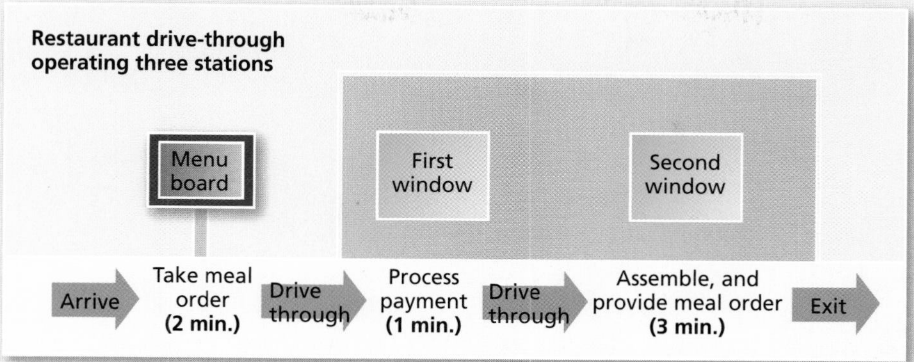

a. What is the maximum rate at which this restaurant can successfully serve arriving cars with this product layout?

b. An average of 15 cars arrive each hour at the restaurant drive-through. What does this imply about the efficiency of this layout?

c. The employee who works at the first window, where the car's payment is processed, has just left the restaurant due to a family emergency. To keep operating, the restaurant has closed the first window and the employee at the second window is now doing the work required at both windows, processing payments and assembling and providing the meal to each of the cars. Now, due to this change, what is the maximum rate at which this restaurant can successfully serve arriving cars?

30. Palms Coast Hospital is designing a new building and has determined the closeness ratings between the eight departments that must be located on the ground floor of that structure. These ratings are as follows:

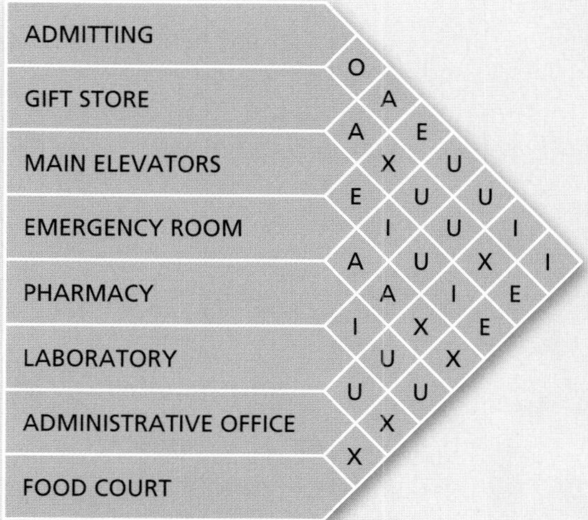

a. Palms Coast considers it absolutely necessary that Admitting be located next to what?

b. What departments should the Emergency Room *not* be next to?

c. Palms Coast is considering a ground floor layout in which the main elevators are next to the pharmacy. Which other departments would be *more* important neighbors to the main elevators?

31. Linlithi Medical provides on-site health screenings for other organizations, and has been hired by the City of Baltimore to conduct the annual health screening of all 250 of Baltimore's bus drivers. The annual health screening for a bus driver consists of the following tasks:

Task Name	Description	Immediate Predecessor	Time Required (minutes)
A	Vision test	none	5 min.
B	Hearing test	none	7
C	Blood pressure test	none	3
D	Lung function test	none	10
E	Draw blood sample	C	4
F	Pulse stress test	B, D, E	8
G	Doctor's consultation	A, F	10

Linlithi Medical has arranged to screen all 250 drivers during one 5-day week. Thus, Linlithi must complete 50 health screenings during each of the 10-hour days. To perform the health screenings efficiently, Linlithi Medical will set up its operation as a product layout, in which the drivers move from station to station until all the tasks of their individual health screening are completed. Please use line balancing to design the most appropriate layout for Linlithi, using the LPT rule to choose among tasks when assigning each task to a particular workstation.

a. What is the cycle time of Linlithi Medical's layout for the Baltimore city bus driver screenings?
b. What is the theoretical minimum number of workstations that Linlithi Medical might have to staff to support this cycle time?
c. At which station will task D, the lung function test, be completed?
d. At which workstation will task F, the pulse stress test, be completed?

CASE STUDY: MYER WINE RACKING AND CELLAR COMPANY

Myer Wine Racking and Cellar Company is a small but growing carpentry job shop that specializes in natural-finish redwood racking systems for storage and display of wine bottles. These racks and cabinets are created by processing redwood lumber through a series of work centers to reduce it to standard components, which are then assembled into seemingly customized goods in an assemble-to-order approach to production. Myer Wine Racking has been so successful in building wine cellars and displays for wine collectors and retail stores, it plans to move to a larger building it has just leased. Myer Wine Racking must organize a layout within the restrictions of that building, which has been divided into the 12 equal-sized zones shown in the Ground Plan of New Building illustration.

Ground Plan of New Building

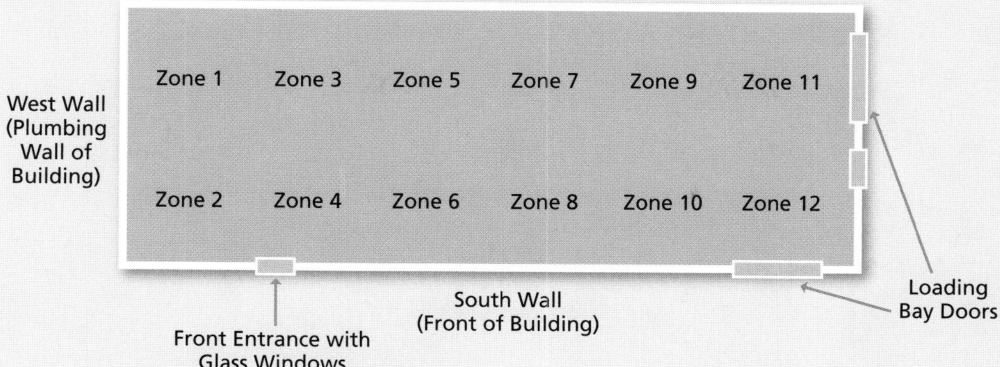

The owner of the building is willing to install interior walls according to Myer Wine Racking's specifications, with some limitations. First, the owner is not willing to change the locations of doors along the exterior of the building. This is important because, of the 12 functional areas within Myer's layout, only the front office or the demo cellar are appropriate locations for the front entrance, meaning that one of these two areas must be assigned to zone 4. Likewise, the shipping department and lumber storage must each be assigned an exterior loading bay door, confining their locations to zones 11 and 12. Second, the building owner wishes to minimize the expense of running water lines and sewer drains. Plumbing enters through the west wall of the building, so the owner is only willing to install restrooms within the first four zones of the building. Because Myer will request restrooms in both its front office and production office areas, these two areas must be located somewhere within zones 1 through 4.

To aid the layout design process further, Myer Wine Racking has determined a closeness rating for each possible pair of neighboring areas within its facility, as organized in the REL diagram shown here.

REL Diagram of Closeness Ratings

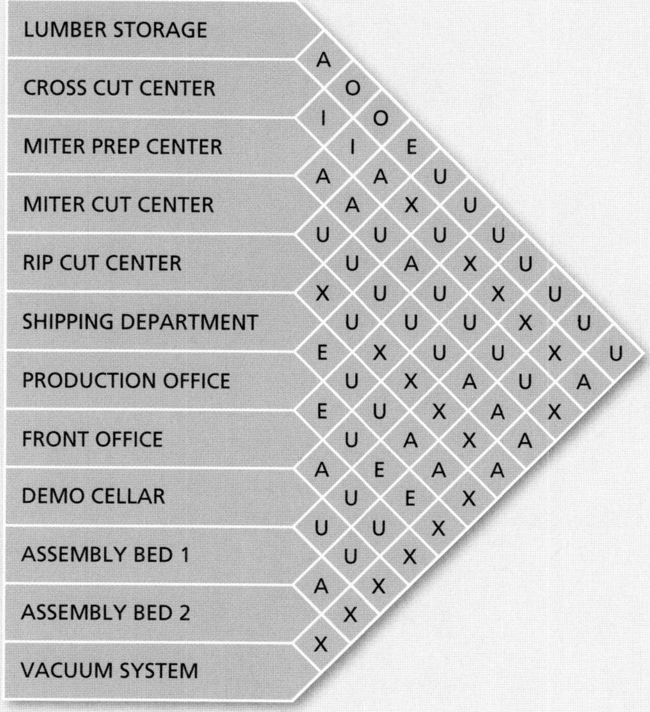

Questions

1. Recommend a good layout for Myer Wine Racking by assigning each of the 12 functional areas to 1 of the 12 zones in the ground plan, working within the building owner's restrictions.
2. Calculate and report the score earned by your recommended layout, based on the following scale: Each pair of areas that share a straight border within the layout earn
   - 100 points if the pair's corresponding closeness rating is A.
   - 50 points if the pair's corresponding closeness rating is E.
   - 25 points if the pair's corresponding closeness rating is I.
   - 5 points if the pair's corresponding closeness rating is O.
   - 0 points if the pair's corresponding closeness rating is U.
   - –100 points if the pair's corresponding closeness rating is X.
3. Can you improve the recommended layout if the building owner could be convinced to run additional water lines and drains, such that the restrooms could be located anywhere in the building? If so, by how much?

BIBLIOGRAPHY

Boysen, N., M. Fliedner, and A. Scholl. 2008. "Assembly Line Balancing: Which Model to Use When?" *International Journal of Production Economics* 111: 509–28.

Francis, R. L. McGinnis, and J. White. 1992. *Facility Layout and Location: An Analytic Approach*. Englewood Cliffs, NJ: Prentice Hall.

Hayes, R., and S. Wheelwright. 1979. "Link Manufacturing Process and Product Life Cycles." *Harvard Business Review* (January/February): 133–40.

PART 2 PLANNING OPERATIONS

CHAPTER 7

Project Management

My personal philosophy is not to undertake a project unless it is manifestly important and nearly impossible.
—Edwin Land

MAJOR SECTIONS

IN THIS CHAPTER, LOOK FOR...

- The essential nature of a project, distinguishing it from all other types of operations.
- Differing methodologies for project analysis.
- Demonstration of network diagrams and Gantt charts.
- Calculation of task timings, and the advantages and disadvantages of differing approaches to assigning task timing within a project.

INTRODUCTION

Most of operations management is dedicated to the ongoing creation of value, such as the daily operation of any manufacturing plant, hospital, or transportation system. However, one of the most challenging areas of operations is not dedicated to sustained creation of value. Projects are, by definition, valuable activities that are completed only once, to produce some unique outcome. Project management is the one sector of operations management dedicated to temporary and one-time operations, where managers have a single opportunity to create the best product possible.

Some projects are monumental undertakings with massive budgets, such as the construction of a dam or the launching of a new satellite. Other projects require only a single entrepreneurial person attempting to create something new. Understanding how to plan a project begins with recognizing what traits all projects share, as well as what distinguishes some projects from others.

THE ESSENTIALS OF A PROJECT

project
A unique collection of activities creating a particular outcome.

A project differs from other operations in that it is created only once, and it shares this characteristic with all other projects. However, projects can differ greatly from one another in their requirements for successful management. So we start our discussion with some general concepts to organize this diversity.

Terminology

WBS
Work Breakdown Structure, a document specifying the tasks required to finish a project.

immediate predecessor
A task that must be completed before another task can start.

milestone
A point of significance in the time line of a project.

Any project consists of a set of activities that must each be completed before the project can be considered finished. These activities are distinct units of work, known as tasks. Thus, project management begins with listing these tasks, creating a document often known as a WBS, or work breakdown structure. Stating the essentials of a project not only requires identifying tasks, but also estimating the potential time required by each task and identifying any dependencies among tasks. These dependencies are usually requirements that some tasks be completed in some certain order, known as *precedence relationships*. In reality, precedence relationships represent logical progress through a set of related tasks, such as the need to obtain a building permit before starting construction, or the need to complete the foundation of a new building before framing its walls on that foundation. In the latter case, the task of completing the foundation is said to be an immediate predecessor of the framing the walls task.

Some industries are project-based, such as building construction, managerial consulting, or the creative arts. Furthermore, almost any business with an ongoing operation will occasionally pursue a project, such as upgrading software or moving to a new facility. While projects have many contexts, they all share another common feature: some deadline on completion. Industrial projects typically have a negotiated deadline that the project manager uses in planning, often with financial penalties for delays. However, some projects suffer such high costs upon missing their deadlines that these projects, for practical purposes, simply cannot tolerate delays in completion. For example, staging a large performance, ceremony, or festival represents a substantial amount of planned work in advance of the scheduled date, but no real option to simply miss the publicized deadline if work does not proceed as planned. These particular projects represent events, and a successful event manager must plan carefully around particular points in time, also known as milestones, wary of any influences on the project that are not within the manager's direct control. Successful staging of an event often involves preparation of multiple interchangeable plans and quick changes to current plans to cope with unpredictable influences in the project's environment, such as the actual size of the attending crowd or

Precedence Relationships Between Tasks

Construction is a project-based industry, and successful construction projects often must navigate many precedence relationships between time-sensitive tasks. Pictured here is the pouring of concrete to create one underground pillar that will support a high-rise building to be constructed later. This underground shaft had to be dug prior to the task in progress, although this precedence relationship was not as time-sensitive as the mixing of the fresh concrete, which must be poured shortly after preparation. Both project management in general and construction in particular rely heavily on good communication and coordination between the people responsible for the various tasks.

the weather on the day of the event. This type of management is known as iterative planning; it requires the manager to plan and replan even as the project is in progress.

Incidents and incident resolution provide even greater challenges. These can be thought of as projects not even known until they are essentially past due for completion. This unannounced urgency is easily recognized in the completion of such tasks as controlling a large wildfire or transporting an accident victim to the hospital, but incident management does not always involve genuine life-threatening emergencies. Successfully restoring a disrupted transportation schedule or addressing the complaints of an unhappy customer are also examples of incident management, requiring managers to plan and implement actions with little or no time to strategize in advance.

iterative planning
Deliberately adjusting plans at short intervals, to reflect emerging information.

incident
An unscheduled event requiring immediate resolution.

Methodologies

By definition, every project is new to even the most seasoned project manager. Successfully completing a complex set of tasks to achieve a unique outcome depends on having a good plan from the outset, so project management provides a methodology to draft these plans from the project's data. At first glance, it appears that there are at least two methodologies for analyzing projects, PERT and CPM. In reality, PERT and CPM represent a single technique developed at the same time by two different organizations. PERT, short for program evaluation and review technique, was developed in the late 1950s by the US Navy during the development and construction of the first Polaris submarines. CPM, or critical path method, was developed by the DuPont Corporation during that same time period, to better coordinate the many activities involved in the overhaul of chemical production plants. Both techniques were designed to

- Identify the activities or tasks associated with the project including duration and precedence relationships.
- Illustrate the tasks and their precedence relationships in a project network diagram.
- Determine, via that diagram, the potential timing of the tasks and the longest overall path, or chain of tasks, through the network that dictates the overall length of the project. (This is the critical path from which CPM draws its name.)

In spite of their consistent goals, PERT and CPM differ on one important dimension: the degree of certainty associated with task times. We discuss CPM, the somewhat simpler of the two methods, first.

PERT
Program Evaluation and Review Technique, a project management methodology developed by the US Navy.

CPM
Critical Path Method, a project management methodology developed by DuPont Corporation.

CRITICAL PATH METHOD (CPM)

deterministic
Fixed and known in advance, representing a high level of certainty when planning.

Because DuPont had considerable experience in plant overhaul, it began its analysis confident of how much time each task would require. Thus, CPM begins with the logical assumption that task times are deterministic, and thus can be listed as known values at the beginning of the analysis. The table embedded in the left-hand side of Figure 7.1 shows typical deterministic data for an example project with four tasks, representing a total of 3 + 2 + 4 + 4 = 13 days of work.

Network Analysis

AON
A style of project network diagram in which nodes represent tasks and the connecting pathways represent precedence relationships.

CPM begins by developing a network illustration of the project, to serve as a visual tool in a more detailed analysis of its inner workings. Figure 7.1 shows two different versions of the example project's network, because there are two different ways to visually encode project data. The top network in Figure 7.1 is an activity-on-the-node, or AON network diagram. Here each task is illustrated as a labeled shape, or node, between milestones representing the start and the finish of the project. Arrows, known as arcs, illustrate precedence relationships between the tasks. Thus, tasks A and B are connected by arcs to the start of the project; they have no immediate predecessor requirements according to the data in Figure 7.1 and may begin immediately. Task A is then connected by an arc to the node representing task C, and task B connected to task D, further illustrating the table data. Tasks C and D are connected to the finish because no other tasks rely upon them as immediate predecessors, highlighting the fact that these are the tasks that would be underway toward the end of the project's timeline.

AOA
A style of project network diagram in which arrows represent tasks and their connections with nodes represent precedence relationships.

The lower network illustration in Figure 7.1 is drawn in the style of activity-on-the-arc, or AOA, network. AOA networks communicate the same information by reversing the visual coding scheme: labeled arcs represent tasks while nodes illustrate the precedence relationships. AOA networks have the advantage of not only illustrating the project's tasks but also the progression of work through each task; the blunt end of the arc represents starting work on the task and the arrowhead at the opposite end represents finishing that work. Neither AOA nor AON is fundamentally better for project analysis, although each

FIGURE 7.1 AOA versus AON Network

Illustrations of an example project consisting of four tasks

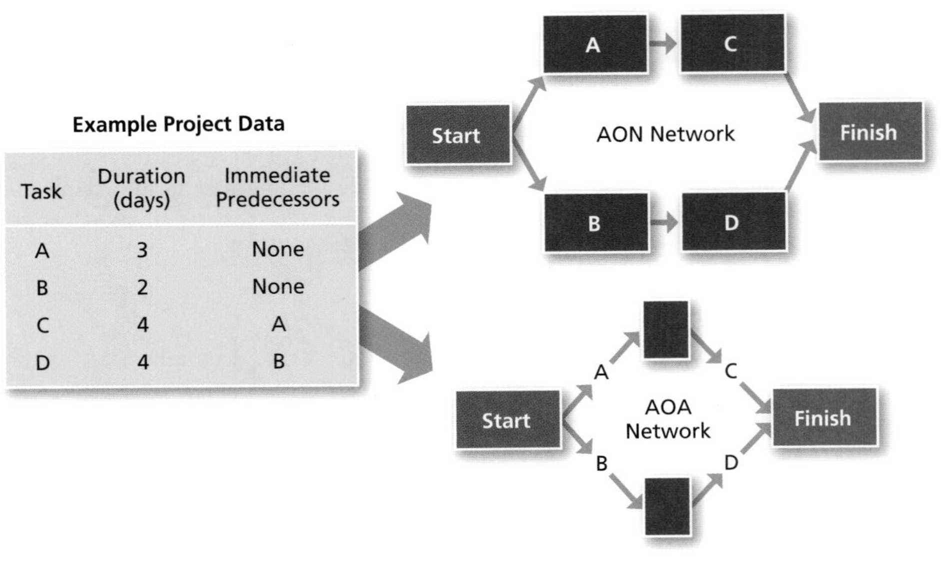

Task	Duration (days)	Immediate Predecessors
A	3	None
B	2	None
C	4	A
D	4	B

has advantages. However, since it is always best to adopt one style before proceeding with any analysis, we will use AON throughout the remaining discussion in this chapter. AON is somewhat more intuitive for most new users of network analysis, which may be why it is usually the default network style drawn by popular software packages such as Microsoft Project or the freeware Open Workbench.

Drawing Networks Drawing an AON network requires representing each activity as a standard shape and joining these shapes with arcs indicating precedence relationships. If done by hand, networks should be sketched in pencil or some erasable medium. The best placement of these shapes within the illustration can be difficult to determine until the network is complete. In Scenario 1a we draw and then revise an AON network.

precedence relationship A dependency between two tasks, usually requiring that one task be completed before the other task is started.

Critical Path Method, Drawing a Network

Scenario 1a

Epic Scenery Studios has just received a contract to build a stage and soft-fabric backdrop for a large trade show display in the San Diego Convention Center (SDCC). This job can be divided into nine tasks, described below:

Task	Description	Duration (days)	Immediate Predecessors
A	Create technical drawings	1	None
B	Purchase and dye fabric	3	None
C	Build stage	4	A
D	Sew fabric and frame backdrop	2	B
E	Rent, deliver, and hang lighting at SDCC	1	A
F	Paint stage	2	C
G	Do trial assembly of stage and backdrop in studio	1	D, F
H	Disassemble and transport to SDCC	1	G
I	Assemble at SDCC, touch-up paint, and adjust lighting	1	E, H

What does this project work look like when illustrated as a network?

Analysis

To create an AON network, we begin by drawing a node that represents the start of the project:

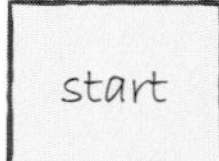

Next, scan the task data and identify any activities that do not have any immediate predecessors. These activities—A and B—can be started immediately, so we add them first:

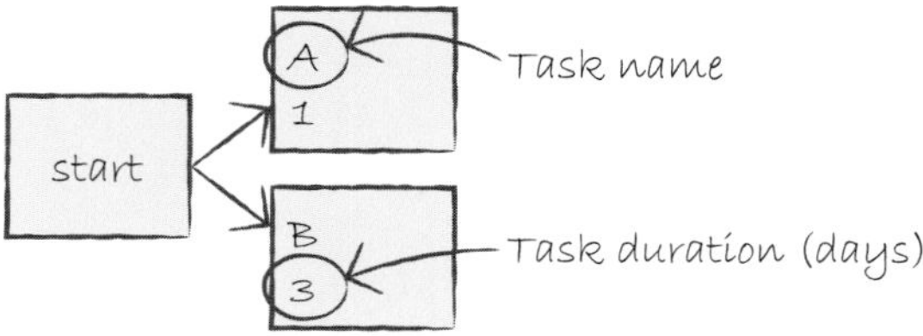

Continues

Note how the labels for tasks A and B are written in the upper left-hand corner of the rectangular nodes, and the duration of each task appears directly below the labels. This is not mandatory when drawing a network but is convenient later in this analysis. Now that A and B are added to the network, scan the task data for any activities that require A and B as immediate predecessors. Since tasks C and E require task A, and task D requires task B to immediately precede it, we now add these relationships to the illustration:

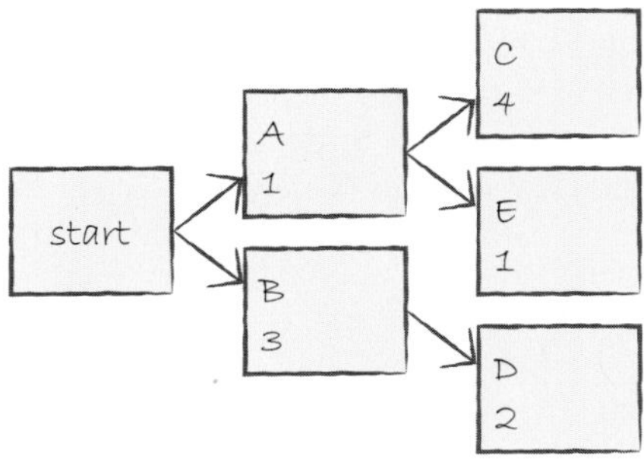

Review the task data again, looking for any task not yet illustrated whose immediate predecessors are nonetheless all present on the current diagram. For Epic, only task F fits this description:

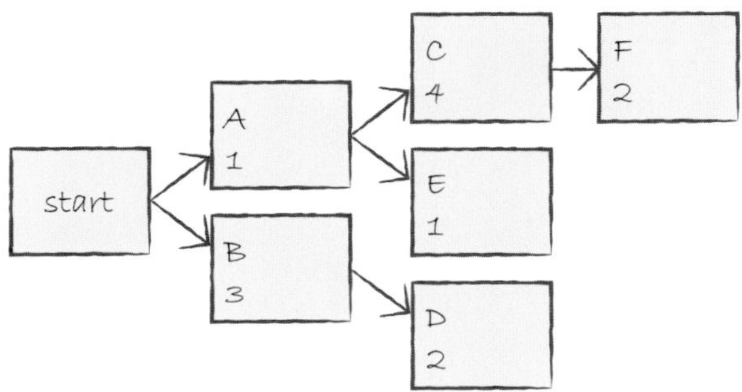

Now we have enough immediate predecessors to add task G, because both tasks D and F must be completed to start G. Task H can then follow G:

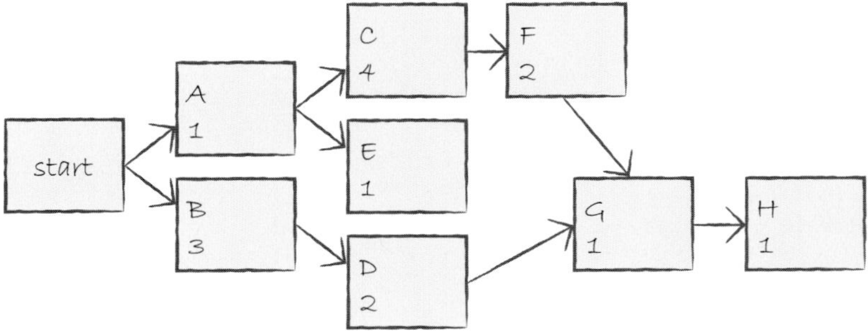

At this point, we need to add only task I. Task I requires tasks E and H as immediate predecessors. Task E is somewhat trapped in the center of this current version of the network, and thus task I cannot be connected without drawing new arcs that cross over existing arcs. This crossing of arcs is not wrong in the strictest sense but is not desirable. Now is a good time to consider revising the illustration to avoid confusion later in the analysis. In this case, if C and E switch locations and F is redrawn somewhat lower in the diagram, we can add task I easily:

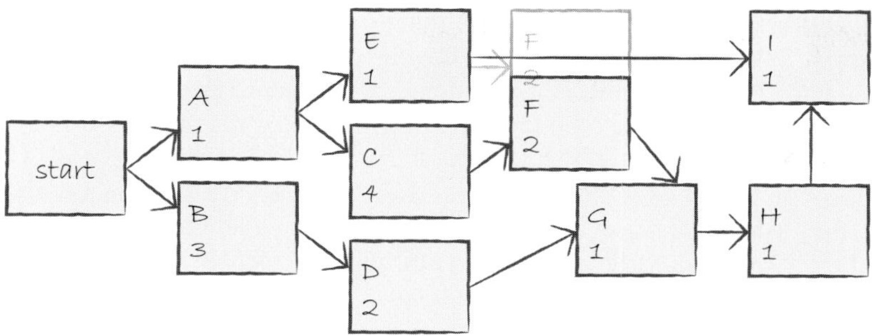

All that remains is to add a finish node. Any task with at least one arc pointing at it but no arcs pointing away should be connected to the finish node. In this case, only task I fits that description:

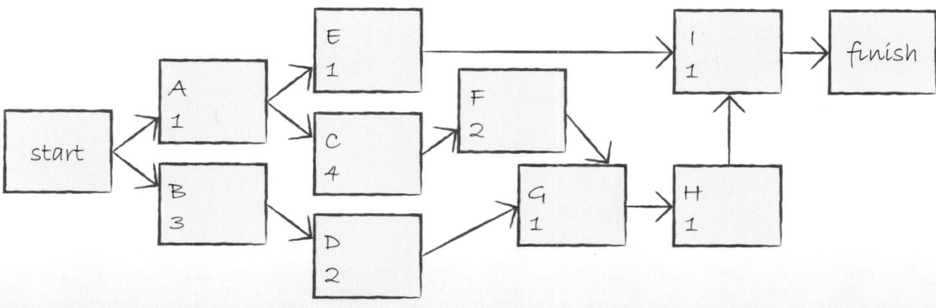

Insight Now the network diagram is a complete illustration of Epic Scenery Studios' project. ■

Paths Once complete, a project network makes visible the paths through that project. Conceptually, a path is any route from the start to the finish node of the project. The simple four-task project in Figure 7.1 has only two paths, A-C and B-D. Epic Scenery Studios' project from Scenario 1a consists of three paths:

path
Any sequence of linked activities that connect the beginning with the end of a project network.

- A-E-I
- A-C-F-G-H-I
- B-D-G-H-I

In reality, paths are strings of activities, each dependent on the completion of the prior activity, and paths themselves often have identities. In Scenario 1a, the project manager might think of path A-E-I as the lighting path, whereas A-C-F-G-H-I concerns the construction and delivery of the stage, and B-D-G-H-I describes construction and delivery of the backdrop. Not surprisingly, the concept of a path is the heart of the Critical Path Method.

Task Timing

Once the network is complete, we can determine the potential timing of each of the tasks. Timing is determined in two stages, the first stage being identification of early start and early finish times of each task.

Early Start/Early Finish Times Early start (ES) and early finish (EF) times express the soonest work may feasibly begin on a given task and the soonest that the task might be completed, respectively. When calculating task timing, remember that CPM measures time as an unbroken number line. On this number line the present moment, or "now," is assigned a value of zero. This is an important milestone, because determining the ES and EF times of tasks begins by identifying only those tasks with no immediate predecessors, thereby declaring their ES to be zero.

Returning to the simple four-task project illustrated earlier in Figure 7.1, tasks A and B have no immediate predecessors, and thus either or both tasks could be started immediately; ES = 0 in both cases. Since CPM assumes the duration of each task is deterministic, calculating the finish time of a task is a matter of logic:

$$\text{Finish time} = \text{start time} + \text{task time}$$

According to the Figure 7.1 data table, task A requires 3 days to complete, while task B requires only 2 days. Since task A requires 3 days, then the earliest task A could be finished would be 3 days from now, so EF = 0 + 3 = 3, while the early finish time of task B would be EF = 0 + 2 = 2 days from now. Since task C in Figure 7.1 has task A as its immediate predecessor, the fact that task A can be finished in 3 days at the earliest means that the soonest task C may start is in 3 days, so ES = 3 for task C. Likewise ES = 2 for task D, because that task cannot start until task B finishes. This reasoning is known generally as the early start time rule:

> **Early start time rule:** The early start time of a task is equal to the *largest* of the early finish times of its immediate predecessors.

By definition, a task cannot start until its immediate predecessors are finished. Therefore, the earliest a task with multiple immediate predecessors can start is determined by the last of its immediate predecessors to finish, or the largest EF time among those predecessors. Figure 7.2 provides an updated version of the four-task AON illustration first appearing in Figure 7.1, complete with these timings.

Figure 7.2 shows that tasks C and D both require 4 days to complete. This would mean that the early finish time of task C would be EF = 3 + 4 = 7 days from now, while the early finish time of task D would be EF = 2 + 4 = 6 days. This raises the question, what is the earliest that the entire project could be finished? Both tasks C and D precede

FIGURE 7.2 **ES/EF and LS/LF Timings**

Example of a project consisting of four tasks

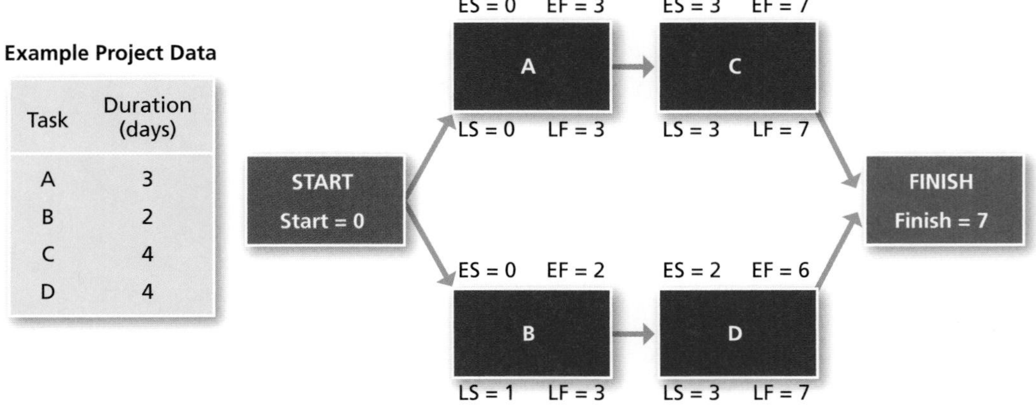

the end of that project, where the earliest task C can finish is in 7 days and the earliest that task D can finish is in 6 days. The project will not be completed until both these ending tasks are concluded; therefore, the earliest the project in Figure 7.2 can finish is the largest of the two EF times, or 7 days.

Note that ES/EF times are determined by using logic to find the ES time of a task, and then arithmetic to find its EF time. We now apply this technique to the example of Epic Scenery Studios, in Scenario 1b.

Critical Path Method, Early Start/Early Finish Times

Scenario 1b

Consider the Epic Scenery Studios project network developed in Scenario 1a. What are the ES and EF times of each of the tasks? How much time will this project require to complete?

Analysis

To determine early task times, it is helpful to grid off each rectangular node into four sectors, leaving the most room for the right-hand boxes within each rectangle:

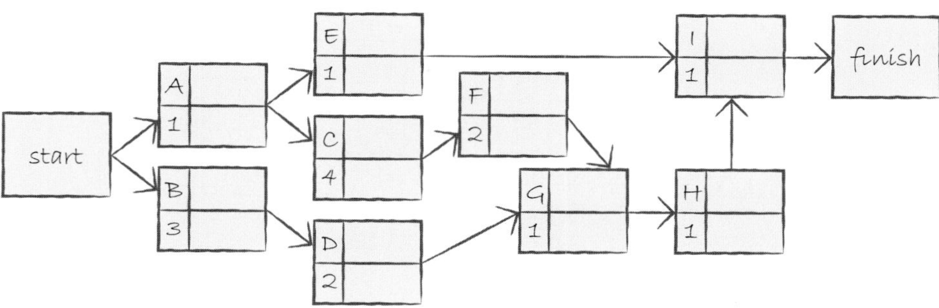

To find ES/EF times, we begin at the start of the project: any task associated with the start is assigned an ES time of zero. This indicates that the earliest that each task can start is immediately, and thus the earliest each could finish (EF) would be the equivalent of their durations:

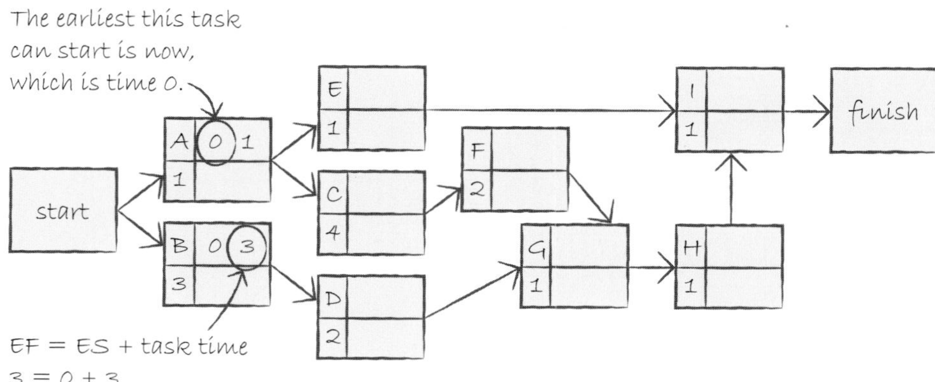

Once the ES/EF times of tasks A and B are established, we use them to determine the ES/EF times for any tasks that require A and B as immediate predecessors. For example, since both tasks C and E cannot start until A is finished, the earliest A can finish (1 day) is the

Continues

earliest that either C or E can start. Loosely speaking, the EF of the immediate predecessor is "handed over" to become the ES of the task depending on its completion:

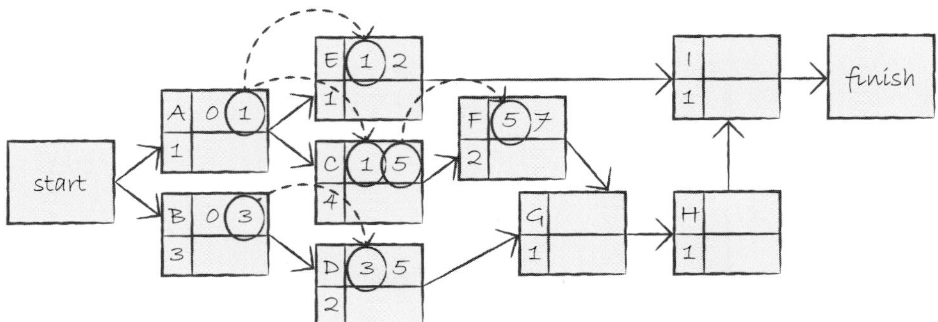

Determining the ES and EF time of task G requires a little more caution, because this task has two immediate predecessors, D and F. Our calculations indicate that the earliest task D can finish is in 5 days and the earliest task F can finish is in 7 days, so the earliest that task G can start is 7 days. Remember: According to the early start time rule, both D and F must finish before task G begins.

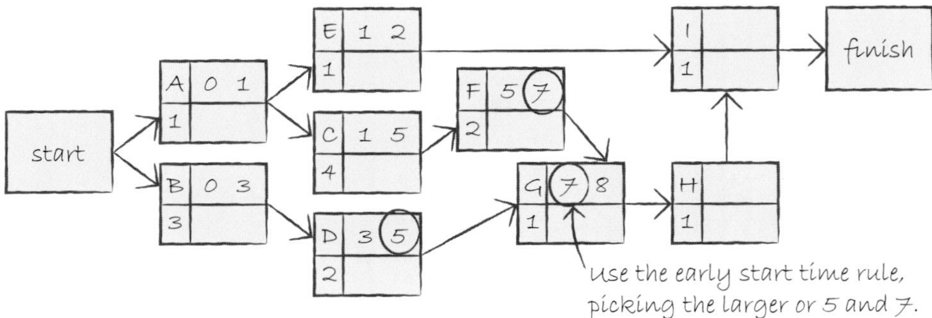

Now that we have determined the ES/EF timings of task G, we can use G's EF time for task H's ES time because G is its only immediate predecessor. This leaves only task I, and another opportunity to employ the early start time rule, by comparing the EF times of E and H before determining task I's ES time:

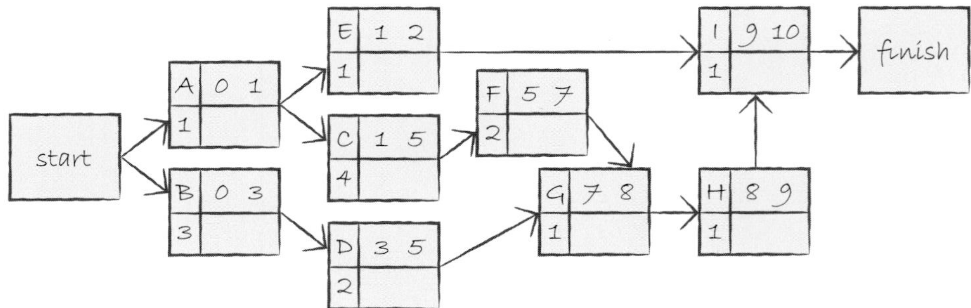

Insight With the ES/EF times determined for all tasks in the project, we look to the timings of task I for the completion time of the project. We see that task I, the final assembly and adjustments of the finished product at the convention center, can be finished as early as 10 days from now, so this project requires 10 days to complete. This result is particularly informative, because summing the task duration data from the WBS in Scenario 1a indicates that this project actually requires 16 days' worth of work. Our analysis here reveals the opportunity to complete the project in as little as 10 days through simultaneous work on some of its tasks. ■

Late Start/Late Finish Times Late start (LS) and Late Finish (LF) timings indicate how long a task can be delayed without creating a delay in the project. Thus, LS/LF times can't be determined until the overall length of the project is known. Returning to the example pictured earlier in Figure 7.2, the earliest this small project could be finished would be in 7 days. This now becomes the deadline for on-time completion, meaning that both ending tasks C and D must be completed in 7 days, or LF = 7. Their LS times are then determined with this logic:

Start time = finish time – task duration

Since both tasks C and D have an LF time of 7 days and both are 4 days long, the LS time for both tasks would be 7 – 4 = 3 days from now. Because task C cannot start before task A is finished, LS = 3 for task C means LF = 3 for task A; otherwise a delay would occur. Likewise, LS = 3 for task D means LF = 3 for task B, a relationship known more generally as the late finish time rule:

> **Late finish time rule:** The late finish time of a task is equal to the *smallest* of the late start times of its immediate followers.

If a task has several tasks immediately following, starting each of the following tasks depends on completion of the first task. To ensure no delays, that task must therefore finish in time to start the one follower with the most urgent, or smallest, LS time. Note that the LS/LF timing technique is the mirror image, or opposite, of finding ES/EF times:

- ES/EF timing begins at the starting node by declaring all tasks associated with the start of the project to have ES = 0, and then works across the network to the finish node. LS/LF timing begins at the finish, declaring LF = project deadline for all tasks there, and works back to the starting node.
- ES/EF timing uses logic to determine start times of tasks, whereas LS/LF uses logic to determine finish times of tasks.
- ES/EF timing uses arithmetic to determine finish times of tasks, whereas LS/LF timing uses arithmetic to determine start times of tasks.

In simple terms, ES/EF timings are calculated by moving forward through time to find the project deadline, whereas LS/LF timings are determined by working back from the deadline. We apply this logic to Epic Scenery Studios' project, in Scenario 1c.

Critical Path Method, Late Start/Late Finish Times — Scenario 1c

Consider the Epic Scenery Studios project network developed in Scenarios 1a and 1b. What are the late start and late finish times of each of the tasks?

Analysis

To calculate late start/late finish times, we begin at the end of the project and work back through time toward the start of the project. From Scenario 1b we know that this project can be finished in 10 days. This becomes the deadline for the project, meaning that any task

Continues

associated with the end of the project must be finished in 10 days. Only one task is associated with the end of Epic Scenery Studios' project, task I, so the LF of task I is 10 days. Since task I requires 1 day to complete, simple arithmetic determines that the latest task I can start is in 10 – 1 = 9 days.

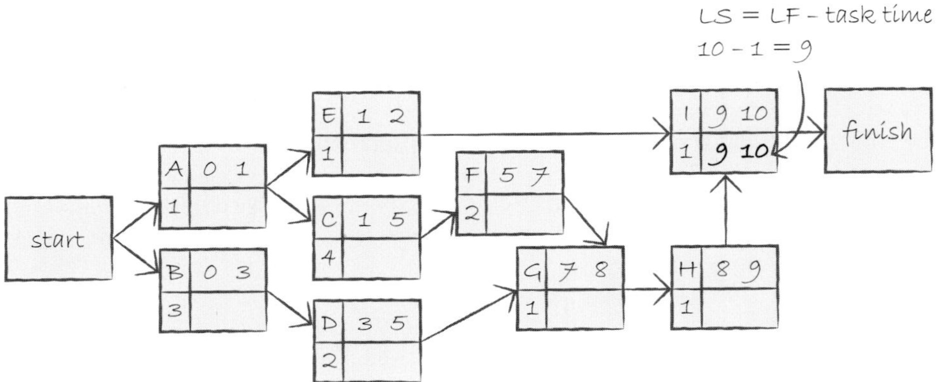

Keep in mind that task I cannot be started until tasks E and H are finished. Therefore, the LS of task I, 9 days, is "passed back" to become the LF time of its immediate predecessors:

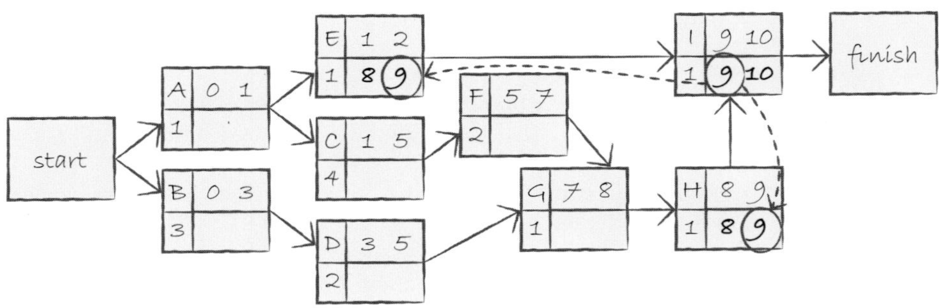

Now that we determined that task H cannot be started any later than 8 days from now, we can pass back this requirement to task G as its late finish time. We subtract task G's duration from that finish time to determine its late start time; this in turn becomes the required late finish time of its immediate predecessors F and D:

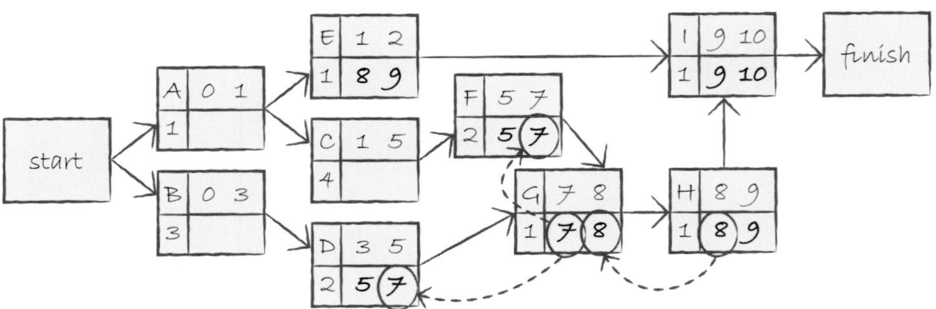

Next, we can pass back the LS time of D to become the LF time of task B, and the LS time of F can likewise become the LF time of task C:

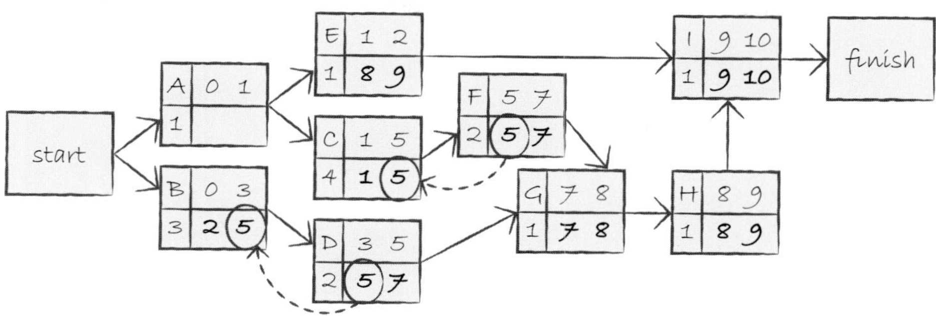

Note that the early start time for task B, purchasing and dyeing the fabric to be used in the backdrop, is zero, indicating that Epic Scenery Studios could start on that task immediately. This step of the analysis reveals that Epic may also wait as late as 2 days from now (LS = 2) to start task B, and the project will nonetheless be completed in 10 days.

We still need to determine late timings for task A, and here we need to be careful, because only task A serves as an immediate predecessor for more than one other task. Both task E and task C cannot start until A is finished, and task E must start at the latest in 8 days while task C must start in 1 day at the latest. To avoid delaying either, the smallest deadline is selected as an LF time for A, in accordance with the late finish time rule.

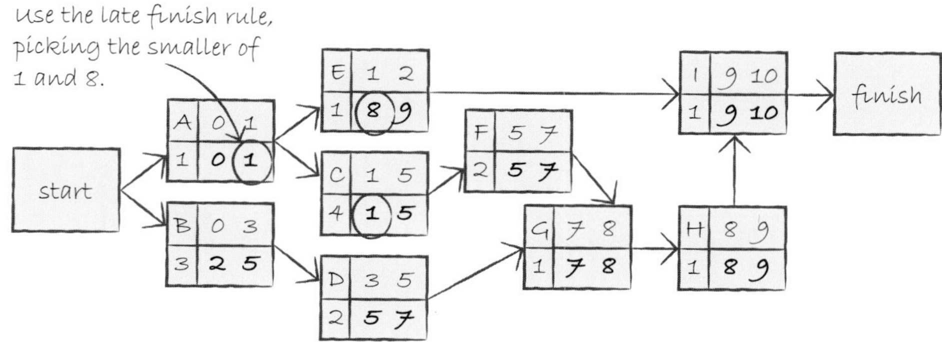

Insight Completing the late start/late finish times of Epic's project reveals some flexibility in the completion times of some, but not all, of the activities. For example, task B, the purchase and dyeing of the fabric, can begin immediately (ES = 0) but can wait as late as 2 days from now (LS = 2) without delaying the project. In contrast, task A, creating the technical drawings, can begin immediately (ES = 0) but can wait no later than immediately (LS = 0), meaning that Epic has no choice in this matter. If Epic Scenery Studios wants to finish on time in 10 days, it must start creation of the technical drawings now. ■

Critical Paths Once a network is drawn and the ES/EF and LS/LF timings are determined, the critical path or paths through the project can be identified. The critical path through a project is the longest path through the project network. A project can have more than one critical path, if a set of paths happen to match in length and this length is the longest among all paths in the project network. This longest path or paths are recognizable once ES/EF and LS/LF timings are available, because the critical path is also the set

critical path
The longest path through a project network; determines the length of the entire project.

slack
The degree to which a task may be delayed from its early start without delaying the project.

of activities with zero slack in their timings. Slack is defined as the difference between a task's ES/EF or LS/LF, and can be calculated using either start or finish times:

$$\text{Slack in a task} = \text{LS} - \text{ES or LF} - \text{EF}$$

Since the critical path is the set of all tasks with zero slack, the critical path is also readily recognized as the set of activities for which early and late timings match, as we see in Scenario 1d.

Scenario 1d

Critical Path Method, Identifying the Critical Path

What is the critical path through the Epic Scenery Studios project? How much slack exists in each task?

Analysis

Because the critical path is formally defined as the set of all tasks with zero slack, we highlight all tasks with matching early and late timings:

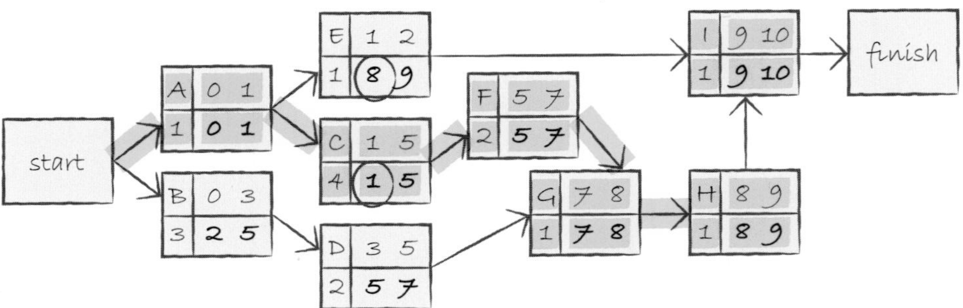

Task	Late Start	Early Start	Slack (days)
A	0	0	0 − 0 = 0
B	2	0	2 − 0 = 2
C	1	1	1 − 1 = 0
D	5	3	5 − 3 = 2
E	8	1	8 − 1 = 7
F	5	5	5 − 5 = 0
G	7	7	7 − 7 = 0
H	8	8	8 − 8 = 0
I	9	9	9 − 9 = 0

Insight The critical path through this project is the set of tasks A-C-F-G-H-I, which each possess zero slack. Both tasks B and D have slack of 2 days, while task E has a slack of 7 days. ■

Identifying the critical path as the set of all tasks with zero slack does not fully explain why this path is critical. Figure 7.3 displays a spreadsheet model of the Epic Scenery Studios project, including the length of each of the three paths through the project. This spreadsheet reveals that not only is path A-C-F-G-H-I the longest path through this project, but its length of 10 days is the length of the project. In listing all the paths,

Sample View of Spreadsheet Model

FIGURE 7.3

Data from Epic Scenery Studios

Task	Description	Duration (Days)	Early Start	Early Finish	Late Start	Late Finish	Slack
A	Create technical drawings	1	0	1	0	1	0
B	Purchase and dye fabric	3	0	3	2	5	2
C	Build stage	4	1	5	1	5	0
D	Sew fabric and frame backdrop	2	3	5	5	7	2
E	Rent, deliver, and hang lighting at SDCC	1	1	2	8	9	7
F	Paint stage	2	5	7	5	7	0
G	Do trial assembly of stage and backdrop in studio	1	7	8	7	8	0
H	Disassemble, transport to SDCC	1	8	9	8	9	0
I	Assemble at SDCC, touch-up paint and adjust lighting	1	9	10	9	10	0

	Length (Days)
Path A-E-I	3
Path A-C-F-G-H-I	10
Path B-D-G-H-I	8
Completion time of the project:	10

Figure 7.3 demonstrates another method for determining the critical path through a project: list all paths through the network, calculate the length of each of those paths, and identify the largest of those lengths.

Because the critical path determines the overall length of the project,

- Any delay in a critical path activity delays the project.
- Any delay in a noncritical path activity does not necessarily delay the project.

Figure 7.4 illustrates these two principles of CPM. The spreadsheet model of Figure 7.3 is revised in two ways: one screen displays the result of delaying noncritical task E and the other screen displays the result of delaying critical path task A. In the case of task E, its

Sample Views of Spreadsheet Model with Simulated Delays

FIGURE 7.4

Data from Epic Scenery Studios

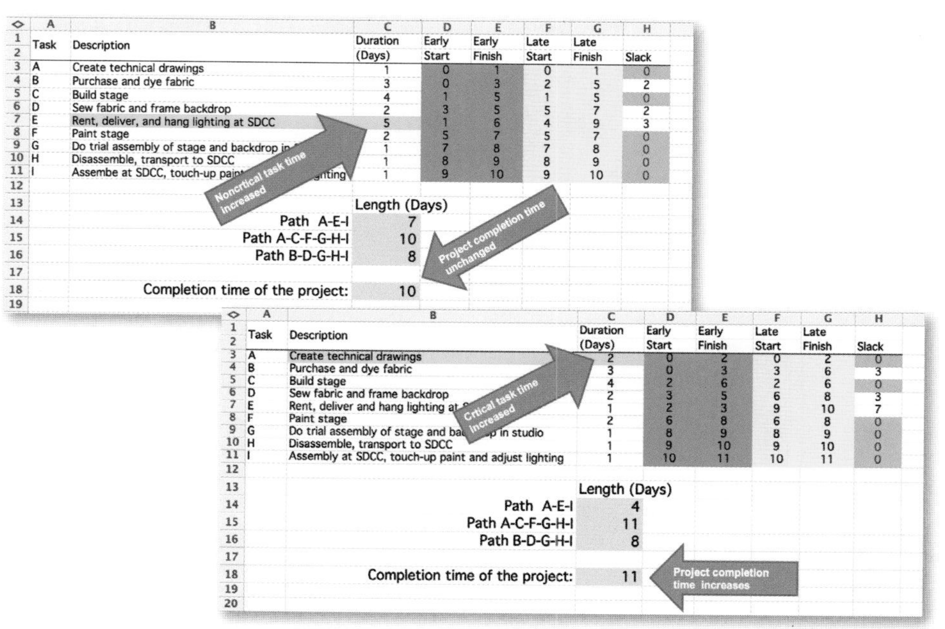

Task	Description	Duration (Days)	Early Start	Early Finish	Late Start	Late Finish	Slack
A	Create technical drawings	1	0	1	0	1	0
B	Purchase and dye fabric	3	0	3	2	5	2
C	Build stage	4	1	5	1	5	0
D	Sew fabric and frame backdrop	2	3	5	5	7	2
E	Rent, deliver, and hang lighting at SDCC	5	1	6	4	9	3
F	Paint stage	2	5	7	5	7	0
G	Do trial assembly of stage and backdrop in [illegible]	1	7	8	7	8	0
H	Disassemble, transport to SDCC	1	8	9	8	9	0
I	Assembe at SDCC, touch-up pai[illegible]ghting	1	9	10	9	10	0

	Length (Days)
Path A-E-I	7
Path A-C-F-G-H-I	10
Path B-D-G-H-I	8
Completion time of the project:	10

Task	Description	Duration (Days)	Early Start	Early Finish	Late Start	Late Finish	Slack
A	Create technical drawings	2	0	2	0	2	0
B	Purchase and dye fabric	3	0	3	3	6	3
C	Build stage	4	2	6	2	6	0
D	Sew fabric and frame backdrop	2	3	5	6	8	3
E	Rent, deliver and hang lighting at [illegible]	1	2	3	9	10	7
F	Paint stage	2	6	8	6	8	0
G	Do trial assembly of stage and ba[illegible]p in studio	1	8	9	8	9	0
H	Disassemble, transport to SDCC	1	9	10	9	10	0
I	Assembly at SDCC, touch-up paint and adjust lighting	1	10	11	10	11	0

	Length (Days)
Path A-E-I	4
Path A-C-F-G-H-I	11
Path B-D-G-H-I	8
Completion time of the project:	11

duration increases from 1 to 5 days, and yet Epic Scenery Studios' project remains 10 days in length. Obviously, task E cannot be delayed indefinitely without causing the project to run longer than 10 days, and the degree to which it can be delayed without causing problems is expressed by its original slack of 7 days. This flexibility is in stark contrast to the result of increasing task A by even 1 day: the length of the project is immediately extended by 1 day. CPM suggests that the tasks on the critical path be given particular priority during the project's implementation, because they are particularly critical to on-time completion.

Gantt chart
A scheduling diagram that illustrates activities across a horizontal time line.

forward scheduling
Starting an activity as soon as possible, regardless of its deadline.

Selecting Task Timing While CPM provides estimates of the project's overall completion time and gives insight into which activities are directly responsible for its duration, CPM does not determine the precise timing of many of the tasks. A project planner has a range of options when scheduling noncritical path tasks, defined by the differing estimates in those tasks ES/EF and LS/LF times. Gantt charts are generally more helpful than network diagrams when considering the issue of tasking timing. Figure 7.5 shows a Gantt chart of the Epic Scenery Studios' project, given that ES/EF timing is implemented for all tasks. Recall that one assumption of CPM is that, given that all precedence relationships are met, any tasks within a project can be scheduled simultaneously. The Gantt chart in Figure 7.5, more so than a network diagram, reveals precisely which tasks would be unfolding simultaneously.

Implementation of ES/EF timing is also known generally as forward scheduling, in that each task is started as soon as possible. Forward scheduling can be thought of as safer or more conservative planning, because it leaves more room for unexpected delays to be absorbed by the slack in some of the tasks. Regardless of whether this is attractive to Epic Scenery Studios or not, Figure 7.5 allows the Epic planner to consider the time line day by day and may reveal problems specific to Epic and unrecognized by

FIGURE 7.5 **Gantt Chart with Early Start/Early Finish Timings**

Data from Epic Scenery Studios project

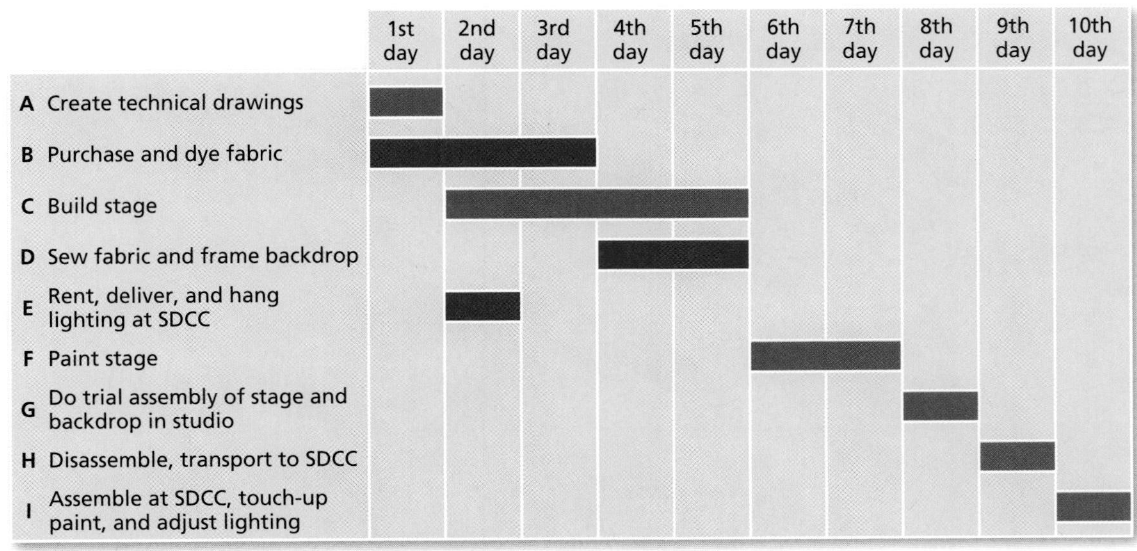

CPM. For example, Figure 7.5 shows that, if ES/EF timings are used, the second of the 10-day project will be unusually busy. This is the only day within the time line in which Epic personnel will be deployed across three tasks (B, C, and E) simultaneously, and Epic may be concerned that it does not have a sufficient number of employees to do so successfully. While this is an issue specific to Epic, it highlights a disadvantage of CPM in general: its inability to recognize shared resources. In reality, it is not uncommon for tasks to be unrelated by precedence relationships and yet incompatible for simultaneous scheduling. Such tasks usually share some certain resource, such as personnel in the case of Epic Scenery Studios. No convenient methodology exists that reliably schedules project tasks while avoiding all issues of shared resources. Rather, the project planner must intervene when necessary, a role made easier with the assistance of project management software such as Microsoft Project or Open Workbench. An alternative to the ES/EF schedule can be generated swiftly by implementing LS/LF timing instead, as illustrated in Figure 7.6.

The timings of tasks A, C, F, G, H, and I are identical between Figures 7.5 and 7.6, visually underscoring the rigid nature of the critical path within the project's time line. However, Figure 7.6 shows noncritical path activities B, D, and E scheduled at the other extreme available to Epic's planner, which happens to result in a time line in which Epic is never working on more than two tasks simultaneously. Use of LS/LF timings is known more generally as backward scheduling, referring to the fact that the latest possible finish times are found first, allowing start times to be identified by working back from these finish times. This approach is risky because any unexpected delay in any task will delay the planned completion time of the project. However, many project planners prefer LS/LF timings, usually for projects spanning many months or even years. In such projects, the timing of tasks correlates closely with the timing of major cash flows associated with the project. Once a task is started and/or completed, the organization must pay for that

backward scheduling Scheduling backward from a project's deadline to its start time.

Gantt Chart with Late Start/Late Finish Timings **FIGURE 7.6**

Data from Epic Scenery Studios project

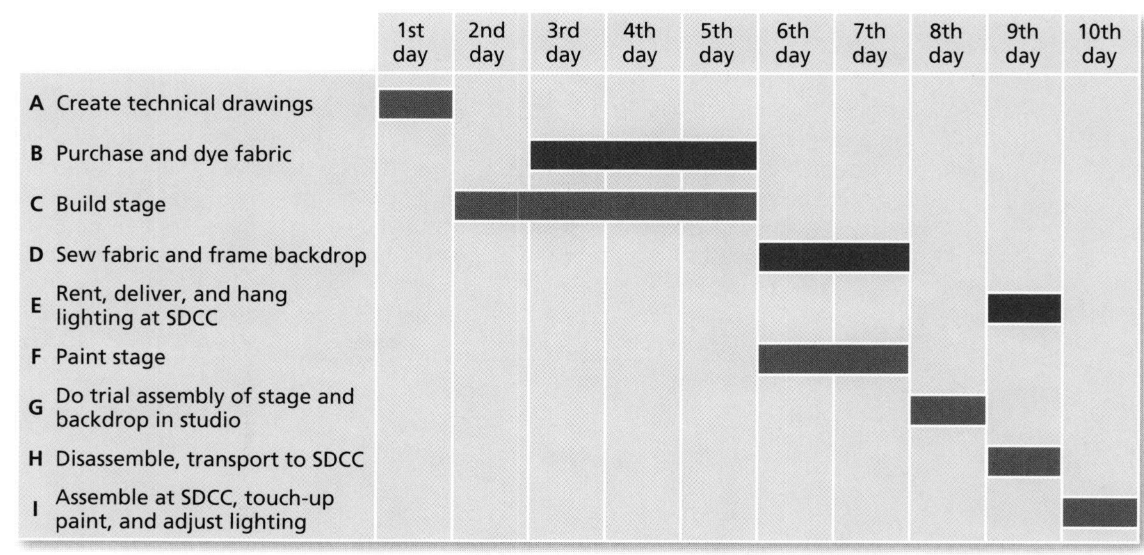

activity, even though that organization will probably not be paid for the project until all tasks are completed. Thus, one powerful advantage of backward scheduling is financial: delaying outgoing cash flows as late as possible maximizes the net present value of the entire project.

Project Crashing

CPM begins with a list of tasks and their durations, deriving an overall estimate of the length of the project from this data. However, even well-known tasks do not always require one certain length of time to complete. Often, a project planner has options allowing some tasks to be completed faster but only at greater expense. As an example, Epic Scenery Studios' project is planned around the assumption that task C, building the stage, will require 4 days. If Epic Scenery Studios paid its carpenters to work overtime or hired enough carpenters to work continuously at task C, it is reasonable to assume that it could complete task C in fewer than 4 days, but at greater expense than if it completed task C at a normal pace. Thus, the economical pace of 4 days is known as the normal time for task C, and devoting extra resources to speed its completion is called crashing task C. To crash any task is to expedite its completion, presumably to meet some deadline set sooner than the project's normal completion time. However, crashing any task within a project does not necessarily shorten the project's completion time; CPM highlights the fact that the project's completion time is the result of the longest path through the project. This introduces two additional CPM principles:

crashing Expediting the completion of a task or group of tasks, to finish a project sooner.

- Crashing a noncritical path activity does not change the length of the project.
- Crashing a critical path activity may shorten the length of the project.

The key to shortening the length of a project is to crash one or more of its critical path activities, but note that the second principle above does not state that doing so is *guaranteed* to shorten the project. This is because any shortening of the longest path through a project network may create more paths with that same distinction, each of which then requires crashing to shorten the project further. This is the case with Epic Scenery Studios' project, as we see in Scenario 2.

Scenario 2

Project Crashing

Consider the Epic Scenery Studios project network analyzed in Scenarios 1a through 1d. This project requires the construction and installation of a stage and soft-fabric backdrop for a trade show display in the San Diego Convention Center (SDCC), and is now known to require 10 days to complete. Unfortunately, Epic has just learned that this trade show display is needed in 7 days, and so plans must be drawn up to meet this new deadline. Of the nine original tasks, four of them could be crashed, but at differing levels of expense:

Task	Description	Normal Duration (days)	Crash Time (days)	Crash Cost, $
B	Purchase and dye fabric	3	2	$1,000
C	Build stage	4	1	2,000 per day
D	Sew fabric and frame backdrop	2	1	500
F	Paint stage	2	1	800

Assuming Epic Scenery Studios begins work right now, how should it proceed to have the trade show display successfully installed at SDCC in only 7 days?

Analysis

We first consider the length of each and every path through Epic's project, provided that each task is completed in a normal amount of time:

PATHS (PROJECT COMPLETION TIME = 10 DAYS)

A-E-I = 1 + 1 + 1 = 3 days
A-C-F-G-H-I = 1 + 4 + 2 + 1 + 1 + 1 = 10 days
B-D-G-H-I = 3 + 2 + 1 + 1 + 1 = 8 days

To determine how Epic should shorten this project to 7 days, we determine how best to shorten the project by *1 day*, which can only be achieved by shortening the critical path by 1 day. Two options exist: shorten task C or task F. Logically, the best option would be the least expensive one, task F. Let's assume that Epic commits to completing task F, painting the stage, in half its normal time, and update the paths accordingly:

PATHS (PROJECT COMPLETION TIME = 9 DAYS)

A-E-I = 1 + 1 + 1 = 3 days
A-C-F-G-H-I = 1 + 4 + 1 + 1 + 1 + 1 = 9 days
B-D-G-H-I = 3 + 2 + 1 + 1 + 1 = 8 days

Next, we determine the least expensive option to shorten the project by *another day*. At this point, there is only one option to shorten the critical path from 9 to 8 days, and that is to shorten the building of the stage, task C, by 1 day:

PATHS (PROJECT COMPLETION TIME = 8 DAYS)

A-E-I = 1 + 1 + 1 = 3 days
A-C-F-G-H-I = 1 + 3 + 1 + 1 + 1 + 1 = 8 days
B-D-G-H-I = 3 + 2 + 1 + 1 + 1 = 8 days

Shortening the project by 1 day more requires somewhat more caution: now the original critical path, A-C-F-G-H-I, is no longer the *only* critical path through the project. While A-C-F-G-H-I can still be shortened by reducing task C another day for $2,000, the project will not be reduced in length unless B-D-G-H-I is shortened as well. The least expensive option for shortening this path would be to shorten task D for $500. Exercising both options allows Epic to meet the 7-day target:

PATHS (PROJECT COMPLETION TIME = 7 DAYS)

A-E-I = 1 + 1 + 1 = 3 days
A-C-F-G-H-I = 1 + 2 + 1 + 1 + 1 + 1 = 7 days
B-D-G-H-I = 3 + 1 + 1 + 1 + 1 = 7 days

Insight Epic Scenery Studios can complete the project by crashing tasks D and F by 1 day and task C by 2 days. The total cost of reducing the project's completion time is $2,000 × 2 + $500 + $800 = $5,300. ■

As Scenario 2 demonstrates, a project is best shortened by several days by first considering how to shorten it by 1 day, and then assessing the impact of this revision on all of the project's paths. Given that the project must be compressed by a considerable amount, it is not uncommon for more than one of its paths to become critical during the crashing process.

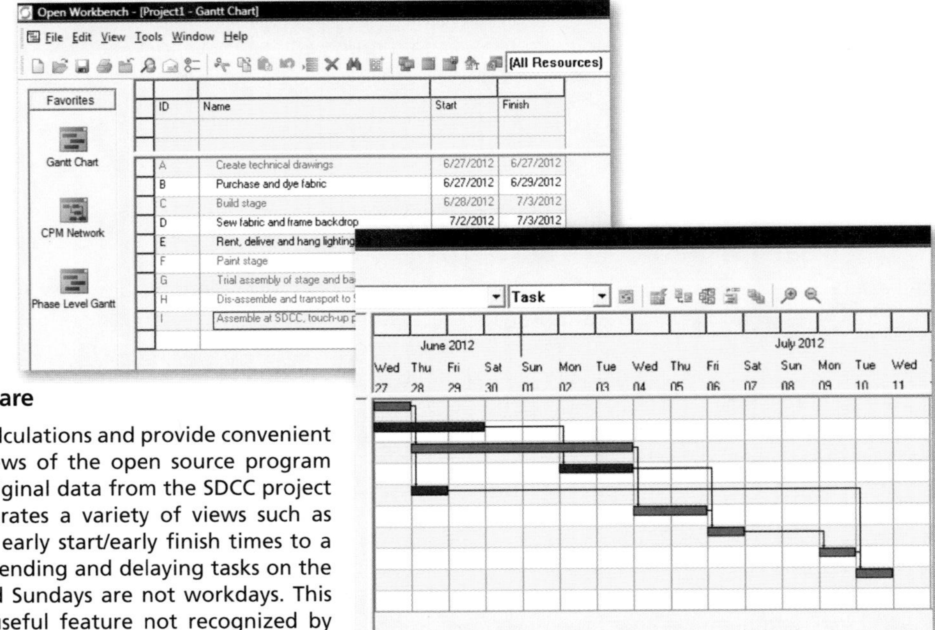

Project Management Software

Software can automate CPM calculations and provide convenient reports, as shown in these views of the open source program Open Workbench. Once the original data from the SDCC project is entered, the software generates a variety of views such as this Gantt chart, mapping the early start/early finish times to a calendar and automatically extending and delaying tasks on the assumption that Saturdays and Sundays are not workdays. This avoidance of weekends is a useful feature not recognized by traditional CPM methodology.

PROJECT EVALUATION AND REVIEW TECHNIQUE (PERT)

While DuPont developed a better methodology for the management of its plant overhauls, the United States Navy was confronted with a large project of a somewhat different nature. The Polaris Missile Project required its organizers to develop and construct a submersible nuclear missile launch platform, now known as a Polaris submarine. The managerial technique developed during this undertaking came to be known as PERT, for project evaluation and review technique.

The Polaris Missile Project involved a complex group of tasks and precedence relationships, similar to DuPont's challenge of coordinating timely plant overhauls.

The Risks in an Unusual Project

The more unusual a project, the less its planners benefit from past experience and the greater its probabilistic elements. Here the space shuttle *Enterprise* is transferred from a sea barge to the deck of the retired aircraft carrier and aeronautical museum that will be its permanent home. As a project, this unusual delivery is exposed to multiple sources of uncertainty and risk, including its uniqueness, the influence of water and weather, and the high value of the historical item being handled.

However, unlike DuPont, the US Navy did not have a wealth of experience completing similar projects, and was thus less certain of how much time would be required by the work involved. Unlike the deterministic nature of DuPont's problem, the time estimates associated with the Polaris Missile Project had a probabilistic nature, better expressed as some range of possibilities than as known values. Thus, unlike DuPont's CPM, PERT works with probabilistic task times, modeling initial uncertainty concerning the tasks ahead.

probabilistic
Varying or not well known in advance; subject to randomness. This represents some uncertainty in planning.

Probabilistic Task Times

PERT analysis assumes that uncertainty concerning each task can be modeled by a beta probability distribution. Figure 7.7 displays an example beta distribution, one that represents some task that will most likely require 0.75 day to complete. The fact that the task may require as little as 0.33 day can be interpreted from the point where the mound-shaped beta distribution begins, also known as the *optimistic time* associated with the task. The most likely duration for the task is the value over which the highest point in the beta's curve is located, indicating that this value is assigned the highest probability and is therefore the *most likely time.* A worst case scenario of about 2 days is suggested by the point at which the beta distribution no longer assigns any significant probability of occurrence, where the curve sinks to zero. This represents the *pessimistic time*, or the longest duration that might be witnessed. These three points suggested by a beta distribution—the optimistic, most likely, and pessimistic times—have proven a useful framework for expressing the range of possibilities associated with uncertain tasks. PERT analysis begins by obtaining estimates for each of these three durations for every task in the project.

Analyzing a Network

Although a PERT analysis starts off with three estimates of each task's duration, it then identifies task timings, expected project length, and the critical path in the same fashion demonstrated earlier for CPM. Each of the three estimates is combined into a single

Beta Distribution of a Task Time — FIGURE 7.7

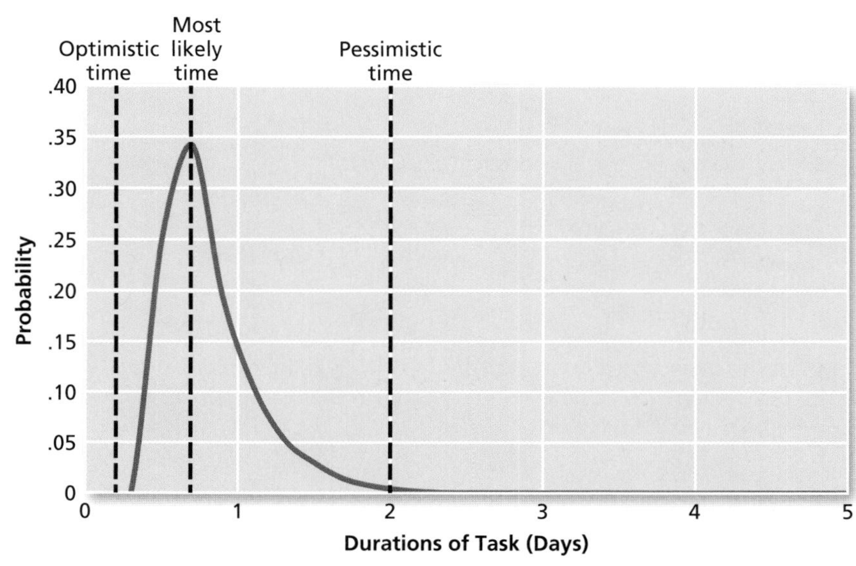

expected value The mathematical expectation of a random variable, calculated as the weighted average of all possible values that may occur.

expected value that represents a task's expected time, which is used in planning. Given an optimistic time (O), a mostly likely time (M), and a pessimistic time (P), we have.

$$\text{Expected task time} = \frac{O + 4M + P}{6}$$

Furthermore, the variance in this distribution of task time can be estimated with the formula:

$$\text{Variance in task time} = \left(\frac{P - O}{6}\right)^2$$

What follows from these calculations is then another application of the technique used in Scenario 1c, as demonstrated in Scenario 3a.

Scenario 3a

PERT Analysis

Epic Scenery Studios is reconsidering its analysis of the San Diego Convention Center (SDCC) trade show project. Epic's technical director has protested Scenario 2's conclusion that Epic must spend an additional $5,300 to complete the project in 7 days. The technical director claims many of the task durations used in the previous analysis represented worst-case estimates and the actual amount of time required is probably less. As a result, the technical director feels the project will "probably take about 7 days to complete" regardless of crashing and thus it is unnecessary for Epic to commit to $5,300 in crashing expenses. The technical director, master carpenter, and lighting director all agree on these more-detailed duration estimates of the nine project tasks:

Task	Description	Optimistic Time (days)	Most Likely Time (days)	Pessimistic Time (days)
A	Create technical drawings	0.5	0.75	1
B	Purchase and dye fabric	1	2	3
C	Build stage	0.5	1.5	4
D	Sew fabric and frame backdrop	1	1.5	2
E	Rent, deliver, and hang lighting at SDCC	0.5	1	1.5
F	Paint stage	1	1.5	2
G	Do trial assembly of stage and backdrop in studio	0.5	0.75	1
H	Disassemble and transport to SDCC	0.5	1	1.5
I	Assemble at SDCC, touch-up paint, and adjust lighting	0.5	1	1.5

Assuming that this project fits the assumptions of PERT analysis reasonably well, what is its expected completion time now? Has the critical path changed from the original path of A-C-F-G-H-I determined in Scenario 1c?

Analysis

The first step in a PERT analysis is to apply the assumption of beta distributed task times to the data provided, calculating an expected time and variance for each task.

PERT CALCULATIONS

Task	Opt. Time (days)	Most Likely Time (days)	Pess. Time (days)	Expected Time (days) $(O + 4M + P)/6$	Variance (days) $((P - O)/6)^2$
A	0.5	0.75	1	$(0.5 + 4 \times 0.75 + 1)/6 = 0.75$	$((1 - 0.5)/6)^2 = 0.0069$
B	1	2	3	$(1 + 4 \times 2 + 3)/6 = 2$	$((3 - 1)/6)^2 = 0.1111$
C	0.5	1.5	4	$(0.5 + 4 \times 1.5 + 4)/6 = 1.75$	$((4 - 0.5)/6)^2 = 0.3403$
D	1	1.5	2	$(1 + 4 \times 1.5 + 2)/6 = 1.5$	$((2 - 1)/6)^2 = 0.0278$
E	0.5	1	1.5	$(0.5 + 4 \times 1 + 1.5)/6 = 1$	$((1.5 - 0.5)/6)^2 = 0.0278$
F	1	1.5	2	$(1 + 4 \times 1.5 + 2)/6 = 1.5$	$((2 - 1)/6)^2 = 0.0278$
G	0.5	0.75	1	$(0.5 + 4 \times 0.75 + 1)/6 = 0.75$	$((1 - 0.5)/6)^2 = 0.0069$
H	0.5	1	1.5	$(0.5 + 4 \times 1 + 1.5)/6 = 1$	$((1.5 - 0.5)/6)^2 = 0.0278$
I	0.5	1	1.5	$(0.5 + 4 \times 1 + 1.5)/6 = 1$	$((1.5 - 0.5)/6)^2 = 0.0278$

At this point, the analysis becomes difficult to distinguish from the earlier work in Scenarios 1a through 1c, consisting of the same basic steps, beginning with the network illustration of the project needed to begin calculation of task timing. Since nothing has changed concerning the identities of the tasks and their precedence relationships, this network will look nearly identical to the one available at the beginning of Scenario 1b. The only difference is highlighted: the duration data staged within each node is the expected completion time calculated earlier.

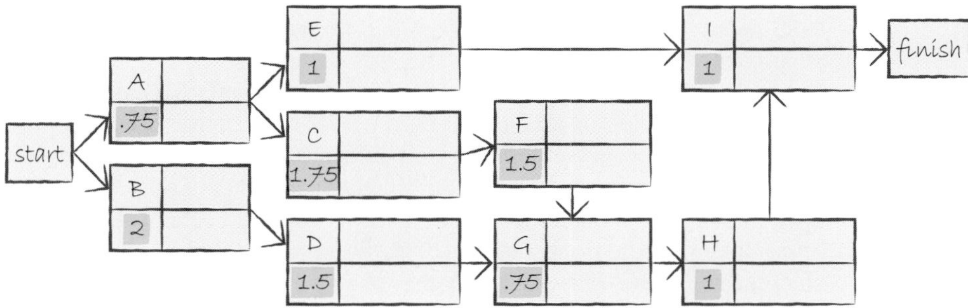

Next, ES/EF times are assigned, although the revised task duration creates somewhat revised timings from those determined earlier in Scenario 1c. As an example, the ES time for task A is still zero, since this task has no immediate predecessors, but the EF time is now 0 + .75 = .75 days. This EF time of A is then passed to tasks E and C to establish their ES times, and the network is completed using the same logic we used during the CPM analysis of Scenario 1c.

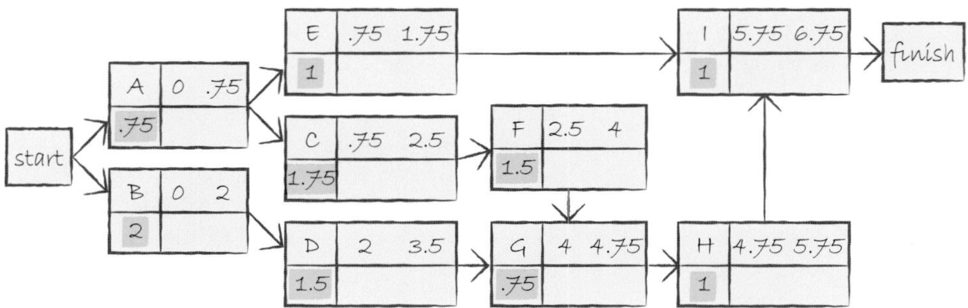

Continues

Insight Since the earliest Epic can expect to finish the project is equivalent to the earliest it can expect to finish task I, the expected completion time of the project, based on this new information concerning task durations, is 6.75 days. To determine the identity of the critical path, the LS/LF times must be determined:

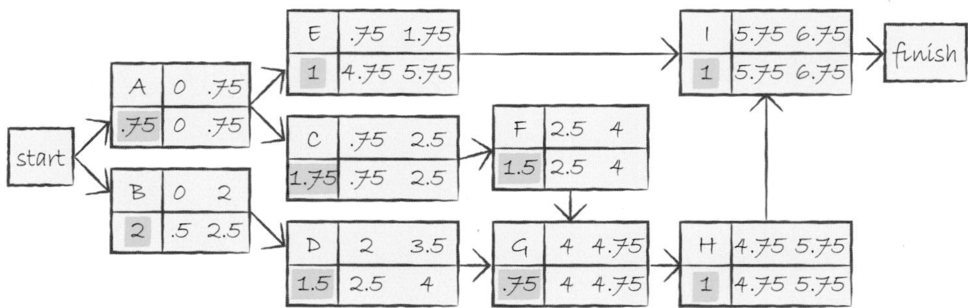

Scanning the diagram reveals those tasks for which early and late timings are identical, which indicates the zero slack of critical path activities. Although the expected completion time of the project is considerably shorter than the 10-day estimate of Scenario 1b, the critical path remains identical to earlier analysis: A-C-F-G-H-I. ■

Estimating Risk

Much of the PERT analysis in Scenario 3a is familiar from the CPM analysis of Epic Scenery Studios' project. Once Epic's technical director revised the task durations, the 7-day deadline on project completion no longer seemed problematic; Scenario 3a concluded that the expected completion time based on the new information was 6.75 days. However, PERT analysis does provide some insight into a project that CPM does not, particularly the risk of not completing a project within given amounts of time. Using Epic Scenery Studios as an example, concluding that the project has an expected completion of 6.75 days does not mean that the project will necessarily be completed in that length of time—it is possible that Epic could be unlucky and experience all pessimistic times when completing tasks, causing it to miss the trade show deadline by several days. What is the risk that Epic might be so unlucky? PERT estimates this risk by harnessing the Central Limit Theorem, which implies that a length of any path through the project, being the combined result of tasks with beta distributed lengths, can itself be represented with a normal distribution. Each path's distribution describes the likelihood of that path requiring a particular length of time to complete, where

Central Limit Theorem The observation that sample values approximate a normal distribution, regardless of the underlying distribution of the population being sampled.

- The mean of the normal distribution that describes a path's length is equal to the sum of the expected times of each task along the path.
- The variance of the normal distribution that describes a path's length is equal to the sum of the variances of each task along the path.

Figure 7.8 displays the three normal distributions suggested by the three paths through Epic Scenery Studios' network, given these two assumptions.

Superimposed on Figure 7.8 is a graphical representation of Epic's 7-day deadline discussed earlier. Although the project's expected completion time of 6.75 days is shorter than the 7-day requirement, Figure 7.8 reveals that a substantial portion of the curve representing potential lengths of critical path A-C-F-G-H-I is to the right of the 7-day deadline, illustrating outcomes in which path A-C-F-G-H-I requires *longer* than 7 days to complete. Since the height of the curve over these values represents the probability of those particular outcomes, the proportion of the total area of A-C-F-G-H-I's normal curve to the

Normal Distributions of the Three Path Lengths

FIGURE 7.8

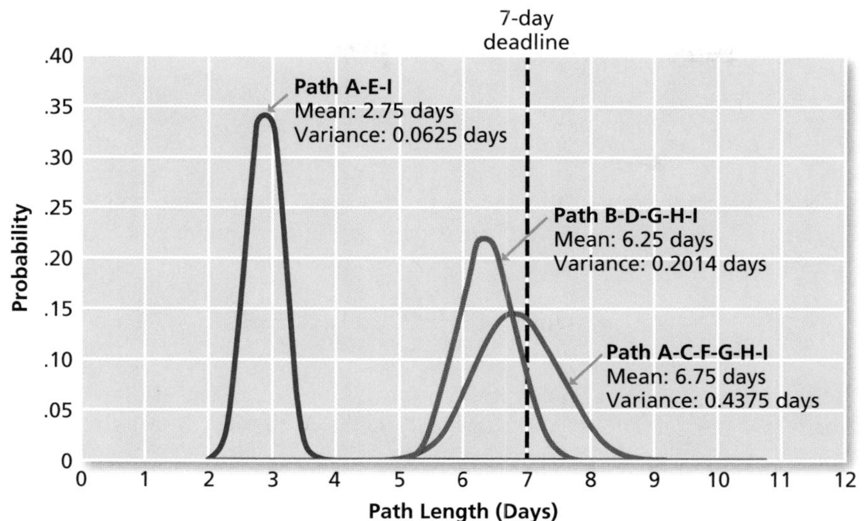

Data from the Epic Scenery Studios project, relative to its 7-day deadline

right of the deadline illustrates the percent risk that the path will run some amount longer than 7 days, missing the deadline. Figure 7.9 illustrates this issue in general, showing that the probability of completing a path within some deadline x can be measured by the area of the curve shaded with tan, to the left of the deadline, while the risk of missing that deadline is represented by the remainder of the normal curves area, shaded in red.

The three normal curves pictured in Figure 7.8 also reveal that critical path A-C-F-G-H-I is not the only path of concern with respect to this deadline; a smaller portion of the curve representing B-D-G-H-I is also on the right-hand side of 7 days, indicating there is a nontrivial risk that this path might violate the deadline.

Epic is concerned with the risk of the project overrunning the 7-day deadline, which is related to the path risk in Figure 7.9 through this principle:

> The probability of completing a project within a certain amount of time is estimated by the *joint* probability of completing all its paths within that certain amount of time.

Normal Distribution of Path Length with Deadline Risk

FIGURE 7.9

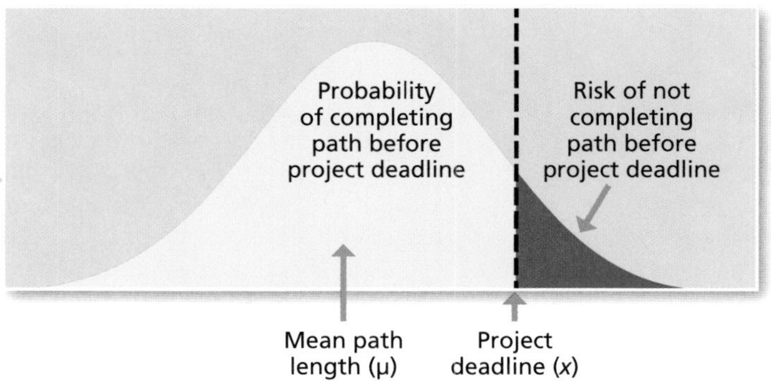

standard normal distribution
A normal distribution with a mean of zero and a variance of 1.

The key to quantifying Epic's overall risk is first calculating the risk associated with each path. This can be determined by translating each normal distribution in Figure 7.8 into its equivalent standard normal distribution, which allows the precise area to the left to be located on any standard normal table. This translation is achieved by calculating the *z*-value of the deadline with the expression

$$z = \frac{x - \mu}{\sigma}$$

where x is the value of interest, μ is the mean of original distribution, and σ is the standard deviation of original distribution (the square root of its variance). In PERT, this general expression can be restated as

$$\text{Path } z\text{-value} = \frac{\text{deadline} - \text{path mean}}{\text{path standard deviation}}$$

To relate these tools to Epic Scenery Studios, recall that path B-D-G-H-I has an expected length of 6.25 days, the sum of the expected lengths of those five tasks. The variance in path B-D-G-H-I is determined by summing the variances of those same five tasks, or $0.1111 + 0.0278 + 0.0069 + 0.0278 + 0.0278 = 0.2014$ days. To compute any *z*-value concerning path B-D-G-H-I requires its standard deviation, determined by taking the square root of 0.2014, or 0.4488. Assuming a deadline of 7 days, the corresponding *z*-value for path B-D-G-H-I would be

$$\text{Path B-D-G-H-I } z\text{-value} = \frac{7 - 6.25}{0.4488} = 1.67$$

Appendix B at the back of this book displays the area of a standard normal curve to the left of any *z*-value between zero and 3.0. This table indicates that .9525, or approximately 95% of the curve, lies to the left of 1.67, which can be interpreted as a 95% probability of path B-D-G-H-I being completed within 7 days. However, the risk associated with the overall project is the combined result of all its paths, not simply B-D-G-H-I. Furthermore, the underlying theory of joint probability assumes that the paths are *independent* of one another, which is not true in the case of Epic's SDCC project. Any paths sharing an activity are linked by their common risk exposure to that activity, and thus these path behaviors cannot be assumed independent. As a result, the joint probability of completing these sorts of paths within a particular deadline is not only an estimate of the project's probability of completion by that same deadline, it is likely to be a somewhat optimistic *over*estimate of that probability. Thus, caution must be exercised when interpreting this estimate, as we see in Scenario 3b.

Scenario 3b

Estimating Risk

Scenario 3a appears to confirm the technical director's argument that there is no need to spend any money on crashing tasks within the SDCC project, because the expected completion time without extra spending is 6.75 days and the client needs the project finished in 7 days. However, there is still concern among Epic Scenery Studios' management, due to the extremely time-sensitive nature of this type of project. The estimate of 6.75 days is based on some uncertainty as to precisely how long many of the tasks will take, and if those tasks actually require pessimistic times to complete, the project would then run much longer. In the case of the SDCC project, missing the 7-day deadline means missing the opening of the trade show being held at SDCC, which would be disastrous for the client.

If Epic proceeds with the project without further arrangements, the expected completion time is 6.75 days. What, however, is the probability that Epic will finish *within* 6.75 days? Furthermore, what is the risk that Epic will *not* finish in time to meet the 7-day deadline?

Analysis

There are two important but similar questions, one concerning the risk associated with 6.75 days and one concerning the risk associated with 7 days. Recalling that, the probability that a project will be completed within a certain amount of time is estimated by the joint probability of all the project paths being completed within that certain amount of time, we must first calculate the probabilities associated with the paths. We do this by calculating a *z*-score for each path and then consulting the appropriate *z*-table for the corresponding probability, such as in the case of 6.75 days.

PERT PATH PROBABILITIES (6.75 DAYS)

Path Name	Path Mean (days)	Path Standard Dev. (days)	z-score	Probability of Completion in 6.75 Days*
A-E-I	2.75	0.25	(6.75 − 2.75)/0.25 = 16	1.0 (100%)
A-C-F-G-H-I	6.75	0.66	(6.75 − 6.75)/0.66 = 0.00	.5000 (50%)
B-D-G-H-I	6.25	0.45	(6.75 − 6.25)/0.45 = 1.11	.8665 (86.65%)

*These probabilities are from the z-table in Appendix B. In the case of path A-E-I, because the z-score is greater than 3.0, the probability is assumed to be 100%.

Since the probability of completing the project in 6.75 days is estimated by the joint probability of completing each of the three paths in that time, we calculate this probability by multiplying each of the individual probabilities together:

ESTIMATED PROBABILITY EPIC PROJECT COMPLETED IN 6.75 DAYS

1.0 × .5000 × .8665 = .4333, or 43.33%

Thus, even though the so-called expected completion time of the project is 6.75 days, there is no better than a 43% chance that Epic will finish in that time. The probability should be better in the case of 7 days (it is a more generous amount of time). We determined this with the same steps:

PERT PATH PROBABILITIES (7 DAYS)

Path Name	Path Mean (days)	Path Standard Dev. (days)	z-score	Probability of Completion in 7 Days
A-E-I	2.75	0.25	(7 − 2.75)/0.25 = 17	1.0 (100%)
A-C-F-G-H-I	6.75	0.66	(7 − 6.75)/0.66 = 0.38	.648 (64.8%)
B-D-G-H-I	6.25	0.45	(7 − 6.25)/0.45 = 1.67	.9525 (95.25%)

ESTIMATED PROBABILITY EPIC PROJECT COMPLETED IN 7 DAYS

1.0 × .648 × .9525 = .6172, or 61.72%

Continues

Before concluding the analysis, we recall that the second question asked above concerned the risk that Epic will *not* finish in 7 days. We can answer this question with one further calculation:

ESTIMATED PROBABILITY EPIC PROJECT *NOT* COMPLETED IN 7 DAYS

1.0 − .6172 = .3828, or 38.28%

Insight If Epic begins immediately, there is no better than a 43% chance it will finish within the project's expected completion time of 6.75 days. Furthermore, there is at least a 38% risk that Epic will not be able to complete the project within the client's 7-day deadline. ■

Even though the expected completion time of Epic's project is 6.75 days, the PERT analysis in Scenario 3b indicates a substantial risk (38%) that the project may take longer than 7 days. Moreover, this risk may be understated by these calculations, because PERT methodology relies on an additional assumption that is not true in the case of Epic's project—path independence. In reality, the three paths in Epic's project network all share tasks with each other. For example, a single delay in task I would impact the length of all three paths in the project, and thus their individual lengths are not strongly independent of each other.

Simulation modeling can explore this risk more accurately, as shown in Figure 7.10, a spreadsheet model of Epic's SDCC project. Simulation models attempt to imitate the actual project by choosing task durations at random and using those values to calculate task timings within the project. This allows the project, a one-time undertaking, to be repeated hundreds or thousands of times in the simulation, and data gathered on outcomes of interest. This also allows path dependencies to be modeled explicitly, something that PERT methodology cannot provide. However, in the case of Epic's SDCC project, the spreadsheet simulation in Figure 7.10 suggests that the traditional PERT estimates are only slightly optimistic, with the actual probability of finishing within 7 days closer to 58%, compared to PERT's original estimate of 61.72%.

Project management might be the most universal form of operations management. Projects appear in all sizes and in all areas, from personal projects to massive industrial constructions. Any product can be argued to have started as a project, as new product development and entrepreneurism are both distinctly project-intensive. In fact, opportunity itself generally appears as a form of project, being an invitation to explore some beneficial direction for the first time. Regardless of whether we work in a project-related industry, the techniques of project management are worthy additions to our toolkit.

FIGURE 7.10 Sample Views of Spreadsheet Simulation

Data from the Epic Scenery Studios project

	A	B	C	D	E	F	G	H	I	J	K	L	M	N	O	P	Q
1		Task A -			Task B -			Task C -			Task D -			Task E -			Task F -
2	Replication	ES	Duration	EF	ES	Duration	EF	ES	Duration	EF	ES	Duration	EF	ES	Duration	EF	ES
3	1	0.00	0.78	0.78	0.00	2.48	2.48	0.78	2.36	3.14	2.48	1.12	3.60	0.78	1.20	1.98	3.14
4	2	0.00	0.72	0.72	0.00	2.07	2.07	0.72	2.08	2.80	2.07	1.20	3.27	0.72	0.84	1.56	2.80
5	3	0.00	0.73	0.73	0.00	1.40	1.40	0.73	1.76	2.49	1.40	1.35	2.75	0.73	1.32	2.05	2.49
6	4	0.00	0.73	0.73	0.00	1.97	1.97	0.73	0.75	1.48	1.97	1.45	3.42	0.73	1.17	1.90	1.48
7	5	0.00	0.69	0.69	0.00	2.06	2.06	0.69	2.05	2.74	2.06	1.33	3.39	0.69	1.11	1.81	2.74
8	6	0.00	0.84	0.84	0.00	1.55	1.55	0.84	1.76	2.61	1.55	1.55	3.10	0.84	0.97	1.81	2.61
9	7	0.00	0.72	0.72	0.00	2.03	2.03	0.72	1.20	1.92	2.03	1.42	3.45	0.72	0.84	1.56	1.92
10	8	0.00	0.59	0.59	0.00	2.25	2.25	0.59	1.11	1.70	2.25	1.43	3.68	0.59	0.89	1.48	1.70
11																	
12																	
13																	
14																	
15																	
16																	
17																	

	P	Q	R	S	T	U	V	W	X	Y	Z	AA	AB	AC	AD	AE	AF
1		Task F -			Task G -			Task H -			Task I -			Length of			
2	EF	ES	Duration	EF	ES	Duration	EF	ES	Duration	EF	ES	Duration	EF	Project			
3	1.60	2.73	1.56	4.29	4.29	0.78	5.07	5.07	0.68	5.75	5.75	0.98	6.73	6.73		Average Length	
4	1.60	2.61	1.77	4.38	4.38	0.70	5.08	5.08	1.05	6.13	6.13	0.91	7.04	7.04		of Project (Days):	
5	1.59	3.55	1.40	4.95	4.95	0.79	5.74	5.74	1.13	6.87	6.87	0.90	7.76	7.76			6.88
6	1.34	3.08	1.38	4.46	4.46	0.58	5.04	5.04	0.81	5.86	5.86	1.17	7.02	7.02			
7	1.97	2.79	1.27	4.06	4.06	0.84	4.89	4.89	1.06	5.95	5.95	0.85	6.80	6.80		Probability of Completion	
8	1.81	1.84	1.75	3.60	3.60	0.86	4.45	4.45	0.83	5.28	5.28	1.00	6.28	6.28		in 7 Days:	
9	1.49	2.41	1.31	3.72	3.72	0.69	4.41	4.41	1.17	5.58	5.58	1.07	6.65	6.65			61%
10	1.38	2.81	1.77	4.58	4.58	0.62	5.20	5.20	0.88	6.08	6.08	1.02	7.11	7.11			
11	1.65	3.48	1.38	4.87	4.87	0.75	5.61	5.61	1.12	6.73	6.73	1.01	7.75	7.75			
12	1.59	2.91	1.65	4.56	4.56	0.69	5.25	5.25	1.10	6.34	6.34	0.98	7.33	7.33			
13	1.52	3.85	1.64	5.49	5.49	0.74	6.23	6.23	0.93	7.16	7.16	1.09	8.25	8.25			
14	1.45	1.83	1.45	3.28	3.28	0.81	4.09	4.09	0.71	4.80	4.80	0.94	5.74	5.74			
15	1.71	1.49	1.29	2.78	4.05	0.76	4.81	4.81	0.98	5.79	5.79	0.92	6.71	6.71			
16	1.97	2.03	1.35	3.37	3.98	0.67	4.65	4.65	0.82	5.47	5.47	1.18	6.65	6.65			
17	1.44	2.83	1.62	4.45	4.45	0.73	5.18	5.18	0.74	5.92	5.92	1.22	7.14	7.14			

SUMMARY

Project management is the one sector of operations not dedicated to the sustained creation of value, but to the successful completion of unique endeavors. Projects are sets of tasks that must be completed to achieve some one-time objective within a limited amount of time, although projects can vary widely in terms of their sensitivity to deadlines and their vulnerability to influences outside of the project manager's control. Event management and incident management are particularly challenging examples of project management in this regard.

While some industries are based on project management, any organization can expect to undertake some form of project periodically. One popular project methodology, the critical path method (CPM), was developed by a manufacturing firm otherwise engaged in ongoing operations. DuPont's CPM provides a useful visual framework for analyzing the many component tasks of a project as well as a convenient means of identifying its critical path, the particular subset of tasks responsible for the project's overall length.

DuPont's high degree of experience with manufacturing overhaul projects is reflected in CPM's treatment of project task times as fixed, extremely predictable values. In reality, task times are not always fixed: options often exist to speed task completion, a treatment known as crashing. Even if the option of crashing is not complicating project planning, there is often less certainty over potential task times than implied by CPM. Higher degrees of uncertainty are incorporated into the otherwise similar project methodology known as PERT (project evaluation and review technique). PERT provides the same insights into project completion as CPM, but also provides a means of estimating overall risks associated with projects subject to greater uncertainty. Selection of an approach is ultimately a judgment made by the project planner, who would have the best sense of the nature of the particular unique endeavor being analyzed.

Key Terms

AOA
AON
backward scheduling
Central Limit Theorem
CPM
crashing
critical path
deterministic
expected value
forward scheduling
Gantt chart
immediate predecessor
incident
iterative planning
milestone
path
PERT
precedence relationship
probabilistic
project
slack
standard normal distribution
WBS

Discussion Questions

1. Critical path methodology allows managers to focus on a group of tasks within a project. What is a potential disadvantage of this methodology?
2. How are projects and customized products related?
3. It is said that a delay in critical path activity will delay the project, while a delay in a noncritical path activity will not necessarily delay the project. Explain the need to specify "not necessarily."
4. Would a project with 100 tasks always be more challenging to manage than a different project with only 20 tasks? Why or why not?

PROBLEMS

Short answers appear in Appendix A. Go to **NoteShaper.com** for full video tutorials on each question.

Minute Answer

1. Is the critical path the shortest or longest path through a project network?
2. If task A is an immediate predecessor of task B, what must be true about the scheduled timing of these two tasks?
3. What is the total amount of slack in all critical path activities?
4. PERT assumes that individual task times can be modeled with what type of probability distribution?
5. PERT assumes that path lengths through a network can be modeled with what type of probability distribution?
6. When crashing a project, a manager generally focuses on which activities first?
7. A point of significance in the time line or history of a project is referred to as a what?
8. Which technique better reflects uncertainty in project management, PERT or CPM?
9. If the early start time of a critical path activity is 7, what is its late start time?
10. If the early start time of a task is 4 days and its early finish time is 6 days, how long is this task?
11. If tasks are always finished on their deadlines and never earlier, is this timing known as forward or backward scheduling?
12. If a noncritical path activity is crashed, what happens to the overall duration of the project?

Quick Start

13. Task C has two immediate predecessors, tasks A and B. Task A has an early finish time of 3 days, and task B has an early finish time of 5 days. What is the early start time of task C?
14. Task C has two immediate predecessors, tasks A and B. Task A has an early finish time of 3 days, and task B has an early finish time of 5 days. Task C is 2 days long. What is the early finish time of task C?
15. Task C has two immediate followers, tasks D and E. Task D has a late start time of 10 days and task E has a late start time of 8 days. What is the late finish time of task C?
16. Task C has two immediate followers, tasks D and E. Task D has a late start time of 10 days and task E has a late start time of 8 days. Task C is 2 days long. What is the late start time of task C?
17. Task E has an early start time of 3 days and an early finish time of 5 days, while it also has a late start time of 10 days and a late finish time of 12 days from now. What is the slack in task E?
18. Task A has an optimistic time of 3 days, a mostly likely time of 4 days, and a pessimistic time of 10 days. What are the expected time and the variance in task A?
19. A project consists of four tasks: A, B, C, and D. Task A must be completed before B and C are started, and task C must be completed before task D is started. How many paths are in this network?
20. A project consists of four tasks: A, B, C, and D. Task A must be completed before B and C are started, and task C must be completed before task D is started. Each task takes 1 day to complete. What is the duration of this project?

Ramp Up

21. A project network has a total of four paths running through it. These four paths vary in length, from a minimum of 4 days long to a maximum of 18 days long. How long will this project take to complete?

22. There are four activities on the critical path, and these activities have standard deviations of 1, 2, 4, and 2 days, respectively. What is the standard deviation of this critical path?

23. A project network has two paths running through it. The first path has an expected length of 10 days and a variance of 2 days. The second path has an expected length of 11 days and a variance of 1 day. What is the probability that this project can be completed in 12 days?

24. A project network has two paths running through it. The first path has an expected length of 10 days and a variance of 2 days. The second path has an expected length of 11 days and a variance of 1 day. What is the probability that this project will require *more than* 14 days to complete?

25. Path A-B-E has a 55% probability of being completed within 3 weeks. Path C-D-F has a 90% probability of being completed within 3 weeks. If these are the only two paths in a project network, what is the probability the project will be completed in 3 weeks?

26. A certain office building must be renovated and then sold. Renovation of similar buildings has taken an average of 4 weeks, with a standard deviation of 1 week. Once placed on the market after renovation, buildings like this one take an average of 10 weeks to sell, with a standard deviation of 2 weeks. Assuming that renovation is started now, what is the probability this office building would be sold within the next 15 weeks?

Scenarios

Reminder: Short answers appear in Appendix A. Go to **NoteShaper.com** for full video tutorials on each question.

27. Consider the following project management problem:

Task	Immediate Predecessor(s)	Duration (days)
A	None	2
B	None	4
C	None	8
D	A	1
E	B, D	6
F	D	2

a. What is the expected completion time of this project?

b. What is the critical path through this project?

28. Consider the project information in the table below:

Activities	Duration (days)	Immediate Predecessor(s)
A	11	None
B	10	None
C	8	None
D	13	A
E	10	B
F	10	B
G	2	B
H	6	C
I	7	G, H
J	8	D, E

Draw and analyze a project network diagram to answer the following questions:

a. If you were to start on this project, which are the activities that you could start on at the very beginning of the project?

b. How many paths are there in this project network?

c. What is the critical path through this network? What is the completion time of this project?

d. What is the earliest that activity G can possibly be completed?

e. What is the most that activity F can be delayed in starting, without delaying the project?

29. Consider the following project, which consists of 10 tasks:

Task	Completion Time (days)	Immediate Predecessors
A	6	None
B	2	None
C	3	A
D	5	A
E	3	A
F	2	C
G	3	E
H	4	B, E
I	2	H
J	2	F, G, I

a. What is the critical path through this network? What is the completion time of this project?

b. What is the slack in task F?

c. Suppose the project has just been started. What is the longest you could delay beginning work on activity A without delaying the completion of the project?

d. Suppose someone tells you they could get activity C done in 1 day, instead of the 3 days you were planning on. Of course, they expect a bonus for this. What is your reaction?

30. Mega Mart Store is a discount department store badly in need of renovation. To avoid loss of sales and disruption of customer shopping habits, Mega Mart wants to complete this renovation without closing the store itself, by temporarily colocating goods from one area of the store into another, creating open spaces for renovation and reoccupation. Mega Mart is divided into four basic areas of goods: clothing, electronics, housewares, and foodstuffs. Each of these areas needs to be temporarily moved, as described in the tasks below:

Activity	Description	Immediate Predecessor(s)	Estimated Length of Activity (days)
A	Colocate clothing in electronics area	None	3
B	Renovate old clothing area	A	4
C	Return clothing to renovated area	B	2
D	Colocate housewares in foodstuffs area	None	5
E	Renovate old housewares area	D	4
F	Return housewares to renovated area	E	1
G	Colocate electronics in clothing area	B	3
H	Renovate old electronics area	C, G	6
I	Return electronics to renovated area	H	2
J	Colocate foodstuffs in housewares area	E	3
K	Renovate old foodstuffs area	F, J	4
L	Return foodstuffs to renovated area	K	3

a. What are the paths through a project network diagram describing Mega Mart's project data?

b. Suppose Mega Mart starts on this project immediately, to finish as soon as possible. How much time will be required to complete this project?

c. What is the critical path through this project?

d. What is the slack in activity C?

e. Assume the project is started immediately. What is the soonest activity H can possibly be started from now?

f. Assume the project is started immediately. What is the latest that Mega Mart can finish returning housewares to its newly renovated area without creating any delay in the overall project completion time?

31. Consider the following project network, with task duration data provided:

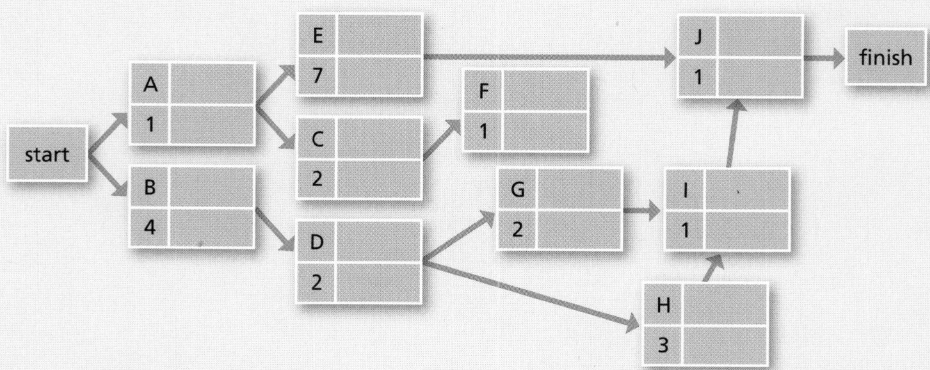

Please answer the following questions, based on your analysis of this diagram.

a. What is the critical path through this network?
b. What is the completion time for this project?
c. What is the slack in activity A?
d. All tasks longer than 1 day can be crashed to as little as 1 day, although prices vary. Task B costs $600 per day to crash, while task H costs $200 per day, and all other eligible tasks cost $100 per day. Which tasks should be crashed to shorten this project to 8 days? How much will this cost?

32. Jersey Warehouse packs and ships customer orders for three large online retailers. Jersey Warehouse normally operates continuously, but is planning to shut down next week to replace its computer servers. This highly sensitive project consists of four tasks, described in the table below:

Task	Description	Immediate Predecessors	Optimistic Time (hours)	Most Likely Time (hours)	Pessimistic Time (hours)
A	Shut down warehouse system and remove old servers from server room	None	1	2	3
B	Install new computer servers in server room	A	2	4	6
C	Reconfigure warehouse terminals	None	2	4	6
D	Reboot warehouse system and run diagnostics	B and C	1	2	9

Please answer the following questions, based on this information:

a. What is the expected completion time of this project?
b. What is the latest that Jersey Warehouse can delay beginning the reconfiguration of the warehouse terminals, without delaying the overall project?
c. Suppose that Jersey Warehouse plans to stop warehouse operations and start this project at 1:00 a.m. next Monday morning. Which of the following is the closest to the probability that Jersey Warehouse will finish the project and be back in operation by 11:00 a.m. the same day?

CASE STUDY: DALVEY POINT STORM WATER UPGRADE PROJECT

Summerline Contracting has just been awarded the Dalvey Point Storm Water Upgrade Project, a major and time-sensitive contract worth several million dollars. The Dalvey Point area is a retail district in a busy city center, drawing its name from the distinctive Dalvey Point Shopping Center at the intersection of Dalvey and Tanglin roads, labeled location 7 in the map below. Each of the three roads pictured must be closed to traffic at some point in the project, as Summerline Contracting installs storm water drainage culverts deep beneath street level to address recent problems with seasonal flooding in the basements of some Dalvey Point area buildings.

Dalvey Point Project Map

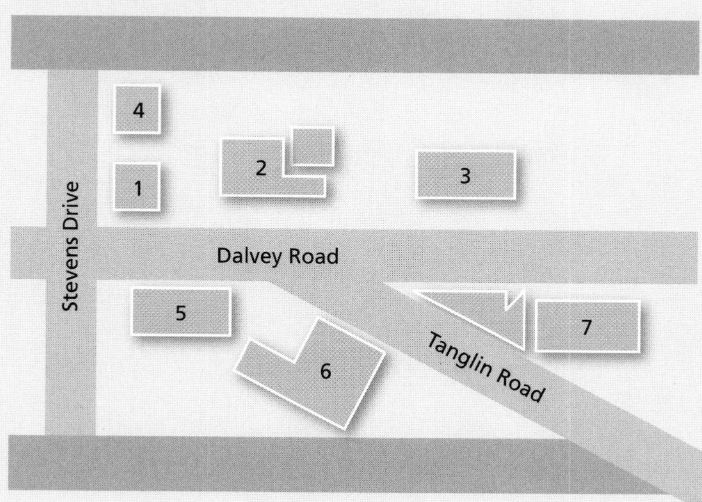

During road closure, Dalvey has agreed in its contract to provide the local vendors hardship payments of $10,000 a day for each weekday their road is closed, and $20,000 for each Saturday or Sunday. Vendors 1 and 4 are each entitled to payments when Stevens Drive is closed, while vendor 6 is entitled to those same payments when Tanglin Road is closed. The remaining four vendors pictured in the map, including Dalvey Point Shopping Center, are entitled to payment from Summerline while Dalvey Road is closed. Each road must be closed while work is completed on three of the four tasks required there:

Typical Four Stages of Activity

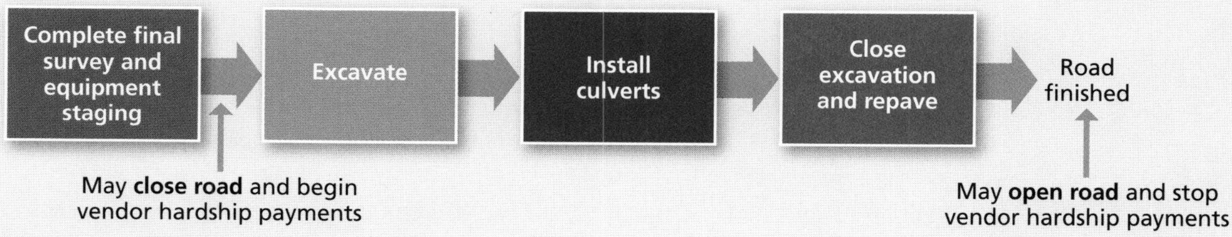

When to close or open a road is usually determined by the start of excavation and the finish of repaving on that road. But there is one important complication: while each road can be shut down separately, Tanglin Road must be closed the entire time Dalvey Road is closed, even if it is not being worked on. (If Tanglin Road were open but Dalvey Road closed, traffic on Tanglin Road would have no way to turn around at Dalvey Point.) Summerline has been experimenting with PERT and has employed its conceptual model to develop the time estimates shown in the Task Data table.

Task Data

Task Abbrev.	Task Description	Immediate Predecessor	Optimistic Time (days)	Most Likely Time (days)	Pessimistic Time (days)
STVNS-1	Complete final survey and equipment staging for Stevens Drive	None	1	2	3
STVNS-2	Excavate Stevens Drive	STVNS-1	2	4	6
STVNS-3	Install Stevens Drive culverts	STVNS-2	1	2	3
STVNS-4	Close excavation and repave Stevens Drive	STVNS-3	1	2	3
DLVY-1	Complete final survey and equipment staging for Dalvey Road	None	1	2	3
DLVY-2	Excavate Dalvey Road	DLVY-1	5	7	9
DLVY-3	Install Dalvey Road culverts	DLVY-2	5	7	9
DLVY-4	Close excavation and repave Dalvey Road	DLVY-3	2	4	6
TNGN-1	Complete final survey and equipment staging for Tanglin Road	None	1	2	3
TNGN-2	Excavate Tanglin Road	TNGN-1	1	3	11
TNGN-3	Install Tanglin Road culverts	TNGN-2	2	4	12
TNGN-4	Close excavation and repave Tanglin Road	TNGN-3	1	3	11

While any work on any of the three roads can be scheduled simultaneously, Summerline would prefer that its own management team perform the final surveys and staging arrangements for each road. As a result, it strongly prefers that the tasks abbreviated STVNS-1, DLVY-1, and TNGN-1 not overlap in time, so that the same team can complete all three.

Questions

1. Using PERT analysis, how long do you estimate the Dalvey Point Storm Water Upgrade Project will require, and what is the probability that Summerline Contracting will be finished in that time?
2. Prepare a Gantt chart indicating your recommendations for the timings for each of the tasks, as well the road closures and reopenings.
3. On what day of the week would you recommend Summerline Contracting begin this project? Based on your recommendation and the expected task times from PERT, how much should Summerline budget for vendor hardship payments?

BIBLIOGRAPHY

Anderson, D., D. Sweeney, and T. Williams. 2005. *An Introduction to Management Science: Quantitative Approaches to Decision Making,* 11th ed. Mason, OH: South-Western/ Thomson Learning.

Austin, R., and L. Devin. 2003. *Artful Making: What Managers Need to Know About How Artists Work.* Upper Saddle River, NJ: FT Prentice Hall.

Bowdin, G., J. Allen, W. O'Toole, R. Harris, and I. McDonnell. 2011. *Events Management,* 3rd ed. Oxford: Elsevier Butterworth-Heinemann.

Crawford, L., and J. Pollack. 2004. "Hard and Soft Projects: A Framework for Analysis." *International Journal of Project Management* 22: 645–53.

Gass, S., and A. Assad. 2005. *An Annotated Timeline of Operations Research: An Informal History.* New York: Kluwer Academic Publishers.

Simpson, N. 2006. Modeling of Residential Structure Fire Response: Exploring the Hyper-Project. *Journal of Operations Management* 24(5): 530–41.

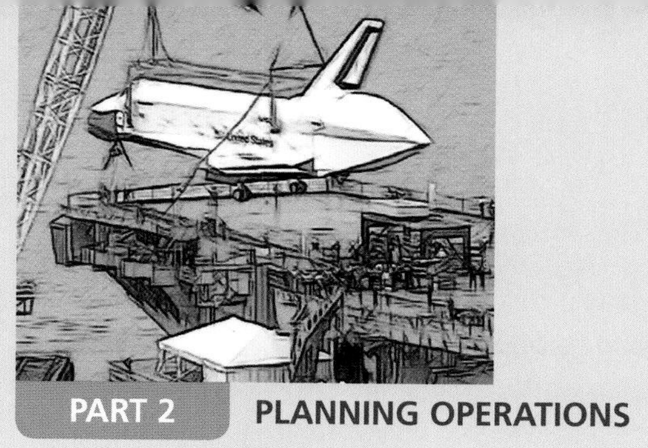

PART 2 PLANNING OPERATIONS

CHAPTER 8

Location Planning and Logistics

You can't have everything. Where would you put it?
—Steven Wright

MAJOR SECTIONS

IN THIS CHAPTER, LOOK FOR...

- Facility location with respect to inputs and outputs, as well as factors specific to the site.
- Three location planning techniques—center of gravity, factor rating, and cost versus volume analysis.
- Logistical links among locations that create larger supply chain networks.
- Various modes of logistics, including their relative strengths and weaknesses.

INTRODUCTION

Planning for location and logistics are two cornerstone activities of strategic operations management, balancing complex and even conflicting concerns that may shape a system for years into the future. Location and logistics also depend heavily on each other. Many existing locations are clear logistical choices, such as how major cities worldwide are located on an ocean shore or a waterway. Businesses face similar issues when deciding where to open, as well as how and what to move to and from what location. Larger supply chains form as business locations link up through logistics, creating larger systems to deliver value to consumers. All this complexity begins with a single organization choosing a certain location.

FORCES INFLUENCING LOCATION

geographic information system (GIS) A database for analyzing and presenting information about a location.

The geographic location of a facility is often best explained as a compromise between differing forces of influence over the original location decision. The increasing sophistication and availability of GIS software assists decision makers in considering the merits of potential locations, allowing many different issues to be visualized and considered simultaneously. These issues of influence can be organized into three categories relating back to the original model of operations, as shown in Figure 8.1.

Input Factors

Input-related factors are issues of resource availability from the perspective of the operation being located. Large hospitals are often colocated with large universities, partially assuring the availability of skilled health care professionals. School districts gather data on the location of their most important input—students—when locating new facilities, while many manufacturing firms seek the availability of low-cost labor when considering locations for a new factory. In extreme cases, the location of an operation may be determined almost exclusively by the issue of input, such as establishing the site of a coal

FIGURE 8.1 Forces Influencing the Location of a Facility

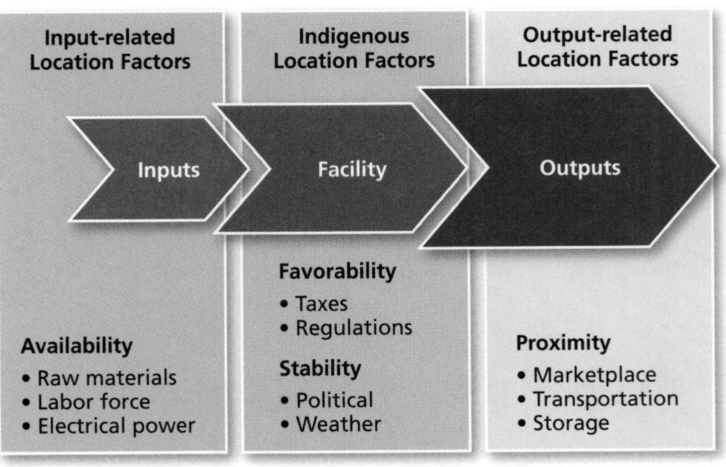

Locating the Global Population

At a strategic level, many operations logically locate in populated areas, and half of the world's population is located within 3% of its land area. This urban concentration is found along rivers or coastal regions, making waterfront a reliable city feature, as in this partial view of Tokyo. Concerns over potential global climate change have highlighted the fact that even a small rise in the world's sea level would severely impact most of its human population.

mining operation or a hydroelectric dam. More often, however, the location is some comprimise between input and other factors.

Output Factors

An output-related location factor is some issue of proximity to demand. Service systems that require the customer as an input are arguably the most heavily influenced by such factors, because the service product must be created in a facility convenient to the customer. This increases the strength of the issue of proximity to clients, such as in the school district example. When locating a facility, a public school district is simultaneously considering the location of school-aged students (input) and which location will benefit best from its service (output), which is identified by the presence of the same group of students. Other examples of this doubled influence of the customer's location are the high concentration of gas stations at the interchange ramps to busy highways and the scarcity of large hospitals in rural areas.

Manufacturers feel the influence of output factors when considering the cost of transporting products to market. As a result, how easily a particular tangible product is shipped often explains the relative distance of its factory to its market. Goods that are delicate, time-sensitive, or otherwise perishable are often produced at a location in close proximity to customer demand. As an example, potato chips purchased at a convenience store will likely have been produced within long-haul driving distance of that store, whereas the electronic components in a tablet computer are more likely to have traveled across the globe before arrival in a retail store. In certain cases, organizations may consider storage of output before sale, such as a natural gas distributor's desire to locate its storage tanks away from densely populated areas, due to the very small possibility of a major accident there.

Indigenous Factors

Indigenous factors are specific to a certain location and are usually issues of favorability of the immediate environment. For example, a location may be logistically convenient and offer abundant resources yet fail to be selected by an organization because the local taxes are deemed too high. Here are some other indigenous factors weighed in site selection:

- Nature and degree of government regulation and taxation required at the site.
- Ecological infrastructure, including the presence of wetlands, wildlife habitat, and aquifer recharge areas.
- Views from the site, scenic or unsightly.
- Favorability of the weather, including the likelihood of future weather-related disruptions, such as hurricanes and severe snowstorms.

In some cases, an organization may consider all factors discussed so far, carefully select the best location for its purposes, and then have this selection disputed by yet another important indigenous factor: the acceptance of local residents. As an example, wind turbine facilities for electrical generation are obviously located where their primary input blows in abundance. However, successfully locating a wind farm is not as simple as securing adequate acreage in a particularly windy area. At some locations, residents have blocked wind farm installation, objecting primarily to the change in the landscape created by the wind turbines. This lack of acceptance of a new facility is often called a NIMBY movement, for not in my backyard. Factories, shopping centers, mental health facilities, highways, and prisons are all examples of new facilities whose potential location might create a substantial NIMBY reaction.

NIMBY
Not in my backyard; a grass-roots political effort to block the planned location of a facility by area residents.

Globalization

Input, output, and indigenous factors in location planning often present themselves in the context of a fourth influence felt by many larger organizations, the increasing opportunities and pressures of globalization. Many large organizations have extended their operations throughout the globe, selecting and linking locations across international borders. The volume of goods crossing the world's oceans has more than tripled since the 1970s, as manufacturers invest in increasingly dispersed sites for production and wholesale purchasers shop a greater diversity of sources. Interestingly, globalization of operations does not appear to be the immediate destiny of all large organizations, as not all industries have met with the same degree of success in linking operations across borders. Retailing is a surprising example of one industry in which even large organizations appear to benefit first from a strong home market, as the top retailers within most countries are local to their respective countries. Nonetheless, location planning is central to success in retailing at the operational level, and the opportunities of global procurement link these national networks with international supply chain networks.

LOCATION PLANNING TECHNIQUES

A location planner must weigh a mix of factors governing the issue of the best location, and a number of analytical techniques can assist in this type of study. We discuss here three well-known location planning techniques: center of gravity, factor rating, and cost versus volume analysis. Each of these techniques has differing requirements, dictating its appropriateness in various situations.

Center of Gravity

Center of gravity is a relatively simple technique that suggests the optimal location for a facility, given a set of known locations that this new facility will serve. Example applications include locating a distribution center to serve retail outlets, locating a central catering facility to serve cafeterias, and locating a specialty medical clinic or lab to serve several different communities.

While the center of gravity technique is convenient, it is best applied only when these requirements are met:

- The entire service area is comfortably represented by a flat map. A service area that spans the globe cannot be relevantly flattened enough to use center of gravity.
- No dramatic changes in service are anticipated in the future.
- The cost of service to each known location is a linear function of distance traveled and degree of service, such as total amount to be shipped.

If the service area is within a certain size and the planning environment is reasonably stable, the first two requirements are met fairly easily. But meeting the third criteria

Measuring Distance in Urban Landscapes

Distance is often the issue in location planning, but distance can be measured in more than one way. Some location planning techniques logically assume Euclidean distance, or the length of the shortest path between two points. Unfortunately, this does not always describe travel between any two points, particularly within a city. This view across a residential sector of Singapore features the grid patterns typical of travel through city streets, which is better measured by rectilinear distance. Center of gravity, ironically, uses neither Euclidean nor rectilinear distance, assuming instead that the squared Euclidean distance between each destination and the optimal center is a reasonable estimate of the inconvenience of travel between them.

of linearity might still prove problematic. Today's broader service areas may span international borders and several modes of transportation. In the case of the distribution of goods, distribution costs can increase sharply at each crossing, due to delays in customs. Likewise, switching modes of transportation (i.e., trucking, rail, air freight, and/or maritime shipping) also changes cost rates, creating nonlinear jumps in expense.

If, however, the service area appears reasonably free from potential complications in linearity of cost, center of gravity can quickly identify a target location for the new facility. We begin by imposing an (X,Y) coordinate grid over the service area and translating the known locations into (X,Y) coordinates. If each location requires the same level of service, then identifying the optimal location for the central facility is accomplished by averaging all location coordinates, as in Scenario 1a.

Center of Gravity (Simple Case)

Scenario 1a

Global Freightways provides airfreight shipping services, operating a fleet of 56 airplanes and 220 freight depots adjacent to airports throughout the world. Currently, Global must identify the optimal location for a new IT Support Center, or ITSC. This new ITSC will house Global's computer network servers and serve as the headquarters for IT field technicians who will travel to five freight depots in the eastern half of North America for computer equipment upgrades and repairs. Figure 8.2 displays a map of this service area, over which a grid is drawn, allowing the assignment of these (X,Y) coordinates to each of the depots:

Freight Depot	*X*	*Y*
YYZ (Toronto Pearson)	2.5	18.5
BUF (Buffalo/Niagara Falls)	3.5	17
RDU (Raleigh/Durham)	5	10.5
ATL (Atlanta Hartsfield)	1	8.5
SFB (Orlando Sanford)	3.5	4

Assuming the degree of service required of the ITSC by each depot is equal, what is the optimal location for the new ITSC?

Continues

Analysis

Since the ITSC will serve all five depots equally, the ideal ITSC location is suggested by averaging the coordinates of the depots:

ITSC LOCATION

X- Coordinate	$(2.5 + 3.5 + 5 + 1 + 3.5)/5 = 3.1$
Y- Coordinate	$(18.5 + 17 + 10.5 + 8.5 + 4)/5 = 11.7$

Insight The resulting coordinate point (3.1, 11.7), illustrated in Figure 8.2, indicates that Global Freightways should investigate potential ITSC locations in the area of Wythe, Virginia. In reality, this is a mountainous region and, given that the technicians will be traveling by air, Global would likely evaluate communities with significant airports within 200 or 300 miles of the target point, such as Greensboro, North Carolina, or Richmond, Virginia. ■

The center of gravity method fits Global Freightways' new ITSC project fairly well. Global has a set of known service locations, these known locations describe an area that can be reasonably flattened into the grid space illustrated in Figure 8.2, and ITSC travel costs appear fairly linear with respect to distance. Note that the most northern depot in Toronto requires the traveling technicians to cross the international border between the US and Canada, but since the technicians are being dispatched to work on equipment and are not themselves transporting freight, this does not suggest the same nonlinearity problems associated with goods distribution. Less realistic, however, is the assumption that each of the depots would require the same degree of service from the ITSC. More common are situations in which the locations to be supported vary in their relative demand for service, such as a distribution center that will routinely ship more to a busy

FIGURE 8.2 Coordinate Grid over Global Freightways Service Area

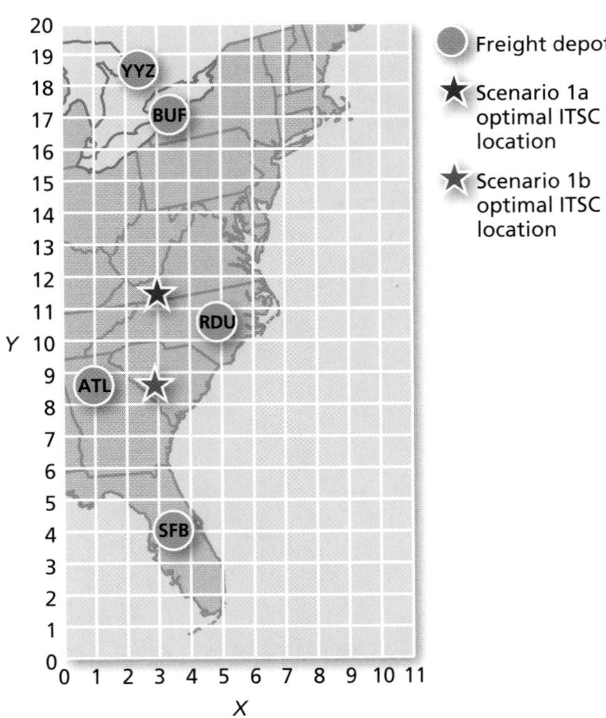

urban retail store than to a quieter rural location. In a case like this, the optimal location for the distribution center is identified by calculating the weighted average of the retail locations. If Q_i represents the amount of service required by the location i at coordinate point (X_i, Y_i), then these weighted averages can be expressed as:

$$X_{OPT} = \frac{\Sigma Q_i X_i}{\Sigma Q_i} \qquad Y_{OPT} = \frac{\Sigma Q_i Y_i}{\Sigma Q_i}$$

In these formulas, each optimal coordinate value is created by first multiplying each location's corresponding coordinate by the amount of service required at that location, adding up these results across all locations and then dividing this sum by the total amount of service. Where the simple averages earlier suggested the location that minimized the combined distances to the destinations, this weighted averaging minimizes the overall load distance of the central location. In Scenario 1b we consider additional information concerning service amounts.

load distance
A quantity multiplied by the distance that the quantity will travel, to create an overall expression of the work required by that action.

Center of Gravity (More Realistic Case)

Scenario 1b

Consider the problem of locating Global Freightways' new ITSC, introduced earlier. While Global anticipates the technicians at the new ITSC to make a total of 800 site visits annually, it now realizes that these visits will not be evenly distributed among the five depots. Three of the depots handle local area freight traffic, but depot ATL processes most inbound and outbound freight for Global's European depots, while depot SFB does the same for most North American/South American freight traffic. As a result, these depots are larger and have more computer equipment, so Global estimates that the annual number of technician site visits would be distributed as follows:

Freight Depot	*X*	*Y*	Annual Site Visits
YYZ (Toronto Pearson)	2.5	18.5	100
BUF (Buffalo/Niagara Falls)	3.5	17	50
RDU (Raleigh/Durham)	5	10.5	100
ATL (Atlanta Hartsfield)	1	8.5	250
SFB (Orlando Sanford)	3.5	4	300

Now what is the optimal location for the new ITSC?

Analysis

To reflect the differing degrees of technician traffic between the ITSC and the five depots, we calculate the weighted average of the five depot coordinates:

ITSC LOCATION (WEIGHTED BY TECHNICIAN VISITS)

Total number of annual visits: 800

X-Coordinate

((2.5 × 100) + (3.5 × 50) + (5 × 100) + (1 × 250) + (3.5 × 300))/800 = 2.8

Y-Coordinate

((18.5 × 100) + (17 × 50) + (10.5 × 100) + (8.5 × 250) + (4 × 300))/800 = 8.8

Insight The resulting coordinate point (2.8, 8.8), illustrated in Figure 8.2, indicates that Global Freightways should investigate potential ITSC locations west of Columbia, South Carolina. While the area described by (2.8, 8.8) on the Figure 8.2 grid is the formal recommendation of center of gravity, Global could consider locating the new ITSC as far west as Atlanta Hartsfield Airport (ATL) if there is any additional benefit to colocating the ITSC at an existing Global Freightways depot site. ■

Figure 8.2 illustrates how incorporating the heavier demands of depots ATL and SFB repositioned the ideal ITSC site southward and somewhat west of the original target in Scenario 1a. As the name of the technique used to determine these points implies, each depot is thought of as influencing the optimal location with a gravitational-like pull proportional to its need for the service. The target area then identified is the center of gravity, the balance among the depots as they pull at the ITSC.

Factor Rating

While factor rating is useful in location planning, this method is not used exclusively for that purpose. Factor rating studies appear elsewhere, such as in the publications *BusinessWeek* and *Fortune* with titles such as "The Top 100 Business Programs" or "The Top 10 Places to Retire." Factor rating ranks a set of candidates, based on their relative merits, making it the likely origin of a Top 10 or Top 100 news article. While the center of gravity technique focuses on outputs, factor rating can incorporate input, output, and/or indigenous factors into location planning with equal ease. Furthermore, factor rating is a far more subjective technique than others discussed here, meaning it can incorporate personal judgments and preferences.

linear averaging
A numerically weighted evaluation method used in situations such as awarding contracts, selecting locations, or ranking candidates.

The factor rating technique, also called linear averaging, involves the following series of steps:

1. Identify a set of candidate locations.
2. Determine factors important in the choice of location.
3. Rate each candidate location based on each of the factors identified. This scoring should be done with a numerical scale, and the same scale should be used for all scoring in the study.
4. Rank the importance of each factor to the choice of the best location. For convenience, use ranking weights that sum to 1.0, so each weight can be interpreted as the percent of influence that each factor has over the final decision.
5. Calculate weighted scores for each location.

The best candidate from the original set of locations is identified by the best score.

We work through the first three steps of this process for Global Freightways in Scenario 2a.

Scenario 2a

Factor Rating, Interpreting Data

Global Freightways must determine the location for a new aircraft maintenance center to support its fleet. The company has identified five airports as candidate locations for the new maintenance center: Narita Airport in Tokyo (NRT), Changi Airport in Singapore (SIN), Los Angeles Airport in California (LAX), Gatwick Airport in London (GAT), or the Buffalo/Niagara Falls Airport in New York (BUF). Global Freightways considers only two issues important when choosing one of these locations. The first issue is the airport's centrality within global network, which refers to how far, on average, any one of its airplanes would need to fly to and from its assigned freight route to receive maintenance at the new center. The second issue is local operating costs, because the cost of operating the center at each of the five airports varies. Global Freightways has created a 10-point scale in which higher scores always indicate more favorable conditions and has rated each of the five airports according to this scale:

Factors	NRT	SIN	LAX	GAT	BUF
Centrality within global network	7	9.5	7	6	4
Local operating costs	3.5	6	4	8.5	9

Which of the five airports is apparently the most favorable in terms of the cost of operating the aircraft maintenance center? How does Singapore's Changi Airport (SIN) compare with the remainder of the group?

Analysis

To answer these questions we must interpret the data. No calculations are necessary. For example, which airport is apparently the most favorable in terms of operating costs is a matter of identifying which airport has the most favorable score; in this case, it is Buffalo/Niagara Falls Airport (BUF) with a score of 9. *One note of caution:* When interpreting data collected for a factor rating study, remain alert for *how* the candidates have been scored. From reading this scenario, we know that

Global Freightways uses a 10-point scale and higher scores mean better-suited airports.

Insight Higher scores for local operating costs indicate lower costs, because lower costs are more favorable. Keeping this in mind, BUF's score of 9 for local operating costs puts it to the head of the pack. Further, even though Singapore's Changi Airport (SIN) is the location most central to Global Freightways' network, operating costs are higher there. A facility located at SIN would be less expensive to operate than a location at Toyko Narita (NRT) or Los Angeles (LAX), but considerably more expensive than BUF or London Gatwick (GAT). ■

Once the important factors have been identified and scored, the relative importance of these factors must be modeled by assigning weights. In some cases, there may be no particular preference among the factors, meaning that all factors are equally important. We would model this condition of indifference among factors by assigning equal weights to each factor, or equally dividing an overall value of 1.0. Then we can rather easily identify the best location, as it will be the candidate with the best average factor score. As with the center of gravity technique, we first try a simple factor rating example, in Scenario 2b.

Factor Rating (Simple Case) — Scenario 2b

Consider the factor rating study of Global Freightways, introduced earlier. If Global Freightways considers the issues of centrality within the global network and local operating costs to be equally important, which of the five airports will it choose for the aircraft maintenance center?

Analysis

This is the simplest case of factor rating, in which there are no preferences between the factors, so equal weights are assigned to them. Since we express weights as a set of values that sum to 1.0, this value is divided equally between them:

Factor	Weight	NRT	SIN	LAX	GAT	BUF
Centrality within global network	1/2	7	9.5	7	6	4
Local operating costs	1/2	3.5	6	4	8.5	9

Score for NRT: (1/2 × 7) + (1/2 × 3.5) = 3.5 + 1.75 = 5.25
Score for SIN: (1/2 × 9.5) + (1/2 × 6) = 4.75 + 3 = 7.75
Score for LAX: (1/2 × 7) + (1/2 × 4) = 3.5 + 2 = 5.5
Score for GAT: (1/2 × 6) + (1/2 × 8.5) = 3 + 4.25 = 7.25
Score for BUF: (1/2 × 4) + (1/2 × 9) = 2 + 4.5 = 6.5

Insight Changi Airport in Singapore (SIN) would be the location selected for Global's new maintenance center, because it has the highest factor rating score (7.75). In this specialized case, assigning each factor an equal weight is the mathematical equivalent of simply averaging all the scores earned by a location. ■

Of course, it is reasonable to assume that some factors may be more important than others. In these cases, the weighted score for a location is calculated:

$$\text{Score} = \Sigma W_i S_i$$

where W_i represents the weight associated with factor i and S_i represents the score that location earned on factor i. While the calculation of scores is mechanical, determining numerical weights that best represent a manager's preferences can require additional thought. In practice, decision makers are not likely to declare, "This factor should have a weight of 0.37," or "That factor should have a weight of 0.63." Rather, these preferences are more likely to be discussed in terms such as "This factor is twice as important as that factor," or "This factor carries triple the weight of that factor." The analyst must then translate these statements into numerical values, as we do in Scenario 2c.

Scenario 2c

Factor Rating (More Realistic Case)

Global Freightways has decided that the two factors discussed earlier are not of equal importance when locating a maintenance facility. Rather, Global Freightways has decided the issue of local operating costs is twice as important as the issue of centrality within Global Freightways' network. Now which location will it choose for its aircraft maintenance center?

Analysis

The only difference between this scenario and the question posed earlier in Scenario 2b is the set of weights associated with the factors. In the first scenario, Global considered the two factors to be equally important, which translates into equal weights when calculating each airport's factor rating score. Now the weight associated with local operating costs must be twice the value of the weight assigned to centrality. In any case where the decision maker expresses preferences between factors, one method of translating these preferences into numerical weights is to list the factors and identify the least important factor(s), assigning it (or them) a preliminary weight of 1.0. Any factor identified as "twice as important" as the least important factor can then be assigned a preliminary weight of 2.0, "three times the importance of" a weight of 3.0, etc. For Global, we would write:

DETERMINING PRELIMINARY WEIGHTS

Factor	Preliminary Weight
Centrality	1
Local operating cost	2 (twice as important)

Next, we set each preliminary weight as the numerator for the corresponding finished weight, while for the denominator of all finished weights we sum the preliminary weights:

DETERMINING FINISHED WEIGHTS

Factor	Preliminary Weight	Finished Weights (Use these)
Centrality	1	= 1/3
Local operating cost	2	= 2/3
Sum of preliminary weights	3	

To select an airport, we use the same calculations used in the simpler Scenario 2b, with the exception that the score for centrality is multiplied by 1/3 and the score for local operating cost by 2/3 (twice the weight):

Score for NRT: $(1/3 \times 7) + (2/3 \times 3.5) = 2.333 + 2.333 = 4.666$
Score for SIN: $(1/3 \times 9.5) + (2/3 \times 6) = 3.167 + 4 = 7.167$
Score for LAX: $(1/3 \times 7) + (2/3 \times 4) = 2.333 + 2.667 = 5$
Score for GAT: $(1/3 \times 6) + (2/3 \times 8.5) = 2 + 5.667 = 7.667$
Score for BUF: $(1/3 \times 4) + (2/3 \times 9) = 1.333 + 6 = 7.333$

Insight Now Global Freightways would select London Gatwick (GAT) as the location for its new maintenance facility, because it has the highest factor rating score at 7.667. ■

Note that while London Gatwick Airport now emerges as the best location for the maintenance facility, it did not earn the highest score in either the centrality or local operating cost categories. Perhaps London Gatwick represents the best balance between these two factors of importance, given the added emphasis on local operating costs. However, this outcome does highlight a vulnerability of this technique when used for long-term planning. Given that Global Freightways is making a strategic decision for many years to come, just how confident is the firm in its statement that local operating costs are "twice as important" than the centrality of the location? In other words, just how sensitive is the selection of London Gatwick to that statement? Asking these questions before implementing a solution is known as performing a *sensitivity analysis*, often achieved with a spreadsheet model like the one displayed in Figure 8.3.

The uppermost screen displays the original decision as stated in Scenario 2c, while the lower screens show the result of modeling other degrees of relative importance for local operating costs. Specifically, the lower screens show points of indifference in this

point of indifference When two alternatives have identical merit.

Spreadsheet Model and Sensitivity Analysis of Factor Weights FIGURE 8.3

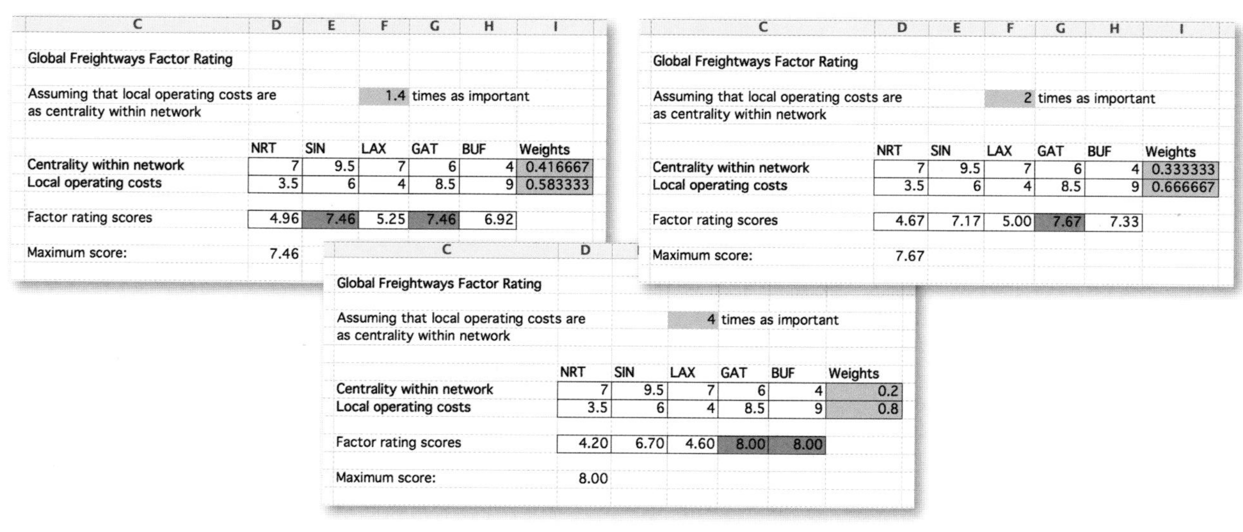

Global Freightways Factor Rating

Assuming that local operating costs are 1.4 times as important as centrality within network

	NRT	SIN	LAX	GAT	BUF	Weights
Centrality within network	7	9.5	7	6	4	0.416667
Local operating costs	3.5	6	4	8.5	9	0.583333
Factor rating scores	4.96	7.46	5.25	7.46	6.92	
Maximum score:	7.46					

Global Freightways Factor Rating

Assuming that local operating costs are 2 times as important as centrality within network

	NRT	SIN	LAX	GAT	BUF	Weights
Centrality within network	7	9.5	7	6	4	0.333333
Local operating costs	3.5	6	4	8.5	9	0.666667
Factor rating scores	4.67	7.17	5.00	7.67	7.33	
Maximum score:	7.67					

Global Freightways Factor Rating

Assuming that local operating costs are 4 times as important as centrality within network

	NRT	SIN	LAX	GAT	BUF	Weights
Centrality within network	7	9.5	7	6	4	0.2
Local operating costs	3.5	6	4	8.5	9	0.8
Factor rating scores	4.20	6.70	4.60	8.00	8.00	
Maximum score:	8.00					

decision, or the tipping points at which Global would begin to prefer a different airport. Essentially, if local operating costs are any less than 1.4 times the importance (or 40% more important) of centrality, Global should locate at Singapore Changi Airport, the outcome of the earlier Scenario 2b. If local operating costs are higher than four times the importance of centrality, the low costs at Buffalo/Niagara Falls (BUF) will make that airport more attractive than London Gatwick. Provided that Global Freightways is comfortable that the range suggested by Figure 8.3 captures its true preference concerning local operating costs, then London Gatwick is confirmed the best selection. One particularly troubling indication from sensitivity analysis is when such a range is revealed to be quite narrow, meaning that the decision is quite sensitive to the precise statement of the weights. In these cases, it is wise to launch a review of all weights selected and perhaps an expansion of the analysis to include more detail in the selection and scoring of the factors, before finalizing the decision.

Cost versus Volume Analysis

fixed cost
Cost incurred regardless of the volume of associated activity.

variable cost
Cost that varies with volume of associated activity.

Like factor rating, cost versus volume analysis evaluates a set of candidate locations to determine the best option. Unlike factor rating, however, cost versus volume analysis allows only two factors to be considered during the selection process: the fixed and the variable costs associated with operating at each location. Fixed costs are expenses that will not vary with the use of the new location, such as debt payments, rent, property taxes, and salary expense. Any cost incurred even when the facility is completely idle would be described as a fixed cost. In contrast, variable costs are proportional to the use of the facility: the higher the activity levels, the greater the cost. Variable costs can be driven by many components, but common sources are the consumption of raw materials, the use of hourly labor, and the expense of utilities at the site. Any organization using cost versus volume analysis believes that the relative merits of the various locations can be expressed solely in terms of differing levels of fixed and variable costs. In addition, the organization expects the facility being located to produce or provide only a single product. Finally, the organization assumes variable costs are a linear function of volume.

aggregate
Combining the creation of many similar products into one relevant measure of activity for the organization.

The requirement of only one product is not as strict as it might sound. Most facilities provide a range of related products, but this technique can be used on their behalf if the organization can aggregate the products into a single expression of volume. Aggregation implies some reasonable simplification of the facility's output, to facilitate longer-term planning. As an example, a hospital can provide a wide variety of services to an individual, but these individual activities can be aggregated into an overall measure of patients served or patient days. Assuming an organization is comfortable with all three assumptions discussed here, cost versus volume analysis becomes a logical choice to select a new location. All that remains is to gather information on fixed and variable costs at each candidate location and then compare the candidates on the combined expense. This is particularly convenient if the organization happens to know precisely what the production volume will be at the new location, such as suggested in Scenario 3a.

Scenario 3a

Cost versus Volume (Simple Case)

Global Freightways must prepare for hurricane season in North America, by contracting for bad weather storage of aircraft that would otherwise be on the ground at one of its freight depots in a hurricane's path. Each airport outside of hurricane-prone areas requires an annual fixed rental fee be paid in advance to allow the emergency parking of aircraft at their facility, plus the airport charges for each plane using its runway to land and later depart again. Global has identified three promising airports for bad weather storage:

Airport	Fixed Rental Cost	Variable Cost (Unscheduled Runway Usage)
Buffalo/Niagara Falls (BUF)	$90,000	$1,400 per plane
Cleveland Hopkins (CLE)	$60,000	$2,000 per plane
Chicago Midway (MDW)	$20,000	$5,000 per plane

If Global believes it will relocate a total of 30 aircraft into bad weather storage during this year's upcoming hurricane season, which airport should it contract with?

Analysis

If Global happens to know that it will be relocating 30 aircraft, then it calculates the total cost at each airport at that volume:

BAD WEATHER STORAGE (30 planes)

Airport	Fixed Cost	Variable Cost	Aircraft
BUF	$90,000 +	1,400 × 30 =	$132,000
CLE	$60,000 +	2,000 × 30 =	$120,000
MDW	$20,000 +	5,000 × 30 =	$170,000

Insight Given only these criteria, Global Freightways should contract with Cleveland Hopkins Airport, at a total cost of $120,000, to relocate 30 aircraft this hurricane season. ■

In reality, a firm cannot be expected to be certain what the volume of activity will be at some future time at a facility not yet established. In Scenario 3a, it is even more suspicious that Global Freightways somehow knows it will be relocating a certain number of aircraft, when it cannot possibly know how many hurricanes will impact its freight network in the upcoming season, let alone to when, where, and to what degree of severity. Under more realistic conditions, we look at the options in terms of ranges of preference, versus the single point of evaluation used in the scenario above. This is best explored graphically, as in the Scenario 3b.

Cost versus Volume, Graphical Case and Points of Indifference — Scenario 3b

Consider the bad weather storage problem of Global Freightways, introduced earlier. Global wishes to retract the statement that it will relocate a total of 30 aircraft during the next hurricane season. The truth is Global cannot possibly know exactly how many aircraft it will need to relocate. How shall Global select a location?

Analysis

This is a more realistic case, requiring the graphing of Global's options to gain more insight. Total cost at each airport varies with the number of planes landed, and since variable landing costs are assumed linear, this total cost function will chart a straight line across a graph. In the case of the Buffalo/Niagara Falls Airport (BUF), we already know one point on its total cost function line from the analysis done in Scenario 3a: (30, 132,000), or a cost of $132,000

Continues

when 30 planes are landed. Another point on the BUF total cost line is very easy to determine: (0, 90,000), representing the fixed cost of $90,000 that will be paid even if Global does not relocate any planes during the upcoming hurricane season. Graphing these two points provides enough information to sketch the straight line that illustrates total cost at BUF for a range of unscheduled plane landings:

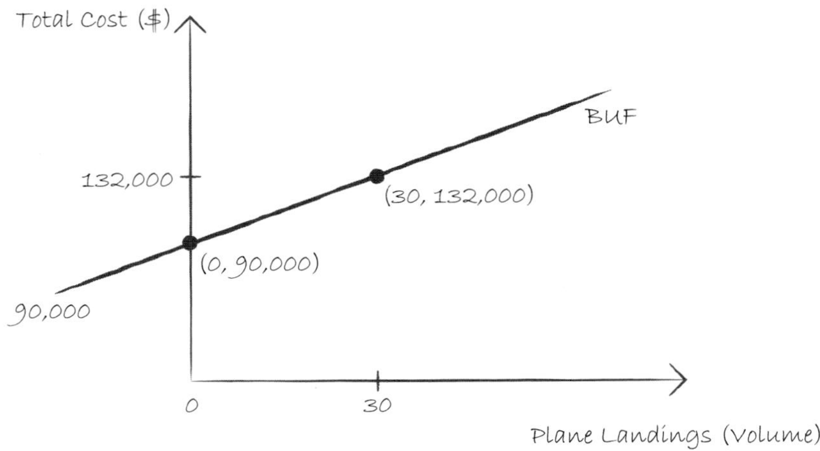

We can add Cleveland Hopkins (CLE) with the same steps, using both the existing calculation at 30 airplanes and the conveniently calculated cost at 0 airplanes.

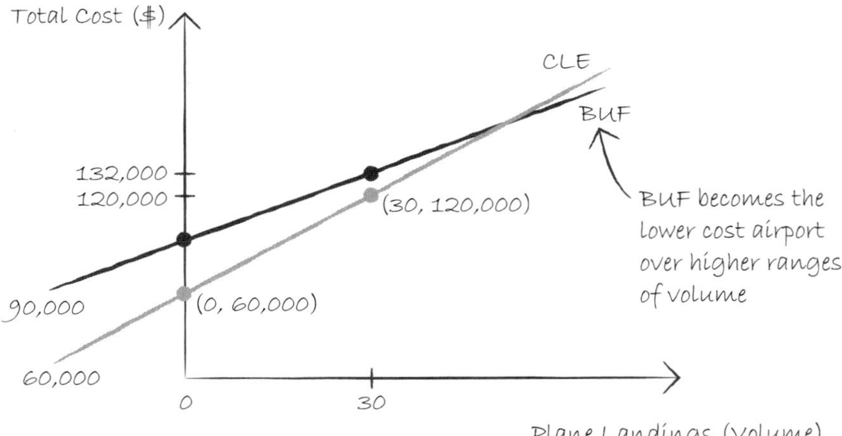

Now the graph illustrates how total costs at CLE are lower than at BUF, except for over a very high volume of landings. While this is useful insight, we should not reach any conclusions before illustrating all locations. Look at Figure 8.4, for example. It clarifies that each airport is the preferable location over a certain range of volume. Even if Global cannot predict exactly how many planes will be relocated in the upcoming hurricane season, if past experience suggests this number will likely be in the single digits, then Chicago Midway (MDW) should be selected. Likewise, it appears that Buffalo/Niagara Falls (BUF) will always be preferable beyond a certain minimum number of plane landings, while Cleveland Hopkins (CLE) is the low-cost airport across some midrange including 30 landings, first explored in Scenario 3a.

To complete our analysis, then, we find the points of indifference between the three locations, where the preferable range of one airport ends and another begins. We do so by solving for when the costs of two airports with neighboring ranges are equal:

POINT OF INDIFFERENCE BETWEEN MDW AND CLE

$$(\text{Cost of MDW} = \text{Cost of CLE})$$
$$20{,}000 + 5{,}000 \times X = 60{,}000 + 2{,}000 \times X$$
$$3000X = 40{,}000$$
$$X = 13.333 \text{ landings}$$

POINT OF INDIFFERENCE BETWEEN CLE AND BUF

$$(\text{Cost of CLE} = \text{Cost of BUF})$$
$$60{,}000 + 2{,}000 \times X = 90{,}000 + 1{,}400 \times X$$
$$600X = 30{,}000$$
$$X = 50 \text{ landings}$$

Insight If no more than 13 plane relocations are anticipated this upcoming hurricane season, Global Freightways should contract with Chicago Midway for bad weather storage this year. If more than 50 plane relocations are anticipated, Global should contract with Buffalo/Niagara Falls. Otherwise Global should contract with Cleveland Hopkins for any relocation forecast in between. ■

Cost versus Volume Analysis

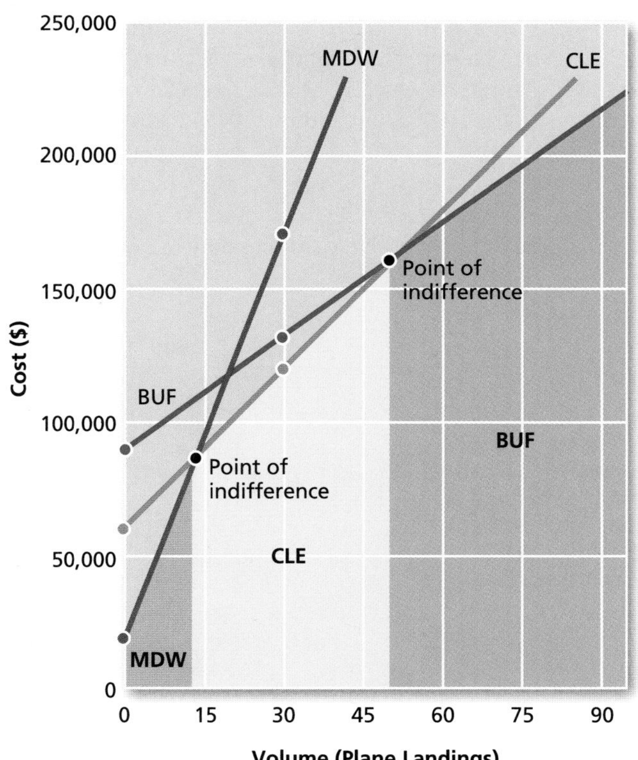

FIGURE 8.4

Graph of data fom Scenario 3b

Precisely which of these three locations will be selected for bad weather storage now rests with Global Freightways, who must select the range it is most comfortable with. The points of indifference are important benchmarks marking the shifting of preference, and the meaning of the term *point of indifference* is easy to visualize. For example, given that Global happens to land precisely 50 planes during the upcoming hurricane season, the organization would be indifferent to whether those landings take place at CLE or BUF. This is because cost versus volume analysis assumes that preferences are based solely on cost, and at a volume of 50 landings, the cost of Cleveland Hopkins (CLE) and Buffalo/ Niagara Falls (BUF) are identical.

SUPPLY CHAIN LOGISTICS

logistics Management of flow between locations, typically the transportation of products, personnel, or other resources.

inbound logistics Management of flow into a facility or other system.

outbound logistics Management of flow departing a facility or other system.

goods Tangible products.

Once locations are established, movement between them becomes an issue of logistics. First, all organizations make logistical decisions within their facilities, such as installing conveyor belts to move packages or relying on employees to walk from a work area to the front counter to greet arriving customers. These issues of internal logistics are linked to facility design, while external logistics link these facilities into larger supply chain systems. For any facility participating in such a system, its inbound logistics describe the transportation of everything to that facility's location, and might differ sharply from its outbound logistics, or transportation of everything away from the facility. The "everything" in these two channels of flow is often assumed to be goods such as inbound supplies and outbound products, but logistics is not just the transportation of goods. Goods, however, are the easiest to recognize as shipments, and are thus a logical starting point for our discussion of logistics between locations.

Transporting Goods

maritime shipping Transportation by sea or other waterway.

Figure 8.5 illustrates four choices for the transportation of goods: maritime shipping, air transport, railroad transport, and road-based ground transportation. Air transport is generally recognized as the quickest but most expensive, whereas maritime or ship transport is generally least expensive but slowest. A logistics manager often has the choice of two or more of these modes of transportation, and may even use combinations of transportation modes when moving goods between locations, to maximize the features of each.

Maritime Logistics Approximately 90% of the world's tangible trade is carried by oceangoing vessels, although this massive maritime network is probably the least visible

The Link Between Maritime and Ground-based Logistical Systems

Intermodal freight containers transformed supply chain management by allowing the seamless transfer of goods between two previously separate logistical systems. Pictured here is that link in operation, as freight containers newly arrived by sea to the south island of New Zealand are fitted to trucks by specialized cranes, sending one loaded truck inland every few minutes.

Transportation Modes of Supply Chain Logistics FIGURE **8.5**

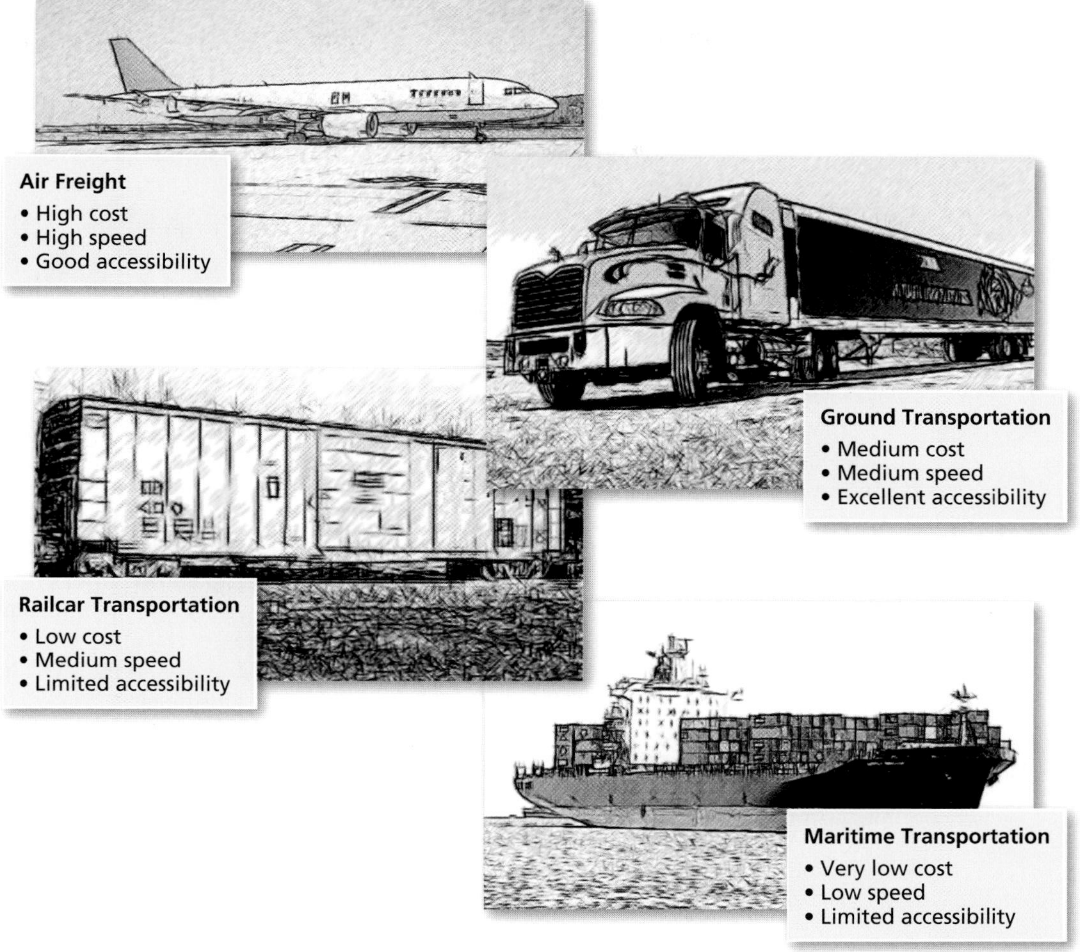

to most of the world's population. Most of this fleet of over 50,000 cargo ships can be divided into three broad categories:

- *Container ships*, which are loaded with standard intermodal containers that can be transferred to trucks or railcars for further shipment inland. Most manufactured products can be containerized for distribution in this fashion.
- *Dry bulk carriers*, which carry large amounts of a loose, unpackaged commodity. Coal, iron ore, and grain are commonly carried as dry bulk, although suppliers of some commodities such as coffee have been switching to intermodal containers in recent years.
- *Oil tankers*, which haul both crude oil for processing and refined petroleum products. This traffic alone accounts for a third of worldwide maritime trade each year.

intermodal container A standard freight container designed to be loaded by the shipper and unloaded at its destination.

Air Transport Shipping goods by air is usually the fastest and the most expensive option for transportation, just as flying is usually the fastest and most expensive means of personal travel. In aviation history, commercial passenger traffic emerged before widespread

Hub-and-Spoke Passenger Networks

Hub-and-spoke networks are common to many forms of passenger transportation. Pictured here is the convergence of activity at a Shanghai train station that serves as a hub within its network, crowded with holiday travelers waiting to switch between spokes in the logistical pattern.

use of airplanes for cargo. As a result, some of the first and some of the largest modern air cargo carriers are better known as passenger airlines, such as Korean Air and American Airlines. Dedicated air cargo fleets such as FedEx and DHL use a hub-and-spokes style of network similar to their passenger airline counterparts', transporting time-sensitive goods such as perishable fruit, cut flowers, and expedited mail. Other options available to the shipper are onboard courier service, the hiring of a courier to escort cargo on a scheduled passenger airline flight, or an air charter, the hiring of an airplane to transport cargo directly. These rapid, short-notice transportation services represent some of the highest costs in logistics, and thus are usually used for extremely high-value, sensitive cargo such as human organs for transplant or diamonds and other precious objects.

hub-and-spokes network A transportation network in which a set of destinations is connected to a central hub, so that any pair of destinations can connect by travel through the hub.

air charter Transportation by an aircraft hired expressly for that trip, operating outside the scheduled flights of an air carrier.

Figure 8.6 shows the locations of the three busiest seaports around the world, as well as the three busiest airports for freight. Although both maritime and air logistics rely heavily on hub-and-spoke network patterns of cargo traffic, the ships and planes themselves often follow looping or even round-the-world routes, stopping to acquire and exchange cargo at these hubs.

FIGURE 8.6 Three Busiest Airports and Seaports by Tons of Freight (2009–2010)

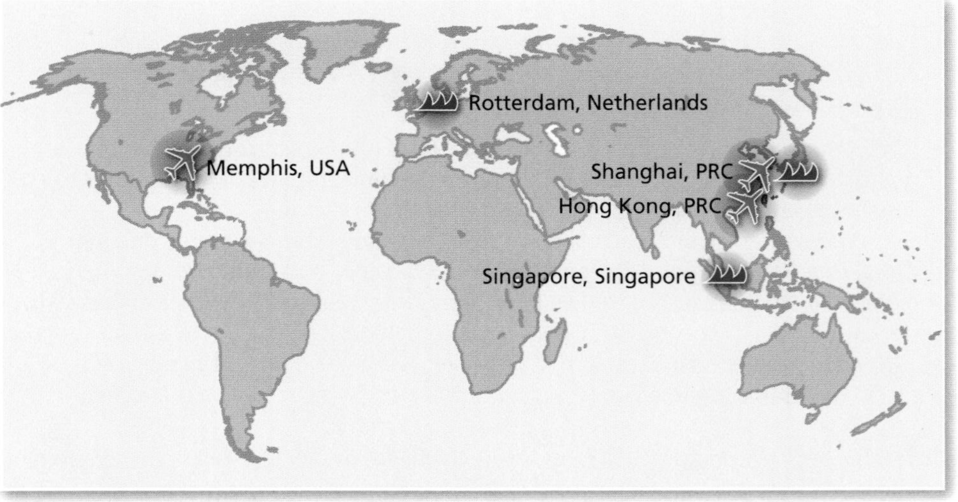

Ground-based Logistics Both the railroad freight car and the over-the-road truck pictured in Figure 8.5 are examples of ground-based modes of transportation. While maritime logistics may transport 90% of the world's trade, it is rare that these vessels ever complete the delivery of goods to consumers. Thus, each shipper is faced with a last-mile problem that requires intermodal containers to be unloaded from ships and delivered inland by truck or rail. However, the same accessibility problems associated with maritime logistics also restrict the choice of rail, reflected in the fact that approximately 80% of shipping load distance in the United States is provided by truck, but less than 5% by railroad. The cost structures of both truck and railroad consist of two major subcategories, dependent on whether the shipper can hire the entire truck or railcar for transportation or requires only a portion of its capacity. Less-than-load (LTL) transportation companies accept smaller shipments and combine them within larger trucks and railcars to provide their transportation, but charge more for this service.

last-mile problem (or last-kilometer problem) The challenge of completing delivery of a good or a service, especially if the destination is remote or disrupted by disaster.

less-than-load (LTL) A shipment sufficiently small so as to not require the entire capacity of a logistical assets, also known as less-than-truckload or less-than-carload.

While trucks and railroad trains do account for most of ground-based logistics, certain products are better transported via these alternate methods:

- **Pipelines.** Crude oil, liquid fuels, natural gas, fresh water, and electricity are examples of products transported through a physical connection between locations, usually a pipeline or its equivalent.
- **Bicycles.** To solve the last-mile problem in congested city centers, small amounts of a good can be transported by bicycle or motorized bike.
- **Couriers on foot.** Small amounts of goods may also be carried on foot by couriers, such as newspapers, mail, or medical supplies for disaster relief.

These additional ground-based choices are rather specialized, although bicycles and couriers are more common to the logistics of service delivery.

Transporting Services

Services differ from goods in that these products are intangible and thus cannot be stored for transportation. Furthermore, services often require the customer as an input to the production process. Some services must bring their productive capability to the customer's location, and these types of services can depend on logistics even more heavily than a shipper of goods. Logistics implies the management of flow, but this flow is not always movement of the product. Some service systems rely on the movement of their personnel and other resources across a service area, including delivery services, police and emergency response, utilities and repair services, landscaping and snow removal, taxi fleets, and garbage collection. All these services rely on various modes of transportation to keep the productive system mobile.

e-commerce Buying and selling product through electronic transactions.

enterprise resource planning (ERP) A strategic information system that integrates all functional areas of an organization.

radio frequency identification (RFID) The tagging of objects with devices that may be detected and interrogated for information by remote electronic readers, allowing identification and tracking without contact.

Transporting Information

Less visible but no less important is the flow of information within and between organizations. E-commerce relies on the seamless electronic transmission of all information required to complete the sale of some good or service, linking organizations to their individual customers. Information must also circulate within the organization, a management information system being a familiar mode of this type of logistics. A large organization may maintain several smaller computer-based information systems to manage different aspects of its business, or it may integrate these functional areas into a single ERP system, establishing a unified logistical network for the flow of information. Information may also be circulated through these modes:

- Radio frequency identification (RFID). Tangible shipments and resources can be tagged with chips that allow their location to be detected remotely, updating this information instantly.

- **Web forms and wireless transmission.** Internet-based documents have replaced the use of paper forms or personal communication in many circumstances, particularly the information flows of e-commerce. Satellite links can move large volumes of information around the world, which handheld devices can acquire and upload almost instantly.
- **Paper forms.** Paper documents such as work orders, catalogues, reports, and requests were once a major carrier of information between decision makers. Electronic systems have reduced but not replaced many organizations' reliance on paperwork.
- **Personal communication.** Personal conversations, phone calls, and e-mail between individuals all represent information flows.
- **Radio dispatch.** Organizations that operate across a landscape and/or under rapidly changing conditions may use the open forum of spoken radio transmission to keep all participants informed. Examples include the dispatching familiar to taxi fleets and emergency services, or the use of radios and hands-free earpieces among crews providing support for banquets, large conferences, concerts, and other events.

dispatching
Assigning work in real-time, often in the context of mobile resources.

electronic data interchange (EDI)
The linking of two information systems from two different organizations to transfer data and conduct transactions.

An organization may create links with other organizations, comparable to tangible inbound and outbound logistical flows, by establishing electronic data interchange (EDI) with suppliers and customers. Since a supply chain relies on the linking of organizations through external logistics, its success often relies on rapid information flows from EDI and RFID systems.

FORCES INFLUENCING LOGISTICS

Both the nature of an organization and its choice of location broadly determine its logistical needs. However, logistics are also influenced by some issues specific to movement between locations. The exact choice of external logistics used to build up a supply chain likely result from a complex combination of all these influences.

Economies of Scale

One factor central to an organization's choice of logistics is cost. Earlier, Figure 8.5 suggested a relative ranking of four transportation modes by cost, but this ranking is not true for every situation. Each mode has differing fixed and variable costs, resulting in differing levels of attractiveness given the volume to be transported. Fixed costs influence this choice in particular; the shipment must be large enough to achieve the economies of scale associated with the mode of transportation. While extremely efficient, maritime shipping has high fixed costs and thus is associated with high-volume shipments. The lower fixed costs of other transportation modes are generally associated with higher variable costs, and thus are more attractive to smaller shipments. Organizations with small shipments may also consider freight consolidation, hiring an agent to arrange for the small shipment to be combined with other small shipments bound for the same destination, increasing the shipment volume and achieving better economies of scale.

economies of scale
Decreasing average unit cost by increasing volume.

freight consolidation
A third-party logistical service that groups small shipments of several clients into a larger shipment to achieve economies of scale in transport.

Speed and Accessibility

An organization's choice of logistics may be heavily influenced by a need for speed. Faster modes such as aviation are more expensive, but an organization may make that choice if the shipment

- **Spoils rapidly.** Cut flowers and fresh seafood are frequently shipped in bulk on airplanes. Plastic flowers and frozen seafood are not.
- **Is needed urgently.** Rush orders can include parts for repair, antivenom and other medical supplies, or materials in unexpected short supply at some location.

- **Is extremely valuable for its size.** Small, high-value shipments such as diamonds are generally transported faster to minimize security risks during transit.

Even if a shipment is not at a particular risk of theft, an organization might choose faster logistics to reduce investment in pipeline stock. The faster the logistical mode of a supply chain link, the less inventory is required to keep that flow constant.

pipeline stock
Inventory currently in transit between locations.

Even if the speed of transport is not important to the shipper, the issue of accessibility to the transportation network might dictate a more expensive mode of logistics. While maritime logistics is the least expensive, cargo ships can only carry shipments from one shoreline to another. A helicopter, in contrast, can pick up and deliver a small shipment virtually anywhere, but represents one of the most expensive means of doing so. Some facilities are located to improve access to efficient logistical networks, such as coal-burning electrical plants and oil refineries near seaports, or food processing plants built along railroad lines.

Supply Chain Linkages

External logistics form the links in a supply chain, existing between supply chain partners. As such, logistics are exposed to issues outside the daily operations at each location, such as the rules and regulations of governments overseeing the linkage routes. As an example, the United States Department of Transportation (US DOT) is responsible for the rules and regulations governing air, water, and ground transport within the US. These rules dictate issues such as the maximum allowable weight of a shipment by truck, what materials may not travel by air or through a public road tunnel, and how many hours a transportation driver may work before requiring a mandatory rest period. Because external logistics often represent exchanges between businesses, these linkages also reflect legal relationships, according to the terms and conditions of the particular shipment.

Terms and Conditions International shipments can be complex in terms of the buyer's and the seller's associated responsibilities. Figure 8.7 illustrates only a few of the questions that must be answered by the terms and conditions of a single international shipment, understood and agreed upon by both the buyer and the seller within the supply chain link.

In international trade, the purchasing organization should specify the International Commercial Terms, or incoterms, for transport, as published by the International Chamber of Commerce. Incoterms are worldwide standard agreements that detail the rights

incoterms®
Standardized sets of terms accepted worldwide for transportation of goods, established and trademarked by the International Chamber of Commerce.

Government Influence on Ground-based Logistics

Pictured here is a tractor trailer, the workhorse of ground-based logistics worldwide. Trucks like this are shaped partially by government policy, such as the US Department of Transportation requirement that cargo trailers be no more than 102 inches wide and 48 feet long to operate on federal interstates. Individual states may impose different rules for state roadways, such as Nevada's tolerance for trailers up to 70 feet in length. The single axle behind the tractor cab of the truck in this picture, followed by three axles beneath its trailer, might look somewhat unfamiliar to motorists in the US. This is the standard format for European tractor trailers, as this truck is moving goods between cities in Sweden.

FIGURE 8.7 Example Questions Addressed in Terms and Conditions

These are but a few of the questions addressed in Terms and Conditions statements for an international maritime shipment.

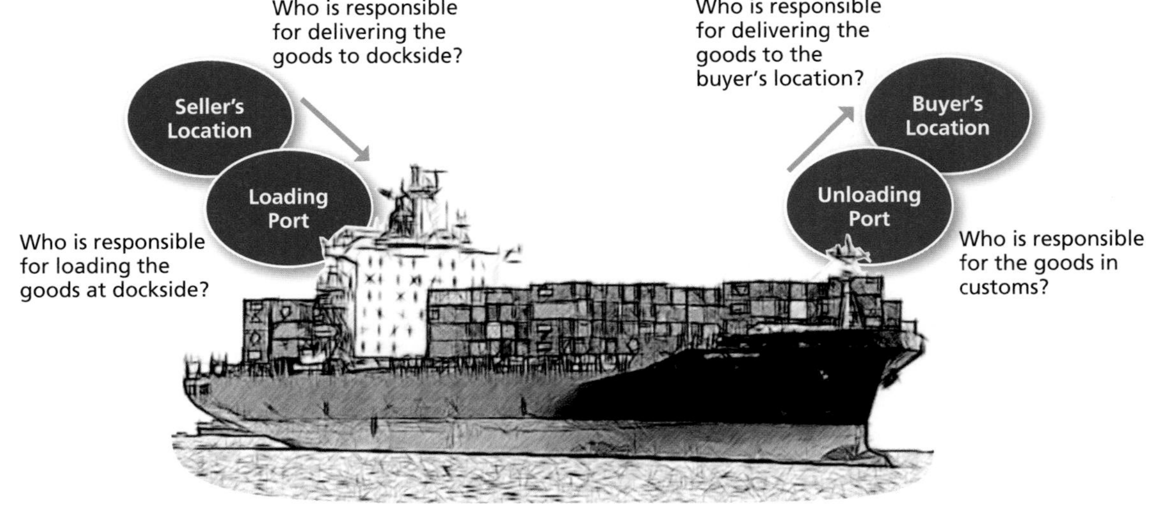
Who is responsible
for delivering the
goods to dockside?
Who is responsible
for delivering the
goods to the
buyer's location?
Seller's
Location
Buyer's
Location
Loading
Port
Unloading
Port
Who is responsible
for loading the
goods at dockside?
Who is responsible
for the goods in
customs?
Who is responsible for the cost of transportation?
When did the ownership of the goods change from seller to buyer?

customs
The governmental agency responsible for controlling the flow of goods in and out of a country, enforcing that country's trade laws and collecting associated taxes.

and obligations of each party in the purchase and shipment of goods, such as who is responsible for the goods' clearing customs and when is ownership of the goods transferred. The answers to questions such as those posed in Figure 8.7 are represented by three-letter abbreviations:

- **EXW** (ex works). EXW indicates that the goods are made available at the seller's premises, and all other arrangements, costs, and risks are the buyer's responsibility. In Figure 8.7, every question that starts with "Who" is answered by "Buyer."
- **FCA** (free carrier). In Figure 8.7, FCA would require the seller to clear the goods for export and deliver them dockside, where the buyer would take over responsibility for all remaining issues.
- **CFR** (cost and freight). CFR is a similar arrangement to FCA except the seller agrees to pay for transportation to the unloading port, although the buyer agrees to assume any risk associated with the shipment as soon as it is loaded.

Figure 8.7 illustrates a single supply chain link as a relationship between two parties, the buyer and the seller. In reality, one or more other organizations are likely at work, providing the logistical assets and other services. While the buyer and seller agree to take on various responsibilities, these two parties are not likely doing all the direct work associated with them. Rather, they then hire third parties to complete some of these tasks.

outsource
To subcontract an internal process to an external provider.

Third- and Fourth-Party Logistics Some organizations own and operate their own logistical assets, such as a bakery that delivers its product to client restaurants with its own vans. These businesses are said to be first-party logistical providers or 1PLs, to distinguish them from organizations that have outsourced their logistics. Many businesses rely on second-party logistical providers (or 2PLs) to transport goods, such as the owners of the cargo ship pictured in Figure 8.5.

Maritime Freight Containers at Dockside

A typical freight container is a steel box approximately 40 feet long, 8 feet wide, and 8 to 9 feet high. Its interior space may be packed with over 40,000 pounds of virtually any good that can endure several weeks of storage, such as electronics, wine, books, clothing, food dye, and spearmint flavoring. Smaller shipments may travel through arrangements with freight forwarders, who fill containers through freight consolidation. In this picture, maritime freight containers wait on land, although not all necessarily contain cargo. Some third- and fourth-party logistical providers specialize in the transfer of empty containers from low-demand regions to high-demand regions, to be loaded again for shipping, repurposed as temporary structures or recycled as scrap steel.

Modern supply chain management has given rise to third-party logistics (3PL), a term now common in supply chain strategy. In addition to the direct transportation service of a 2PL carrier, a 3PL provider offers additional services that can include warehousing, order packing, tracking, tracing, and security. Many 3PLs are also known as freight forwarders, facilitating transportation with services such as freight consolidation mentioned earlier. Freight forwarders and similar 3PLs are often non–asset based, meaning that they offer expertise in arranging for shipment, but do not themselves own any trucks, ships, or other logistical assets. More recently, non–asset based consulting firms specializing in supply chain integration are sometimes referred to as fourth-party logistics (4PL) providers. This term, first proposed by the management consulting firm Accenture, depends heavily on its non–asset based distinction, as 4PLs are intended to be neutral advisers unaffiliated with any particular choice of logistical mode, software, or carrier.

third-party logistics (3PL) Outsourcing logistics activities to a provider.

freight forwarders Third-party logistics providers that facilitate shipments for clients.

fourth-party logistics (4PL) Logistical consulting provided by a firm without logistical assets.

Some of the most interesting and successful examples of 3PL and 4PL providers are actually spin-offs from 1PL companies whose internal logistical divisions grew so skillful that they went into business for themselves. For example, Caterpillar, manufacturer of the distinct yellow heavy equipment often found at construction sites, long possessed a particular expertise in handling orders for service parts with remarkable speed and accuracy, which enhanced the reputation of its overall brand. Recognizing this ability, Land Rover, a manufacturer of sports utility vehicles, was the first to approach Caterpillar about acquiring some of its inventory and logistical exptertise, eventually becoming the first client of Caterpillar Logistics. Like many 3PL providers, Caterpillar Logistics now serves a wide variety of clients in several different industries, many of them quite distant from its parent company's business of building heavy equipment.

Logistics has shaped the world's map since the dawn of human history, influencing the location of cities, the availability of resources, and the transfer of knowledge. Once thought of as a rather mundane business topic, logistics is now recognized as a discipline unto itself, and a powerful source of competitive advantage in a global marketplace.

SUMMARY

All organizations are confronted with at least one location and/or logistical decision at some point in their histories. These critical decisions are not formulaic; no single model or procedure works for every organization, every time. Organizations are often influenced by a wide variety of forces when selecting a location, and highly adaptable techniques such as factor rating allow such diversity to be incorporated into the decision-making process. However, other organizations view the issue of a good location as driven mostly by travel distance and/or production costs, making more specialized location planning techniques such as center of gravity or cost versus volume analysis attractive. A diversity of logistics may then link these locational decisions, moving both tangible goods, resources, and vital information among facilities to create larger supply chain networks.

Key Terms

aggregate
air charter
customs
dispatching
e-commerce
economies of scale
electronic data interchange (EDI)
enterprise resource planning (ERP)
fixed cost
fourth-party logistics (4PL)
freight consolidation
freight forwarders
geographic information system (GIS)
goods
hub-and-spokes network
inbound logistics
incoterms
intermodal container
linear averaging
last-mile problem/last-kilometer problem
less-than-load (LTL)
load distance
logistics
maritime shipping
NIMBY
outbound logistics
outsource
pipeline stock
point of indifference
radio frequency identification (RFID)
third-party logistics (3PL)
variable cost

Discussion Questions

1. How does a NIMBY argument potentially relate to the issues of productivity and sustainability?
2. Where is your college or university located and what factors best explain this? What *types* of factors are these?
3. What impact did introduction of the intermodal container to logistics have on location planning?

PROBLEMS

Short answers appear in Appendix A. Go to **NoteShaper.com** for full video tutorials on each question.

Minute Answer

1. Costs incurred at a facility even when it is idle are called what?
2. What is the viewpoint of someone nicknamed a NIMBY?
3. What are costs that vary with volume of associated activity called?
4. Which does not support the flow of information between supply chain partners, intermodal containers or paper forms?
5. If goods are available under standard terms EXW is the buyer or seller responsible for the goods' clearing customs?
6. Would passenger airlines or a bicycle courier service be an example of a hub-and-spoke network?

7. Which is less accessible, air freight or maritime shipping networks?
8. Which logistical mode is most appropriate for a small shipment that must be somewhere very fast and far away?
9. In center of gravity, if all destinations require the same degree of service, should their coordinates be added or averaged?
10. If factor A is given a weight of 0.2 and factor B a weight of 0.4, what does that imply about factor B when compared to factor A?
11. Which technique is more subjective, center of gravity or factor rating?
12. Which alternative is preferable at a point of indifference?

Quick Start

13. ART Contractors must locate an equipment staging area to serve three construction sites, located at coordinates (0, 2), (0, 4), and (5, 5). Traffic between the staging area and each of the three sites will be equal. What is the best set of coordinates for the equipment staging area?
14. ART Contractors must locate an equipment staging area to serve three construction sites, located at coordinates (0, 2), (0, 4), and (5, 5). Traffic between the staging area and each of the three sites is 30 trips a week, except for the site located at (5, 5), which is only 10 trips a week. What is the best set of coordinates for the equipment staging area?
15. A manufacturing firm is considering two locations for a plant to produce a new product. Location A has a fixed cost of $80,000 and a variable cost of $20 per unit. Location B has a fixed cost of $120,000 and a variable cost of $15 per unit. The firm plans to manufacture 20,000 units a year at the plant. Where should the plant be located?
16. A manufacturing firm is considering two locations for a plant to produce a new product. Location A has a fixed cost of $80,000 and a variable cost of $20 per unit. Location B has a fixed cost of $120,000 and a variable cost of $15 per unit. What is the firm's point of indifference between these locations?
17. You are reading a magazine article with the title "The Top 100 Undergraduate Business Programs." The article mentions that the magazine's staff collected data on various undergraduate programs including enrollment, average class size, and average starting salary at graduation. The staff then used these facts about each program to create the overall ranking. The staff has most likely used what technique to create the ranking?
18. If location A scored 1127.2 in a factor rating study and location B scored 903.9, which location would be selected as a superior choice?
19. If a location received a score of 60 for appearance and 40 for access, what would its factor rating score be if each factor were assigned a weight of 1/2?
20. If a location received a score of 60 for appearance and 40 for access, what would its factor rating score be if appearance were assigned a weight of 1/4 and access a weight of 3/4?

Ramp Up

21. A manufacturing firm is choosing a new location based on five factors. It considers all these factors to be equally important. What weights should it assign each factor in a factor rating analysis?

22. PowerBright must decide between two locations on which to build a new power station to provide 60 megawatt-hours of electricity a month. Location A would have a variable cost of $1,000 per megawatt-hour and location B would have a variable cost of $1,500 per megawatt-hour. A power station at location A would also require a fixed cost of $50,000 a month, although an estimate of the monthly fixed cost at location B has not been made available yet, due to ongoing negotiations with a landowner there. At what fixed cost for location B would PowerBright be indifferent to the choice of either of these two locations?

23. Best Purchase must select a location for a new store. Best Purchase has identified five factors as important to store location: land cost, road access, population density, average income, and zoning laws. Best Purchase feels that each of these factors has the same importance to a new store location decision, with the exception of land cost, which it feels is twice as important as any one of the other four factors. In a factor rating analysis, what weight would Best Purchase attach to land cost?

24. A manufacturing firm is choosing between two locations based on factors A and B. The first location scored 10 for factor A and 90 for factor B. The second location scored 90 for factor A and 10 for factor B. Over what range of weights for factor A would this firm select the first location?

Reminder: Short answers appear in Appendix A. Go to **NoteShaper.com** for full video tutorials on each question.

Scenarios

25. E-Me, a chain of personal electronics superstores, distributes merchandise to its 300 retail outlets from five regional warehouses. E-Me wants to locate a new central distribution center that would supply each of these five regional warehouses. E-Me has determined these coordinates of each regional warehouse:

Warehouse	*X*	*Y*
A	2	7
B	–8	2
C	0	1
D	2	6
E	5	–4

a. Assuming that the amount of merchandise shipped from the new distribution center to each regional warehouse is equal, what should be the coordinates of the new distribution center?

b. Now assume that E-Me has provided the following additional information: 50 tons of personal electronics will be shipped to regional warehouse A annually, 100 tons will be shipped to regional warehouse B, 100 tons will be shipped to regional warehouse C, 200 tons will be shipped to regional warehouse D, and 400 tons will be shipped to regional warehouse E. What should be the coordinates of the new distribution center?

c. Unfortunately, regional warehouse E has just burned down, and E-me does not plan to replace it. Rather, E-me will split the merchandise formally shipped to warehouse E equally among the remaining four warehouse locations. Given this new four-warehouse system, what should be the coordinates of the new distribution center?

26. Garysburg Fire Rescue (GFR) is considering three different locations for a new fire station. Using factor rating, GFR has created the following table:

Factor	Weight	Location 1: SW 34th Street	Location 2: SW 23rd Terrace near Williston Road	Location 3: SW 63rd Avenue
Cost of available land parcel	0.3	4	2	1
Accessibility (road size and traffic)	0.5	5	2	4
Size of available land parcel	0.2	1	5	3

When rating these locations, GFR used a 5-point scale, where 1 means unfavorable and 5 means excellent.

a. Which of the following statements are true and which are false?

   i. The cost of the available land parcel is of the greatest importance in this analysis.

   ii. Location 2 has better accessibility than location 3.

   iii. GFR considers the size of the available land parcel to be the least important factor.

b. According to the analysis above, where will GFR locate the new fire station?

c. Suppose Meera at GFR said that the current weights given to the factors in the table above were wrong. She said that there isn't any difference between the cost of the available land parcel and the size of the available land parcel when compared on the issue of importance. Basically, those two factors are equally important. But, according to Meera, the accessibility factor is three times more important than either of those other two factors. According to Meera, what weight should have been given to each of the three factors?

d. Given the new set of weights expressed in part c of this scenario, now where should GFR locate the new fire station?

27. Tom, David, Dale, and Murdock are four business students who want to rent a four-bedroom apartment together for the fall semester. They have identified the three factors important to them in choosing a location for their apartment: proximity to campus, cost of rent, and quality of common areas (pool, clubhouse, fitness facility). Based on information supplied by real estate agents, the friends have rated three possible apartment locations on these factors, where 1 means worst and 10 means best:

Factor	The Courtyard Apartments	The Garden Apartments	La Mancha Apartments
Proximity to campus	10	1	9
Cost of rent	7	10	8
Quality of common areas	5	5	8

While the four friends can agree on what factors are important, they don't agree on which of the three factors is more important than the remaining factors. Using a weighting scale in which all three factor weights add up to 1.0, Tom and David agree that the quality of common areas is the most important factor and should receive a weight of 0.6. Tom and David both agree that proximity to campus should have a weight of 0.2 and cost of rent a weight of 0.2. Dale, however, doesn't own a car, so he gives proximity to campus a weight of 0.75. Dale then weights cost of rent at 0.2 and quality of common areas at 0.05. Murdock says that all three factors are equally important to him; he has no favorites.

a. What weighted score would Tom or David give to La Mancha Apartments?
b. What weighted score would Murdock give The Garden Apartments?
c. Which apartment location would Dale prefer?
d. Does anyone other than Tom and David agree on which apartment to rent?

28. West Calder Fabrication is trying to decide in which of the following three cities to locate a new production facility, and has gathered the following information about each:

City	Annual Fixed Cost	Variable Cost (per unit)
Singapore	$30,000	$2
Hong Kong	$20,000	$3
Niagara Falls	$10,000	$6

a. If this facility will produce 5,000 units annually, where should West Calder locate it?
b. What is the point of indifference between Singapore and Hong Kong?
c. Over what range of production levels would West Calder Fabrication prefer to be in Niagara Falls?

29. Consider the following map of six cities, indicated by the six dark-numbered points. The five light-colored points labeled A through E indicate five candidate locations for a new warehouse that will ship to each of the six cities:

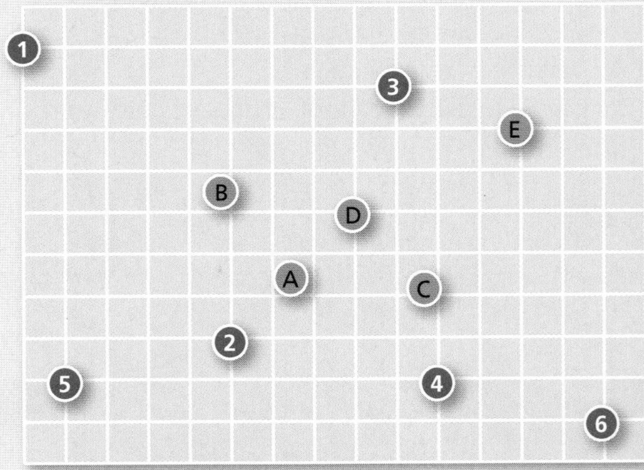

a. If the amount to be shipped from the new warehouse is equal for each of the six cities, which candidate location should be selected for the new warehouse?
b. Suppose that the monthly amount to be shipped to each of the cities is as follows: 500 tons to city 1; 200 tons to city 2; 500 tons to city 3; 100 tons to city 4; 300 tons to city 5; and 100 tons to city 6. Given this shipping information, now which candidate location should be selected for the new warehouse?

CASE STUDY: CELVIN FOODSTUFF

Celvin FoodStuff operates a chain of mini convenience stores in downtown city settings, offering beverages, snack food, and some fresh food items to passing pedestrian traffic. A typical Celvin Foodstuff is half the size of the average convenience store, with no customer parking and almost no backroom area, as Celvin delivers stock directly to store shelves early each morning. The ideal FoodStuff store includes 100 square meters of space, with a busy city sidewalk passing immediately in front of its display windows. Because a FoodStuff store relies on impulse purchases from walk-in traffic, it is better located farther from similar stores that might reduce this traffic or invite price comparisons by shoppers. Locating on the corner of a city block is considered particularly beneficial, as this doubles the visibility of the FoodStuff to passing customers.

Celvin FoodStuff rents each of its 27 current locations and is now considering adding a 28th store. Celvin management has identified three promising locations, each owned by a different commercial real estate company. The Factor Data table provides data on each location, designated by the name of the real estate rental company.

Factor Data for Celvin FoodStuff

Factor	Bay Holding Co. Location	Lin Agency Location	Martin & LeBlanc Location
Distance to nearest competitor	300 meters	50 meters	400 meters
Size	90 sq. meters	180 sq. meters	80 sq. meters
Rent	$3,100/month	$2,200/month	$2,500/month
Corner site	yes	no	no

Questions

1. Prepare this data for a factor rating analysis by converting the information provided into appropriate scores. Explain any assumptions you made during this process.
2. If each of these factors is equally important to Celvin FoodStuff, which location should it choose to rent?
3. If rent were twice as important a factor as any of the other three, would your previous recommendation change? If so, to what location?
4. If you could ask Celvin two questions for clarification before you finished your analysis and committed to a location, what would those questions be?

BIBLIOGRAPHY

Collins, J., and E. Jack. 2012. "Here or There? Deciding Where to Put Your Operations." *APICS Magazine* 22(3): 12.

Corstjens, M., and R. Lal. 2012. "Retail Doesn't Cross Borders: Here's Why and What to Do About It." *Harvard Business Review* April: 104–11.

Francis, R., L. McGinnis, and J. White. 1992. *Facility Layout and Location: An Analytic Approach.* Englewood Cliffs, NJ: Prentice Hall.

Kaluza, P., A. Kölzsch, M. Gastner, and B. Blasius. 2010. "The Complex Network of Global Cargo Ship Movements." *Journal of the Royal Society Interface* 7(48): 1093–103.

Kuo, C,. and R. White. 2004. "A Note on the Treatment of the Center-of-Gravity Method in Operations Management Textbooks." *Decision Sciences Journal of Innovative Education* 2(2): 219–27.

LaGro, J. 2008. *Site Analysis: A Contextual Approach to Sustainable Land Planning and Site Design.* Hoboken, NJ: John Wiley and Sons, Inc.

Small, C., and J. Cohen. 2004. "Continental Physiography, Climate, and the Global Distribution of Human Population." *Current Anthropology* 45(2).

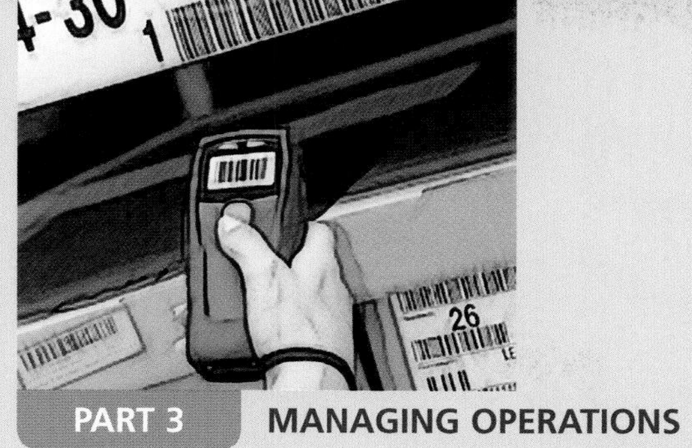

PART 3 MANAGING OPERATIONS

CHAPTER 9

Purchasing and Supply Chain Partnering

An oral contract isn't worth the paper it's written on.
—Samuel Goldywn

MAJOR SECTIONS

IN THIS CHAPTER, LOOK FOR...

- Formation and management of supply chains
- The complex environment within which supply chains operate
- Models for selecting purchasing partners and building supply chain networks.

INTRODUCTION

When one organization depends on another to provide something needed to serve its customers, this dependency creates one link in a supply chain network. In modern times, an organization that operates without supplies or assistance from any outside party would be a curiosity, as supply chains now cover the globe with complex webs of purchasing and partnering to bring products to market. Some of these networks are created and coordinated with great care, giving retailers like Walmart and manufacturers like Hewlett-Packard distinct competitive advantages in their markets. Others result from circumstance, such as a small business purchasing from a nearby store due to its convenience. Like any aspect of operations, supply chains can always be improved, and strengthening these vital webs begins by understanding their formation.

supply chain
A system consisting of all organizations that play some role in supplying a particular product to a customer.

downstream
Closeness to the end customer in the supply chain.

upstream
Closeness to the supplier in the supply chain.

SUPPLY CHAIN BASICS

By definition, supply chains connect individual businesses into networks that provide consumers with goods and services. Multiple suppliers, manufacturers, and/or service providers may be involved in any product, with each business relying on other suppliers and providers, resulting in a network of linked relationships that can grow quite complex. Figure 9.1 shows a simplified supply chain illustration, presenting terminology helpful when navigating these networks.

Organizations and activity positioned between a business and the end consumer of a product are said to be downstream of that business. Figure 9.1 positions its labels from the manufacturer's viewpoint, so that the distributor is logically downstream, although the retailer in Figure 9.1 would consider the distributor to be an upstream supply chain partner. While the boxes in Figure 9.1 represent organizations, arrows symbolize flow of goods and

FIGURE 9.1 Example Supply Chain, Manufacturer's Viewpoint

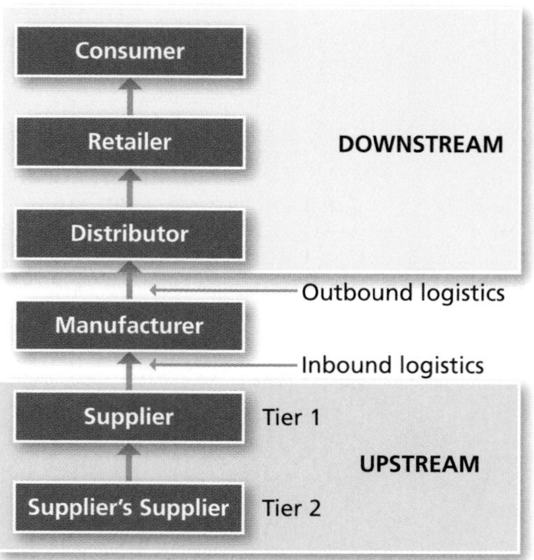

Upstream Inventory in the Restaurant Supply Chain

As a consumer product passes through B2B supply chain links, it often bears little resemblance to the product as seen by the ultimate customer. Pictured here are ready-to-eat cold salads awaiting outbound shipment from the warehouse of a tier 1 supplier of delis and restaurants. These downstream customers will repackage the contents of the buckets for B2C sales.

services, with most arrows representing both outbound logistics for a sending organization and inbound logistics for a receiving organization. Thus, these arrows also represent the purchasing process creating this flow between suppliers and buyers along the chain.

Inbound logistics connect an organization to its first tier or tier 1 suppliers, the businesses from which it purchases the materials and support it needs to participate in the supply chain. These first tier suppliers are then likely to rely on their own set of tier 1 suppliers, which become the tier 2 suppliers of the original organization. Almost all transactions governing the logistical flow suggested in Figure 9.1 would be called B2B (business-to-business) activity. In fact, all nonconsumer supply chain members in Figure 9.1 could be called B2B suppliers with the exception of the retailer, whose role in this chain is B2C (business-to-consumer) sales.

Ironically, supply chains will exist whether they are managed or not. For any organization to function effectively, it must secure goods and services from some external source at the right time, in the right place, and for the right price. In turn, the organization takes these inputs, adds value, and makes available a product for its downstream customer. Organizations operating without attempting to communicate or coordinate with fellow supply chain participants risk losing competitiveness against organizations that do. Unmanaged supply chains not only miss opportunities to supply the end customer more effectively, they can even inflict damage upon themselves, such as suffering harsh cycles of high and low inventory levels touched off by exaggerated chain reactions to changes in the end customer's buying pattern, known generally as the *bullwhip effect*.

The practice of supply chain management includes several areas, all sharing a common thread of coordination and flow along the links illustrated in Figure 9.1. Major areas include purchasing and sourcing, materials planning, inventory management, distribution planning and logistics, product development, and quality management. As a business function, supply chain management is distinctive in that it interfaces with the external world of downstream customers and upstream suppliers, while simultaneously serving the internal organization. Achieving this balance begins at the strategic level, with long-term decisions on how the supply chain function should best be structured and to whom it should link.

outbound logistics
Management of flow departing a facility or other system.

inbound logistics
Management of flow into a facility or other system.

tier 1 supplier
An organization's immediate supplier.

tier 2 supplier
The supplier of an organization's immediate supplier.

business-to-business (B2B)
Commercial transactions between organizations.

business-to-consumer (B2C)
Commercial transactions between an organization and individual consumers.

STRATEGIC SUPPLY CHAIN PARTNERING

Organizations often compete to obtain resources and sell products in a global marketplace. Few can afford to focus solely on their internal operations, making active supply chain management critical to their success. This success begins by first determining how the supply chain function is integrated into the organization, which often reflects issues seemingly unrelated to topics such as inventory management. Rather, study of the supply chain function often begins with assessing organizational policy, culture, and even the shape of the business's organizational chart.

Structuring the Supply Chain Function

centralized organizational policy Assigning decision making and authority to one individual or set of individuals within a larger organization.

functional organizational structure An organization of specialists grouped into distinct departments.

Overall organizational structure and policy can strongly influence supply chain management. Any multisite or multidivisional organization must determine the degree of centralization of the supply management function that will best support its corporate goals. Centralized organizational policy assigns decision-making authority and responsibility to a single center, typically a head office or headquarters. Organizations following this policy usually adopt a functional organizational structure, grouping individuals according to their area of expertise and assigning authority over that area to that group. In the case of supply management, this approach creates a single purchasing department within the larger organization, which in turn effects these:

- Buying leverage created by consolidation of purchases.
- Standardization of purchasing policies and procedures.
- Specialized buying expertise and better communication with outside suppliers due to single point of contact.
- Enhanced ability to implement e-procurement solutions such as e-auctions and electronic data interchange (EDI).

Each of these advantages of centralized supply management lowers costs by increasing purchasing volume through a single department, allowing greater up-front investment in the purchasing process itself. Consolidating all purchasing requirements also enables optimization of procurement; one department gathers all the information necessary to identify the best plan across the entire organization.

decentralized organizational policy Distributing decision making and authority to individuals or groups throughout a larger organization.

matrix organizational structure An organization that groups differing functions together according to requirements of the work.

Centralized supply management works well with smaller organizations but, as an organization grows and becomes more complex, the centralized decision-making process may grow cumbersome and inefficient. If a decentralized organizational policy is adopted for supply management, decision-making authority and responsibility are assigned to managers throughout the organization. This can take the form of small purchasing departments in different divisions or geographic locations, or the organization may adopt a matrix structure, creating collaborative, cross-functional teams that each have a procurement specialist as a member. Distributing supply management throughout a larger organization achieves these benefits:

- Better communication with internal customers due to closer proximity.
- Faster decision making due to flatter organizational structure.
- Fostered relationships with smaller and more local suppliers at each of the larger organization's sites, due to smaller purchasing needs.

Any compromise between the centralization and decentralization creates a hybrid policy where authority and responsibility are shared between some central department and individual sites. In supply management, one common hybrid policy uses a decentralized philosophy except for certain common purchases, which must be procured through one central department. This creates the buying leverage for common items, but leaves open the opportunity for smaller local purchases of less common ones. The goal of any form of hybridization is to find the best mix of benefits from both centralization and decentralization supporting the needs of that particular organization.

Selecting Supply Chain Partners

In addition to supporting internal customers such as engineering, design, information technology, operations, and marketing, supply chain management looks outward and interacts with suppliers and other outside parties, enabling its internal customers to create value for the organization's external customers. These external interactions can range from a simple one-time purchase to a long-term strategic partnership with a trusted supplier.

Looking upstream, strategic supply chain management begins with an understanding of what must be purchased there. A spend analysis reveals what the organization has been purchasing previously and from whom. One of the objectives of this report is to determine whether any goods or services would benefit from consolidation into larger categories of purchasing, to pursue savings when approaching a supplier upstream. Grouping individual purchases together to create buying power, such as consolidating all purchases of milk, butter, and cheese into dairy products, creates the foundation of a commodity or category plan. Commodity/category planning continues by considering how each purchasing category should be managed in the future, using tools such as supplier positioning and supplier preferencing.

spend analysis Collecting, classifying, and reporting the expenditures of an organization.

commodity/category plans Consolidating related products or services to increase buying leverage.

Supplier Positioning Supplier positioning (also known as a *Kraljic matrix,* after its author) classifies purchasing to gain better insight into how each category should be managed by the buying organization. Graphing the cost of purchasing relative to its total risk creates the supplier positioning matrix in Figure 9.2, labeled with each of the four classifications into which any purchasing category might fall.

supplier positioning Classifying purchases according to the buyer's annual procurement cost versus relative risk.

Across the horizontal axis of Figure 9.2, the annual expense of purchasing measures the influence this purchasing has on the overall profitability of the buying organization. This issue alone is used to prioritize attention to purchasing in a simpler ranking scheme known as an ABC policy. However, supplier positioning also recognizes the vulnerability of the supply, determined by a variety of factors that can include limited availability and shortages of the item being purchased, the reliability of delivery, the number of potential suppliers, and even environmental concerns. Purchases positioned in the bottom left-hand quadrant of Figure 9.2 are described as *tactical acquisitions*, being of both low value and risk. A minimum amount of time should be spent on purchasing in this category, because there is little benefit to focusing energy on these items. Items in the bottom

ABC policy Prioritizing the management of inventory according to the significance of each item's annual dollar volume to the organization.

Supplier Positioning Matrix — **FIGURE 9.2**

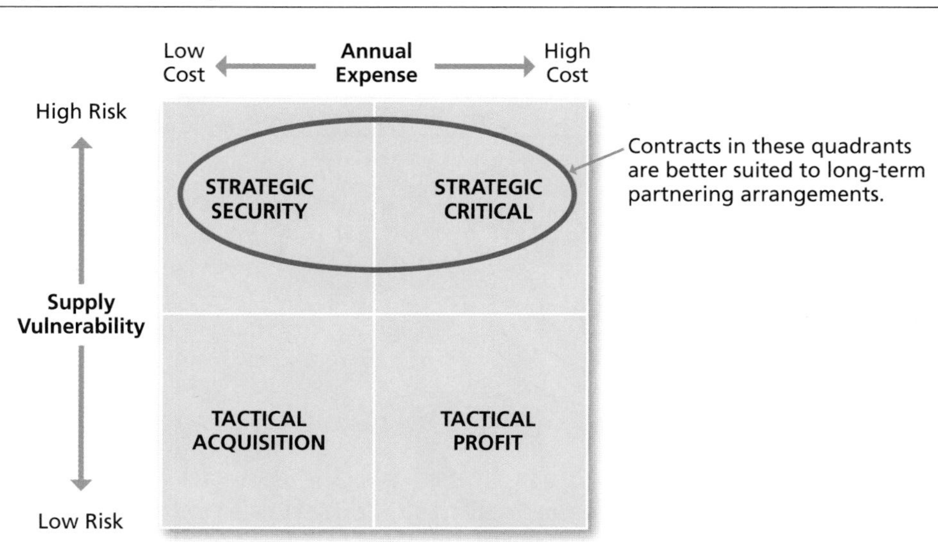

right-hand quadrant, the *tactical profit* category, are relatively high value but their low risk implies the presence of several competitive suppliers, so the buying organization should focus on leveraging its purchasing power when selecting a supplier. Purchases in the top left-hand quadrant, described as *strategic security,* are of lower monetary value but do represent a critical risk to the organization, so the objective here should be to ensure continuity of supply, even at a premium price, and developing relationships with potential suppliers. Finally, *strategic critical* purchases in the top right-hand quadrant are both high in value and in risk to the organization. These items are the natural focus of the organization, requiring the most time and effort devoted to purchasing decisions, contingency planning, and maintaining close supply chain partnerships.

Scenario 1a

Supplier Positioning

Fields of Green is a busy vegetarian restaurant located near a large university campus. The dayshift manager of this restaurant is responsible for purchasing the many different goods and services required to operate Fields of Green. Currently, the manager is considering four purchasing categories: fresh vegetables, security system monitoring, office supplies, and after-hours cleaning services. Usually, the Fields of Green dayshift manager takes the same approach to selecting any tier 1 supplier, although the restaurant does spend far more on purchasing vegetables and cleaning services than on office supplies or security system monitoring.

What does the supplier positioning model suggest about these four purchasing categories? What does this suggest about how the dayshift manager at Fields of Green should approach purchasing?

Analysis

Although it could be useful to know the details of a spend analysis at Fields of Green, the four categories mentioned do strongly suggest the four different positions on the supplier positioning matrix, a sketch of which might look like this:

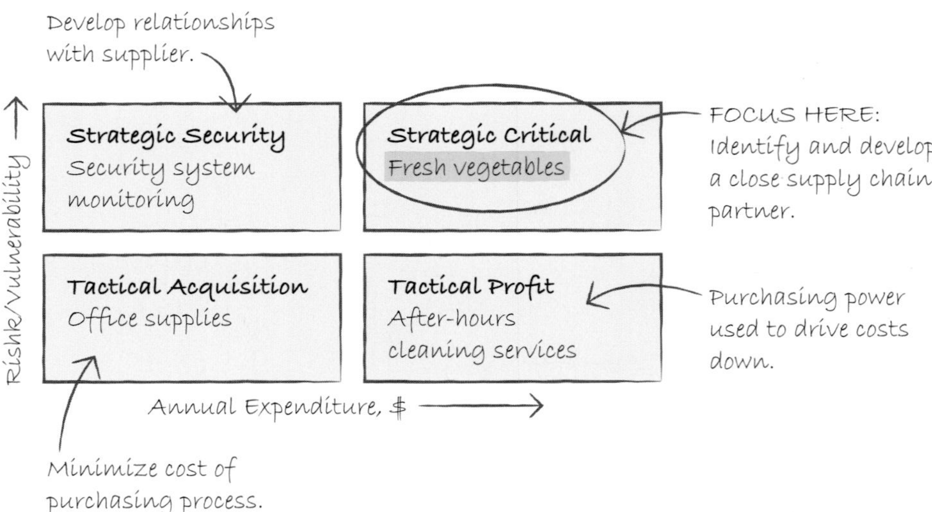

Insight This matrix suggests that the dayshift manager should take a different approach to each of the four purchasing categories mentioned. The dayshift manager should consider focusing on the purchasing of fresh vegetables for Fields of Green, since the vegetarian restaurant spends a significant amount of money on vegetables and is also the most vulnerable to any disruption in its fresh vegetable supply. While Fields of Green also spends heavily on after-hours cleaning services, this is less central to its core operations and the likely availability of several potential suppliers suggests that the Fields of Green manager should leverage its purchasing power to lower costs. The security systems contract, due to high sensitivity but low relative cost, means that if Fields of Green currently has a reliable security provider, the manager should work to maintain a good relationship with that provider and may even tolerate a small premium in price. Finally, the dayshift manager should invest the least energy in identifying suppliers for Fields of Green office supplies. The relatively low cost and low risk that office supplies present in a restaurant operation suggest that the manager could rely on purchasing these supplies as needed at the nearest discount store. ■

Supplier Preferencing The supplier positioning matrix clarifies what strategy a buying organization should adopt for purchasing a certain item or category of items. Before proceeding, that same organization must consider how each supplier in the marketplace might view that same purchasing opportunity. This is captured in the supplier preferencing matrix illustrated in Figure 9.3. Here the buyer's potential purchasing is evaluated for its relative value versus its relative attractiveness to a potential supplier, creating four different viewpoints that the supplier is likely to take of the buyer. Generally, the value of the buyer's business is determined by factors such as the size of the buyer's potential purchasing account, the overall size of the supplier, and the number of suppliers competing for that same business. The attractiveness of the buyer's business concerns its potential profitability, which includes issues as varied as the cost of maintaining the buyer's business, the buyer's reputation for on-time payment, whether the supplier believes the buyer's account will grow in the future, and even the perceived prestige of association with the buyer.

supplier preferencing Classifying a supplier by how it would likely view the buyer.

A supplier whose viewpoint places it within the bottom half of the matrix is generally not a good business match for the buyer. A potential supplier in the bottom left-hand quadrant of Figure 9.3 would consider the opportunity of little value relative to its other accounts and relatively unattractive for other reasons, and thus merely a nuisance. As a result, this supplier would likely have little interest in the opportunity and provide little support, implying that the buying organization should avoid such a supplier if possible.

Supplier Preferencing Matrix **FIGURE 9.3**

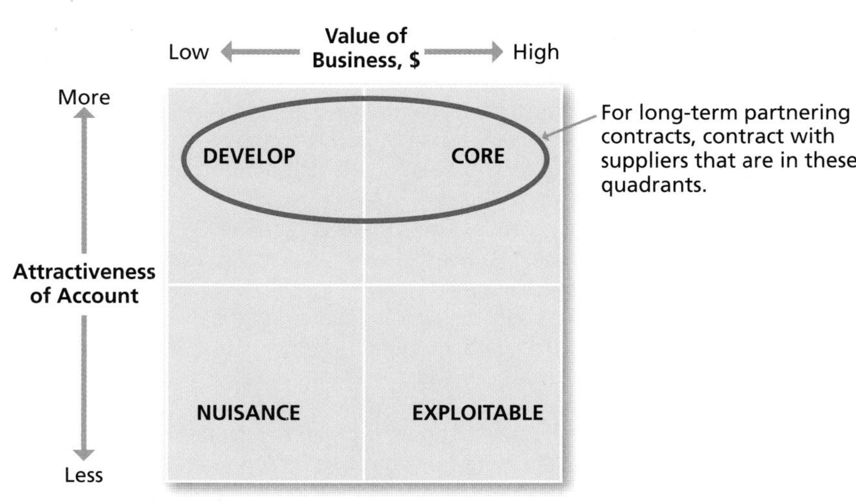

Information Technology as Strategic Security

Even though a business may only occasionally spend on installation or repair of communication and information infrastructure, services like the one pictured here are very often prioritized as strategic security. While the expense is not the majority of the business's overall operation, the risk associated with access to information and potential disruption of communication may give the client business reasons to pick an information technology provider carefully and develop an enduring relationship.

The bottom right-hand quadrant represents the view that the buyer's business is valuable but is nonetheless distinctly unattractive, such as requiring tight delivery windows or other unfavorable conditions for the supplier. Here the buyer should be aware that the supplier would likely view this business as exploitable, asking a high price with little concern for losing the opportunity.

The upper half of Figure 9.3 represents better matches to the buyer. A supplier in the top left-hand quadrant would view the buyer as a relatively low value but otherwise highly attractive opportunity, so the supplier would likely work hard to develop the buyer's business, at least in the short term. Finally, the best match to the buyer would be located in the top right-hand core quadrant, where the buyer's account is considered both a valuable and attractive account to the supplier, who would likely offer a high level of service and work vigorously to retain the buyer's future business. This is also the most logical group from which the buyer could select candidates for developing strategic alliances and partnerships.

Scenario 1b

Supplier Preferencing

The dayshift manager at Fields of Green in Scenario 1a now realizes that the vegetarian restaurant's supply of fresh vegetables deserves special attention. The manager decides that a partnering arrangement is suitable, due to the strategic importance of fresh vegetables to Fields of Green's operation. Fields of Green has done business with four fresh vegetable suppliers in the past:

- Global Fruit Supplies—a very large company that sells almost every kind of fresh fruit imaginable and can deliver a narrower range of fresh vegetables as well. Global Fruit Supplies specializes in supplying food-processing plants, supermarket chains, and other high-volume institutional buyers.
- Total Veg, Inc.—a vegetable wholesaler similar to its competitor Global Fruit Supplies, although not quite as large. Total Veg boasts many major supermarket chains as clients for both fresh and canned vegetables.
- Fresh Veggies, Inc.—a multinational company specializing in the on-time delivery of large quantities of fresh vegetables directly to restaurant kitchens. Fresh Veggies prefers to negotiate with restaurant franchises, and supplies many well-known restaurant chains across North America and Asia.
- All About Veg LLC—a local company that partners with nearby farms to offer a wide variety of freshly picked vegetables and fruits throughout the year. Like the larger Fresh Veggies, Inc., All About Veg specializes in small daily deliveries directly to commercial kitchens.

Where would each of these suppliers fall on the supplier preferencing matrix? What does this suggest the manager should do?

Analysis

Each of the four suppliers suggests a different quadrant on the supplier preferencing matrix, which might be sketched like this:

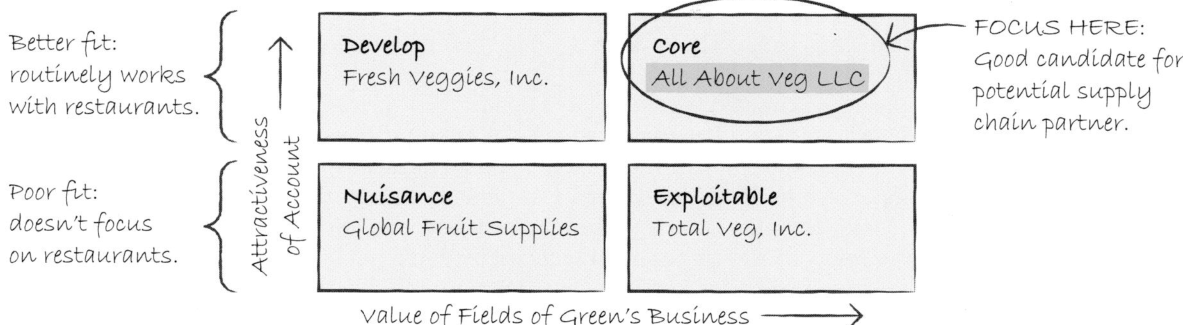

Insight Supplier preferencing suggests that the manager focus first on All About Veg LLC as a supply chain partner. All About Veg would consider Fields of Green a core business, since this fresh vegetable supplier is adapted to the rigors of commercial kitchen delivery, and securing Fields of Green as a client would be a valuable expansion of All About Veg's own small business. All About Veg could be expected to work the hardest toward a successful partnership, where its larger competitor Fresh Veggies, Inc., would not be as impressed with the opportunity to serve one restaurant, and thus not as attentive. Fresh Veggies, Inc., remains a possibility, and might develop a partnership with Fields of Green if Fresh Veggies felt that Fields of Green would expand into a larger chain in the future.

The analysis also clarifies which of Fields of Green's previous suppliers are not the best fit for the restaurant. Global Fruit Supplies and Total Veg, Inc., both specialize in high-volume delivery of fresh foods to other large organizations, and thus neither would consider the opportunity to deliver small amounts directly to a kitchen to be attractive. Being smaller than Global Fruit Supplies, Total Veg, Inc., would perceive this account as more valuable, but may ask premium prices and remain relatively indifferent to being awarded the business. Global Fruit Supplies should be deselected as a viable partner if possible; while fully capable of supplying Fields of Green with fresh vegetables, this supplier would likely consider the opportunity to be nothing more than a nuisance, distracting it from its mission of high-volume fruit distribution. ■

Tools for Global Supply Chain Partnerships

A strategic supply chain partnership can be loosely defined as a close relationship between a buyer and a seller to pursue a mutual advantage. The importance of accurate forecasting and the value of sharing reliable information quickly are critical to ensure orders are accurate and on-time. To underscore this, business models such as collaborative planning, forecasting, and replenishment (CPFR) emphasize this aspect of inventory management, particularly in partnerships between manufacturers and retailers. The CPFR process adopts an end-customer viewpoint and focuses on information sharing by manufacturer and retailer through joint planning, demand, and supply management activities.

Once established, supply chain partnerships can be enhanced in a variety of ways. One technology often critical to successful CPFR is electronic data interchange, or EDI. Organizations who partner through EDI create links between their internal information systems, allowing the seamless transfer of data and instant logging of transactions. While

collaborative planning, forecasting, and replenishment (CPFR) A business model where supply chain partners share information and plan jointly in inventory management.

electronic data interchange (EDI) The linking of two information systems from two different organizations to transfer data and conduct transactions.

this requires up-front investment, benefits such as better communication and quicker access to information can translate into substantial savings, including a distinct reduction in the bullwhip effect mentioned earlier. Supply chain partnerships may also rely on these tools:

- **Web-forms and Internet-based transactions.** Two organizations may decide against EDI due to concerns such as the up-front cost or a security issue in data sharing. Those organizations may still pursue EDI's greater transaction speed by creating web-based forms for use in the partnership, speeding the processing of requests and allowing greater visibility for a limited amount of information through web-based reports.
- **Vendor-managed inventory.** In a vendor-managed inventory (VMI) arrangement, a buyer entrusts all aspects of the management of some good to its supplier, including ordering and stocking the good in the buyer's facility. Generally, this inventory is not considered purchased until it is then resold or consumed by the buyer.
- **Third-Party Logistics** and **Fourth-Party Logistics.** In a third-party logistics (3PL) agreement the transportation required by outbound logistics is frequently outsourced to another firm in major supply chains. 3PL service providers not only provide such transportation, these potential partners offer additional services such as warehousing, inventory management, and freight forwarding. The rise in popularity of 3PLs has motivated fourth-party logistics (4PL) partners, consulting firms dedicated to greater integration of supply chains through logistical opportunities.

vendor-managed inventory (VMI) Transferal of ownership and management of inventory within a system to its external provider, who will be compensated after its use by the system.

third-party logistics (3PL) Outsourcing logistics activities to a provider.

fourth-party logistics (4PL) Logistical consulting provided by a firm without logistical assets.

Global trade has become more prominent in recent years as many international trade barriers have relaxed. Some organizations market and distribute their products and services worldwide, while other smaller firms may work as local agents or suppliers of multinational companies elsewhere. Producers in regions with particular productive advantages, such as Saudi Arabia for oil, China for labor, or Canada for timber, can leverage these abilities in the global marketplace. A single manufactured item such as an automobile may consist of components purchased from the Middle East, Asia, Europe, Canada, and South America.

Increasing competitive advantage through cost reduction has been a key driver in the recent expansion of global trade. In countries where the cost of labor and associated benefits are much lower, savings on manual processes such as the assembly of finished goods can quickly exceed the cost of the transportation of those products between countries and continents. Technological advances, such as the use of radio frequency identification (RFID) tagging to provide seamless tracking of pipeline inventory between

radio frequency identification (RFID) The tagging of objects with devices that may be detected and interrogated for information by remote electronic readers, allowing identification and tracking without contact.

Handling Inventory as a Third Party

When an organization centralizes its buying to save on the cost of some purchases, it must also invest in the ability to safely handle bulk shipments. This includes equipment and skilled operators such as the forklift and driver in this picture, as well as sufficient storage space and control methods to keep the inventory organized. Where once the phrase *third-party logistics* was assumed to mean outsourcing the transportation of goods, increasing numbers of organizations rely on these companies to also manage warehouses and provide all these associated services.

locations, have reduced the complexity of inventory management in this setting. RFID technology has been a particular boost to smart seals that allow businesses to streamline customs procedures, when inventory crosses between nations. Still global sourcing carries numerous potential risks, such as longer lead times and heavier pipeline inventory burdens, unfavorable currency fluctuations and differing tax policies, differing international accounting and shipping laws, and increased exposure to potential supply disruption due to natural disasters or even bad weather. The benefits of going global, however, often outweigh these disadvantages for mid- to large-sized businesses, and support companies continue to emerge to offer specialist advice to smaller firms considering this opportunity.

smart seals
Tamper-evident seals that guarantee shipments have not been tampered with after inspection at the port of origin.

OPERATING A SUPPLY CHAIN

Many external factors may impact the operation of an organization's supply chain. First, complex interaction between supply chain partners is subject to the legal environment in which they interact. Since supply chain management links an organization with the world outside, this function also provides powerful opportunities to draw in a greater diversity of cultures and ideas to enrich the organization, but simultaneously raises new issues of ethical behavior and sustainability. Operating a supply chain with careful attention to these issues enables each organization to pursue a triple bottom line of economic prosperity, environmental quality, and social equity—all of which begin with the supply chain contract.

Legal and Regulatory Considerations

Most organizations are legal entities, conducting business with other organizations through contracts. These contracts shape the links within a supply chain and govern the activity among organizations, so it is important to understand both the contracts themselves and who creates them.

Terms and Conditions of Contract In the business world a contract is the total legal obligation between two or more parties, normally expressed in writing and usually defining goods to be purchased or services to be performed for a certain sum of money. A contract is made when an offer is accepted between two capable parties. Offers may be rejected by the party receiving them, or that party may make a counteroffer for the first party to consider.

For the lower-value, lower-risk purchases represented as tactical acquisitions in the supplier positioning matrix, a seller's or buyer's boilerplate terms and conditions are usually sufficient to create a contract, although care must be taken that both parties understand whose boilerplate is to be used. For other purchases, both parties should fully explore potential risks and jointly create a set of terms and conditions that incorporates the final positions of both parties under a single contract. Such a contract often reflects these specific issues:

contract
The total legal obligation among two or more parties.

offer
To present a proposal for acceptance or rejection.

counteroffer
An offer that is made in response to a previous offer.

boilerplate
In purchasing, standard terms and conditions of contract, covering major generic risks.

- **Variation to contract price**—defining when and how the supplier's price might change during a longer-term contract, often stated in relation to a publicly tracked statistic such as the consumer price index.
- **Service levels or service credits**—defining a level of service, such as on-time delivery, and what the buying organization shall receive if that level of service is not met, such as a discount on the price. Occasionally, the seller may be entitled to some form of credit if the service level is exceeded, such as a bonus for early completion of a critical construction project.
- **Provision of labor**—specifying the level of professionally trained and qualified staff to be provided through the contract. For example, a commercial ambulance company may sign a contract to supply ambulances staffed with two licensed

paramedics each, yet negotiate another contract in which each ambulance is staffed with one licensed paramedic and one ambulance driver who does necessarily have medical credentials.
- **Termination**—defining the conditions under which the contract may be terminated by either party. Unless these terms are exercised, the contract terminates naturally upon completion.

Once both parties agree on terms and conditions, they create and sign a contract, creating a link within a supply chain.

purchasing agent A person empowered to buy on behalf of an organization.

sales agent A person empowered to bind a selling organization in contracts with buyers.

sales representative A person who solicits orders but cannot bind the selling organization in contracts with buyers.

actual authority Authority specified explicitly, often in the job description.

implied authority Authority an organization intends the agent to have.

apparent authority Giving the impression of actual authority without having actual authority.

Authority and Regulation Although an organization is a legal persona, it cannot negotiate and sign a contract personally. If the contract is an agreement to buy, any person with the authority to contract on behalf of the organization is called a purchasing agent. Although this is an important distinction, purchasing agents are not necessarily called that by name, often having titles such as buyer, senior buyer, purchasing manager, or even vice president. While the purchasing agent acts on behalf of a buying organization, a sales agent acts on behalf of the selling organization. In contrast, sales representatives solicit orders for signing by sales agents, but do not have the authority to bind their organization into agreements.

Authority is an important concept; it dictates what a particular individual can actually do on behalf of an organization. The actual authority delegated by an organization to a purchasing agent is an explicit statement of the agent's power, such as the authority to enter into contracts up to $500,000 for the organization. Actual authority is documented in writing, often contained in the individual's job description or legal documents such as a power of attorney. The implied authority of purchasing agents is their power to carry out what is stated in their actual authority, such as the authority to request bids and negotiate contracts up to $500,000. However, it is not uncommon for individuals to use apparent authority, where it appears they have the actual authority of a purchasing agent when in fact they do not. This occurs when personnel without actual authority act anyway, such as an engineer by-passing official purchasing channels to buy a small component for a project, and then seeking reimbursement from the organization. Also known as *maverick buying,* individuals in this instance are personally liable for such purchases unless a purchasing agent in the organization ratifies the purchase by accepting it for and on behalf of the company.

Agents bind their business into contracts that must conform to the regulatory environment in which they operate. For example, in the United States, numerous laws govern interstate trade, including these:

- The Sherman Anti Trust Act (1890) made it illegal to conspire or collude to restrict competition (such as price fixing among suppliers or group boycotts). Later, the Clayton Act (1914) plugged loopholes in the Sherman Act by making it illegal to substantially lessen competition through the creation of a monopoly or by tying in the sale of one product with another.
- The Federal Trade Commission Act (1914) established a regulatory authority (FTC) in the United States, and made illegal unfair and deceptive methods of competition. This includes issues of advertising and consumer protection.
- The Robinson-Patman Act (1936) requires a supplier to sell a product at the same price in each state within the US, all other factors being equal. The supplier must justify any price variances among states by citing issues such as lower price through lower local costs, liquidating obsolete or damaged products or matching a competitor's lower price.

Many governments have specific regulations and laws for different business sectors, and thus agents developing international agreements must be aware of these distinctions.

Border Delays in Global Sourcing

Delivery of goods from outside a country is subject to complexity that local sources do not suffer. In most areas, trucks crossing an international border must stop for customs inspection, sometimes adding considerable time to their trip. As a result, the trucks queuing here are a familiar sight in border cities around the world. These trucks are entering Canada from the United States, but their transition through Canadian customs may be further complicated by the fact that their cargo could be from anywhere in the world.

For example, standards of workplace safety relevant to service and employment contracts are outlined by the Occupational Safety and Health Act (1970) in the United States, while similar but not identical principles are covered by the Health and Safety at Work Act (1974) in the United Kingdom. Doing business globally also exposes a transaction to a variety of international regulatory agreements. These are some of the best known:

- The United Nations Convention on Contracts for the International Sale of Goods (CISG, 1988) is a treaty ratified by 76 countries (as of 2010), allowing exporters to avoid choice of country law issues. The CISG represents a standard, accepted set of rules for international transactions and these rules automatically apply to an international purchasing contract unless expressly excluded by the document.
- The World Trade Organization (WTO, 1995) replaced the General Agreement on Tariffs and Trade (1948), providing a framework for negotiating and formalizing trade agreements between its member countries. It currently has 153 members representing 97% of world trade.
- The North American Free Trade Agreement (NAFTA, 1994) is a regulatory agreement among the United States, Canada, and Mexico, reducing barriers to trade between the three largest countries of the North American continent.

Purchasing agents must ensure their organization complies with all appropriate laws and regulations and often consult with specialist attorneys in the countries in which they do business.

Diversity and Ethics

In business strategy, the supply chain function can play a powerful role in the development of corporate diversity initiatives. As goods and services are bought and sold on an increasingly global scale, the issue of diversity often expands from a key goal of social responsibility to an imperative for competitiveness. Cultivating external links with a diverse group of supply chain partners enables the supply chain function to draw fresh ideas and new competencies into the internal core of an organization. Diversity of membership also strengthens a supply chain's resilience by lessening its dependency on any single supplier, region, mode of transportation, or other issue that might otherwise disrupt its operation.

resilience
The ability of a system to adjust to or recover from a shock or sudden change.

Historically, governments around the world have led the way in pursuing supply chain diversity, demonstrating its multiple benefits to the private sector through government procurement. As an example, passage of the Small Business Act (1953) in the United States created the Small Business Administration (SBA) to aid, assist, and protect the interests of small businesses, ensuring their inclusion in a fair share of government contracts. Both the act and the agency further recognize and promote the interests of businesses owned and controlled by women, racial minorities, veterans, and several other socially or economically disadvantaged groups. Organizations that champion supplier diversity between nations include the United Nations, the Asia Pacific Economic Cooperation, the World Bank, and the Organization for Economic Cooperation and Development.

In certain instances resistance to a supplier diversity initiative may occur internally, often from conflict between the short-term costs versus the longer-term benefits. A strongly centralized supply chain function often has the advantage in championing the early stages of any initiative, although a decentralized supply chain function often has an advantage when recruiting smaller suppliers and drawing in local knowledge. An organization's supply chain function is also uniquely positioned to influence other organizations. Every organization should have a written policy stating its corporate code of ethics, or what conduct it deems acceptable versus unacceptable. The supply chain function of an organization should communicate this policy to others and evaluate potential suppliers for the degree of fit between that policy and the suppliers' ethics. If, for example, the organization believes the use of prison labor is unethical, that organization is not a good fit with a supplier who uses prison labor in production. If the buying organization is true to its stated ethics, it may either offer the supplier the opportunity to cease the activity it deems unethical in exchange for its business or decline the business opportunity to that supplier.

ethics
Principles governing conduct, delineating good from bad.

Strong ethical leadership downstream in supply chains can cascade back through tier 1, tier 2, and beyond, spreading ethical change through multiple organizations upstream. However, an organization may state a certain activity is unethical and choose not to practice it, yet make no such demands on its supply chain partners. This weak adherence to ethics, or turning a blind eye toward the supplier's activities, does allow practices that end consumers might consider unacceptable to exist, essentially hidden from view, farther upstream in their supply chains.

In general, impartiality and fairness are two ethical principles central to both successful supply chain operation and business transactions in general. In the context of supply chain management, organizations maintain impartiality and fairness through these efforts:

- Implementing policies and procedures for business processes that are fair, unbiased, and applied consistently.
- Encouraging prompt and fair communication, including problem resolution.
- Maintaining fully transparent processes, such as bidding for contracts, bid evaluation, and feedback for suppliers.
- Publishing the organization's explicit policy for reporting those suspected of unlawful or unethical practices.

Traditionally, professional organizations also maintain similar ethical codes that they expect to be practiced by their members. In the case of supply chain management, the Institute for Supply Management (ISM) and The Association for Operations Management (APICS) provide such guidelines.

Sustainability

sustainability
The degree to which activity with immediate benefit does not incur greater costs in the long term.

Sustainability in supply chain operation refers to replenishing resources as they are consumed, maintaining a steady environmental state, reducing waste, reducing pollution, and managing risk. These activities all allow continuous operation of the supply chain, as current activities will not be conducted at the expense of future operation. Historically, sustainability has been associated with conserving the consumption of limited natural resources, such as coal, oil, and lumber. Recycling is included in these efforts, as is the development of renewable resources. Concern for the environment, particularly global climate change, created recognition for the need to consider pollution as well as conservation when considering sustainability. As an example, Dell Computer announced a successful effort to reduce its carbon emissions and fund other reductions through the purchase of environmental credits, such that its operations do not increase current levels of greenhouse gases. While this is a worthy effort, the reality of carbon neutrality is made far more complex by modern supply chain practices. In the case of Dell, it is estimated that Dell's own operations represent as little as 10% of the total carbon-producing activity involved in the creation of one of its computers, when considering production and shipping among all Dell's component suppliers.

Practices that assure sustainability are often referred to as green, or as greener supply chain management. However, not all issues of sustainability are directly related to the natural environment. For example, one unsustainable practice of a large organization would be to use its extreme purchasing power to force key suppliers to lower their prices such that their businesses are profoundly weakened in the long run. Under these conditions, the suppliers would likely fail during an inevitable future downturn, breaking the supply chain. This is an ethically questionable use of power on behalf of the first organization and it creates conditions that will disrupt that organization's operation in the future, particularly if those suppliers were members of the strategic security/critical quadrants of the supplier positioning model. The failure in these suppliers would be a violation of the principles of sustainability. Lean practices are another good example of the concept of sustainability not strictly linked to the environment. An operation is said to be lean when it operates without waste, such as without unnecessary packaging, idle stocks of valuable goods, or avoidable delays. A lean supply chain, therefore, focuses the best use of its resources, which lessens its adverse environmental impact while simultaneously maximizing its financial attractiveness. The longer the planning horizon, the more difficult it can be to distinguish the issues of sustainability and profitability from one another.

green
Assures sustainability.

lean
Operating without waste.

Supply Chain Risks

The supply chain is the lifeblood of an organization and consequently any changes to it can pose great risks. Supply chain disruption can cause lost business opportunities, damage to the company's reputation, and loss of profit and share value. In domestic supply chains, risk management is centered on ensuring a supplier can indeed provide what is ordered and on developing contingencies should requirements not be met. A supply chain professional should have a good understanding of the domestic marketplace and with good category management may mitigate many of these risks, often by maintaining awareness of a healthy selection of preferred suppliers for important but noncritical goods.

In global supply chains these risks are exacerbated as the goods and services are generally strategic critical in nature to start with, and this condition alone means it is not easy to find a substitute supplier quickly should problems arise. Global supply partnerships are also exposed to the following risks and difficulties particular to international trade:

- **Cultural differences**—which can lead to cultural misunderstandings between individuals and organizations based in different countries.
- **Differences in intellectual property laws between countries**—which may result in sensitive information being forwarded to tier 2 suppliers (and beyond) without appropriate protection of the interests of the original company.

- **Greater complexity of communication**—translators, time differences, and diverse cultures come into play, resulting in greater opportunity for expensive mistakes.
- **Difficulties in problem solving and expediting**—due to the distance between parties and the complexity of communication.
- **Greater exposure to political and environmental threats**—leaving open the possibility of supply disturbances from bad weather, natural disaster, and even pirates half a world away.

Supply chain risks cannot be managed until they are identified. The many approaches to risk management begin with identification of a potential threat, followed by estimates of the likelihood of that threat and the magnitude of its impact. Methods of monitoring and possibly mitigating the risk are then identified, and accountability delegated. This is done for all identified risk events and a prioritized report card showing the trends of those risks is developed for senior management. This holistic approach attempts to identify risks and report their movements back to stakeholders and decision makers for corrective action before any major disruption is evidenced.

THE PURCHASING PROCESS

Money saved by a purchasing agent has a powerful influence over the organization's bottom line. If, for example, a business operates with a 10% profit margin, every dollar saved in purchasing has the same impact on profitability as a $10 increase in sales. Thus, an appropriate and well-defined purchasing process is not only vital to successful supply chain operation, but it is also vital to the financial well-being of the organization linking into the supply chain. Purchasing is also known as procurement, but not all procurement is necessarily purchasing. The term *procurement* refers to all acquisitions of outside goods and services, and thus includes both purchasing and other forms of acquisition, such as trading, recycling, or extracting.

procurement
The acquisition of goods and services on behalf of an organization.

The exact steps in a generic procurement process often depend on the value and risk of the goods or services being aquired, the same two issues illustrated in the supplier positioning matrix earlier. For the strategic security, strategic critical, and tactical profit quadrants in Figure 9.2, this process generally includes these steps:

1. **Develop specifications.** Ideally, these technical specifications should be developed through consultation with all internal stakeholders in the purchase. In some cases, the buying organization may also request information from candidate suppliers concerning what the marketplace can reasonably provide, before finalizing its own specifications.
2. **Structure an invitation to tender and a tender evaluation model.** This decides the process through which potential suppliers submit tenders, bids to supply the good or service described in the buyer's specifications. For large, complex contracts, the buying organization may host pretender meetings to discuss these specifications with all interested bidding parties.
3. **Issue the invitation to tender and collect responses.** This must be done in a manner that ensures the integrity of the process and communicates equal information in a timely manner to all potential bidders. Widespread advertising of the opportunity also supports multiple tender offers from a greater diversity of organizations.
4. **Evaluate tender responses with the tender evaluation model.** Tenders for large contracts may be evaluated by several different groups internally, such as an engineering team evaluating the technical components, a procurement team evaluating the commecial components, and a finance team researching the apparent financial health of each bidding organization.

tender
Bid or cost provided to a potential buyer.

5. **Select a supplier from among the tender responses, negotiate, and award a contract.** Procurement teams usually award, monitor, and manage the finished contract throughout its lifespan with input from those using the contract.

Tender Evaluation Methods

At the core of the procurement process is the selection of a supplier's offer. Evaluations may be conducted through a variety of methods, and the same supplier is not necessarily favored under all evaluation methods. For this reason, special attention should be placed on the careful selection of the method itself. Two of the most commonly used tender evaluation methods are linear averaging and lowest price.

linear averaging A numerically weighted evaluation method used in situations such as awarding contracts, selecting locations, or ranking candidates.

Linear Averaging

Linear averaging is the most common method for tender evaluation. In linear averaging, various criteria important to the purchasing organization are identified first, then refined into descriptive categories such as price, quality, and delivery. These categories are weighted with percentages reflecting their relative importance, such as price: 45%, quality: 45%, and delivery, 10%. Each tender offer is scored in each category, and a total performance rating is then calculated by using these percentages. Linear averaging is reliable, easy to understand, and considers multiple factors important to the buying organization. In the European Union this method is commonly called the Most Economically Advantageous Tender (MEAT) and is one of two allowable evaluation methods for government contracts—the other being lowest price. Linear averaging allows whole life costs or total cost of ownership to be evaluated for asset purchases. This cradle-to-grave evaluation of an asset over its lifetime includes not simply the up-front financial cost, but also social, environmental, operating costs and disposal costs, to name but a few.

Lowest Price

Lowest price selects an offer solely on the price offered by the supplier, provided that the offer complies with the specifications and the terms and conditions outlined in the original invitation to tender. While simple to understand, this method of evaluation must specify very clearly what is required of the supplier and what does not meet minimum criteria for consideration based on price.

Regardless of what method is used to select a tender offer, any shortlisted supplier, typically the best two or three tenders, should be invited for further discussion of the

Contract Monitoring and Compliance in Construction

The greater the expense, complexity, and/or risk associated with a purchase, the greater the necessity of careful development of the purchasing contract, to protect both the purchasing organization and the vendors who must estimate associated costs to bid accurately. Large construction projects fit this description, so it is not surprising to find detailed contracts governing this activity. In this picture, remote sensing equipment is used to verify the position of storm water infrastructure to be embedded deep underground. The complexity of this project requires that adherence to sensitive contract specifications be monitored throughout the production process.

potential contract and site visits arranged to check that what is written in the tender offer is what happens in practice at the supplier's facility. It is also important to investigate the financial stability of a candidate supplier. Any new information should be reflected in the scores given to that candidate in the tender selection process.

We evaluate a tender in Scenario 2.

Scenario 2

Tender Evaluation

The dayshift manager at the Fields of Green restaurant is proceeding with the selection of a fresh vegetable supplier for a strategic supply chain partnership. The manager issued four invitations to tender to the four suppliers first described in Scenario 1b, and received three responses. Working closely with the Fields of Green owner, its business manager, and the Fields of Green chef, the dayshift manager scored each of the three responses on a 100-point scale in three critical categories:

Tender Offer from	Quality	Delivery	Price
Total Veg, Inc.	85	60	87
Fresh Veggies, Inc.	85	75	100
All About Veg LLC	95	80	95

Assuming that Fields of Green weights quality at 30%, delivery at 25%, and price at 45%, which supplier would be selected with linear averaging? Does this selection differ from the one suggested by the lowest price method?

Analysis

Using linear averaging, each supplier's overall score is the result of its individual category scores multiplied by each category's weight:

Score for Total Veg, Inc.

$$(0.30 \times 85) + (0.25 \times 60) + (0.45 \times 87) = 25.50 + 15.00 + 39.15 = 79.65$$

Score for Fresh Veggies, Inc.

$$(0.30 \times 85) + (0.25 \times 75) + (0.45 \times 100) = 25.50 + 18.75 + 45.00 = 89.25$$

Score for All About Veg LLC

$$(0.30 \times 95) + (0.25 \times 80) + (0.45 \times 95) = 28.50 + 20.00 + 42.75 = 91.25$$

Insight According to linear averaging, All About Veg LLC's tender offer scores the highest and thus should be selected. Interestingly, All About Veg LLC would not be selected based on the lowest price evaluation method: price scoring indicates that Fresh Veggies, Inc., offered the lowest price, as it received the highest score in that category (100 out of 100 points). While All About Veg LLC is not the lowest price supplier, linear averaging recognizes that it offers both the highest-quality product and the best delivery terms to meet the demands of a busy commercial kitchen. Furthermore, its price score of 95 indicates that its price is not far off the lowest bid by its larger competitor Fresh Veggies, Inc.

The lack of competitiveness in the pricing and delivery offers of Total Veg, Inc., is consistent with the findings of the supplier preferencing model in Scenario 1b. Being both the largest of the three organizations to answer Fields of Green's invitation of tender and accustomed to supplying retail chains with a full range of food supplies, Total Veg, Inc., was not likely to consider supplying only fresh vegetables to a single restaurant an attractive opportunity. ■

Tactical Acquisitions

Purchasing that falls into the lower left-hand tactical acquisitions quadrant of the supplier positioning matrix represents relatively small amounts of money spent with little risk to the buying organization. Here the purchasing process should be as simple and efficient as possible. An incidental transaction such as the posting of a letter may be completed instantly with the use of petty cash, although somewhat greater expenses are good candidates for submitting a request for quotation (RFQ) to upstream suppliers. RFQs are sent to three suppliers typically, and the resulting best priced quote is accepted, providing that it meets specifications. Once a quote is accepted, a contract may be drawn up for that particular purchase, but is often created instead through the supplier's acceptance of a simple purchase order (PO) from the buyer.

Even this simple type of transaction, however, has a potential pitfall, often referred to as a battle of the forms. A buyer's PO is an offer stating the *buyer's* boilerplate terms and conditions of contract, while the supplier's response to the initial RFQ, the supplier's delivery paperwork, and even the supplier's invoice all contain references to the *supplier's* terms and conditions. If these two sets of terms differ substantially, a complex legal case can emerge in which a court may eventually decide whose terms and conditions of contract apply. This is very serious in cases where injury or death result from use of machinery and the seller has limited their liability for such events. Thus, purchasing agents, even when completing low-value/low-risk purchases, must have a basic understanding of such legal factors, to avoid potentially entering into an expensive battle of the forms over some relatively minor purchase that goes wrong.

petty cash
A very small fund supporting incidental purchases.

request for quotation (RFQ)
An invitation to offer a price for a particular product or service.

purchase order (PO)
A written offer to a supplier to buy a particular product in a particular quantity at a particular price.

battle of the forms
Determining which version of a contract has precedence.

Simple cash transactions, complex contracts, and enduring alliances between partners all represent supply chain relationships. Failure to appropriately structure purchasing and those partnering relationships among businesses is equivalent to failure to install appropriate connections among elements of some physical structure. The resulting structure, despite the value of its components, is doomed to suffer and may ultimately fail in its purpose. A supply chain formed from appropriate relationships, however, should emerge strong and ideally suited to purpose, providing greater value to the end consumer than could otherwise be achieved by its individual participants.

SUMMARY

Operations management is about the conversion of inputs into outputs, and supply chain management is concerned with obtaining inputs and providing outputs that are cost-effective, sustainable, and resilient in the presence of risk. Supply chain management is integral to how an organization organizes itself and has a significant role in being competitive by bringing the expertise from a diverse supply chain into its key business processes. Contracts create these beneficial links between organizations, ideally shaping these interactions to the mutual benefit of supply chain partners.

Key Terms

ABC policy
actual authority
apparent authority
battle of the forms
boilerplate
business-to-business (B2B)
business-to-consumer (B2C)
centralized organizational policy
collaborative forecasting, planning, and replenishment (CPFR)
commodity/category plan
contract
counteroffer
decentralized organizational policy
downstream

Continues

Key Terms (continued)

electronic data interchange (EDI)
ethics
fourth-party logistics (4PL)
functional organizational structure
green
implied authority
inbound logistics
lean
linear averaging
matrix organizational structure
offer
outbound logistics
petty cash
procurement
purchase order
purchasing agent
radio frequency identification (RFID)
request for quotation (RFQ)
resilience
sales agent
sales representative
smart seal
spend analysis
supplier positioning
supplier preferencing
supply chain
sustainability
tender
third-party logistics (3PL)
tier 1 supplier
tier 2 supplier
upstream
vendor-managed inventory (VMI)

Discussion Questions

1. How does the analysis from the supplier position and supplier preferencing models affect how a purchasing manager plans to do business with suppliers?
2. Why is the organization's structure important in how the supply chain management function operates?
3. How can good boilerplate terms and conditions of contract still fail to protect an organization against some risk?
4. Do the steps of a procurement process differ, depending on the risk and/or value of what is being purchased?

PROBLEMS

Short answers appear in Appendix A. Go to **NoteShaper.com** for full video tutorials on each question.

Minute Answer

1. Is the end customer upstream or downstream from a manufacturer?
2. Is a tier 1 supplier associated with the inbound or outbound logistics of another firm?
3. In the supplier positioning model, the *X* and *Y* axes are composed of what?
4. In the supplier preferencing model what does *core* represent?
5. Does a centralized supply management function have purchasing decisions assigned to individual functions or managers at each of the organization's locations?
6. Who has greater authority, a sales representative or a sales agent?
7. In purchasing, a bid or cost estimate provided by a potential supplier is commonly called a what?
8. In purchasing, when someone acts with authority that they don't formally possess, is this known as apparent or actual authority?
9. In purchasing, a PO is understood to be what?
10. Are standard terms and conditions for a contract often referred to as boilerplate or as ABC policy?

Quick Start

11. Using the supplier positioning/preferencing models you identify that the goods to be purchased fall within the strategic critical/core quadrants of the models. What sort of contract should you consider entering into?

12. You are a recently appointed purchasing manager who is overseeing terms and conditions of contract for an important international purchase with a UN country. What rules should you be particularly aware of, and why?

Ramp Up

13. You are reviewing a tender evaluation that is to be awarded on lowest total price. The bid evaluations follow:

Company	Capital Cost	Maintenance	Disposal
A	$7,500	20% of capital cost	5% of capital cost
B	$6,700	25% of capital cost	5% of capital cost
C	$6,500	30% of capital cost	5% of capital cost

To which company should the contract be awarded?

14. You are analyzing bids from two companies. Company A has scored 85 points on the quality evaluation (out of a scale of 100 points), while company B has scored 95 points. The overall weighting your company uses is 60% for price and 40% for quality. To translate quality into dollar amounts to compare with price, each point *not* earned in the quality evaluation is considered equal to $200. Assuming that company A has just finalized its bid at $10,000, what is the maximum price in whole dollars that company B could have bid to win the contract?

Full Scenarios

Reminder: Short answers appear in Appendix A. Go to **NoteShaper.com** for full video tutorials on each question.

15. Pegasus Veterinary Hospital (PVH) is a partnership of five veterinarian surgeons who specialize in treating horses. PVH is located in a $25 million facility on 20 acres of land, employing over 40 full-time staff members. The business manager of PVH had conducted the following spend analysis of last year's purchasing expenses at PVH:

Category	Total Expenditures in Previous Year	Percent of Previous Year's Expenditures
Surgical supplies and pharmaceuticals	$215,111	52%
Horse transportation services	$25,100	6%
Commercial-grade horse supplies, not including hay and grain	$10,154	2%
Hay and grain	$130,200	31%
Veterinary-grade horse supplies, including special feed and sterile bedding	$35,010	8%

PVH's approach to purchasing in each of these five categories has always been the same, but the business manager suspects that PVH could benefit from taking a more sophisticated approach, recognizing some key differences between the categories. As an example, surgical supplies and pharmaceuticals are critical to the care that PVH provides, and most of these items are highly specialized to the treatment of horses and not easily located on short notice. Hay and grain, in contrast, can be purchased from a variety of vendors for immediate delivery. Veterinary-grade horse supplies are available from several national suppliers who offer overnight shipping, making this category of purchasing only slightly less convenient than commercial-grade horse supplies, which can be bought at any one of a dozen nearby farm and pet supply stores. Horse transportation service is a surprisingly problematic category of expense, considering how little PVH spends in this category. Most PVH clients prefer to transport their horses to and from the PVH facility themselves, to avoid the additional expense of being billed by PVH for transportation. Occasionally, however, a PVH client requests that PVH provide transportation as well as treatment for the horse, meaning that PVH must then hire a transportation service. While PVH is not a frequent user of this service, it must be able to hire transportation for a sick or injured horse on very short notice.

a. Which category would PVH most likely consider core to its business, and thus invest the most effort in securing a long-term strategic supply partner?

b. In which category should PVH focus most strongly on competitive bidding and award its business based on the lowest-cost bid, viewing these purchases as tactical decisions only?

c. If petty cash were to be used for any of PVH's purchasing, it would be most appropriate to which category?

16. Main Street Cinema is a single-screen movie theater in a residential area. Main Street Cinema is a licensed exhibitor of Mega Pictures Distribution Company, meaning that it receives all its movies from and pays all rental fees to this larger corporation, as per the license agreement. Otherwise, Main Street Cinema is a small business that spends a considerable amount of money each year purchasing a wide variety of products from suppliers. Last year's spend analysis revealed the following:

Main Street Cinema Purchasing Categories (Excluding Exhibition Fees to Mega Pictures)	Annual Expenditure
Daily janitorial services	$83,000
Upholstery and carpet cleaning, quarterly	$28,000
Soft drinks	$25,000
Popcorn and candy	$33,000
Toilet paper and liquid soap for public restrooms	$750

The two contract services listed at the top of this table are particularly important to Main Street Cinema in that they require Main Street to entrust its facility to personnel sent by the other companies it hires for these services. Upholstery and carpet cleaning, while only purchased four times a year, is particularly worrisome to Main Street Cinema, because the supplier of this service must work overnight to complete the cleaning, and any problems during that work can force Main Street Cinema into closing the following business day and losing all sales revenue.

a. In the spend analysis, which category of spending best fits the description of strategic critical purchasing in the supplier positioning model?

b. In the spend analysis, which category of spending best fits the description of strategic security purchasing in the supplier positioning model?

c. In the spend analysis, which two categories of spending best fit the description of tactical profit purchasing in the supplier positioning model?

d. In the spend analysis, which category of spending best fits the description of tactical acquisition purchasing in the supplier positioning model?

17. Main Street Cinema invited three firms to bid on its daily janitorial services contract, and then scored those tenders based on quality, reliability/risk, and price (using a 100-point scale in each case). The scores are listed here:

Tender Offer from . . .	Quality	Reliability/Risk	Price
Dawson Commercial Cleaning Services	70	60	100
Fulton Maintenance and Facilities Service	100	100	70
SteadyBrite Contract Cleaning	70	90	80

a. If Main Street Cinema were to use lowest price to award the contract, who would receive it?

b. If Main Street Cinema were to use linear averaging to then choose a supplier for its janitorial services contract, who would it choose if it felt that quality, reliability/risk, and price were all equally important aspects of the contract?

c. Assume that quality and reliability/risk are equally important to Main Street Cinema. However, the issue of price is twice as important to Main Street Cinema than either quality or reliability/risk. What score would Dawson Commercial Cleaning Services earn under this weighting scheme?

d. Assuming the weighting scheme described in part b, which janitorial service supplier does linear averaging suggest?

CASE STUDY: CHAMPIONS' GATE SPORTS CAMP

Champions' Gate Sports Camp operates four consequective 8-week residential training sessions for young athletes. Each sports camp session hosts 150 student athletes and 30 staff members at the Champions' Gate Sports Complex, which provides athletic facilities, classroom space, dormitories, and a picnic area. Unfortunately, what the Champions' Gate Sports Complex lacks is a commercial kitchen, so breakfast is limited to cold items that Champions' Gate stocks in the dormitory refrigerators, while lunch and dinner are delivered fresh each day by an outside catering company. A spend analysis (shown below) of the nonpayroll operating costs of last year's camp season reveals outside catering to be both a substantial portion of overall spending and a high-risk purchasing category.

Spend Analysis of Last Year's Operating Expenses

Category	Expense, Overall $ and Percent of Total (%)	Risk Level of Category
Sports equipment, including maintenance	$750,000 (30%)	High
Accommodation supplies (laundry, bedding, etc)	$500,000 (20%)	Low
Outside catering (buffet dinners and packed lunches)	$375,000 (15%)	High
Facilities management, including contract janitorial and security services	$250,000 (10%)	High
Communications and computing	$175,000 (7%)	Low
Utilities, including water	$125,000 (5%)	Low
Vehicles and transportation	$125,000 (5%)	High
Other (20 items)	$200,000 (8%)	Low

This year, Champions' Gate has budgeted $65 per person per day for outside catering. This budget includes all student athletes and all staff for all four 8-week camp sessions. Champions' Gate's longtime catering company closed during its off-season, so a new company must be chosen for that contract. Champions' Gate has identified the six candidates, shown in the table below, with business locations no more than 50 miles from the Champions' Gate Sports Complex.

Candidate Catering Companies

Company	Notes on Company Size	Estimated Average Contract Size, in Terms of Champions' Gate's Catering Budget
Salem Food Service	Multinational—uses network of local suppliers to deliver locally	20 times larger
A&V Food Services	Large corporate—strong presence in state, subcontracts delivery to meet each contract	10 times larger
Great Plains Catering	Largest market share in state—has own fleet of vehicles that are fully employed in current contracts	7 times larger
Best Foods and Beverage	Local to area—has own underutilized fleet of vehicles	Half of Champions' Gate's budget
Home-Cooked Sales and Service	Large—specializes in home delivery, subcontracts fleet of delivery vehicles to meet each contract	Same as Champions' Gate's budget
Dragon Meals	Small—new company developing local market share; has own underutilized fleet of vehicles	0.3 times Champions' Gate's budget

Proceeding with this information, Champions' Gate prepared a comprehensive invitation to tender, and received tenders from each of the six companies.

Tenders for Catering Contract

Company	Bid on Contract	Food Quality Score (out of 30 points)	Delivery Risk Score (out of 30 points)
Salem Food Service	$383,250	29	25
A&V Food Services	$372,000	27	23
Great Plains Catering	$401,500	25	15
Best Foods and Beverage	$372,000	27	20
Home-Cooked Sales and Service	$397,850	26	22
Dragon Meals	$365,000	29	20

The food quality and delivery risk scores were awarded by Champions' Gate's resident manager, who serves as the point of contact for outside catering. In the case of either score, higher numbers of points indicate a better score.

Questions

1. Consider the purchasing categories in Champions' Gate's spend analysis. How would you chart each category within the supplier positioning matrix?

2. Where would each of the six candidate suppliers' views on Champions' Gate's contract be located within the supplier preferencing matrix?
3. Convert the bid information into a price score. Explain any assumptions you make. If Champions' Gate considers price, food quality, and delivery risk to be equally important to the contract decision, which company should be chosen for the outside catering contract?

BIBLIOGRAPHY

Ball, J. 2008. "Green Goal of 'Carbon Neutrality' Hits Limit." *The Wall Street Journal,* December 30, p. A1.

Benton, W. C., Jr. 2007. *Purchasing and Supply Management.* Burr Ridge, IL: McGraw-Hill/Irwin.

Bromberger, S., and S. Hoover. 2003. "Supply Chain Challenges: Building Relationships." *Harvard Business Review,* July: 64–73.

Handfield, R. B., and E. L. Nichols, Jr. 1999. *Introduction to Supply Chain Management.* Upper Saddle River, NJ: Prentice-Hall.

Kraljic, P. 1983. "Purchasing Must Become Supply Management." *Harvard Business Review,* September: 109–17.

Steele, P. T., and B. H. Court. 1996. *Profitable Purchasing Strategies.* Burr Ridge, IL: McGraw-Hill/Irwin.

PART 3 MANAGING OPERATIONS

CHAPTER

10

Inventory Management

I went to a general store, but they wouldn't let me buy anything specific.

—Steven Wright

MAJOR SECTIONS

IN THIS CHAPTER, LOOK FOR...

- Inventory as idle stock waiting to achieve value.
- Classifying inventory based on where it is waiting in a system and why.
- Differing inventory management policies.
- Three models of the best order quantity.
- The reorder point, with its associated issues of safety stock, service level, and stock out risk.

INTRODUCTION

Inventory can be thought of as an idle stock of anything destined for use and can be found in virtually any organization. It is not exclusive to manufacturing. Retailing operations are service systems dedicated to inventory, beginning with the procurement of goods from suppliers through to the promotion and delivery of those goods to customers. Other operations such as hospitals may provide highly complex and intangible services, yet must keep inventories of important supplies supporting their activities. Inventory management is not important simply because inventory is everywhere, but also because of its sensitive nature as something that will create greater value, but has not achieved that status yet. Good inventory management assures that these tangible stocks do achieve their full potential and begins by understanding inventory itself.

THE NATURE OF INVENTORY

inventory
Tangible items awaiting sale or use.

tangibility
The degree of perceivable, physical essence of a product.

SKU (stock keeping unit)
A particular item of inventory.

Inventory can refer to anything tangible that is waiting to provide value to an organization. Since the term *inventory* can literally refer to anything, the exact identity of any particular stock of inventory is important to good inventory management. This seemingly simple issue can present surprising challenges in some situations, particularly retailing. As an example, a typical supermarket must manage the stocks of over 10,000 different items sold from its shelves. Each of these unique items, from fresh oranges to chicken soup in microwavable containers, must be managed to maintain its availability to shoppers. For this reason, organizations rely on a unique SKU (pronounced *skew*), short for stock keeping unit, for each particular item. For example, a single SKU might be a bottle of water or it might be a case of 24 bottles of water, depending on how that water is packaged for sale. A SKU may belong to one or more categories, or recognizable types, of inventory. This stock also brings with it a set of costs that the organization must pay for the privilege of owning it. These costs combine with the basic dynamics of inventory management to shape the policies the organization develops to manage that particular SKU.

Types of Inventory

Inventory can be divided into types, primarily by observing where it waits within the operation and why it is being kept there. The issue of where is not literally its exact location,

Retail SKUs

Stores usually sell many different items and must monitor and manage each of these SKUs. Differing SKUs may be very similar in appearance, but their individual identities are important to accurate stock keeping. A detailed description of each SKU, often barcoded, often appears attached to the shelf that supports it.

Types of Inventory

FIGURE 10.1

although knowing the exact location of a particular SKU is important to good inventory management. Instead, where in this context refers to the inventory's location within a theoretical model of the operation. Figure 10.1 displays the three-stage model of any operation, as well as the names of the three types of inventory that map to each of the stages.

The left-hand side of Figure 10.1 represents the inputs required by any given operation, or what is drawn from the environment outside the operation in supporting the creation of valuable outputs. If goods are brought in for future use, these stocks are known as raw materials, whereas finished products not yet sold to the outside world are known as finished goods. Raw materials are generally purchased from suppliers and may literally be raw ingredients such as wood, steel, or flour, but not necessarily so. One operation's raw materials can be the intricate finished goods of some other operation, such as a circuit board being purchased by a tablet manufacturer. As a result, two different organizations may perceive the same tangible object as two different types of inventory: the circuit board manufacturer considers the circuit board to be a finished good, while the tablet manufacturer considers it a raw material. These differing perspectives on inventory type sometimes lead to conflicting perspectives on how best to coordinate the movements of the circuit board through the supply chain and into the hands of the customer.

raw materials
Inventory brought in from outside the system.

finished goods
Inventory awaiting sale to consumers.

Work-in-process inventory, or WIP, is not usually the subject of supply chain tension between organizations, but nonetheless brings concerns of its own. As pictured in Figure 10.1, WIP is inventory at any stage between raw materials and finished goods, residing within the transformation process itself. WIP is essentially unfinished work, which makes it the riskiest type of inventory in a certain sense. While all inventories represent idle goods waiting to be used or sold, WIP represents partial investment in a good that cannot be redeemed for its value until even more investment is made to finish it. Should something go wrong before transformation is complete, the value invested up to that point

WIP (work in process)
Inventory resulting from transformation of raw materials, but not yet ready for sale to consumers.

Raw Materials as Finished Goods

Inventory classification depends on the perspective of the organization conducting the analysis. Lumber, for instance, would seem an excellent example of raw material inventory. However, the lumber in this picture is a finished good from the perspective of its producer and its current owner, the retailer offering it up for sale. The builder who purchases lumber in this setting will consider it raw materials.

may be lost. Recognizing these concerns, some inventory management systems focus on minimizing or even avoiding the creation of WIP, operating as lean as possible.

Inventory can also be classified according to why it is kept in stock. An organization might choose to keep a large stock of some particular SKU on-hand for many different reasons, but most of them stem from a few basic motivations:

economies of scale Decreasing average unit cost by increasing volume.

price break A discount for orders of a certain minimum size.

cycle stock Inventory held to gain economies of scale.

stockpiling Producing or securing goods in advance of demand, building up substantial inventory.

safety stock Inventory held to protect against uncertain supply or demand.

pipeline stock Inventory currently in transit between locations.

- **Achieve economies of scale.** An organization may invest in inventory to save money through economies of scale. As one example, this savings might be the result of a price break offered by the organization's supplier for large orders. Alternatively, scheduling the delivery of new inventory might have some inconvenient cost attached to it, regardless of how much is purchased, so the organization seeks to save money by ordering large amounts that last longer and reduce the frequency of deliveries. The resulting inventory that will be stored and used between deliveries is then known as cycle stock.
- **Produce a stockpile.** An organization may be deliberately stockpiling goods in anticipation of future demand for that inventory. The motivation for stockpiling is usually to produce at a level rate despite varying demand for the finished goods output. Assembly lines operate best at level rates of production, and thus those manufacturers prefer to work steadily, accumulating finished goods during slower demand periods, to sell off later when demand increases.
- **Create safety stock.** An organization may have invested in inventory simply because it is uncertain about either the future demand or the future availability of that SKU. Inventory that is held to protect against uncertainty is known as safety stock.
- **Ensure pipeline stock.** An organization might be in possession of a large stock of some SKU because it has chosen to transfer that stock between two geographic locations. Examples include purchasing goods from a remote supplier or shipping between different facilities operated by the same organization. This inventory, sitting idle on its journey between locations, is known as pipeline stock, and global supply chain logistics can involve significant investment in it. For example, a single standard 40-foot cargo container can hold over 12,000 boxes of shoes, ready for sale, and a large seagoing cargo ship can carry over 3,000 of these 40-foot containers. Loaded with cargo containers, the ship then generally requires 2 weeks or more to move between ports, housing a substantial amount of a shoe retailer's pipeline stock as it travels.

Costs of Inventory

While inventory may be vital to an operation, it also costs the operation in a variety of ways. First, raw material inventory must be purchased, a significant expense. Next, some costs of idle inventory of any type varies with how much is actually waiting, while other costs are incurred by simply acquiring inventory, regardless of how much or how little.

Pipeline Stock

Longer supply chains require greater pipeline stock to keep product flowing. Cargo ships offer dramatic visual examples of this, such as these two vessels entering the Panama Canal as they cross between the Pacific and Atlantic oceans. Their combined loads include thousands of full-sized containers filled with in-transit inventory owned by multiple organizations. This inventory may sit idle at sea or dockside for several weeks.

These two categories represent two contrasting factors that are familiar from other settings: variable versus fixed costs.

Variable Costs Variable costs vary with some level of activity, and variable inventory costs vary with the amount of inventory idle in the system. Large order sizes result in large deliveries, which in turn result in higher inventory levels before the stock is used. In contrast, small order sizes imply many small deliveries and lower stock levels. One of the principle costs associated with inventory is its holding cost, or the cost of having inventory. The more inventory, the greater holding costs the system can expect to pay. In turn, this cost is generally determined by a mix of component costs.

variable cost
Cost that varies with volume of associated activity or, in inventory planning, the size of the order.

holding costs
Variable costs associated with having inventory.

Direct storage costs are probably the most easily recognized components of holding cost. Higher inventory levels require more square footage of storage space to shelter the inventory stock. For example, automobile dealerships are rarely located in expensive downtown areas but are common to suburban areas where the ready availability of property means lower storage costs for the dealership's substantial inventory. Automobile dealers that do locate in city centers rarely store their entire inventory at the city retail location, but maintain a showroom with fewer cars on display while keeping the bulk of automobile inventory at some second, lower-cost location. However, direct storage costs are not always linked to the literal cost of the real estate needed for storage. Inventory that requires special storage conditions such as subfreezing temperatures or extremely high security can incur significant direct storage costs, regardless of the affordability of the storage property itself.

Although direct storage costs are easy to recognize, opportunity costs are often the majority of an organization's holding cost. Opportunity costs refer to the real and yet indirect financial burden that inventory places on an organization. Inventory represents investment in some tangible good, waiting to be redeemed through sale or use in some beneficial manner. Thus, inventory represents a lag in time between investing money in a necessary input for the operation, and then regaining that money in some sense. As inventory sits idle, the organization loses the interest that money could have earned if invested in a financial institution instead. If the organization does not have cash to purchase inventory, it must borrow this money and it will pay interest on the borrowed funds until it is able to repay the debt. In either case, the cost of holding inventory is linked to the cost of capital for the organization, because the inventory represents capital tied up in idle goods.

opportunity cost
Cost of an alternative foregone. In inventory planning, this is often the cost of capital.

cost of capital
The cost of funding for an organization, such as the interest rate on borrowed funds.

Holding costs may include the cost of spoilage, a risk that varies with the amount of inventory an organization chooses to hold. As the name suggests, spoilage can take the form of literally spoiling, such as a large amount of fresh bakery goods failing to sell while still fresh. Inventory that does not sell in a timely fashion cannot later be sold for its original value, and the organization loses that value. However, inventory does not have to physically transform to spoil. Idle inventory can suffer spoilage simply by becoming obsolete before its use, such as a stock of clothing going out of fashion in the marketplace or a stock of consumer electronics abruptly losing appeal to customers due to the release of an upgraded version of that device.

spoilage
Unintended transformation of inventory before sale or use, rendering it inappropriate for its original purpose.

Perhaps the most specialized holding cost component is shrinkage. In some cases, the decision to invest in inventory must be weighed against the fact that a certain amount of that inventory will simply disappear before it is used. This shrinkage may be due to consistent theft by employees or other individuals, but not necessarily so. Certain products naturally shrink over time, such as industrial gases and dry ice. A plumbing firm might decide to purchase a large batch of dry ice to assist in certain types of well repairs, but must consider that this extremely cold substance will steadily evaporate even when kept in cold storage, eventually disappearing even if never used.

shrinkage
Physical loss of inventory before sale or use.

But holding costs are not the only variable costs associated with inventory. Choosing to *not* have inventory may also prove costly. For example, if an organization chooses not to hold some SKU in inventory and then a customer arrives with the intention of purchasing

Inconvenient Direct Storage Costs

Although financial costs often drive a firm's holding costs, certain kinds of inexpensive inventory can have very high holding costs for other reasons. The building insulation in this picture is an example, as this item is not particularly expensive and does not spoil, yet its retailer must keep stock levels to a careful minimum. This particular item has high holding costs simply because it is unusually bulky, occupying large amounts of valuable retail space that could otherwise be serving more profitable items.

stock out
To fail to meet customer demand due to inadequate supply.

that SKU, the firm is said to have suffered a stock out. Stock outs result from lower inventory levels combined with unexpected demand, and the cost to the organization is the loss of the sale that could have been made on that SKU. Stock outs can also be suffered internally when an organization does not have adequate stock of some raw material or WIP needed to proceed with some desired work, creating disruption and delay.

backorder
To delay order fulfillment due to inadequate supply.

If an organization does not have a desired SKU in stock, it may be able to place the item on backorder. In that case, the customer agrees to wait until the organization can supply the item and presumably will not purchase from a competitor instead. The cost of backordering can include the cost of administering the waiting list, the cost of expediting the missing inventory, and the loss of goodwill with the delayed customer.

Purchasing costs are also variable costs associated with inventory, but this can be a surprisingly complex issue. First, the purchasing costs of an item may influence the strategy an organization chooses to use to best govern that item's inventory, as we will see later in the discussion of ABC analysis. However, once an appropriate strategy is chosen, purchasing costs aren't usually considered relevant to the developing the detailed inventory policy unless how much the organization pays in purchasing depends in some way on its chosen inventory levels, not its purchasing needs. Why an organization's inventory levels and its overall purchasing needs would be two different issues is described by inventory dynamics, discussed at the end of this section. Generally, purchasing costs directly influence inventory policy if the supplier offers discounts for large orders, providing an incentive to keep higher inventory on-hand (economies of scale).

Retail Stock Out

Stock outs are a lack of inventory. This absence may be the result of unexpected demand for the item or it may be deliberately created by the retailer, who wishes to draw inventory levels down.

Fixed Costs Fixed costs do not vary with the amount of inventory but come from a variety of sources. For example, a supplier may charge a fixed fee. Cash machines often charge such a fee, billing the same amount regardless of whether the customer withdraws a small or a large amount of the machine's stock of cash. In addition, fixed costs are often associated with receiving and stocking a delivery, regardless of size. Delivery vehicles often create these costs; the truck and driver needed for a delivery cost the same whether the truck is partially loaded with a small order or completely loaded with a large order. Finally, production of some items may involve fixed setup costs. Often setting up machinery to produce an order for the item must be paid in full regardless of how much or how little of the item is then produced.

fixed costs
Cost incurred regardless of the volume of associated activity. In inventory planning, this is understood to be costs incurred regardless of the size of the order.

While a fixed cost does not vary with the amount of inventory ordered, this category of cost can be heavily influenced by inventory decisions. Many small orders would create many fixed cost charges, thus substantial fixed costs make large orders look attractive. Large orders then drive up holding costs, however, and finding the best balance between these issues is the purpose of the inventory management techniques demonstrated later in this chapter.

Inventory Policies

Inventory management is conducted according to some policy the organization established to control that inventory. The differing approaches to inventory management can be summarized as differing answers to two questions:

- *How much* should be ordered?
- *When* should it be ordered?

Figure 10.2 illustrates how two sets of answers define two different approaches to inventory policy.

Fixed Order Quantity Policies Fixed order quantity policies rely on the identification of a single best amount to order whenever more of an item is required. As the name implies, this amount is predetermined and fixed, to be used each time a new order is placed. This fixed amount might be a simple rule-of-thumb, such as "every time we need more paper, we always order two boxes" or it might be the result of some more sophisticated math model such as the economic order quantity, discussed later in this chapter. Regardless of how the fixed amount is determined, all fixed order quantity policies are marked by the fact that they do not specify precisely when orders should be placed. In this type of policy, the issue of *when* varies with demand for that item. If demand for an item has been heavy, the stock on-hand will drop fast and the need for replenishment will arrive soon. Therefore, when is not an actual point in time, but rather an amount of stock that signals when a new order should

fixed order quantity policy
An inventory system in which the amount of replenishment is predetermined at some economical value and its timing is then determined by the rate of previous demand.

Inventory Policies FIGURE **10.2**

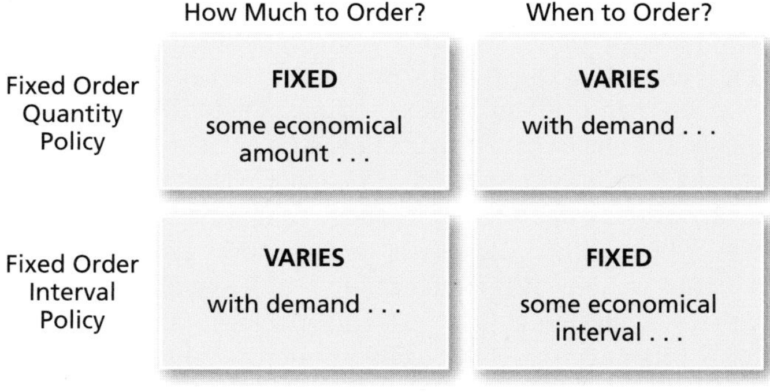

be placed, such as "when we open our last ream (500-sheet package) of paper, we always order more paper." Opening the last ream means that only 500 sheets are now left in stock, an important amount referred to as a *reorder point*.

fixed order interval policy
An inventory system in which the amount of replenishment is determined by the rate of previous demand and its timing is predetermined at an economical interval.

periodic review system
An inventory system operated according to a fixed order interval policy.

Fixed Order Interval Policies A fixed order interval policy states when new inventory should be ordered, allowing the amount to fluctuate according to how much has been used. Also known as a periodic review system, this policy specifies the frequency of ordering, such as "place a new order on the first and third Tuesday of every month." This policy requires a review of the amount of inventory actually present on that date, so that an order might be placed for an amount that brings inventory back up to some target level. The ordering amount then varies according to how much of the item is actually left in inventory on the ordering date. If there has been little demand for that item during the previous time interval, stock remains and only a small order will be placed to bring the stock level up to target. If demand has been heavy, however, less will be left in stock on the review date and a larger order will then be placed.

One disadvantage of a fixed order interval policy is the possibility that demand is so strong between orders that the organization suffers a stock out. This vulnerability is balanced, however, by the opportunity to synchronize the ordering of many different items, by assigning them all the same fixed order interval policy. As Figure 10.2 illustrates, fixed order quantity and fixed order interval policies are reflections of the same approach: carefully predetermining and fixing one-half of the overall issue of how much and when, while letting the other half be driven by demand. Since the differences between the two policies mirror each other, we will focus on the numerical techniques associated with only one of the pair, the fixed order quantity policy.

ABC policy
Prioritizing the management of inventory according to the significance of each item's annual dollar volume to the organization.

ABC Policy Organizations such as supermarkets, catalogue warehouses, and large manufacturers manage thousands of different SKUs. In these settings, it would be highly unusual for each individual SKU to be of the same strategic importance to the organization. An ABC policy of inventory management recognizes that some SKUs are more important to the organization and therefore should receive a higher degree of attention and control in inventory management. This issue of importance is usually expressed as some form of annual dollar volume, whether that is the annual amount spent on the SKU in purchasing costs or the annual amount of sales of that SKU to customers. ABC analysis requires four steps:

1. Calculate the annual dollar volume of every SKU.
2. Sort this list of dollar amounts from largest to smallest.
3. Calculate the cumulative (running total of) dollar volume, starting with the top of the sorted list.
4. Divide the list into three groups, known as the class A, B, and C items of the ABC policy.

Pareto analysis
The use of statistics to identify which factors are the most influential in a particular outcome of interest.

The formation of the three groups in step 4 relies on Pareto analysis, named after the nineteenth-century Italian economist Vilfredo Pareto, credited with observing that there are usually a critical few and a trivial many in any long list of factors. Pareto analysis is a tool for identifying those critical few factors, accomplished in ABC analysis by reviewing the cumulative dollar volume of the sorted list of SKUs. While there are no strict rules for where to place the dividing lines for classes A, B, and C, class A items are always the largest dollar volume items at the top of the list, whose combined cumulative dollar volume is often 70% to 80% of the *total* dollar value of the entire list, even though the SKUs themselves are usually 15% to 20% of the total number of items on the list. These items are the critical few SKUs, which should be managed very closely according to ABC inventory management. Class B items are then the medium priority items, generally accounting for another 15% to 20% of sales, while the largest group of items will be those at the bottom

The C Items from an ABC Policy

Thousands of different SKUs are being held in stock here, although their combined usage only accounts for a small portion of this custom manufacturer's cost of goods sold. These inexpensive C-ranked items are carefully organized, but otherwise receive little attention during daily inventory planning. They are what the economist Vilfredo Pareto would have called the trivial many for this manufacturer.

of the list. The majority of all SKUs falls in low-priority class C, with their combined annual dollar volume accounting for the remaining 15% to 20% of total dollar volume.

Once all SKUs are assigned to one of these three classes, an ABC policy is implemented by establishing different inventory policies for each of the three classes. For example, class A SKUs receive the greatest priority in inventory management, such as individualized ordering policies, frequent replenishment, and careful monitoring of use. In contrast, all class C items might be controlled through a single, fixed order interval policy that requires new orders be placed once a month.

Inventory Dynamics

An inventory policy shapes both inventory levels and inventory-related activity within a system, and these dynamics result from a series of linked relationships, some of which have been mentioned in earlier discussion:

- The larger the order size specified in a policy, the higher the average inventory level. Smaller order sizes result in lower average inventory levels.
- The larger the order size, the less frequently orders must be placed and deliveries received. Smaller order sizes require more frequent ordering.
- Less frequent ordering implies higher average inventory levels. More frequent orders and deliveries result in lower average inventory levels.
- Higher average inventory incurs higher holding costs. Thus, larger order sizes and infrequent ordering are likewise associated with higher holding costs.
- More frequent ordering incurs higher fixed ordering costs. Thus, smaller order sizes and lower inventory levels are associated with higher fixed ordering costs.

Figure 10.3 summarizes these linked relationships.

Inventory Dynamics FIGURE 10.3

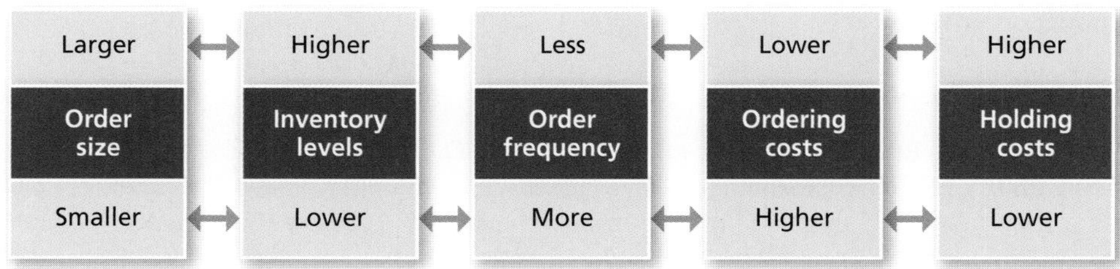

FIGURE 10.4 Sawtooth Diagram

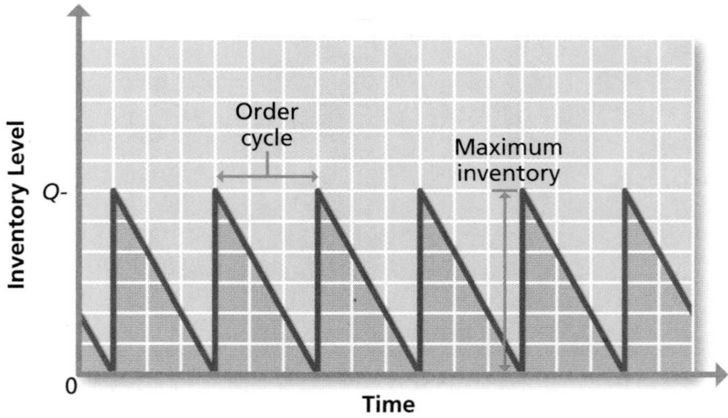

sawtooth diagram
A graph of inventory levels over time.

A sawtooth diagram, a graph of inventory levels over time, reveals much of the behavior of a particular policy. Figure 10.4 displays an example for some fixed order quantity policy with an order size of *Q*. By examining this diagram, we see that this system apparently receives this item as a single delivery of size *Q*, which always arrives just as the last item from the previous delivery of *Q* is consumed and no more inventory remains. This condition is also known as *instantaneous replenishment* and is indicated by the vertical lines on the graph, where inventory goes from its minimum of zero to its maximum of *Q* instantly and at regular intervals. These regular intervals represent the frequency of replenishment, creating the teeth of the sawtooth diagram. The length of the base of any single tooth in Figure 10.4 illustrates how much time is required to consume an order for *Q* items completely, a feature of the policy also known as the order cycle.

order cycle
The time required for average demand to consume an order, triggering another order for replenishment.

Figure 10.4 also suggests that this system experiences level demand for the item being illustrated. This is indicated by the fact that after each delivery, the inventory level falls back to zero at a perfectly constant rate, completing the identical right triangles that are the teeth in the diagram. This can only be created by steady consumption or sale of the item throughout the time line in Figure 10.4.

FIXED ORDER QUANTITIES

A fixed order quantity policy depends on identification of the optimal order size for an item, to be used when ordering that item in the future. Inventory brings with it many different costs, so what is optimal or best is usually determined by what costs the least. These costs, however, vary with the item and the situation in question. The three techniques most commonly used for the optimization of a fixed order quantity are the economic order quantity, the economic order quantity with pricebreaks, and the economic production quantity.

optimization
Identification of the best alternative.

Economic Order Quantity

As its name implies, the *economic order quantity*, or *EOQ*, is an order size that minimizes the inventory-related costs incurred by the fixed order quantity policy. The original EOQ has a long history of use, having first been published in 1905 by economist F. W. Harris. This mathematical model recommends an optimal order size, assuming the situation meets the following conditions, some of which were illustrated earlier in the sawtooth diagram of Figure 10.4:

- A fixed order quantity policy for a single SKU is being planned.
- This SKU experiences constant demand, being consumed or sold at a constant rate.
- This SKU experiences instantaneous replenishment, meaning an order of any size arrives in its entirety, instantly increasing stock levels by the order amount. This is typical of anything delivered to a system.
- A fixed ordering cost is incurred every time an order is placed. Let that fixed cost be denoted by S.
- Inventory holding costs are linear. Let H denote the cost of holding one unit of this SKU in inventory for 1 year.

Given these assumptions, we can model the total annual cost of any order size Q. Note that the two costs of concern—ordering and holding costs—do not appear in any sawtooth diagram. Instead, total annual ordering costs are determined by the fixed cost S of each order and the actual number of orders during the year. If D denotes total annual demand for the SKU, then

$$\text{Total annual ordering cost} = (D/Q) \times S$$

For example, if 1,000 of some SKU are sold during the year (D) and the order size for this SKU is 200 (Q), then the system would place $D/Q = 1{,}000/200 = 5$ orders a year, experiencing five order cycles. This makes the ratio D/Q a simplistic estimate of the important issue of inventory turnover, or the number of times that inventory is replaced each year. If the cost of placing an order is always \$50 (S), then this system will spend $5 \times 50 = \$250$ a year on ordering costs. If a smaller Q is used, more orders will result and ordering costs will rise, whereas a larger choice for Q would produce the opposite effect.

inventory turnover The number of annual inventory cycles, sometimes referred to as *turns*.

Holding costs are partially determined by H, the cost of holding one unit in inventory for 1 year, but reviewing the inventory levels in Figure 10.4 suggests that there aren't any units that stay in inventory throughout the year. Rather, holding costs in the EOQ model are based on the assumption that these costs can be estimated from average inventory levels. Inventory is assumed to peak at the order size Q each time a new order arrives and it is assumed to be as low as zero at the end of the order cycle. Since the stock level drops evenly between these two values and this pattern repeats itself for as long as the policy is in use, average inventory for the system can be determined by averaging these two extreme values, or $(Q + 0)/2 = Q/2$. Holding cost can then be modeled as

average inventory The average of the beginning and the ending inventory of a particular time period.

$$\text{Total annual holding cost} = (Q/2) \times H$$

In the case of the example just mentioned, ordering $Q = 200$ implies that a maximum of 200 will be present in inventory at the start of each order cycle, and an average of $Q/2 = 200/2 = 100$ of this SKU will be inventory throughout the year. If it costs \$0.50 to hold one unit in inventory for an entire year (H), then the total annual inventory costs associated with holding an average of 100 throughout the year is $(Q/2) \times H = 100 \times 0.5 = \$50$. This cost, combined with the annual ordering costs calculated earlier, indicate that the total cost of a policy of $Q = 200$ would be \$250 (ordering) + \$50 (holding) = \$300. We can calculate the total annual cost of any size of Q with the combined expression

$$\text{TC} = \frac{D}{Q}S + \frac{Q}{2}H$$

However, this does not indicate what would be the best choice for Q. While \$300 is the total cost of $Q = 200$, there is likely another value for Q with a lower total cost. This could be investigated through trial and error, but a more efficient method of identifying

FIGURE **10.5** The Economic Order Quantity

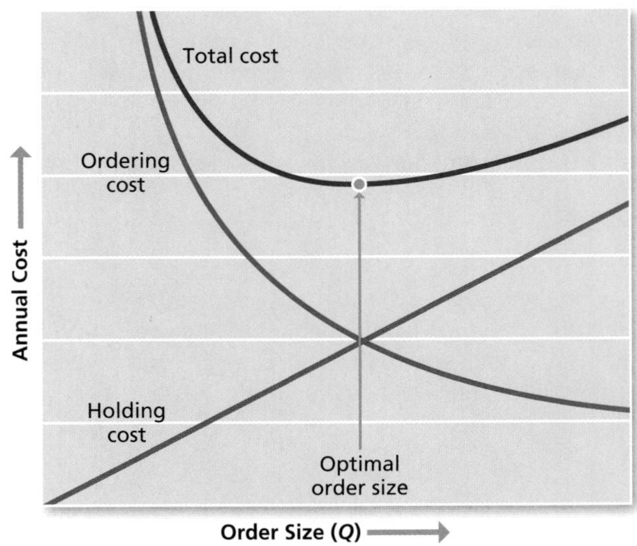

the lowest-cost order size begins by considering the nature of the general cost expression stated above. Holding costs increase with order size, while ordering costs decrease with order size, so their combined influences create a total cost curve with a distinct minimum corresponding to some particular order size, as illustrated in Figure 10.5. This optimal order size is known as the economic order quantity, or EOQ, and can be determined directly from the data. Using calculus to identify the value of Q that minimizes the total cost formula reveals that this EOQ is

$$\text{EOQ} = \sqrt{\frac{2DS}{H}}$$

In the case of the example discussed earlier, where $D = 1{,}000$, $S = \$50$, $H = \$0.50$, the best order size would be

$$\text{EOQ} = \sqrt{\frac{2 \times 1{,}000 \times 50}{0.5}} = \sqrt{200{,}000} = 447.21$$

Exactly how much better an order size of $Q = 447$ is than the previous order size of $Q = 200$ can only be determined by calculating the total cost of 447 for comparison. We apply the general total cost formula and the EOQ, including this type of comparison, in Scenario 1a.

Scenario 1a

EOQ, Determining an Order Size

Adventure Center is a 1,500-acre theme park in southern Florida. Like many well-known tourist attractions, one portion of Adventure Center's income is earned from themed merchandise sales through retail areas operated within the park. One example is the Adventure Center branded book bag, designed primarily for use by children. This particular item sells at a fairly steady rate throughout the year, and Adventure Center sells a total of 5,000 book bags annually. Adventure Center currently orders and receives new book bags in lots of

1,000, and estimates the cost of ordering and receiving branded merchandise from its supplier to be $100, regardless of how much or how little is ordered. Adventure Center pays $16 per book bag and estimates its holding cost of all branded merchandise to be 25% annually.

How much is Adventure Center paying in ordering and holding costs for these book bags annually? What can Adventure Center do to reduce these costs?

Analysis

Adventure Center already has a book bag inventory policy of $Q = 1{,}000$. To determine the combined holding and ordering costs of that policy, we first identify the relevant parameters of the total cost formula:

BOOK BAG POLICY PARAMETERS

$Q = 1{,}000$ (current order size)
$D = 5{,}000$ (annual demand)
$S = \$100$ (fixed setup cost)
Unit cost = $16
$H = \$16 \times 0.25 = \$4$ (annual holding cost)
Carrying rate = 0.25 (25%)

Note that holding cost parameter H was derived from the item's purchasing cost and Adventure Center's carrying rate ("Adventure Center . . . estimates its holding cost of all branded merchandise to be 25% annually"). This is a common approach to expressing holding cost, meaning that the cost of holding one item in inventory for 1 year (H) is known to be some proportion (25%) of its unit cost to the organization ($16).

Once we identify the parameters, we can calculate the total relevant cost of the current policy ($Q = 1{,}000$) with the appropriate formula:

CURRENT BOOK BAG POLICY TOTAL COST ($Q = 1{,}000$)

$$\begin{aligned}\text{Total annual cost} &= (D/Q) \times S + (Q/2) \times H \\ &= (5{,}000/1{,}000) \times 100 + (1{,}000/2) \times 4 \\ &= 500 + 2{,}000 = \$2{,}500\end{aligned}$$

Thus, Adventure Center currently pays $2,500 annually in combined ordering and holding costs of branded book bags. To reduce these costs we use the EOQ formula, to identify the order size that minimizes this combination of costs:

$$\text{EOQ} = \sqrt{\frac{2 \times D \times S}{H}} = \sqrt{\frac{2 \times 5{,}000 \times 100}{4}} = 500 \text{ book bags}$$

Note that the EOQ is substantially different from Adventure Center's current policy, but the benefit gained by switching to this order size cannot be stated until its total cost is calculated for comparison:

EOQ BOOK BAG POLICY TOTAL COST ($Q = 500$)

$$\begin{aligned}\text{Total annual cost} &= (D/Q) \times S + (Q/2) \times H \\ &= (5{,}000/500) \times 100 + (500/2) \times 4 \\ &= 1{,}000 + 1{,}000 = \$2{,}000\end{aligned}$$

$$\text{Improvement over current policy} = \$2{,}500 - \$2{,}000 = \$500 \text{ annually}$$

Insight Adventure Center can reduce the ordering and holding costs associated with book bags by $500 annually by reducing its order size to 500. $Q = 500$ is the economic order quantity for book bags, meaning that no other order size will result in lower combined costs. ■

In Scenario 1a, calculation of the total cost associated with the EOQ revealed that the annual ordering costs of $1,000 and the annual holding costs of $1,000 were matching values, creating the combined minimized total cost of $2,000. This was not a coincidence: any EOQ not only minimizes the total cost of its policy, but it also simultaneously locates the order size that balances the opposing forces of ordering and holding costs, as illustrated in Figure 10.5.

Once a policy is created, the total cost formula can be used to evaluate the policy in detail. For example, for any fixed order policy with an order size of Q, an analyst can determine

- Maximum inventory, Q.
- Average inventory, $Q/2$.
- Total annual number of order cycles, D/Q.
- Length of order cycle, Q/D. This expression is not a visible component of the total cost formula but calculating Q/D reveals how much time passes between orders, expressed as a fraction of the year.

Scenario 1b demonstrates this style of follow-up analysis on an inventory policy.

Scenario 1b

EOQ, Analyzing a Policy

Adventure Center intends to adjust its current inventory policy for branded book bags by reducing the order size to 500, based on the analysis in Scenario 1a. However, some employees have expressed concern about this new policy, worried that this smaller order size will result in too few book bags available for sale at the park.

If Adventure Center makes this change to $Q = 500$ when ordering its branded book bags, what is the maximum number of book bags that would ever be available for sale? What is the average number of book bags that would be available for sale? How frequently will book bags need to be ordered?

Analysis

Of the three questions asked above, the first two are easier to answer. The maximum and the average number of book bags available for sale are:

BOOK BAG INVENTORY LEVELS ($Q = 500$)

$$\text{Maximum inventory} = Q = 500 \text{ book bags}$$

$$\text{Average inventory} = Q/2 = 500/2 = 250 \text{ book bags}$$

Thus, Adventure Center's new book bag inventory policy will result in a maximum of 500 book bags available for sale throughout the park, and an average of 250 book bags available for sale. Now we can answer the question of how frequently book bags will need to be ordered by determining both the number of orders that will be placed each year and the cycle time of the policy:

BOOK BAG ORDERING FREQUENCY ($Q = 500$)

Number of orders a year $= D/Q = 5{,}000/500 = 10$ orders a year

Cycle time $= Q/D = 500/5{,}000 = 0.1$ years

Assuming Adventure Center operates 365 days a year: 0.1 years $\times$ 365 $=$ 36.5 days

Insight Assuming that Adventure Center is open year-round, this new book bag policy will result in 10 orders to be placed a year, or an order for new book bags being placed every 36.5 days. ■

Economic Order Quantity with Price Breaks

Note that the original EOQ model assumes that purchasing costs are unaffected by the choice of order size. For example, Scenario 1a confirmed that the EOQ of 500 was a distinct improvement over Adventure Center's policy of $Q = 1{,}000$ for branded book bags, although this merchandise was assumed to cost Adventure Center \$16 per book bag in either case. This assumption is not always valid in reality; a supplier may offer a discount for purchase of a certain minimum amount, known as a price break quantity. If this offer is made, direct purchasing costs are no longer independent of the manager's choice of order size. Use of the EOQ formula becomes more complex under these conditions, and it may not necessarily provide the best order size. We saw one complicating factor in Scenario 1a, where holding cost H depended on the unit purchase cost (the cost of holding one unit in inventory for a year was cited as 25% of its value, or $16 \times 0.25 = \$4.00$ for a branded book bag). If Adventure Center were offered one or more price breaks as incentives to order larger quantities, these alternate prices would suggest different values of H, which in turn suggest multiple EOQ values. Furthermore, since the total annual purchasing cost now varies with the choice of Q, it is no longer appropriate to leave it out of total policy cost. If C_Q is the price, or purchasing cost per unit when Q are ordered, then the total annual relevant costs of the choice of Q should now read:

price break quantity The minimum order size that qualifies for a quantity discount.

$$\text{TC} = \frac{D}{Q}S + \frac{Q}{2}H + \text{D}C_Q$$

The combined result of these price break complications is illustrated in Figure 10.6, showing the total cost of any policy of order size Q where two different price breaks have been offered. Unlike the total cost curve that appeared earlier in Figure 10.5, the equivalent total cost illustration in Figure 10.6 is not a single curve, but the complex result of multiple curves. Each price break discount creates its own total cost curve, but each individual curve is only relevant over a limited range of values for Q, determined by the price break scheme.

Economic Order Quantity with Price Breaks — FIGURE 10.6

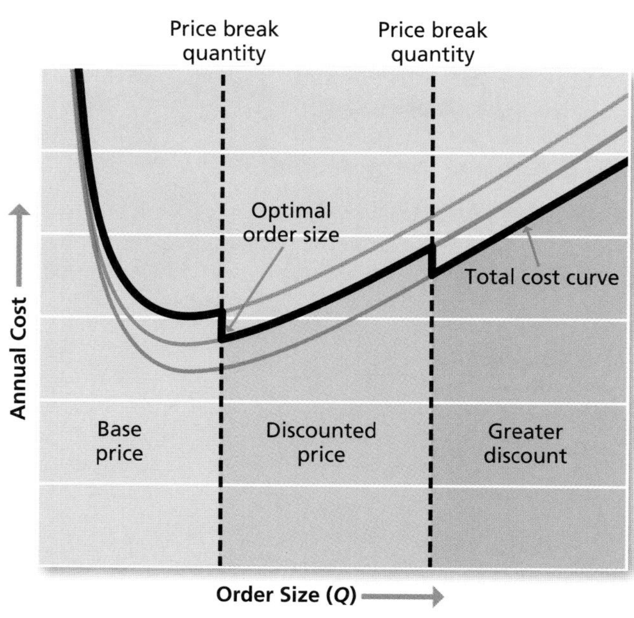

Figure 10.6 also illustrates a case in which the optimal order size occurs not at the low point of any of the three curves, but rather at one of the two price break quantities. Generally, the best order size in this situation may result from the EOQ formula, or it may result from the price breaks offered by the supplier. Thus, the best order size is not found by using a single formula, but rather by completing an algorithm involving EOQ calculations. To find the most economic order size with price breaks we complete these steps:

algorithm
A procedure described by a series of steps.

1. Calculate the EOQ in the case of each potential purchase price.
2. Review the results of step 1 and eliminate all invalid EOQs. An invalid EOQ will be an order size that does not actually fall within the range of Q that the purchase price used to calculate parameter H that the EOQ formula requires.
3. If the only EOQ that remains qualifies its purchaser for the lowest price offered by the supplier, then this is the optimal order size and the analysis is complete. If not, proceed to step 4.
4. Calculate the total relevant annual cost of the valid EOQ remaining from step 2. This total cost should include ordering costs, holding costs, and the purchasing costs resulting from using this EOQ as the ordering size policy.
5. Calculate the total annual cost of any price break quantity that qualifies the purchaser for a lower price than the price associated with the valid EOQ.
6. Compare the total annual costs obtained from both steps 4 and 5. The order size with the lowest cost is the optimal order size.

Scenario 1c introduces a discount for bulk orders of Adventure Center's branded book bags, changing its original EOQ problem into an EOQ with price breaks problem.

Scenario 1c

EOQ with Price Breaks

The supplier of Adventure Center's branded merchandise has learned Adventure Center's plans to decrease the order size of its branded book bags. Since smaller order sizes are less convenient to the supplier, that supplier has offered two price breaks to Adventure Center to make larger orders more attractive. Specifically, the cost charged to Adventure Center for one book bag remains $16, unless Adventure Center orders at least 1,000 book bags, at which point the supplier is willing to drop the price to $15 each. Furthermore, if Adventure Center is willing to order at least 5,000 book bags at a time, the supplier will reduce the purchase price of the book bags to $14 each. Given this new pricing schedule, what would be the best order size for Adventure Center branded book bags?

Analysis

We begin a price break analysis by calculating the EOQ associated with each price offered. Three prices are offered here and thus we should calculate three order sizes, although the only difference among the three will be the changing unit cost C_Q embedded in H, the cost of holding one unit in inventory for a year.

BOOK BAG PRICE BREAK ANALYSIS

EOQ when unit cost (C_Q) is $16 ($Q$ less than 1,000): $H = 16 \times .25 = 4$

$$EOQ_{16} = \sqrt{\frac{2 \times D \times S}{H}} = \sqrt{\frac{2 \times 5{,}000 \times 100}{4}} = 500 \text{ book bags}$$

EOQ when unit cost (C_Q) is $15 ($Q$ at least 1,000, less than 5,000): $H = 15 \times .25 = 3.75$

$$EOQ_{15} = \sqrt{\frac{2 \times D \times S}{H}} = \sqrt{\frac{2 \times 5{,}000 \times 100}{3.75}} = 516.40 \text{ book bags}$$

EOQ when unit cost (C_Q) is \$14 (Q at least 5,000): $H = 14 \times .25 = 3.50$

$$EOQ_{14} = \sqrt{\frac{2 \times D \times S}{H}} = \sqrt{\frac{2 \times 5{,}000 \times 100}{3.50}} = 534.52 \text{ book bags}$$

Only one of these suggested order sizes will be a valid suggestion, so the next step is to identify the valid EOQ:

BOOK BAG PRICE BREAK ANALYSIS

EOQ when unit cost (C_Q) is \$16 (Q less than 1,000): $H = 16 \times .25 = 4$

$$EOQ_{16} = \sqrt{\frac{2 \times D \times S}{H}} = \sqrt{\frac{2 \times 5{,}000 \times 100}{.4}} = 500 \text{ book bags}$$

VALID EOQ: 500 is less than 1,000, which is what C_Q = \$16 assumes.

EOQ when unit cost (C_Q) is \$15 (Q at least 1,000, less than 5,000): $H = 15 \times .25 = 3.75$

$$EOQ_{15} = \sqrt{\frac{2 \times D \times S}{H}} = \sqrt{\frac{2 \times 5{,}000 \times 100}{3.75}} = 516.40 \text{ book bags}$$

NOT VALID: 516.40 is *not* between 1,000 and 5,000, which is what C_Q = \$15 assumes.

EOQ when unit cost (C_Q) is \$14 (Q at least 5,000): $H = 14 \times .25 = 3.50$

$$EOQ_{14} = \sqrt{\frac{2 \times D \times S}{H}} = \sqrt{\frac{2 \times 5{,}000 \times 100}{3.50}} = 534.52 \text{ book bags}$$

NOT VALID: 534.52 is *not* above 5,000, which is what C_Q = \$14 assumes.

At this point, we can identify the best order size for book bags by comparing the one valid EOQ with any price break quantity that qualifies for a price lower than the one associated with the valid EOQ. Since \$16 is the price associated with the valid EOQ of Q = 500, two price break quantities deliver lower prices: C_Q = \$15 (Q = 1,000) and C_Q = \$14 (Q = 5,000). This comparison is based on the total annual relevant cost of each of these three potential order sizes, to determine which would be less expensive. Unlike the total cost calculations in the earlier Scenario 1a, the annual cost of purchasing 5,000 book bags must be included here, because this now varies with the order size.

BOOK BAG PRICE BREAK ANALYSIS (Annual Costs)

Potential Order Size (Q)	Ordering Costs (D/Q) × S	Holding Costs (Q/2) × H	Purchasing Costs D × C_Q	Total Annual Costs
500	(5,000/500) × 100 = \$1,000	(500/2) × 4 = \$1,000	5,000 × 16 = \$80,000	\$82,000
1,000	(5,000/1,000) × 100 = \$500	(1,000/2) × 3.75 = \$1,875	5,000 × 15 = \$75,000	\$77,375 (Lowest cost)
5,000	(5,000/5,000) × 100 = \$100	(5,000/2) × 3.50 = \$8,750	5,000 × 14 = \$70,000	\$78,850

Insight Since the price break quantity Q = 1,000 has the lowest relevant annual costs, Adventure Center should order 1,000 branded book bags each time it places an order. This, in fact, represents a continuation of its older policy of ordering 1,000 book bags at a time, but with the understanding now that Adventure Center will be paying \$15 for each book bag, per the vendor's offer. ■

Economic Production Quantity

The original EOQ minimizes ordering and holding costs, provided that new orders are added to inventory instantaneously upon delivery to the system. While this assumption of the EOQ model is a good fit for procurement from an outside supplier, in some organizations the ordering of a particular SKU is an internal transaction; that organization is both the producer and the consumer or the seller of that SKU. Consider, for example, manufacturers producing component items for the assembly of complex products or businesses such as bakeries producing finished goods for sale to consumers. In such cases, the assumption of instantaneous replenishment is unreasonable—an order placed internally cannot appear suddenly and completely. An order in a production environment, sometimes referred to as a *batch*, requires a certain amount of time to complete. During this time inventory of the SKU climbs steadily as the batch is under production. Since the SKU is assumed to be completed one by one until the batch is complete, this batch size is sometimes referred to as a run size, and the time required to finish the batch is then known as its run time. The steady climb in accumulating inventory during the run time is what creates the case of noninstantaneous replenishment.

run size
A batch or order size associated with the production of an item.

run time
The time required to produce a batch of some item.

We can determine an economic order quantity for the case of noninstantaneous replenishment through modeling similar to that for the original EOQ. This optimal order/batch/run size is also known as the *economic production quantity*, or *EPQ*, and identifying this amount begins by recognizing what has changed and what remains the same when comparing the EPQ to the EOQ. Figure 10.7 displays the sawtooth diagram corresponding to the use of some fixed order size Q in a production environment.

Like Figure 10.4, Figure 10.7 shows the distinct teeth created by minimum and maximum inventory levels across repeating order cycles. However, a single order cycle in Figure 10.7 is more complex than in Figure 10.4; it is split into two intervals: a run time during which the item is being produced and inventory is climbing, followed by an interval of inventory consumption only. Both Figures 10.4 and 10.7 illustrate situations in which demand for the item is perfectly constant, meaning that some of the items produced during the run time in Figure 10.7 were consumed *before* the order for Q was completed. Thus, unlike in the EOQ model, the maximum inventory level in the EPQ environment is *not* simply Q, the size of batch ordered. Let p represent the daily production rate of an item, or how fast it is being produced, and let d represent the daily demand rate for that

FIGURE 10.7 Sawtooth Diagram with Noninstantaneous Replenishment

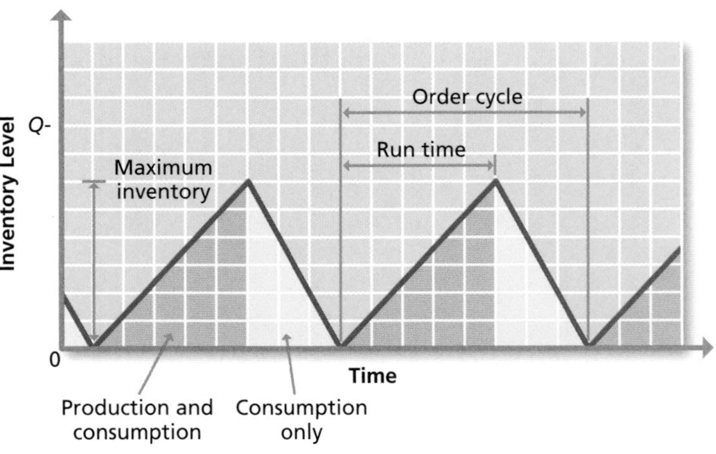

same item, or how fast it is being consumed or sold. The somewhat lower peaks in Figure 10.7 can then be calculated by

$$\text{Maximum inventory} = \frac{Q(p-d)}{p}$$

In the case of both the EOQ and EPQ models, average inventory is assumed to be one-half of maximum inventory and annual holding costs are assumed to be average inventory level multiplied by the cost of holding one unit in inventory throughout the year. These commonalities combined with the EPQ's modified maximum inventory level result in the following expression for the total combined cost of any batch size Q:

$$\text{TC} = \frac{D}{Q}S + \frac{Q(p-d)}{2p}H$$

Note that S remains the fixed ordering cost, although this cost is often called a setup cost in production environments, because it usually represents the fixed expense of setting up machinery and work areas to begin production. Note also that any per unit purchasing cost is once again omitted from the calculation of total cost, because it is assumed that this per unit cost does not vary with the choice of Q. Fixed setup costs and variable holding costs still work against each other in response to variations in batch size Q, and these costs are balanced and minimized when the batch size is set to this amount:

$$\text{EPQ} = \sqrt{\frac{2 \times D \times S}{H}} \times \sqrt{\frac{p}{p-d}}$$

We now use these formulas to determine an order size in Scenario 2a.

EPQ, Determining an Order Size

Scenario 2a

All casual dining restaurants, night clubs and food stalls within Adventure Center's park grounds are supplied by the central kitchen of Adventure Center's catering service. Among its many menu items, this kitchen prepares all fresh salads sold throughout the park. Salad consumption (demand) is virtually constant and known to be about 40,150 plates annually during Adventure Center's 365-day year. It costs \$8.00 to set up the salad workstation, regardless of how many plates of salad are then prepared, and each salad costs \$0.80. Once set up, staff at the salad station can assemble 400 salads per day. The appropriate annual holding cost of a salad is estimated at 300% of the cost of the salad, due to the risk of spoilage.

What order size for setup and salad assembly would minimize the total annual cost of salads? What would that cost be?

Analysis

To develop an inventory policy for salads we first identify the parameters needed by the EPQ model. From the discussion, we know that

SALAD POLICY PARAMETERS

$D = 40{,}150$ (annual demand)   Operating days $= 365$
$S = \$8$ (fixed setup cost)
Unit cost $= \$0.80$ Carrying rate $= 3.00$ (300%)
$H = \$0.80 \times 3.00 = \$2.40$ (annual holding cost)
$p = 400$ (daily production rate) $d = 40{,}150/365 = 110$ (daily demand rate)

Continues

Using this information and the EPQ formula, we can now determine the salad order size that minimizes all relevant costs discussed:

SALAD POLICY ORDER SIZE (EPQ)

$$EOQ = \sqrt{\frac{2 \times D \times S}{H}} \times \sqrt{\frac{p}{p-d}} = \sqrt{\frac{2 \times 40{,}150 \times 8}{2.40}} \times \sqrt{\frac{400}{400-110}}$$

$$= 517.3651 \times 1.1744 = 607.6 = 608 \text{ salads}$$

Finally, to calculate the total cost of this policy, we combine $Q = 608$ with the appropriate total cost formula:

SALAD POLICY TOTAL COST ($Q = 608$)

$$TC = (D/Q) \times S + ((Q \times (p-d))/(2 \times p)) \times H$$

$$= (40{,}150/608) \times 8 + ((608 \times (400 - 110))/(2 \times 400)) \times 2.4$$

$$= 528.29 + 528.96 = \$1{,}057.25$$

Insight Employees preparing salads in the Adventure Center central kitchen should prepare 608 salads each time they set up salad production. This will minimize Adventure Center's combined setup and holding costs associated with salads to $1,057.25 annually. ■

While the issue of determining the order cycle is the same for an EOQ or EPQ policy, the issue of determining the length of either of the two EPQ subintervals is new. Dividing the run size Q by the production rate p gives the length of the run time, while the length of the consumption only interval is the balance of the overall length of the cycle time. We analyze an EPQ policy in Scenario 2b.

Scenario 2b

EPQ, Analyzing a Policy

Consider the optimal inventory policy for salad production in Adventure Center's central kitchen, assembling salads in batches of 608. Keeping to this policy, how often would the staff set up and assemble salads? How long does it take to complete a batch of 608 salads? What is the maximum number of salads that would ever be in chilled storage throughout Adventure Center, awaiting sale to a visitor?

Assume that Adventure Center food service staff always serves the oldest salads first, to make certain that none of the salad inventory sits around for an unnecessarily long time. (This habit is also known as a FIFO policy, for first-in, first-out.) If salad is selling evenly through all the park's outlets, what is the oldest any given salad served to a visitor could potentially be?

Analysis

All the questions posed above concern a policy in which $Q = 608$. The first question of how often the staff will set up and assemble salads is a question of the cycle time associated with the policy:

SALAD POLICY ($Q = 608$)

Cycle time $= Q/D = 0.0151$ years
$0.0151 \times 365 = 5.5$ days

The question of how long a batch will require to complete is a question of run time:

SALAD POLICY ($Q = 608$)

Run time $= Q/p = 608/400 = 1.5$ days

To determine the maximum number of salads that would ever be in chilled storage, we calculate the maximum inventory level:

SALAD POLICY ($Q = 608$)

Maximum inventory $= (Q \times (p - d))/p = (608 \times (400 - 110))/400 = 440.8$ salads

Insight Adventure Center's optimal salad policy will require the central kitchen staff to set up salad assembly every 5.5 days, and each batch of 608 salads will require 1.5 days to complete. This will result in a peak inventory of approximately 440 salads in chilled storage during each 5.5 day cycle.

If Adventure Center follows a FIFO policy in the sale of salads, then the oldest salad would be the 608th salad produced. We can determine the age of this salad by calculating the length of the consumption-only phase of the order cycle, as pictured in Figure 10.8, because we assume that this salad is sold just before Adventure Center begins a new batch of salad. Using the information developed so far:

SALAD POLICY ($Q = 608$)

Potential age of oldest salad = Length of consumption-only phase of order cycle
Length of consumption-only phase = Length of order cycle − length of run time
= 5.5 days − 1.5 days = 4 days

Insight Adventure Center's policy implies that a salad sold to a customer in the park could be at most 4 days old. ■

REORDER POINTS

Formulas such as the EOQ and EPQ provide an answer of how much should be ordered under certain conditions, but they do not provide any recommendation as to when an order should be placed. In fixed order quantity systems, the issue of when to order is determined by a reorder point (ROP). When inventory drops to its reorder point, a new order is placed. The timing of this new order is important, because the item is assumed to require some lead time between placement of the new order and actual receipt of that order. Thus, the reorder point needs to be set at a level that leaves enough of the item in inventory to satisfy demand while waiting for the new order to arrive.

reorder point
An inventory level that triggers replenishment of an item.

lead time
Any delay between requesting a product and receiving it.

If the issues of demand and lead time are purely deterministic, then setting a reorder point is relatively straightforward. If d units are always needed each day and the lead time between placing an order and receiving it is always LT days, then the reorder point (ROP) under these conditions should be:

deterministic
Fixed and known in advance, representing a high level of certainty when planning.

$$\text{ROP} = d \times \text{LT}$$

For example, if the lead time on some item is always 3 days and this item is consumed or sold at a rate of exactly 10 per day, then a new order for this item should be placed when its current stock level drops to $10 \times 3 = 30$ units on-hand. These 30 units will be exactly enough to satisfy demand during lead time, and the new order will arrive just as stock runs out. While this deterministic example is not very realistic, it does highlight the nature of reordering under any conditions: a reorder point must anticipate demand during lead time (DDLT).

Demand During Lead Time

If demand during lead time can vary, it is said to be probabilistic, or naturally subject to some randomness. This is more realistic than the deterministic case, because actual

probabilistic
Variable or not well known in advance; subject to randomness. This represents some uncertainty in planning.

FIGURE 10.8 Reorder Point with Normally Distributed Demand

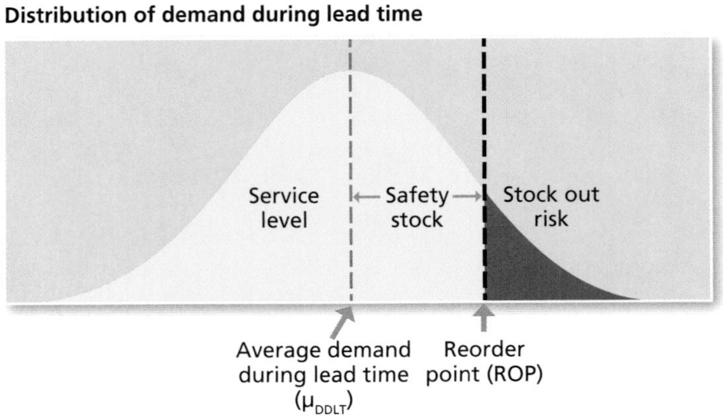

demand for an item might vary each day, or the lead time on an order may not always be the same for every order. Nonetheless, past experience usually offers clues as to how much will be needed during lead time. Average past demand during lead time is important, although actual demand in the future is expected to vary around this average. We assume that this variation is normally distributed, as illustrated in Figure 10.8.

Under these assumptions, actual demand during lead time is expected to be greater than average demand during lead time during half of all lead times. If average demand during lead time were used as a reorder point, new orders would not arrive fast enough in half of all cases of ordering, because actual demand would exceed available supply during lead time and a stock out would occur. Since it is probably not acceptable to be stocking out so frequently, an effective inventory manager sets a reorder point at some amount higher than the average amount needed during lead time—creating safety stock to avoid stock outs. If an average of μ_d is needed each day and the lead time between placing an order and receiving it is an average of LT days, then the reorder point (ROP) under probabilistic conditions can be described as

$$\text{ROP} = (\mu_d \times \text{LT}) + \text{safety stock}$$

For example, if the lead time on ordering some item is an average of 3 days, and this item is consumed or sold at an average of 10 per day, then the average demand during lead time would be $10 \times 3 = 30$ units. If the reorder point for this same item is 33 units, this policy implies a safety stock of $33 - 30 = 3$ units. Whether this is a desirable reorder point or a desirable amount of safety stock depends on how well it performs as a policy.

Performance Measures

When demand during lead time is not perfectly predictable, setting a reorder point requires accepting some risk. This risk can be reduced by setting the reorder point higher, thus increasing the safety stock. Safety stock, however, brings its own costs to the reorder point decision. In the long run, actual demand during lead time for a series of order cycles averages to the known average demand during lead time. Any reorder point that includes safety stock represents a decision to keep that equivalent amount of inventory throughout the year, as if a blanket of that thickness had been layered over the sawtooth diagram for the item. The cost of the safety stock in a reorder point policy is the annual cost of keeping this amount of stock in inventory throughout the year. The higher the reorder point, the higher the safety stock, and thus the higher these safety stock holding costs.

However, if the reorder point is too low, the risk is greater that it will not trigger new orders soon enough for on-time arrival. The inventory manager must determine whether this risk is acceptable relative to the cost of the reorder point. Evaluating a reorder point requires judging its performance on two dimensions related to the issue of safety stock: service level and stock out risk.

Service Level The service level of a reorder point is the probability that demand will not exceed supply during lead time, each time the reorder point triggers placement of a new order. Figure 10.8 illustrates service level as the combined area of the demand during lead time distribution that is to the left-hand side of the reorder point. Since all points to the left represent instances in which demand during lead time was less than the reorder point, and the height of the curve over these points represents the probability of those particular levels of demand, their combined area then represents the likelihood of *not* stocking out during lead time.

service level
The probability that demand for an item will be met during the lead time on replenishment of that same item.

A reorder point can be evaluated for its service level by translating the existing demand during lead time distribution into a standard normal distribution, and then using a standard normal table to estimate the area to the left-hand side of the reorder point. Any ROP used with average demand during lead time of μ_{DDLT} and a deviation of σ_{DDLT} can be translated into a corresponding point z on a standard normal curve by computing a z-score:

standard normal distribution
A normal distribution with a mean of zero and a variance of 1. Any other normal distribution can be converted to this standard, allowing the use of standard normal tables to analyze the original distributions.

$$z = (\text{ROP} - \mu_{DDLT})/\sigma_{DDLT}$$

This z-score can then be located on any z-table, such as the one available in Appendix B. For example, if average demand during lead time (μ_{DDLT}) were 30 units and the standard deviation of demand during lead time were 2 units (σ_{DDLT}), then the z-score corresponding to an ROP of 33 units would be $(33 - 30)/2 = 3/2 = 1.50$. Looking up the value of the row corresponding to 1.5 and the column corresponding to 0.00 in Appendix B indicates an area of 0.9332 or 93.32% of the normal curve. Restated, the ROP of 33 units provides a service level of 93.32%.

Stock Out Risk Figure 10.8 labels the area of the demand during lead time distribution to the right-hand side of the reorder point as its stock out risk. Stock out risk is the probability of demand exceeding the on-hand supply during lead time. This makes stock out risk the complement of service level: if a policy has a 93.32% service level, it has a stock out risk of 6.68%. Thus, all three of these reorder point measures are related as follows:

- The higher the reorder point, the higher the safety stock and its costs, but the lower the stock out risk.
- The lower the reorder point, the lower the safety stock and its costs, but the higher the stock out risk.

We use these three measures in Scenario 3a to evaluate a reorder point.

Evaluating a Reorder Point — Scenario 3a

Adventure Center sells bottled water to visitors at refreshment kiosks throughout its park. Each kiosk is supplied by a central warehouse that takes delivery of large shipments of bottled water and other refreshments purchased in bulk. When the Adventure Center warehouse orders a new shipment of bottled water from its beverage vendor, it usually sells an average of 1,500 bottles from its existing stock while it waits for the newly placed order to be delivered. This demand during lead time for bottled water varies according to a normal distribution, with a standard deviation of 200 bottles during lead time. Adventure Center had been reordering when 1,500 bottles were left in stock at the warehouse, but kiosk employees are unhappy with that reorder point. Based on their feedback, Adventure Center is considering

Continues

increasing the ROP to 2,000 bottles of water. What are the safety stock, service level, and stock out risk associated with the policy of ROP = 2,000?

Analysis

To begin, we determine the safety stock for ROP = 2,000 by calculating the difference between the proposed reorder point and the average demand during leadtime:

PROPOSED WATER BOTTLE REORDER POLICY (ROP = 2,000)

Demand during lead time: $\mu_{DDLT} = 1{,}500$, $\sigma_{DDLT} = 200$ bottles
Safety stock = ROP − μ_{DDLT} = 2,000 − 1,500 = 500 bottles

To determine the service level associated with ROP =2,000, we determine the combined area of the normal curve representing demand during lead time to the left of ROP = 2,000:

PROPOSED WATER BOTTLE REORDER POLICY (ROP = 2,000)

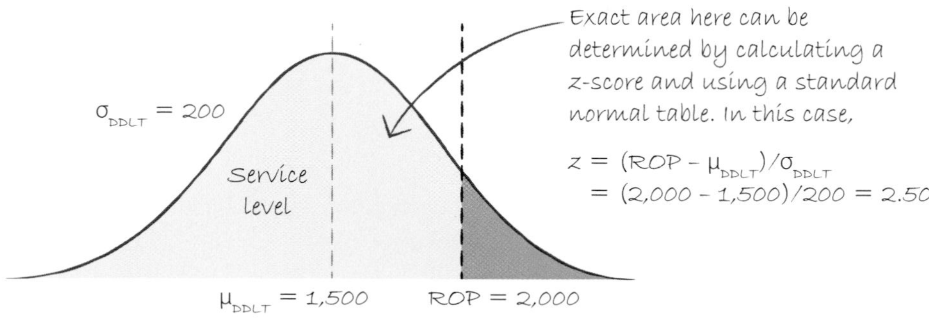

$\sigma_{DDLT} = 200$
Service level
$\mu_{DDLT} = 1{,}500$
ROP = 2,000
Exact area here can be determined by calculating a z-score and using a standard normal table. In this case,
$z = (ROP - \mu_{DDLT})/\sigma_{DDLT}$
$= (2{,}000 - 1{,}500)/200 = 2.50$

This *z*-score of 2.50 corresponds to an area of 0.9938 in Appendix B at the back of this text, as a value of 0.9938 lies at the intersection of the table row labeled 2.5 and the table column labeled 0.00. Thus

PROPOSED WATER BOTTLE REORDER POLICY (ROP = 2,000)

Service level = 0.9938, or 99.4%

Now we can calculate stock out risk from the service level:

PROPOSED WATER BOTTLE REORDER POLICY (ROP = 2,000)

Stock out risk = 1 − 0.9938 = 0.0062, or 0.6%

Insight Adventure Center's proposed reorder point of 2,000 water bottles implies that the equivalent of 500 bottles will be kept as safety stock throughout the year, supporting a service level of 99.4%. Thus, a reorder point of 2,000 water bottles has a stock out risk of 0.6%. ■

Note that in Scenario 3a we evaluated a potential reorder point of 2,000 water bottles, but that does not necessarily indicate that Adventure Center should use this new reorder point. This proposal of ROP = 2,000 is certainly better than ROP = 1,500 in terms of service level, because Adventure Center's current policy of reordering when the average amount needed during lead time is left in stock provides a service level of only 50%. Whether ROP = 2,000 is better overall than ROP = 1,500 can only be determined by Adventure Center's expressing a preference between carrying an average 500 extra water bottles in inventory versus not doing so, but stocking out more frequently.

Determining Reorder Points

A business often determines the service level it considers necessary to operate effectively, and then determines reorder points for various SKUs based on that service level. Under these circumstances, it is easiest to think of ROP as an equation:

$$\text{ROP} = \mu_{\text{DDLT}} + (z \times \sigma_{DDLT})$$

This formula expands the expression discussed earlier in which ROP equals average demand during lead time plus a certain amount of safety stock. In this formula, the amount of safety stock is expressed as $(z \times \sigma_{\text{DDLT}})$ or z standard deviations in demand during lead time. This z links a chosen service level to an appropriate ROP for any given item. A standard normal table reports how much area of a normal curve is associated with a boundary placed z standard deviations from its mean (μ). Appendix B provides the area to the left of z, which corresponds to the service level of a reorder point. To determine what z-value corresponds to a particular service level

1. Locate the value closest to this result within the body of the table in Appendix B.
2. Trace the row on which this value is located to its label, to identify the first two digits of the z-value required.
3. Trace from the value upward to its column label, to identify the third digit in the z-value required.

For example, if a service level of 90% is required, the value closest to 0.9 within Appendix B is 0.8997. This value of 0.8997 is on the row of the table labeled 1.2 and the column labeled 0.08. This indicates that a value of 1.2 + 0.08 = 1.28 should be used for z when determining any reorder point with a 90% service level. With this in mind, we can determine a reorder point in Scenario 3b.

Determining a Reorder Point

Scenario 3b

Adventure Center's management was surprised to find out that an ROP of 2,000 water bottles would provide a service level of 99.4%, as revealed in Scenario 3a. Management feels that 99.4% is a bit excessive for water bottles. Basically, management believes the service level when reordering any bottled beverage or packaged snack item should be closer to 90%. Given this clarification, what should be the ROP for water bottles?

Analysis

We expect this new ROP to be less than 2,000, because its service level is less. To determine its precise value, we first retrieve the same demand during lead time data used earlier in Scenario 3a, and note that this ROP will divide that curve such that 90% is to the left of the correct ROP.

PROPOSED WATER BOTTLE REORDER POLICY

Demand during lead time: $\mu_{DDLT} = 1{,}500$, $\sigma_{DDLT} = 200$ bottles
Target service level: 90%

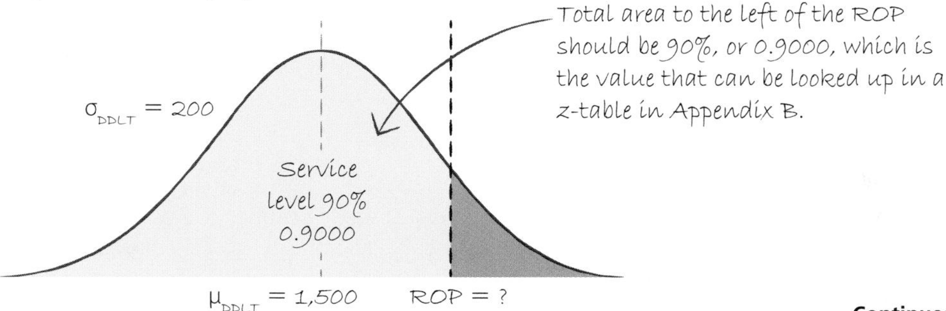

Total area to the left of the ROP should be 90%, or 0.9000, which is the value that can be looked up in a z-table in Appendix B.
σDDLT = 200
Service level 90% 0.9000
μDDLT = 1,500
ROP = ?

Continues

We find the z-value needed to determine a reorder point providing an overall service level of 0.90 by first inspecting the body of the standard normal table in Appendix B for the one value closest to 0.9000.

PROPOSED WATER BOTTLE REORDER POLICY

The value within the standard normal table in Appendix B that most closely corresponds to an area of 0.9000 to the left of z is 0.8997. This value lies on the table row labeled 1.2 and the column labeled 0.08, which indicates a z of $1.2 + 0.08 = 1.28$. We can now calculate the ROP:

$$ROP = \mu_{DDLT} + (z \times \sigma_{DDLT}) = 1{,}500 + (1.28 \times 200) = 1{,}756$$

Insight To maintain a 90% service level when reordering water bottles, Adventure Center should place a new order when there are 1,756 water bottles left in stock. ■

Deriving Distributions for Demand During Lead Time

The reorder point technique discussed here assumes that demand during lead time is normally distributed, and requires its average (μ_{DDLT}) and its standard deviation (σ_{DDLT}) for further analysis. However, overall demand during lead time does not always vary for the same reasons in every situation. For example, demand during lead time might vary because the length of the lead time is uncertain, or it might vary because daily demand varies, or both. In each of these three cases, it is relatively easy to determine how the resulting overall demand during lead time is distributed, given certain details.

Variable Demand with Constant Lead Time Sometimes demand varies naturally, although lead times are fixed and certain. Let μ_d represent average daily demand (also assumed to be normally distributed) and σ_d represent the standard deviation in daily demand. If the known length of the lead time is *LT*, then the distribution of overall demand during lead time can be identified by

- $\mu_{DDLT} = LT \times \mu_d$
- $\sigma_{DDLT} = \sqrt{LT} \times \sigma_d$

For example, if average daily demand (μ_d) for some SKU is 50 units, the standard deviation in daily demand (σ_d) for that SKU is 5 units, and lead time on orders of that SKU is always 9 days (LT), then the average demand during lead time would be $50 \times 9 = 450$ units (μ_{DDLT}). Furthermore, the standard deviation in the distribution of demand during lead time would be $\sqrt{9} \times 5 = 3 \times 5 = 15$ units (σ_{DDLT}).

Constant Demand with Variable Lead Time Demand for an item may be constant, such as parts being used by an assembly system working at a steady rate. However, if the lead time on resupply of those parts varies, then the resulting overall demand during lead time is probabilistic as well. In this situation, let d be the unvarying amount that is needed each day and let LT represent the average lead time for that item, where σ_{LT} is the standard deviation in that varying lead time. Demand during lead time parameters can be then identified:

- $\mu_{DDLT} = LT \times d$
- $\sigma_{DDLT} = d \times \sigma_{LT}$

For example, suppose demand for some SKU is always 50 units a day (d), the average lead time on orders of that SKU is 9 days (LT), and the standard deviation in lead time variability is 2 days (σ_{LT}). Then, average demand during lead time would be $50 \times 9 = 450$ units (μ_{DDLT}), while the standard deviation in demand during lead time would be $50 \times 2 = 100$ units (σ_{DDLT}).

Variable Demand with Variable Lead Time Demand during lead time may vary because both daily demand and the length of the lead time are not certain. Assuming both are normally distributed, let μ_d and σ_d represent the average and standard deviation in daily demand, where LT and σ_{LT} represent the average and standard deviation in the uncertain length of the lead time. The distribution of demand during lead time is:

- $\mu_{DDLT} = LT \times \mu_d$
- $\sigma_{DDLT} = \sqrt{(LT \times \sigma_d^2) + (\mu_d^2 \times \sigma_{LT}^2)}$

For example, if demand for some SKU is an average of 50 units a day (μ_d) and the average lead time on orders of that SKU is 9 days (LT), then average demand during lead time is $50 \times 9 = 450$ units (μ_{DDLT}). Furthermore, if the standard deviation in demand (σ_d) is 5 units and the standard deviation in lead time variability (σ_{LT}) is 2 days, then standard deviation in demand during lead time is $\sqrt{9 \times 25 + 2{,}500 \times 4} = 101.12$ units (σ_{DDLT}).

In Scenario 3c we derive demand during lead time.

Deriving Demand During Lead Time

Scenario 3c

Adventure Center instructs its refreshment kiosk workers to reorder crushed ice and cubed ice when their kiosk has only 15 pounds remaining in stock. Crushed ice and cubed ice have been assigned the same reorder point because both are used at the same rate of about 5 pounds an hour, and both take about 3 hours to deliver to the kiosk requesting more ice. These types of ice are either used or otherwise melt at a steady rate, and thus the demand/usage of 5 pounds an hour is constant.

Refreshment kiosk workers have complained about the 15 pound reorder point policy, however, stating that crushed ice and cubed ice delivery are not the same. Both are produced by Adventure Center's central catering facility, which reliably delivers fresh bags of cubed ice in about 3 hours. Crushed ice production, however, is a slower process on less reliable equipment, so central catering tries to prioritize these requests in case of problems with the machinery, but cannot always do so. The result is that the wait for fresh bags of crushed ice is less predictable: lead time is usually between 2 and 4 hours, but sometimes the crushed ice arrives in only an hour or takes 4 to 5 hours to appear. Even though demand for crushed ice is the same as cubed ice, the workers who do the reordering feel that it is not appropriate to use the same reorder point.

How do the distributions of demand during lead time differ for crushed ice and cubed ice? If Adventure Center maintains a 99% service level for the delivery of ice, what should these two reorder points be?

Analysis

Cubed ice is the simpler of the two distributions, being constant at 15 pounds during lead time:

CUBED ICE DDLT DISTRIBUTION

Demand is constant: $d = 5$ pounds per hour
Lead time is contant: $LT = 3$ hours
DDLT is constant: $d \times LT = 5 \times 3 = 15$ pounds

Continues

This confirms that the current reorder point is appropriate:

CUBED ICE REORDER POINT
(Deterministic DDLT)

$$ROP = d \times LT = 5 \times 3 = 15 \text{ pounds}$$

However, the issue of the distribution of demand during lead time for crushed ice is more detailed, and does require that an assumption be made:

CRUSHED ICE DDLT DISTRIBUTION

Demand is constant: $d = 5$ pounds per hour
Lead time is NOT constant:

- Assume from description of "between 2 and 4 hours" that the *average* is 3 hours, thus $LT = 3$ hours.
- Assume from description that the variation in lead time is *normally* distributed.
- Assume from description "usually 2 to 4 hours" means "about two-thirds of the time," or two standard deviations from the mean. Thus, one standard deviation from the mean, (σ_{LT}) is 2.5 to 3.5 hours, or $\sigma_{LT} = 0.5$ hours.

DDLT is variable (normally distributed):
Constant demand/variable lead time case

$$\mu_{DDLT} = LT \times d = 3 \times 5 = 15 \text{ pounds}$$

$$\sigma_{DDLT} = d \times \sigma_{LT} = 5 \times 0.5 = 2.5 \text{ pounds}$$

We find the *z*-value needed to determine a reorder point providing an overall service level of 0.99 by first inspecting the body of the standard normal table in Appendix B for the one value closest to 0.99, which is .9901, corresponding to $z = 2.33$. Then, based on these descriptions and assumptions, the reorder point for crushed ice is

CRUSHED ICE REORDER POINT

(Probabilistic DDLT)
$z = 2.33$ (for a 99% service level)
$ROP = \mu_{DDLT} + (z \times \sigma_{DDLT}) = 15 + (2.33 \times 2.5) = 15 + 5.825 = 20.825$ pounds

Insight There is merit in the kiosk workers' objections to using the same reorder point for both cubed and crushed ice. For cubed ice, distribution of demand during lead time is reliably constant at 15 pounds, indicating that the current reorder point of 15 pounds is appropriate. However, even though crushed is used at an *average* rate of 15 pounds during lead time, its variable nature requires that kiosk workers place orders for new crushed ice when 20.825 pounds are left in stock, so that the kiosk does not run out of crushed ice 99% of the time it waits for deliveries. ■

All organizations make inventory management decisions. In some cases, inventory management is a relatively minor matter, such as keeping a professional service stocked with the office supplies necessary to conduct daily business. In other cases, inventory management defines the very purpose of the organization, such as the sourcing activities of any large retail chain. Regardless of its scale, inventory management is a challenge that threads together organizations and individuals, as it challenges us to make thoughtful use of our own capital when investing in what resources we need to create greater value.

SUMMARY

The term "inventory" can describe any stock of tangible good waiting for use. Since inventory represents potential value, it must be managed carefully to assure that it actually achieves this value through successful use or sale. Inventory can be categorized according to where in the system it is waiting, such as among the inputs as raw materials, as work in process, or among the outputs as finished goods. Inventory can also differ on why it is waiting, such as to gain some other savings or to protect the system from uncertainty. A stock of inventory can even fall into more than one category simultaneously, such as a retailer's stock serving as both raw materials and finished goods from the perspective of the store.

While there are many different approaches to inventory management, its fundamental mission is the same: determine and control how much and when to order more inventory. Differing choices of answers for these two questions influence a host of related issues, including the frequency of ordering, the average amount of inventory present in the system, and the risk of stock outs. Analytical models recommend best answers in terms of what quantity minimizes the total relevant costs under certain conditions. Thus, these models are called the *economic* order quantity and the *economic* production quantity, each better suited to a particular situation. Choosing a reorder point answers the question of when to order, although the inventory manager must weigh the cost of safety versus the risk of stock outs to determine whether that reorder point is best for successful operation.

Key Terms

ABC policy
algorithm
average inventory
backorder
cost of capital
cycle stock
deterministic
economies of scale
finished goods
fixed costs
fixed order interval policy
fixed order quantity policy
holding costs
inventory
inventory turnover
lead time
opportunity cost
optimization
order cycle
Pareto analysis
periodic review system
pipeline stock
price break
price break quantity
probabilistic
raw materials
reorder point
run size
run time
safety stock
sawtooth diagram
service level
shrinkage
SKU (stock keeping unit)
spoilage
standard normal distribution
stock out
stockpiling
tangibility
variable cost
WIP (work-in-process)

Discussion Questions

1. Mathematically, when would the EOQ and the EPQ recommend nearly identical order sizes? How does this relate to the concepts of instantaneous and noninstantaneous relationships?
2. Why would inventory holding costs be higher for a new business than for a similar business that has been operating for many years?
3. What type of business sells a tangible product and yet has no WIP inventory?
4. If annual demand suddenly fell by half, would the EOQ likewise be reduced by half? Explain.
5. If annual demand suddenly fell by half, would the ROP likewise be reduced by half? Explain.
6. Two items both have reorder points with service levels of 99%. One of the items is ordered 10 times a year, and the other item is ordered 20 times a year. Do these two items have the same overall risk of stocking out at least once during the year?

PROBLEMS

Short answers appear in Appendix A. Go to **NoteShaper.com** for full video tutorials on each question.

Minute Answer

1. If a reorder point is increased, what happens to its service level?
2. If a reorder point is increased, what happens to its safety stock?
3. If a reorder point is decreased, what happens to its stock out risk?
4. In a fixed order quantity policy, if the policy's order size is decreased, what happens to average inventory level?
5. In a fixed order quantity policy, if the policy's order size is decreased, what happens to the frequency of ordering?
6. In a fixed order quantity policy, if the policy's order size is increased, what happens to the reorder point?
7. Assuming perfectly constant demand, if lead time increases from 5 to 10 days, what happens to the reorder point?
8. In an ABC classification scheme, which groups of items will be least tightly controlled?
9. The two basic issues in inventory are how much to order and what else?
10. A company that was using the EOQ formula to determine batch sizes realizes it has made a mistake and must recalculate those batch sizes using the EPQ formula. What will happen to batch sizes at this company?
11. What is SKU short for?
12. Is a transaction fee mostly likely an example of a fixed or a variable cost?

Quick Start

13. Lead time for some SKU is always 5 days, and demand for that SKU is always 50 per day. What is the reorder point for this SKU?
14. A gift shop sells 400 boxes of scented candles a year. The ordering cost is $60 for scented candles, and holding cost is $24 per box per year. What is the economic order size for scented candles?
15. A car rental agency uses 96 boxes of staples a year. The boxes cost $4 each. It costs $10 to order staples, and it costs $0.80 to hold a box of staples in inventory for 1 year. How many boxes of staples should the car rental company order each time it needs staples, to minimize the combined ordering and holding costs for staples?
16. A car rental agency uses 96 boxes of staples a year. The boxes cost $4 each. It costs $10 to order staples, and it costs $0.80 to hold a box of staples in inventory for 1 year. Using the order size that minimizes the car rental agency's combined ordering and holding costs for staples, how long will a single order of staples last the agency, before it must receive more staples? (Assume there are 52 weeks in the year for the car rental agency.)
17. A car rental agency uses 96 boxes of staples a year. The boxes cost $4 each. It costs $10 to order staples, and it costs $0.80 to hold a box of staples in inventory for 1 year. Using the order size that minimizes the car rental agency's combined ordering and holding costs for staples, how much does the car rental agency actually spend on holding costs for staples each year?
18. A gift shop sells 2,000 musical greeting cards each year. The ordering cost for musical greeting cards is $100 per order and the holding cost is $10 per musical greeting card per year. If the gift shop always orders 100 musical greeting cards when it places an order from its supplier, how many musical greeting cards does the gift shop have in inventory, on average?

19. The reorder point for SKU 303 is 102 units, while average demand during the lead time on an order for SKU 303 is 97 units. How much safety stock is implied by SKU 303's reorder point policy?

20. A certain company reorders envelopes when its stock drops to 12 boxes, although demand for envelopes during lead time is normally distributed with a mean of 10 boxes and a standard deviation of 3 boxes. What is the probability of this company's stocking out before a new order of envelopes arrives?

Ramp Up

21. A carpet cleaning firm uses an average of 20 gallons of cleaning fluid a day. Usage tends to be normally distributed with a standard deviation of 2 gallons per day. Lead time is 4 days, and the desired service level is 92%. What is the most appropriate reorder point for this carpet cleaning firm?

22. A gift shop sells 400 boxes of scented candles a year. The ordering cost is $60 for scented candles, and holding cost is $24 per box per year. What is the minimum annual amount of these combined costs the gift shop could pay?

23. The Office of Environmental Studies uses a reorder point system to govern its ordering of new shipments of public information flyers. Demand for public information flyers varies, depending on the number of public visitors that the Office of Environmental Studies receives each day, and the delay between when the office requests a new shipment of flyers and when it actually receives that shipment can also vary slightly. Thus, based on past experience, the Office of Environmental Studies estimates that demand for flyers during the lead time on a new shipment is normally distributed, with an average of 200 flyers and a variance of 50 flyers. If the Office of Environmental Studies reorders when its stock of flyers falls to 215, what is the chance that the new shipment will arrive before the office runs out completely and must disappoint a visiting member of the public?

24. If demand for an item is 10 per *month*, the cost of placing an order is $15, and the cost of holding one item in inventory for 1 *year* is $25, what is the EOQ?

25. Suppose that annual demand for a certain item has decreased dramatically this year, although the store that stocks this item has not updated its inventory policy, so the store is still using the same order size and reorder point established for that item when it was selling better in previous years. What will happen to frequency of ordering?

Scenarios

26. The demand for a particular part called SKU 005 is 1,500 units a year. The cost of one SKU 005 is $50.00. It costs $60.00 to place an order for SKU 005, and the user of SKU 005 has a per year inventory carrying cost of 25% of unit cost. Assume 250 working days in the year where SKU 005 is used.

a. What is the combined annual holding and ordering cost of an order size of 200 units for SKU 005?

b. How many of SKU 005 should be ordered, to minimize combined ordering and holding costs?

c. The vendor who sells SKU 005 has just offered a 5% discount for orders of 500 or more. Now how many should be ordered?

d. Once the purchasing manager for SKU 005 places an order, the vendor requires 5 working days to deliver that order. What should be the purchasing manager's reorder point?

Reminder: Short answers appear in Appendix A. Go to **NoteShaper.com** for full video tutorials on each question.

27. The Sun Up Convenience Store is open 365 days a year. Sun Up sells 25 bottles of Electric Energy Drink each day. It costs $8.00 for Sun Up to order Electric Energy Drink, regardless of the size of the order. The distributor of Electric Energy Drink sells Electric Energy to Sun Up for $0.25 a bottle, and the distributor delivers Electric Energy exactly 3 days after Sun Up places an order. If Sun Up were to hold one bottle of Electric Energy Drink in inventory for 1 year, it would cost Sun Up four times (or 400% of) the bottle's cost.

a. What order size will minimize Sun Up's costs? What is the total cost of this order size?

b. Using the order size that minimizes Sun Up's total costs, how many bottles of Electric Energy Drink, on average, will be in inventory?

c. Using the minimum cost order size, how frequently will Sun Up order Electric Energy Drink?

d. When should Sun Up order Electric Energy Drink?

e. Now suppose that the Electric Energy Drink distributor has just made Sun Up an offer: if Sun Up orders at least 1,000 bottles at a time, then the distributor will charge only $0.22 for each bottle. What should Sun Up do now?

28. The Fine Crate Company uses 14,600 wooden slats a year, building wooden crates at a constant rate. The Fine Crate Company can produce 160 wooden slats a day when it sets up to produce wooden slats. The company only sets up and produces wooden slats five times a year, and it always produces the same number of wooden slats each time it sets up production (in other words, a fixed batch size). The Fine Crate Company is open 365 days a year.

a. What is the run time of one of the Fine Crate Company's batches of wooden slats?

b. What run size is Fine Crate using when building wooden crates? What is the run time on this order size?

c. What is the most number of wooden slats that the Fine Crate Company would ever have in inventory, waiting to be used for wooden crates?

29. A large hotel serves banquets and several restaurants from a central kitchen in which labor is shifted among various stations and jobs. Dessert consumption is virtually constant and known to be 30,000 desserts a year. Desserts can be produced at a rate of 125 a day, and the hotel is open 365 days a year. It costs $4.00 to set up the dessert preparation station, regardless of how many deserts are then prepared, and each dessert costs $0.40. The appropriate annual holding cost of a dessert is estimated at 300% of the cost of the dessert, due to the risk of spoilage. Unfortunately, the refrigerated pantry that the kitchen uses to store desserts only stores a maximum of 300 desserts, so the kitchen always makes a batch of 300 desserts every time it needs new desserts.

a. How much does the hotel central kitchen pay in total annual holding and ordering costs on dessert? How often does it produce desserts under its current policy?

b. What is the order size, or run size, that would minimize the total annual cost of desserts? How much savings could be achieved by using this order size?

c. By how much would the central kitchen have to expand the capacity of the refrigerated pantry that stores desserts to implement the lowest cost policy?

30. A warehouse stocks three different items: SKU 1, SKU 2, and SKU 3. Information on each of these items is provided in this table:

SKU	Daily Demand	Lead Time
1	Constant at 25 units per day.	Normally distributed with an average of 4 days and a standard deviation of 1 day.
2	Normally distributed with an average of 25 units per day and a standard deviation of 5 units.	Constant at 4 days.
3	Normally distributed with an average of 25 unit per day and a standard deviation of 5 units.	Normally distributed with an average of 4 days and a standard deviation of 1 day.

The warehouse uses the same reorder point for all three items: it always places an order when 120 units are left in stock.

a. How much safety stock is implied by this reorder point?

b. What is the service level provided by this reorder point, in the case of each of these three items?

31. Consider the sawtooth diagram below, which illustrates the inventory issues associated with SKU 0012, a small, stamped metal part produced by the ConAm Company, over the last 40 days. Answer the following questions, based on this sawtooth diagram.

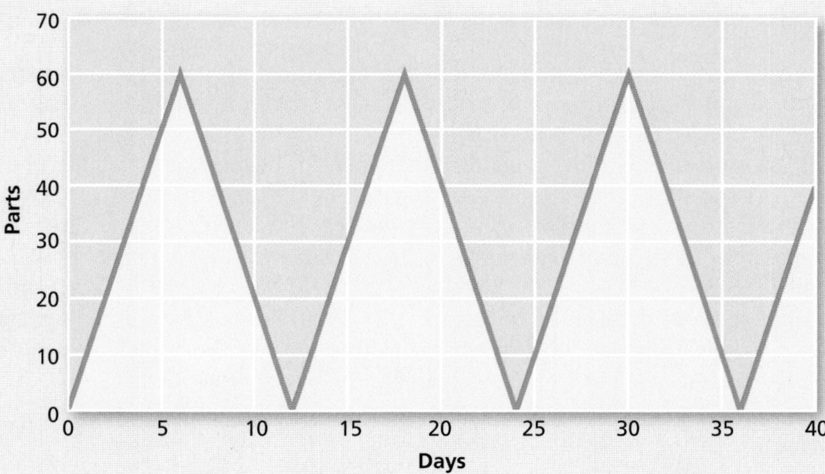

a. What is the maximum inventory level of SKU 0012?

b. How long can ConAm Company operate on a single order of SKU 0012?

c. What is the run time on a single order of SKU 0012?

d. If demand for SKU 0012 is 10 parts per day, what order size is ConAm Company apparently using?

e. If demand for SKU 0012 is 10 parts per day, at what rate is ConAm apparently producing these parts?

CASE STUDY: DENTON PET CLINIC

Denton Pet Clinic is a small business owned by two veternarians who employ two full-time staff members and a new part-time business manager. The business manager believes that Denton could save money by improving its inventory management, even though Denton Pet Clinic stocks very little except pharmaceuticals, cleaning supplies, and some miscellaneous products. In the case of pharmaceuticals, Denton purchases most drugs from a supply company who offers very good prices and who ships to veterinarians overnight for a flat fee of $15. Using this overnight service, Denton Pet Clinic has been in the habit of simply ordering a dozen boxes of any drug when only a few doses of that drug remain in stock near the end of a business day. The business manager has gathered the information, shown in the table below, on the three most common drugs purchased routinely from this supply company, whose prior purchasing accounts for nearly 70% of all money spent on pharmaceuticals by Denton Pet Clinic.

Three Most Common Pharmaceuticals

Drugs Purchased	Average Monthly Usage by Denton Vets	Unit Cost
Rabies booster vaccine, feline, 10 doses per box	4 boxes	$120 per box
Distemper booster vaccine, feline, 10 doses per box	20 boxes	$210 per box
Broadband antibiotic,100-ml ampoules, 50 per box	20 boxes	$400 per box

The business manager estimates that Denton's holding costs for these small but expensive supplies is best estimated by the business's cost of capital, 15%. Interestingly, the business manager suspects that Denton's habit of always ordering one dozen boxes probably isn't a bad rule-of-thumb, although somewhat better order sizes might be identified if this issue were treated more scientifically. Rather, the business manager is troubled by the fact that Denton has always treated the issue of ordering each of the three drugs separately, never taking advantage of the fact that the supply company will deliver overnight for $15, regardless of the number of different drugs in the order. Coordinating the replenishment of these three important supplies to Denton Pet Clinic might provide substantial savings on that delivery fee, given that the business manager can devise a plan that at least partially synchronizes the ordering of two or more drugs.

Questions

1. Assuming constant demand for the three drugs and the historical ordering policy described, how much has Denton Pet Clinic been paying annually in holding costs and ordering costs for these supplies?
2. If the business manager were to use the EOQ model, what should the order size of each drug be changed to? How much will be saved annually by changing to this more scientific order size, in the case of each drug?
3. Consider the business managers idea of coordinating of inventory policies to avoid the $15 fee being charged to each drug in at least some cases. How would this work? Design and describe a lower-cost inventory policy that saves additional money by making use of this coordination.
4. If Denton Pet Clinic were to follow your improved plan, how much would Denton pay annually in holding costs and ordering costs for these supplies? How great a savings is that, compared to what it is paying now with its historical rule-of-thumb ordering?

BIBLIOGRAPHY

Blackstone, J. ed. 2010. *APICS Dictionary,* 13th ed. Chicago: APICS, The Association for Operations Management.

Crowther, J. 1964. "Rationale for Quantity Discounts." *Harvard Business Review*, March/April: 121–27.

Gass, S., and A. Assad. 2005. *An Annotated Timeline of Operations Research: An Informal History.* New York: Kluwer Academic Publishers.

Silver, E., D. Pyke, and R. Peterson. 1998. *Inventory Management and Production Planning and Scheduling*, 3rd ed. New York: Wiley & Sons.

Turbide, D. 2012. "Too Much or Not Enough? The Balance Between Inventory Levels and Customer Service." *APICS Magazine* 22(3): 15.

Vollmann, T. E., W. L. Berry, D. C. Whybark, and F. B. Jacobs. 2005. *Manufacturing Planning & Control Systems for Supply Chain Management,* 5th ed. Chicago: McGraw-Hill.

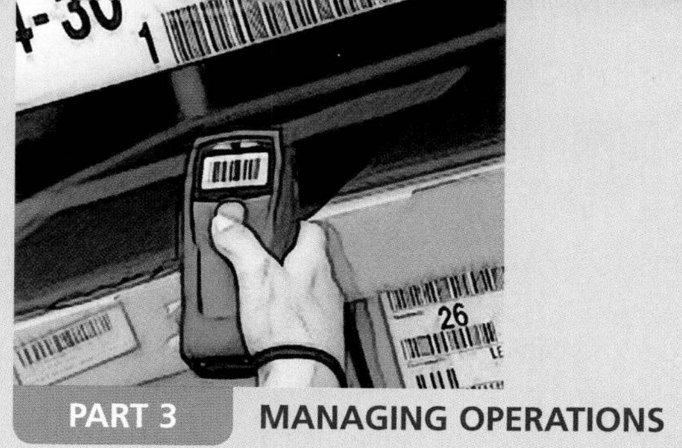

PART 3 MANAGING OPERATIONS

CHAPTER 11

Aggregate and Material Requirements Planning

I bought some batteries, but they weren't included.
—Steven Wright

MAJOR SECTIONS

IN THIS CHAPTER, LOOK FOR...

- Three essential aggregate planning strategies: chase demand, level production, and leveling demand.
- Explanation and demonstration of a product structure tree.
- Three components of an MRP system: master production schedule, bill of materials, and inventory records.
- Advantages and disadvantages of using an MRP system.

INTRODUCTION

An operation exists to provide value. If the amount of value required from that operation never varied, it would not be difficult to determine how best to produce it. However, it is difficult to identify a realistic example of any such operation that serves only perfectly constant demand for its valuable output. Consumers, customers, clients, and constituents can all be expected to vary in what they require and when. Hospitals expect fluctuations in both the number and the needs of patients, retailers understand that shoppers will crowd into stores during certain seasons of the year, and airlines know that fewer passengers will travel during the middle of any given week. All these organizations must create plans to meet dynamic, ever-changing demand for their output.

Once future levels of demand on the operation or system are forecast, aggregate planning identifies the best overall operating levels to support that fluctuating forecast. Material requirements planning (MRP) then determines how to coordinate internal production to best support the aggregate plan. Figure 11.1 summarizes the relationship of aggregate planning and MRP to the overall success of the planning process. Because aggregate planning must be completed before MRP can begin, we begin our discussion with aggregate planning.

AGGREGATE PLANNING STRATEGIES

aggregate planning
Medium-term tactical capacity planning in response to changing demand.

dynamic
Actively and continuously changing.

Aggregate planning identifies a strategy to meet dynamic demands on a system. It relies on a forecast of demand for exactly one product, to develop a strategy to meet that pattern. But just as it is difficult to find an operation serving unchanging demand for its product, it is also difficult to identify an operation that produces only one product. Even mass manufacturers focused on creating high volumes of standardized goods usually produce a small variety of finished products. For example, a typical beverage bottling plant processes several different beverages, often sold under multiple brand names. As another example, the manager of a large retail store, concerned about demand on that operation, is actually concerned about demand for thousands of different items available for sale

FIGURE 11.1 Hierarchy of Aggregate and Material Requirements Planning

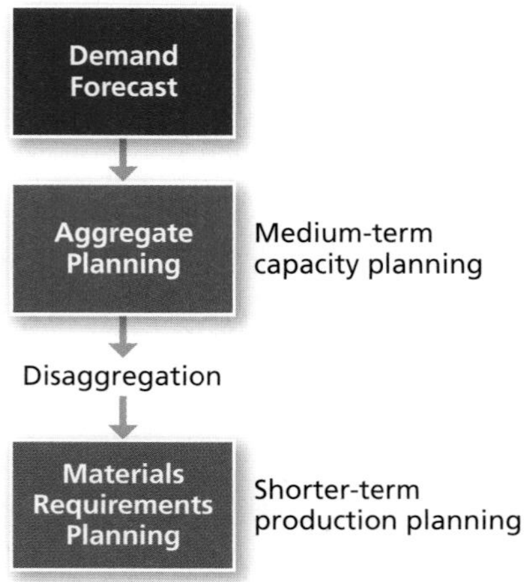

within that facility, each representing a distinct service to its customers. Aggregate planning can be conducted in either case, but only after aggregation of all items involved.

Aggregation

Aggregation is a process in which a variety of products or services are logically simplified into one measure of production activity, for the purpose of planning. Here are some typical examples:

aggregation
To combine the creation of many similar products into one relevant measure of activity for the organization.

- A beverage bottling plant produces different bottled beverages bearing several brand labels, but these products can be aggregated together as bottles of production, regardless of beverage type or brand label.
- A retail store manager would likely express overall demand for the store's variety of merchandise by projecting dollars of sale across future time periods, grouping together the different items sold by combining their retail values.
- Hospitals, which provide highly individualized services to each of their patients, can aggregate these services into overall patient days of care, aligning many different types of patients with many different requirements.

Each organization must identify the measure that best aggregates the variety of valuable products it creates. Once this measure is recognized and the future demands on the system are expressed in terms of this measure, the organization can then proceed to select an approach to best meet those changing demands.

Essential Approaches

Aggregate planning is considered medium-term planning, because aggregate plans rarely address planning horizons greater than 1 year into the future. Thus, aggregate planning typically begins with a forecast of the changing demand for the organization's output over the next few months. With this forecast in place, the organization must consider which of several basic approaches to adopt to meet this fluctuating demand. Three strategic paths can be explored at this point, often referred to as chasing demand, leveling production, or leveling demand.

planning horizon
The farthest point in the future considered in decision making.

Chasing Demand A chase demand strategy requires the productive capacity of an organization to vary, reflecting its forecast demand pattern. If a low demand period is forecast at some point in the future, the organization plans for low levels of operation, whereas a peak in demand in the future requires arrangements for intensive production at

chase demand strategy
Aggregate planning approach that relies on changing capacity to match demand.

Chasing Demand by Renting Temporary Locations

In the United States, tax preparation services suffer sharp peaks in customer demand during spring months, in anticipation of the April tax deadline. These firms often use the option of renting facilities during these busy months, to quickly expand their capacity. The temporary business signs in this picture are clues that the facility itself is only operational during peak periods.

that same point in the future. In either case, this variation in the pace of operation can be accomplished through one or more medium-term capacity options, like these:

- Working overtime hours during peak periods and tolerating employee idle time during low-demand periods.
- Hiring part-time or temporary employees during peak periods.
- Expanding the size of the full-time workforce through hiring, and/or conducting layoffs to reduce the size of the full-time workforce.
- Renting additional machinery or facility space during peak periods.
- Adding additional production shifts or extending store hours during peak periods.
- Subcontracting some portion of production to outside firms during peak periods.

subcontract
To engage a third party in the provision of value to a customer.

Each of these options represents an opportunity to temporarily boost or reduce the productive capacity of an operation, which is what distinguishes these options from long-term capacity decisions such as whether to build a new facility or sell an existing one. These options might be used to match the future demand pattern precisely, known as pursuing a perfect chase demand strategy, or to simply mimic the pattern closely, as demonstrated in Scenario 1a.

Scenario 1a

Aggregate Plan, Chase Demand Strategy

Main House Gaming is a small but agile company specializing in the rapid development and sale of packaged board games for retail and educational markets. These games include entertainment strategy games for children and adults, role-playing games scripted to support employee training, and a broad range of games for schools, sold with suggested readings and lesson plans. Main House Gaming assembles all these games at a central facility and has developed a 6-month demand forecast and a potential production strategy to meet this demand. A unit of sale at Main House Gaming is a single boxed game of any type, for any market.

Month	Demand Forecast (Units of Sale)	Proposed Chase Demand Plan (Units of Sale)
1	10,000	10,000
2	35,000	40,000
3	15,000	10,000
4	5,000	10,000
5	5,000	0
6	50,000	50,000

If Main House Gaming uses this production plan, what production and inventory conditions will be experienced at the central assembly facility over the next 6 months?

Analysis

We can quickly illustrate the conditions created by the proposed production plan by converting both the demand forecast and the strategy to cumulative monthly amounts, or running totals over the 6-month time horizon.

CUMULATIVE DEMAND AND PRODUCTION PLAN

Month	Demand Forecast (Units of Sale)	Cumulative Demand	Proposed Chase Demand Plan (Units of Sale)	Cumulative Production
1	10,000	10,000	10,000	10,000
2	35,000	45,000	40,000	50,000
3	15,000	60,000	10,000	60,000
4	5,000	65,000	10,000	70,000
5	5,000	70,000	0	70,000
6	50,000	120,000	50,000	120,000

Cumulative numbers are running totals. For example, the cumulative demand for the third month is the combined demand for the first 3 months, or 10,000+35,000+15,000= 60,000.

To illustrate this 6-month history, we graph the cumulative demand values first:

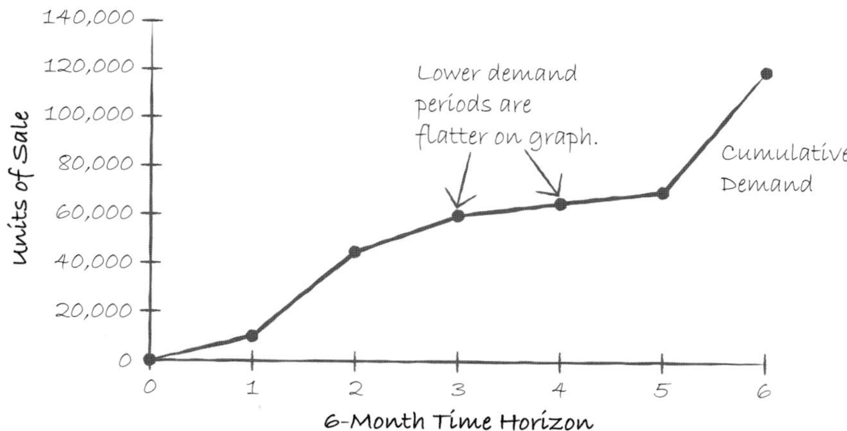

We interpret the graph by looking at its slope over time. A graph of cumulative demand that is near level or flat indicates low or no demand during that part of the time horizon, such as in the fourth and fifth months in Main House Gaming's forecast. If the graph grows steeper, climbing at a more aggressive rate, this indicates higher demand during that part of the forecast. The conditions created by pursuing a particular strategy can then be illustrated by comparing cumulative production against cumulative demand on the same graph.

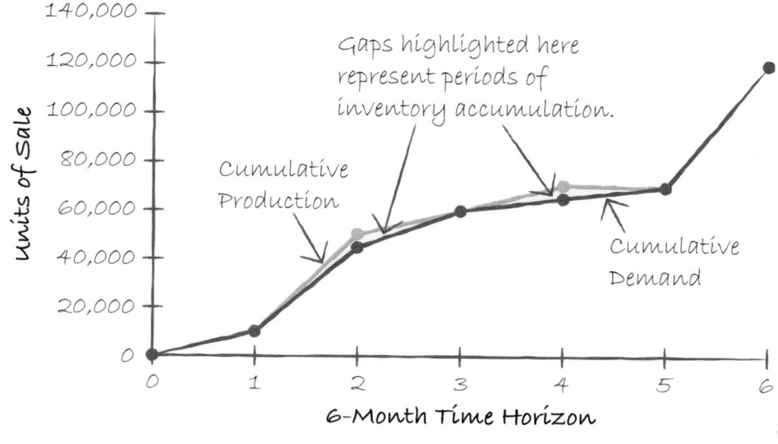

Continues

In this illustration, any gaps created by cumulative production rising above cumulative demand indicate that more units of sale are being produced than are required at that time, and thus inventory is accumulating. As this graph illustrates, there are relatively few instances of inventory associated with the proposed chase demand production strategy.

Insight If Main House Gaming follows the proposed chase demand strategy, monthly production rates will vary from as little as zero to as much as 50,000 units of sale, but resulting inventory levels will be low overall. Following this strategy results in a small accumulation of inventory by the end of month 2, which is depleted by the end of the next month, and similar accumulation again at the end of month 4, which will be depleted during the proposed shutdown of production during month 5. ■

Scenario 1a illustrates a strategic advantage of chasing demand: as resources are matched to current demand across the time horizon, very little inventory is accumulated for storage. One challenge is accurately predicting future demand so that this balance might be planned in advance. Another challenge of chasing demand concerns exactly how this fluctuating production pattern will be accomplished, an issue that Scenario 1a did not comment on. Nonetheless, concerns over which capacity options should be exercised and when might cause an organization to reconsider its chasing strategy.

level production strategy Aggregate planning approach that relies on fixed capacity despite changing demand.

Leveling Production Compared to chasing demand, a level production strategy avoids changing a production facility's output, despite the changing demand conditions. We consider this contrasting approach in Scenario 1b.

Scenario 1b

Aggregate Plan, Level Production Strategy

The production manager at Main House Gaming is concerned with the chase demand aggregate strategy proposed in Scenario 1a. The production manager is particularly concerned with the complete shutdown of production during month 5, followed by record production levels in month 6. The production manager would strongly prefer to assemble Main House Games at a steady pace throughout the next 6 months and has proposed this aggregate plan as an alternative to Scenario 1a:

Month	Demand Forecast (Units of Sale)	Proposed Level Production Plan (Units of Sale)
1	10,000	20,000
2	35,000	20,000
3	15,000	20,000
4	5,000	20,000
5	5,000	20,000
6	50,000	20,000

If Main House Gaming uses this level production plan, what production and inventory conditions will be experienced at the central assembly facility over the next 6 months?

Analysis

We first convert both the demand forecast and the strategy itself to cumulative monthly amounts over the 6-month time horizon:

CUMULATIVE DEMAND AND PRODUCTION

Month	Demand Forecast (Units of Sale)	Cumulative Demand	Proposed Level Production Strategy (Units of Sale)	Cumulative Production
1	10,000	10,000	20,000	20,000
2	35,000	45,000	20,000	40,000
3	15,000	60,000	20,000	60,000
4	5,000	65,000	20,000	80,000
5	5,000	70,000	20,000	100,000
6	50,000	120,000	20,000	120,000

Now we graph this cumulative data to determine the level strategy:

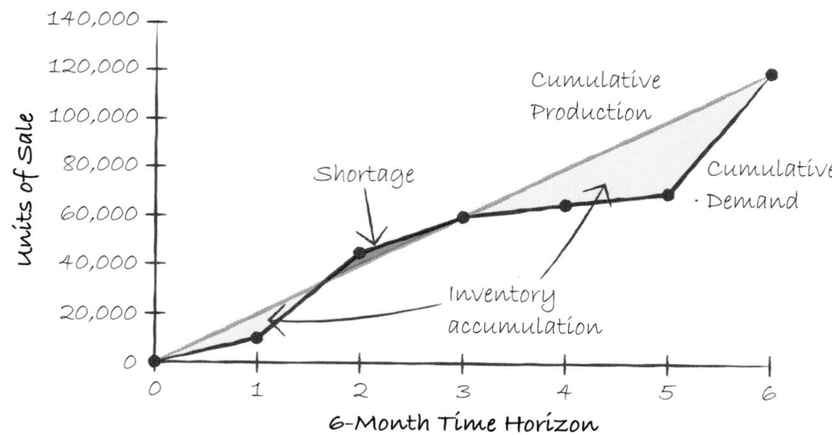

Insight The production manager's level plan involves substantial inventory accumulation during the second half of the planning horizon, when the steady monthly production pace combined with the low demand of months 3 and 4 results in a large stockpile of inventory. This inventory is then used to meet peak demand during month 6. Ironically, this plan also features a brief period of shortage at the end of month 2, where the steady pace fails to produce enough units to meet all demand by the end of that month. ■

The graph of the plan in Scenario 1b reveals a feature of most level production strategies: significant inventory. While a level plan may ignore the long list of medium-term capacity options associated with chasing demand, the level strategy usually creates a build up of inventory during slow periods to meet demand during peak periods without increasing production activity during those periods. This steady accumulation of inventory is also known as stockpiling. Insistence on a steady rate of production despite fluctuating demand can also create a risk of shortages, another feature revealed by the graph in Scenario 1b. A planner implementing a level production strategy may opt to

stockpiling
Producing or securing goods in advance of demand.

allow shortages, although it is not clear that the Main House Gaming production manager intended for the Scenario 1b production plan to fall behind demand at the end of month 2. Whether deliberate or accidental, these shortages may take the form of production delays, lost sales, and/or backorders, depending on the situation.

utilization
Percent of design capacity in use.

efficiency
Percent of a resource in productive use.

capacity cushion
Largely idle capacity maintained beyond the expected load level of a system, often to absorb unexpected demand.

level demand strategy
Aggregate planning approach that relies on influencing demand to match capacity.

Increased inventory and potential shortages aside, the steady pace of level production provides a powerful advantage over chasing demand, because it usually allows higher utilization of the production system throughout the planning horizon, yielding greater efficiency in the use of resources. As an example, note that many service organizations have little choice but to chase demand, because their products simply cannot be produced earlier and stored away for future consumption. This ongoing matching of production to fluctuating demand often requires a service organization to maintain a capacity cushion that stands largely idle outside of distinctly busy periods, such as the lunchtime rush at a restaurant and the lull in activity that generally follows before dinner.

Leveling Demand The third approach to the problem of meeting changing demand is not related to production. Rather, a level demand strategy is an attempt to fix the aggregate planning problem at its source, the fluctuating demand for the product. Leveling demand refers to any attempt to influence or manipulate demand to create a flatter pattern, one that is presumably more convenient to the operation of the system. Efforts to level demand may use one or more of the following approaches:

- **Identify a counterseasonal product and add it to the production mix.** A counterseasonal product possesses a customer demand pattern that moves in the opposite direction from the original product and can be created with most of the same resources as the original product. As an example, universities often host sports camps and high school band camps during summer semesters. These products earn revenue from the use of campus facilities at a time when demand on these facilities from university education is lower.
- **Level demand through pricing.** The use of pricing may appear to the customer as increased fees to obtain the product during a peak period, or off-season discounts on products selected during nonpeak periods. Airline ticket pricing provides rich examples of attempts to influence customers to avoid peak periods and thus flatten overall demand patterns. Any single ticket price may include incentives for the customer to consider travel during a less popular time of day, a less popular day of the week, and outside of a holiday travel season. Restaurants also use this approach, offering happy hours and early-bird specials to encourage some customers to visit earlier than the usual mealtime rush.

Leveling the Demand for Roadways with Pricing

Toll roads do not always represent attempts to level demand, but some toll road systems are designed to do exactly that. Pictured here is part of the electronic road pricing system in the city of Singapore, which automatically charges a toll to each vehicle driving under this gantry and changes the amount of the toll according to a schedule that is intended to flatten demand for the road by pricing it more heavily during its usual peak hours.

- **Use promotion to influence demand.** Organizations that attempt to level demand through promotion advertise with particular intensity during nonpeak periods, often targeting a particular customer base for this purpose. As an example, tourist areas with national or international appeal may focus on raising awareness in their local vicinity during nonpeak travel periods, as local customers with short travel times do not require holidays to complete a visit. Promotion is often used in conjunction with pricing, such as when restaurants and attractions within a tourist area advertise discount deals to the local market during the area's off season.

It is not a coincidence that the examples cited for leveling demand are all service industries. Manufacturers such as Main House Gaming have the option of attempting to level demand, but also have the options of chasing demand or leveling production. In contrast, leveling production is generally not a sensible approach for most service systems, because service products cannot be built up as inventory. Furthermore, some service systems such as airlines are doubly disadvantaged because chasing demand is not an attractive approach either. Airlines are good examples of production systems that cannot adjust their production capacities as easily and rapidly as many other organizations can. Each flight within the airline's production schedule represents a sizable block of capacity and safety concerns alone prevent an airline from continuously adding, rerouting, and removing these blocks as customers purchase tickets. Thus, it is not surprising to find that airlines pursue level demand strategies with particular creativity, as they have few other choices when approaching the problem of demand fluctuation.

Most organizations, however, have at least some choice in the selection of an aggregate planning approach, and may choose to pursue some combination of the three strategies outlined here. Making this choice requires developing the potential plan in more detail.

DEVELOPING AGGREGATE PLANS

Aggregate plans cannot progress beyond basic strategies without developing the details of a potential plan. Once an overall strategy is identified, development continues by determining how best to implement the strategy's suggested production levels, using the options available to the organization. Since more than one way to implement the strategy may exist, and the organization may wish to consider more than one strategy, aggregate plan development continues by evaluating each plan for its total cost, ultimately allowing selection of the most appropriate plan.

Introducing Inventory Logic

Scenarios 1a and 1b demonstrated charting cumulative demand and production to visually assess a production plan, revealing periods of inventory accumulation and shortages. However, these illustrations do not specify precisely how much inventory is in storage at any given time, or exactly how far the Scenario 1b production plan falls behind demand at the end of month 2. These exact inventory levels must now be calculated to determine the total cost of each plan. Inventory levels in any given period can be expressed in three different ways: beginning inventory, ending inventory, and average inventory.

beginning inventory The level of inventory as measured at the beginning of a particular time period. This level is assumed to be the ending inventory of the previous time period.

ending inventory The level of inventory as measured at the conclusion of a particular time period. This level is assumed to be the beginning inventory of the next time period.

Beginning and Ending Inventory Beginning inventory is measured at the start of a time period, while ending inventory is measured at the end of the period. Ending inventory is simple to calculate if a plan has already been charted, as in Scenarios 1a and 1b. Ending inventory for any month t, or EI_t, is determined by the difference between cumulative production and cumulative demand in that month:

$$EI_t = \text{Cumulative production in } t - \text{cumulative demand in } t$$

assuming the organization began with nothing in stock, as was the case with Main House Gaming. Thus, we can now calculate the small amount of inventory accumulated at the end of month 2 by the chase demand strategy in Scenario 1a: 50,000 (cumulative production in month 2) minus 45,000 (cumulative demand in month 2) equals 5,000 units of inventory. Once we know the ending inventory of any time period (EI_t), we also know the beginning inventory of the next time period (BI_{t+1}) because

$$EI_t = BI_{t+1}$$

In other words, the amount remaining in inventory at the end of a certain time period is assumed to be the same as the amount then available in inventory at the beginning of the next time period.

Note that identifying ending inventory by comparing cumulative production and demand is convenient only if the cumulative amounts are available, and is only accurate if the organization held no initial inventory. In the absence of that, ending inventory can be more reliably found through the application of inventory logic. If P_t represents the planned amount of production in period t and D_t represents the demand in period t, the ending inventory for that period can be reasoned to be:

$$EI_t = BI_t + P_t - D_t$$

Restated, how much remains in inventory at the end of a certain time period is the result of how much inventory is available at that start of that time period (BI_t) combined with how much is created during that time period (P_t), minus how much is used or removed (D_t). As an example, the beginning inventory of month 1 in Scenarios 1a and 1b can be assumed to be zero, because the initial scenario did not mention any current available inventory. In the case of the level production plan in Scenario 1b, the ending inventory of month 1 would then just be how much was produced that month (20,000) minus demand that month (10,000):

$$EI_{\text{Month 1}} = 0 + 20{,}000 - 10{,}000 = 10{,}000 \text{ units of sale}$$

These 10,000 units then become the beginning inventory for month 2, or $BI_{\text{Month 2}}$. We can then calculate inventory levels for the remaining months of Scenario 1b through a chain of logic, linked by beginning and ending inventory levels:

$$EI_{\text{Month 2}} = BI_{\text{Month 2}} + P_{\text{Month 2}} - D_{\text{Month 2}} = 10{,}000 + 20{,}000 - 35{,}000 = -5{,}000 = BI_{\text{Month 3}}$$

$$EI_{\text{Month 3}} = BI_{\text{Month 3}} + P_{\text{Month 3}} - D_{\text{Month 3}} = -5{,}000 + 20{,}000 - 15{,}000 = 0 = BI_{\text{Month 4}}$$

$$EI_{\text{Month 4}} = BI_{\text{Month 4}} + P_{\text{Month 4}} - D_{\text{Month 4}} = 0 + 20{,}000 - 5{,}000 = 15{,}000 = BI_{\text{Month 5}}$$

$$EI_{\text{Month 5}} = BI_{\text{Month 5}} + P_{\text{Month 5}} - D_{\text{Month 5}} = 15{,}000 + 20{,}000 - 5{,}000 = 30{,}000 = BI_{\text{Month 6}}$$

$$EI_{\text{Month 6}} = BI_{\text{Month 6}} + P_{\text{Month 6}} - D_{\text{Month 6}} = 30{,}000 + 20{,}000 - 50{,}000 = 0$$

Note that inventory logic also reveals the instance of shortage at the end of month 2, indicated by a negative ending inventory level. In reality, this amount represents delayed demand, not idle stock.

holding costs Variable costs associated with having inventory.

average inventory The average of the beginning and the ending inventory of a particular time period.

Average Inventory Beginning and ending inventory levels are useful measurements at distinct points in time during a plan. However, these measurements are not always preferred when calculating holding costs. Holding costs represent the expense incurred by keeping inventory, so holding costs are often charged against the average inventory within a particular period. Average inventory refers to the average of the beginning and ending inventory of a certain time period t:

$$\text{Average inventory for time period } t = (BI_t + EI_t)/2$$

For example, recall that month 5, the stockpiling period of Scenario 1b, had a beginning inventory of 15,000 and an ending inventory of 30,000 units of sale. Average inventory in month 5, therefore, would be (15,000 + 30,000)/2 = 22,500 units of sale.

Implementing Other Options

Calculating inventory levels does not require further decision making, only accurate information on production and demand levels. In contrast, determining how production will be met can require expert judgment from the planner. Constructing a detailed aggregate plan requires that these particular options be implemented in a logical fashion:

- **Determining the size of the workforce in each period.** This decision begins with determining whether the workforce will be varied throughout the planning horizon and, if so, by how much. This also requires information on how large a workforce is needed to support the suggested production level.
- **Determining how the workforce will work.** This decision can include using overtime or tolerating idle employee time in any certain period, or perhaps coordinating some mix of full-time and part-time workers to complete production in that certain time period.
- **Determining what amount of production, if any, to subcontract to another firm each period.**

While distinct formulas for calculating inventory levels exist, there are no distinct procedures for developing other details of an aggregate plan. Rather, these details are identified by first collecting technical information on each of the relevant options. The planner then uses logic to determine how each option would be activated during each period of the plan, to support the overall proposed production levels. Since the planner is tracking a variety of issues and options across a span of periods, this type of planning is most easily organized into a table-style format with columns representing those time periods. We demonstrate this process in Scenario 1c.

Aggregate Planning, Implementing Options — Scenario 1c

The general manager of Main House Gaming feels that the production manager's concerns over the chase demand strategy proposed Scenario 1a are unfounded. Main House Gaming can vary its monthly production rate in a variety of ways, including working overtime or changing the size of its workforce of production employees. The general manager has collected the following information on these options:

Main House Gaming Workforce Information:

- Each production employee will work 150 hours of regular time (RT) each month.
- Each production employee can work up to 50 hours of overtime (OT) each month.
- It takes 1 production employee 1 hour to produce 10 units.
- Current workforce size is 7 production employees.

The general manager wishes to proceed with the chase demand strategy first proposed in Scenario 1a, putting these options to work. While changing the size of the workforce is an option, the general manager would prefer to avoid these changes as much as possible. Therefore, the general manager wants an implementation plan that both minimizes hiring by using overtime to its maximum benefit during busy months and minimizes layoffs by reducing the size of the workforce only when one or more employees would be left completely idle for the month.

How should Main Street Gaming implement the Scenario 1a chase demand strategy?

Continues

Analysis

Constructing a detailed aggregate plan of any type requires the organization of substantial information. This organization usually begins by creating a table that describes the use of each of the options during each of the future periods. In the case of Main House Gaming, a blank table that represents the start of the analysis could look like this:

CHASE DEMAND AGGREGATE STRATEGY

	Month 1	Month 2	Month 3	Month 4	Month 5	Month 6
Forecast (units of sale)	10,000	35,000	15,000	5,000	5,000	50,000
Overall production	10,000	40,000	10,000	10,000	0	50,000
Ending inventory						
Average inventory						
Regular-tme production						
Overtime production						
New hires						
Layoffs						
Size of workforce 7						
Idle regular-time hours						

The blank cells represent the decisions that now need to be made.

Now we calculate inventory levels.

CHASE DEMAND AGGREGATE STRATEGY

	Month 1	Month 2	Month 3	Month 4	Month 5	Month 6
Forecast (units of sale)	10,000	35,000	15,000	5,000	5,000	50,000
Overall production	10,000	40,000	10,000	10,000	0	50,000
Ending inventory	0	5,000	0	5,000	0	0
Average inventory	0	2,500	2,500	2,500	2,500	0
Regular-time production						
Overtime production						
New hires						
Layoffs						
Size of workforce 7						
Idle regular-time hours						

Ending inventory = beginning inventory (ending inventory of the previous month) + production − demand
Example: Ending inventory for month 2 = 0 + 40,000 − 35,000= 5,000

Average inventory = (beginning inventory + ending inventory)/2
Example: Average Inventory for month 3 = (5,000 + 0)/2 = 2,500

Now that we identified the ending and average inventory levels, we can determine the details of meeting the proposed production plan. We begin by determining how best to support production in month 1. One issue important to the decision making in month 1 is the productive capacity of Main House Gaming's current workforce of seven production employees:

Monthly Regular-Time Productive Capacity (1 employee)

10 units of sale per production employee hour × 150 RT hours a month per employee
= 1,500 units of sale per month per production employee working regular time

Monthly Overtime Productive Capacity (1 employee)

10 units of sale per production employee hour × 50 OT hours a month per employee
= 500 units of sale per month per production employee working overtime

MONTHLY PRODUCTIVE CAPACITY OF CURRENT WORKFORCE

Size of current workforce: 7 employees
Regular-time production capacity: 7 × 1,500 = 10,500 units of sale
Overtime production capacity: 7 × 500 = 3,500 units of sale
Total productive capacity of current workforce: 10,500 + 3,500 = 14,000 units of sale

Recall that the general manager prefers overtime to increasing the size of the workforce. In month 1 the current workforce's regular-time capacity of 10,500 units is enough to cover planned production of 10,000 units. Furthermore, the general manager will reduce the workforce only if an employee would otherwise be completely idle in regular time, meaning that the current workforce size supplies more than 150 surplus hours, which is the equivalent of 150 × 10 = 1,500 unused units of sale produced in regular time. The regular-time capacity of the current workforce of seven employees supports only 10,500 – 10,000 = 500 more units of sale than required, which means that 500/10 = 50 hours of regular time will go idle when the workforce of seven produces only 10,000 units of sale. This is not enough to motivate a layoff, so we can add the details of month 1 to the table:

CHASE DEMAND AGGREGATE STRATEGY

	Month 1	Month 2	Month 3	Month 4	Month 5	Month 6
Forecast (units of sale)	10,000	35,000	15,000	5,000	5,000	50,000
Overall production	10,000	40,000	10,000	10,000	0	50,000
Ending inventory	0	5,000	0	5,000	0	0
Average inventory	0	2,500	2,500	2,500	2,500	0
Regular-time production	10,000					
Overtime production	0					
New hires	0					
Layoffs	0					
Size of workforce 7	7					
Idle regular-time hours	50					

7 employees means 7 × 150 = 1,050 RT hours available, but 10,000 units produced in RT means only 10,000/10 = 1,000 RT hours used. Thus, 1,050 – 1,000 = 50 RT hours are left idle.

Continues

However, the workforce size clearly needs to be increased to meet the higher production levels of month 2. If hiring must take place, the general manager prefers to minimize it by using as much overtime as possible. Thus, determining the hiring for month 2 begins by determining how many employees would be required overall, and how much regular time versus overtime would then result:

MINIMUM WORKFORCE NEEDED FOR MONTH 2

Production target: 40,000 units of sale
Maximum capacity of one employee (RT + OT): 1,500 + 500 = 2,000 units of sale
Minimum workforce needed: 40,000/2,000 = 20 employees
RT units of sale from 20 employees: 20 × 1,500 = 30,000 units of sale
OT units of sale needed from 20 employees: 40,000 (total needed) – 30,000 (RT) = 10,000 units of sale

A workforce of 20 employees at work in month 2 implies that 20 – 7 = 13 new employees would be hired for that month.

CHASE DEMAND AGGREGATE STRATEGY

	Month 1	Month 2	Month 3	Month 4	Month 5	Month 6
Forecast (units of sale)	10,000	35,000	15,000	5,000	5,000	50,000
Overall production	10,000	40,000	10,000	10,000	0	50,000
Ending inventory	0	5,000	0	5,000	0	0
Average inventory	0	2,500	2,500	2,500	2,500	0
Regular-time production	10,000	30,000				
Overtime production	0	10,000				
New hires	0	13				
Layoffs	0	0				
Size of workforce 7	7	20				
Idle regular-time hours	50	0				

Seven employees from month 1 plus 13 hired results in a workforce of 7 + 13 = 20 employees. These employees can then create 20 × 1,500 = 30,000 units in RT, and then complete production in overtime, as calculated previously.

Proceeding to month 3, note that monthly production returns to 10,000 units, the same target as month 1. This means that no more than 7 employees are appropriate, requiring the layoff of 13 employees. This month-by-month logic, implementing the preferences of the general manager, can then be completed for the entire 6-month planning horizon.

CHASE DEMAND AGGREGATE STRATEGY

	Month 1	Month 2	Month 3	Month 4	Month 5	Month 6
Forecast (units of sale)	10,000	35,000	15,000	5,000	5,000	50,000
Overall production	10,000	40,000	10,000	10,000	0	50,000
Ending inventory	0	5,000	0	5,000	0	0
Average inventory	0	2,500	2,500	2,500	2,500	0
Regular-time production	10,000	30,000	10,000	10,000	0	37,500
Overtime production	0	10,000	0	0	0	12,500
New hires	0	13	0	0	0	25
Layoffs	0	0	13	0	7	0
Size of workforce 7	7	20	7	7	0	25
Idle regular-time hours	50	0	50	50	0	0

A production target of 50,000 divided by 2,000 units per employee means 50,000/2,000= 25 employees are needed. They can then provide 25 × 1,500 = 37,500 units in RT and the remainder in OT.

Insight The detailed aggregate plan relies on regular-time production in five of the six months, with overtime being worked only in the peaked production periods of months 2 and 6. Main House Gaming should retain its current workforce and hire 13 more employees for month 2, although it should lay off 13 employees at the end of that month, and lay off the original 7 employees during the scheduled shutdown of month 5. This will then necessitate hiring 25 employees to complete production in month 6. ■

Selecting a Plan and Replanning

Note that in Scenario 1c we developed a detailed plan supporting the original chase demand strategy proposed for Main House Gaming in Scenario 1a, but did not comment on whether this is the plan that Main House Gaming should actually use. The desirability of a plan can be judged by comparing it to an alternate plan, and the basis of this selection is usually cost. In Scenario 1d we continue with the aggregate planning process by introducing the costs of each of the options used in Scenario 1c. We calculate these costs and then sum them for the Scenario 1c plan, determining an overall cost that can then be used for comparison.

Aggregate Planning, Calculating Total Cost — Scenario 1d

The production manager of Main House Gaming has seen the detailed chase demand aggregate plan developed in Scenario 1c, and remains unconvinced that this is the best plan. The production manager has located the following costs associated with the options used:

Aggregate Planning Production Costs

- Hiring 1 production employee: $1,000
- Laying off 1 production employee: $500
- Producing 1 unit of sale in regular time: $15
- Producing 1 unit of sale in overtime: $25

Continues

- An idle regular-time hour (nothing is produced): $10
- Carrying 1 unit of sale in inventory for 1 month: $0.50

What is the total cost of the chase demand plan developed in Scenario 1c?

Analysis

Recall the detailed plan from Scenario 1c:

		Month 1	Month 2	Month 3	Month 4	Month 5	Month 6
Forecast (units of sale)		10,000	35,000	15,000	5,000	5,000	50,000
Overall production		10,000	40,000	10,000	10,000	0	50,000
Ending inventory		0	5,000	0	5,000	0	0
Average inventory		0	2,500	2,500	2,500	2,500	0
Regular-time production		10,000	30,000	10,000	10,000	0	37,500
Overtime production		0	10,000	0	0	0	12,500
New hires		0	13	0	0	0	25
Layoffs		0	0	13	0	7	0
Size of workforce	7	7	20	7	7	0	25
Idle regular-time hours		50	0	50	50	0	0

Calculating the total cost of an existing aggregate plan is like preparing an invoice, charging for all the options used in the plan. As an example, one option heavily used in this plan is regular-time production:

REGULAR-TIME PRODUCTION COSTS

10,000 + 30,000 + 10,000 + 10,000 + 0 + 37,500 = 97,500 units of sale produced in RT

97,500 × $15 each = $1,462,500 regular-time production cost

The total cost of the plan is then the combined cost of each of the options, including this $1,462,500 in production costs:

CHASE DEMAND PLAN TOTAL COST

Regular-time production: $1,462,500
Overtime production: (10,000 + 12,500) × $25 each = $562,500
Inventory cost: (0 + 2,500 + 2,500 + 2,500 + 2,500 + 0)
× $0.50 per unit per month = $5,000
Hiring cost: (13 + 25) × $1,000 each = $38,000
Layoff cost: (13 + 7) × $500 each = $10,000
Idle regular-time cost: (50 + 0 + 50 + 50 + 0 + 0) × $10 per hour = $1,500

TOTAL COST OF PLAN

$1,462,5000 + $562,500 + $5,000 + $38,000 + $10,000 + $1,500 = $2,079,500

Insight The chase demand aggregate plan has a combined total cost of $2,079,500. Whether or not this is acceptable to Main House Gaming depends on whether another plan with a lower cost can be identified. ■

Spreadsheet Models of Aggregate Planning Scenarios | **FIGURE 11.2**

Data from Main House Gaming scenarios

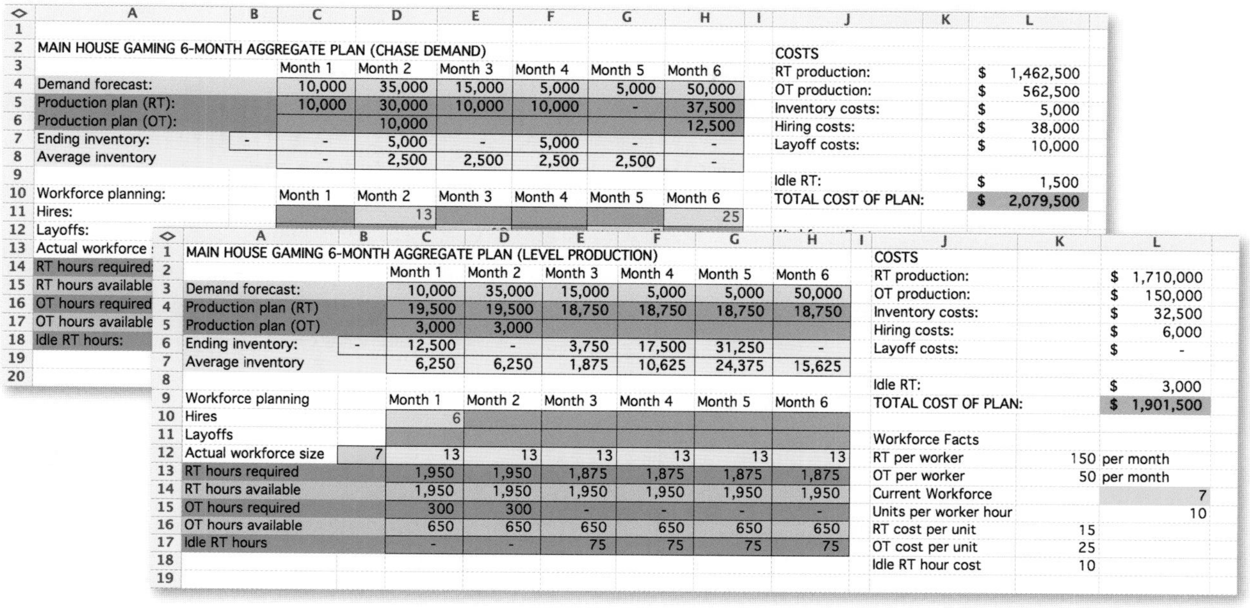

MAIN HOUSE GAMING 6-MONTH AGGREGATE PLAN (CHASE DEMAND)

	B	Month 1	Month 2	Month 3	Month 4	Month 5	Month 6
Demand forecast:		10,000	35,000	15,000	5,000	5,000	50,000
Production plan (RT):		10,000	30,000	10,000	10,000	-	37,500
Production plan (OT):			10,000				12,500
Ending inventory:	-	-	5,000	-	5,000	-	-
Average inventory		-	2,500	2,500	2,500	2,500	-
Workforce planning:		Month 1	Month 2	Month 3	Month 4	Month 5	Month 6
Hires:			13				25
Layoffs:							
Actual workforce :							
RT hours required:							
RT hours available							
OT hours required							
OT hours available							
Idle RT hours:							

COSTS		
RT production:	$	1,462,500
OT production:	$	562,500
Inventory costs:	$	5,000
Hiring costs:	$	38,000
Layoff costs:	$	10,000
Idle RT:	$	1,500
TOTAL COST OF PLAN:	$	2,079,500

MAIN HOUSE GAMING 6-MONTH AGGREGATE PLAN (LEVEL PRODUCTION)

	B	Month 1	Month 2	Month 3	Month 4	Month 5	Month 6
Demand forecast:		10,000	35,000	15,000	5,000	5,000	50,000
Production plan (RT)		19,500	19,500	18,750	18,750	18,750	18,750
Production plan (OT)		3,000	3,000				
Ending inventory:	-	12,500	-	3,750	17,500	31,250	-
Average inventory		6,250	6,250	1,875	10,625	24,375	15,625
Workforce planning		Month 1	Month 2	Month 3	Month 4	Month 5	Month 6
Hires		6					
Layoffs							
Actual workforce size	7	13	13	13	13	13	13
RT hours required		1,950	1,950	1,875	1,875	1,875	1,875
RT hours available		1,950	1,950	1,950	1,950	1,950	1,950
OT hours required		300	300	-	-	-	-
OT hours available		650	650	650	650	650	650
Idle RT hours		-	-	75	75	75	75

COSTS		
RT production:		$ 1,710,000
OT production:		$ 150,000
Inventory costs:		$ 32,500
Hiring costs:		$ 6,000
Layoff costs:		$ -
Idle RT:		$ 3,000
TOTAL COST OF PLAN:		$ 1,901,500
Workforce Facts		
RT per worker	150	per month
OT per worker	50	per month
Current Workforce		7
Units per worker hour		10
RT cost per unit	15	
OT cost per unit	25	
Idle RT hour cost	10	

While Scenario 1d provides a method to compare the chase demand aggregate plan to other plans for Main House Gaming, it does not conclude that this plan should necessarily be selected for use. This final phase of the aggregate planning process can occur when the total cost of at least one other plan, such as the proposal of the production manager in Scenario 1b, is calculated for comparison. The tablelike format of detailed aggregate planning fits with the construction of spreadsheet models to accomplish the work demonstrated in Scenarios 1c and 1d, as shown in Figure 11.2.

The screenshot in the background of Figure 11.2 is a spreadsheet model of the same problem discussed in the previous scenarios, complete with a total cost of $2,079,500. The screenshot in front, however, is an alternate aggregate plan similar to one proposed by the production manager, but with the use of some overtime to lift the production rate in the first 2 months and avoid the shortage first spotted in Scenario 1b. This particular plan has a total cost of $1,901,500, which is lower than the total cost identified in Scenario 1d. Therefore, Main House Gaming would most likely prefer this new level plan over the chase demand plan explored so far.

Although the level production spreadsheet model displayed in Figure 11.2 has a lower cost, this does not suggest it is necessarily the best plan for Main House Gaming. Main House Gaming could continue to explore new plans by revising production levels and modelling in a heuristic fashion, seeking an even lower total cost through trial and error, or by using optimization software, an example of which is shown in Figure 11.3.

heuristic
A procedure to develop a good, though not necessarily optimal, solution.

The total cost of $1,840,500 is the lowest possible cost of meeting demand over these 6 months of demand, given all the technical data supplied in Scenarios 1c and 1d. This plan is neither strongly chase demand nor level production, but appears to balance these approaches, with the formal planning horizon broken into three distinct 2-month intervals and the workforce size adjusted for each of these intervals, although production is kept level and within regular time within the smaller interval. If Main House Gaming has

optimization
Identification of the best alternative.

FIGURE 11.3 Optimal Solution for Main House Gaming

	A	B	C	D	E	F	G	H	I	J	K	L
1												
2	MAIN HOUSE GAMING 6-MONTH AGGREGATE PLAN									COSTS		
3			Month 1	Month 2	Month 3	Month 4	Month 5	Month 6		RT production:		$ 1,800,000
4	Demand forecast:		10,000	35,000	15,000	5,000	5,000	50,000		OT production:		$ -
5	Production plan (RT):		22,500	22,500	15,000	15,000	22,500	22,500		Inventory costs:		$ 25,000
6	Production plan (OT):		-	-	-	-	-	-		Hiring costs:		$ 13,000
7	Ending inventory:	-	12,500	-	-	10,000	27,500	-		Layoff costs:		$ 2,500
8	Average inventory:		6,250	6,250	-	5,000	18,750	13,750				
9										Idle RT:		$ -
10	Workforce planning:		Month 1	Month 2	Month 3	Month 4	Month 5	Month 6		TOTAL COST OF PLAN:		$ 1,840,500
11	Hires:		8	0	0	0	5	0				
12	Layoffs:		0	0	5	0	0	0		Workforce Facts		
13	Actual workforce size:	7	15	15	10	10	15	15		RT per worker:	150	per month
14	RT hours required:		2,250	2,250	1,500	1,500	2,250	2,250		OT per worker:	50	per month
15	RT hours available:		2,250	2,250	1,500	1,500	2,250	2,250		Current Workforce		7
16	OT hours required:		-	-	-	-	-	-		Units per worker hour:		10
17	OT hours available:		750	750	500	500	750	750		RT cost per unit:	15	
18	Idle RT hours:		-	-	-	-	-	-		OT cost per unit:	25	
19										Idle RT hour cost:	10	
20										Monthly Inventory		
21										Cost per unit:	0.5	
22										Cost of hire:	1000	

no further costs or concerns relevant to this situation, then this Figure 11.3 plan should be selected for implementation over the next 6 months.

Once Main House Gaming puts this plan into action, it will not begin planning again for another 6 months, the length of its formal planning horizon. However, note that the newer level plan in Figure 11.2 and the optimal plan in Figure 11.3 make adjustments to production at the end of month 2, the same point in time that the perfectly level plan proposed by the production manager in Scenario 1b failed to keep pace with demand and created a shortage. This point in time has particular significance, particularly in replanning, and is referred to as the natural planning horizon. Figure 11.4 illustrates the natural planning horizon in Main House Gaming's case, giving some insight into its name.

natural planning horizon A point of time within a forecast where aggregate demand dictates the minimum level production rate necessary to fulfill all demand specified by that forecast.

As the name suggests, the natural planning horizon is the distance the planner can see when looking across the surface of cumulative demand, standing on the current moment and gazing toward the formal planning horizon. This particular feature in any

FIGURE 11.4 Natural Planning Horizon for Main House Gaming

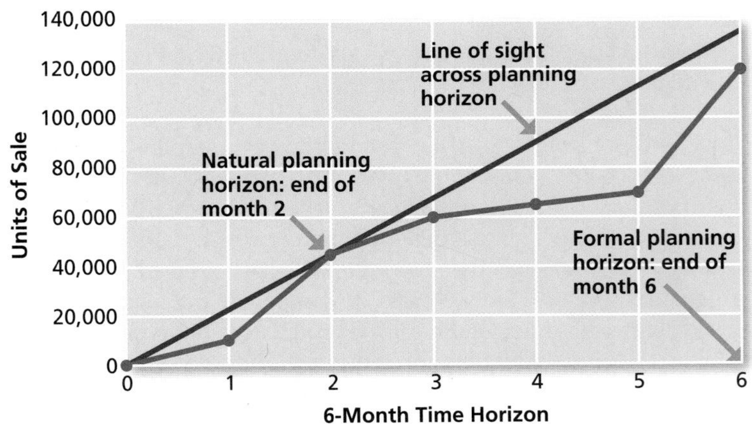

forecast can be located by graphing cumulative demand and pivoting a straight edge on the bottom of the graphed line until it makes first contact with the demand curve when lowered from above. The natural planning horizon might be the same as the formal planning horizon at the end of the graphed line, but for Main House Gaming it is not. Here, the natural planning horizon occurs much earlier at the end of month 2, and this becomes significant to any planner interested in leveling production. Note that the production planner in Scenario 1b selected 20,000 units a month as the production rate, which was likely identified by taking cumulative demand at the formal planning horizon, 120,000 units of sale, and dividing that total requirement evenly over the 6 months within the plan. This resulted in a shortage at the end of month 2, however, which can only be avoided with a level rate by taking the cumulative demand at the end of month 2 and dividing it by the number of months until the end of month 2, or 45,000/2 = 22,500 units of sale a month. This is known generally as the minimum constant production (MCP) rate:

minimum constant production (MCP) rate The lowest speed of perfectly level production that will not produce any shortages within a demand forecast.

$$\text{MCP rate} = \frac{\text{Cumulative demand at the natural planning horizon}}{\text{Number of periods until the natural planning horizon}}$$

The MCP rate of 22,500 units a month for the first 2 months of a plan is featured both in the level plan of Figure 11.2 (divided between regular time and overtime) and in the optimal plan in Figure 11.3 (completed in regular time only). In both cases, the plans adjust this production rate after the natural planning horizon has passed. In general, the natural planning horizon often suggests a good point in time to divide a longer formal planning horizon into shorter intervals with more specific plans, particularly if the planner is interested in level production rates. At this time, the organization may turn to material requirements planning (MRP) techniques to address shorter-term production needs.

material requirements planning (MRP) A technique for scheduling the production of multiple items related by both independent and dependent demand.

MATERIAL REQUIREMENTS PLANNING

Aggregate planning draws its name from the fact that all productive activity is treated as a single output. This simplification is useful for making broad decisions on how to best meet changing demands on that system, but when this level of decision making is complete, aggregation has reached the end of its usefulness. Once an aggregate plan is selected, its overall production levels must then be translated back into various amounts of specific products that are, in reality, the true outputs of the system. This challenging process of breaking a larger aggregate production value into smaller distinct estimates of actual products is known as disaggregation.

disaggregation Translation of an aggregated value into smaller individual estimates corresponding to specific products.

Disaggregating an aggregate plan creates the foundation for a master production schedule (MPS). However, the process of disaggregation is seldom the only complication during implementation. While the MPS provides the details of how much of certain products should be created and when, these products may themselves be composed of multiple components that must also be recognized and scheduled. Material requirements planning (MRP) begins where disaggregation ends, and introduces the internal issues of material requirements into the overall production planning process.

In a manufacturing environment, MRP means ensuring that the right part is received at the right time. For Main House Gaming, this would require having the right number of components such as dice, playing boards, or plastic figures available when producing any certain type of game. This in turn requires having a detailed understanding of how each type of board game is assembled. Thus, the technique known as MRP begins with recognition of the distinction between independent versus dependent demand, featured within a key document known as a bill of materials.

Independent and Dependent Demand

independent demand Requirements for an item from outside the system, also known as customer demand.

finished goods Inventory awaiting sale to consumers.

dependent demand Requirements for child items; also known as component demand.

Independent demand is demand from outside a system, which can usually be described as customer demand. Finished goods experience independent demand, although not all independent demand is necessarily for finished goods. In the case of Main House Gaming, independent demand for its various units of sale takes the form of orders for its various types of board games.

Dependent demand is the need for a particular item that was created by a request for some *other* item. Dependent demand is sometimes described as component demand, although the component experiencing dependent demand can take on many different forms, such as a simple part required for assembly, a highly complex subassembly required to create a finished good, an otherwise finished good undergoing customization, or an ingredient needed for blending. In each case, the dependent demand item "goes into" a more complex item, and it is demand for the more complex item that creates the need for the dependent demand item. While Main House Gaming sells board games to customers, its resulting need for game components such as dice is an example of dependent demand.

parent An item created from one or more other items, known as its children.

child An item required for immediate transformation into another item, known as its parent.

In dependent demand, when an item such as a finished board game creates demand for another item such as dice, the first item is said to be the parent of the second item, which is said to be its child item. These distinctions within any pair of items linked by a dependent demand relationship are important to describing how complex finished goods are ultimately created.

Bill of Materials

bill of materials A description of all raw materials and intermediate assemblies required to create a finished product.

A bill of materials is a document describing all components needed to create a particular finished good. This information file is a necessary input to MRP, because the bill of materials outlines all dependent demand that might result from any independent demand for an item. Figure 11.5 displays an example of a Main House Gaming independent demand item, a finished unit of sale called the Environmental Response Game, with several of its dependent demand components labeled. If a customer requests the particular game pictured, Main House Gaming must secure related items such as the playing board, dice, and box to create a finished unit of sale for the customer. The bill of materials would specify precisely what must be secured and in what amount, to successfully assemble one unit of the Environmental Response Game. This information can be organized into several formats, from simple lists to coded illustrations of assembly known as product structure diagrams.

product structure diagram A particularly visual format for a bill of materials, in which parent/child relationships among inventory items are illustrated as a network of connected shapes.

Product Structure Diagrams A product structure diagram is a format of bill of materials that visually outlines the relationships between components. In this illustration, each distinct item is represented by a labeled shape, with branching lines representing the

Dependent Demand Items within an External Hard Drive

Manufactured goods provide the best examples of dependent versus independent demand. Pictured here are the major subassemblies of an external computer hard drive, made visible by dismantling one unit of finished good. To fulfill independent demand for external hard drives, the manufacturer must plan for the production or purchasing of each of these dependent demand items.

One Unit of Sale for Main House Gaming

FIGURE 11.5

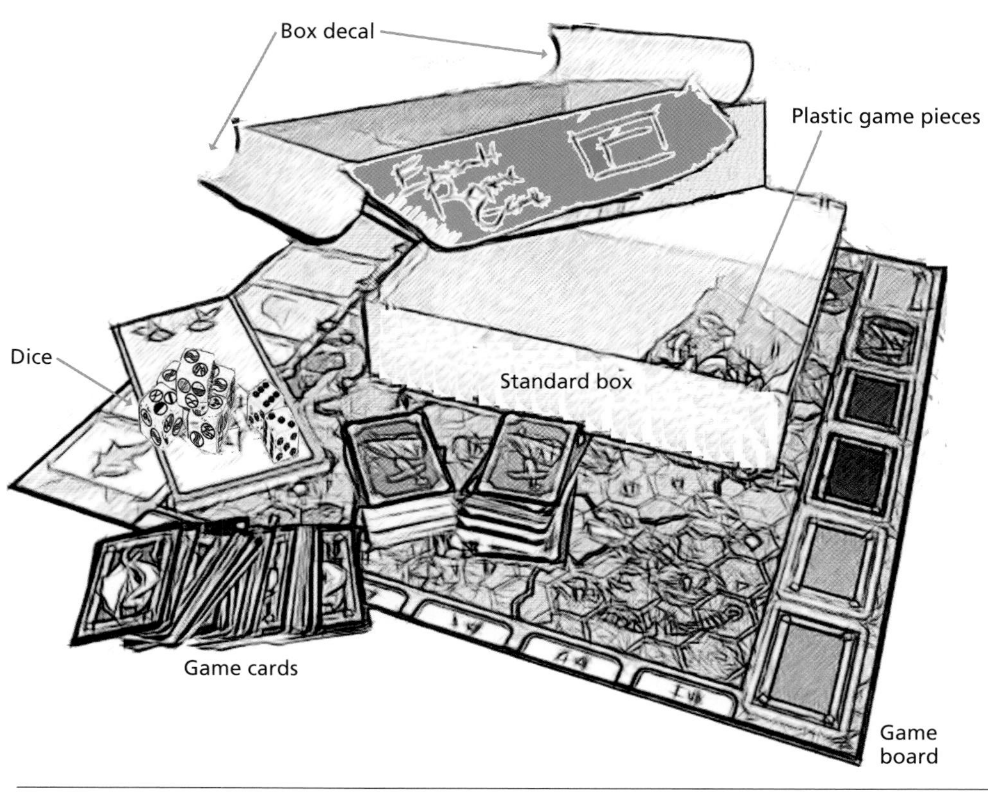

A bill of materials would list these component parts, among others.

parent/child relationships. If a finished good A is created from some other item B, which was in turn created from some material C, Figure 11.6 displays the resulting product structure diagram. In any product structure diagram, finished goods such as item A in Figure 11.6 are assigned to level 0, the topmost portion of the illustration. We create a product structure diagram for Main House Gaming's Environmental Response Game as the finished good in Scenario 2a.

Example Bill of Materials as a Product Structure Diagram

FIGURE 11.6

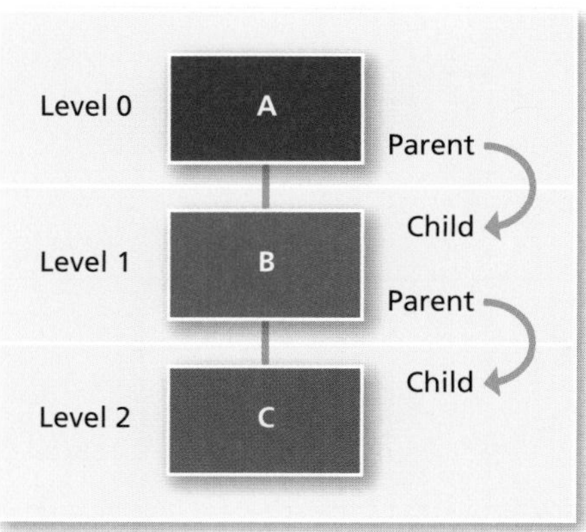

This product structue diagram illustrates a three-item, three-level bill of materials.

Scenario 2a Bill of Materials, Creating a Product Structure Diagram

Main House Gaming has developed the Environmental Response Game, for sale to schools for use in science instruction with students aged 10 to 12. This game, pictured earlier in Figure 11.5, is created by mixing items standard to many Main House Gaming products with other items it has fabricated specifically for the Environmental Response Game (ERG). The ERG bill of materials is provided below:

Item Name	Item Description	Parent Item	Number Needed Per Parent Item
SKU ERG001	ERG finished unit of sale	None	
SKU ERG101	ERG packed set	ERG001	1
SKU GNRL06	Standard die cube	ERG001	2
SKU ERG102	ERG branded game box	ERG001	1
SKU ERG201	ERG card set	ERG101	1
SKU ERG202	ERG branded playing board	ERG101	1
SKU ERG203	ERG plastic game piece packet	ERG101	1
SKU PAPR01	Standard game box	ERG102	1
SKU ERG204	ERG box decal	ERG102	1
SKU PAPR25	Standard foldable playing board	ERG202	1
SKU ERG301	ERG game board laminate top	ERG202	1

How does this bill of materials appear as a product structure diagram? How many levels are within this bill of materials?

Analysis

Before we sketch a product structure diagram from the ERG bill of materials, we identify all items that do not have parent items. These items are finished goods and should be drawn on level 0 at the top of the diagram. In the ERG case, only the finished game SKU ERG001 has no parent item. So we draw this item first:

ERG PRODUCT STRUCTURE DIAGRAM

To continue building the diagram, we review the bill of materials for all items that have ERG001 as a parent. There are three such items, so we draw their dependent demand links to ERG001 as branches downward to the next level of the diagram:

ERG PRODUCT STRUCTURE DIAGRAM

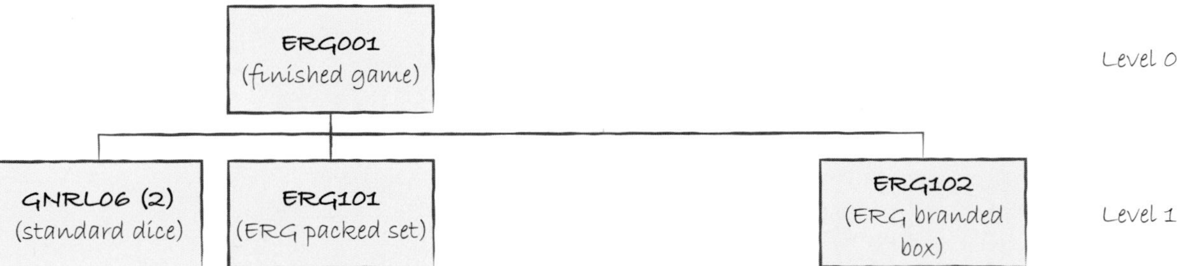

At this point, we look back at the bill of materials for any children of the three items on level 1. ERG101, the ERG packed set, consists of three components, listing it as a parent.

ERG102, the ERG branded box, is composed of two child items, a standard box PAPR01 and the adhesive decal ERG204. We now draw all five of these children as members of level 2. A slight repositioning of the previously drawn ERG102 on level 1 makes these additions more convenient:

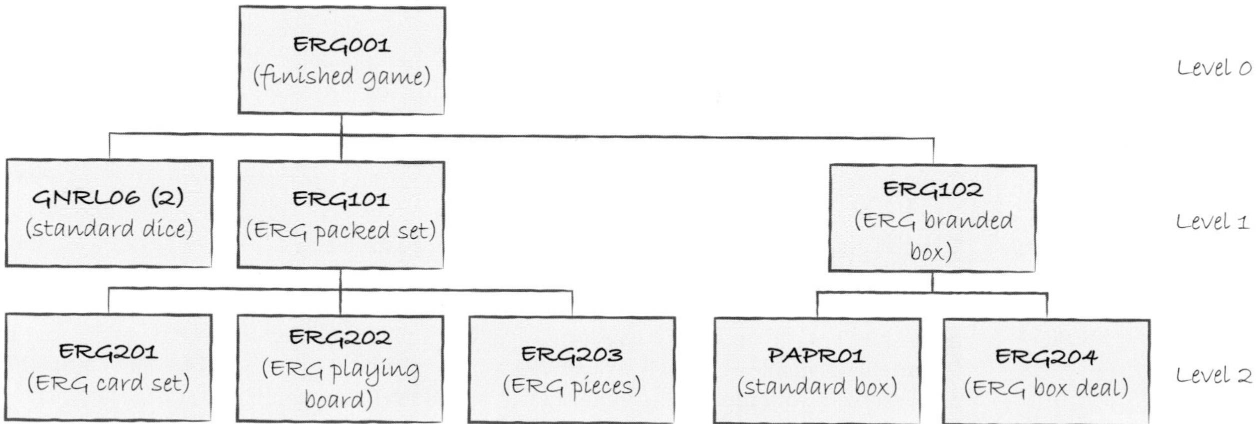

Now the only two items remaining to be added to the structure are PAPR25, a standard foldable game board, and SKU ERG301, the printed laminate game board top. These level 3 items create ERG202, the ERG branded playing board:

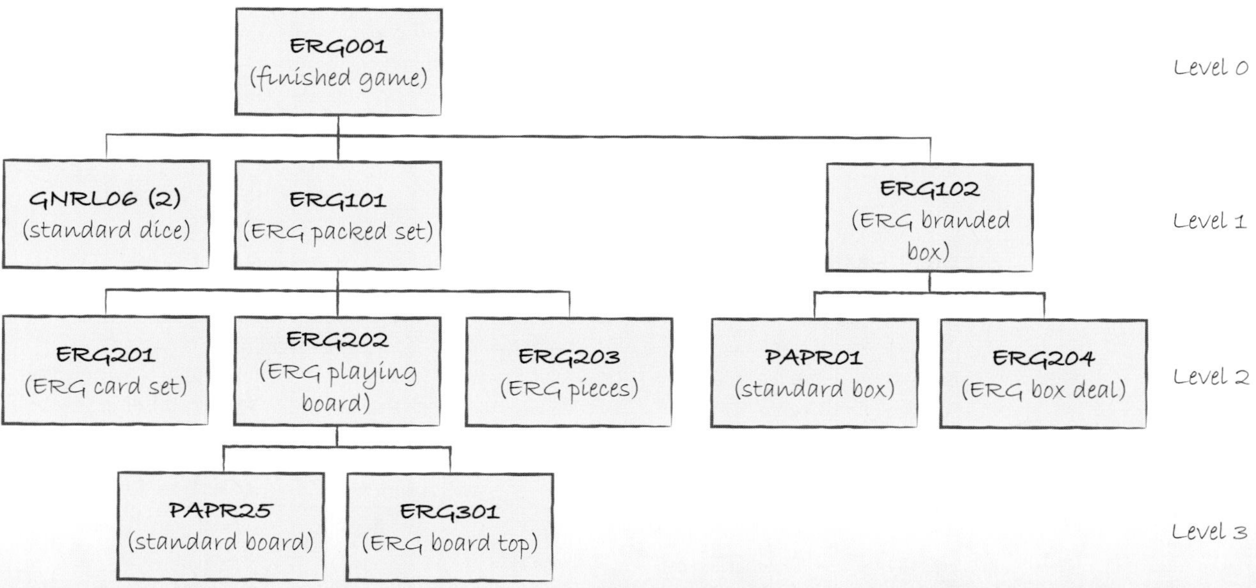

Insight The Main House Gaming product structure diagram for the Environmental Response Game consists of 11 distinct inventory items, distributed across four levels. ■

Product structure diagrams not only illustrate component requirements and parent/child relationships, but they also clarify what type of inventory is required throughout the production process. More specifically, finished goods inventory, on level 0, has no parent items, experiencing only independent demand. In contrast, raw materials of any sort always have a parent item, although this type of inventory never has any child items. Raw material items always populate the lowest level of the diagram, such as the two

raw materials
Inventory brought in from outside the system.

components PAPR25 and ERG301 needed to create an ERG playing board in Scenario 2a, but can be found on any level other than level 0.

work-in-process (WIP) Inventory resulting from transformation of raw materials but not yet ready for sale to consumers.

A third type of inventory found in product structure diagram is work-in-process (WIP). WIP represents partially transformed inventory that is not yet ready for sale to the customer. Any item in a bill of materials that possesses a parent item and at least one child item is work-in-process. Three instances of WIP inventory appear within the ERG product structure diagram: ERG101, ERG102, and ERG202. These represent the entire packed set of ERG-specific playing pieces (ERG101) of which the ERG playing board is one component (ERG202), and the empty ERG labeled game box (ERG102) that will house them. At any given time, Main House Gaming may build a stock of any or all three of these items, although none of them can be sold to the customer directly.

lead time Delay between requesting a product and receiving it.

backward scheduling Starting an activity so it will finish on its deadline.

Gantt chart A scheduling diagram that illustrates activities across a horizontal timeline.

Time Phasing MRP introduces two complexities into planning that aggregate planning ignores. The first is the familiar issue of dependent demand. The second issue is lead time. Specifically, MRP recognizes that each item in a bill of materials may have a lead time associated with it, creating a gap in time between when the item is ordered and when it is actually available for use. This gap can represent time spent producing the item or the delay expected in ordering the item from an outside vendor. Planning an order sufficiently ahead of time so that it might be completed or received when needed is referred to as *time phasing*, and is one of the defining features of MRP. MRP time phasing is an example of backward scheduling, where the timing of the start of an activity is determined by scheduling back from when it must be finished.

A time-phased product structure diagram shows how delays on receiving the various items interact to create the overall lead time on producing a finished good. This diagram is usually drawn horizontally, with its items drawn to a scale that reflects their actual lead times. In a sense, a time-phased product structure diagram is a special form of a general scheduling tool known as a Gantt chart. We will create one for the Environmental Response Game in Scenario 2b.

Scenario 2b

Bill of Materials, Time Phasing

Main House Gaming estimates that the 11 distinct items listed on the bill of materials of the Environmental Response Game (ERG) each have differing fixed lead times, representing the delay between placing an order for any amount of the item, and then actually receiving that order. The reasons why these lead times vary between the items are described in the following table:

Item Name	Item Description	Lead Time	Lead Time Description
ERG001	ERG finished unit of sale	1 day	Final game assembly
ERG101	ERG packed set	1 day	Assembly
GNRL06	Standard die cube	7 days	Procurement
ERG102	ERG branded game box	2 days	Assembly
ERG201	ERG card set	5 days	Procurement
ERG202	ERG branded playing board	4 days	Assembly
ERG203	ERG plastic game piece packet	3 days	Procurement
PAPR01	Standard game box	5 days	Procurement
ERG204	ERG box decal	3 days	Procurement
PAPR25	Standard foldable playing board	3 days	Procurement
ERG301	ERG game board laminate top	3 days	Procurement

How does this information appear as a time-phased product structure diagram? What does this diagram indicate about the overall time required to produce the ERG, if Main House Gaming begins with nothing in inventory?

Analysis

Sketching a time-phased product structure diagram is similar to sketching a standard product structure diagram, except the illustration develops from right to left, instead of from the top downward. It helps to organize the work area in columns and rows, to represent time periods (days) and items. Similar to Scenario 2a, we begin charting by illustrating the single level 0 item on the far right-hand side of the diagram, scaled to represent the exact length of lead time:

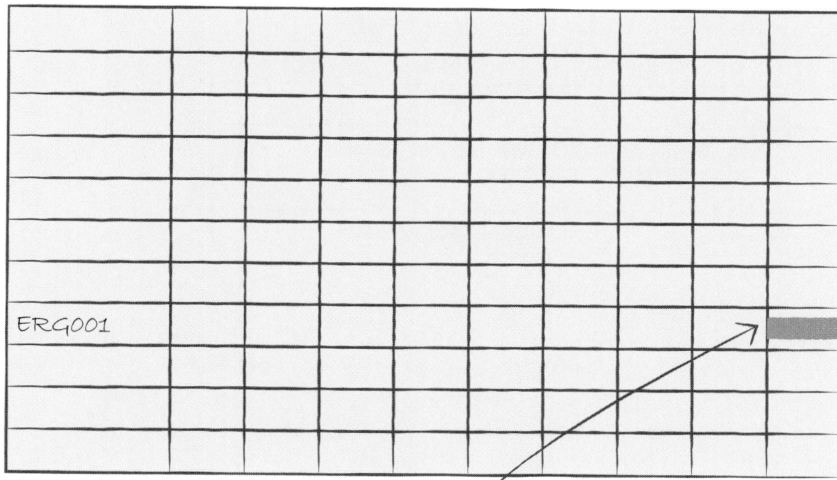

Each column in this grid represents a day. Since the lead time on final assembly of finished game ERG001 is 1 day, it is drawn to the far right, blocking out one column of the grid.

As we did in Scenario 2a, we continue here by adding all items that have ERG001 as a parent. Unlike the standard diagram in Scenario 2a, however, we draw these times to the left of their parent, and scale to the length of their individual lead times.

GNRL06
ERG101
ERG001
ERG102

Continues

Now we can add all items that appeared on level 2 of the Scenario 2a diagram, followed by the remaining items on level 3. Once we chart all items on the time-phased product structure diagram, we can label the time line itself by locating the leftmost point on the diagram and labeling that point "0" to indicate the start of the time line.

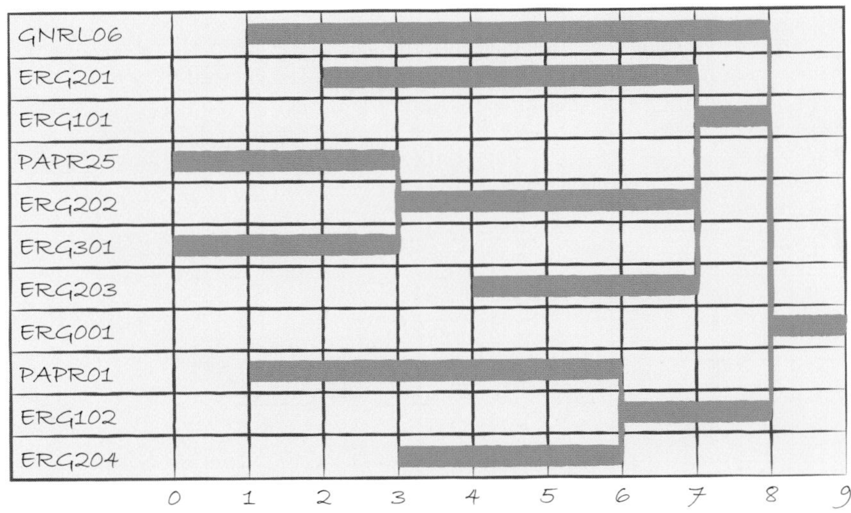

Insight From inspection of the diagram we see that the overall lead time on production of the ERG is 9 days, provided that Main House Gaming has no components in stock. Such production would begin with the ordering of PAPR25 and ERG301, the standard playing board and the printed laminate cover required to create an ERG playing board. ■

In Scenario 2b we represented the lead times graphically but we also need to consider the assumptions made in doing so. For example, the lead time on PAPR25, the standard folding bases from which Main House Gaming's boards are created, is 3 days. MRP applies this information under the following assumptions:

- **Lead time is fixed and constant.** Each time standard foldable playing boards are ordered, Main House Gaming will always wait exactly 3 days to receive them.
- **Lead time is independent of order size.** If Main House Gaming orders 30 standard foldable playing boards or 3 million standard foldable playing boards, the wait for delivery of either amount will be exactly 3 days.
- **Any children are available in inventory when the order for the parent item is placed.** This is not problematic in the case of PAPR25, because this item has no children. However, this item and ERG301 are both children of ERG202, the finished game board. ERG202 has a lead time of 4 days, meaning that any amount of finished game boards can be completed in 4 days, provided that enough standard boards (PAPR25) and ERG laminate tops (ERG301) are ready in inventory to assemble that amount when the order is placed.

Later in the chapter we discuss these assumptions further, disclosing their advantages and disadvantages in practice.

Master Production Schedule

master production schedule (MPS) A statement of independent demand for all inventory items in an MRP system.

The master production schedule (MPS) is a second major input required by the MRP process. Derived from the broader aggregate plan, the MPS specifies precisely how much of what must be produced and by when, to satisfy all independent demand on the system.

Since the MPS is a statement of independent demand, it is usually populated with customer orders or projected customer sales for various finished goods. However, any item in a bill of materials might be mentioned at least occasionally on the MPS, given that some customer wishes to purchase it specifically. An organization may sell small amounts of raw materials or WIP inventory directly to the outside world, typically as replacement parts for previously purchased finished goods. For this reason, the MPS cannot be strictly defined as a set of orders for finished goods, although that is often an accurate description.

Like the bill of materials, the MPS brings issues of its own into MRP. Generally, the MPS is more detailed than its parent aggregate plan, but has a shorter formal planning horizon, reflecting only an early portion of the original aggregate plan. This shortened interval, sometimes a month or less, is broken up into even smaller time buckets for more detailed timing of activity. Where aggregate planning usually outlines the future in terms of weeks, months, or quarters, an MPS describes an early portion of that same future with hourly, daily, or perhaps weekly time buckets. The size of time bucket depends on the level of detail needed to coordinate production and the speed at which the system needs to react to changes in the plan. These issues also influence the choice of length of the MPS planning horizon, because too short a horizon does not leave the system enough time to react to new information, a condition sometimes referred to as *myopia* to liken it to human shortsightedness. However, too long a planning horizon can result in unnecessary planning: a lengthy plan is often changed before its later portions are implemented, the passage of time having brought new information.

time bucket
The smallest interval of time used in planning, such as hourly, daily, or weekly.

MRP itself is known as a nervous procedure, meaning that a small revision to its input data can set off dramatic changes to the detailed plans it generates with that data. We return to this condition and its consequences in greater detail later in this chapter but for our purposes now we note that changes to the MPS are a common cause of undesirable effects in MRP. Remember, the MPS consists of customer orders and customer demand, and it is not uncommon for customers to revise their plans and change their requests. So, to protect an MRP system from nervousness, organizations often establish one or more time fences within the planning horizon, freezing at least the earliest portion of the MPS. Figure 11.7 illustrates such a policy, where the first 3 days of a 7-day planning horizon are frozen, meaning that no changes will be tolerated, even if late-arriving information concerning customer demand suggests a revision. In this frozen zone, new requests cannot be accommodated and any cancelled or reduced orders may be produced according to the original MPS despite this new information.

nervous
In management science, a condition in which a small change to input data can create major revisions to the conclusions suggested by a particular technique.

time fence
A point in time specified by a policy to protect an MPS from near-term changes, dividing the planning horizon into shorter intervals with varying levels of protection.

Setting a time fence and freezing some portion of the MPS is a matter of operational policy making, and this decision should be made carefully. While freezing does protect the system from nervous revisions to its detailed plans, it tends to work against responsiveness and customer service. Thus, if freezing is judged necessary, the MPS may be divided into multiple sections, allowing differing degrees of flexibility through time, to

freezing
In planning, a policy that does not allow changes to the MPS within a protected interval.

Example MPS with Time Fences FIGURE **11.7**

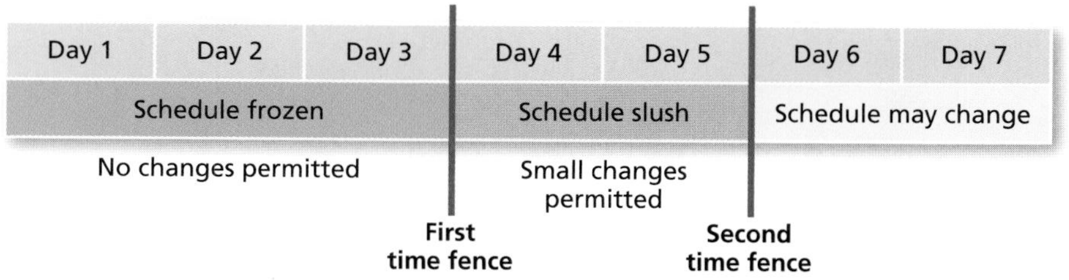

better serve late-arriving customer requests while nonetheless shielding the system from some nervousness. Figure 11.7 displays such a policy; the frozen portion of the MPS is followed by 2 days of "slush," where small changes to the MPS will be tolerated.

DEVELOPING MATERIAL REQUIREMENTS PLANS

MRP is essentially an information system that draws from three distinct files of information to generate detailed plans. The planner or planning system must have access to these three resources to begin MRP:

- A master production schedule, specifying what outputs should be created, and by when.
- A bill of materials, specifying how outputs are created through dependent demand relationships with other items.
- Current inventory records, specifying how much of what items are available.

Moving forward with this information, MRP creates a set of linked production and ordering plans involving all the various items mentioned in the bill of materials, a process also known as backflushing.

backflushing
Determining the overall inventory requirements of a finished good by combining information on amount of the good produced with the requirements information in its bill of materials.

MRP as an Information System

An MRP system can be thought of as a set of linked data tables generated from the three input files described above. Each table within the information system is an MRP record dedicated to one of the items within the bill of materials. The links between the records represent parent/child relationships also found within that bill of materials. Backflushing generates new material requirements plans by taking the information from the MPS and current inventory records and disseminating it across all the records through these links.

MRP Records An MRP system maintains and updates one MRP record for each distinct item within a bill of materials. Figure 11.8 shows an example record with its important features labeled. These features include the identity of the item and any information that

FIGURE 11.8 Features of an MRP Record

Each MRP record has an identity. It refers to a single, unique item.

Each MRP record is linked to inventory records of its item. It displays the relevant information needed for further planning for that item.

Example Item | Lead time: 2 days | Lot size: 50

		Day 1	Day 2	Day 3	Day 4	Day 5	Day 6	Day 7
Gross requirements			10			40		
Planned order receipts						50		
Available balance	15	15	5	5	5	15	15	15
Planned order release				50				

Each MRP record ultimately displays how much of the item should be ordered and when it should be ordered, to meet the gross requirements of the item.

may be useful when planning for that item. The record reflects the same number of time buckets as the MPS.

The uppermost line of the planning table displays the gross requirements for that item over the planning horizon. Gross requirements are demands for that item that must be supplied by certain points in time, such as the 10 units on day 2 of the example item in Figure 11.8, followed by 40 units on day 5. Gross requirements may be actual customer orders or dependent demand from parent items or the combined effect of both. An MRP record also displays precisely how and when these requirements will be supplied, labeled planned order receipts in Figure 11.8. Here a planner has decided how to support the gross requirements with the arrival of new orders, given current inventory levels and that item's lot size, if any. In the case of the first gross requirement on day 2 in Figure 11.8, nothing has been scheduled for receipt because 15 units of this item have been available in inventory since the beginning of the plan. After day 2, however, this available balance will be reduced to 15 – 10 = 5 units of ending inventory, and the record reflects this change. These 5 units will not be adequate to meet the demand for 40 units in day 5, so a planned order receipt for another 50 units has been scheduled to assist.

gross requirements The combined, overall demand for an item.

planned order receipts A schedule of the arrival of a particular item within a planning horizon, to supply its gross requirements over that same time interval.

While only 40 – 5 = 35 units were needed to meet the gross requirement in day 5, 50 units have been scheduled for receipt to recognize the item's lot sizing requirement, visible in the upper right-hand side of Figure 11.8. A lot size requirement restricts the size of an item's orders to a multiple of the lot size number. In the case of the example, ordering in multiples of 50 units may be necessary because this item is purchased in boxes of 50 units, meaning that the planned order release in Figure 11.8 is an arrangement to receive another box. If no such restrictions exist, planned order receipts can be sized to fit gross requirements exactly, commonly known as ordering lot-for-lot, LFL or L4L.

lot-for-lot (LFL) An ordering policy in which orders are sized to match individual demands exactly, theoretically accumulating no inventory.

The bottom line of an MRP record displays the plan that results from coordinating all the information staged above it, in planned order releases. Planned order releases dictate exactly how much of the item to order and when to order it, by taking the planned order receipts and phasing them forward in time. This is the time phasing discussed earlier as a central feature of MRP, in which it is assumed that any amount of the item, if ordered at a certain time, will arrive after a fixed delay known as its lead time. The lead time on the example item in Figure 11.8 is 2 days, so the 50 units that must be received on day 5 should be ordered on day 3.

planned order releases A schedule of the ordering of a particular item within a planning horizon, to supply its gross requirements over that same time interval.

Linking the Records Links between MRP records represent dependent demand relationships within the bill of materials. Specifically:

> Planned order releases of each item are linked to the gross requirements of each of that item's children. The quantity passed along this link is multiplied by the number of the child item required to create one parent item.

Figure 11.9 displays a set of linked records, assuming the example item in Figure 11.8 is a finished good in a three-item bill of materials similar to Figure 11.6. Planned order releases of parent items are passed down level by level and incorporated into the gross requirements of child records to support an assumption discussed earlier: the lead time on every item is a fixed delay, provided that all the item's children are in stock when the parent item is ordered. Thus, the example item's order for 50 units placed on day 3 in Figure 11.9 will arrive 2 days later as planned, provided that 50 units of its child item are ready for use on day 3.

Now familiar with each of its components, we can generalize the MRP technique itself, coordinating each of the components in these general steps:

1. **Set up the records.** Set up a blank MRP record for each item in the bill of materials, entering all data supplied by the current inventory records. Enter any amounts scheduled on the MPS into the gross requirements of those items' records.

FIGURE 11.9 MRP Records Linked to Example Item

Because 50 of the parent item are ordered (planned order releases), 50 of the child item must be ready for use (gross requirements) at the time of ordering.

Example Item — **Lead time: 2 days** — **Lot size: 50**

		Day 1	Day 2	Day 3	Day 4	Day 5	Day 6	Day 7
Gross requirements			10			40		
Planned order receipts						50		
Available balance	**15**	15	5	5	5	15	15	15
Planned order release				**50**				

Child of Example Item — **Lead time: 1 day** — **Lot size: LFL**

		Day 1	Day 2	Day 3	Day 4	Day 5	Day 6	Day 7
Gross requirements				50				
Planned order receipts				50				
Available balance	**0**	0	0	0	0	0	0	0
Planned order release			**50**					

Child of Child of Example Item — **Lead time: 1 day** — **Lot size: LFL**

		Day 1	Day 2	Day 3	Day 4	Day 5	Day 6	Day 7
Gross requirements			50					
Planned order receipts			50					
Available balance	**0**	0	0	0	0	0	0	0
Planned order release		**50**						

2. **Calculate the planned order releases for the current level.** At the beginning, this will be level 0, the top level. Complete the records on that level.
3. **Enter those planned order releases into the gross requirements of all child records.** When determining the gross requirements of a child, multiply the parent's planned order release by the number of the child item required to create one parent unit.
4. **Move to the next level, and return to step 2.**

Completing these steps until all records are completed on all levels creates a set of planned order releases for all items, a material requirements plan that supports the original MPS. In the case of planning production of the ERG for Main House Gaming, 11 MRP records would be created and linked according to the ERG parent/child relationships, as illustrated in Figure 11.10.

To develop a material requirements plan for Main House Gaming, these 11 records would be completed by moving through general steps of the technique four times, for each of the four levels first revealed in Scenario 2a. We do so now in Scenario 2c.

The Linked MRP Records for the Environmental Response Game | **FIGURE 11.10**

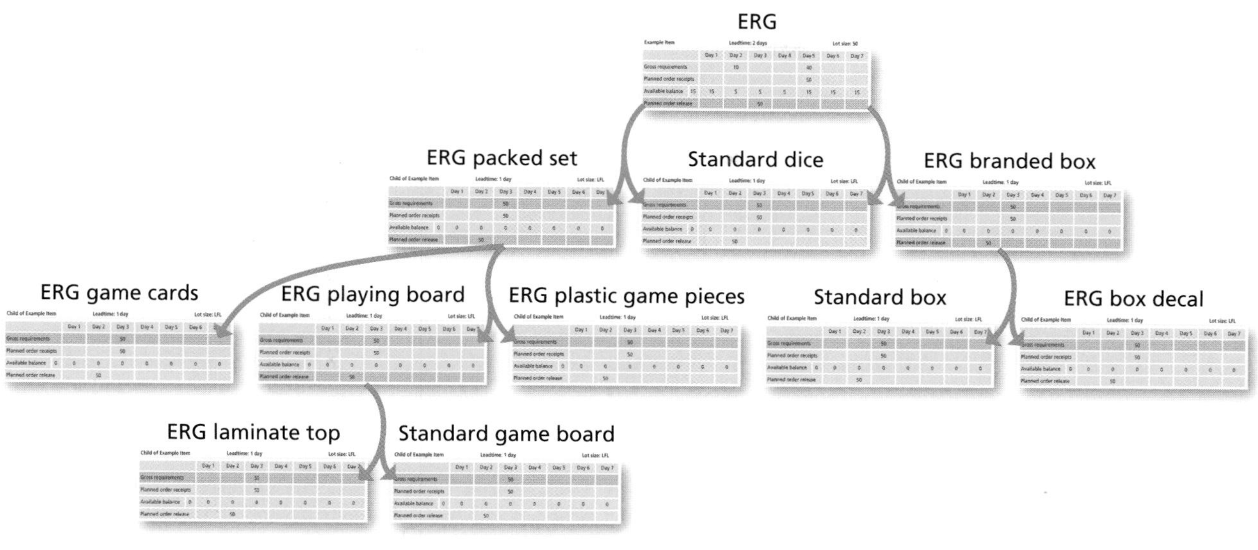

MRP, Creating a Plan

Scenario 2c

The production manager of Main House Gaming now needs a detailed material requirements plan to support the following MPS, which contains four orders for the ERG over the next 14 days:

Master Production Schedule (MPS)

Day:	1	2	3	4	5	6	7	8	9	10	11	12	13	14
ERG001 (finished ERG game)				50					60	70				75

The production manager has available the ERG bill of materials developed in Scenario 2a, and the following current inventory records:

Current Inventory Records

Item Name	Item Description	Lead Time	On-hand Inventory	Lot Size
ERG001	ERG, finished unit of sale	1 day	0	LFL
ERG101	ERG packed set	1 day	0	LFL
GNRL06	Standard dice (2 six-sided die cubes)	7 days	244	500
ERG102	ERG branded game box	2 days	0	LFL
ERG201	ERG cards set	5 days	50	20
ERG202	ERG branded playing board	4 days	50	LFL
ERG203	ERG plastic game pieces packet	3 days	50	40
PAPR01	Standard game box	5 days	203	100
ERG204	ERG box decal	3 days	50	30
PAPR25	Standard folding game board	3 days	60	30
ERG301	ERG game board laminate top	3 days	60	20

How many of these items should to be ordered and when should they be ordered, to fulfill the orders on this MPS?

Continues

Analysis

These two questions of how much and when are answered by calculating the planned order releases for all the items in the bill of materials. We begin by setting up a blank MRP record for each item, providing the same number of planning periods as the MPS. We need 11 records in the case of Main House Gaming's problem, the first of which is pictured below:

ERG001 Lead time: 1 day Lot size: LFL

		Day 1	Day 2	Day 3	Day 4	Day 5	Day 6	Day 7	Day 8	Day 9	Day 10	Day 11	Day 12	Day 13	Day 14
Gross requirements					50					60	70				75
Planned order receipts															
Available balance	0														
Planned order release															

The values entered for initial available balance, lead time, and lot size appeared in the current inventory records at the beginning of the scenario. This record is for the finished game ERG001, which is the only item mentioned on the MPS and thus the only record of the 11-record system that begins with entries in the gross requirements line. These numbers, passed from the MPS into the gross requirements of the ERG001 record, begin the process of backflushing. The next step is to complete all the records on level 0 of the bill of materials.

ERG001 Lead time: 1 day Lot size: LFL

		Day 1	Day 2	Day 3	Day 4	Day 5	Day 6	Day 7	Day 8	Day 9	Day 10	Day 11	Day 12	Day 13	Day 14
Gross requirements					50					60	70				75
Planned order receipts					50					60	70				75
Available balance	0	0	0	0	0	0	0	0	0	0	0	0	0	0	0
Planned order release				50					60	70				75	

Orders sized lot-for-lot and phased forward 1 day for on-time ordering, as specified in the initial information.

Now that we completed the planned order releases for level 0, we enter this pattern of ordering into the gross requirements of the three children of ERG001. Two of these children, ERG101 and ERG102, have one-to-one parent/child relationships. This means that exactly one ERG101 (the ERG packed set) and exactly one ERG102 (the ERG box) are required to create exactly one ERG001 (the finished ERG unit of sale). This also means that we can enter the pattern of numbers on the bottom row of ERG001's record directly into the top line of the ERG101 and ERG102 records:

ERG101 Lead time: 1 day Lot size: LFL

		Day 1	Day 2	Day 3	Day 4	Day 5	Day 6	Day 7	Day 8	Day 9	Day 10	Day 11	Day 12	Day 13	Day 14
Gross requirements				50					60	70				75	
Planned order receipts															
Available balance	0														
Planned order release															

ERG102 Lead time: 2 days Lot size: LFL

		Day 1	Day 2	Day 3	Day 4	Day 5	Day 6	Day 7	Day 8	Day 9	Day 10	Day 11	Day 12	Day 13	Day 14
Gross requirements				50					60	70				75	
Planned order receipts															
Available balance	0														
Planned order release															

The third record on level 1, GNRL06 (dice), requires more calculation because more than one child is required to create one unit of the parent. According to the bill of materials, two GNRL06 die cubes must be included in each finished unit of sale, so the planned order releases of ERG001 must be multiplied by two, to correctly estimate the gross requirements for dice:

50 × 2 = 100. All gross requirements here are the planned order releases for ERG001, multiplied by two.

GNRL06 — Lead time: 7 days — Lot size: 500

		Day 1	Day 2	Day 3	Day 4	Day 5	Day 6	Day 7	Day 8	Day 9	Day 10	Day 11	Day 12	Day 13	Day 14
Gross requirements				100					120	140				150	
Planned order receipts															
Available balance	244														
Planned order release															

Now that the transfer of the newly calculated planned order releases from level 0 to all child items is complete, we move to level 1, the next level down. These same three records inhabit level 1, so we can now complete them to determine the planned order releases of these three items.

ERG LEVEL 1

ERG101 — Lead time: 1 day — Lot size: LFL

		Day 1	Day 2	Day 3	Day 4	Day 5	Day 6	Day 7	Day 8	Day 9	Day 10	Day 11	Day 12	Day 13	Day 14
Gross requirements				50					60	70				75	
Planned order receipts				50					60	70				75	
Available balance	0	0	0	0	0	0	0	0	0	0	0	0	0	0	0
Planned order release			50					60	70				75		

ERG102 — Lead time: 2 days — Lot size: LFL

		Day 1	Day 2	Day 3	Day 4	Day 5	Day 6	Day 7	Day 8	Day 9	Day 10	Day 11	Day 12	Day 13	Day 14
Gross requirements				50					60	70				75	
Planned order receipts				50					60	70				75	
Available balance	0	0	0	0	0	0	0	0	0	0	0	0	0	0	0
Planned order release		50					60	70				75			

GNRL06 — Lead time: 7 days — Lot size: 500

		Day 1	Day 2	Day 3	Day 4	Day 5	Day 6	Day 7	Day 8	Day 9	Day 10	Day 11	Day 12	Day 13	Day 14
Gross requirements				100					120	140				150	
Planned order receipts										500					
Available balance	244	244	244	144	144	144	144	144	24	384	384	384	384	234	234
Planned order release			500												

With level 1 complete, we transfer these new planned order releases into the gross requirements of any child items below. When the transfer is finished for all level 1 items, we move on to complete all records on Level 2. On level 1, both ERG101 and ERG102 have child

Continues

items, appearing on level 2. ERG102 is the simpler of the two level 1 parents; the resulting records for its two children would then appear as

ERG LEVEL 2

Gross requirements of PAPR01 passed from planned order releases of ERG102.

PAPR01 Lead time: 5 days Lot size: 100

		Day 1	Day 2	Day 3	Day 4	Day 5	Day 6	Day 7	Day 8	Day 9	Day 10	Day 11	Day 12	Day 13	Day 14
Gross requirements		50					60	70				75			
Planned order receipts												100			
Available balance	203	153	153	153	153	153	93	23	23	23	23	48	48	48	48
Planned order release							100								

ERG204 Lead time: 3 days Lot size: 30

		Day 1	Day 2	Day 3	Day 4	Day 5	Day 6	Day 7	Day 8	Day 9	Day 10	Day 11	Day 12	Day 13	Day 14
Gross requirements		50					60	70				75			
Planned order receipts							60	90				60			
Available balance	50	0	0	0	0	0	0	20	20	20	20	5	5	5	5
Planned order release				60	90				60						

ERG101, the ERG packed set, is composed of three child items whose planned order releases we can now calculate.

Gross requirements came from planned order releases of ERG101.

ERG201 Lead time: 5 days Lot size: 20

		Day 1	Day 2	Day 3	Day 4	Day 5	Day 6	Day 7	Day 8	Day 9	Day 10	Day 11	Day 12	Day 13	Day 14
Gross requirements			50					60	70				75		
Planned order receipts								60	80				80		
Available balance	50	50	0	0	0	0	0	0	10	10	10	10	15	15	15
Planned order release			60	80				80							

ERG202 Lead time: 4 days Lot size: LFL

		Day 1	Day 2	Day 3	Day 4	Day 5	Day 6	Day 7	Day 8	Day 9	Day 10	Day 11	Day 12	Day 13	Day 14
Gross requirements			50					60	70				75		
Planned order receipts			50					60	70				75		
Available balance	50	50	0	0	0	0	0	0	0	0	0	0	0	0	0
Planned order release				60	70				75						

ERG203 Lead time: 3 days Lot size: 40

		Day 1	Day 2	Day 3	Day 4	Day 5	Day 6	Day 7	Day 8	Day 9	Day 10	Day 11	Day 12	Day 13	Day 14
Gross requirements			50					60	70				75		
Planned order receipts								80	80				80		
Available balance	50	50	0	0	0	0	0	20	30	30	30	30	35	35	35
Planned order release					80	80				80					

With level 2 complete, we need only pass planned order releases down to level 3 and complete the records there. On level 2, ERG202 is the only parent item, requiring one each of child items PAPR25 and ERG301.

ERG LEVEL 3

Gross requirements came from planned order releases of ERG202.

PAPR25 — Lead time: 3 days — Lot size: 30

		Day 1	Day 2	Day 3	Day 4	Day 5	Day 6	Day 7	Day 8	Day 9	Day 10	Day 11	Day 12	Day 13	Day 14
Gross requirements				60	70				75						
Planned order receipts					90				60						
Available balance	60	60	60	0	20	20	20	20	5	5	5	5	5	5	5
Planned order release		90				60									

ERG301 — Lead time: 3 days — Lot size: 20

		Day 1	Day 2	Day 3	Day 4	Day 5	Day 6	Day 7	Day 8	Day 9	Day 10	Day 11	Day 12	Day 13	Day 14
Gross requirements				60	70				75						
Planned order receipts					80				80						
Available balance	60	60	60	0	10	10	10	10	15	15	15	15	15	15	15
Planned order release		80				80									

Finally, with all records completed, we can summarize the planned order releases of each item as a single table, answering the questions of when Main House Gaming should order these items and in what amounts:

PLANNED ORDER RELEASES

Item	Level	Day 1	Day 2	Day 3	Day 4	Day 5	Day 6	Day 7	Day 8	Day 9	Day 10	Day 11	Day 12	Day 13	Day 14
SKU ERG001	0			50					60	70				75	
SKU GNRL06	1		500												
SKU ERG101	1		50					60	70				75		
SKU ERG102	1	50					60	70				75			
SKU PAPR01	2						100								
SKU ERG201	2		60	80				80							
SKU ERG202	2			60	70				75						
SKU ERG203	2				80	80				80					
SKU ERG204	2			60	90				60						
SKU PAPR25	3	90				60									
SKU ERG301	3	80				80									

Insight To fill the four orders for the Environmental Response Game in the original master production schedule, Main House Gaming must order all 11 items in the ERG bill of materials over the next 14 days, in the amounts and times indicated by the table of planned order releases. This 14-day plan begins with ordering 90 units of PAPR25 (standard game boards), 50 units of ERG102 (branded game box), and 80 units of ERG301 (ERG game board laminate tops) immediately (day 1), to begin on-time production.

Continues

Furthermore, this 14-day plan also assumes no other games are under production at Main House Gaming, or they would appear on the MPS. If other games are under production during this time, the planned order releases for some of the standard components shared with these games can be expected to be higher. Since other games could share components such as the standard game box PAPR01 as child items, the planned order releases for these other parents would be added into the gross requirements of those child records, collecting the combined dependent demand of all games being assembled. ■

Advantages and Disadvantages of MRP

Most any technique has advantages and disadvantages, and MRP is no exception.

Advantages The principal advantage of an MRP system is its versatility. MRP was developed primarily for manufacturing, but the technique can be adapted to scheduling most any dependent demand environment, provided that the assumption of fixed lead times is a reasonable fit to the situation. MRP's interface with the aggregate plan, its links with customer requests through the MPS, and its links with procurement through planned order releases all invite greater integration of production with other functional areas such as sales, purchasing, and human resources. MRP modules often serve as production planning engines embedded in broader enterprise resource planning (ERP) systems, creating bridges between these functional areas. Here MRP can be informed by data passed through the ERP system, seamlessly generating detailed plans for distribution back to the same system.

enterprise resource planning (ERP) A strategic information system that integrates all functional areas of an organization.

infinite loading A scheduling approach that ignores capacity constraints.

Disadvantages MRP has two major disadvantages, the first and greatest being that it is an infinite loading technique. An infinite loading technique creates schedules without any consideration of capacity constraints, loading a system as heavily as is necessary to complete all known demand. Within MRP, infinite loading takes the form of its optimistic assumption that lead times are fixed and independent of order size. Thus, the time required to process an order for one item or 1 million items is assumed to be the same. In reality, this time would likely vary due to capacity constraints. Restated, MRP's greatest weakness is that the detailed plans it produces are not guaranteed to be feasible, given the size of the orders.

finite loading A scheduling approach that recognizes capacity constraints.

When capacity constraints are included during scheduling, the much more difficult problem known as finite loading results. The finite loading problem has not yet been resolved by any particular known technique, although various attempts to regulate the capacity-blind MRP approach by adding routines that check planned order releases for unreasonable amounts with respect to actual capacity, and then repair any violations by rescheduling the overscheduled production, have emerged. This integration of capacity constraints and limited resources into the development of planned order releases creates a broader production planning system with MRP logic at its center, one of which is sometimes referred to as a manufacturing resource planning or MRP II system. Like MRP, any MRP II system can then function as a component of the organization's overarching ERP system.

manufacturing resource planning (MRP II) A broader information system embedding MRP logic in a set of modules that integrate input from other areas of the organizations and enforce relevant capacity constraints on the development of schedules.

The second disadvantage of MRP is its nervousness, mentioned earlier in discussion of the MPS. In Figure 11.11, the MRP problem in Scenario 2c is set up as a spreadsheet model. The uppermost screenshot of this model displays the MPS and the resulting planned order releases from Scenario 2c, while the lower screenshot shows the result of making a single change to the original problem, simulating a request to consolidate one order on the MPS with an earlier order. MRP nervousness is apparent in the widespread changes to both the sizes and the timings of the planned order releases, as well as the warnings that this change creates multiple instances of items that simply cannot

Spreadsheet Model for the ERG, Exhibiting Nervousness FIGURE **11.11**

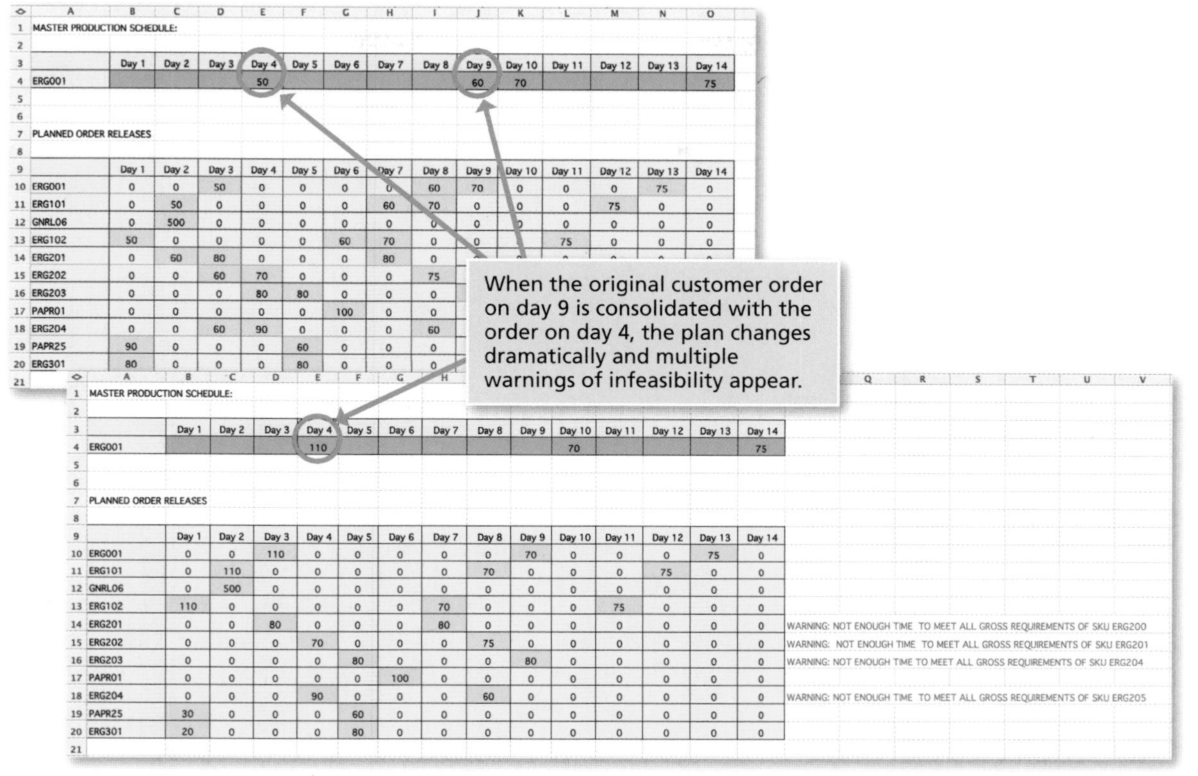

MASTER PRODUCTION SCHEDULE:

	Day 1	Day 2	Day 3	Day 4	Day 5	Day 6	Day 7	Day 8	Day 9	Day 10	Day 11	Day 12	Day 13	Day 14
ERG001				50					60	70				75

PLANNED ORDER RELEASES

	Day 1	Day 2	Day 3	Day 4	Day 5	Day 6	Day 7	Day 8	Day 9	Day 10	Day 11	Day 12	Day 13	Day 14
ERG001	0	0	50	0	0	0	0	60	70	0	0	0	75	0
ERG101	0	50	0	0	0	0	60	70	0	0	0	75	0	0
GNRL06	0	500	0	0	0	0	0	0	0	0	0	0	0	0
ERG102	50	0	0	0	0	60	70	0	0	[illegible]	75	0	0	0
ERG201	0	60	80	0	0	0	80	0	[illegible]	[illegible]	[illegible]	[illegible]	[illegible]	[illegible]
ERG202	0	0	60	70	0	0	0	75	[illegible]	[illegible]	[illegible]	[illegible]	[illegible]	[illegible]
ERG203	0	0	0	80	80	0	0	0	[illegible]	[illegible]	[illegible]	[illegible]	[illegible]	[illegible]
PAPR01	0	0	0	0	0	100	0	0	[illegible]	[illegible]	[illegible]	[illegible]	[illegible]	[illegible]
ERG204	0	0	60	90	0	0	0	60	[illegible]	[illegible]	[illegible]	[illegible]	[illegible]	[illegible]
PAPR25	90	0	0	0	60	0	0	0	[illegible]	[illegible]	[illegible]	[illegible]	[illegible]	[illegible]
ERG301	80	0	0	0	80	0	0	0	[illegible]	[illegible]	[illegible]	[illegible]	[illegible]	[illegible]

MASTER PRODUCTION SCHEDULE:

	Day 1	Day 2	Day 3	Day 4	Day 5	Day 6	Day 7	Day 8	Day 9	Day 10	Day 11	Day 12	Day 13	Day 14
ERG001				110						70				75

PLANNED ORDER RELEASES

	Day 1	Day 2	Day 3	Day 4	Day 5	Day 6	Day 7	Day 8	Day 9	Day 10	Day 11	Day 12	Day 13	Day 14	
ERG001	0	0	110	0	0	0	0	0	70	0	0	0	75	0	
ERG101	0	110	0	0	0	0	0	70	0	0	0	75	0	0	
GNRL06	0	500	0	0	0	0	0	0	0	0	0	0	0	0	
ERG102	110	0	0	0	0	0	70	0	0	0	75	0	0	0	
ERG201	0	0	80	0	0	0	80	0	0	0	0	0	0	0	WARNING: NOT ENOUGH TIME TO MEET ALL GROSS REQUIREMENTS OF SKU ERG200
ERG202	0	0	0	70	0	0	0	75	0	0	0	0	0	0	WARNING: NOT ENOUGH TIME TO MEET ALL GROSS REQUIREMENTS OF SKU ERG201
ERG203	0	0	0	0	80	0	0	0	80	0	0	0	0	0	WARNING: NOT ENOUGH TIME TO MEET ALL GROSS REQUIREMENTS OF SKU ERG204
PAPR01	0	0	0	0	0	100	0	0	0	0	0	0	0	0	
ERG204	0	0	0	90	0	0	0	60	0	0	0	0	0	0	WARNING: NOT ENOUGH TIME TO MEET ALL GROSS REQUIREMENTS OF SKU ERG205
PAPR25	30	0	0	0	60	0	0	0	0	0	0	0	0	0	
ERG301	20	0	0	0	80	0	0	0	0	0	0	0	0	0	

be scheduled in time to meet the new demand pattern. Such widespread revisions can be quite disruptive to complex systems once production is underway, motivating some organizations to protect the system by freezing the MPS.

Completely freezing an MPS does not necessarily prevent MRP nervousness, however. This nervous behavior can also be triggered by modifying any other input data that the MRP technique uses, such as its current inventory records. If an MRP schedule is based on inaccurate estimates of current inventory, correcting even a single on-hand inventory mistake may touch off nervous corrections throughout the schedule. Thus, through its nervous nature, MRP is also vulnerable to poor-quality data.

Both aggregate planning and MRP emerged from manufacturing, where they are still in active use today. However, neither of these concepts is confined to manufacturing. All organizations must look ahead and determine how best to meet demand forecasts, weighing options when formulating their responses. Whether staffing a hospital, establishing a college course schedule, or readying a fleet for the next busy shipping season, aggregate planning threads through each. Many organizations translate their plans with the logic of MRP to plan the quantity and timing of components required, though few planners outside manufacturing speak of a bill of materials. for example, commercial kitchens routinely translate finished meals back into component ingredients and surgery centers translate scheduled procedures into personnel and materials required. Nonetheless, the need to anticipate component requirements to match the planned, broader goal is a challenge in almost any complex system—and one that is vital to its ultimate success.

SUMMARY

The questions of how much and when to order are cornerstones of inventory management and both aggregate planning and material requirements planning address these decisions. Aggregate planning provides the broader view, requiring selection of an overall strategy for production during a time of changing demand, such as chasing that demand or leveling production despite it. Our focus in strategy selection here has been to minimize cost, typical of an organization making tactical plans. However, any one of a number of other concerns may influence this decision in reality, specific to the organization making the decision. For example, an organization may prefer to build up inventory as a marketing strategy, ensuring an oversupply of some good to prevent newcomers from entering that market, and this will ultimately be reflected in the aggregate plan even if it is not the least costly solution that meets the current demand forecast.

Material requirements planning follows from aggregate planning, creating detailed schedules of ordering for the many items that can be involved in the production of a single finished product. This linking and time-phasing technique is the equivalent of an information system within itself, and many choices in commercial MRP software are readily available. Whether calculated electronically or manually, MRP is nonetheless a highly nervous technique, which makes it vulnerable to inaccurate input data and often causes organizations using MRP to freeze portions of their master production schedules to protect the MRP-scheduled system from multiple disruptive changes when planning. MRP is also an infinite loading procedure, and thus there may not be enough production capacity in reality to carry out its plans in a timely fashion. MRP is nonetheless a useful and adaptable procedure for coordinating dependent demand relationships within production, particularly when a planner interprets it with careful consideration of its weaknesses.

Key Terms

aggregation
aggregate planning
average inventory
backflushing
backward scheduling
beginning inventory
bill of materials
capacity cushion
chase demand strategy
child
dependent demand
disaggregation
dynamic
efficiency
ending inventory
enterprise resource planning (ERP)
finite loading
finished goods
freezing
Gantt chart
gross requirements
heuristic
holding costs
independent demand
infinite loading
lead time
level demand strategy
level production strategy
lot-for-lot (LFL)
minimum constant production (MCP) rate
manufacturing resource planning (MRP II)
master production schedule (MPS)
material requirements planning (MRP)
natural planning horizon
nervous
optimization
parent
planned order receipts
planned order releases
planning horizon
product structure diagram
raw materials
stockpiling
subcontract
time bucket
time fence
utilization
work-in-process (WIP)

Discussion Questions

1. What is more important, aggregate or material requirements planning?
2. Material requirements planning was developed for manufacturing. How might this system be put to work for a service organization?
3. Newer, smaller businesses are more often observed chasing demand than leveling production. Why would these businesses prefer that particular strategy?

4. What is an Achilles' heel and why would a certain assumption about lead times be considered the Achilles' heel of MRP?

PROBLEMS

Minute Answer

Short answers appear in Appendix A. Go to **NoteShaper.com** for full video tutorials on each question.

1. Aggregate planning can also be thought of as what kind of capacity planning?
2. The process of translating an aggregated value into individual estimates corresponding to specific products is referred to as what?
3. What is an aggregate planning approach that relies on adjusting capacity to reflect current demand called?
4. Largely idle capacity maintained beyond the expected load level of a system, often to absorb unexpected demand, is described as what?
5. What type of inventory has a parent and at least one child item?
6. What type of inventory is childless?
7. Finished goods always appear on what level in a product structure diagram?
8. If a product structure diagram has five levels, what is the number of its lowest level?
9. When performing MRP calculations, the planned order releases of an item are incorporated into the gross requirements of any child of that item, multiplied by what?
10. A scheduling approach that recognizes capacity constraints is described as what?
11. What is a strategic information system that integrates all functional areas of an organization called?
12. Are level production strategies associated with lower or higher utilization of resources, compared to other approaches?

Quick Start

13. Consider the following product structure: Each A consists of one B and three Cs. Each B consists of one D, 2 Es, and 5 Fs. Each C consists of one E and one F. How many Es are necessary to produce a single finished good A?
14. Consider the following product structure: Each A consists of one B and three Cs. Each B consists of one D, two Es, and five Fs. Each C consists of one E and one F. How many Fs are necessary to produce a single finished good A?
15. Maynard Associates has 62 units of a certain product on hand currently. The demand forecast for next week is 25 units, and Maynard plans to produce an additional 10 units of the product during that week. What will be the ending inventory of this product next week?
16. Maynard Associates has 62 units of a certain product on hand currently. The demand forecast for next week is 25 units, and Maynard plans to produce an additional 10 units of the product during that week. What will be the average inventory of this product next week?
17. Brightlin has 50 steel wheels in stock and needs 332 to complete an upcoming project. If Brightlin creates its own steel wheels in batches of 25, how many steel wheels should it order from itself to cover the requirements of this project?
18. If a shipment is needed in week 8 and the lead time on its arrival is always 3 weeks, when should the shipment be ordered?
19. If item Y is the parent of Z and item X is the parent of Y, which item is the finished good?
20. Given no starting inventory, cumulative production of 2,000 units at the end of a certain month by which cumulative demand is up to 2,500 units implies what?

Ramp Up

21. Maynard Associates has 62 units of a certain product on hand currently. The demand forecast for the next two planning periods is 25 units each period. Maynard Associates has no plans for production of this product in the first planning period, but does plan to build 120 units of this product in the period after that. How much of this item would be in stock at the end of period 1?
22. Maynard Associates has 62 units of a certain product on hand currently. The demand forecast for the next two planning periods is 25 units each period. Maynard Associates has no plans for production of this product in the first planning period, but does plan to build 120 units of this product in the period after that. How much of this item would be in stock at the end of period 2?
23. Maynard Associates has 62 units of a certain product on hand currently. The demand forecast for the next two planning periods is 25 units each period. Maynard Associates has no plans for production of this product in the first planning period, but does plan to build 120 units of this product in the period after that. What is the average inventory level during period 1?
24. A finished good A consists of two child items, one B and one C. Lead time on each of these three items is 1 week, and 10 of each of these three items are available in inventory currently, available for use. How much of each item should be ordered and when should it be ordered, so that 50 A's might be finished in 3 weeks?
25. Customer demand for some finished good is forecast at 1,000 units for January, 2,000 units for February, and 3,000 units for March. If the company that produces this finished good has nothing in inventory at the beginning of January, how much should it plan to produce during the month of March, if it wants to follow a level production schedule that leaves it with nothing in inventory at the end of March?
26. The XYZ Firm has 56 units of SKU001 available in inventory right now. The forecast of demand for SKU001 is 20 units per week for the next 4 weeks. If XYZ Firm plans to produce 100 units of SKU001 this week, how much of SKU001 will be left in inventory at XYZ Firm by the end of this week?
27. A warehouse began the month of October with 300 tons of goods, but its inventory had fallen to 100 tons at the beginning of November, before increasing again to 200 tons at the beginning of December. What was the percent change in average inventory between October and November?

Reminder: Short answers appear in Appendix A. Go to **NoteShaper.com** for full video tutorials on each question.

Scenarios

28. Brightland Tech must develop an aggregate plan to meet the following 5 months of demand:

Month	1	2	3	4	5
Demand (Units)	200	50	200	200	150

Brightland has 50 units in inventory at this time, and the company intends to produce 150 units a month for the next 5 months, following a perfectly level aggregate plan.

a. Based on the Brightland Associates plan, what would the ending inventory be at the end of month 4?

b. Based on the Brightland Associates plan, what would the average inventory be during month 2?

c. What are the total inventory holding costs over these 5 months of the Brightland Associates plan, given that it costs $0.50 to hold one unit in inventory for 1 month?

29. The manufacturing company Highlands Archery has forecast the demand for the Grizzly compound bow for the next 4 months. The production manager at Highlands Archery has already created an aggregate production plan, based on that information:

	Month 1	Month 2	Month 3	Month 4
Demand	10,000 bows	5,000 bows	30,000 bows	50,000 bows
Managers production plan	Produce 25,000 bows	Produce 25,000 bows	Produce 25,000 bows	Produce 25,000 bows

a. If Highlands Archery uses the manager's production plan, how many bows would be in inventory at the end of the fourth month?

b. Following this plan, which month has the highest average inventory?

c. If Highlands Archery pays $1 per bow to keep a bow in inventory, what is the total inventory cost of the manager's plan?

30. Livingston Fabrication has created the following aggregate plan for the next 5 months:

	August	September	October	November	December
Forecasted demand (units of finished goods)	1,000,000	1,000,000	2,000,000	4,000,000	1,000,000
Production plan	2,000,000	2,000,000	2,000,000	2,000,000	2,000,000

Assume that Livingston will have nothing in inventory at the end of July. Livingston employs 500 production assembly workers and it takes one production assembly worker 3 minutes to assemble one unit of finished good. (The unit is complete at that point.) Each production assembly worker can provide 160 hours of assembly time a month without requiring overtime pay.

a. Livingston wants to complete this plan without working any overtime in assembly. How many additional production assembly workers does Livingston need to hire to accomplish this? When should they be hired?

b. Using this production plan, how many units will be in inventory at the end of October?

c. What will the average inventory level be each month?

31. General Food Stuffs packages a variety of breakfast cereals and snack bars, which it aggregates as simply units of sale when doing medium-term planning. General Food Stuffs has created the following aggregate plan for the next 6 months:

	Month 1	Month 2	Month 3	Month 4	Month 5	Month 6
Forecast (units of sale)	25,000	35,000	15,000	5,000	5,000	20,000
Overall production	35,000	40,000	0	10,000	0	20,000
Ending inventory						
Regular time production						
Overtime production						

General Food Stuffs can produce up to 30,000 units of sale a month in regular time, when production costs are only $1.50 per unit of sale. When General Food Stuffs plans to exceed 30,000 units of sale produced in a single month, all units of sale in excess of 30,000 must be produced in overtime production at a cost of $2.50 per unit of sale. General Food Stuffs actually has 5,000 units of sale available in inventory at the start of month 1, and it will cost $0.50 to hold one unit of sale for 1 month.

a. What is the ending inventory for month 3 in this plan?
b. What is the *average* inventory for month 5 in this plan?
c. Logically, what is the total amount that General Food Stuffs plans to produce in overtime production in this plan?
d. Assuming that General Food Stuffs calculates inventory holding costs based on ending inventory levels, what is the total cost of this plan?

32. Williston Technologies wishes to use MRP methodology to develop a plan for the next 9 weeks. Williston Technologies has gathered the following information:

Bill of materials

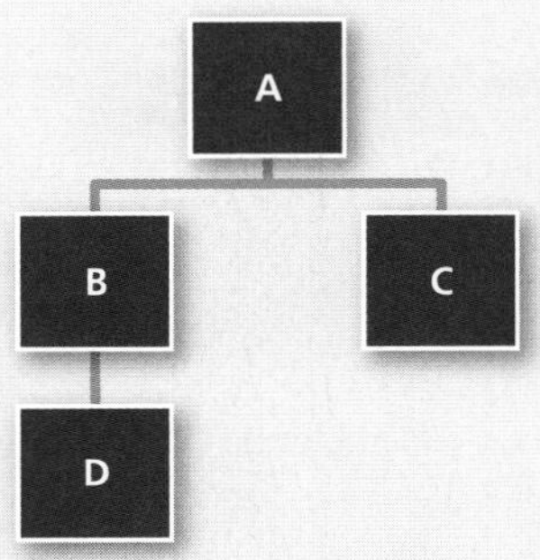

Current Inventory Records

Part	Lead Time (Weeks)	Lot Size	Inventory Currently on Hand
A	1	LFL	100
B	2	50	150
C	2	25	50
D	3	LFL	150

Master Production Schedule

	Weeks								
Part	1	2	3	4	5	6	7	8	9
A	50	0	50	200	0	0	100	0	100

a. Using MRP methodology, how much of parts A, B, C, and D should be ordered, and when should they be ordered?
b. Based on the material requirements plan developed for Williston Technologies, how much of parts A, B, C, and D will remain in inventory at the end of week 9?
c. Williston Technologies has just learned that the order for 200 As appearing in week 4 has been cancelled. How does this change the material requirements plan?

33. Dumfries Industries is generating a materials requirement plan for the next 6 weeks. Here is its most current information:

Master Production Schedule

Week:	1	2	3	4	5	6
Item A	10	0	20	20	10	10

Other Information

Item	Item's Parent	Item's Lead Time	Item's Lot Size	Item's Current On-Hand Inventory
A	None	1 week	LFL	20
B	A	1 week	20	20
C	B	1 week	50	20

a. How many levels does a product structure for Dumfries' item A have?

b. Using MRP methodology, how much of parts A, B, and C should be ordered, and when should they be ordered?

c. Which item will experience the highest ending inventory, following this plan?

34. Consider the following product structure diagram, representing a bill of materials required to assemble some finished good A:

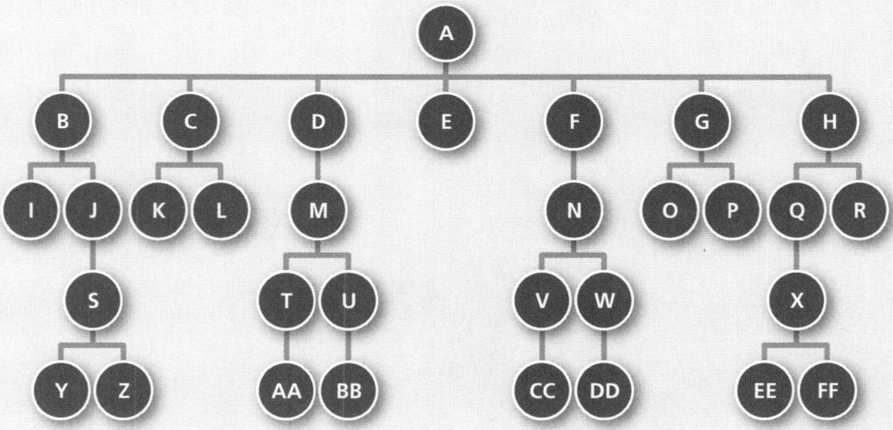

(Items A through FF have been sketched as circles for convenience, but represent the same information as a product structure diagram sketched with squares, or any other shapes.) Please answer the following questions, based on this information.

a. Who is the parent of item N?

b. Who are the children of item B?

c. List all raw material items.

d. Item S belongs to what level?

e. Suppose you have absolutely no inventory on hand, but you want to assemble one unit of finished good A. The lead time associated with each and every item pictured in the product structure is exactly 1 week. How long would it take you to complete the one unit of A?

CASE STUDY: MYER WINE RACKING AND CELLAR COMPANY, REVISITED

Recall from Chapter 6 that Myer Wine Racking and Cellar Company is a small but growing carpentry job shop specializing in natural-finish redwood racking systems for storage and display of wine bottles. In addition to building customized wine cellars, Myer offers two sizes of standard box rack set, or preassembled wine racks roughly the size of book cases. Box rack sets hold wine bottles in precise 20-bottle high columns, with the smaller box rack set storing 10 columns for a total capacity of 200 bottles, while the larger set stores 20 columns. These products are popular purchases for retail stores and restaurants, and are marketed through catalogs and websites as beginner's kits for private wine collections. Myer Wine Racking refers to the two sizes as BOX2010 for the smaller and BOX2020 for the larger set, assembling them both as described in the illustration below:

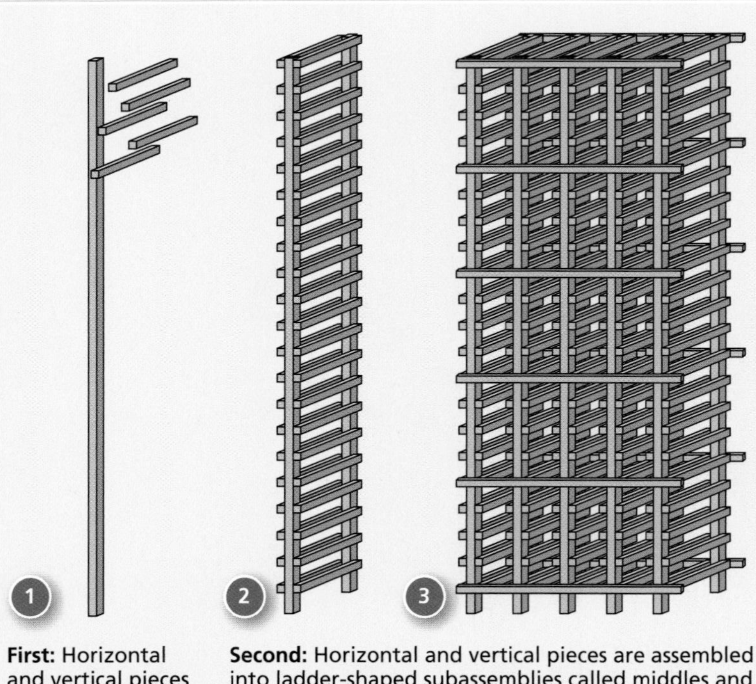
1
First: Horizontal and vertical pieces are cut to precise lengths.
2
Second: Horizontal and vertical pieces are assembled into ladder-shaped subassemblies called middles and ends.
Each middle requires 2 vertical pieces and 42 horizontal pieces. Each end also requires 2 vertical pieces but only 21 horizontal pieces, because ends only have horizontal pieces on one side.
3
Third: The freestanding box rack set is created by attaching 6 horizontal trim pieces across the front edges of a set of middles and ends, and another 6 horizontal trim pieces across the back edges of those same subassemblies.
The number of middles and the length of the horizontal trim determine the size of the box rack set. Each BOX2010 consists of 9 middles and 2 ends, while each BOX2020 consists of 19 middles and 2 ends. This illustration shows four complete columns.

Myer has just received an order for this popular product line from one of its retail distributors, who is requesting that 10 units of BOX2010 and 10 units of BOX2020 be shipped out as soon as possible. This order arrives at an awkward time, in that the employees in Myer's job shop are busy working on a large custom wine cellar and none of the pieces or subassemblies that might speed the assembly of a BOX2010 or BOX2020 are currently in stock. Nonetheless, this retail distributor has been a valuable supply chain partner in the past, so Myer Wine Racking would like to fill this unexpected order for BOX2010 and BOX2020 as quickly as possible. Lead time on any item varies with how many of the item is needed, as Myer produces all items within its job shop:

Bill of Materials Data for Box Set

SKU	Description	Parent SKU	Lead Time/Production Rate
BOX2010	20 high × 10 column wide box rack set	None	5 sets per labor-hour
BOX2020	20 high × 20 column wide box rack set	None	5 sets per labor-hour
RACK20M	20 high middles	BOX2010, BOX2020	10 middles per labor-hour
RACK20E	20 high ends	BOX2010, BOX2020	20 ends per labor-hour
PART20V	20 high vertical pieces	RACK20M, RACK20E	160 pieces per labor-hour
PART1H	Horizontal rack piece	RACK20M, RACK20E	600 pieces per labor-hour
PART10T	10 wide horizontal trim pieces	BOX 2010	60 pieces per labor-hour
PART20T	20 wide horizontal trim pieces	BOX 2020	60 pieces per labor-hour

Questions

1. Draw standard product structure diagrams for the two finished goods discussed here, BOX2010 and BOX2020. Be certain to note the correct parent-to-child ratio required between each of the items in the diagram.
2. Draw time-phased product structure diagrams for a single BOX2010 and a single BOX2020, using the production rate information to estimate lead times for each item in the structure. Under the assumption of material requirements planning that work on a parent item cannot begin until all work on all child items is finished, how long does your diagram suggest Myer needs to produce one BOX2010 from nothing in stock? How long to produce one BOX2020?
3. How many labor-hours will be required in total to fill the retail distributor's order?
4. Myer Wine Racking and Cellar Company is willing to reassign three employees to build this order, which it wishes to ship within three 8-hour days. Work out a schedule for these three employees to accomplish this goal, outlining the timing of the production of all the items in the bill of materials. State any assumptions you make concerning how the Myer job shop works.

BIBLIOGRAPHY

Blackstone, J. ed. 2010. *APICS Dictionary*, 13th ed. Chicago: APICS, The Association for Operations Management.

Hopp, W. J., and M. L. Spearman. 1996. *Factory Physics: Foundations of Manufacturing Management*. Burr Ridge, IL: McGraw-Hill/Irwin.

Miller, J., and L. Sprague. 1975. "Behind the Growth in Materials Requirements Planning." *Harvard Business Review*, September: 83–91.

Silver, E., D. Pyke, and R. Peterson. 1998. *Inventory Management and Production Planning and Scheduling*, 3rd ed. New York: Wiley & Sons.

Thurston, P. 1972. "Requirements Planning for Inventory Control." *Harvard Business Review*, May/June: 67–71.

Vollmann, T. E., W. L. Berry, D. C. Whybark, and F. B. Jacobs. 2005. *Manufacturing Planning & Control Systems for Supply Chain Management*, 5th ed. Chicago: McGraw-Hill.

CHAPTER 12

Lean Operations

Intellectuals solve problems, geniuses prevent them.
—Albert Einstein

MAJOR SECTIONS

IN THIS CHAPTER, LOOK FOR...

- Just-in-time inventory management and its development from older forms of inventory control.
- The distinction between push and pull systems and implicit versus explicit planning.
- The mechanics of a lean system, including the use of kanban loops to control inventory levels.
- Elimination of waste and focus of flexibility, visibility, and continuous improvement.

INTRODUCTION

An operation is said to be lean if it is operating with minimal waste of any kind. At first, it might seem ironic that an organization would strive for anything else, but the mechanical principles and the underlying philosophy of lean operation are relatively young, beginning with Toyota Motor Company's innovative transformation of production control and inventory management starting in the 1950s. Lean operations are now practiced worldwide by many types of organizations.

EVOLUTION OF INVENTORY SYSTEMS

lean
Operating without waste.

inventory
Tangible items awaiting sale or use.

Lean operations can be thought of as the latest chapter in an evolving understanding of inventory management, building upon reorder point and material requirements planning systems. Figure 12.1 summarizes this progression.

Reorder Point Systems

reorder point
An inventory level that triggers replenishment of an item.

pull system
A production system that reacts to signals of demand, relying on internal coordination instead of the implementation of explicit plans to achieve outcomes.

Reorder point systems control production activity by monitoring inventory levels, reacting when the stock available drops to a certain minimum level, known as a reorder point. It is not known precisely how old reorder point systems are, but some of the oldest examples of written language are 5,000-year-old Egyptian and Sumerian inventory records. Further, published descriptions and analysis of reorder point systems have been available for more than a century.

Traditional reorder point systems are examples of implicit and signal-based planning, meaning that their operation requires only that participants understand the minimum levels to watch for; there are no further specific instructions concerning when to take that action. A traditional reorder point operation is also known as a pull system, because it allows demand to consume existing inventory and then reacts to the lower stock level by ordering replacements, pulling new inventory into the system.

FIGURE 12.1 Historical Development of Inventory Management

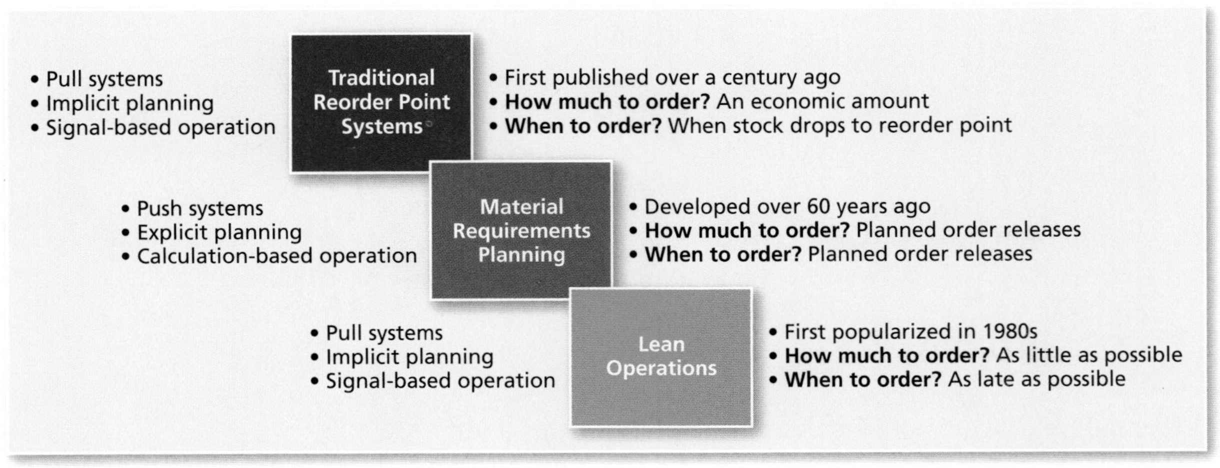

Material Requirements Planning

Material requirements planning, or MRP, emerged in the 1970s as an alternative to pull-style inventory management. MRP combines information on product structure and current inventory levels with forecasts of future demand, calculating precise amounts and exact timings for orders of raw materials, components, subassemblies, and finished goods. These explicit plans for all items in production are called planned order releases, providing detailed answers to the questions of how much and when any certain item should be ordered.

material requirements planning (MRP) A technique for scheduling the production of multiple items related by both independent and dependent demand.

planned order releases A schedule of the ordering of a particular item to meet its requirements over a specific time interval.

While the older reorder point systems are considered pull systems, MRP-based systems are often referred to as push systems. MRP relies on central planning to calculate and distribute instructions to everyone involved in production. In that sense, the production system is "pushed" to act by the central planner, instead of being triggered to act by dropping inventory levels. Moreover, in a multistage environment, when an order for any item is finished, it is then moved or "pushed" to the area where it will be processed next. In the more passive reorder point system, orders simply wait wherever they appear, to be retrieved by users as needed.

push system A production system that calculates and anticipates demand, relying on the implementation of explicit plans instead of internal coordination to achieve outcomes.

The complex, layered, and logical calculations of the MRP technique can be traced back to the 1940s, but MRP systems did not become popular until computer and information technology allowed companies to conveniently generate planned order releases with MRP software. A traditional reorder point approach requires its participants to scan their environment for signals to act, whereas participants in MRP usually consult a computer for direction. The older system's reliance on heads-up system visibility and MRP's transformation of this into heads-down software-based activity may have partially set the stage for the changes that would later become known as JIT and then lean operation.

Lean Operations/JIT

Toyota Motor Corporation faced daunting financial, technological, and competitive pressures during the 1950s. This organization and this era are now widely recognized as the genesis of what would become the youngest of the production systems illustrated in Figure 12.1. To address its early difficulties, Toyota sought to make the absolute most efficient use of its resources, eliminating any unnecessary inventory or activity within its production system. Ideally, any operation would only produce exactly what was needed exactly when it was needed; it would produce one at a time, only when requested and only when nothing was otherwise available in stock. The Toyota Production System that evolved over the next three decades gained global attention under the more general name of just-in-time or JIT in the 1980s. While this approach to production was always lean, the terms *lean* and *lean production* followed afterward.

just-in-time (JIT) An earlier and alternate term for *lean operation*, in which a system implicitly operates with minimum of inventory and waste.

Toyota's vision of lean resisted the separation of planning from production that had grown with the popularity of MRP systems. Contrary to the heavy emphasis on explicit, push-style schedules, lean production emphasizes implicit signaling to trigger production only when needed. This approach is not only another form of pull system, it can be argued to be a return to the traditional reorder point approach illustrated at the top of Figure 12.1. Although a JIT/lean system is, by definition, a form of reorder point system, it is a very particular reorder point system in which the reorder point has deliberately been set to zero or near-zero. How Toyota created a production system whose success is based on the fact that it only reacts when it is on the verge of running out is explained by both the mechanics of the system and the philosophy that governs it.

MECHANICS OF LEAN SYSTEMS

Being the youngest of the production systems, lean operations are often formed from some older system, similar to how lean production resulted from Toyota's self-study over a half century ago. Creation of a lean production system, whether original or transformed, requires an understanding of the internal mechanics of a pull-style operation. Specifically, to implement lean production, organizations must adopt the following mechanical principles:

- Plan smaller lot sizes to support lower inventory levels.
- Employ effective signaling to support implicit planning.
- Smooth production to support efficient operation.

Each of these principles brings its own set of related issues into the system, so we will discuss each in detail.

Reducing Lot Sizes

Little's law
The average number of some item in a system equals its average arrival rate multiplied by the average time each unit spends in the system.

A lean system acquires as little as possible and only when necessary. The ideal lean order size is one unit, being the theoretically smallest possible amount of anything that can be acquired. This very particular focus is explained by a mathematical rule-of-thumb known as Little's law, an observation that the overall amount of some item in a system is the result of its average arrival rate (pulled in by demand) multiplied by its average wait in the system. Any item ordered in extremely small amounts will not wait long before use, and thus the overall average inventory level of that item will be quite lean.

However, ordering and delivering some item one by one is seldom practical in reality, and keeping lot sizes at a practical minimum should not be pursued without having investigated two related issues: potential reduction of any fixed costs associated with ordering and preparation for the frequent deliveries that will result from smaller lot sizes.

economies of scale
Decreasing average unit cost by increasing volume.

Reducing Fixed Costs A more traditional approach to ordering focuses on identification of an economic order size, regardless of whether this amount is large or small. This perspective seeks economies of scale, increasing an order size if this reduces the overall cost of the inventory policy. Given that inventory costs consist of S, a fixed cost associated with any order, and H, an annual per unit holding cost, Figure 12.2 displays the landmark formula that answers the question of how much to order, given that D units are needed throughout the year.

Note that the lot size recommended by the traditional economic order quantity formula may be a large or a small amount, depending on the relative values of the inputs S, D, and H. At first glance, it might appear that this recommendation conflicts with lean operation, because lean insists that order sizes simply be as small as possible. However, lean operation also requires that any fixed costs associated with ordering likewise be reduced as much as possible. This attention to fixed costs, S, makes lean operation consistent with the earlier inventory model. Reducing the value of S in the numerator of the economic order quantity naturally reduces the amount recommended for ordering.

FIGURE 12.2 The Link Between Traditional and Lean Order Size Philosophies

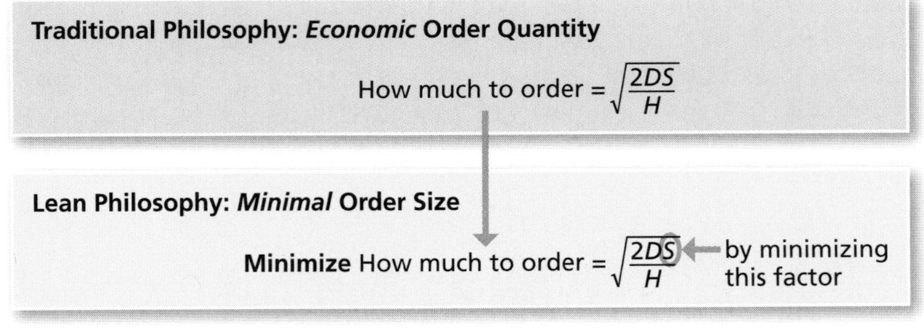

Traditional Philosophy: *Economic* Order Quantity
How much to order = $\sqrt{\frac{2DS}{H}}$
Lean Philosophy: *Minimal* Order Size
Minimize How much to order = $\sqrt{\frac{2DS}{H}}$
by minimizing this factor

Efforts to reduce fixed costs associated with ordering and replenishment can take on many forms, depending on the situation. These common improvements reduce the value of *S*:

- Eliminating the paperwork traditionally associated with ordering and receiving through electronic data interchange (EDI) with suppliers.
- Streamlining order stocking, retrieval, and handling through bar coding and radio frequency identification (RFID) tagging of inventory.
- Investing in the process of machine setup, to make frequent changeovers quicker and more efficient.

RFID and EDI technology are good examples of tools that have emerged after the economic order quantity formula was first published in 1913, supporting the natural evolution of lean operation.

electronic data interchange (EDI) The linking of two information systems from two different organizations to transfer data and conduct transactions.

radio frequency identification (RFID) The tagging of objects with devices that may be detected and interrogated for information by remote electronic readers, allowing identification and tracking without contact.

Enabling Frequent Deliveries If order sizes from suppliers are reduced to minimal amounts, then delivery of new orders from suppliers becomes more frequent. To function well, a lean system must accommodate these frequent deliveries and should consider making the following changes as well:

- **Eliminate the warehouse.** Many organizations maintain a warehouse to receive and store large shipments of raw materials and supplies. If such an organization plans to go lean, it might consider eliminating this facility and arranging for the smaller deliveries to be made straight to the production facility itself.
- **Deliver directly to the user.** A small order for replenishment should ideally be delivered to where it is needed, instead of to an official reception area, to be retrieved after its arrival. The smaller and more frequent the ordering, the more time the user spends retrieving these orders from an older-style reception area, and thus the user would have less and less time for production.
- **Reduce lead times.** Cultivating relationships with local suppliers and/or seeking more efficient means of small order transportation and handling can greatly reduce lead times.

lead time Delay between requesting a product and receiving it.

Frequent delivery of small orders directly to users within a large facility can create complex traffic patterns unknown to an older-style operation. One elegant solution for enabling the frequent delivery supporting work along a production line is illustrated in Figure 12.3. Here, the U-shaped cellular layout replaces the traditional linear layout of the

The Presence of High Fixed Costs

Some industrial processes have high fixed costs even with the use of the most advanced technology, so larger batch sizes still prevail in these settings. Cheese is an example of a product that can be produced in very small amounts, but it simply is not economical to do so. Thus, when a commercial production facility creates a product such as the premium mozzarella in this picture, it typically prepares a sizable batch, even if the plant is otherwise practicing lean operation.

FIGURE 12.3 Advantage of Cellular Layout with Frequent Delivery of Supplies

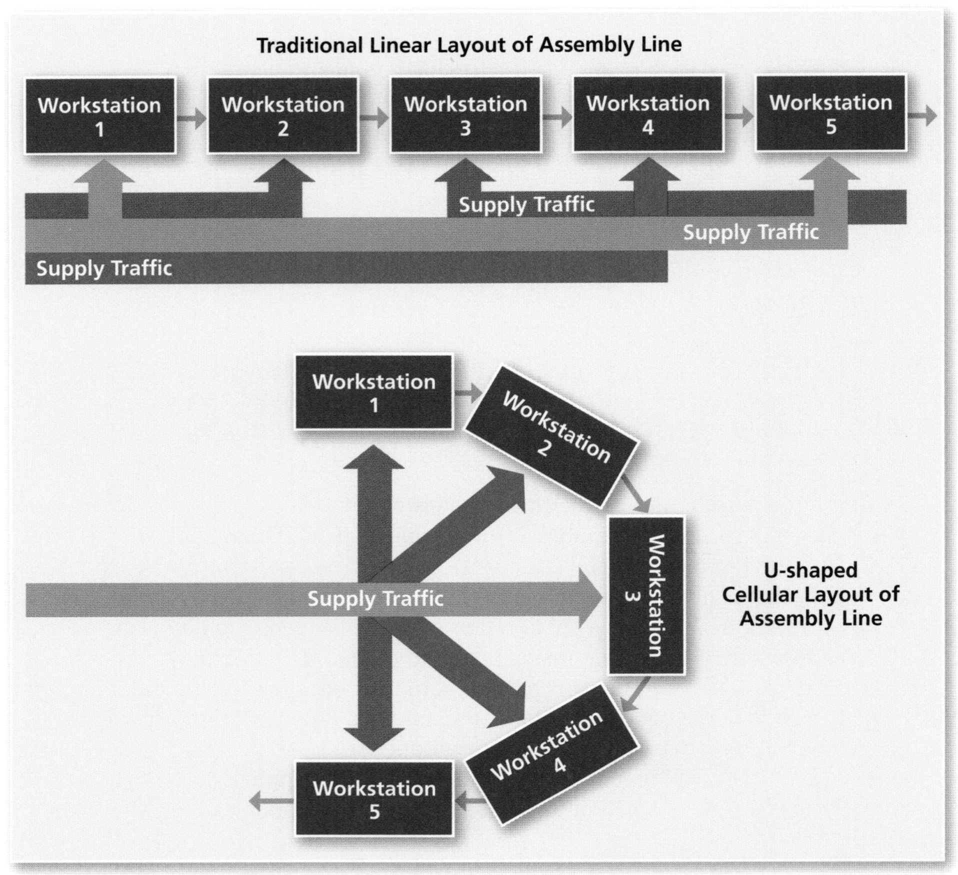

same production system. This revision allows the supplies required by each workstation to be delivered to a single central point, eliminating the need for delivery traffic to move back and forth across the length of a traditional layout. A cellular layout has a variety of advantages, but one benefit attractive to lean operation is its ability to shape supply traffic patterns such that they are less likely to interfere with themselves and with the operation of the line.

Signaling Replenishment

Since a lean system represents a return to implicit planning without strong centralized coordination and control, this system relies on internal signals to function properly. Signaling the need for replenishment of some item is critical not only because no central planner is responsible for replenishment, but also because a lean system, by its very nature, can be expected to keep only the smallest amounts of the item in stock. In practice, signaling replenishment can be accomplished several ways, and which methodology is best often depends on the complexity of the pull-style environment. In small, rapidly moving systems such as commercial kitchens, verbal signals among workers may be sufficient to coordinate these needs. Beyond this, however, an organization should consider tools that can be used to signal replenishment once verbal signaling becomes less reliable. This is often the case in factory settings, where verbal signals to trigger

Bakery Bin-Based Signaling Systems

Although the industrial principles of lean operation were first popularized by automotive manufacturers, small firms with perishable goods have long used similar techniques to operate with a minimum of stock. As an example, bakeries often use bin-based signaling systems to control replenishment, such as the one pictured here. When one bin of time-sensitive product is emptied by demand, this signals the bakery to create another small batch.

replenishment would be impractical because workers are not all confined to one room, noise levels are too high for spoken words, and the number of differing items that might be needed is too long to rely on spoken words and human memory to express and track.

Bin-based Systems One simple but powerful technique for signaling replenishment is a bin-based system. Here an organization dedicates bins and storage areas to individual items. For each item, the signal for replenishment is simple: more is needed if the bin is empty. These bins can be labeled storage containers or labeled shelf space in a storage area. In the case of very large items or large containers of items, footprints can be painted on the floor to outline where the item should rest while waiting in inventory. If a worker sees an empty bin, empty shelf space, or an empty footprint on the floor, the worker then takes action to fill it again with that item. Exactly how much of that item is sitting idle in inventory is loosely determined by the organization, by deciding how much bin capacity to label on behalf of that item.

Kanban Systems Reacting to an empty bin by refilling it is a good signaling system, provided the person or people who can refill the bin can also watch it while production is underway. However, if the inventory is not stored in the same area where it is created, or stored across several locations for easy access by multiple users, the builders of that inventory will not be able to monitor the state of all bins effectively. This problem is typical of any large production plant, and one that is readily solved with another tool for signaling: the kanban. A kanban is usually some type of card, highly visible, transportable, and readily recognizable by everyone involved in production. Each kanban is understood to be a signal that a bin of inventory is being consumed, and thus another needs to be filled to replace it. Figure 12.4 illustrates a typical kanban system, signaling replenishment of some item that is being consumed at some other, distant work center.

kanban
In operations, a Japanese term for a signal, often a card. Kanban systems use these signals to regulate production.

When a kanban is found by the producing work center to the left of Figure 12.4, it is attached to an empty bin and that bin is then filled with the inventory specified by the kanban. This brightly colored work ticket then remains attached to the bin as it is transferred to some inventory storage area. When the bin is later removed from storage by a consuming work center, its kanban is detached and immediately returned to the producing work center, to signal the need to create another bin of inventory. If the producing work center cannot locate any cards returned without their bins, then the producing work center remains deliberately idle, as this is the signal that the system does not require any

FIGURE 12.4 Single Card Kanban System

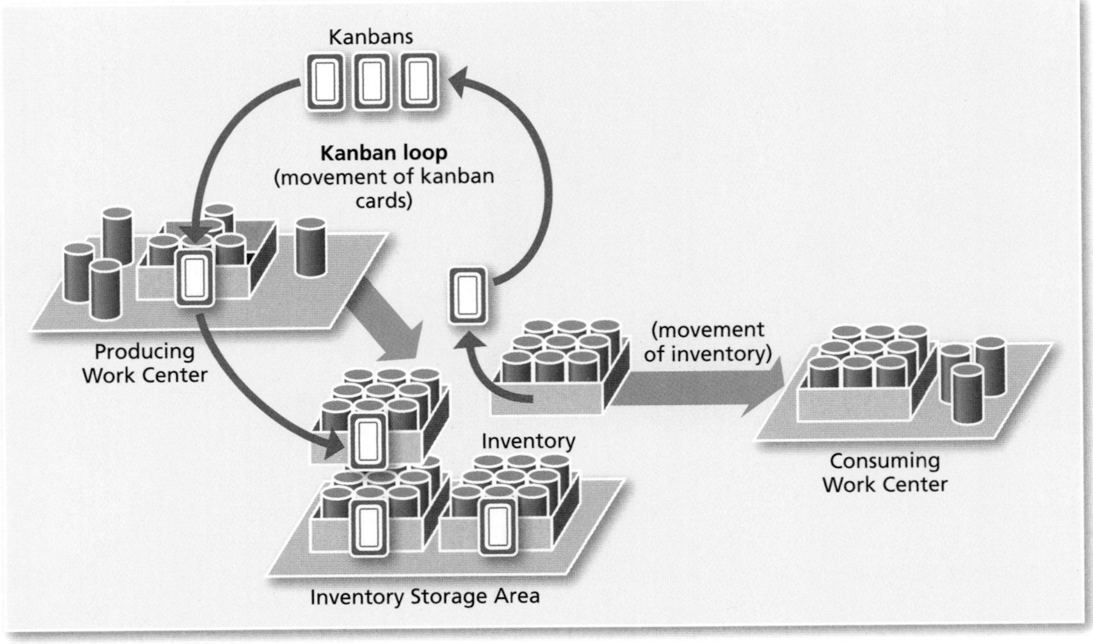

new inventory. Thus, while inventory is moving from left to right between the producing and the consuming work centers in Figure 12.4, the kanbans are not following that same path. Rather, the kanbans are circulating in their kanban loop, traveling from the producing work center to the inventory storage area and returning repeatedly for reuse each time inventory is claimed for consumption.

kanban loop
The continuous path of travel of a set of kanbans, governing the production or consumption of some inventory item.

A kanban system does not explicitly plan production, but it offers a means to explicitly plan inventory levels, by manipulating the number of kanbans circulating in the loop. Figure 12.5 illustrates the range of choices when designing a kanban loop, beginning with a single card circulating between the producing work center and the inventory area and ranging upward with no technical limit.

Issuing few kanbans into a loop obligates the system to run lean, allowing only a minimal amount of inventory to be pulled into existence at any time. However, too few cards may drop the inventory level too low to operate effectively, in that the producing work center may not be able to refill bins fast enough to prevent a delay if multiple users

FIGURE 12.5 Selecting the Number of Kanbans to Circulate in a Kanban Loop

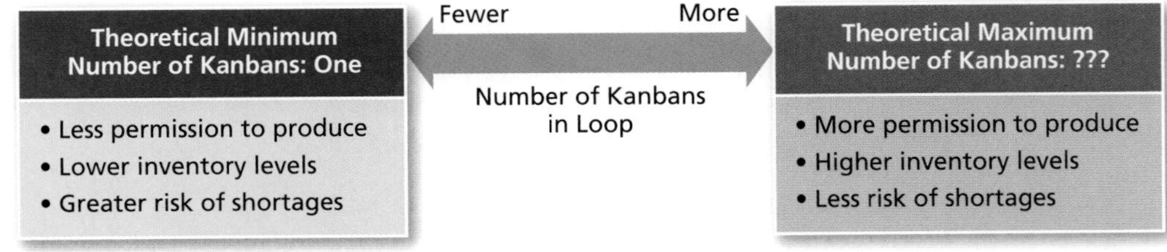

need that inventory item. Adding more cards, however, increases the inventory burden on the system, and risks the wasteful creation of unnecessary inventory.

Designing a Signaling System Figure 12.4 illustrates a single card kanban system, but the word "single" does not refer to the number of kanban cards in the loop. Rather, a single card kanban system refers to only one loop in which kanbans circulate, limiting the overall level of inventory in the system. In establishing lean production, Toyota Motor Company developed a formula to determine the optimal number of kanbans that should be circulating in such a loop. To use this formula, four pieces of data must be collected:

single card kanban A kanban control arrangement consisting of a single kanban loop, controlling production and limiting inventory levels of some item.

- D, the demand rate for the item. This would be the equivalent of how fast the consuming work center in Figure 12.4 is using the items pictured.
- L, the lead time of a single container of inventory. This would be the delay between a signal for replenishment at the producing work center and the successful filling of a container to answer that signal.
- C, the capacity of a single container.
- X, a policy variable or safety factor supplied by management. This factor is not visible in Figure 12.4, expected to be a value between 0 and 1, and thus often expressed as a percent.

Toyota's formula for N, the optimal number of kanban cards to circulate in the loop, is

$$N = \frac{DL(1 + X)}{C}$$

We use this formula in Scenario 1.

Determining the Number of Kanban Cards

Scenario 1

The welding shop of Dumfries Fabrication supports that organization's production of industrial equipment by cutting thick sheets of steel into small square blanks used by other work centers. Since steel blanks are used continuously, Dumfries Fabrication has decided to create a kanban loop to control this item, eliminating the need to specifically schedule steel blank production in the future. Finished steel blanks have always been stored and transported in metal baskets that hold 40 blanks each. Dumfries Fabrication will implement the kanban system by adding bright orange detachable tags to the baskets, to act as kanbans. Everyone who uses these blanks now understands that they should detach this bright orange tag and return it to the welding shop every time they retrieve a basket of blanks from storage. Everyone in the welding shop understands that they should never fill a basket with new blanks unless they have a bright orange tag to attach to that basket. What is not certain, however, is how many bright orange tags should be circulating in this loop between the welding shop and the storage area. The combined use of steel blanks throughout Dumfries Fabrication averages 160 per 8-hour day. Dumfries would also prefer a 10% safety factor be included in the kanban loop, to buffer against small uncertainties concerning steel blank usage. The welding shop needs 7 hours to fill one metal basket with blanks, including the time necessary for the blanks to cool enough for safe handling by users.

How many bright orange tags should Dumfries manufacturing release into the kanban loop?

Continues

Analysis

We can answer this question directly by applying Toyota's formula. First, we gather the input parameters to plug into that formula.

INPUT PARAMETERS FOR KANBAN FORMULA

$C = 40$ blanks (container size) $D = 160$ per 8-hour day (demand)
$X = 0.1$ ("safety factor") $L = 7$ hours

Before using the kanban formula, however, the input data requires a small but important adjustment. Toyota's formula assumes that the demand rate *D* and the lead time *L* are stated in the same time units. The current values for *D* and *L* here are referring to different units of time: *D* refers to an 8-hour day and *L* simply to hours. The easiest solution is to adjust the value of *D* to match *L*:

$$D = 160 \text{ per 8-hour day} = 160/8 = 20 \text{ per hour}$$

Now all the parameters for the formula are ready:

KANBAN CALCULATIONS

$$N = (D \times L \times (1 + X))/C = (20 \times 7 \times 1.1)/40 = 3.85 \text{ kanbans}$$

Insight The numerical result of 3.85 kanbans isn't useful to Dumfries Fabrication, because Dumfries cannot literally release 3.85 bright orange tags into circulation. Rather, the results of the kanban analysis suggest Dumfries should release either 3 or 4 bright orange tags into the kanban loop governing the production of steel blanks. Three tags will minimize the inventory of idle blanks, but may prove too lean to protect production elsewhere from delays due to the unavailability of blanks. Four tags are safer in that respect, although slightly higher inventory levels result. ■

Design of the signaling system as discussed so far has assumed that only production needs to be controlled by the signaling mechanism, such as the production of steel blanks in Scenario 1. However, in complex production environments, the system designer may also wish to control the consumption of the item, particularly when multiple work centers or parties may have reason to withdraw that item from the storage area, and these groups do not otherwise coordinate with each other. In this environment, a second loop may be established, creating the dual card kanban system pictured in Figure 12.6.

dual card kanban A kanban control arrangement consisting of two kanban loops. The first kanban loop signals and limits production of an item, while the second loop signals and limits withdrawals for consumption of the item.

In the simpler single card system pictured in Figure 12.4, a person withdrawing a container from the inventory storage area needs only to detach the kanban on the container and return it to a designated place, where the producing work center will retrieve it as a signal to produce another container. In the dual card arrangement, this person must swap that production kanban with a consumption kanban that essentially claims the container as its own. This card can then be detached only when the container is empty, the inventory inside having been completely used by the consuming work center. Since the consuming work center can only withdraw as many containers as it has consumption kanbans to claim them, withdrawals for consumption are effectively controlled by the number of consumption cards circulating in the second loop.

Smoothing Production

The third mechanical principle in successful lean operation is the smoothing of finished goods production, enabling a rapid, even flow of inventory throughout a system. This issue of smoothing has two different forms, the first being the general leveling of the production schedule and the second being mixed model scheduling.

Dual Card Kanban System

FIGURE 12.6

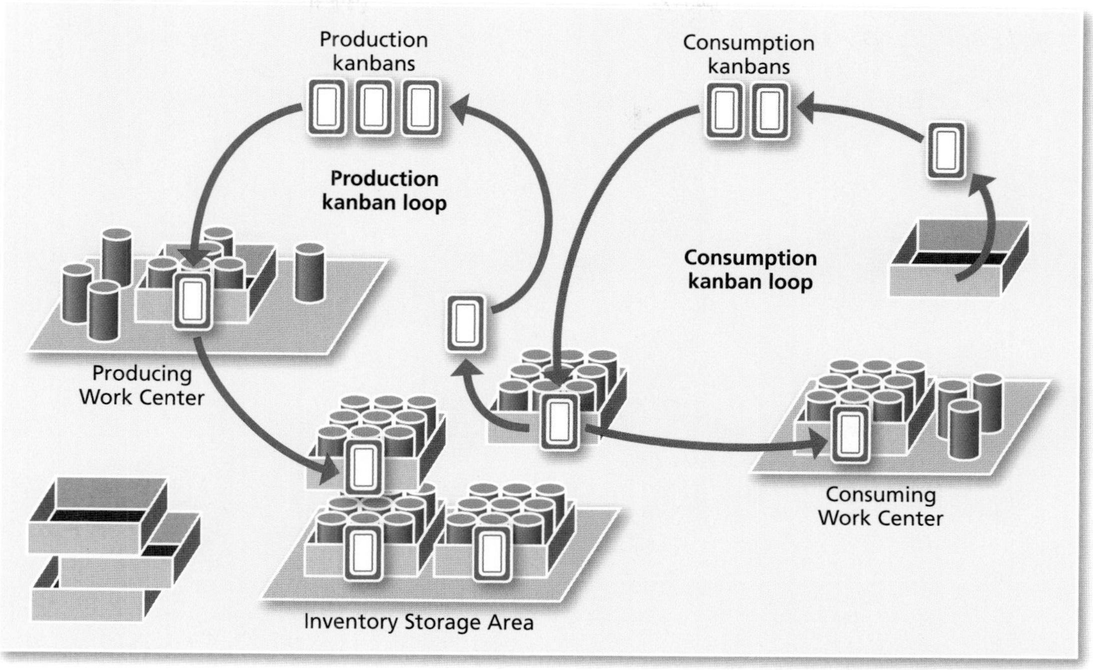

Level Scheduling Lean production works best when used in conjunction with a level production strategy, producing finished goods at a steady rate across time. This allows kanban loops to operate with minimal disruption and maximum efficiency, enabling rapid conversion of low levels of input materials into a steady stream of finished goods. This may seem counterintuitive, because the theory behind pull systems is that nothing is produced until the customer requests it, yet a level production schedule deliberately freezes the production rate, even if customer demand for the product fluctuates. This contradiction is resolved by acknowledging that the pull-style mechanics within lean production are focused primarily on keeping raw materials and work-in-process inventory, but not *necessarily* finished goods, to minimal levels. When customer demand fluctuates, such as the annual cycling of some seasonal product, lean operations may prefer to absorb that fluctuation by stockpiling finished goods inventory during the low-demand periods, to be stored until sale during peak demand periods. This allows the lean operation to follow a level production schedule throughout the cycling of finished goods demand.

level production strategy Aggregate planning approach that relies on fixed capacity despite changing demand.

work in process (WIP) Inventory resulting from transformation of raw materials, but not yet ready for sale to consumers.

stockpiling Producing or securing goods in advance of demand.

Mixed-Model Scheduling Rarely does a production system produce only one distinct type of product. Even mass manufacturing, the setting for some of the most significant accomplishments in lean operation, usually involves production of several different models of a finished good. Traditionally, these differing models were produced in economically sized batches, also known as run sizes. If, for example, a manufacturer knew of demand for 24 of model A, 36 of model B, and only 12 of some luxury model C, a traditional production schedule for that manufacturer might adopt these demand requirements as run sizes. Thus, the traditional production schedule would focus first on producing all 24 of model A, then all 36 of model B, and finally 12 of model C. Each of these runs then requires a significant amount of time to finish, known as the run time of each batch. If it happened that this manufacturer could build model A at a rate of 24 per week, model B at a rate of 36 a week,

run size A batch size, or order size, associated with the production of an item.

run time The time required to produce a batch of some item.

FIGURE 12.7 Traditional versus Mixed-Model Scheduling

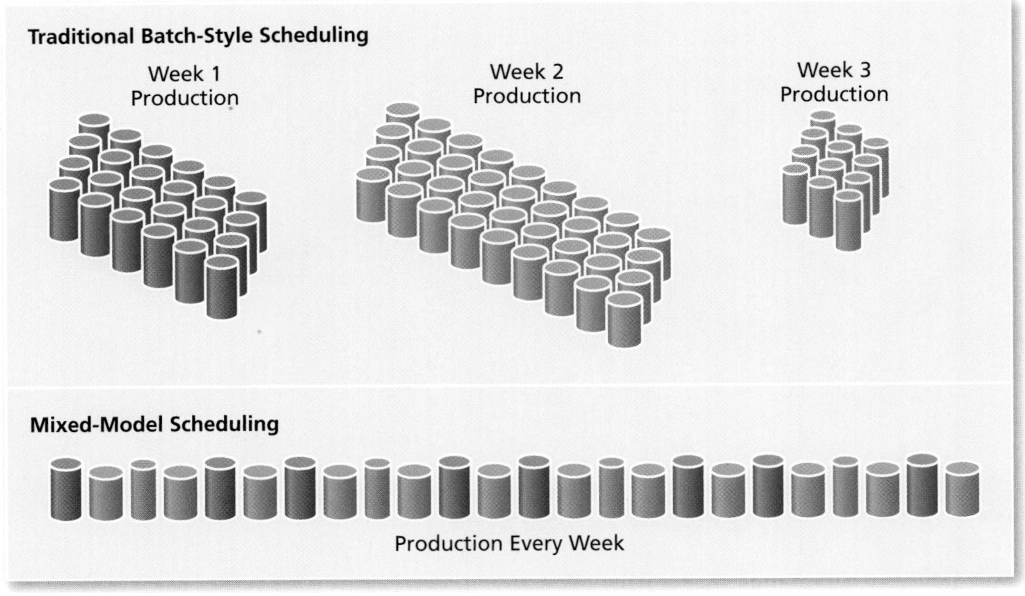

and model C at a rate of 12 a week, then the run time of each batch would be conveniently 1 week. This example is illustrated across the top half of Figure 12.7.

However, to smooth production for optimal performance of a lean operation, this traditional batch-style approach must end. Since the different models do vary somewhat in their material requirements, batching them together creates fluctuation in demand for those components the models do not share. To smooth out this component demand, the overall production requirements for the models should be blended evenly in a *mixed-model schedule*. Mixed-model scheduling requires that a pattern be found such that each model type is produced at a steady rate, such as the weekly pattern supporting the example manufacturer pictured in the lower half of Figure 12.7. Since 24 of model A must be produced over the course of a 3-week schedule, then 24/3 = 8 of model A should be produced every week, mixed in with 36/3 = 12 of model B, and 12/3 = 4 of model C.

mixed-model assembly Production of a range of products with a single assembly line, primarily by varying features on an otherwise standardized product.

Finding a repeating pattern that blends product models into one smooth sequence then enables mixed-model assembly, or the use of a highly efficient assembly line to create a mix of different products. However, the challenge of mixed-model scheduling and mixed-model assembly isn't simply locating the smoothest pattern possible from various model requirements. Rather, the lean operation must confront why the traditional batch-style scheduler judged the larger run sizes as economical and thus preferable. This returns the discussion to the issue of reducing fixed costs, in this case the cost of switching between models, which the traditional scheduler minimized.

PHILOSOPHY OF LEAN SYSTEMS

Mechanical tools such as kanban loops enable leaner operation of a system but do not in and of themselves ensure lean operation. Overall, lean operation is better described as the pursuit of an ideal state, outlined by this set of broader philosophical principles:

- Eliminate waste.
- Strive for visibility and flexibility in the system.

- Pursue closer relationships with outside suppliers.
- Seek continuous improvement.

Each of the mechanical principles discussed earlier is linked with one or more of these philosophical principles, providing a practical method supporting the philosophical argument. Since the mechanical principles are narrower in focus than the corresponding philosophy, limiting discussion to the tools alone would leave out much of the value of lean operation.

Elimination of Waste

Currently, approximately 10% of everything (by weight) extracted from this planet is transformed into finished goods, the remainder being discarded as waste. Elimination of such waste is the defining principle of lean operation. Waste in this context of lean/JIT is also known as muda, and can be thought of as the enemy of value-added, the goal of any operation. Muda represents anything that the customer would not care to pay for, inflating input values without increasing output value and thus reducing value-added. One of the major offenders in this category is inventory, the natural focus of much of the mechanics of a lean system.

muda
Japanese term for waste, particularly anything a customer is not willing to pay for.

value-added
The difference between the total value of the outputs and the total value of the inputs associated with an operation.

Inventory as Muda Inventory, by definition, is idle value waiting for use, and it is the holding costs created by this idleness that the customer does not value. Reducing fixed costs, reorder points, and lot sizes supports the reduction of inventory levels.

Safety stock is one kind of inventory common to traditional production systems, yet particularly troublesome to the philosophy of lean operation. Contrary to the spirit of just-in-time, safety stock represents idle goods being held just-in-case. This inventory is intended as protection against some uncertainty in the future, such as an unexpected surge in demand or a possible future failure in supply. Not only does safety stock represent muda because of its idle costs, the philosophy of lean sees this type of inventory as hurting the system. Figure 12.8 illustrates an allegory often used to clarify how safety stock can hurt an operation even as it protects it.

safety stock
Inventory held to protect against uncertain supply or demand.

Here, the production system is symbolized by a boat operating on a lake. The water in the lake is symbolic of inventory in the system, so the boat in the upper left-hand image of Figure 12.8 is where the story begins, the equivalent of a traditional system operating with high levels of safety stock. The high water level at the beginning of the story keeps the boat safely away from hazardous rocks on the lake bottom, symbolic of the uncertainties from which the production system requires protection. Lean operation calls for the equivalent of draining the lake, but this will then expose the boat to the

Allegory of the Lake FIGURE **12.8**

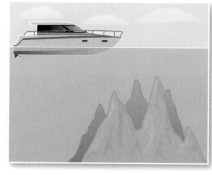

hazards below. This is where traditional inventory management and lean philosophy take starkly different views: while the traditional view of the second image in Figure 12.8 is one of danger and crisis, lean philosophy considers the second image a positive situation. At the beginning, the problems and uncertainties plaguing the system were hidden by the high inventory levels, but now they are being exposed by carefully dropping those levels, with the most significant problems emerging first. Although successful operation is in jeopardy in the short term, these problems can now be named, confronted, and fixed. In the allegory of the lake, this is the equivalent of destroying those rocks that have been exposed, allowing the boat to continue operating across the shallower—leaner—lake.

It is tempting to interpret the allegory of the lake as a demonstration of the need to eliminate inventory in the pursuit of lean operation. But that is a dangerous oversimplification. Note that the muda in Figure 12.8 exists in the rocks, not the lake level, and thus the greatest achievement in the symbolic story is the removal of the exposed rocks, not the draining of the lake. This demonstrates that successful pursuit of a lean philosophy does not dictate the elimination of inventory, but rather the elimination of the reason for inventory. For example, reducing fixed costs reduces the motivation to order or produce in large lot sizes, which naturally reduces inventory. Safety stock may be held just-in-case disruptions occur in deliveries from a distant supplier. If this reason can be eliminated, such as by switching to a local source, then the safety stock is no longer necessary and can be eliminated.

This distinction between eliminating inventory versus eliminating the *reason* for inventory becomes crucial when the pursuit of lean operation exposes a need for inventory that cannot be eliminated. Some operations are naturally exposed to high levels of uncertainty, and simply eliminating the inventory that traditionally buffers against this turbulent environment will only damage the operation. As an example, a hospital may be able to smooth the flow and reduce the levels of idle supplies to many of its treatment areas, but its emergency room will always be subject to unpredictable and irregular demands for critical supplies, which should remain in stock within that particular area. This can be thought of as a rock in the allegory of the lake that simply cannot be removed, and thus a certain amount of water should remain in the lake to enable safe operation. This is also an issue that is not exclusive to emergency services, as even tools developed by Toyota, the original champion of lean operation, contain careful provisions for a controlled amount of inventory. Embedded in the formula for the optimal number of kanbans is the input parameter X, explained as a policy variable. The function of X in the numerator of that formula is to increase the resulting recommended number of kanbans by a certain percentage, effectively increasing operating inventory by a controlled amount. This slight increase represents safety stock, added to absorb any natural fluctuations in actual demand or production rates.

Other Forms of Muda While inventory is a major offender in pursuit of lean operation, it is not the only form of waste that may be in the system. Muda can exist in the following forms as well:

- **Conveyance and transportation.** Moving product through a system does not create value, so unnecessarily lengthy or complex traffic patterns can create a waste of resources and effort. Revised layouts such as the cellular pattern first suggested in Figure 12.3 are practical suggestions to minimize this.
- **Overprocessing.** Ideally, a product should provide the customer with exactly and only what the customer desires. Any unused features are considered wasteful. This principle refers to both the product itself and the processes that create it; this form of muda can include overpackaging, unnecessary automation, and unnecessary control and computerization.
- **Delays and waiting.** When tangible goods are made to wait, they become inventory. When a customer is made to wait, another damaging form of muda emerges,

as this is of no value to the customer. Employees can also be delayed by a poorly designed or unpredictable system, wasting productivity.

- **Defects.** Defective work that reaches the customer can be costly to any operation. Even defects that are detected and corrected before reaching the outside world represent muda, in that these efforts require resources but do not add value. Thus, one emphasis of lean operation is on poka yoke, or revisions to the system to make any outcome other than the desired outcome impossible. Such fail-safe solutions eliminate both the defects and the need to monitor for, retrieve, and fix them.

poka yoke
Japanese term for process improvements striving to make the desired outcome of a process inevitable, largely by preventing mistakes.

Recognizing noninventory forms of muda clarifies how lean philosophy can be useful to service organizations. While a service organization might manage some inventory to support its operations, the broader test of waste as what the customer does not value reveals many noninventory opportunities for improvement to that system.

Visibility and Flexibility

Visibility, or transparency, is a philosophical thread running through many different aspects of lean operation. Visual systems communicate information through their appearance, and even the concept of safety stock as muda is partially related to a desire for visibility, as stocks of unnecessary inventory can literally hide problems in the system. Kanban loops are an example of lean operation's preference for visual signalling, making visible the need to produce. Visual systems can be designed for signalling other types of information as well, such as an andon system that signals when assistance is required in a certain area. Highly visual systems have the advantage of being able to keep large groups of people continuously well-informed, a condition that promotes good situational awareness.

andon
Japanese term for a signaling system announcing problems encountered and assistance requested, often implemented as sets of lights over workstations.

situational awareness
An individual or organization's comprehension of the surrounding environment and its potential near-future states.

Situational awareness is critical to successful pursuit of another broad goal of lean operation, that of developing and practicing flexibility. This need for flexibility was first suggested in the mechanical principle of mixed-model scheduling, in which a lean system resists batching together identical production items, switching between different models during production instead. A broader form of this flexibility are systems that encourage and enable participants to assist others in the system, such as workers leaving their usual work area to investigate and assist with the problem indicated by an andon signal elsewhere. Cellular layouts, mentioned earlier as a good means of minimizing wasteful traffic patterns, also facilitate this type of flexibility.

Close Relationships with Suppliers

A lean/JIT operation requires many small deliveries, often creating more activity and greater pressure on purchasing in general. For this reason, a lean system should develop a closer relationship with the supplier providing the deliveries, viewing that supplier as a partner in production. Such a relationship is often necessary to implement some JIT mechanisms, such as linking the two organizations' information systems through a paperless EDI ordering arrangement, or trusting the supplier to move unsupervised through the facility and deliver straight to the worker who is using the item. To encourage the supplier to participate in this more rigorous arrangement, a lean perspective suggests that the organization consider a longer-term sole-sourcing arrangement with one supplier, rather than adopting the traditional perspective requiring various suppliers to continuously bid for the organization's business.

partnering
Long-term strategic alliances that benefit both parties.

sole sourcing
Relying on a single supplier.

The pursuit of seamless supplier partnerships can even be taken to the extreme of inviting suppliers to locate operations *within* the lean operation being supplied, so that raw material inventory might travel in the smallest amounts over the shortest distances to arrive at the moment of use. This colocation of user and supplier was first popularized by the Bose Company as JIT II, suggesting it as the next chapter in the development of JIT. JIT II usually implies implementation of a broader arrangement known as

JIT II
A phrase first popularized by the Bose Company, emphasizing vendor-managed inventory and colocation of those vendors within a production facility.

Wireless Devices for Inventory Tracking

The rapid movement of minimum amounts of inventory though a lean system makes real-time inventory information critical. Wireless, handheld devices are common tools guiding this type of inventory flow, such as the portable barcode reader in this picture. Not only does the device reveal detailed information concerning the contents of the box, it can remotely report this information to a central information system, supporting good situational awareness among all system users.

vendor-managed inventory (VMI) Transferal of ownership and management of inventory within a system to its external provider, who will be compensated after its use by the system.

vendor-managed inventory (VMI). VMI not only requires a close relationship in which the lean organization trusts all aspects of its inventory management to the supplier, but it also allows ownership of the inventory to remain with the supplier, usually until such time as the lean operation actually withdraws the inventory for use. This is an important distinction: the holding costs of the inventory are transferred back to the supplier.

Continuous Improvement

kaizen Japanese term for a focus on continuous improvement.

quality circle A group of employees that meets regularly to discuss and develop opportunities for continuous improvement of their operation.

Because lean systems are often created from existing systems that had operated previously under an older style of production planning and control, outside consultants are often brought in to initiate the transformation process. These consultants assess the operation for early opportunities to eliminate waste and educate participants on the underlying principles so that they may carry the transformation further. The latter is critical, because a lean philosophy sees the transformation to lean operation as never being finished. One compelling philosophical principle of lean is its emphasis on continuous improvement, or kaizen. While improvement is desirable in any production philosophy, a traditional view of this process usually considers improvement as an undertaking separate from normal operation. A system would proceed normally according to its design, but the organization might choose to improve upon that design periodically in a separate initiative, a project with a definite start and completion. In contrast, kaizen sees the process of improvement very differently, as a daily part of the system's operation. The result is a system that is constantly evolving toward an ideal state, but one that is likewise never completely designed. Ideally, its evolution is guided by the participants in that system, often organized into teams of employees known as quality circles. Quality circles meet regularly as part of the normal operation of the system, brainstorming the constant stream of new opportunities to pursue in the spirit of continuous improvement.

Ultimately, lean operation banishes waste, including less obvious forms such as unnecessary action and delay. In this sense, lean is not simply a higher form of efficiency, but rather pursuit of the larger goal of sustainability. Trading safety stock and explicit scheduling for quality circles and kanban signaling may result in a remarkable transformation of production toward that goal, yet it is a trade that must be considered carefully. A lean operation is sustainable only if it can make the best use of resources and effectively cope with surprises in its environment, which is when a small amount of safety stock may prove itself valuable after all.

SUMMARY

Lean operation, also known by its earlier and more inventory-focused name of just-in-time, is the youngest form of production planning and inventory management. The powerful combination of system mechanics and philosophical principles that would become known as lean were developed initially by Toyota Motor Corporation, beginning with a self-study over a half century ago. Lean has emerged globally as a style of operation devoted to the elimination of waste in all forms, including unnecessary inventory, unnecessary processing, and even unnecessary motion and travel. At its heart, lean relies on the older pull-style logic of a reorder point system, operating with the minimum materials necessary in a highly visual and flexible production environment. This same production environment is under constant revision for continuous improvement, as the mission of creating only what the customer wants is believed never to be finished.

Key Terms

andon
dual card kanban
economies of scale
electronic data interchange (EDI)
inventory
JIT II
just-in-time (JIT)
kaizen
kanban
kanban loop
lead time
lean
level production strategy
Little's law
material requirements planning (MRP)
mixed-model assembly
muda
partnering
planned order releases
poka yoke
pull systems
push systems
quality circle
radio frequency identification (RFID)
reorder point
run size
run time
safety stock
single card kanban
situational awareness
sole sourcing
stockpiling
value-added
vendor-managed inventory (VMI)
work-in-process (WIP)

Discussion Questions

1. A system held inventory to protect it from uncertainties in supply. In an effort to be lean, this inventory is used and not replaced, although the uncertainties in supply remain unchanged. What is likely to happen to the operation of the system now?
2. Why is vendor-managed inventory considered a lean practice? Does VMI reduce inventory?
3. Why does Toyota's kanban formula contain a safety factor? When is it appropriate for X to be a smaller value? When should it be a larger value?
4. Just as lean systems are also called just-in-time systems, earlier approaches to inventory control are sometimes called just-in-case systems. The phrase just-in-case refers to what?
5. The emergence of JIT and lean operation are relatively recent when compared to other styles of production and inventory control, but what exactly is new about JIT/lean? What are its defining features, separating it from previous styles of operation?
6. What does the lean principle of level scheduling imply about finished goods inventory? Is this a contradiction to the philosophy of lean?

PROBLEMS

Short answers appear in Appendix A. Go to **NoteShaper.com** for full video tutorials on each question.

Minute Answer

1. Does lean operation rely on implicit or explicit production planning?
2. Is a lean operation considered a push or a pull system?
3. Does lean operation rely more on precise calculations or reaction to signals?
4. Push versus pull refers to pushing or pulling what?
5. Muda is another term for what?
6. In a dual card kanban system, one kind of card represents permission to produce. What does the second type of card represent permission to do?
7. What does reducing the number of kanban cards circulating in a single card kanban loop reduce?
8. Lean refers to less what?
9. An employee says, "I've got to get back to work now. I've got to calculate how many of each kind of part the factory needs to make next week. Then I've got to fill out all those work orders and make sure everybody out in the factory gets one." What word or words best describe the type of inventory control system this employee supervises?
10. What is the ideal order size in a lean/JIT environment?
11. Revising a process such that its desired outcome is the only outcome possible, also known casually (and rather inaccurately) as "dummy proofing" or "mistake proofing," is a principle known formally as what?
12. Will implementing leaner practices likely increase or reduce the frequency of ordering materials?

Quick Start

13. The usage rate D of a component is 200 an hour, the lead time L on a container of the component is 1 hour, and each container holds 110 components. Assuming a policy variable X of 0.10, how many kanban cards should be used to control production?
14. The usage rate D of a component is 200 an hour, the lead time L on a container of the component is 1 hour, and each container holds 22 components. Assuming a policy variable X of 0.10, how many kanban cards should be used to control production?
15. The usage rate D of a component is 200 an hour, the lead time L on a container of the component is 1 hour, and each container holds 22 components. Assuming a policy variable X of 0.21, how many kanban cards should be used to control production?
16. Five hundred of part A and 2,000 of part B are used annually. If the job shop that creates and uses these parts operates 250 working days a year, level scheduling requires the shop to create how many of each part each day?

Ramp Up

17. One common illustration used to demonstrate the philosophy of just-in-time inventory management shows a lake in which sharp rocks are hiding beneath the water's surface. What do the rocks represent?

18. One common illustration used to demonstrate the philosophy of just-in-time inventory management shows a lake in which sharp rocks are hiding beneath the water's surface. What does the water represent? Why should the lake be drained?

19. The usage rate of a component is 600 an hour, the lead time on a container of the component is 30 minutes, and each container holds 110 components. Assuming a policy variable of 10%, how many kanban cards should be used to control production?

20. A kanban system has just been introduced into a machine shop to control the production of a common part used by many different subassemblies at many different workstations. The kanban system has been operating for 2 weeks, but workers have made many complaints about it. Apparently workers who build the subassemblies cannot always find that part in stock exactly when they need it. How can the kanban system be adjusted to address these complaints?

21. Three kanban cards are hanging on a board next to a work area, while another identical kanban card is attached to the container that an employee is busy filling with parts created in that work area. Five more matching kanban cards are already attached to full containers placed in a convenient waiting area near this work area. A supervisor walks over, removes two of the kanban cards from the board, and puts them in her pocket. The supervisor then walks away. Which is the best explanation for why the supervisor did that?

Scenarios

Reminder: Short answers appear in Appendix A. Go to **NoteShaper.com** for full video tutorials on each question.

22. The Belmont Company must produce 1,500 boxes of product A each year, 2,000 boxes of product B each year, and 500 boxes of product C each year. The Belmont Company works 250 days a year, and it can make a total of 16 boxes of product a day (any mix of the products A, B, and C). In the past, Belmont would spend the first of the year producing just product A, then producing just product B when all 1,500 boxes of product A were finished, and then switch over late in the year to produce product C. However, the president of Belmont has decided that the company should follow the principles of lean operations, including smoothing production of the demand requirements of these three products into mixed-model scheduling.
    a. When Belmont uses its traditional schedule, how many days does it spend making product A at the beginning of the year? When it switches then to product B, how many days does it spend producing that product? How many days are then required to finish the batch of product C?
    b. If Belmont implements a perfectly smooth, mixed-model schedule, it will produce the same mix of three products every day. How many of each product should be in this daily mix?
    c. Ideally, in what order should this new daily mix be completed during the day?

23. The fabrication department provides a component for the assembly department. The assembly department's usage of the component is 4,800 units per 8-hour day. The fabrication department fills each container with 60 units in 40 minutes. Management has built a 20% cushion into the system.
    a. How many containers (or kanban cards) should be used for this component?
    b. Next month, the fabrication department expects its own usage of the component to fall by half, due to an expected decrease in sales of the finished goods requiring that component. Assuming that this change is permanent, how should the number of containers (or kanban cards) used to control this component be adjusted?

CASE STUDY: ROTHERA POINT POWER PLANT

Rothera Point Utilities operates Rothera Point Power Plant, a coal-fired generation facility that operates continuously, providing electricity to nearly 700,000 households in its service area. Rothera Point Plant consumes coal at a steady rate of 350 tons an hour, supplied through a contract with a coal mine over 1,500 miles from Rothera Point. Coal is delivered over this distance by rail, in dedicated coal trains rented by Rothera Point Utilities. Each railcar in the train carries 110 tons of coal and can be loaded at the mine or unloaded into Rothera Point's coal stockpile in about 2 minutes. However, travel of that railcar between the coal mine and Rothera Point Plant requires an average of 30 hours to complete.

Rothera Point determines the overall lengths of its dedicated coal trains, also known as unit trains, by determining how many railcars to rent from its logistics provider. Historically, Rothera Point has rented and operated two maximum-length, 150-railcar unit trains, dispatching each train to the mine as needed, to keep the plant stocked with coal. This results in a complex delivery schedule, during which each train is sometimes operating and sometimes idle. Recently, managers at Rothera Point decided to convert this complex push-style scheduling of the unit trains into a leaner, pull-style operation in which Rothera Point unit trains circulate continuously between the mine and the Rothera Point plant. With this change, the round-trip travel of the unit trains becomes a form of kanban loop, in which the mine loads trains that arrive empty, the Rothera Point plant unloads trains that arrive with coal, and the trains themselves require no scheduling or other explicit instructions, as they simply keep moving. However, operating the current two 150-unit railcar trains in this fashion delivers coal to the plant faster than the plant consumes it, so the managers at Rothera Point realize the two Rothera Point unit trains must be shortened to implement this leaner system.

Operating the coal supply and unit trains as a leaner, pull-style system has other advantages. Idle coal in inventory is relatively easy to store, but it poses environmental concerns. Rothera Point's coal inventory consists of pipeline inventory stored in its open railcars in transit, and its own outdoor coal stockpile where the arriving coal is deposited for use by the plant. When coal is stored outside, coal dust can be carried by windy weather and deposited in other areas. While Rothera Point maintains systems to suppress this potentially harmful dust as much as possible, management has resolved to reduce overall average coal inventory levels to curtail it further. There has even been discussion of renting a third unit train, which would allow all unit trains to be even shorter, hauling coal in lesser amounts and reducing average inventory further. Each unit train brings with it the substantial fixed cost of operating its engines, so the benefit of adding an additional train would have to outweigh its additional fixed cost.

Questions

1. Assume that Rothera Point will always operate unit trains of equal length, to achieve the smoothest flow of coal delivery possible. Recommend the number of railcars that should be in each of its two unit trains to achieve a lean but adequate flow of coal between the mine and the Rothera Point plant.
2. In your two-train pull-style system, what is the average pipeline inventory? What is the average size of the coal stockpile at the Rothera Point plant? How much smaller is this stockpile than the one Rothera Point must have under its current 150-railcar unit train delivery system?

3. Recommend the number of railcars that should be in each of its unit trains if Rothera Point were to add a third unit train to its coal delivery system. By how much does this improve inventory levels, compared to the two unit train system?

BIBLIOGRAPHY

Flinchbaugh, J., and A. Carlino. 2006. *The Hitchhiker's Guide to Lean: Lessons from the Road.* Dearborn, MI: Society of Manufacturing Engineers.

Karmarkar, U. 1989. "Getting Control of Just-in-Time." *Harvard Business Review,* September: 122–31.

Pascal, D. 2007. *Lean Production Simplified,* 2nd ed. Boca Raton, FL: CRC Press.

Simpson, N. 2001. "Inventory by Any Other Name: Lessons from the Emergency Room." *APICS: Performance Advantage,* June: 80.

Sprague, L. 2007. "Evolution of the Field of Operations Management." *Journal of Operations Management* 25: 219–38.

Vollmann, T. E., W. L. Berry, D. C. Whybark, and F. B. Jacobs. 2005. *Manufacturing Planning & Control Systems for Supply Chain Management,* 5th ed. Chicago: McGraw-Hill.

CHAPTER 13

Quality Control

Only the mediocre are always at their best.
—Jean Giraudoux

MAJOR SECTIONS

IN THIS CHAPTER, LOOK FOR...

- Natural versus assignable variation, dictating whether a process is or is not in control.
- The Central Limit Theorem as the foundation for statistical process control.
- How control charts reveal assignable variation in a process.
- Four different types of control charts.

INTRODUCTION

Successful operation requires a product that meets or exceeds customer expectations. When customers are not directly involved in production, their expectations are nonetheless reflected in the design of any successful product. This design is adopted as the producer's expectation of the product, and adhering to that design during production achieves quality of conformance. Quality control is the process of maintaining quality of conformance, monitoring the product in question for conformance to design specifications.

THE NATURE OF VARIATION

Even seemingly identical objects possess small differences. For example, the contents of two bottles of the same beverage, when measured closely, could be expected to vary by a very small amount, just as the width or alignment of the bottles' labels might also vary slightly. For this reason, successful organizations monitor the quality of conformance, or degree to which a good or service meets their expectations, to ensure their customers' ultimate satisfaction.

quality of conformance The degree to which the output of an operation meets the producer's expectations.

Figure 13.1 displays an example product, expected to conform to detailed specifications provided by an underlying design. The strategy board game in Figure 13.1 provides a good illustration of this conformance in that it contains many detailed pieces required by the design of the game, and failure to include any one of these pieces when assembling this game would create a defect in that unit of sale, one which might interfere with the functionality of the game itself.

defect A single identifiable deviation from acceptable conformance.

While defects are a damaging form of product variation, not all instances of variation are defects. If two boxes of the Strata game in Figure 13.1 were opened and studied, many small differences might be found between them that have no impact on the functionality of the game. If the square playing pieces were each measured closely enough, they might be found to vary slightly in size, but the differences would be too small to detect simply by looking at them. Likewise, the square pieces might also vary slightly in thickness, but this issue would be unimportant to the game's players. The contrast over serious concern

FIGURE 13.1 An Example Product

Strata, by Main House Gaming, is a strategy board game that requires cardboard tiles and other playing pieces. Main House Gaming monitors game assembly to ensure defects do not interfere with the functionality of the game.

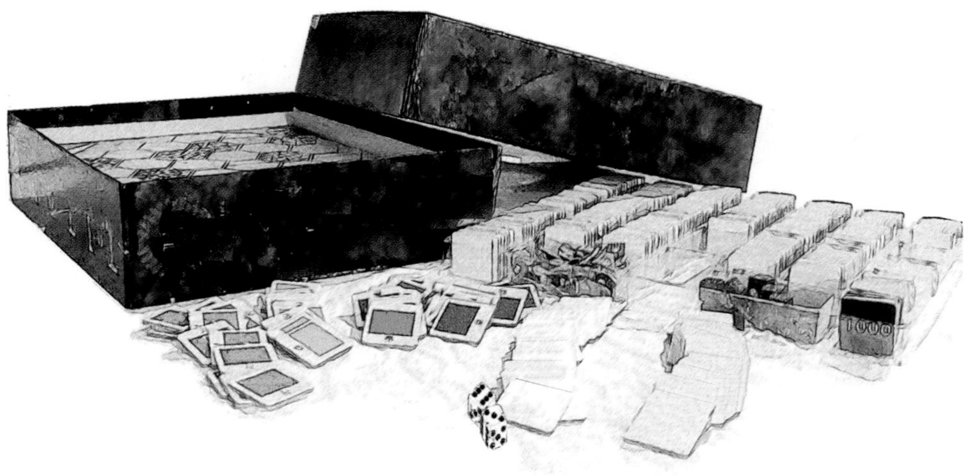

for missing pieces versus indifference to subtle variation highlights the dual nature of variation itself, also known as natural versus assignable variation.

Natural Process Variation

Natural variation in a process, also called random variation, is variability that cannot be avoided. In the context of the example Strata board game in Figure 13.1, the subtle differences in the thickness of the square pieces is a good example of the natural variation in the process that produces them. Since natural variation represents randomness that is always present in production, it should be relatively easy to observe, document, and describe. Generally, natural randomness occurs within a process or between samples.

natural variation The randomness inherent in a process; also known as random variation.

Variation within a Process The natural variation within a process is observed directly by measuring each and every outcome created by that process under normal conditions. When recorded as historical data, this variation should describe a stable probability distribution, based on the frequencies of particular measurements observed. For example, a process under observation creates outcomes of some average value, and these recorded outcomes vary between a historical minimum and maximum value. However, variation between the minimum and maximum values might then take one of a variety of forms. The variation related to natural phenomena is often normally distributed, such as the height of adults or the average daily air temperature at a certain location on a certain day. In contrast, the natural variation between service times required by customers standing in line for individual assistance often follows a skewed beta or exponential distribution, as most customers require a certain minimum amount of time but a few customers require substantially more assistance. The outcomes of processes that are subject to extreme randomness can even describe flat, uniform distributions, with no particular outcome appearing any more or less likely than any other particular outcome.

Variation between Samples While the variation of a process can be observed by monitoring it continuously, this is seldom practical. Rather, the output of an ongoing process is usually sampled at regular intervals, and the contents of these samples are closely measured. When sampling from a larger population, it is important to recognize that the natural variation among the population will not be the same as the natural variation between the samples. In Figure 13.2, the large population of individual observations plotted as circles are randomly distributed with a mean value of 80.0. The square data points in Figure 13.2 result from gathering samples of 10 observations from that same population and charting the mean value of each sample. While these sample means vary around the same central value as the original population, Figure 13.2 reveals that the degree of variation between the sample means is considerably less than the variation among the individual observations, creating a narrower band across the graph.

Figure 13.2 illustrates what is known generally as the Central Limit Theorem, a set of principles helpful for anticipating the natural variation of samples. Given a large population with an overall mean of μ and a standard deviation of σ, the following will be true for the natural variation of samples from that population:

Central Limit Theorem The observation that sample values approximate a normal distribution, regardless of the underlying distribution of the population being sampled.

- Samples will be distributed around the population mean, as seen in Figure 13.2. In other words, the mean of the sample means equals the mean of the population: $\bar{\bar{X}} = \mu$.
- Samples will vary less than the population itself, as also seen in Figure 13.2. Specifically, if n is the sample size, then the standard deviation in the sample means is equal to the population's standard deviation divided by the square root of the sample size: $\sigma_{\bar{X}} = \sigma/\sqrt{n}$.
- Samples will follow an approximation of the normal distribution, regardless of the distribution of the original population.

FIGURE 13.2 Random Observations versus Sample Means of the Same Observations

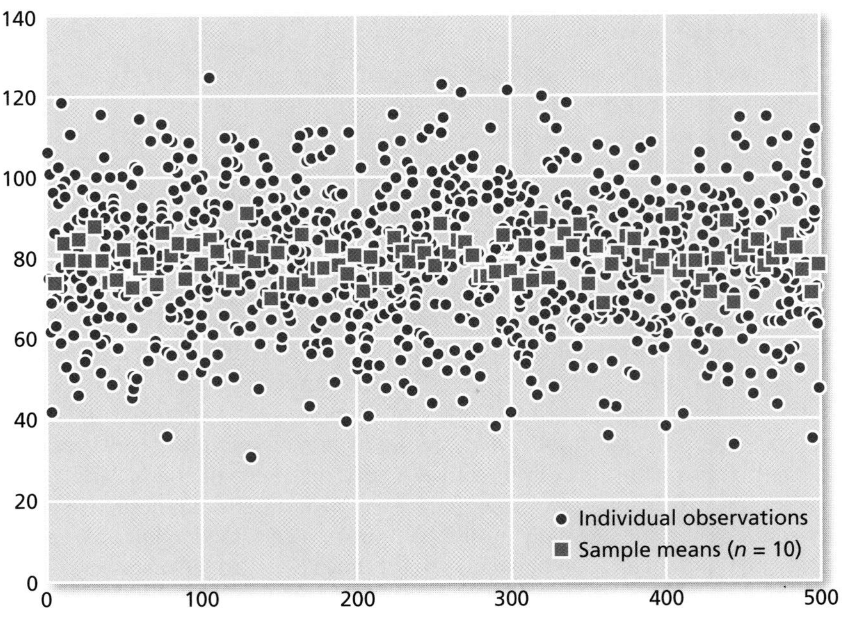

Many tools of quality control rely on these principles to monitor the ongoing natural behavior of samples, watchful for yet another form of variation—assignable process variation.

Assignable Process Variation

assignable variation Deviations with a specific cause or source.

Nonnatural variation in a process is called assignable variation, named after the fact that this type of variation can be assigned to a specific cause. This distinction is important for two reasons, the first being that this type of variation creates defects, or unacceptable units of product. Once created, defects must be located and destroyed or repaired, otherwise these defective products will likely be returned by or recalled from those customers unlucky enough to receive them. All these activities represent additional costs to the operation, including loss of the customer's good opinion of the product.

Assignable variation is also significant because it has a source, implying that if assignable variation is detected, it can then be traced to and fixed at its source. In other words, assignable variation is a signal that a problem is emerging somewhere within the system, which serves as an invitation to stop normal production and locate and resolve the problem before it grows worse. Upon investigation, this problem might be a single machine that has become misaligned; a sensor, scanner, or card reader that is malfunctioning; or one person who is not consistently following instructions. In each case, the problem can likely be solved, but not before it is noticed and investigated. Monitoring production for evidence of emerging assignable variation is the central purpose of statistical process control.

Statistical Process Control

statistical process control (SPC) The monitoring of overall conformance through the ongoing evaluation of samples.

Much of quality control is known formally as statistical process control (SPC), a set of concepts, tools, and procedures that monitor active processes by sampling output. If this sampling suggests only natural variation is present in the output, the process is said to be

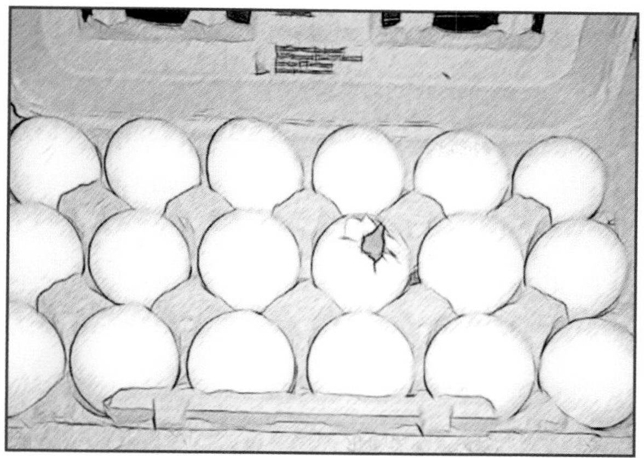

Assignable Variation in Fresh Eggs

This picture displays both natural and assignable variation common in fresh eggs. Individual egg size and weight will vary slightly within acceptable standards, but the damaged egg varies in an unacceptable manner, an example of a product defect. Being assignable variation, this particular nonconformance suggests a problem with a specific source, such as damage during shipment.

in control. However, if this sampling indicates the presence of assignable variation, the process is then declared *out of control*, and the decision to stop production and search for its cause usually follows. This distinction between in control and out of control is often signaled through the use of graphical tools.

SPC Tools Sampling is a concept critical to statistical process control, as are the principles of the Central Limit Theorem, outlining the natural behavior of samples. One of the oldest and most common tools to monitor samples for potential assignable variation is the control chart, like the one pictured in Figure 13.3.

control chart Graph illustrating observed values in relationship to the allowable limits on those values.

Control charts are graphs that are actively updated, by plotting the values of samples taken at regular intervals during operation. Thus, the chart pictured in Figure 13.3 is nearly finished (there is only enough room on the right for a few more sample values), and this process will need a blank chart soon. While the process operates, each member of the sample is measured for the particular specification the chart is designed to

Example Control Chart FIGURE 13.3

This process is in control—all values plotted fall within the upper and lower control limits and are distributed evenly about the mean.

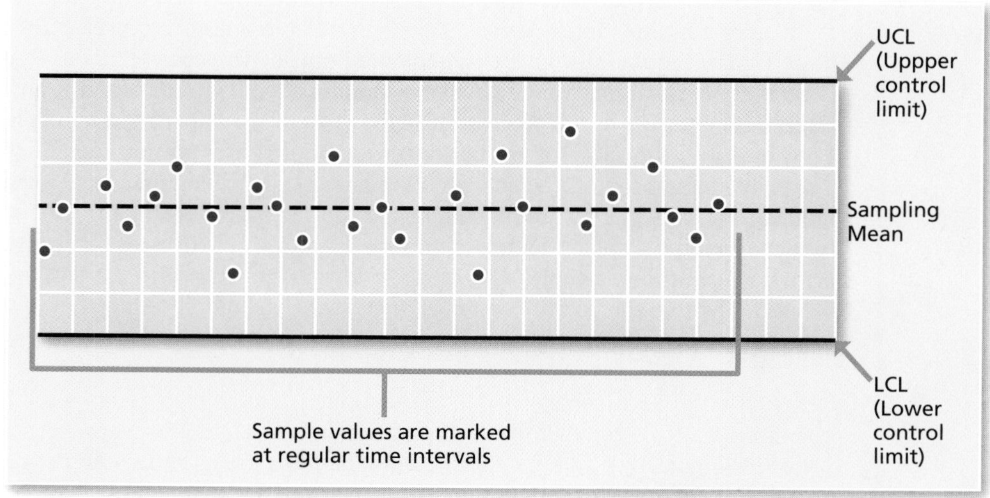

FIGURE 13.4 Example Control Charts with Various Out-of-Control Signals

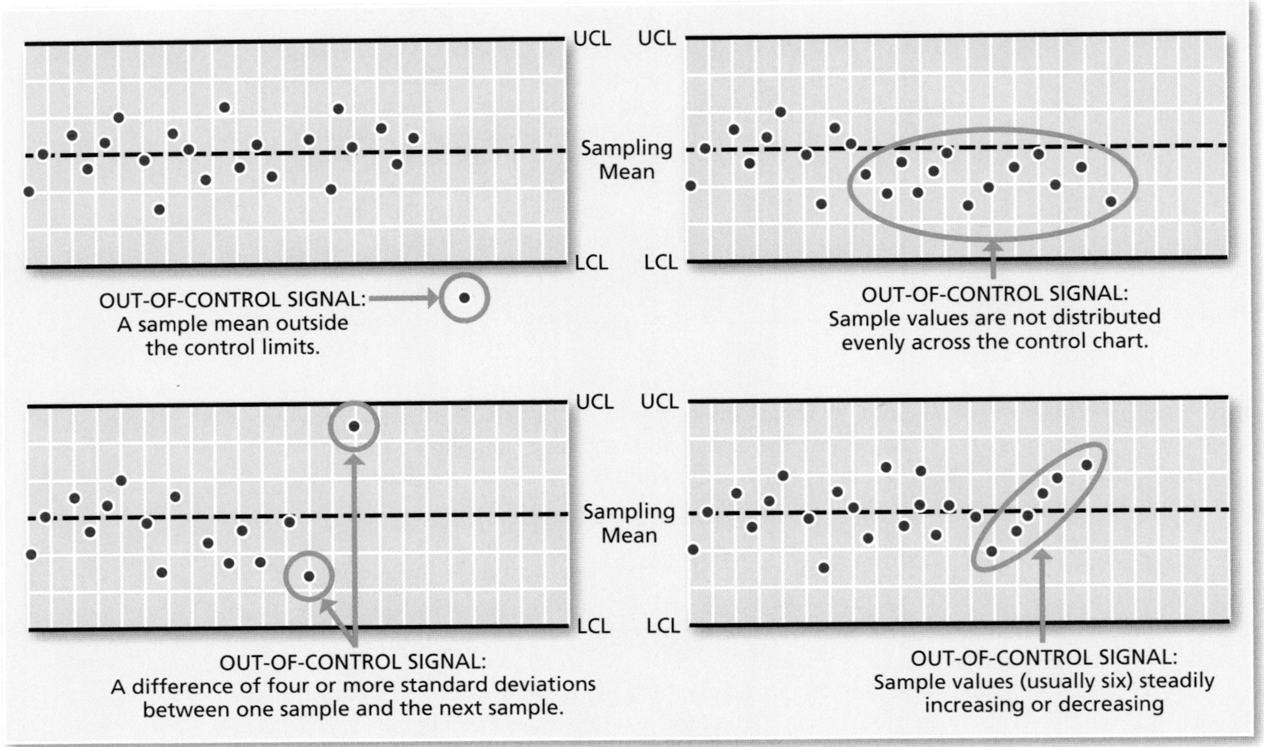

monitor. These measurements are then summarized as a single sample value, such as the sample's mean measurement, and this is plotted on the chart. The samples means in Figure 13.3 indicate that the process is in control, as they all fall appropriately within the chart's control limits. If a sample falls outside these limits when plotted on the chart, this is interpreted as a signal that assignable variation is now present in the process. At this point, the process is declared out of control, and production should be stopped, so that the cause of the assignable variation can be located and removed or fixed.

control limit
A control chart boundary, where values observed beyond this limit signal the process is not in control.

Figure 13.4 illustrates various signals of trouble within a process, although not all these signals require a sample to actually fall outside the control limits. Drawing on the Central Limit Theorem to anticipate how samples should group naturally, any grouping of samples to one side of the process mean, such as in the upper right-hand chart in Figure 13.4, indicates the samples are no longer distributed around that mean and thus some assignable influence must be acting on the process. Following that same logic, it is highly unlikely that a sample value would vary by four or more standard deviations between two consecutive samples naturally (Figure 13.4, lower left) or visually trend over six or more consecutive samples (Figure 13.4, lower right). Despite the fact that all sample values are within the acceptable range, the process should be stopped in these cases and evaluated for a potential problem.

Risks Control charts make visible the ongoing variation in a process, enabling a process operator to recognize when the process may be out of control. However, the in-control pattern in Figure 13.3 and the out-of-control patterns in Figure 13.4 do not guarantee that the underlying process is either in or out of control. Use of a control chart always implies some small risk that the actual state of the process is *not* being reflected by the signals

Control Chart Risks

FIGURE 13.5

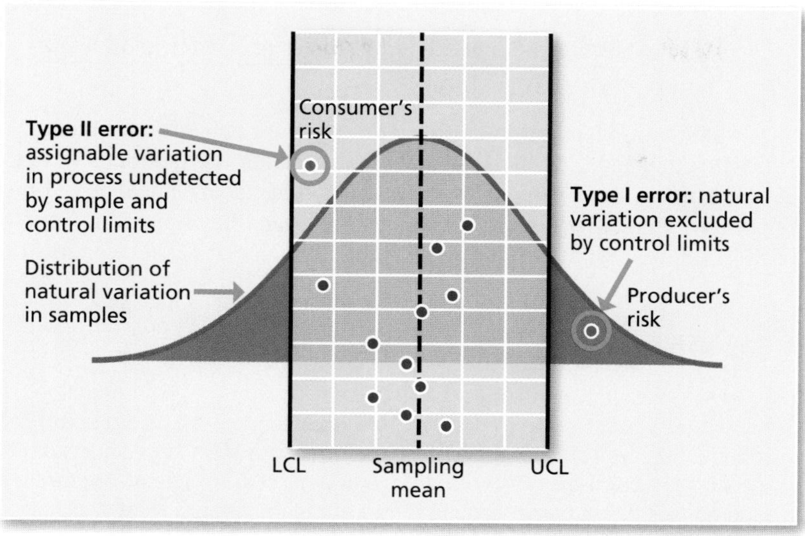

from the chart. Figure 13.5 illustrates this danger by superimposing an example control chart, rotated vertically, against the distribution of the natural variation of its samples.

Because the sampling distribution is normal, it theoretically extends to infinity in both directions, although the probability of observing any sample value farther than four standard deviations from the sampling mean is almost nonexistent. In reality, a small but ever-present chance exists that the process could create an unusually small or large sample observation even while in control. Since the upper and lower control limits must be set at some certain finite values, these limits exclude at least a small part of the natural distribution, where this unusual natural sample would fall outside those limits. This would then signal that the process is out of control, when in fact it is not, a condition known in statistics as a type I error. In the context of control charts, this danger is also known as the producer's risk, because of the likelihood that production will be stopped upon seeing the signal but the producer will be unable to find any assignable cause.

type I error
In quality control, concluding the process is out of control when in fact it is not.

producer's risk
The likelihood of a type I error.

Widening the span of the control limits decreases this risk to the producer, but will increase another risk, known as type II error. As Figure 13.5 illustrates, a possibility exists that assignable variation might corrupt the process, but the particular sample taken during that time nonetheless falls inside the control limits, sending a false signal of control. Wider control limits, which reduce producer's risk, also allow more variation of any type to fall within the limits. This danger of undetected assignable variation is the consumer's risk, implying defects are escaping detection and will be passed along to the customer.

type II error
In quality control, concluding the process is in control when in fact it is not.

consumer's risk
The likelihood of a type II error.

Designing a good control chart is primarily an issue of locating its limits (discussed in more detail later in this chapter). Setting these limits is partially an issue of balancing producer's and consumer's risk. However, no successful balance will be found if the process itself is not capable of supporting production. As an example, consider the numerous square cardboard tiles required by the Strata board game pictured earlier in Figure 13.1. While very small variations in the dimensions of these playing pieces might be unimportant to the game, larger variations create tiles that do not fit in the storage tray pictured, and thus are unacceptable. The Strata manufacturer will have a process for cutting these tiles, but if that process does not cut the square tiles precisely enough to stay within the Strata design specifications, no control chart can enable this process to successfully support the production of Strata board games. This issue of whether the process

process capability The natural variation in an existing process, stated relative to the allowable variation specified in a product's design.

is appropriate given the requirements of the design is known as process capability. Process capability is often measured as an index value (C_p) comparing the variation tolerated by the design to the variation inherent in the process:

$$C_p = \frac{\text{design specification width}}{\text{natural width of the process}} \quad \text{or} \quad \frac{\text{design specification width}}{6\sigma}$$

where σ is the standard deviation in natural process variation. An index value C_p greater than 1.0 indicates that the process is capable of supporting the product's design specifications. A value of less than 1.0, however, indicates that the specifications of the design are more restrictive than what the process is generally capable of providing, and thus the process itself is not appropriate to this application. We calculate C_p in Scenario 1a.

Scenario 1

Process Capability Index

Main House Gaming designs and manufactures strategy board games. These games require multiple playing pieces called game tiles, visible in the contents of the Strata board game in Figure 13.1. Game tiles are cut to a variety of shapes and sizes from large sheets of printed cardboard, creating the particular pieces that support a particular game. While Strata relies mostly on squared tiles, other games require round or triangular tiles, all of which can be stamped from large sheets of cardboard by Main House Gaming's tile-cutting machine.

The production manager has decided to use statistical process control to monitor the tile-cutting machine. This manager is particularly concerned about the production of round tiles, as these appear to vary when the machine is working at its highest speed settings. According to the firm that built this machine, "When in control, the game tile cutter produces round tiles with a standard deviation in tile diameter of 0.1 millimeters." The machine can be set to produce round tiles ranging from 10 to 50 mm in diameter, but the standard deviation in the process remains 0.1 mm. Most of Main House Gaming's products featuring round tiles use 20-mm tiles. Tiles less than 19.5 mm or greater than 20.5 mm in diameter create problems in packing the game, and thus should be rejected.

What is the process capability index value (C_p) for the current production of 20-mm round tiles? What does this value indicate?

Analysis

The process capability index is the ratio of the specification width to the natural width of the process variation. We calculate these widths from the information provided:

20-MM ROUND TILE PROCESS CAPABILITY

- Upper limit of diameter specified: 20.5 mm
- Lower limit of diameter specified: 19.5 mm
- Specification width: 20.5 − 19.5 = 1.0 mm
- Standard deviation (σ) in process: 0.1 mm
- Natural width of process (6σ): 6 × 0.1 = 0.6 mm

The index value is then the ratio of specification to natural process width:

20-MM ROUND TILE PROCESS CAPABILITY

Process capability index value = C_p = 1.0/0.6 = 1.667

Insight Because this value is greater than 1, the existing tile-cutting process appears capable of supporting the design requirements for 20-mm round tiles. If this number had been less than 1, that would have indicated that the tile-cutting machine was not capable of producing large amounts of 20-mm tiles without consistently creating some tiles either too big or too small for packing in a finished game. ■

TRADITIONAL QUALITY CONTROL

Perceiving quality as an issue of conformance to standards dates back to ancient craft guilds. This outlook developed further during the Industrial Revolution in the late eighteenth century, but many of the current methods to measure quality emerged with the concept of scientific management in the early twentieth century. In fact, much of the design of control charts can be traced back to the efforts of a group of engineers at Western Electric in the 1930s, including the world's first control chart, sketched in a one-paged memo written by quality pioneer Walter Shewhart in 1924. Modern systems or quality subsystems that focus on statistical process control follow this long tradition, employing an approach outlined in Figure 13.6.

scientific management
A methodology stressing the use of data collection and analysis to redesign processes and improve efficiency.

Distinguishing Features

As Figure 13.6 suggests, traditional statistical process control is often organized across the three segments of the classic model of an operation, divided among the operation's inputs, transformation process, and outputs. As the pattern of words across Figure 13.6 suggests, *inspect* and *conformance* are key features of this system.

Focus on Conformance The oldest understanding of the concept of quality is the degree to which a product conforms to the producer's standards. Traditional quality management supports this vision, employing tools such as control charts to monitor for conformance at all stages of production. Ironically, focus on conformance is also an excellent example of outcome bias, the sometimes mistaken assumption that a good outcome automatically indicates a good system.

outcome bias
A tendency to assume a process is acceptable if its output is acceptable.

Reliance on Inspection and Inspectors A traditional view of quality focuses on conformance to specifications, so implementation relies heavily on sampling and inspection. Since inspection is the cornerstone of this style of quality management, such a program often employs full-time inspectors. Thus, employees conducting quality inspections are not the same employees creating the product, and may even be organized into a quality control department wholly separate from production personnel in a functional organizational structure. While this separation of production and inspection is not strictly harmful, it is generally the trademark of an older quality management program and often deliberately avoided by more modern programs.

functional organizational structure
An organization of specialists grouped into distinct departments.

Traditional Quality Management | **FIGURE 13.6**

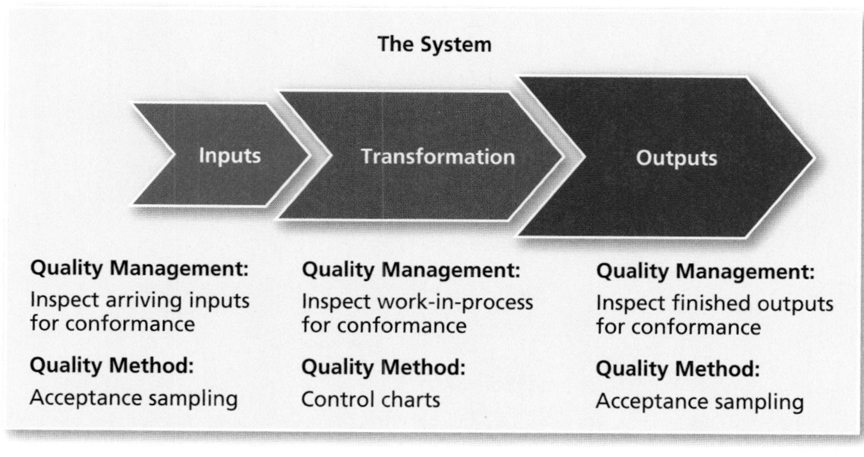

An Ideal Amount of Inspection A traditional approach to quality is also founded on the idea that an ideal amount of inspection exists, some optimal amount of inspection that those full-time inspectors should be providing. Figure 13.7 illustrates this idea as a trade-off between two opposing forces: the cost of the inspection versus the cost of undetected defects.

As Figure 13.7 shows, the cost of inspection is driven by the amount of inspection conducted: the greater the percent of output that must be inspected, the greater the cost. However, less inspection implies that more defects go undetected, and the traditional view assumes that each creates a certain cost when released into the marketplace, such as the cost of repairs or returns. Theoretically, if 100% of output is inspected, no defects will ever escape detection and thus there will be no cost of undetected defects. In Figure 13.7, the total cost of a quality management program is the combination of these two opposing cost functions, implying a distinct low point in total cost signaling the ideal amount of inspection. The quality manager in a traditional program must determine what this amount is, given knowledge of the actual costs of inspection and undetected defects, and then organize enough full-time inspectors to enforce that policy.

Vulnerabilities

total quality management (TQM) Simultaneous and continuous pursuit of improvement in both the quality of design and conformance through the involvement of the entire organization.

This traditional mindset is neither incorrect nor obsolete, but is usually considered incomplete for managing quality in modern times. Broader approaches such as total quality management (TQM) evolved from this strong foundation, motivated by its distinct vulnerabilities. One weakness of the traditional approach is its heavy reliance on inspection. Inspection is a process that only catches mistakes that have already been suffered; inspection does not solve problems or make any correct product more valuable. Thus, a quality management program devoted to a non-value-adding process creates a contradiction when viewed from the strategic level. Furthermore, the idea that this program can locate an ideal amount of inspection to optimize quality and that this ideal will never

FIGURE 13.7 The Optimal Inspection Policy, or Ideal Amount of Inspection

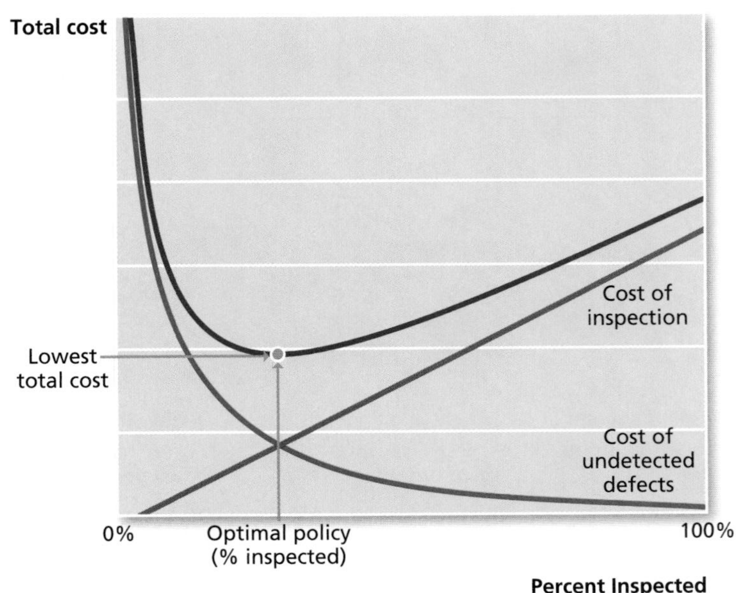

require modification when implemented raises further doubts concerning this approach in any dynamic environment.

An inspection-intensive program also brings up the issue of tolerance, or setting the boundaries on permissible variation. Tolerances are at least partially determined by the cost of nonconformance, which is traditionally assumed a linear function of the degree of nonconformance. For example, if the difference between an actual measurement and its specification were found to be twice as large for one unit of product versus the next unit, it would be assumed that the previous unit would cost the organization twice as much as the next unit due to its nonconformance.

tolerance
Allowable variation from a standard.

In the 1970s, Genichi Taguchi introduced the idea that this linear assumption may in fact be a very poor explanation of the true cost of quality. Rather, the true combined cost of nonconformance is more likely to rise sharply with the degree of nonconformance, in a nonlinear fashion. This model is now described as the Taguchi loss function, illustrated in Figure 13.8. Because the Taguchi loss function suggests that all but the smallest deviations from target are likely to result in unacceptable loss, it further suggests that tolerances should be set much tighter than assumed necessary by the traditional perspective.

Taguchi loss function
A proposed model of the cost of nonconformance that penalizes even small degrees of deviation from a target specification.

Even if an organization is producing products that minimize the Taguchi loss function through tight adherence to specifications, this does not guarantee that the organization is producing value. Perhaps the greatest vulnerability of focusing exclusively on conformance concerns the origins of the specifications defining that conformance. While specifications represent the producer's expectations of the product, this does not necessarily mean that the product will meet the customer's expectations. Bridging this potential gap between the producer's and the consumer's views of product quality serves as one of the central pillars of many modern quality programs, but even these programs rely on statistical process control in the implementation of product designs. As a result, tools such as control charts and acceptance sampling remain critical components in the operations of many complex production systems.

Taguchi Loss Function

FIGURE 13.8

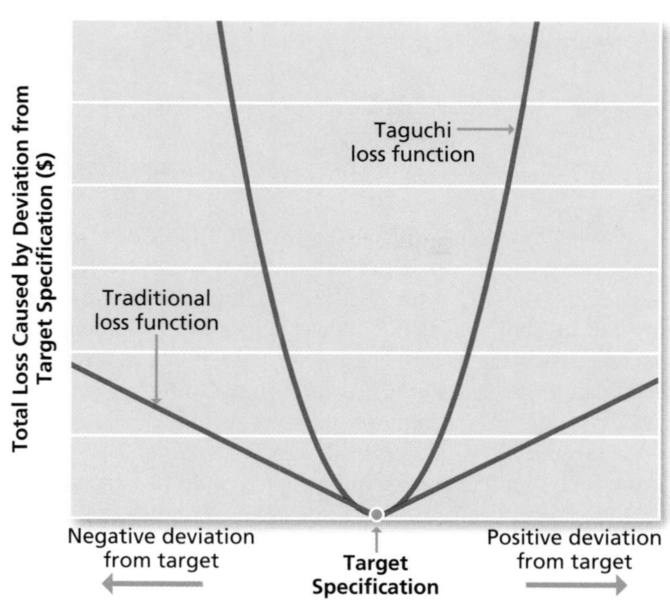

DESIGNING CONTROL CHARTS

On one level, designing a control chart to monitor a process helps to determine appropriate values for control limits. However, the method used to set these limits must be appropriate for the particular situation. Correctly determining the limits on a control chart depends on the following factors:

- **The issue being monitored.** A mean chart, for example, monitors a measurement of interest, tracked as the average measurement within a sample. *C*-charts and *p*-charts, in contrast, monitor the count or proportion of something of interest, while *R*-charts monitor the range of values present in a sample.
- **The quality of information about the natural variation in the process.** Sometimes the exact nature of this distribution is known, but often not. In other cases, natural variation is known to exist, but its precise mean, standard deviation, and distribution type are not available to the chart's designer.
- **The degree of producer's risk deemed acceptable.**

Mean Charts with Known Variation

mean chart
Control chart used in monitoring the central tendency of some characteristic within a sample, also known as an *x*-bar chart in reference to the plotting of averages.

Mean charts are the most common type of control chart; the earlier illustrations in Figures 13.3, 13.4, and 13.5 are all mean charts. Mean charts are designed to display sample averages and so are also known as *x*-bar charts, referring to the charting of $\overline{x}$ each time a sample is taken. Mean charts monitor the central tendency of some measurable characteristic of a product. The most basic type of mean chart is one in which this natural variation is known and understood completely before the chart is ever drawn. Scenario 1 provided an example of such a situation, in which Main House Gaming was aware that its round-tile-cutting machine, when operating normally, could produce round tiles with an average diameter of 20 mm ($\mu = 20$) and a standard deviation in diameter of 0.1 mm ($\sigma = 0.1$). This information might be supplied by the manufacturer of the equipment, as implied in Scenario 1, or it might be gleaned from a long history of experience with the process.

When natural variation is known, the control chart designer must decide how many standard deviations of normal sampling behavior to include within the chart limits, a factor known traditionally as *z*, or the *z*-value. Drawing on the Central Limit Theorem, future observations of sample means are expected to be normally distributed and display less variation than individual measurements from the process output. Thus, the control chart limits can be defined as

$$\text{Upper control limit (UCL)} = \mu + z\frac{\sigma}{\sqrt{n}} = \mu + z\sigma_{\overline{x}}$$

$$\text{Lower control limit (LCL)} = \mu - z\frac{\sigma}{\sqrt{n}} = \mu - z\sigma_{\overline{x}}$$

The selection of a particular *z*-value when setting control limits determines the producer's risk associated with the chart. The most common value observed in practice is $z = 3.0$, also known as a *three-sigma chart*. Because the sampling distribution is assumed normal, the chart designer can be confident that 99.7% of all samples will actually fall within the three-sigma limits when the process is in control, because 99.7% of any normal distribution falls within three standard deviations of its mean. This also represents a slight producer's risk that 1.0 – 0.997 = 0.003 = 0.3% of future samples will fall outside those control chart's limits even though the process is in control. If $z = 2.0$ were chosen instead, the control limits would narrow such that 95.5% of sample means could be expected to fall within the limits when in fact the process is in control, decreasing consumer's risk through tightening the boundaries on tolerated variation. However, this corresponds to an increased producer's risk of 1.0 – 0.955 = 0.045 = 4.5% of samples naturally falling outside the limits when the process is operating normally. We consider both standards in Scenario 2a.

Mean Chart (Known Natural Process Variation)

Scenario 2a

The production manager of Main House Gaming plans to use a mean chart to monitor the production of 20-mm round tiles, discussed earlier in Scenario 1. When the tile-cutting machine is producing these tiles, the production manager will require the machine operator to measure four round tiles at random every hour, and plot the average of the four diameters on the mean chart.

What would this mean chart look like if the production manager wishes 99.7% of all four-tile samples to fall within its limits, given that the machine is in control? What would the chart look like if the manager is willing to reduce this requirement to 95.5% of all samples falling within the limits, given that the machine is in control?

Analysis

The production manager requested two mean charts, but the only difference is two different levels of producer's risk, expressed as 99.7% versus 95.5% of all in-control samples, being captured by the control limits. In both cases, the two charts will have the same centerline (μ), the same sample size (*n*), and reflect the same degree of natural variation (σ). In the case of σ, this information can be retrieved from the earlier discussion of tile cutting in Scenario 1; specifically, "When in control, the game tile cutter produces round tiles with a standard deviation in tile diameter of 0.1 millimeters."

20-MM ROUND TILE MEAN CHART PARAMETERS

- $\mu = 20.0$ mm (process mean)
- $\sigma = 0.1$ mm (the standard deviation in process)
- $n = 4$ tiles (sample size)

The two different levels of producer's risk translate into two different *z*-values chosen for the control limit formula:

20-MM ROUND TILE MEAN CHART

- $z = 3.0$ provides for 99.7% of all sample means t o fall within the limits when the process is in control.
- $z = 2.0$ provides for 95.5% of all sample means to fall within the limits when the process is in control.

Now we can use the formulas to calculate for the upper and lower control limits for both levels of producer's risk:

20-MM ROUND TILE MEAN CHART LIMITS

For the case of $z = 3.0$ (99.7% of all in-control samples within limits)

$$\begin{aligned} UCL &= \mu + z\frac{\sigma}{\sqrt{n}} = \mu + z\sigma_{\bar{x}} \\ &= 20.0 + 3.0 \times (0.1/2) = 20.0 + 3.0 \times 0.05 \\ &= 20.15 \text{ mm} \end{aligned}$$

$$\begin{aligned} LCL &= \mu - z\frac{\sigma}{\sqrt{n}} = \mu - z\sigma_{\bar{x}} \\ &= 20.0 - 3.0 \times (0.1/2) = 20.0 - 3.0 \times 0.05 \\ &= 19.85 \text{ mm} \end{aligned}$$

Continues

For the case of $z = 2.0$ (95.5% of all in-control samples within limits)

$$UCL = \mu + z\frac{\sigma}{\sqrt{n}} = \mu + z\sigma_{\bar{x}}$$
$$= 20.0 + 2.0 \times (0.1/2) = 20.0 + 2.0 \times 0.05$$
$$= 20.1 \text{ mm}$$

$$LCL = \mu - z\frac{\sigma}{\sqrt{n}} = \mu - z\sigma_{\bar{x}}$$
$$= 20.0 - 2.0 \times (0.1/2) = 20.0 - 2.0 \times 0.05$$
$$= 19.9 \text{ mm}$$

Insight When drawn to scale, the two mean charts look like these:

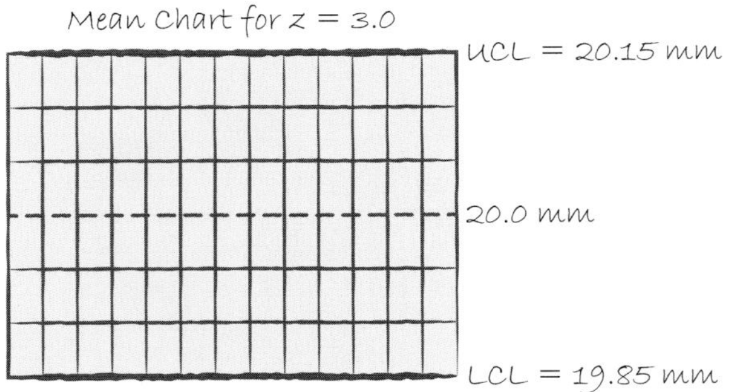

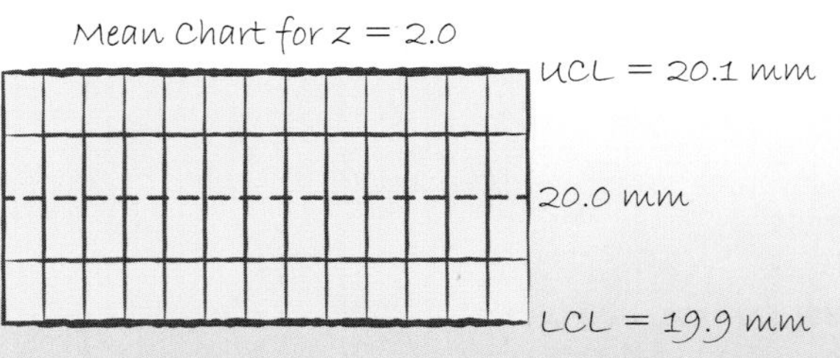

standard normal distribution
A normal distribution with a mean of zero and a variance of 1.

Although $z = 3.0$ is a common z-value in practice, the producer's risk inherent in any value of z can be determined by recognizing the link between this value in the control limit formula and its general meaning to the standard normal distribution. Since a standard normal distribution has a mean of $\mu = 0.0$ and a standard deviation of $\sigma = 1.0$, the z-value and the resulting upper control limit would be the same value for any process that happened to have standard normal sampling distribution. Thus, the exact area of *any* sampling distribution included or excluded by a set of control limits can be estimated by locating its chart's z-value on a standard normal table, such as the one provided in Appendix C at the back of this text. Figure 13.9 demonstrates this process for an example in which a z-value of 1.35 was chosen to create the control limits.

Mean Charts with Unknown Variation

Although mean charts are the most common type of control chart, most organizations drawing up a mean chart do not know μ and σ, the exact parameters associated with the distribution of natural variation in the process. Rather, the designer of the mean chart must estimate the chart's underlying sampling distribution by observing samples taken when the process is known to be in control. Ideally, this initial data gathering includes no

Producer's Risk for a Mean Chart with $z = 1.35$

FIGURE **13.9**

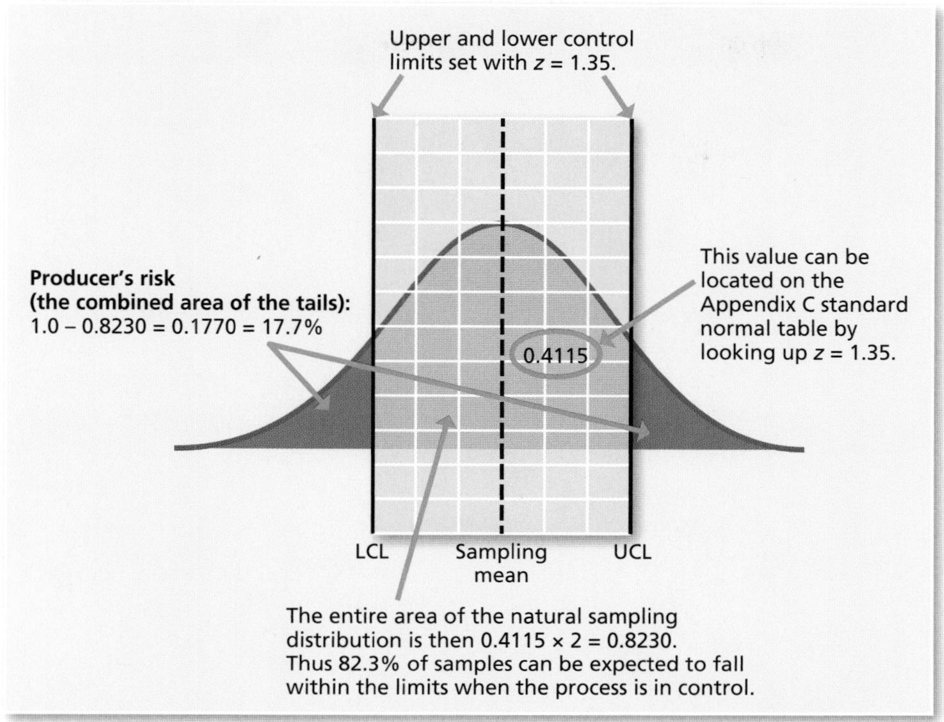
Upper and lower control limits set with z = 1.35.
Producer's risk (the combined area of the tails): 1.0 – 0.8230 = 0.1770 = 17.7%
This value can be located on the Appendix C standard normal table by looking up z = 1.35.
0.4115
LCL
Sampling mean
UCL
The entire area of the natural sampling distribution is then 0.4115 × 2 = 0.8230. Thus 82.3% of samples can be expected to fall within the limits when the process is in control.

less than 25 samples to ensure statistical significance. When these samples are taken and the individual sample means $\bar{x}$ are calculated, the Central Limit Theorem indicates that μ can be estimated by the mean of those means:

$$\bar{\bar{x}} = \mu$$

To estimate the degree of variation that would normally be observed around that center value, the range of each sample belonging to this in-control group is calculated:

range
The difference between the largest observed value of some characteristic within a sample and the smallest observed value of that same characteristic.

$$\text{Sample range } (R) = \text{maximum observation in sample} - \text{minimum observation in sample}$$

These ranges are summarized as $\bar{R}$, the average sample range, which can then function in a role similar to the true standard deviation in the process when determining upper and lower control limits:

$$\text{UCL} = \bar{\bar{x}} + A_2\bar{R} \qquad \text{LCL} = \bar{\bar{x}} - A_2\bar{R}$$

Note that the issue of selecting a z-value and its impact on producer's risk has now disappeared from the calculation of the mean chart's limits. In its place is the so-called A_2 factor, a value that has been derived to work with the average range $\bar{R}$ to approximate a three-sigma control chart. The correct value for A_2 for any given mean chart depends upon n, the size of the sample being used, and can be located according to that size on the table provided in Figure 13.10.

Because of the natural variation in the samples estimated with sample means and sample ranges, it is wise to continue to monitor both issues. Thus, mean charts created

FIGURE 13.10 Mean (x-bar) and Range (R) Chart Factors

Sample Size (n)	Mean chart (A_2)	Range Chart	
		D_4	D_5
2	1.88	0	3.27
3	1.02	0	2.57
4	0.73	0	2.28
5	0.58	0	2.11
6	0.48	0	2.00
7	0.42	0.08	1.92
8	0.37	0.14	1.86
9	0.34	0.18	1.82
10	0.31	0.22	1.78
11	0.29	0.26	1.74
12	0.27	0.28	1.72
13	0.25	0.31	1.69
14	0.24	0.33	1.67
15	0.22	0.35	1.65
16	0.21	0.36	1.64
17	0.20	0.38	1.62
18	0.19	0.39	1.61
19	0.19	0.40	1.60
20	0.18	0.41	1.59

***R*-chart**
Control chart used in monitoring the range of some characteristic within a sample.

under conditions of unknown variation are often used in conjunction with *R*-charts, where future sample ranges can be recorded. The bounds of an *R*-chart are based on the original *R* obtained when the process was known to be in control:

$$\text{UCL} = D_5\bar{R} \qquad \text{LCL} = D_4\bar{R}$$

When the exact nature of natural variation is unknown, the *R*-chart is at least as important as the mean chart, if not sometimes more important. If, in fact, the variation in a process is growing, this highly troublesome condition can go completely undetected by watching only average values on a mean chart. Similar to the mean chart's A_2 factor, both the D_4 and D_5 values needed to calculate these range chart limits can be located according to sample size in Figure 13.10. Scenario 2b demonstrates these calculations for both types of charts.

Scenario 2b **Mean and Range Charts (Unknown Natural Process Variation)**

The production manager of Main House Gaming is worried about the assumption that "When in control, the game tile cutter produces round tiles with a standard deviation in tile diameter of 0.1 millimeters." This assumption is based on a claim made by a company that built the tile cutting machine several years ago, and the production manager is not comfortable with setting up current quality control tools based on that aging claim. Instead, the manager feels that Main House Gaming should base its tools on actual observation of game tile production. The production manager gathered 10 samples consisting of four round tiles each during a period in which the machine was known to be operating correctly, cutting 20-mm round tiles:

Round Tile Sample Data (exact diameter of each round tile, in millimeters)

Sample	Tile 1	Tile 2	Tile 3	Tile 4	Sample Mean
1	20.01	19.98	19.95	19.98	19.98
2	19.99	20.03	19.97	20.05	20.01
3	19.97	19.93	19.98	19.91	19.95
4	20.09	20.01	20.01	19.97	20.02
5	20.05	20.02	19.97	20.00	20.01
6	19.95	20.03	19.97	19.94	19.97
7	19.96	19.98	20.09	20.04	20.02
8	19.97	20.02	20.00	19.94	19.98
9	20.01	19.93	20.03	19.97	19.99
10	19.94	20.00	20.01	20.00	19.99

Given that the production manager treats true process variation as unknown, what would the appropriate mean and range chart look like to monitor 20-mm round tile production in the future? What does this set of samples look like when charted against those limits?

Analysis

The data gathered by the production manager includes sample means—the average of the four diameters recorded in each sample. To create a mean chart under these circumstances, however, the ranges of each sample should also be calculated:

ROUND TILE SAMPLES FOR MEAN AND RANGE CHARTS

Sample	Tile 1	Tile 2	Tile 3	Tile 4	Sample Mean	RANGE (Max – Min)
1	20.01	19.98	19.95	19.98	19.98	20.01 – 19.95 = 0.06
2	19.99	20.03	19.97	20.05	20.01	20.05 – 19.97 = 0.08
3	19.97	19.93	19.98	19.91	19.95	19.98 – 19.91 = 0.07
4	20.09	20.01	20.01	19.97	20.02	20.09 – 19.97 = 0.12
5	20.05	20.02	19.97	20.00	20.01	20.05 – 19.97 = 0.08
6	19.95	20.03	19.97	19.94	19.97	20.03 – 19.94 = 0.09
7	19.96	19.98	20.09	20.04	20.02	20.09 – 19.96 = 0.13
8	19.97	20.02	20.00	19.94	19.98	20.02 – 19.94 = 0.08
9	20.01	19.93	20.03	19.97	19.99	20.03 – 19.93 = 0.10
10	19.94	20.00	20.01	20.00	19.99	20.01 – 19.94 = 0.07

Once the ranges are determined, we can calculate two of the three input parameters needed for the mean chart, the mean of the sample means ($\bar{\bar{X}}$) and the mean of the sample ranges ($\bar{R}$):

ROUND TILE MEAN AND RANGE CHARTS

Mean of the sample means

$$\bar{\bar{X}} = (19.98 + 20.01 + 19.95 + 20.02 + 20.01 + 19.97 + 20.02 + 19.98 + 19.99 + 19.99)/10$$
$$= 19.992 \text{ mm}$$

Mean of the sample ranges

$$\bar{R} = (0.06 + 0.08 + 0.07 + 0.12 + 0.08 + 0.09 + 0.13 + 0.08 + 0.10 + 0.07)/10$$
$$= 0.088 \text{ mm}$$

Continues

To plot the charts, we must determine the appropriate input values for the factors A_2, D_5, and D_6 from the table in Figure 13.10. To do so, we locate n, the size of each sample, in the chart's first column; $n = 4$ in the case of this data:

ROUND TILE MEAN AND RANGE CHARTS

Values needed from chart in Figure 13.10 (looking up $n = 4$)

- $A_2 = 0.73$
- $D_4 = 0$
- $D_5 = 2.28$

Now everything required for calculation of the control limits on both the mean and the range chart is available, and we can determine the bounds:

ROUND TILE MEAN AND RANGE CHARTS

Upper and Lower Control Limits for Mean Chart

$$UCL = \bar{\bar{X}} + A_2\bar{R} = 19.992 + 0.73 \times 0.088 = 19.992 + 0.064 = 20.056 \text{ mm}$$

$$LCL = \bar{\bar{X}} - A_2\bar{R} = 19.992 - 0.73 \times 0.088 = 19.992 - 0.064 = 19.928 \text{ mm}$$

Upper and Lower Control Limits (UCL and LCL) for Range Chart

$$UCL = D_5\bar{R} = 2.28 \times 0.088 = 0.201 \text{ mm}$$

$$LCL = D_4\bar{R} = 0 \times 0.088 = 0 \text{ mm}$$

To create the charts we graph these limits to scale, so that future samples may be accurately marked for comparison. Remember that this scenario specifically requests that the original 10 samples be plotted.

ROUND TILE MEAN CHART

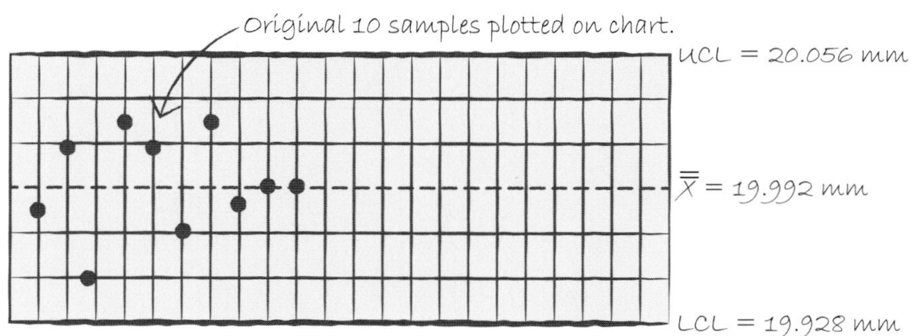

ROUND TILE RANGE CHART

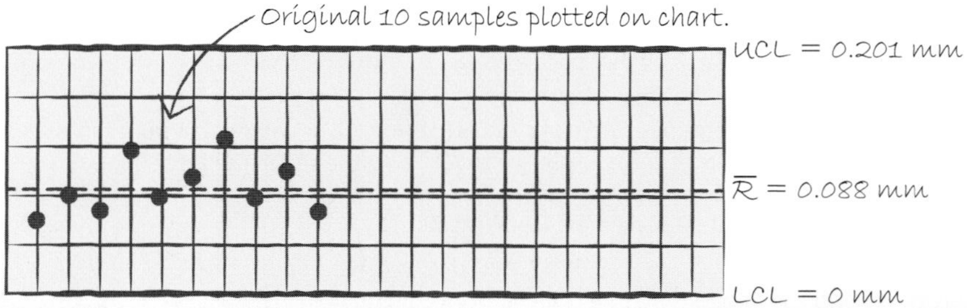

Insight This mean chart with unknown variation has narrower control limits than either of the mean charts drawn up in Scenario 2a. However, all sample data so far falls well within the control limits, supporting the production manager's assumption that the round tile cutting process is currently in control. ■

Disclaimer: Scenario 2b's use of only 10 original samples to establish the charts is not good practice; a minimum of 25 such samples is generally considered acceptable to achieve statistical significance. Scenario 2b's risky use of only 10 samples was for convenience of demonstrating the steps of the chart design process.

Control Charts for Attributes

Mean charts monitor the average of some measurable characteristic of a product. However, a characteristic of interest might not be a quantitative issue, but rather a simpler yes or no qualitative question: Is this unit defective? Is this pellet orange in color? Did the shipment arrive late? If a yes or no question such as these is being asked of each member of a sample of known size, then the issue of interest is usually the proportion of yes answers earned by that sample, monitored with a *p*-chart.

***p*-chart**
Control chart used in monitoring the proportion of some characteristic within a sample.

***p*-Charts** The central parameter of interest in a *p*-chart is $\overline{p}$, the average proportion of some attribute present in output when the process is in control. This might be known in advance, but is most likely confirmed by drawing several samples of size n while the process is operating normally, assessing the exact proportion in each sample and averaging those sample proportions to estimate $\overline{p}$. With this parameter in hand, the only other parameter requiring estimation is the standard deviation in the distribution of those sample proportions (σ_p) calculated with this expression:

$$\sigma_p = \sqrt{\frac{\overline{p}(1-\overline{p})}{n}}$$

The upper and lower control limits on a *p*-chart are then established by these equations:

$$\text{UCL} = \overline{p} + z\sigma_p \qquad \text{LCL} = \overline{p} - z\sigma_p$$

The value of z chosen to set the bounds brings the same issues discussed earlier in creating mean charts with known variation: how many standard deviations of natural variation does the control chart designer wish to include within the chart's limits? A value of $z = 3.0$ yields the common three-sigma control chart, as demonstrated in Scenario 3a. The general recommendation for the number of samples to be taken when estimating p is at least 25 samples, but note that Scenario 3a fails this particular requirement just as Scenario 2b did, for the sake of convenient presentation.

p-Charts

Scenario 3a

Several of Main House Gaming's strategy games rely on two colors of round tiles representing two types of resources earned by the players of the game. The games are shipped with a total of 100 tiles in each box, split between the two color themes of that game's artwork, usually red and blue. Loose tiles of the two different colors are loaded into a counting machine that quickly releases 100 round tiles into each box, based on tile weight. This machine is set to release an equal weight of each tile type, creating a color mix of 50% red and 50% blue. However, since the machine is working at high speed, the exact proportion of red and blue tiles in each box varies slightly. While small variations are acceptable, the production manager of Main House Gaming wants to use a *p*-chart to monitor this mix in the future. The manager opened 10 game boxes packed when the counting machine was known to be in control and counted the exact number of each color of round tile.

Continues

Box	Red Tiles	Blue Tiles	Total Round Tiles
1	50	50	100
2	48	52	100
3	52	48	100
4	54	46	100
5	44	56	100
6	42	58	100
7	52	48	100
8	56	44	100
9	50	50	100
10	54	46	100

The production manager wishes for 99.7% of all future boxes sampled to fall inside the control limits when the counting machine is operating normally. What then should a *p*-chart to monitor future proportions of red tiles in each game box look like? How would this current data appear when charted on that *p*-chart?

Analysis

Each game box is functioning as a sample, and that sample's size is 100 tiles. The production manager's wish for 99.7% of all future boxes to fall within the control limits when the counting machine is operating normally is the equivalent of 99.7% of all samples falling within the control limits when the process is in control. This is the same level of confidence first explored in Scenario 2a, meaning that a *z*-value of 3.0 should be used in calculating the limits. To summarize:

RED TILE p-CHART INPUT PARAMETERS

- $n = 100$ (each box contains 100 tiles)
- $z = 3.0$ (as specified by the production manager)

To calculate the control limits, we analyze the data to determine *p*, the mean sample proportion of red tile:

RED TILE p-CHART INPUT PARAMETERS

Box	Red Tiles	Proportion of Red Tiles (p)
1	50	50/100 = 0.50
2	48	48/100 = 0.48
3	52	52/100 = 0.52
4	54	54/100 = 0.54
5	44	44/100 = 0.44
6	42	42/100 = 0.42
7	52	52/100 = 0.52
8	56	56/100 = 0.56
9	50	50/100 = 0.50
10	54	54/100 = 0.54

Mean proportion of red tiles, $\bar{p} = 0.50$

Next we can calculate standard deviation in this sampling distribution, σ_p:

$$\sigma_{\bar{p}} = \sqrt{\frac{\bar{p}(1-\bar{p})}{n}} = \sqrt{\frac{0.5(1-0.5)}{100}} = 0.05$$

Now we have values for all variables required to calculate the upper and lower bounds:

RED TILE *p*-CHART CONTROL LIMITS

$$UCL = \bar{p} + z\sigma_{\bar{p}} = 0.50 + 3.0 \times 0.05 = 0.50 + 0.15 = 0.65$$

$$LCL = \bar{p} - z\sigma_{\bar{p}} = 0.50 - 3.0 \times 0.05 = 0.50 - 0.15 = 0.35$$

We draw the *p*-chart by graphing these limits, so that the proportion of red tiles found in future boxes sampled can be charted for comparison. This scenario specifically requested that the original 10 sample boxes be plotted, as pictured below:

RED TILE *p*-CHART

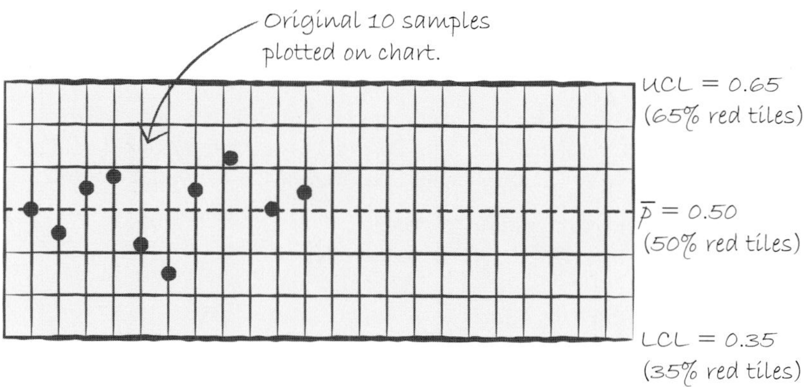

Insight The 10 boxes charted here fit well within the limits set by the *p*-chart, which tolerates as much as 65% or as few as 35% red tiles found in a game box. If the production manager believes the limits should be tightened somewhat, the *z*-value can be reduced and the chart redrawn with narrower control limits around the desired proportion of 50% red tiles, although this change will increase the theoretical risk that some future sampled box does fall outside those limits even though the counting machine is actually operating normally. ■

c-Charts Sometimes occurrences, such as the number of complaints about cold food at a restaurant, are tracked without taking samples. Without a fixed sample size, this attribute cannot be calculated as a proportion. When the issue is a simple count of yes answers to an attribute question, a c-chart can be used, assuming that this count is taken at regular intervals. If *c* is the average number of occurrences in each interval, the limits of a *c*-chart are determined by

c-chart Control chart used in monitoring the count of some characteristic within a sample.

$$UCL = \bar{c} + z\sqrt{\bar{c}} \qquad LCL = \bar{c} - z\sqrt{\bar{c}}$$

Similar to a *p*-chart, a *c*-chart requires its developer to adopt some level of producer's risk by choosing a *z*-value, and may require the developer to estimate $\bar{c}$ by averaging past counts under acceptable conditions, and may initially suggest a negative lower limit, which will be logically reset to zero. We demonstrate all these issues in Scenario 3b.

Scenario 3b

c-Charts

Each month, a few strategy board games are returned to Main House Gaming due to quality problems. These problems include incorrect contents, poorly cut playing pieces, or damage during shipment. The production manager has 20 months of past data concerning the number of games returned:

Month	Returns	Month	Returns	Month	Returns	Month	Returns
1	3	6	1	11	5	16	1
2	3	7	5	12	1	17	0
3	0	8	2	13	0	18	1
4	1	9	1	14	5	19	1
5	2	10	2	15	2	20	2

The production manager wishes to construct a c-chart for these returns, setting the limits such that 99.7% of all future monthly returns fall inside the control limits when game production is functioning as it has over these past 20 months. What should this c-chart look like? How would this data appear when charted on that c-chart?

Analysis

The production manager's concern for 99.7% of future returns falling within the limits is the same level of confidence as adopted in Scenarios 2a and 3a, meaning that we should use a z-value of 3.0 to calculate the limits. To estimate $\bar{c}$, we average the return data for all 20 months:

RETURNS c-CHART INPUT PARAMETERS

- $z = 3.0$ (as specified by the production manager)
- $\bar{c} = (3 + 3 + 0 + 1 + 2 + 1 + 5 + 2 + 1 + 2 + 5 + 1 + 0 + 5 + 2 + 1 + 0 + 1 + 1 + 2)/20 = 1.90$

Now we can calculate the limits:

RETURNS c-CHART LIMITS

For the case of $z = 3.0$

$$UCL = \bar{c} + z\sqrt{\bar{c}}$$

$= 1.90 + 3 \times 1.38 = 6.04$ returns (round to 6 monthly returns)

$$LCL = \bar{c} - z\sqrt{\bar{c}}$$

$= 1.90 - 3 \times 1.38 = -2.24$ returns (reset to 0 monthly returns)

Finally we draw the c-chart by graphing these limits to scale and plotting the historical data, as requested:

MAIN HOUSE GAMING RETURNS c-CHART

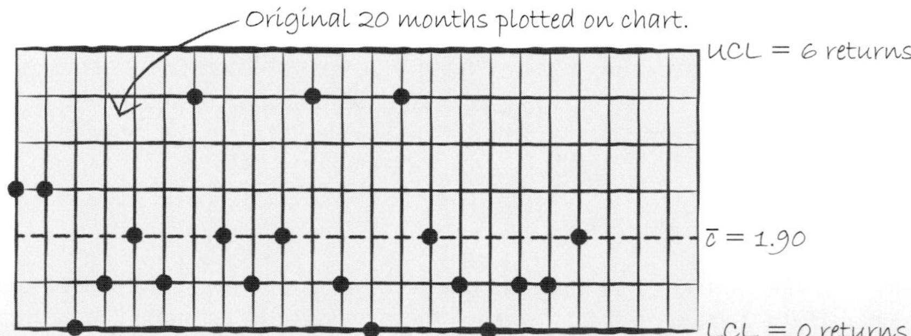

Insight Main House Gaming should expect future monthly returns to fall between zero and six each month, although clustering below the midline of the chart is not problematic in this case, since a lower count for returned games would be a desirable condition. ■

ACCEPTANCE SAMPLING

Control charts monitor transformation processes as they operate. Earlier, Figure 13.6 suggested that statistical quality control includes monitoring the conformance of an operation's inputs and outputs. Similar to the setting for control charts, inputs and outputs are not likely to be inspected completely, but rather sampled for conformance. Unlike control charts, the decision in this setting is not whether to stop production but whether to declare a larger batch of input and output as acceptable, based on the smaller sample. Thus, this process is known as acceptance sampling, and this critical acceptance/rejection decision is made according to a sampling plan developed for that operation. Sampling plans are based on the following criteria:

acceptance sampling Estimating the quality of conformance of large batches through inspection of smaller samples.

sampling plan Defined procedure for conducting acceptance sampling, including the criteria that determines rejection of the batch being sampled.

- **The size of the samples (*n*).**
- **The size of the lots or batches being sampled (*N*).**
- **The number of samples to be taken.** For example, a large batch might be judged on one sample, but should a sample fail to pass some test, a second sample is taken.
- **The rule for acceptance versus rejection.**For example, if no more than a certain number of defects (*c*) are found in the sample, the batch is accepted.

The design of the sampling plan influences both its costs and its risks, suggested earlier by the Figure 13.7 trade-off. The larger and more numerous the samples required by the plan, the greater the cost of implementing it. However, judging large batches by studying small samples brings the risk of missing bad batches. In acceptance sampling, these risks and their combined result are expressed in the operating characteristics (OC) and the average outgoing quality (AOQ) curves of the sampling plan.

operating characteristic (OC) curve A graph of the likelihood of accepting a batch, given an increasing proportion of defects within that batch.

Operating Characteristic Curves

An operating characteristic (OC) curve illustrates a particular plan's response to a range of defectiveness, as shown for an example sampling plan in Figure 13.11. This curve illustrates the chance a batch will be accepted when the sampling plan requires a sample of

Example OC Curve (n = 20, c = 1)

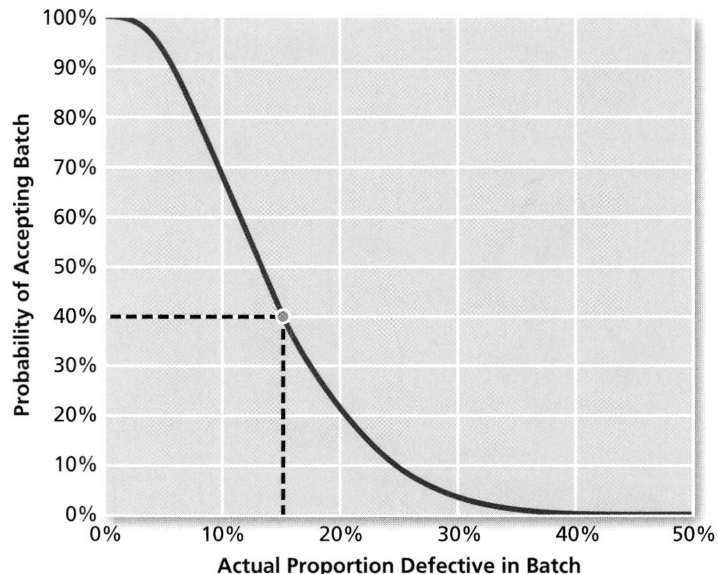

FIGURE 13.11

With n = 20 and c = 1 a batch faces rejection if more than 10% of a sample of 20 units is defective. Here, a batch that is 15% defective has a 40.4% chance of being accepted, based on one sample.

20 items ($n = 20$) be drawn at random from the batch, and the batch be rejected if more than one defect ($c = 1$) is found in the sample. Under this plan, a batch with 15% defective has a 40% chance of being accepted, even though this proportion defective is actually higher than the portion defective tolerated in its random sample.

Poisson distribution
A discrete probability distribution describing the likelihood of a particular number of independent events within a particular interval.

OC curves are generated with a cumulative binomial or Poisson distribution, and thus all start at a 100% chance of acceptance when there are in fact no defects anywhere in the batch, dropping to 0% chance of acceptance when the batch is 100% defective. The precise shape of the curve results from choices made in the sampling plan, as illustrated in Figure 13.12. Here the Figure 13.11 OC curve is pictured with the OC curves of two other plans that both tolerate up to 10% defective in a sample, but require different-sized samples.

In general, steeper OC curves indicate plans that are less likely to mistake the quality of a batch based on the quality of a sample. Figure 13.12 illustrates that larger sample sizes reduce this risk: there is very little chance that the plan with sample size $n = 1{,}000$ will mistake a batch with no more than 10% defective as unacceptable or more than 10% defective as acceptable. However, this safeguard must be weighed against the increased costs of inspecting larger samples.

acceptable quality level (AQL)
Proportion of defects a consumer considers acceptable.

Selecting an appropriate sampling plan requires declaration of an acceptable quality level, or AQL, indicating what percent defective is considered reasonable. Given a certain AQL, the producer's risk can be determined from the sampling plan's OC curve, as illustrated in Figure 13.13. If, for example, the user is willing to tolerate up to 5% defective, the original sampling plan from Figure 13.11 has a 92% chance of accepting any batch of that description, based on one sample. The risk to the producer is the remaining 8% chance that a batch will be rejected based on one "unlucky" sample, even though its actual quality is acceptable to the consumer.

Interestingly, what the consumer considers reasonable and what the consumer will tolerate are two different issues in acceptance sampling. It is often assumed that the consumer who declares a particular AQL will nonetheless accept up to a higher amount occasionally, recognizing the randomness in sampling and in the process. Thus, the consumer

FIGURE 13.12 Three OC Curves of Three Different Sample Sizes

Here, a batch is rejected if more than 10% of the sample is defective.

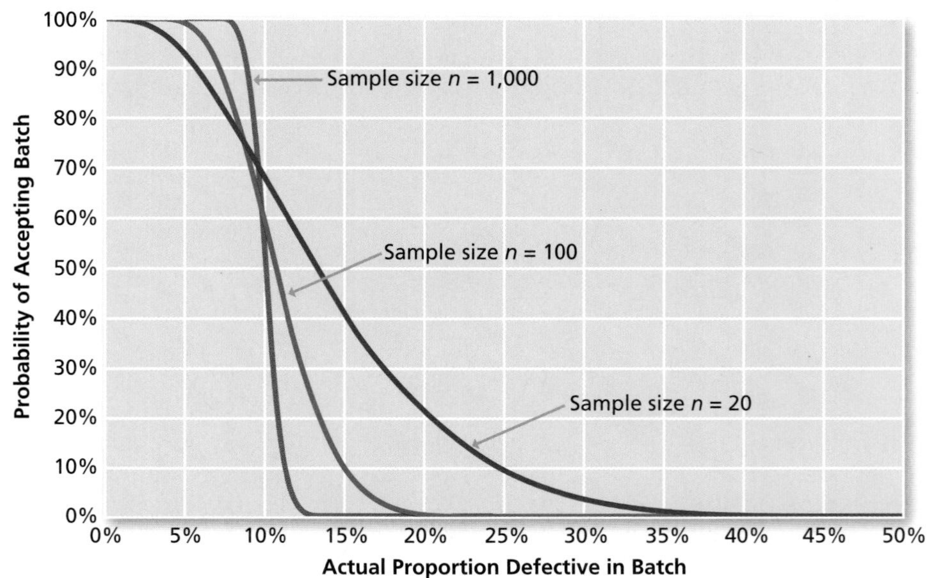

Example Policies of AQL and LTPD and Producer's versus Consumer's Risk (n = 20, c = 1) FIGURE **13.13**

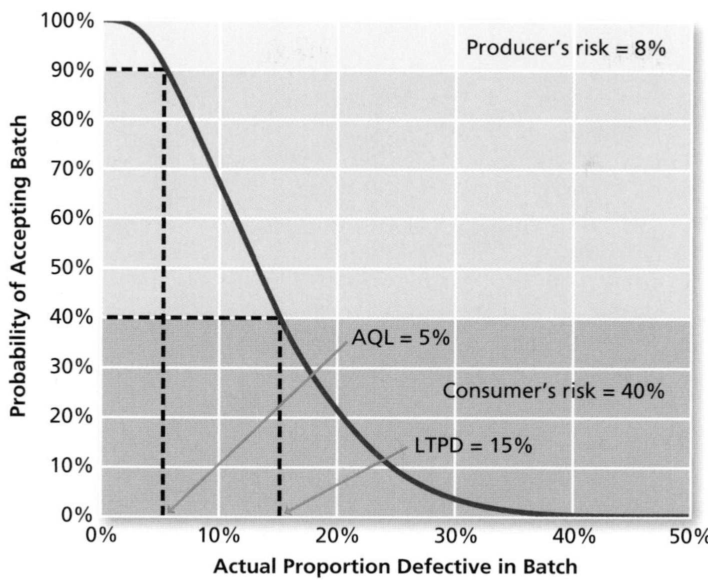

has a second, higher limit on what is usable, known as a lot tolerance percent defective, LTPD. It is the height of the curve at this LTPD that expresses the consumer's risk of accidentally accepting an unacceptable batch under the sampling plan. For example, the consumer's LTPD is 15% in Figure 13.13, where there remains a 40% chance of accepting batches with greater amounts defective under this plan.

lot tolerance percent defective (LTPD) Maximum proportion of defects that a consumer can tolerate.

Average Outgoing Quality

Just as each sampling plan has its particular OC curve, each plan is assumed to result in a certain level of average outgoing quality (AOQ), the average proportion of defects that is actually passed to the consumer under the plan. Using a sampling plan's OC curve, the AOQ achieved at a particular actual proportion defective of p can be calculated by first retrieving P_{AC}, the probability of accepting a batch at that level of p, and completing this formula:

average outgoing quality (AOQ) Estimate of the proportion of defects that pass an acceptance sampling plan.

$$\text{AOQ} = P_{AC} \times p \times \left(\frac{N-n}{N}\right)$$

where n is the sample size and N is the batch size. For example, Figure 13.11 shows that $P_{AC} = 20\%$ when $p = 20\%$, using samples of size $n = 20$. Assuming that the batch size being sampled is 5,000, the resulting AOQ of the plan would be

$$\text{AOQ} = 0.20 \times 0.20 \times \left(\frac{5{,}000 - 20}{5{,}000}\right) = 0.04 = 4\%$$

This indicates that the sampling plan, when taking in an average of 20% defective, will pass an average of 4% defective to the consumer. The plan's apparent improvement of quality is based on a critical assumption of the AOQ formula: all rejected batches are 100% inspected and all rejects found there are fixed. Thus, the greater the number of rejected batches, the greater the number of 100% fixed batches passed into the system, and the lower the combined percentage of defects being passed by the sampling plan.

FIGURE 13.14 An Example AOQ Curve (n = 20, c = 1)

If the batches are 20% defective, the plan accepts 4% defective into the system.

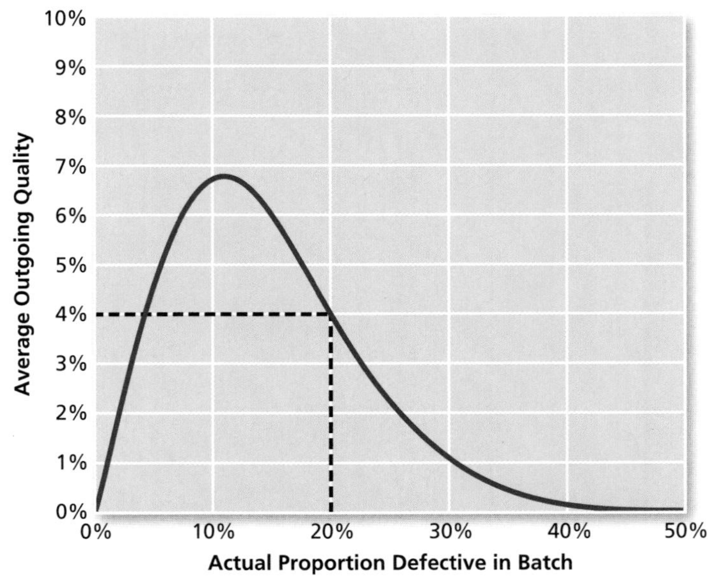

While this is a doubtful long-term response in reality, calculating the AOQ at various levels of incoming defective does give another reading on the responsiveness of the sampling plan. Plotting a range of these readings creates an AOQ curve, such as the example in Figure 13.14.

After discussing techniques such as control charting and acceptance sampling, we should note an irony: the "control" in "quality control" does not refer to direct control over product quality. Whatever direct control over quality does exist is found in the choices made during product design and in the most appropriate operation of the system. In contrast, quality control techniques grant a manager control over some, but not all, variation in that product. The challenge answered by quality control is the recognition of when observed variation is assignable, implying it can be controlled, versus when it is random and beyond control. Given that nothing can be absolutely perfect, successful quality control makes clearer what can be changed from what can't be changed, inviting us to focus on those changes over which our own actions would be most effective.

SUMMARY

Any ongoing process provides a background of natural variation into which troublesome assignable variation can easily blend. The highly visual tools of statistical process control are means of making assignable variation more apparent to any observer of the process, allowing that observer to stop the production process when it appears to go out of control. The most popular of these tools is the mean chart, a control chart allowing sample means to be graphed as they become available, illustrating any changes in the central tendency of the issue being measured. Designing such a chart requires setting limits on how much variation is acceptable in production, a task that requires balancing the producer's risk of stopping production when in fact nothing is wrong with the process with the consumer's risk of receiving unacceptable product because the limits are spaced too generously and assignable variation has gone undetected. Similarly, any acceptance sampling plan requires its designer to make that same choice between consumer's and producer's risk when deciding how frequently to sample and how harshly to assess sample results, decisions that determine the risk of mistaking a bad shipment for a good one or a good shipment for a bad one.

Key Terms

acceptable quality level (AQL)
acceptance sampling
assignable variation
average outgoing quality (AOQ)
c-chart
Central Limit Theorem
consumer's risk
control chart
control limit
defect
functional organizational structure
lot tolerance percent defective (LTPD)
mean chart
natural variation
operating characteristic (OC) curve
outcome bias
p-chart
Poisson distribution
process capability
producer's risk
quality of conformance
R-chart
range
sampling plan
scientific management
standard normal distribution
statistical process control (SPC)
Taguchi loss function
tolerance
total quality management (TQM)
type I error
type II error

Discussion Questions

1. Which represents the greatest threat to the success of an operation, the producer's or the consumer's risk?
2. What types of operations exhibit the greatest natural variation in their output? How useful is statistical process control to these operations?
3. If the Central Limit Theorem were to suddenly become invalid, how would the current use of control charts then be misguided?
4. Suppose the range within a sample was calculated and then plotted on an *R*-chart, but this sample range fell outside the *lower* control limit on the *R*-chart. Does this necessarily represent defective production?
5. Why would a consumer tolerate a certain amount of defectiveness in a product? When is this more common?

PROBLEMS

Minute Answer

Short answers appear in Appendix A. Go to **NoteShaper.com** for full video tutorials on each question.

1. A production process that exhibits only natural variation would be considered what?
2. Another term or description for natural variation is what?
3. If a point plotted on a control chart falls outside one of the control limits, what does this suggest?
4. Producer's risk refers to what potential mistake?
5. To what potential mistake does consumer's risk refer?
6. Will the variation in sample means be greater or less than the variation in the process being sampled?
7. A process capability index value greater than 1.0 indicates what?

8. Will widening the distance between the control limits on a mean chart increase or decrease producer's risk?
9. How does decreasing the sample size influence the producer's risk in acceptance sampling?
10. Theoretically, how does an increasing proportion of defects in incoming product influence the probability of accepting a batch?
11. Do larger sample sizes lead to narrower or wider control limits on a process?
12. Do larger sample sizes increase or decrease consumer's risk?

Quick Start

13. Five cans are measured from the recent output of a high-speed bottling line. The weights of each of these cans are 12.23, 12.55, 12.01, 12.26, and 12.17 ounces. What is the mean weight of this sample of five cans?
14. Five cans are measured from the recent output of a high-speed bottling line. The weights of each of these cans are 12.23, 12.55, 12.01, 12.26, and 12.17 ounces. What is the range in this sample of five cans?
15. Samples of five cans are to be selected periodically from a canning process that has a standard deviation (σ) of 0.2 ounces when in control. What will the standard deviation in the sampling distribution be?
16. A certain product can weigh no more than 1.001 and no less than 0.998 ounces by design. A machine being considered to produce this product has natural standard deviation of 0.0004 ounces in its output. What is the process capability index for this use of the machine?
17. Thirty samples of 16 cans each are measured from a canning process while it is in control. The mean of the 30 sample means is 12.03 ounces and the average range is 0.04 ounces. What should the upper and lower control limits be on a mean chart to monitor this canning process in the future?
18. Thirty samples of 16 cans each are measured from a canning process while it is in control. The mean of the 30 sample means is 12.03 ounces and the average range is 0.04 ounces. What should the upper and lower control limits be on a range chart to monitor this canning process in the future?
19. The average proportion defective is known to be 1%. What should the upper and lower control limits of a p-chart be if $n = 25$ and $z = 3.0$?
20. The average number of defects is 35 per day. What should the upper and lower control limits of a c-chart be if $z = 3.0$?
21. If a sampling plan used a sample size of $n = 100$ for batches of $N = 1{,}000$ units with a 58.3% chance of accepting batches that have an actual proportion defective of $p = 10\%$, what AOQ would result from this plan?

Ramp Up

22. Suppose a manager must construct either a mean chart with known variation or a p-chart to monitor some process. When the process is in control, the manager wants only 0.6% of the samples taken to fall outside these limits. What z-value should be used when calculating the limits for this chart?
23. Suppose a manager must construct either a mean chart with known variation or a p-chart to monitor some process. When the process is in control, the manager wants only 12.6% of the samples taken to fall outside these limits. What z-value should be used when calculating the limits for this chart?

24. Samples of five cans are to be selected periodically from a canning process that has a variance (σ^2) of 0.2 ounces when in control. What will the standard deviation in the sampling distribution be?

25. A certain product can weigh no more than 1.001 and no less than 0.998 ounces by design. What is the maximum natural variation a process can have to be considered capable of supporting these design specifications?

26. Suppose a manager must construct either a mean chart with known variation or a *p*-chart to monitor some process. When the process is in control, the manager wants only 1.92% of the samples taken to fall outside these limits. What *z*-value should the manager use when calculating the limits for this chart?

27. An office supply company manufactures paper clips, and even tolerates a small proportion of those paper clips being defective (incorrectly shaped and/or twisted) in its outgoing product. (The company reasons that paper clips are so cheap, users will simply discard the occasional defective paper clip they might find in a box.) The average proportion of defective paper clips is known to be 2% when the paper clip manufacturing process is in control. To monitor this issue, what should be the value of the upper control limit of a *p*-chart if the company plans to include 100 paper clips in each of its samples and uses a *z*-value of 3.0 to construct the chart?

Full Scenarios

Reminder: Short answers appear in Appendix A. Go to **NoteShaper.com** for full video tutorials on each question.

28. A beverage company would like to use a mean chart to monitor how much liquid beverage it puts into each 500-ml bottle. They know from past experience that whenever this process is under control, bottle weight is normally distributed with a mean of 500 ml and a standard deviation of 2 ml. The company plans to measure samples of 25 bottles from the production line every hour, and record the mean weight of liquid beverage in the bottles.
    a. If the company uses $z = 3.0$ as its standard for establishing the mean chart, where will the upper and lower control limits be on that chart?
    b. For legal reasons, the company cannot tolerate more than 501 or less than 499 ml in each bottle. What is the process capability index value for this bottling process? What does it indicate about the process?

29. A large beverage company would like to use statistical process control to monitor a new bottling machine designed to load liquid into 350-ml bottles. This company knows that the exact amount the machine places in each bottle can naturally vary by a small amount, but does not have any more specific information about the process. The company operated this new machine under careful supervision, confident that the machine was under complete control, for 7 hours. Each hour, a sample of six bottles was taken off the line and the amount of liquid in each bottle was carefully measured. This is the resulting data:

Sample	Sample Mean	Sample Range
1	350.85 ml	0.6 ml
2	350.80 ml	0.8 ml
3	351.20 ml	0.5 ml
4	351.00 ml	1.0 ml
5	350.62 ml	0.8 ml
6	351.12 ml	0.7 ml
7	351.50 ml	0.8 ml

a. Where should the control limits be placed on a mean chart intended to monitor this machine in the future, using the same sampling procedure that produced this data?

b. Where should the control limits be placed on a range chart intended to monitor this machine in the future, using the same sampling procedure that produced this data?

c. A new sample is taken from the machine's output, and these are the exact weights of liquid in each bottle: 350.82 ml, 350.07 ml, 350.10 ml, 350.50 ml, 349.75 ml, and 349.90 ml. According to the charts created in parts a and b of this question, does this sample indicate the process is in control?

30. A manager wants to monitor the proportion of red candies present in a five-color candy mix. For 8 hours, the manager has gathered exactly 50 candies every hour, by randomly selecting and emptying one 50-candy bag produced by the the candy mix packaging machine. During this 8-hour shift, the manager was assured the candy color mix was under appropriate control. Examining the eight samples gathered revealed these amounts of red candy:

Sample	Red Candy (number in sample)
1	10
2	12
3	11
4	10
5	8
6	13
7	11
8	9

a. What are the mean and the standard deviation of the natural variation in this sampling process for the proportion of red candy?

b. If the manager uses $z = 3.0$ to create a p-chart to continue monitoring the proportion of red candy in the five-color mix, what will be its upper and lower control limits?

c. Suppose the manager is mistaken in the belief that each bag contains 50 candies. In reality, the number of candies in each bag can vary quite a bit, so the manager has resolved to use a c-chart instead. Assuming the same level of confidence as in part b, what are the upper and lower control limits of this chart? How does this chart compare to the p-chart in part b?

CASE STUDY: EXIT 53 WMA FAST LANE TOLL SYSTEM, REVISITED

Recall from Chapter 5 that Western Motorway Authority (WMA) operates a network of toll roads connecting three urbanized areas. Each of its toll collection plazas offers a choice of payment methods to approaching drivers, including WMA FAST, a subscription service that allows drivers to pay wirelessly as they pass through a special toll lane without stopping. Exit 53 toll plaza is a typical WMA facility, equipped with five toll lanes, one of which is dedicated to WMA FAST subscribers only. Each day, the dedicated WMA FAST lane automatically debits the FAST accounts of thousands of passing vehicles, although occasionally a vehicle will pass without transmitting billing information to the FAST system. This is referred to as FAST lane violation and high-speed cameras record the rear license plate of that vehicle as it exits the toll plaza. The WMA FAST system automatically processes these photos and mails a billing statement to the registered owner of the vehicle, requiring this person to pay both the exit 53 toll and a small penalty for incorrect usage of the WMA FAST lane.

A WMA FAST lane toll violation is usually caused by a nonsubscription vehicle incorrectly choosing the FAST lane when passing the toll plaza, although sometimes it is caused by inadequate funds in the FAST account of a subscription vehicle. Another possible but less common cause is a malfunctioning onboard FAST transceiver in a passing subscription vehicle, failing to identify itself to the WMA FAST lane wireless system. All of these scenarios are natural outcomes in a system used by thousands of vehicles a day, appropriately addressed by the automatic paper billing of the registered owner. However, one other potential cause of a FAST lane violation is that the FAST system itself malfunctioned, failing to record the signals from a correctly functioning onboard transceiver. This causes failure to debit any account, which automatically triggers the lane violation system. This scenario is the most troublesome to WMA management, in that the automatic billing for FAST lane violation assumes the vehicle was at fault, not the FAST lane system itself.

A FAST lane system should not malfunction if it is properly maintained, although a small possibility exists that some part of it could fail between maintenance cycles. This disturbing possibility was the subject of heated discussions at a recent toll plaza managers' meeting, after a FAST lane installation malfunctioned and issued over a thousand billing statements to unsuspecting vehicle owners before employees recognized the problem and closed the malfunctioning lane. Some managers at the meeting pointed out WMA's need for some tool to monitor the number of FAST lane violations each day, to make any unusual change in that activity more visible. Other managers at the meeting remembered previous attempts to use control charts, particularly *c*-charts, to plot the daily number of violations issued by a FAST lane, and how those pilot projects failed. "We've been over this before," said one of those managers. "The usual quality control *c*-chart stuff doesn't work for FAST lanes. Every time we draw up a chart from the data of a flawlessly functioning lane, it just indicates that lane is out of control. We're stuck before we even start using the chart."

The manager at exit 53 volunteered its FAST lane as the site for yet another pilot project to develop a relevant tool to monitor FAST lane violations, one that would correctly signal any unusual changes, to be acted on quickly by closing the lane. Exit 53's FAST lane equipment was upgraded less than a year ago, and preventative maintenance was conducted in late May, so the following 30 days of past data from exit 53 represents the behavior of a system that is in complete control:

Recent 30 Days of Data for Exit 53 WMA FAST Lane Activity

Date	Day	FAST Lane Tolls Successfully Collected	FAST Lane Violations Issued	Date	Day	FAST Lane Tolls Successfully Collected	FAST Lane Violations Issued
1-Jun	Monday	9,395	25	16-Jun	Tuesday	9,793	28
2-Jun	Tuesday	10,325	26	17-Jun	Wednesday	9,499	23
3-Jun	Wednesday	8,978	26	18-Jun	Thursday	9,300	27
4-Jun	Thursday	9,916	24	19-Jun	Friday	9,603	27
5-Jun	Friday	9,418	26	20-Jun	Saturday	940	8
6-Jun	Saturday	2,637	20	21-Jun	Sunday	3,053	27
7-Jun	Sunday	3,736	30	22-Jun	Monday	9,168	27
8-Jun	Monday	9,866	29	23-Jun	Tuesday	10,386	27
9-Jun	Tuesday	8,412	25	24-Jun	Wednesday	8,499	24
10-Jun	Wednesday	9,213	23	25-Jun	Thursday	8,784	25
11-Jun	Thursday	8,371	22	26-Jun	Friday	9,183	25
12-Jun	Friday	8,045	20	27-Jun	Saturday	2,264	20
13-Jun	Saturday	6,087	52	28-Jun	Sunday	275	2
14-Jun	Sunday	4,599	35	29-Jun	Monday	8,076	22
15-Jun	Monday	9,343	24	30-Jun	Tuesday	7,678	19

Questions

1. Use this data to create a *c*-chart for daily FAST lane violations issued, assuming $z = 3.0$. This is the method that WMA attempted to use earlier. Mark the past data on the chart. Does your *c*-chart indicate that the FAST lane system was in control over these past 30 days?
2. One employee at exit 53 remembers the previous pilot project and says, "That wasn't ever going to work. You can't just watch the number of violations, because that varies with the number of cars each day." This employee is referring to the choice of a *c*-chart versus a *p*-chart, but WMA management assumed that a *p*-chart couldn't be used because there is no fixed sample size n. Propose a logical adaptation of the *p*-chart methodology and create a chart to track the proportion of vehicles in the FAST lane that are issued violations each day. Does this chart indicate the current system is in control?
3. Now create a charting system that solves WMA's monitoring problem. The secret to this lies in the employee's previous statement and in an additional remark about the earlier unsuccessful pilot project: "Why did they think that we'd be able to use the same chart all week?"

BIBLIOGRAPHY

Blackstone, J. ed. 2010. *APICS Dictionary,* 13th ed. Chicago: APICS, The Association for Operations Management.

Evans, J., and W. Lindsay. 2002. *The Management and Control of Quality,* 5th ed. Cincinnati, OH: South-Western/Thomson Learning.

Hoyle, D. 2009. *ISO 9000 Quality Systems Handbook,* 6th ed. Oxford, UK: Elsevier.

McClave, J. E., P. G. Benson, and T. Sincich. 2009. *Statistics for Business and Economics.* Upper Saddle River, NJ: Prentice Hall.

Tague, N. 2005. *The Quality Toolbox,* 2nd ed. Milwaukee, WI: ASQ Quality Press.

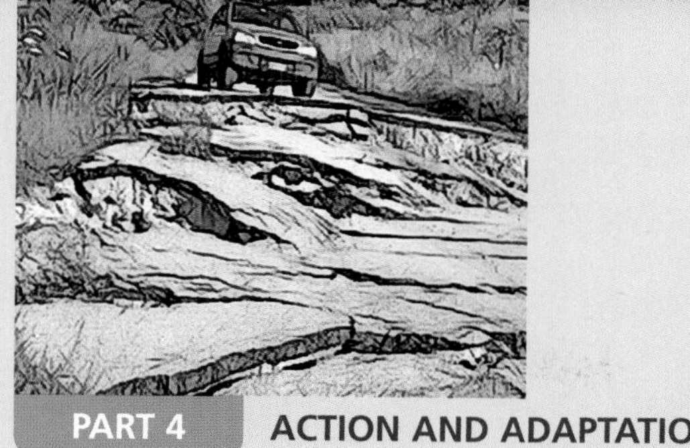

PART 4 ACTION AND ADAPTATION

CHAPTER 14

Scheduling and Real-Time Operations

I love deadlines. I like the whooshing sound they make as they fly by.

—Douglas Adams

MAJOR SECTIONS

IN THIS CHAPTER, LOOK FOR...

- Scheduling in many different aspects of operations planning and applied to short-term decisions.
- A variety of priority rules to create various scheduling sequences.
- Scheduling for a single work center, a bottleneck work center, several work centers simultaneously, personal time management, and in real-time.
- Gantt charts.

INTRODUCTION

To schedule is to determine timing. This seemingly simple task is a cornerstone of successful operations management, apparent almost anywhere a person or organization is striving to create value. Finished schedules are everywhere in daily life; you have no doubt been exposed to class schedules, conference schedules, and building schedules; bus, train, and airline schedules; television broadcast and theater schedules; and scheduled appointments with professional services. In each case, an organization has determined the timing of valuable activities, for access by you—the customer. Organizations also create and revise schedules for internal use, such as production scheduling and employee schedules. The discussion in this chapter is dedicated to the process of scheduling, although most of operations management might be argued as some form of determining timing. Therefore, we first consider all forms of timing, to clarify what kinds of scheduling may present the greatest challenge to the operations manager.

SCHEDULING ENVIRONMENTS

scheduling
To determine timing.

planning horizon
The farthest point in the future considered in decision making.

Most of operations management is theoretically related to scheduling, because timing is a thread that runs from broad issues such as selecting capacity strategies through to detailed calculations such as ordering raw materials. The nature of scheduling varies, however, with the length of planning horizon allowed to the scheduler. Events such as new facility construction can be scheduled years in advance, but this type of scheduling is usually referred to as *planning*. Likewise, an airline traffic controller could be said to be planning the safe arrival of aircraft in the area around an airport, but this short-term problem in planning is more likely to be associated with the word *scheduling*. Figure 14.1 organizes this range of planning horizons, to expose the continuum of various scheduling environments.

Long Planning Horizons

make-to-stock
A system that produces high volumes of standardized product.

Scheduling in a long-term environment involves the timing of activities a year or more in advance. This form of scheduling often involves timings permanently designed into a system, supporting make-to-stock production. Large-scale projects can also require scheduling years in advance, such as the construction of a new train line through a crowded city center. Successful project management is heavily dependent on good scheduling, and example project schedules can be found for planning horizons of many different lengths.

FIGURE 14.1 Various Scheduling/Planning Horizons

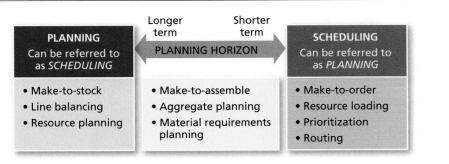

PLANNING Can be referred to as *SCHEDULING*	Longer term ⟵ PLANNING HORIZON ⟶ Shorter term	SCHEDULING Can be referred to as *PLANNING*
• Make-to-stock • Line balancing • Resource planning	• Make-to-assemble • Aggregate planning • Material requirements planning	• Make-to-order • Resource loading • Prioritization • Routing

Medium Planning Horizons

Scheduling over a midrange planning horizon determines the timing of activities over the course of a month to a year. This could be the aggregate planning or more detailed material planning for an assemble-to-order system, mapping much of its activities reasonably far in advance. Large projects, such as the renovation of an existing structure or the preparations for an important event, inhabit this particular environment as well. Medium-term environments can be considered the border between when timing decisions are most likely to be considered planning versus when such decisions are more likely to be called scheduling by name.

assemble-to-order (ATO)
A system that produces standard modules to be modified and/or combined into a customizable product.

Short Planning Horizons

Scheduling in the short term presents challenges distinct from other forms of planning. Thus, this form of scheduling is most likely to be called scheduling by name and is the focus of this chapter. Short-term scheduling is usually associated with make-to-order production, managing the ever-changing traffic patterns through facilities often called job shops. For this reason, short-term scheduling is sometimes referred to as *job shop scheduling*, although this type of scheduling does not necessarily take place in an industrial shop building customized goods. Figure 14.2 lists scheduling issues any machine shop or custom cabinetry shop would share with what might appear to be a very dissimilar operation, the busy airport in the illustration.

make-to-order
A system that produces low volumes of customized product.

job shop
A process layout.

Short-term scheduling may map out the timing of activities for several weeks into the future, or it may look only hours ahead. In fact there may be no planning horizon at all, requiring a decision maker to guide activity through the changing conditions of real-time. Since all scheduling involves timing, certain decisions form common threads through different short-term scheduling situations, including the airport in Figure 14.2. Scheduling often involves the issue of sequencing, prioritizing activities to create a desirable order for their completion. Scheduling can also require careful loading of a system by assigning activities to its resources, such as directing arriving planes to gates. The creation of sequences and assignments often create the issues of routing and traffic through the system, which in turn may require monitoring and updating through some type of supervisory control.

sequencing
To determine the order in which requirements are met.

loading
Assigning work to resources.

Job Shop Scheduling Issues — **FIGURE 14.2**

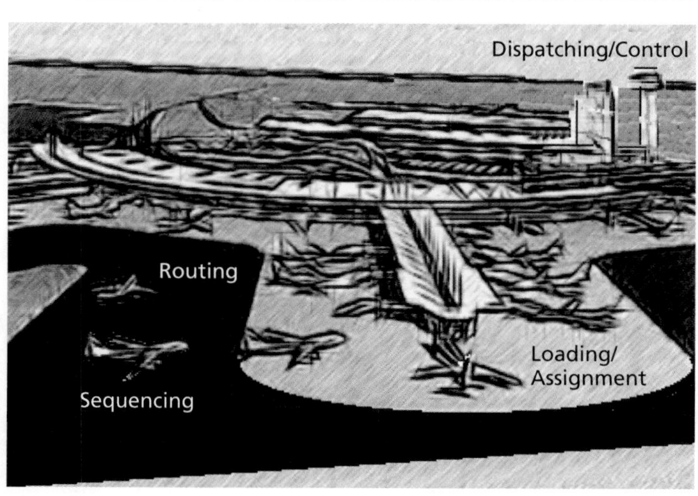

While these issues can be identified at an airport, a machinery repair shop, a walk-in medical clinic, and even in personal time management, the challenge of scheduling is not identical in each of these settings: it varies dramatically with the complexity of the system being scheduled.

SINGLE WORK CENTER SCHEDULING

A single work center is the simplest system in scheduling. It is an entity that processes arriving work and can only work on one arrival at a time. This entity might be a single industrial machine, such as a metal press, or a single person, such as a physician or a court judge. In any case, the work center at the heart of the situation completes one requirement at a time, and a queue may form for the work center's services. While the loading of a work center influences the length of this queue, so too does the sequencing within that queue. If the amount of work required of the work center has been predetermined, selection of a good sequence for that work becomes the scheduler's primary concern.

queue
A waiting line.

Evaluating Sequences

Individual requirements of a work center are known as *jobs*. Jobs might be custom orders moving between machines in an industrial job shop, or they might represent individual patients waiting to consult a physician, or individual court cases waiting to go before a judge. Regardless of the situation, each job requires some time from that work center, and the duration of this requirement could vary dramatically between jobs. Summing these requirements together for a group of jobs determines the makespan of that group, or the total amount of time required to finish all the jobs. Scheduling in this context is primarily an issue of choosing a sequence to arrange the jobs within this makespan.

makespan
The length of time required to complete a finished schedule.

All sequences at the single work center possess the same makespan, because jobs must be completed one-at-a-time, regardless of their order. What varies between different sequences is the flowtime associated with each job, or how much time passes before each job is finished. The flowtime of any job consists of two parts:

flowtime
The length of time a job spends in the system.

$$\text{Flowtime} = \text{waiting time (or flowtime of previous job)} + \text{processing time}$$

We can evaluate a sequence by calculating its average flowtime, a measure of general efficiency. Flowtimes can also determine whether the sequence completes jobs in a timely fashion, because each job may have some form of due date, an expectation of when the

Four Work Centers in an Industrial Job Shop

While the concept of a work center can be applied to many different situations, work centers are usually easy to identify in industrial settings, as distinct groups of machinery with bright boundary lines painted between them. Painted borders, such as those in this picture, are intended to help guide traffic safely among the activities in the work centers.

job will be finished. If a job's flowtime is less than its due date, this job will be completed before it is due. However, if a job's flowtime is greater than its due date, this job will not be completed on time. The amount of time by which a job misses its deadline is called its tardiness; should the job be completed early or on time, that job is said to have no tardiness, or a tardiness of zero. Thus, a sequence can also be evaluated by calculating average tardiness across all its jobs, which can then be interpreted as a measure of customer service. We demonstrate these calculations in Scenario 1a.

tardiness The length of time a job is late. If a job is finished early or on time, its tardiness is zero.

Single Work Center: Evaluating a Sequence

Scenario 1a

Global Freightways, an international air freight company, operates a small satellite center in Edinburgh, Scotland. Each day, a large plane from Amsterdam, Netherlands lands at the Edinburgh airport, bringing inbound packaged freight to be delivered across the United Kingdom. As this plane is unloaded, five small courier jets arrive in Edinburgh, bringing outbound freight collected from across the UK and Ireland. Once the large plane is unloaded, each of the small courier jets is unloaded and then reloaded with their portion of the newly arrived inbound freight. These small jets then leave, while the crew at the satellite center loads the large jet with the outbound freight collected from the courier jets. The larger jet then departs, returning to Global Freightways' central cargo center in Amsterdam. This entire cycle repeats daily.

While the large jet must be unloaded first and loaded last, there is flexibility in the courier jet sequence. These five jets vary somewhat in the time required to turn them around—unload and then reload them—releasing them for departure from Edinburgh:

Jet	Processing Time (hrs.)	Scheduled Departure (hrs.)
Belfast	0.50 hr.	1.0 hr.
Birmingham	0.25	2.6
Dublin	0.65	2.0
Manchester	0.75	1.5
London	1.50	3.0

For convenience, departure times are stated as the number of hours after start of work on the courier planes. This work on the courier plane sequence usually begins at 9:30 p.m. GMT, meaning that Belfast's scheduled departure of 1 hour indicates it is expected to be turned around and then to depart by 10:30 p.m. GMT.

The five courier planes are usually processed in alphabetical order. Is this a good sequence?

Analysis

It is difficult to determine whether an alphabetical sequence is good or bad without another sequence for comparison, but we can evaluate it in terms of flowtime and tardiness. We begin by calculating the flowtime of each jet, starting with the first jet in the sequence. Since Belfast is processed first and Belfast requires 0.5 hour to turn around, then Belfast will be finished in 0.5 hour:

COURIER JET SEQUENCE (ALPHABETICAL)

Jet	Flowtime (hrs. from start)	Tardiness (hrs.)
Belfast	0.50 hr.	
Birmingham		
Dublin		
London		
Manchester		

Continues

The next jet in the sequence, Birmingham, must wait until the jet from Belfast is finished. Therefore, the flowtime for Birmingham is equal to its own processing time, 0.25 hour, plus the 0.50 hour it waited.

COURIER JET SEQUENCE (ALPHABETICAL)

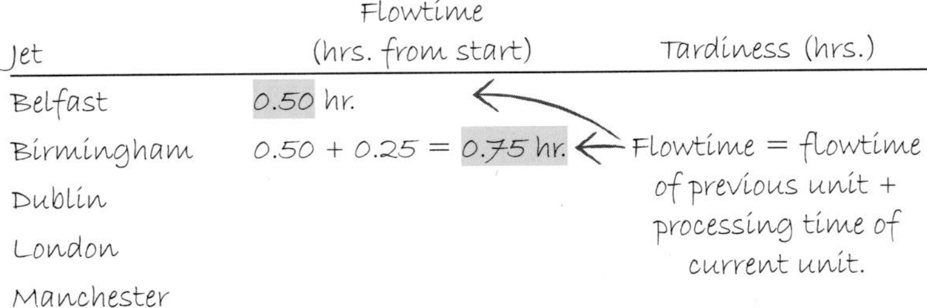

Jet	Flowtime (hrs. from start)	Tardiness (hrs.)
Belfast	0.50 hr.	
Birmingham	0.50 + 0.25 = 0.75 hr.	
Dublin		
London		
Manchester		

Flowtime = flowtime of previous unit + processing time of current unit.

We extend this logic to each of the other jets, revealing the point in time at which each will be finished and ready for departure.

COURIER JET SEQUENCE (ALPHABETICAL)

Jet	Flowtime (hrs. from start)	Tardiness (hrs.)
Belfast	0.50 hr.	
Birmingham	0.50 + 0.25 = 0.75	
Dublin	0.75 + 0.65 = 1.40	
London	1.40 + 1.50 = 2.90	
Manchester	2.90 + 0.75 = 3.65	

Once flowtime is determined, we can then calculate the potential tardiness of each jet by comparing the flowtime of a jet to its scheduled departure time. Belfast's flowtime is 0.5 hour, while its original scheduled departure time is 1 hour, so this jet will be ready 1.0 – 0.5 = 0.5 hour early. In the event that a jet is early, it is not tardy, so its tardiness is 0.

COURIER JET SEQUENCE (ALPHABETICAL)

Jet	Flowtime (hrs. from start)	Scheduled Departure (hrs.)	Tardiness (hrs.)
Belfast	0.50 hr.	1.0 hr.	0 hrs.
Birmingham	0.50 + 0.25 = 0.75	2.6	
Dublin	0.75 + 0.65 = 1.40	2.0	
London	1.40 + 1.50 = 2.90	3.0	
Manchester	2.90 + 0.75 = 3.65	1.5	

When we compare flowtime to scheduled departure time on the remaining jets, we see only one problem at the end of the sequence:

COURIER JET SEQUENCE (ALPHABETICAL)

Jet	Flowtime (hrs. from start)	Scheduled Departure (hrs.)	Tardiness (hrs.)
Belfast	0.50 hr.	1.0 hr.	0 hrs.
Birmingham	0.50 + 0.25 = 0.75	2.6	0
Dublin	0.75 + 0.65 = 1.40	2.0	0
London	1.40 + 1.50 = 2.90	3.0	0
Manchester	2.90 + 0.75 = 3.65	1.5	3.65 − 1.50 = 2.15

Manchester is scheduled for departure in 1.5 hours, but won't be finished for 3.65 hours, so it will be 2.15 hours late.

To summarize these findings, we calculate average flowtime and average tardiness:

COURIER JET SEQUENCE (ALPHABETICAL)

Average flowtime = (0.50 + 0.75 + 1.40 + 2.90 + 3.65)/5 = 1.84 hrs.

Average tardiness = (0 + 0 + 0 + 0 + 2.15)/5 = 0.43 hr.

Insight While we cannot determine how good the alphabetical sequence is without another sequence for comparison, we now know this sequence has an average flowtime of 1.84 hours and an average tardiness of 0.43 hour. In the case of tardiness, this average represents four courier jets that are ready for departure early, but the fifth jet departs over 2 hours late. ■

Priority Rules

Scheduling a single work center requires selecting a desirable sequence for its queue of jobs, which in turn may require generating multiple sequences for evaluation. A sequence can be created by employing a priority rule, a policy that specifies how jobs should be sorted into order. For example, the sequence evaluated in Scenario 1a was created by the rule of alphabetical order. While this is a logical rule for organizing objects for storage and retrieval, alphabetical order is not a common priority rule, because it addresses neither the processing needs of a job nor the urgency of its due date. Two priority rules for generating sequences do address these issues directly, known by their abbreviations SPT and EDD.

priority rule A rule determining the sequence in which requirements will be met.

SPT and EDD One rule for prioritizing work into a sequence is shortest processing time first, or the SPT rule. As the name implies, the SPT rule sorts jobs by their processing times, with the shortest jobs being placed at the beginning of the sequence. Because the shortest jobs are completed first, an SPT sequence finishes more jobs within a given amount of time. Thus, the SPT rule is known for minimizing average flowtime, although it requires the same makespan as any other sequence.

While known for its efficiency, the SPT rule ignores any information concerning promised due dates. In contrast, another common priority rule is earliest due date first, or the EDD rule. EDD creates a sequence by sorting according to due date, ignoring the processing time information. We apply and evaluate both these rules in Scenario 1b.

SPT Abbreviation for the priority rule of shortest processing time, or scheduling the task that requires the least amount of processing time first.

EDD Abbreviation for the priority rule of earliest due date, or scheduling the task with the most imminent deadline first.

Scenario 1b

Single Work Center: Priority Rules

The cargo manager at the Global Freightways Edinburgh satellite center is concerned that processing the center's five courier jets in alphabetical order isn't necessarily the best sequence and asks for an evaluation of the SPT and EDD rules instead.

What sequence does SPT suggest? What sequence does EDD suggest? How do these compare with processing in alphabetical order, examined in Scenario 1a?

Analysis

To create the SPT sequence, we sort flights by the processing times given in Scenario 1a, from smallest to largest:

COURIER JET SEQUENCE (SPT)

Jet	Processing Time (hrs.)
Birmingham	0.25 hr.
Belfast	0.50
Dublin	0.65
Manchester	0.75
London	1.50

To evaluate this sequence, we calculate the resulting flow times first:

COURIER JET SEQUENCE (SPT)

Jet	Flowtime (hrs. from start)
Birmingham	0.25 hr.
Belfast	0.25 + 0.50 = 0.75
Dublin	0.75 + 0.65 = 1.40
Manchester	1.40 + 0.75 = 2.15
London	2.15 + 1.50 = 3.65

With this data we can calculate any tardiness, and then determine summary averages for that sequence:

COURIER JET SEQUENCE (SPT)

Jete	Flowtime (hrs. from start)	Scheduled Departure (hrs.)	Tardiness (hrs.)
Birmingham	0.25 hr.	2.6 hrs.	0 hrs.
Belfast	0.25 + 0.50 = 0.75	1.0	0
Dublin	0.75 + 0.65 = 1.40	2.0	0
Manchester	1.40 + 0.75 = 2.15	1.5	2.15 − 1.5 = 0.65
London	2.15 + 1.50 = 3.65	3.0	3.65 − 3.0 = 0.65

Average flowtime = (0.25 + 0.75 + 1.40 + 2.15 + 3.65)/5 = 1.64 hrs.

Average tardiness = (0 + 0 + 0 + 0.65 + 0.65)/5 = 0.26 hr.

SPT has a lower average flowtime and lower average tardiness than the alphabetical sequence in Scenario 1a, although the SPT sequence does delay two jets, whereas the alphabetical sequence delays the departure of only one jet.

Next, we evaluate the EDD sequence by first sorting the jets by their scheduled departures, from smallest to largest:

COURIER JET SEQUENCE (EDD)

Jet	Scheduled Departure (hrs.)
Belfast	1.0 hr.
Manchester	1.5
Dublin	2.0
Birmingham	2.6
London	3.0

Then as we did with the SPT sequence, we calculate flowtimes and tardiness for EDD:

COURIER JET SEQUENCE (EDD)

Jet	Flowtime (hrs. from start)	Scheduled Departure (hrs.)	Tardiness (hrs.)
Belfast	0.50 hr.	1.0 hr.	0 hrs.
Manchester	0.50 + 0.75 = 1.25	1.5	0
Dublin	1.25 + 0.65 = 1.90	2.0	0
Birmingham	1.90 + 0.25 = 2.15	2.6	0
London	2.15 + 1.5 = 3.65	3.0	3.65 − 3.0 = 0.65

Average flowtime = (0.50 + 1.25 + 1.90 + 2.15 + 3.65)/5 = 1.89 hrs.

Average tardiness = (0 + 0 + 0 + 0 + 0.65)/5 = 0.13 hrs.

Insight The SPT sequence has the lowest average flowtime of all three sequences, indicating that each jet will be turned around and ready for departure in an average of 1.64 hours. However, the EDD sequence has the lowest average tardiness of 0.13 hour, enabling on-time departures for all but the London flight, which is delayed 0.65 hour. Both the EDD and the SPT sequence have better average tardiness than the alphabetical sequence, although the alphabetical sequence does have a slightly better average flowtime than EDD. ■

Note that the flowtime of the fifth and last courier jet in each of the sequences in Scenarios 1a and 1b is identical: 3.65 hours. This highlights the fact that the flowtime of the final job in any sequence is, by definition, also the makespan of the sequence, determined by the sum of all the processing times.

Other Rules Despite SPT's strength for minimizing average flowtime and EDD's strength for minimizing tardiness, neither SPT nor EDD is common in situations where people are the jobs waiting on a single work center. When people queue for a service, FCFS—or first-come, first-served—is usually the rule in operation to sequence the arrivals, a process also known as queue discipline. FCFS is not a particularly reliable rule for minimizing flowtime nor for avoiding tardiness, yet it is probably the best known of all priority rules because it is perceived as fair by the arrivals joining the queue.

Other priority rules include putting the longest jobs first or sorting by a combination of processing requirement and due date known as a critical ratio, discussed later. Still other rules may prioritize based on a factor particular to that situation, not expressed by the simple measures of processing time and due date. For example, triage is a priority rule familiar to disaster response, where only those who could benefit most from a limited resource are placed at the front of a sequence, similar to the more everyday logic of the emergencies-first rule.

FCFS
First-come, first-served sequencing rule.

queue discipline
A rule or rules determining the order in which waiting individuals will be served.

triage
A priority rule creating sequences intended to yield the most value from distinctly limited resources.

The Challenge of FCFS

Although FCFS sounds simple, it is not always easy to create this sequence in practice. This overhead view of the random arrivals at a tour assembly point for the Eiffel Tower in Paris demonstrates the difficulties of accurately maintaining an FCFS sequence once the queue outgrows the facility. Free-forming serpentine lines such as this are often forced to wrap back on themselves, at which point the location of the end of the line may be hidden to new arrivals, and the accuracy of FCFS is lost. This may or may not impact the efficiency of the system, but it will interfere with the customers' perception of service because deviating from FCFS sequencing of an on-demand service is considered distinctly unfair in many cultures.

Personal Time Management

multitasking
Simultaneous completion of multiple tasks by a single processor.

Personal time management can be thought of as single work center scheduling. Despite the popularity of the term multitasking, it is generally not possible for one person to actively process more than one task at any single moment in time. When examined closely, successful human multitasking is usually the skillful switching between two or more tasks, blending together smaller episodes of attention to each task so that all tasks appear to proceed simultaneously. Thus, an individual's time management, even when multitasking, still fits the description of a single work center.

People who prefer SPT when scheduling their time complete small tasks first, often expressing a desire to "cross those off the list quickly" and thus enjoy the sense of minimizing average flowtime. EDD also suggests a logical way to sequence personal work, prioritizing what is needed soonest. However, personal time management involves complexity that the industrial view of a single work center does not always recognize. When sequencing multiple tasks, time management consultants often advise people to prioritize a task based on these criteria:

- Focus on its importance, recognizing the difference between the urgency and the importance of a task. Urgency, as expressed in due dates, is a more reliable indicator of relative importance in an industrial setting than in a personal calendar. At the individual level, prioritizing strictly by due date or FCFS is less likely to create the best sequence to support an individual's effectiveness.
- Balance attention to production with attention to productive capacity. In an industrial setting, the issue of maintaining productive capacity is easily recognized in the scheduling of preventative maintenance and the replacing of equipment, but maintaining personal effectiveness is not as tangible. Proper attention to productive capacity in personal time management includes scheduling some time for personal improvement and maintaining a good work/life balance among activities.
- Strive to be proactive, but be aware of what tasks you have good control over and what tasks are heavily influenced by issues outside your control. Tasks heavily influenced by external forces may not be avoidable, but should be recognized as not the best choice for the use of limited time and more likely to create delays in any sequence.

While an individual person is a far more complex resource than any single machine, many of the concepts and some of the general tools of scheduling work in personal time management. Gantt charts, discussed in the next section, are particularly useful in mapping out personal work.

MULTIPLE WORK CENTER SCHEDULING

Most organizations do not consist of one and only one distinct work center. By definition, systems and organizations usually consist of sets of resources that interact and cooperate to provide value to an outside customer. Single work center scheduling concepts are still useful, because each resource within a complex system becomes a single work center when studied individually. However, these multiple internal work centers are often linked by precedence relationships, passing work from one center to another before completion. As a result, the sequence chosen at one work center has a direct influence on the sequence available to any downstream work center, creating a complex scheduling problem. In single work center scheduling the issue of makespan is not influenced by the sequence of work. However, in multiple work center scheduling precedence relationships between centers create situations in which makespan can be strongly influenced by sequencing, even in the simplest case of two work centers. In this simplest of multiple work center environments, the scheduler who wishes to minimize a schedule's makespan should use Johnson's rule to create the sequence.

precedence relationship A dependency between two tasks, usually requiring that one task be completed before the other task is started.

Johnson's Rule

If a system consists of two unique work centers, most or all of its jobs will require both centers, always starting at one particular work center and then finishing at the other. This could describe any product or service that is provided in two phases, such as preparation and then painting, emptying and then reloading, or examination and then treatment. While both work centers can operate simultaneously, they cannot work on the same job simultaneously, and the second work center cannot begin work on any job until the first work center has completed its work on that job. One of the most influential findings in job shop scheduling is Johnson's rule, named after the researcher who identified how to minimize the makespan of any schedule in this environment.

To generate a sequence with Johnson's rule,

1. Identify the shortest processing requirement of any job at either work center; that is, find the smallest number in the processing data.
2. If that shortest requirement (or smallest number) occurs at the first work center, schedule that job into the earliest available slot in the sequence. If that shortest requirement occurs at the second work center, schedule that job into the latest available slot in the sequence.
3. Discard the data associated with the job that has been scheduled, and return to the first step. Repeat until all jobs are scheduled into the sequence.

The five courier jet problem of the Global Freightways Edinburgh satellite center would become a Johnson's rule problem if each jet were processed in two distinct phases to complete its turn around for departure, as we do in Scenario 2a.

Two Work Centers: Johnson's Rule — Scenario 2a

The cargo manager at Global Freightways' Edinburgh center is concerned about the analysis of the five courier jets in Scenarios 1a and 1b. Each sequence had a makespan of 3.65 hours, which the cargo manager feels is not an accurate estimate of the time needed to turn those five jets around. The cargo manager believes the actual makespan should be less, and suspects that the sequences in Scenarios 1a and 1b overestimate this time because they do

Continues

not include the fact that the total time each courier jet requires is split between two phases, unloading and loading the jet:

Jet	Total Duration (hrs.)	=	Unloading Time (hrs.)	+	Loading Time (hrs.)
Belfast	0.50 hr.		0.20 hr.		0.30 hr.
Birmingham	0.25		0.15		0.10
Dublin	0.65		0.30		0.35
Manchester	0.75		0.50		0.25
London	1.50		1.00		0.50

One crew unloads a jet while another crew loads a previously unloaded jet, a detail missing from the earlier analysis.

How should the cargo manager schedule these five jets, to minimize the total amount of time required to accomplish all loading and unloading?

Analysis

The question above is the equivalent of asking, What sequence for the five jets would minimize makespan? This is the sequence found by using Johnson's rule. To begin, we create a blank sequence in which to add decisions made during the use of this rule:

EDINBURGH SATELLITE COURIER JET SEQUENCE

______	______	______	______	______
1st jet	2nd jet	3rd jet	4th jet	5th jet

Now review the original data concerning the two work centers—unloading and loading—to locate the smallest number and identify the jet that number refers to:

Jet		Unloading Time (hrs.)		Loading Time (hrs.)
Belfast	Plane with	0.20 hr.		0.30 hr.
(Birmingham) ←	smallest	0.15	Smallest →	(0.10)
Dublin	number	0.30	number	0.35
Manchester		0.50		0.25
London		1.00		0.50

If the smallest number had referred to unloading, then the Birmingham plane would have been scheduled first in the sequence. However, this number referred to loading, the second work center, and thus we schedule Birmingham as late as possible in the sequence.

EDINBURGH SATELLITE COURIER JET SEQUENCE

______	______	______	______	Birmingham
1st jet	2nd jet	3rd jet	4th jet	5th jet

Now that Birmingham has been scheduled, we cross out its data and repeat the process of finding the smallest number among the remaining values:

Jet	Unloading Time (hrs.)	Loading Time (hrs.)
Belfast	0.20 hr.	0.30 hr.
~~Birmingham~~	~~0.15~~	~~0.10~~
Dublin	0.30	0.35
Manchester	0.50	0.25
London	1.00	0.50

Plane with smallest number: Belfast. Smallest number: 0.20.

Belfast is selected for scheduling, and since its value of 0.20 hour refers to unloading, we schedule this plane as early as possible.

EDINBURGH SATELLITE COURIER JET SEQUENCE

1st jet	2nd jet	3rd jet	4th jet	5th jet
Belfast				Birmingham

Now we cross Belfast off the list, and repeat the process of finding the smallest remaining number:

Jet	Unloading Time (hrs.)	Loading Time (hrs.)
~~Belfast~~	~~0.20 hr.~~	~~0.30 hr.~~
~~Birmingham~~	~~0.15~~	~~0.10~~
Dublin	0.30	0.35
Manchester	0.50	0.25
London	1.00	0.50

Plane with smallest number: Manchester. Smallest number: 0.25.

Manchester's smallest value of 0.25 refers to loading, so we schedule Manchester as late as possible. Since Birmingham is already scheduled last, Manchester is scheduled fourth:

EDINBURGH SATELLITE COURIER JET SEQUENCE

1st jet	2nd jet	3rd jet	4th jet	5th jet
Belfast			Manchester	Birmingham

This time we cross Manchester off the list, and locate the smallest remaining number :

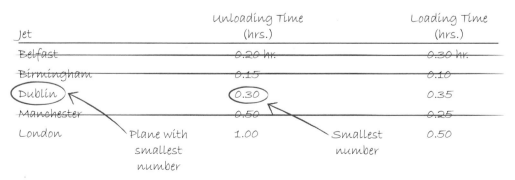

Jet	Unloading Time (hrs.)	Loading Time (hrs.)
~~Belfast~~	~~0.20 hr.~~	~~0.30 hr.~~
~~Birmingham~~	~~0.15~~	~~0.10~~
Dublin	0.30	0.35
~~Manchester~~	~~0.50~~	~~0.25~~
London	1.00	0.50

Plane with smallest number: Dublin. Smallest number: 0.30.

Continues

Next we schedule Dublin as early as possible, and then finally schedule London by default in the only remaining position, finishing the sequence:

EDINBURGH SATELLITE COURIER JET SEQUENCE

Belfast	Dublin	London	Manchester	Birmingham
1st jet	2nd jet	3rd jet	4th jet	5th jet

Insight To minimize the total amount of time spent unloading and loading these five courier planes, they should be completed in this order: Belfast, Dublin, London, Manchester, and then Birmingham. ■

Note that Johnson's rule identifies the sequence of five courier jets that minimizes the makespan of the schedule, but it does not supply any information as to how much time will be required or precisely when each jet will be finished. A Gantt chart, one of the oldest management science tools still in popular practice, can reveal this timing.

Gantt Charts

Gantt chart
A scheduling diagram that illustrates activities across a horizontal time line.

project scheduling Gantt chart
A Gantt chart in which the horizontal bars represent distinct tasks or activities.

A Gantt chart illustrates the timing of activities as rectangular bars drawn to scale across a time line. This illustration was first popularized by its namesake Henry Gantt in the early 1900s, and remains in use today in many different forms, including project plans, classroom schedules, and appointment books. Gantt charts typically, although not always, represent time as the horizontal axis of the chart, illustrating progression of planned activities from left to right. Most Gantt charts can be loosely classified as one of two types, either project scheduling or loading charts. Figure 14.3 displays an example of a project scheduling Gantt chart, where each activity is broken out into a separate row of the chart.

FIGURE 14.3 Example Project Scheduling Gantt Chart

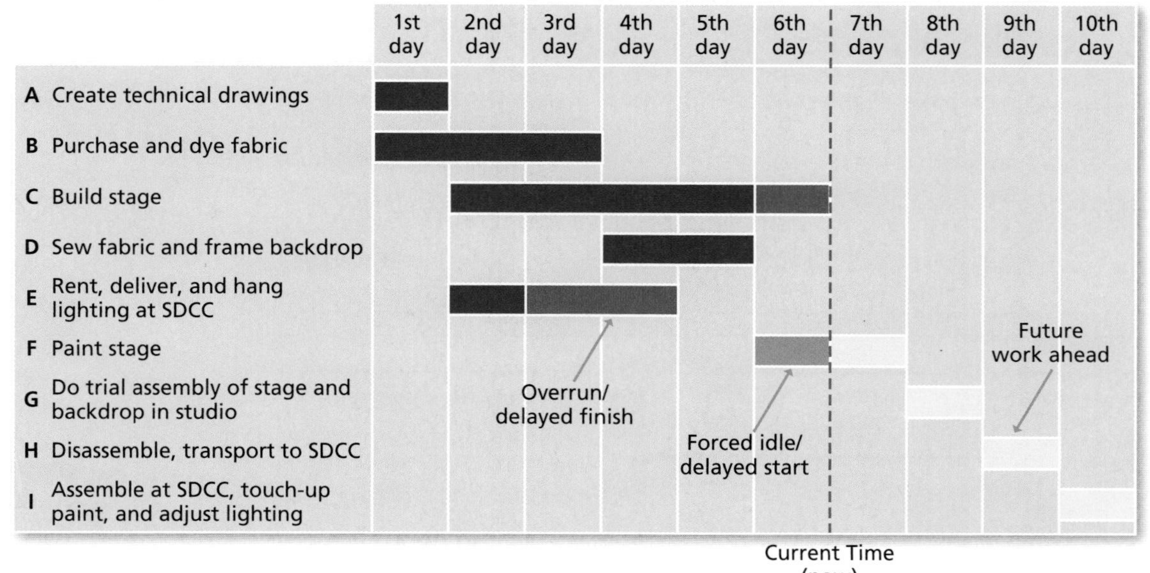

Example Loading Gantt Chart FIGURE **14.4**

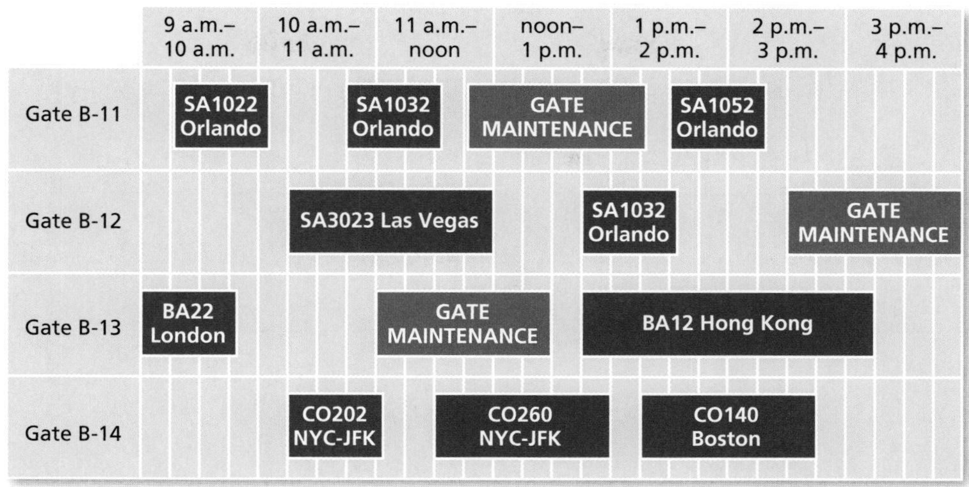

These Gantt charts emphasize the activities themselves and highlight any relevant milestones in the progress of the project. Milestones are points in time important to the schedule, such as the planned start and finish times of each activity in Figure 14.3, marked with brackets. The Gantt chart in Figure 14.3 has apparently been in use for 6 days, as the current time is marked in a line across the chart. Plotting these milestones against planned timings allows the scheduler to rapidly assess progress and incorporate new information, such as the graphing of unplanned overruns in two of the activities' completion times, one of which appears to be delaying the start of a third activity.

milestone
A point of significance in the time line of a project.

A second format of Gantt chart is popular when the most important issue is not the interdependencies of activities, but rather the successful scheduling of finite resources. Loading Gantt charts usually illustrate each distinct resource across one row of the chart, assigning activities to resources by graphing their timings across the appropriate rows. Figure 14.4 displays an example Gantt chart for work center loading, suggesting the assigning of passenger planes to gates at an airport.

loading Gantt chart
A Gantt chart in which the horizontal bars represent utilization of work centers or finite resources.

When used for resource loading, Gantt charts can prevent conflicts in the timing of activities requiring the same resources. Furthermore, if precedence relationships exist among these resources, this type of chart clarifies when activity assigned to a downstream resource may begin by making visible when the upstream resource is finished. While the assigning of arriving planes to gates pictured in Figure 14.4 does not suggest any upstream and downstream dependencies among the gates, the unloading and reloading problem of Global Freightways in Scenario 2a does fit this description. Thus, construction of a Gantt chart is a key to understanding the five courier jet sequence created by Johnson's rule, as we now demonstrate in Scenario 2b.

Two Work Centers: Gantt Chart — Scenario 2b

The cargo manager at Global Freightways' Edinburgh center is considering the five courier jet sequence created in Scenario 2a, but continues to have concerns. If the five jets are scheduled as recommended in Scenario 2a, how much time will be required to complete the sequence? Will any of the courier jets then be late for departure from Edinburgh?

Continues

Analysis

To investigate, we illustrate the sequence identified in Scenario 2a as a Gantt chart. First we draw the chart itself, representing the two work center structure by two rows on the chart, and using columns to represent a time line.

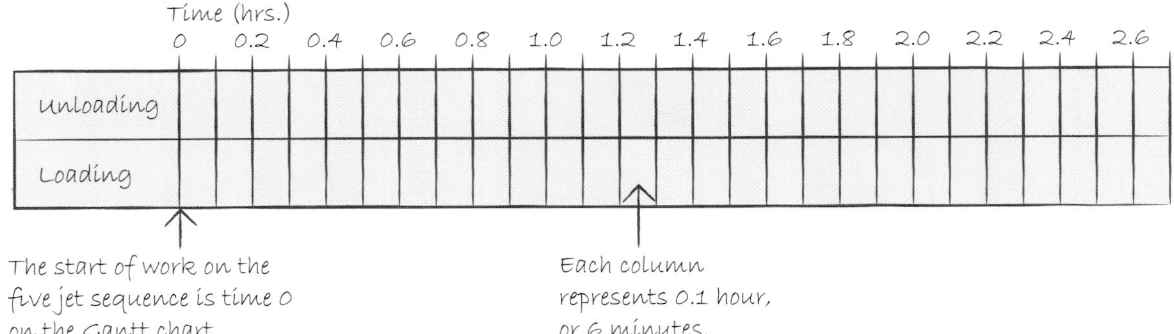

Recall from Scenario 2a that the sequence identified was Belfast, Dublin, London, Manchester, and then Birmingham. The jet arriving from Belfast requires 0.2 hour of unloading followed by 0.3 hour of loading, so this is scheduled first across the Gantt chart, by blocking out those lengths of time:

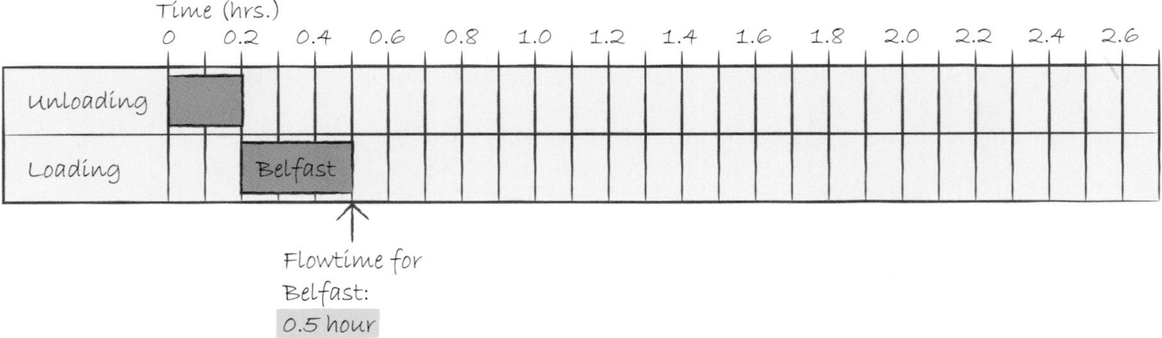

Now the flowtime for the Belfast flight is visible: if it is started immediately, it will turn around in 0.2 + 0.3 = 0.5 hour. Next we schedule Dublin, requiring 0.3 hour of unloading and 0.35 hour of loading to turn around for departure.

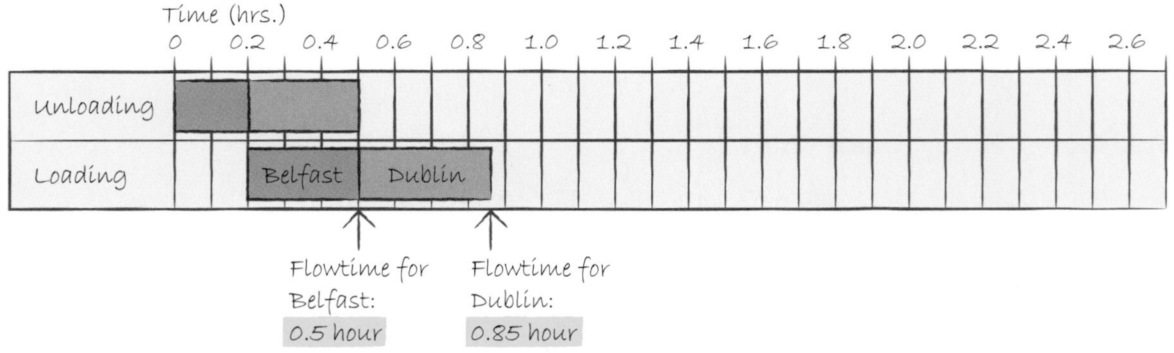

Following Dublin is the jet from London, requiring 1 hour of unloading and 0.5 hour of loading:

EDINBURGH GANTT CHART (JOHNSON'S RULE SEQUENCE)

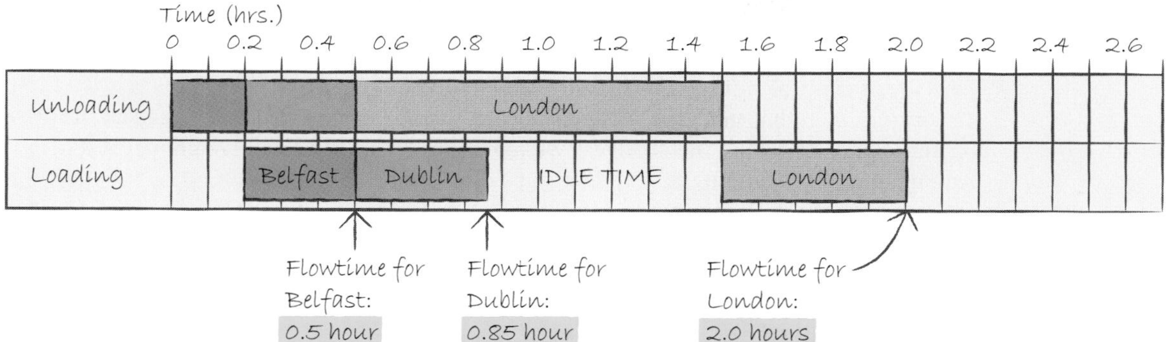

Here the Gantt chart reveals a feature of the schedule not otherwise visible in the sequence. The loading crew will finish with the Dublin flight in 0.85 hour, but the London flight will not be unloaded and ready for loading until 1.5 hours from start of work. Thus, this sequence creates a 0.65-hour stretch of time that the loading crew is forced idle, waiting for the unloading of the London flight to finish. To complete the Gantt chart, the Manchester (0.5 hour unloading and 0.25 hour loading) and Birmingham (0.15 hour unloading and 0.1 hour loading) jets may be added:

EDINBURGH GANTT CHART (JOHNSON'S RULE SEQUENCE)

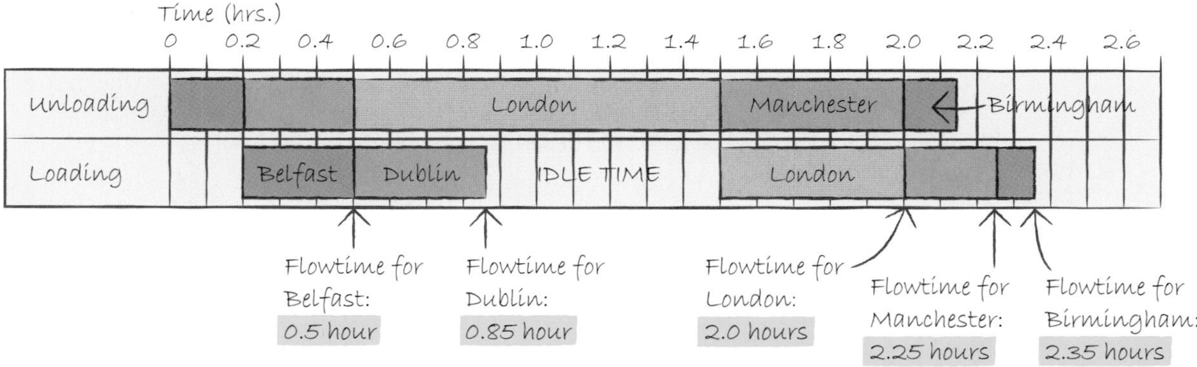

With the Gantt chart complete, the makespan of the schedule is now apparent from the flowtime of the last jet in the sequence, or 2.35 hours from the start. To determine if any courier jet will be late for departure, we calculate the tardiness of each jet.

EDINBURGH SATELLITE CENTER JET TARDINESS

Jet	Flowtime (hrs. from start)	Due Date (hrs.)	Tardiness (hrs.)
Belfast	0.50 hr.	1.0 hr.	0 hrs.
Dublin	0.85	2.0	0
London	2.00	3.0	0
Manchester	2.25	1.5	2.25 - 1.5 = 0.75
Birmingham	2.35	2.6	0

Insight A total of 2.35 hours, or 2 hours and 21 minutes, will be required to complete this sequence of five courier jets. However, the Manchester jet will be late for its scheduled departure, with a tardiness of 0.75 hour, or 45 minutes behind schedule. ■

Critical Ratio

critical ratio Time remaining until due date divided by work remaining to be done.

All priority rules discussed so far focus on one feature of a job, such as its processing time or its due date. Critical ratio is a rule that blends the issues of processing time and due date together into a single value used to sort through waiting jobs. Critical ratio is an adaptable rule, but its general formula requires time remaining until a job's due date be divided by the time required to complete all work remaining on a job. The job with the lowest critical ratio is then selected for processing next. Critical ratio is a dynamic priority rule, in that this value changes as time passes, so the scheduler must continually update ratios to reflect the changes. We look once again at Global Freightways' scheduling dilemma, considering this cycle of job selection and recalculation ratios to reflect the passage of time in Scenario 2c.

Scenario 2c

Two Work Centers: Critical Ratio Rule

The cargo manager at Global Freightways' Edinburgh satellite center is displeased that the sequence discussed in Scenarios 2a and 2b causes the Manchester courier jet to depart 45 minutes late. The cargo manager feels that a good sequence for all five jets cannot be developed without considering both the processing requirements and planned departure times of the jets, and wonders if critical ratio would be a better priority rule in this situation.

If the Edinburgh center uses critical ratio to select courier jets for processing, what sequence would result? How much more time will this schedule require than the Johnson's rule schedule? Will any of the planes be late for departure now?

Analysis

We begin exploring these issues by first generating the sequence and drawing a Gantt chart to illustrate its timings. To identify the first jet in the sequence, we must calculate the critical ratio of all five jets. Since critical ratio is time remaining divided by work remaining, these initial ratios are simply the scheduled departure times divided by the total processing times:

Jet	Unloading Time (hrs.)	+	Loading Time (hrs.)	=	Total Duration (hrs.)	Scheduled Departure (hrs.)	Initial Set of Critical Ratios
Belfast	0.20 hr.		0.30 hr.		0.50 hr.	1.0 hr.	1/0.5 = 2.0 ←
Birmingham	0.15		0.10		0.25	2.6	2.6/0.25 = 10.4
Dublin	0.30		0.35		0.65	2.0	2/0.65 = 3.1
Manchester	0.50		0.25		0.75	1.5	1.5/0.75 = 2.0 ←
London	1.00		0.50		1.50	3.0	3/1.5 = 2.0 ←

The jet with the lowest critical ratio at the current time should be scheduled first, which happens to be a three-way tie among Belfast, Manchester, and London. There is no formal rule for which of these three jets should be chosen, so we resolve this three-way tie by making a logical choice. In the case of Global Freightways, it is logical to select Belfast from among the three jets, because it has the earliest scheduled departure time and it has the shortest unloading time, so processing it first would allow the unloading crew to start on a second jet sooner.

COURIER JET SEQUENCE (CRITICAL RATIO)

Belfast				
1st jet	2nd jet	3rd jet	4th jet	5th jet

If, however, we had chosen Manchester or London as the first jet, these alternate choices would not have been incorrect with respect to the Critical Ratio rule. With Belfast first, we must simulate the passage of time and recalculate the critical ratios. If Belfast is processed first, the next point in time where a decision needs to be made is when Belfast is finished. If operation of the Edinburgh center were a classic single work center problem, then this new point in time would be 0.50 hour from the start, because that is the total duration of processing required by the Belfast jet. However, the operation unfolds in two stages, meaning that the next decision point will be even earlier than 0.50 hour, because the Belfast jet only takes 0.20 hour to unload, after which the unloading crew needs to know which jet is unloaded next. To select this second jet, we simulate the passage of 0.20 hour by subtracting this amount from the time remaining in the critical ratio of the remaining four jets.

Jet	Unloading Time (hrs.)	+	Loading Time (hrs.)	=	Total Duration (hrs.)	Scheduled Departure (hrs.)	Second Set of Critical Ratios
Birmingham	0.15 hr.		0.10 hr.		0.25 hr.	2.6 hrs.	(2.6 − 0.2)/0.25 = 2.4/0.25 = 9.60
Dublin	0.30		0.35		0.65	2.0	(2 − 0.2)/0.65 = 1.8/0.65 = 2.77
Manchester	0.50		0.25		0.75	1.5	(1.5 − 0.2)/0.75 = 1.3/0.75 = 1.73
London	1.00		0.50		1.50	3.0	(3 − 0.2)/1.5 = 2.8/1.5 = 1.87

Each critical ratio is adjusted to reflect waiting for the Belfast flight to unload (0.2 hour).

Now the Manchester jet has the lowest critical ratio, and thus we select it to follow Belfast in the sequence:

COURIER JET SEQUENCE (CRITICAL RATIO)

Belfast	Manchester			
1st jet	2nd jet	3rd jet	4th jet	5th jet

The critical ratios of the remaining flights must now be adjusted forward by 0.5 hour, to reflect the unloading time of the Manchester flight.

Jet	Unloading Time (hrs.)	+	Loading Time (hrs.)	=	Total Duration (hrs.)	Scheduled Departure (hrs.)	Third Set of Critical Ratios
Birmingham	0.15 hr.		0.10 hr.		0.25 hr.	2.6 hrs.	(2.4 − 0.5)/0.25 = 1.9/0.25 = 7.60
Dublin	0.30		0.35		0.65	2.0	(1.8 − 0.5)/0.65 = 1.3/0.65 = 2.00
London	1.00		0.50		1.50	3.0	(2.8 − 0.5)/1.5 = 2.3/1.5 = 1.53

Continues

With the lowest adjusted ratio, London is scheduled third and the ratios of the remaining two jets are updated to reflect waiting for this jet to unload as well.

COURIER JET SEQUENCE (CRITICAL RATIO)

Belfast	Manchester	London		
1st jet	2nd jet	3rd jet	4th jet	5th jet

Jet	Unloading Time (hrs.)	+	Loading Time (hrs.)	=	Total Duration (hrs.)	Scheduled Departure (hrs.)	Fourth Set of Critical Ratios
Birmingham	0.15 hr.		0.10 hr.		0.25 hr.	2.6 hrs.	(1.9 – 1.0)/0.25 = 0.9/0.25 = 3.60
Dublin	0.30		0.35		0.65	2.0	(1.3 – 1.0)/0.65 = 0.3/0.65 = 0.46

Note that the lowest ratio, corresponding to the Dublin jet, has been reduced to a value less than 1.0. Since this is a ratio of time remaining to work remaining, a value less than 1.0 signals that less time is available than work remains, and that this jet will be tardy. We continue the procedure according to the rule, placing Dublin fourth, which places Birmingham at the back of the sequence:

COURIER JET SEQUENCE (CRITICAL RATIO)

Belfast	Manchester	London	Dublin	Birmingham
1st jet	2nd jet	3rd jet	4th jet	5th jet

To evaluate this sequence, we can draw a Gantt chart similar to the one in our earlier analysis in Scenario 2b.

SATELLITE CENTER GANTT CHART (CRITICAL RATIO SEQUENCE)

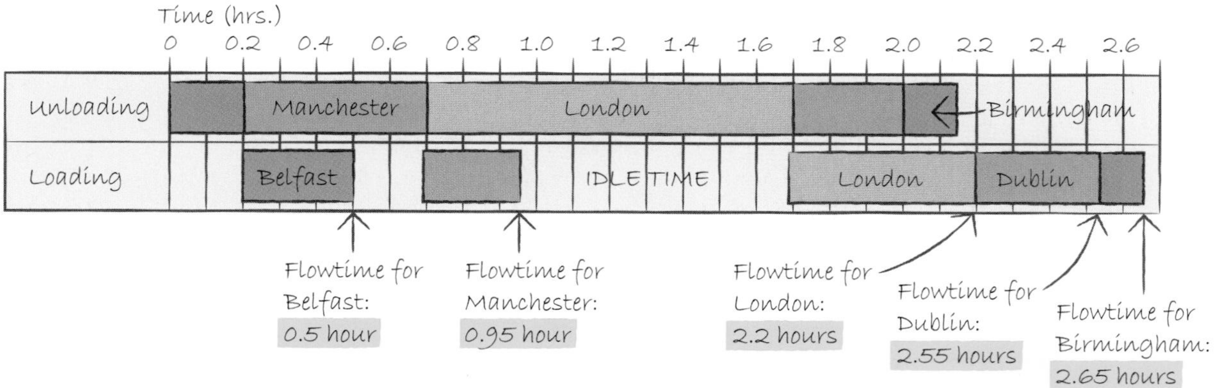

The makespan of the sequence is now apparent, visible as the flowtime of the last jet, or 2.65 hours. Using these flowtimes, we can identify tardiness.

SATELLITE CENTER FLIGHT TARDINESS

Jet	Flowtime (hrs. from start)	Due Date (hrs.)	Tardiness (hrs.)
Belfast	0.50 hr.	1.0 hr.	0 hrs.
Manchester	0.95	1.5	0
London	2.20	3.0	0
Dublin	2.55	2.0	2.55 − 2.00 = 0.55
Birmingham	2.65	2.6	2.65 − 2.6 = 0.05

Insight As expected, the critical ratio sequence's makespan of 2.65 hours is longer than that of the Johnson's rule sequence, causing 2.65 − 2.35 = 0.30 hour more idle time for the loading crew. This new sequence does have slightly better average tardiness than the Johnson's rule sequence, but this sequence creates delayed departures for two jets instead of the one longer delay in the Johnson's rule sequence. Whether or not two smaller delays are better than one larger delay should be decided by the cargo manager. ■

While Scenario 2c simulated normal operating conditions at the Edinburgh center, critical ratio might prove particularly useful to the cargo manager when conditions are not normal. In Scenario 2c, critical ratio was used to rank the five courier jets on the assumption that they were all present at the center and loaded normally. If, on some particular evening, one or more jets were delayed or arrived with unusually little or unusually heavy cargo, then the manager could calculate ratios based on this current information. This would then suggest a sequence to proceed through the unloading and reloading of the jets on that unusual evening.

General Approaches

Beyond the simple two work center environment of Johnson's rule, few definitive procedures exist for creating multicenter schedules. Individual work centers within a complex system can still be viewed as a set of simpler single work center problems, but this view might lead to substantial inefficiencies from local optimization, particularly when the work centers depend on each other's actions for successful operation.

local optimization Localized problem solving that ignores any larger problem of which the local decision is a component.

Although scheduling multiple work centers within a complex job shop system is a problem largely unsolved by management science, many tools and principles are available for guidance. Loading Gantt charts are often useful in the finite loading of work centers, creating schedules within the limited amount of time available within the planning horizon. This scheduling approach contrasts sharply with infinite loading, the optimistic assignment of work to resources without any regard for time available or other form of capacity constraint. Generally, infinite loading is not a preferred approach, because simply assigning work to resources without calculating capacity can overload a system, although this simplification is sometimes necessary to achieve a quick solution to a complex problem. Infinite and finite loading approaches may also be used together, with the infinite loading assignments made to create an initial systemwide schedule that is then broken down through the more detailed finite loading of individual work centers.

finite loading A scheduling approach that recognizes capacity constraints.

infinite loading A scheduling approach that ignores capacity constraints.

Two other general approaches, however, are not likely to be used in conjunction with each other—forward and backward scheduling. In forward scheduling, the timing of an activity is determined by locating the earliest point possible to start that activity.

forward scheduling Starting an activity as soon as possible, regardless of its deadline.

The activity is scheduled starting at that point and, as a result, is completed as soon as possible. In contrast, backward scheduling uses the deadline or due date of the activity to determine its timing. Backward scheduling assumes that each activity must be completed at a certain point, and thus starts with just enough time to finish by that point in time. A forward schedule is attractive in that it is safe, leaving the greatest room to recover from unexpected delays in processing time, and likely finishes most activities early. Since backward scheduling does not leave any extra just-in-case time, it is the most prone to disruption from unexpected delays in activities. However, the fact that backward scheduling does not finish work early may sometimes be attractive to the scheduler, because early is not always desirable. Consider, for example, preparing freshly cooked food for a scheduled event or delivering bulk materials to a highrise construction site with very limited storage space. In personal time management, backward scheduling is sometimes referred to as deadline-driven behavior.

backward scheduling Scheduling backward from a project's deadline to its start time.

Bottleneck Scheduling

Another approach to scheduling multiple work centers builds a schedule around one select work center, the bottleneck of the group. A bottleneck is the busiest work center in a system; the greater the imbalance in work between a bottleneck and its companion nonbottleneck resources, the greater the constriction and delay at the bottleneck. This is pictured as inventory buildup queuing before the bottleneck work center in Figure 14.5.

bottleneck The most heavily utilized resource within a system.

Because all work must squeeze through the bottleneck, unfinished work may be delayed there, similar to traffic congestion that forms upstream of lane closures on an otherwise wide road. Another indication of a bottleneck is the presence of work centers forced to stand idle, waiting to continue work delayed at the bottleneck resource. Such symptoms are important, because the first step in bottleneck scheduling is to identify which work center is indeed the current bottleneck. Once located, a schedule for the system is then created by focusing on this work center as the highest priority, mindful of the following principles:

- **The bottleneck is setting the pace of the system.** While the system consists of many resources and the bottleneck might be embedded deep within this network, the system cannot complete work any faster than the bottleneck is working. Therefore, anything that can be done to increase the productive capacity of the

FIGURE 14.5 Bottleneck within a System

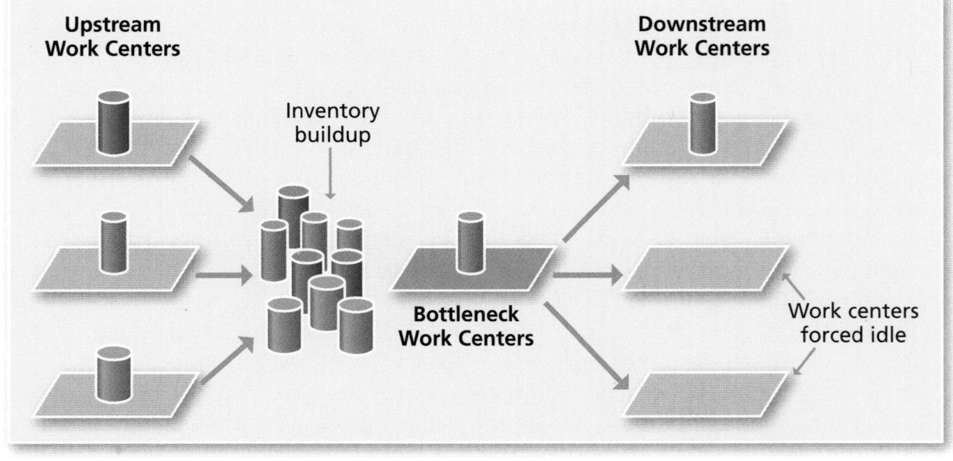

bottleneck, such as scheduling overtime, should increase the overall productivity of the system.

- **An hour lost by the bottleneck is an hour lost by the system.** Any idleness at the bottleneck work center, scheduled or unintentional, represents a gap in the system's overall productivity. Therefore, the bottleneck's schedule should avoid forced idle time and a controlled amount of inventory buildup at the bottleneck is considered desirable, because this creates a buffer that assures the bottleneck always has work available.
- **Activation and utilization of any resource are not the same.** *Activation* refers to scheduling activity, whereas *utilization* refers to creating value for the system. Scheduling activity does not guarantee creation of value at a nonbottleneck work center. If this work center is upstream of the bottleneck, overactivating it may create too much work accumulating at the bottleneck, burying it in inventory buildup. Idle time scheduled at an upstream nonbottleneck work center to avoid this wasteful condition is more valuable than activity scheduled to simply keep that work center busy.

drum-buffer-rope (DBR) Central principle of bottleneck scheduling, evoking the bottleneck (drum) ideally protected by a buffer of waiting work produced by upstream work centers whose activities are constrained to the bottleneck's pace (rope).

Theory of Constraints (TOC) A body of knowledge focused on managing the limitations on a system for continuous improvement.

These scheduling principles are often summarized as drum-buffer-rope, or DBR. This phrase refers to the pace-setting bottleneck as the beating drum, the desirable inventory buildup as the buffer, and the careful restraint of upstream activities to avoid undesirable levels of buildup as the rope. First popularized in the 1980s by physicist Eli Goldratt, this scheduling model grew rapidly into the broader management philosophy now known as the Theory of Constraints (TOC). Whereas bottleneck scheduling focuses on finding a bottleneck and building the best possible schedule around it, TOC extends this concept to the strategic level, stressing improvement of a bottleneck constraint until it is no longer a bottleneck, renewing the need to seek out the new bottleneck constraint and begin the cycle of improvement again.

REAL-TIME OPERATIONS

real-time The present point in time; now.

on-demand Products provided with zero lead times.

All plans and schedules are implemented in real-time, and thus all organizations and all managers ultimately operate in real-time. However, the decision making that preceded an activity may have been made in real-time, or it may have been carefully determined several months earlier, owing to the organization's longer planning horizon. Thus, the "real-time" in "real-time operations management" does not refer to the operation itself as much as it refers to the decision making guiding that operation. Detailed plans cannot be created in advance if customer requirements are not known, so on-demand services rely

Bottleneck Problems with Real-Time Traffic

Busy roads are on-demand service systems, and good traffic management must respond in real-time to changing conditions, such as the need to block available lanes in this picture, routing traffic around a car-and-bus accident. This reduction in lane capacity creates a bottleneck at this intersection, and local dispatchers are likely advising all nearby taxis, delivery vans, and passenger buses to avoid this route.

incident
An unscheduled event requiring immediate resolution.

heavily on real-time operation. Successful incident management, whether the incident is a complaining guest or a wildfire, is heavily dependent on good real-time decision making for the same reason. Creative endeavors such as rapid software development also depend on real-time, because it is not possible to plan precisely for a project that will not be fully defined until it is finished. Real-time operations represent the extreme in short-term scheduling, where issues such as loading or sequencing must be done in the moment. Real-time operation depends partially on recognizing what makes this process difficult, and what supports its success.

Uncertainty and Criticality

deterministic
Fixed and known in advance, representing a high level of certainty when planning.

probabilistic
Varying or not well known in advance; subject to randomness. This represents some uncertainty in planning.

known unknown
A source of uncertainty known to a decision maker, usually evident in past experience or data.

Short-term scheduling assumes both demand and the scheduler's environment are deterministic, meaning that everything the scheduler needs to create a sequence is known in advance. This includes precisely what is needed and when it is needed, as well as the availability of resources required to meet those needs. While deterministic decision making may be complex, it is unlikely to be real-time because the information necessary is available in advance. In contrast, all real-time operations share some degree of probabilistic demand, requiring decision making and action as new information arises. What real-time operations may differ on, however, is the degree of uncertainty concerning the probabilistic environments. For example, the chef and staff of a restaurant kitchen cannot know exactly what meals must be prepared and by when on a certain evening. However, this operation is highly aware of its own menu and is likely to have some past knowledge of the relative popularity of those menu items. Thus, the restaurant kitchen's real-time performance deals with primarily known unknowns, similar to the examples of taxi fleets and hotel guest services that are grouped within the upper left-hand corner of Figure 14.6.

FIGURE 14.6 Uncertainty versus Criticality for Real-Time Operations

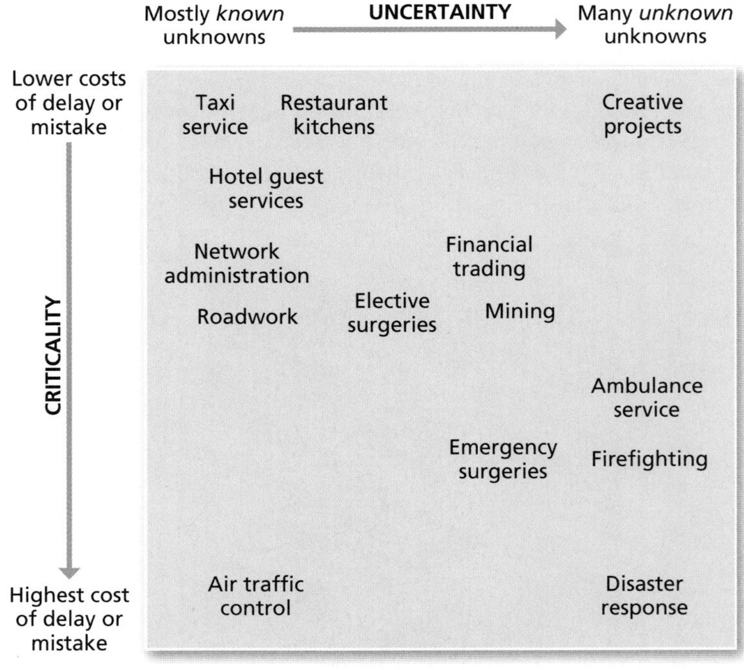

Other real-time operations must answer unexpected demand or respond to unexpected changes in their operating environments. Any creative project begins with the uncertainty of where it will end, while any organization might experience an incident unlike anything in its past history. These examples represent a differing type of uncertainty sometimes referred to as unknown unknowns, which places greater pressure on real-time performance. Maintaining a high level of performance also avoids differing magnitudes of cost in different real-time settings. Figure 14.6 suggests both a range of uncertainty and a range of criticality, referring to the higher costs of delays or mistakes for real-time settings such as these:

unknown unknown
Uncertainty omitted from planning because the decision maker is unaware of its presence.

- *Health and safety products.* Real-time operations that support human health and safety, such as air traffic control or emergency surgery, are extremely adverse to delay and production failure.
- *Dangerous environments.* Operations in dangerous work environments such as mining or construction have criticality concerns similar to those operations that support human health and safety, and similar dependence on real-time performance.
- *Large investments.* The greater the potential monetary loss from a failure in real-time decision making, the greater the criticality of real-time operation of the organization.

Successful Practices

Dynamic environments are the logical settings for real-time operations, requiring operations managers to make decisions continuously, as production happens. Thus, one issue vital to successful real-time operation is the situational awareness of the real-time decision makers, or the degree to which their mental model of a situation fits its changing reality. The importance of situational awareness is demonstrated by the obvious case of an air traffic controller: if the actual number of aircraft approaching an airport is different from the controller's understanding of that section of the sky, any decision the controller makes may have devastating consequences. Because situational awareness depends on the acquisition of both accurate and relevant information, it may be strengthened by the following factors:

dynamic
Actively and continuously changing.

situational awareness
An individual or organization's comprehension of the surrounding environment and its potential near-future states.

- **Decision support systems.** Real-time operations are often supported by a decision support system (DSS), specialized software that acquires and displays relevant information, and may even make recommendations to managers. The most successful examples of DSSs, however, are usually found on the left-hand side of Figure 14.6, embedded in operations with the greatest proportion of known unknowns in real-time.
- **Proximity and visibility.** Real-time operations are rarely managed remotely. Providing views of the facility from overlook areas and careful placement of heads-up

decision support system (DSS)
Software that assists human decision making in a particular setting.

Making Work Center Assignments Obvious in Dynamic Systems

A fast-moving system with many participants may display seemingly exaggerated signage, such as the labeling of these loading docks at a busy warehousing and cross-docking operation. The dramatic visibility of the oversized signs enhances situational awareness among the arriving truck drivers, a key to success when the facility's complex schedule changes continuously in real-time.

Telecommunications in Event Management

Event management requires good situational awareness, as many uncontrollable conditions can change in real-time. Telecommunications, particularly through open-channel radio frequencies, allows a group of observers to share their views from across a changing landscape, giving the entire event greater combined visibility to anyone monitoring their communications. Here an employee uses a radio to update his coworkers on the length of the queue of vehicles forming at the entrance to an outdoor musical event.

displays support situational awareness by keeping the surrounding environment visible to a decision maker. Large displays of the changing data of common interest to a group of participants, such as the number of orders currently waiting, are not uncommon in real-time operations.

- **Control of information and noise.** Good situational awareness requires acquisition and comprehension of information most relevant to the situation. Ironically, good-quality information that is not helpful to a particular problem can harm situational awareness by crowding out more relevant signals and distracting the decision maker. Thus, real-time operations may deliberately restrict the number of channels of information to a decision maker from those that might be browsed by an analyst with longer lead times.

Here are some other common real-time practices not necessarily related to situational awareness:

dispatching
Assigning work in real-time, often in the context of mobile resources.

iterative planning
Deliberately adjusting plans at short intervals, to reflect emerging information.

- **Dispatching.** By dispatching, assigning work in real-time, incoming demand is effectively distributed across a system.
- **Teamwork.** Since requirements are not known in advance, real-time operations often rely on teams of individuals with different skill sets, who routinely collaborate on solutions.
- **Iterative planning.** Real-time operations often use iterative planning to create plans with very short horizons, formally known as iterations, that are repeatedly revised and replaced as time progresses. Each iteration reflects any new information that has since become available, as well as any feedback from the previous iteration.

Successful managers may employ any combination of these practices to meet real-time needs, based on environment, cost, availability, and other restrictions.

To schedule something is to determine its timing. In that broad sense, almost all of operations management and planning can be called scheduling. Whether it goes by that name or not, scheduling is a process embedded in all organized activity. In fact success itself may depend largely on good timing.

SUMMARY

Although scheduling can be found in all types of operations, the most intense form of this process is short-term, job shop scheduling, as it requires a manager to constantly update the timing of activity throughout a complex system. Sequencing of work and loading of work centers through job assignments are important tasks in this type of scheduling, determining flow times and tardiness throughout the system. Priority rules can be used to generate sequences waiting at work centers, just as they can be employed in effective personal time management.

Scheduling multiple work centers that must coordinate with one another is particularly challenging. If the combined efforts of two work centers must be coordinated, Johnson's rule can be employed to identify a sequence that results in the minimum overall makespan, but few procedures exist to prescribe schedules for any system more complex. While Gantt charts do not suggest schedules, these visual illustrations of timing can be helpful in understanding and guiding complex schedules toward completion. The principles of bottleneck scheduling suggest that a complex system might be simpler than it first appears, if a distinct bottleneck within its interior is in fact dictating the overall successful output of the system. Real-time operations may be simple or complex in structure, but always represent the shortest of all possible planning horizons, requiring decision making be completed in the moment.

Key Terms

assemble-to-order (ATO)
backward scheduling
bottleneck
critical ratio
decision support system (DSS)
deterministic
dispatching
drum-buffer-rope (DBR)
dynamic
EDD
FCFS
finite loading
flowtime
forward scheduling
Gantt chart
incident
infinite loading
iterative planning
job shop
known unknown
loading
loading Gantt chart
local optimization
makespan
make-to-order
make-to-stock
milestone
multitasking
on-demand
planning horizon
precedence relationship
priority rule
probabilistic
project scheduling Gantt chart
queue
queue discipline
real-time
scheduling
sequencing
situational awareness
SPT
tardiness
Theory of Constraints (TOC)
triage
unknown unknown

Discussion Questions

1. How could bottleneck management's recommendations concerning the distinction between activation and utilization relate to personal time management?
2. How can work be urgent without being important?
3. Consider an incentive system that simply rewards production output. How can this system hurt an organization with a distinct bottleneck operation? What part of the organization will be hurt the most?
4. A major advantage of using SPT is the minimization of average flowtime. What is a disadvantage of the use of SPT?
5. Give an example in which more than one priority rule is used simultaneously to create a sequence.

PROBLEMS

Short answers appear in Appendix A. Go to **NoteShaper.com** for full video tutorials on each question.

Minute Answer

1. The total amount of time required to complete a schedule is called what?
2. Line balancing is a technique for scheduling for a system that produces at what level of volume?
3. Do deadlines determine the timing in forward or backward scheduling?
4. Critical ratio is calculated as the time remaining divided by what?
5. What does using Johnson's rule to schedule two work centers minimize?
6. Does scheduling according to shortest processing time tend to minimize average flowtime or average tardiness?
7. Does scheduling according to earliest due date tend to minimize average flowtime or average tardiness?
8. If a job is finished 4 days early, what is its tardiness?
9. Dispatching involves the assigning of what?
10. Is recognizing capacity constraints when developing a schedule called finite or infinite loading?
11. The length of time a job spends in the system is referred to as what?
12. What priority sequencing rule is usually used to order customers standing in a line?

Quick Start

13. Job Alpha requires 2 weeks of work and is due in 4 weeks. What is the critical ratio for this job?
14. Job Alpha is due in 4 weeks. If the flowtime for this job is 2 weeks, what is this job's tardiness?
15. Job Alpha requires 2 weeks of work and job Beta requires 3 weeks of work. If job Alpha is completed first and job Beta is completed next, what is the flowtime for job Beta?
16. The flowtime of the last job in a single work center's schedule is 7 days. What is the makespan of this schedule?
17. Job Tango is due in 4 weeks. If the flowtime for this job is 6 weeks, what is this job's tardiness?
18. Job Victor requires 8 weeks of work and job Tango requires 2 weeks of work. If job Victor is completed first and job Tango is completed next, what is the tardiness for job Tango if it is due in 4 weeks?
19. All work orders at a bakery require prep and then baking. An order for a single birthday cake requires the least amount of baking of all orders for the day. Assuming the bakery wishes to minimize the makespan of the daily schedule, when should that birthday cake be scheduled?
20. All work orders at a bakery require prep and then baking. An order for a batch of baked apples requires the least amount of prep of all orders for the day. Assuming the bakery wishes to minimize the makespan of the daily schedule, when should that batch of baked apples be scheduled?

Ramp Up

21. Consider the following three jobs: Job Alpha requires 2 weeks of work and is due in 4 weeks. Job Beta requires 3 weeks of work and is due in 5 weeks. Job Carlos requires 1 week of work and is due in 3 weeks. If these jobs are completed in alphabetical order, how late will job Beta be?

22. Consider the following three jobs: Job Alpha requires 2 weeks of work and is due in 4 weeks. Job Beta requires 3 weeks of work and is due in 5 weeks. Job Carlos requires 1 week of work and is due in 3 weeks. If these jobs are sequenced with SPT, how late will job Beta be?
23. Suppose you have three jobs waiting to be completed, and you must determine the sequence in which these jobs should be worked on. You calculated the critical ratio for each of the jobs and the results were that job A has a critical ratio of 1.27, job B has a critical ratio of –0.89, and job C has a critical ratio of 0.15. Which of these jobs is already late?
24. Suppose you have three jobs waiting to be completed, and you must determine the sequence in which these jobs should be worked on. You calculated the critical ratio for each of the jobs and the results were that job A has a critical ratio of 1.27, job B has a critical ratio of –0.89, and job C has a critical ratio of 0.15. Which of these jobs is not late at this moment, but will be late?

Full Scenarios

25. Jack, the owner of Jack's Electronic Repair, currently has five jobs to be scheduled:

Job	Processing Time (hrs.)	Due (hrs.)
A	3 hrs.	5 hrs.
B	1	1
C	4	9
D	2	3
E	5	7

a. If Jack uses SPT to schedule these jobs, what will be the average job tardiness?
b. If Jack uses EDD to schedule these jobs, what is the flowtime of job A?
c. If Jack uses EDD to schedule these jobs, when will job E be finished?

26. Consider the following three jobs: Job Oscar requires 2 weeks of work and is due in 4 weeks. Job Lima requires 3 weeks of work and is due in 5 weeks. Job Denver requires 1 week of work and is due in 3 weeks.
    a. If these jobs are completed in alphabetical order, what is the tardiness associated with job Oscar?
    b. If these jobs are completed in alphabetical order, what would be the makespan of the schedule?
    c. If shortest processing time were used to sequence these three jobs, what would be the average flowtime of that sequence?
27. The operations manager of a body and paint shop has five cars to schedule for repair. He would like to minimize the time needed to compete all work on these cars. Each car requires body work prior to painting. The estimates of the times required to do the body and paint work on each car are as follows:

Car	Body work (hrs.)	Paint (hrs.)
A	10 hrs.	2 hrs.
B	5	4
C	7	5
D	3	6
E	1	7

a. If the cars are processed in alphabetical order, how long will it require to complete all five cars?
b. In what sequence should the cars be processed to minimize the makespan of the schedule, and how long will that be?
c. According to the schedule found in part b, what is the flowtime of each car?
d. The owner of car D will arrive to pick up his car in 3 hours. Will car D be ready and, if not, how long will the owner be forced to wait?

28. Pristine Aircraft Maintenance has received four Boeing 737 airplanes that require maintenance. Airplane SW-023 will require 4 days of hull inspection and 3 days of painting, Airplane DL-040 will require 1 day of hull inspection and 4 days of painting, Airplane SA-009 will require 5 days of hull inspection and 1 day of painting, while Airplane AA-887 will require 5 days of hull inspection and 5 days of painting. (Hull inspection must always be completed before painting can begin.) Assume that Pristine Aircraft Maintenance uses Johnson's rule to minimize the overall time needed to complete maintenance on these three airplanes.
a. In what order will Pristine Aircraft Maintenance complete these three airplanes?
b. When should Pristine Aircraft tell each airplane owner that the airplane will be completed and available for flying?
c. When will Pristine Aircraft Maintenance be finished with all the work described in this scenario?

29. The owner/operator of an in-home meal catering company has four jobs to deliver today, shown in the order in which they were received:

Job	Processing Time (hrs.)	Due (hrs.)
W	4 hrs.	5 hrs.
X	3	9
Y	2	2
Z	1	1

a. Suppose the owner uses FCFS to schedule these jobs. How long, on average, will be required before each job is finished?
b. If the owner uses SPT to schedule these jobs, which jobs will be late and what will be the average job tardiness?
c. If the owner uses EDD to schedule these jobs, which jobs will be late and what will be the average job tardiness?
d. Which sequence is the most efficient, FCFS, SPT, or EDD?

30. The table below contains information about five jobs waiting to be processed at stamping machine 307 in the MetalBright Job Shop.

Job	Processing Time (hrs.)	Hours Until Due
A	3 hrs.	4 hrs.
B	5	9
C	1	3
D	2	6
E	4	1

a. Which of these three rules provides the best sequence in terms of average flow-time: EDD, critical ratio, or SPT?
b. Which of these three rules provides the best sequence in terms of average tardiness: EDD, critical ratio, or SPT?
c. In each of the three sequences, when will job C be finished?

CASE STUDY: TIGER STRIPE COPY CENTER, REVISITED

Recall from Chapter 4 that Tiger Stripe Copy Center is a small business located near a large university campus. Tiger Stripe Copy offers a range of services to walk-in customers, including passport photos, self-service copy machines, packaging and shipping, and the sale of course packs. Course packs are bound documents manufactured by Tiger Stripe Copy for purchase by students enrolled in particular classes at the nearby university.

Each semester, Tiger Stripe Copy receives either electronic files or paper originals from professors requesting course packs be prepared for sale to their students. Sometimes these course packs consist of one or more original documents that Tiger Stripe cannot legally copy until someone on its staff contacts the publishers of those documents for permission. This process of obtaining copyright permission generally takes about 20 minutes for each document in question. Regardless of copyright permissions, all paper documents submitted to Tiger Stripe Copy Center must first be converted into electronic files, a process that takes about 20 minutes to set up for each course pack, but then runs at a speed of 40 original pages scanned per minute. Once all files for a course pack are in electronic form, Tiger Stripe can instantaneously transmit these files to a pair of high-speed copiers, each of which prints at a rate of 120 pages per minute. Tiger Stripe covers and binds all course packs in a separate process that requires about 10 minutes to set up with the correct course pack covers, but then can operate at a comfortable pace of four course packs covered and bound per minute. Once the cover and binding process is complete, the course pack is ready for sale.

Speed is often crucial, because some professors request course packs on very short notice. Today is the day before the first day of classes, and five professors have just dropped off course packs to be made available for sale by tomorrow morning, the details of which are given in the Last-Minute Course Pack Orders table.

Last-Minute Course Pack Orders

Course	Pages in Each Course Pack	Original Documents Requiring Copyright Permission be Obtained before Copying	Pages of Paper Originals to be Scanned	Production Batch Size (Number of Course Packs)
AC 225	300	3	300	180
AC 405	250	none	250	25
EC 201	100	none	none	250
ES 330	50	6	50	300
WA 330	450	4	450	65

Although the Tiger Stripe production shop is caught up on all other work and everyone is available to begin production on these five orders, the regular work shift for the shop ends in 6 hours. Tiger Stripe Copy Center relies on its reputation for fast and convenient service to university classes, so the day manager is willing to pay overtime and the staff is willing to work as long as necessary to finish these five course pack batches before leaving this evening. However, the manager would prefer to minimize this overtime expense as much as possible, and the production staff would likewise prefer to go home as early as possible.

Questions

1. Prepare a schedule to complete these five course pack production batches. Use a Gantt chart to illustrate the work processes (obtaining copyright permissions, scanning, copying, and binding) associated with each order. Rounding to the nearest half hour for each block of work is sufficient for scheduling Tiger Stripe's production shop, but do not split up any single requirement for any one of the four processes.
2. What is the makespan of your schedule? What is the average flowtime of this schedule?
3. How much overtime is required by your schedule?

BIBLIOGRAPHY

Austin, R., and L. Devin. 2003. *Artful Making: What Managers Need to Know About How Artists Work*. Upper Saddle River, NJ: FT Prentice Hall.

Covey, S. 1990. *The Seven Habits of Highly Effective People.* New York: Simon & Schuster.

Cox, J., and E. Goldratt. 1986. *The Goal: A Process of Ongoing Improvement.* Great Barrington, MA: North River Press.

Gass, S., and A. Assad. 2005. *An Annotated Timeline of Operations Research: An Informal History.* New York: Kluwer Academic Publishers.

Johnson, S. 1954. "Optimal Two- and Three-Stage Production Schedules with Setup Times Included." *Naval Research Logistics Quarterly* 1(1).

Pinedo, M. 2002. *Scheduling: Theory, Algorithms, and Systems.* Upper Saddle River, NJ: Prentice Hall.

Véronneau, S., and S. Cimon. 2007. "Maintaining Robust Decision Capabilities: An Integrative Human-Systems Approach." *Decision Support Systems* 43: 127–140.

PART 4 ACTION AND ADAPTATION

CHAPTER 15

Incident and Disruption Management

Our greatest glory is not in never falling, but in rising every time we fall.

—Confucius

MAJOR SECTIONS

IN THIS CHAPTER, LOOK FOR...

- How to characterize incidents and disruptions.
- Ways to assess reliability and resiliency of operations, and to design for the unexpected.
- The processes of temporary organization, continuity planning, and workarounds.
- Disaster logistics, and how an operation may mirror such techniques to succeed under difficult conditions.

INTRODUCTION

Ideally, operations management would always proceed according to thoughtful and accurate plans. In reality, this rarely if ever happens. Surprises and disruptions appear in all sizes and forms, and one characteristic of a talented manager is an ability to succeed despite this ongoing interference.

Most modern companies are more exposed to such interference than in earlier history, as global supply chains and heavily networked operations risk disruption from naturally occurring disasters across the planet. Operations that do react and adapt when routine conditions abruptly change benefit both themselves and their communities, and successful navigation of these sudden murky waters represents one of the highest achievements in operations management. The journey to achieving this level of readiness and ability begins by confronting the unavoidable nature of disruption.

UNDERSTANDING DISRUPTION

A disruption is any interruption of normal operation that is caused by an unforeseen incident. Global supply chains can be disrupted by natural disaster, convention planning can be disrupted by a flu epidemic, and personal plans can be disrupted by a punctured car or bike tire. Nonetheless, plans must be made, and when disruptions block the paths through those plans, new plans and paths must be found.

incident
An unscheduled event requiring immediate resolution.

Despite their apparent diversity, all disruptions share certain features, such as probability, loss, and magnitude. Preparedness and agile response to disruption relies on recognizing these features, beginning with the established frameworks of decision theory.

Traditional Decision Theory

In traditional decision theory, a planning decision is a choice of options, although the desirability of each option is obscured by an issue of uncertainty, or chance event. In this model, the chance event may disrupt by presenting some unfavorable condition after a particular option is chosen. For example, a retailer orders and stocks some item according to a forecast. One chance event is customer demand itself, because if the item proves to be more popular than the retailer expected, the amount in stock will prove insufficient to supply all customers. Another chance event could be an unexpected interruption in supply of an item, as featured in Figure 15.1. Here, a traffic accident causes roads to be temporarily closed, which in turn causes a local delivery van to be delayed. The van's delay in turn creates a stock out of produce at a local grocery store, and ultimately to lost sales and dissatisfied customers.

chance event
A distinct source, cause, or issue of uncertainty.

Known Unknowns and Future States of Nature Although actual customer demand is not precisely known in advance, the issue of customer demand is very familiar to a retailer. Much of business analysis is built on this concept of the known unknown, or a source of uncertainty that a decision maker is aware of and may even have some suspicions as to its actual outcome. These are probabilistic problems for the decision maker, where what is known about the chance event can be harnessed analytically to develop a solution.

known unknown
A source of uncertainty known to a decision maker, usually evident in past experience or data.

probabilistic
Variable or not well known in advance; subject to randomness. This represents some uncertainty in planning.

One concept critical to this traditional model of uncertainty is future states of nature. Here uncertainty is represented as a known set of possible outcomes, although it is unknown which will actually come to pass. In the case of the retailer, the future might be separated into three categories: low demand, normal demand, and high demand. While the retailer does not know which of these future states of nature will actually occur, the retailer is aware of the potential of each when choosing an order size for the item in

future states of nature
A set of distinct conditions associated with a chance event, only one of which will actually occur.

Component Features of a Small Disruption

FIGURE **15.1**

Probability?

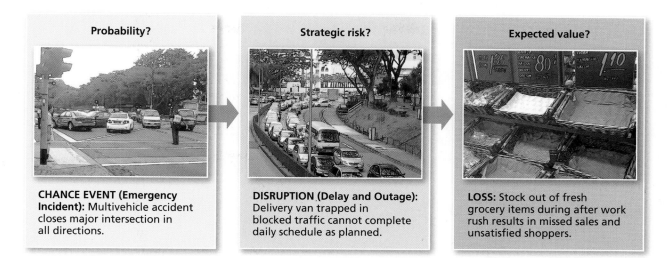

CHANCE EVENT (Emergency Incident): Multivehicle accident closes major intersection in all directions.

Strategic risk?

DISRUPTION (Delay and Outage): Delivery van trapped in blocked traffic cannot complete daily schedule as planned.

Expected value?

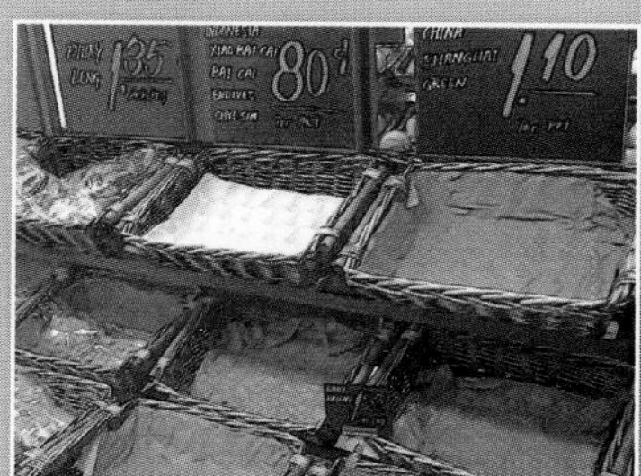

LOSS: Stock out of fresh grocery items during after work rush results in missed sales and unsatisfied shoppers.

question. Furthermore, the retailer might recognize the possibility of a disruption like the one shown in Figure 15.1 by further dividing the future into a normal traffic day versus a bad traffic day, which then implies a total of *six* future states; that is, the retailer might experience a normal traffic day with low demand or a bad traffic day with normal demand or any other combination of the two chance events. Regardless of the number of futures identified, this awareness of distinct futures helps us to structure the problem logically and make informed decisions, as we see in Scenario 1a.

Future States of Nature

Scenario 1a

Regional Disaster Relief Services (RDRS) provides emergency assistance to the victims of large-scale natural disasters. Upon news of a disaster within its logistical reach, RDRS activates both its permanent staff and groups of volunteer workers to deploy from one or more of its warehouse headquarters and provide disaster relief. Volunteers are particularly helpful during the early phase of deployment, known as the load out, when supplies and equipment are pulled from the warehouse and loaded into RDRS cargo containers and trucks. More volunteers at a load out greatly speeds the packing of RDRS's resources, shortening the overall time until emergency assistance.

The incident manager at RDRS warehouse 4 has instructions to deploy emergency shelter for several hundred people displaced by a fast-moving wildfire. The local agency placing that request has indicated great urgency, asking for RDRS's ETA (expected time until arrival) at the shelter site. Travel time to the site will be 7 hours, but load out depends on the number of volunteers responding to the incident manager's call for assistance. RDRS alerts its volunteers through an e-mail and text messaging system, and waits about an hour for those who can help to arrive at the warehouse, an interval known as turnout time. If the usual number of volunteers appears for load out, counting and packing takes about 4 hours. However, occasionally the turnout is rather poor, due to conflicting demands on the volunteers' time, and the load out takes twice as long. Sometimes the turnout is distinctly good, yielding a surplus of volunteers, and the load out is completed in half the usual amount of time.

Continues

What is the chance event with distinct future states of nature that concerns this RDRS incident manager? What are the consequences of those future states of nature?

Analysis

Even though the wildfire is a classic source of uncertainty, the chance event that concerns the RDRS manager at this moment is the issue of volunteer turnout:

EVACUATION SHELTER RESPONSE

- Chance event: RDRS volunteer turnout at load out (can't know in advance)
- Future states of nature: three distinct levels of volunteer turnout, described as rather poor, usual, and distinctly good.
- Consequences: time spent completing load out influences ETA. This is what varies among the future states of nature.

To assist the incident manager in answering the local agency, we organize the details concerning the consequences into a table format:

EVACUATION SHELTER RESPONSE

Future States of Nature (Volunteer Turnout)	Consequences (ETA)
Rather poor	1 + 8 + 7 = 16 hours
Usual	1 + 4 + 7 = 12 hours
Distinctly good	1 + 2 + 7 = 10 hours

Turnout time + load out + travel = ETA

Insight RDRS should expect to be operational at the evacuation shelter site 10 to 16 hours from the activation of the volunteer alert system. Use of the word "usual" suggests that this particular turnout level is more likely to happen than the other two future states, so the RDRS manager could give the local agency an ETA of 12 hours, and promise to contact the agency in an hour if that estimate needs updating. ■

expected value The mathematical expectation of a random variable, calculated as the weighted average of all possible values that may occur.

Expected Values After an uncertain event is expressed as a set of possible values, these values can be combined into a single mean value, referred to as the expected value of that uncertain event. This single value is treated as a rational summary of the various possibilities and used as an input to further decision making. If a chance event has N possible future states, where the outcome of each future state i is symbolized as χ_i and its probability as P_i, then the expected value of that chance event is

$$\text{Expected value} = \sum_{i=1}^{N} P_i \chi_i$$

This expression requires that each possible value χ_i be multiplied by the probability that value will actually occur (P_i), and this result summed with the corresponding results from all other possible future values. You can think of a lottery ticket as an example of this technique, because its future states of nature are quite clear: either the lottery ticket wins a prize or it does not. Consider drawing a lottery ticket at random from a set of 100 tickets and awarding that particular ticket a prize of $2,500. If the drawing is random, each ticket has 1 chance in 100 of being drawn, or a 1/100 = 1% probability of winning, with a consequence of a $2,500 reward, less the cost of the ticket. Otherwise, it has a 99% probability of not winning, which has a consequence of a $0 reward and loss of the money spent on the ticket. If the cost of each ticket is $25, the expected value of that ticket is

$$P_{\text{winning}} \times \chi_{\text{winning}} + P_{\text{not winning}} \times \chi_{\text{not winning}} = (.01) \times (2{,}500 - 25) + (.99) \times (0 - 25) = \$0$$

Prior to the lottery drawing, each ticket in this example is said to have an expected value of $0, or no value. We demonstrate this same pattern of calculation in the context of the incident manager's problem at RDRS in Scenario 1b.

Expected Values

Scenario 1b

The RDRS incident manager has activated the alert systems for volunteers to report to warehouse 4 for the load out discussed in Scenario 1a. If the incident manager simply waits, the usual number of volunteers will arrive within an hour about 70% of the time. If the turnout is not usual, it is then equally likely to be distinctly good or rather poor.

The incident manager knows that volunteer turnout for a load out can be boosted by organizing a "phone tree" among the early arriving volunteers, who personally contact other past volunteers and ask them to report to warehouse 4. The manager reserves the phone tree protocol for only the most urgent responses, partially because volunteers arriving for disaster logistics aren't always happy to be asked to phone other people and partially because the complexity of phone tree operations means that the start of packing is delayed by a half hour. Even with more volunteers, this delay until the start of packing makes the incident manager nervous. Nonetheless, phone tree operation guarantees no "rather poor" turnout, bringing in "distinctly good" volunteer turnout half of the time.

What is the expected value of the ETA at the shelter site, with and without the phone tree protocol in operation? Should the incident manager ask the arriving volunteers to begin making phone calls?

Analysis

To calculate expected value, both the actual consequence and the probability of each future state of nature must be identified. Combining the information here with the earlier data in Scenario 1a, our summary of ETA without the phone tree looks like this:

RDRS ETA WITHOUT PHONE TREE DATA

Future States of Nature (Volunteer Turnout)	Consequences (ETA)	Probability
Rather poor	16 hours	.15, or 15%
Usual	12 hours	.70, or 70%
Distinctly good	10 hours	.15, or 15%

Probability of poor or good = (1 − .7)/2 = 0.3/2 = 0.15, or 15%.
They are equally likely, and the set of three probabilities must sum to 1.

To calculate expected value, we pair each probability with its consequence, multiply each pair, and sum the results:

RDRS ETA WITHOUT PHONE TREE

Expected value of ETA: 16 × .15 + 12 × .70 + 10 × .15
= 12.30 hours, or 12 hours and 18 minutes

Continues

We repeat this process for the case of phone tree operation, with careful adjustments to the input data:

RDRS ETA WITH PHONE TREE DATA

Future States of Nature (Volunteer Turnout)	Consequences (ETA)	Probability
Rather poor	16.5 hours	.0, or 0%
Usual	12.5 hours	.5, or 50%
Distinctly good	10.5 hours	.5, or 50%

ETA has increased by 0.5 hour in each case, due to the use of the phone tree delaying the start of packing.

Expected value of ETA: $16.5 \times .0 + 12.5 \times .50 + 10.5 \times .5$
$= 11.50$ hours, or 11 hours and 30 minutes

Insight The expected value of RDRS's ETA at the shelter site is 12.3 hours without use of the phone tree, and 11.5 hours with the phone tree, a reduction of 0.8 hours (48 minutes). Whether the manager uses the tree depends on how costly its disadvantages are when compared to this expected savings on time. One advantage of the phone tree not directly reflected by expected value is the fact that it assures ETA will be no worse than 12.5 hours, as compared to the potential of 16 hours if not used. ■

Expected value is a popular tool of business analysis, being found in some form within financial analysis, project management, inventory planning, and many other applications. However, the term "expected value" is itself misleading, because to expect something is to believe that it might happen, but the expected value might be impossible in reality. The earlier lottery ticket example provides an excellent example of this paradox: Each ticket has an expected value of $0. In reality, no ticket owner will break even on the purchase of a ticket, recovering exactly $25 to restore its purchase cost but gaining nothing. Rather, one ticket holder will profit by much more, and the remaining ticket

Planning Volunteer Operations

Volunteers work for reasons other than monetary compensation, motivated by a desire to make life better for others. Medicine, carpentry, education, and emergency response are all examples of services in which volunteers are active around the world. Volunteers can also temporarily boost the limited capacity of community resources such as the city park cleanup in this picture. Planning a volunteer operation differs from planning a project for paid employees, because volunteers are not necessarily practiced in the work required, may not be familiar with the location of the event, and may have never met anyone they will be working with. Furthermore, volunteer labor is probabilistic in many cases, as a planner does not know precisely how many people to include in the plan before the event starts. All these conditions can be overcome with managerial effort, to assure good utilization of the volunteers' valuable time.

owners will lose $25 each. The expected value of the ticket purchase, however, does not offer this cautionary advice.

Unknown Unknowns Another disadvantage of expected value is its dependence on a future containing only known unknowns. This style of analysis is most useful within a limited range of uncertainty, one that does not include the possibility of unexpected futures, or unknown unknowns. Unknown unknowns cannot be incorporated into traditional probabilistic analysis by virtue of the fact that the decision maker has no knowledge of these random elements. Yet the future can be expected to contain the unexpected, making unknown unknowns no less significant than known unknowns when planning for disruption. Unknown unknowns may not necessarily disrupt when they appear, but those that do cause extreme disruption are designated Black Swans, a term referring to existing birds once widely believed to be impossible. These unknown unknowns can even be positive; the rapid rise of the Internet and its transformation of society is an example of a largely beneficial Black Swan in business strategy. Positive Black Swans are usually examples of disruption innovation, in which a game-changing product or process abruptly transforms an industry or market in a direction previously unforeseen by long-term planners.

unknown unknown Uncertainty omitted from planning because the decision maker is unaware of its presence.

Black Swan An incident of extreme consequence, unexpected or considered highly improbable.

disruptive innovation A technological change that profoundly alters an existing market unexpectedly.

Common Cognitive Biases One simultaneous strength and weakness of traditional decision theory is its rationality. In theory, a rational decision maker reasons through all relevant data and selects the best option from that clinical analysis. In reality, people make decisions, and even when using the tools of decision theory, people are prone to certain patterns of mistaken reasoning, known as cognitive biases. For example, use of expected value implies that every possible future is known in advance, weighted by its probability. Use of this tool in a situation where actual outcomes are highly difficult to anticipate is an example of framing, a common cognitive bias in which the analyst oversimplifies a problem and is not likely to reach a useful conclusion. If an analyst does anticipate a potential event such as a large hurricane striking a city, framing the issue of preparedness as an expected value multiplies the enormous damage to an unprepared city by the extremely small probability of a direct hit. In reality, either the city suffers a direct hit from a large hurricane or it does not, and scaling the damage of this event proportional to its original probability provides little insight into the value of advance preparation.

framing Adopting too narrow a view in the analysis of a problem.

Disruptive Innovation in Steel Making

The term *disruptive innovation* brings to mind wireless devices and social media, but this type of Black Swan is not confined to consumer electronics or the Internet. Steel making, once dominated by massive manufacturing plants, underwent a wave of transformation touched off by the appearance of steel mini-mills. Mini-mills redefined steel making by using small, electrically powered furnaces to produce relatively small amounts of product, often from recycled scrap. This disruptive innovation traded the efficiencies of a large traditional mill for newfound flexibility, distributing small plants across large markets that could each be shut down and restarted easily, to better match the rise and fall of demand for steel.

In addition to framing, psychology has cataloged numerous cognitive biases that may distort decision making. Four in particular are closely associated to business disruption:

outcome bias
A tendency to assume a process is acceptable if its output is acceptable.

- **Outcome bias.** Outcome bias is a common and yet dangerous assumption that a system is problem-free if its output is problem-free. While it is appropriate to monitor output closely for deviation from accepted standards, lack of these deviations in end products is not confirmation that all is well in the production system.
- **Commission versus omission.** An act of commission, such as advice to do something, is often given more weight by a decision maker than an equally valaubleact of omission, such as advice *not* to do something. As a result, a decision maker consistently prioritizes an opportunity to earn a certain amount over the opportunity to prevent a loss of equal value, despite the fact that the two actions have equal benefit. This discrimination is related to a tendency for decision makers to underestimate their own risks in general, as witnessed in a 2010 survey of small US business owners by insurance carrier Travelers. Over 90% of those owners indicated they were adequately prepared for disaster, although historical evidence indicates that at least one in every four of such businesses do not survive actual disasters.

normalization
A tendency to accept anomalies as normal events, particularly over time.

- **Normalization.** Normalization is a tendency to accept unexplained anomalies as normal. When this condition combines with outcome bias, decision makers often ignore multiple warnings of impending disaster. For example, oil-drilling rig *Deepwater Horizon* was notoriously plagued with problems as it worked a particular site in the Gulf of Mexico. Most of these incidents, in hindsight, were warnings of circumstances that led to its explosion in April 2010, killing 11 people and creating the largest oil spill in history. However, other Gulf of Mexico drilling rigs had suffered seemingly similar incidents and yet completed their drilling successfully, leading to a mistaken acceptance of the warning signs aboard the *Deepwater Horizon* as normal.

confirmation bias
A tendency to favor information that supports a hypothesis and to suppress or neglect information that refutes it.

- **Confirmation bias.** Confirmation bias is seeing what you want to see, another good description of normalization. Normalization, however, refers specifically to not seeing what you do not want to see, whereas confirmation bias refers to both seeking information supporting what you want to see and suppressing information that does not fit. Decision makers are suffering confirmation bias when they pay closer attention to information that supports their current conclusions, and ignore or trivialize

Cognitive Bias against Black Swans

For centuries, Black Swan was a well-known metaphor for the impossible in Europe. Ironically, black swans are quite common in the southern hemisphere, and when European explorers and whalers first returned with eyewitness accounts of these creatures, experts in Europe "knew" these stories were either exaggerated or mistaken. However, this confirmation bias against the eyewitnesses only lasted until travelers returned with actual black swans, shocking the scientific community. As a result, the black swan remains a powerful symbol, not for the impossible but for the game changer—the ever-present possibility of the completely unexpected.

anything that does not fit their desired understanding of the situation. This tendency may be worse if decision makers are participating as a group, as some viewpoints may be suppressed or unvoiced in favor of conflict avoidance and quick agreement, a collective phenomenon known as groupthink.

groupthink
A tendency to neglect full critical evaluation of a decision in favor of minimizing conflict within a group of decision makers.

Confirmation bias is also related to the phenomenon of *narrative fallacy*, a very human and not entirely negative tendency for observers to create stories around what facts they happen to observe. If these stories are explaining away the presence of a hazard, however, the observers are then unknowingly at risk.

Types of Risk

Risk indicates potential loss. Any danger of loss has two important features, the chance event posing this danger and the likelihood of the actual loss. Interestingly, *risk* refers to both, as the phrase "stock out risk" refers to likelihood of loss, while the statement, "he's a security risk" labels someone as a potential cause of loss. Risk management integrates both causes and likelihoods in planning against the possibility of loss, and this process begins with considering the type of risk at hand.

risk
The possibility of loss or the source of such a possibility.

Preventable Risk A preventable risk is usually an internal issue, with no benefit associated with its presence. To be preventable, a risk must be a known unknown of a controllable nature, and thus can be managed through compliance with rules to minimize exposure to its danger. Almost all workplace safety programs, for example, address this type of risk. Avoiding preventable risk is considered the most basic level of all risk management, sometimes referred to as proaction.

proaction
Avoidance of preventable risk, the first and most basic stage of risk management.

Strategic Risk Strategic risks are similar to preventable risks with one all-important difference: a strategic risk has at least some benefit associated with exposure, and thus an organization *chooses* this risk. Credit risk is a natural example from this category, in that financial institutions routinely accept the possibility of loss from investments in return for a greater probability of income. Successful risk management in this category focuses on mitigating the accepted risk as much as possible, such as purchasing insurance policies. However, no effective decision concerning strategic risk can be made if the decision maker underestimates the scope of that risk, making confirmation bias particularly dangerous in this setting.

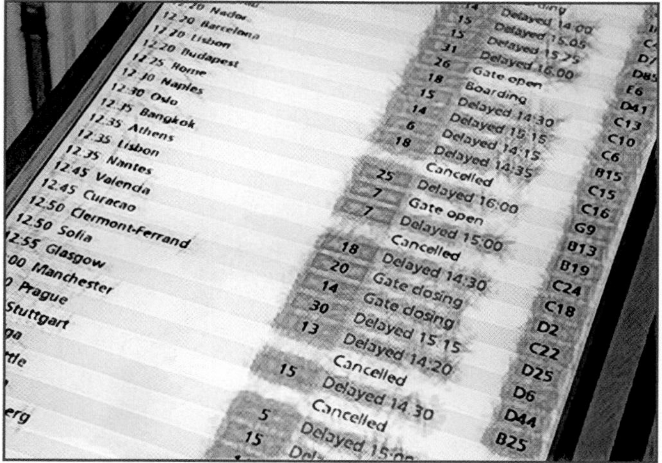

Strategic Risks in Airline Schedules

Travel delays are routine incidents worldwide. Fleet sizes, flight schedules, and booking and cancellation policies of passenger airlines all reflect calculated amounts of strategic risk, as an airline does not expect to fly 100% on time. One delay may affect only a small part of the airline's complex schedule, such as maintenance problems with one aircraft, and might be prevented if the airline chose to maintain expensive redundant aircraft at that location in its network. However, the widespread delays and cancellations pictured here indicate a systemic disruption, where one external cause is affecting all airlines at this location. This type of incident in air travel is usually weather-related.

External Risk External risks are posed by incidents beyond the influence or control of an organization, such as natural disasters or shifts in economic or political environments. External risk management focuses on identification of the potential event, and then seeks ways to protect against its projected impact. However, this approach is limited by the organization's ability to at least broadly identify an event before it actually occurs. That ability has practical limits created by both the cognitive biases of planners and the fact that some events are simply not identifiable in advance.

Modeling Risk Modern risk management identifies risk as the first step in developing a strategy to lessen or control its influence. After this step, the risk manager must describe the risk as a probability distribution, similar to how the manager in Scenario 1b estimated a 70% chance of the usual volunteer turnout without use of a phone tree, with the lower and higher turnout numbers balanced at 15% each. In this context, the distribution models the actual uncertainty in the situation, and one of the most popular distributions used for this purpose is the normal distribution, pictured at the center of Figure 15.2. The assumption of normally distributed uncertainty is embedded in widely used techniques for forecasting, financial analysis, quality control, inventory planning, and project scheduling, to name only a few.

Selection of a distribution, however, can have unintended consequences. For example, suppose an energy planner is concerned with supplying an industrial facility with reliable electrical power. A key concern is the peak demand for electricity, because the energy planner must weigh the costs of arranging capacity against the risk of inadequate capacity and service failure. If the facility is new, the planner would identify similar existing facilities and gather data on their historical daily peak demands. If this long list of readings had a mean value of 3.0 megawatts (MW) and a standard deviation of 1.6 MW, then both curves appearing in Figure 15.2 theoretically fit this uncertainty so far. To explore the strategic risk of service, the energy planner picks one probability distribution to model the uncertainty associated with the new facility's peak needs, and uses it to estimate the risk of failure at certain levels of capacity. For instance, based on the popular assumption of normal distribution, the energy planner would conclude that a service of

FIGURE 15.2 A Normal and a Heavy-Tailed Probability Distribution ($\mu = 3.0$, $\sigma = 1.6$)

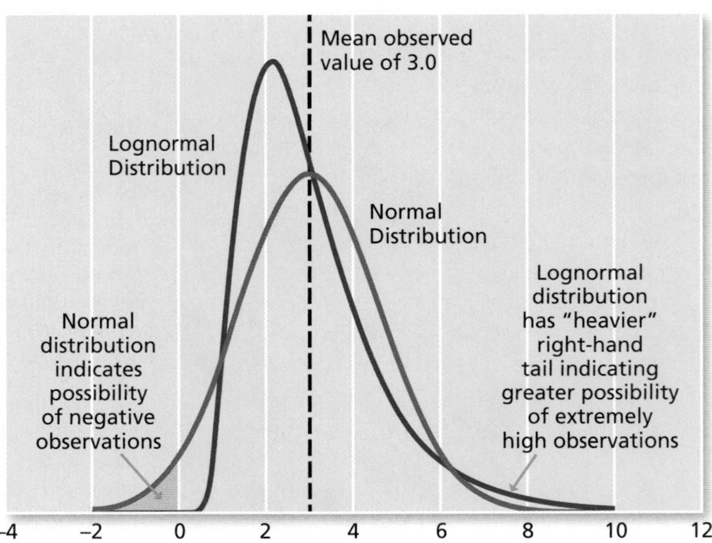

6.0 MW maximum has a 3% risk of being inadequate during peak daily demand, based on the fact that 3% of the area of the normal curve is associated with values greater than 6.0 MW.

Despite its popularity, assuming a normal distribution assumes possibilities that might not, in fact, make any sense in reality. In the energy planner's case, using a normal distribution also assumes that there is a 3% chance of a *negative* peak in daily demand, although there is 0% chance of that in reality. Furthermore, a normal distribution assumes that the mean value observed is the equivalent of the most frequently observed value, which gives this bell-shaped curve its peak. In the case of the energy planner's data, it is more likely that a mean value near 3.0 MW is the result of averaging a large group of smaller values such as 2.0 MW with a smaller group of much larger values, each representing the occasional substantial spike in electrical demand. This behavior is more accurately modeled by a skewed distribution such as the lognormal curve also pictured in Figure 15.2. This lognormal curve assigns 0% chance to any negative outcomes and double the probability of an outage with service limited to 6.0 MW, when compared to its normal counterpart.

The lognormal distribution belongs to a group known as the *heavy-tailed probability distributions,* often better choices for modeling high degrees of uncertainty, although somewhat less convenient to work with. In the energy planner's case, missing any skewness in the historical data would be a needless oversight, but note that such data is not necessarily available to a risk manager. In the absence of stable data, use of analytical tools based on the assumption of normally distributed likelihoods brings the danger of underestimating the real chance of extreme values, and thus the real risk in the actual situation.

Types of Disruption

Disruption creates loss, but disruption, like the risk of loss, can take different forms. Some forms of disruption are routine, such as delays in travel systems. Other categories of disruption are, by definition of the category, relatively rare. Overall, these categories differ most strongly in terms of magnitude, outlined here from least to greatest potential loss.

Outage and Delay Shortages, outages, delays, and other failures of planned activity are probably the most familiar form of disruption in operations management. These disruptions are frequently failures in coordination, either within an organization or between it and external parties. Project management, supply chain management, and scheduling all offer analytical tools that recognize this type of risk. In some cases these disruptions are deliberately tolerated as strategic risks, such as the occasional stock out of some retail item when its inventory is held to a lean level that its retailer otherwise benefits from. Thus, this class of disruption is usually expected by the organization, at least over long planning horizons, distinguishing it from true emergencies.

Emergency An emergency is an unexpected incident requiring immediate response. An emergency may disrupt an organization directly, such as a fire destroying a warehouse within a supply chain, or it may disrupt indirectly, such as a vendor called upon to suddenly double production to resupply the organization that lost its warehouse. Thus, the word *emergency* is used in many different ways, usually but not always signaling a threat to human life and property. Nonetheless, an emergency is a sudden unanticipated disruption that requires immediate response, which distinguishes it from a crisis.

Crisis A crisis is frequently described as a turning point in which a change, usually for the worse, is imminent. Thus, a crisis differs from an emergency in that it is not necessarily unexpected, and the organization is not necessarily disrupted while this change grows closer in time, but presumably will be if that change is not addressed. Use of the term

crisis
The critical time prior to an impending change of great significance.

Structure Fires as Emergencies

An uncontrolled fire in a manmade structure is a classic emergency, in that it is unexpected, highly dangerous, rapidly evolving, and requires immediate action to prevent further harm. However, this action is not always firefighting, in that the best response to some structure fires is to focus on issues other than attacking the fire. In the case of this unoccupied shed, arriving emergency units would first confirm the safety of people nearby and next stop the spread of fire across the ground to the right of the structure. Although still standing at the moment of this picture, the building itself is fully involved with accidental fire and no intervention can rescue it at this point.

crisis generally implies that the approaching disruption will be devastating, threatening the future viability of the organization itself.

Disaster Disaster, surprisingly, is a political declaration. While hurricanes and earthquakes may be well-known causes of disaster, disaster itself does not exist until a government agency declares the hurricane or earthquake's aftermath to be a disaster zone. Even the largest hurricane ever witnessed, if it were to remain at sea throughout its lifespan, would not likely be declared a disaster. This hurricane might create significant disruption to maritime activities, but it would not impact enough human population or infrastructure to warrant a large-scale response to its impact. Although the term *disaster* is assigned by a government, it generally represents a disruption too large to be answered by any single organization, creating the need for a broader authority to declare a special condition that allows multiple organizations to coordinate and combine their resources.

Urban Flooding Crisis

Almost all cities are located near coastlines or other bodies of water, making flooding an ever-present chance event. Cities are also vulnerable due to the higher proportion of solid surface covering a cityscape, holding flood waters in place. This asphalt expressway provides a dramatic example of that effect, as these residents wade down what would otherwise be a busy street. Fortunately, urban flooding does not usually pose the same immediate threat to human life when compared to some other sudden onset disasters, as most flooding does not occur instantly and city structures often create a means to escape the water. However, urban flooding shuts down utilities and distribution systems, prevents normal travel, and disables sanitation. These disruptions create a humanitarian crisis and second disaster if the response to the initial flooding is inadequate.

Vulnerabilities of Modern Operations

One criticism of risk management is its emphasis on predicting future outcomes based on past experience. While seemingly rational, this habit can in fact create new risks if the manager or the industry does not recognize instances in which the present day has changed such that past data does not reflect future conditions. History has witnessed many recent changes in operations, often positive and even exciting, that nonetheless create new weaknesses and vulnerabilities that can go unrecognized in traditional decision making.

Complexity and Interdependency Both the Internet and the distinct trend of globalization are relatively recent events from a historical perspective, and both have transformed operations worldwide. Systems and even societies are now vastly more interconnected, creating complex interdependent networks without historical precedent. While these networks have brought much value, they have also introduced new risks into operations. Increasing complexity makes forecasting more difficult, which reduces the chances of successfully anticipating a critical event and its consequences. Furthermore, the interconnectivity of modern systems can propagate a single problem far more readily than earlier operations. As an example, one strain of the H1N1 flu virus appeared in Veracruz, Mexico, in late 2008, yet killed over 14,000 people around the world within another year, a testimony to the modern-day mobility of the human population. Similarly, computer viruses were largely unheard of until the 1970s, but now cause hundreds of billions of dollars in damage annually in the United States alone, exploiting the propagation properties of the Internet itself.

propagate To increase or spread elsewhere.

Nonlinearity Much of business analysis is based on symmetrical and stable distribution of variable outcomes, as reflected in the popularity of the normal distribution. However, modern operations work in the presence of increasing nonlinearities that are not well-recognized by these older models, such as the wild swings of fortune in winner-take-all schemes that concentrate success in a small part of an overall market. Increasing nonlinearity also reflects increasing dependency on particular sets of resources, introducing more vulnerability. As a broad example, worldwide food production has had tens of thousands of edible plants to work with, but modern agricultural operations concentrate almost exclusively on four varieties: corn, rice, wheat, and soybeans. The resulting high-carbohydrate commodities combined with modern transformation

Risk Management in Maritime Shipping

Most global trade travels by ship at some point in its journey to market. The cargo vessel in this picture carries an average of 4,500 freight containers across the ocean, exposed to risks such as extreme weather, mechanical difficulties, ice, and even piracy. Manufacturers send out over 100 million of these containers annually, and some 10,000 accidently wash overboard before arrival. Not surprisingly, marine insurance is believed to be the original insurance industry, tracing its history back to financial risk management among shippers and importers in ancient Greece.

systems support highly efficient global food production, but this extreme dependency on a few plants raises new concerns, particularly in the context of a potential shift in the world's climate.

Degree of Exposure Despite the growing complexity of global trade and supply chain networks, supply chain risk management is a relatively new topic, and many businesses engaged in these practices do not have any particular person assigned to this issue. Global supply chains are both more complex than their counterparts from history and more likely to contain concentrated dependencies to achieve greater cost savings in production or distribution. In addition to these strategic risks, these operations are literally more exposed to external risks such as unfavorable weather patterns, natural disasters, and fluctuating currency rates. Such factors create a turbulent operating environment, one in which interference by forces beyond a manager's control are more likely to influence the success of operation. Disruptive innovation, in which the marketplace itself is transformed by new product development, is yet another form of this turbulence. Although examples of disruptive innovation can be traced throughout history, recent breakthroughs in information technology have accelerated the pace of product innovation, a positive force that nonetheless further increases the turbulence around planning for these products.

PLANNING FOR DISRUPTION

Former US President Dwight Eisenhower said, "Plans are nothing, but planning is everything." This paradox is a particularly good description of planning for disruption, because the reality of any disruption includes elements that could not have been foretold in a preexisting plan. However, the act of planning builds a strong foundation from which an agile response may spring, adapting and resolving those unforeseen elements. This response is an act of resilience, demonstrating the organization's ability to recover from the unexpected. Despite its uncertain nature, disruption planning begins with developing some solutions in advance of incidents.

resilience
The ability of a system to adjust to or recover from a shock or sudden change.

Business Continuity Planning

Every organization should have a business continuity plan, outlining how it intends to continue in the face of disruption. The Travelers 2010 study revealed that while 90% of small businesses may believe they are adequately prepared for a disaster, less than half report having a business continuity plan. This optimism despite lack of preparation is even more disturbing when considering the history of business failure in the wake of actual incidents. Since business continuity planning is vital to an organization's survival, it is a social responsibility as well. When businesses recover quickly from disaster, that recovery also benefits employees, customers, and thus the community, all of whom are likely to be suffering the impact of that same disaster.

business continuity plan
Guidelines and arrangements for response to disruption of critical business functions, to restore and maintain operation.

Effective business continuity plans result from four key steps, starting with assessment and ending with implementation.

Risk Assessment Like general risk management, business continuity planning begins with identifying potential hazards to a business. These hazards can be external, such as the risk of hurricanes and flooding, or internal, such as a business's reliance on one particular supplier or even one particular employee to maintain its computer network. As always, continuity planners must recognize that not all risks to the business are identifiable in advance.

Business Impact Analysis To draft the continuity plan, the organization must understand itself, so business impact analysis starts with a self-study of what functions and processes are vital to its operation. These findings are then combined with those of the earlier risk assessment to estimate the impact each risk may have on those functions, and thus the resulting impact on the business. In some cases, multiple hazards may be found to have similar impacts, such as an airline recognizing its reliance on its real-time flight reservation system, and then determining that a fire in the computer server room or a cyber attack disabling its connectivity would each have similar impact on its operations.

Hazard Prevention and Risk Mitigation A third stage of work is the true "planning" in business continuity planning, in which a strategy is developed for each impact identified, to either prevent or minimize that disruption. An example of outright prevention would be a hospital that realizes its emergency generators can be flooded at their current basement location, and thus arranges to move the generator room several floors above ground level. For impacts that cannot necessarily be prevented, contingency plans are often developed at this phase, outlining alternatives to the process that will be impaired. For example, a business may realize its dependence on a single supplier can be mitigated by compiling information on alternative suppliers, ready to go if and when something happens to its preferred source.

contingency plan An alternate plan developed in anticipation of a possible obstacle to the original plan.

Contingency planning may also include research into older, seemingly less-efficient processes, to substitute during temporary loss of current business functions. As an example, a supermarket might address total loss of its electronic cashier system by developing a method using teams of two cashiers per lane, one to look up item prices manually while the other records those prices on paper and sums them with a calculator.

Implementation and Maintenance Business continuity planning then requires implementation, a phase that occurs *before* disruption. As an example, the supermarket mentioned will have wasted its check-out contingency plan if it does not purchase calculators suitable for this use and store them where cashiers can find them easily during an incident that disables the supermarket's electronic systems. Furthermore, the cashiers must be educated in the alternative process, and ideally allowed to practice the plan in a training environment, feedback from which may further improve the contingency plan.

Finally, like all strategic planning, business continuity plans are never finished. The details of existing strategies must be updated continuously to reflect changes in personnel and contact information, while the entire cycle of planning should repeat periodically to detect and incorporate new risks and mitigation schemes.

Reliability and Redundancy

Planning for disruption includes assessment of the current strength of the underlying system, often examined during business impact analysis. A *system* is broadly defined as any set of interdependent elements with a common purpose. An electronic good such as a computer tablet is a system, being an intricate set of components that all contribute to its functioning. Likewise, the factory that manufactured that tablet is a system, consisting of the people and machines that participated in its assembly, as is the broader supply chain that brought that tablet to market. In each case, the reliability of the system is the likelihood that it will actually perform as expected, such as the probability the tablet will function correctly or the supply chain will successfully deliver it to market.

reliability The probability that an element or a system will perform as specified.

The reliability of any system is a combination of the reliabilities of its elements. Given that the reliabilities of the elements are independent of one another and the system depends on each of them to function, then the system's reliability is the joint probability of the elements' reliabilities. If a system has N elements and the reliability of element i is denoted R_i, then

$$\text{Reliability of system} = R_1 \times R_2 \times R_3 \times \cdots \times R_N$$

For example, suppose two employees work in the field and must remain in contact with one another throughout the day, to exchange updated information. To do so, each carries a phone that is 97% reliable, meaning that it will successfully sustain a connection to the cellular network 97% of the time. Furthermore, the cellular network is itself 97% reliable, making communication between the two employees a three-element system, as illustrated in Figure 15.3.

Although each element of this three-part network is itself 97% reliable, Figure 15.3 indicates that these employees can only expect to reach one another 91% of the time. If more elements are added to the system, the reliability will continue to drop, such as if the cellular network forwards the call to a different network of towers to reach the second phone. If the second network also has a reliability of 97%, the overall reliability of communication then sinks to 88.5%. This is the same effect discussed earlier as a general vulnerability of some modern operations: increasing system complexity usually works against reliability.

redundancy Duplication of an element within a system.

Highly reliable systems, however, do not necessarily have the option of being simple. In these cases, redundancy can be added to strengthen overall reliability, adding one or more duplicate features to back up existing elements. The greater the need for high reliability, the more likely a system will contain exact duplicates just in case, such as the twinning or mirroring of computer servers and storage within information networks. If an element is duplicated, then the resulting reliability of the element and its duplicate is the

FIGURE 15.3 Reliability of Communication between Two Employees

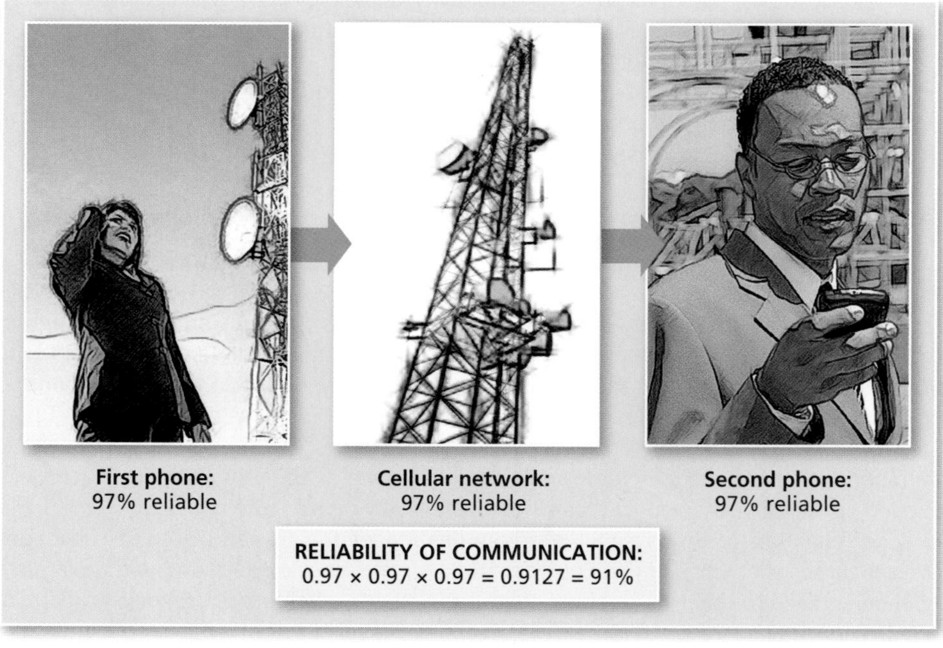

opposite of the joint probability that both *fail*. If a system relies on a set of N redundant elements, with the reliability of element i denoted R_i, then

$$\text{Reliability of redundant set} = 1 - ((1 - R_1) \times (1 - R_2) \times (1 - R_3) \times \cdots \times (1 - R_N))$$

Adding redundancy is not limited to adding exact duplicates. Returning to the example of Figure 15.3, redundancy can be introduced into this communication system if each employee agrees to a policy that, if a call does not go through, the caller then attempts to borrow the use of another phone at their current location and repeat the process. This presence of an alternative phone is redundant to the capabilities of the caller's original phone, although reliability is lower because there may not be a phone to borrow under all circumstances. Assuming that the reliability of borrowing a functioning phone is 85%, Figure 15.4 shows how the policy boosts the caller's reliability to nearly 100%, which raises the overall chance of successful communication to 94%.

Adding unlike elements that act as backups has an added advantage of potentially enhancing the robustness of the system as well as its reliability. A system is said to be robust if its reliability is reliable, that is, unchanging despite fluctuating conditions. As an example, both satellite and land-based cable services have reliability issues when providing digital entertainment, but satellite service is typically the less robust of the two systems because it is less reliable in poor weather, whereas land-based cable transmission is largely unaffected by those same external conditions. Adding unlike substitutes to a system favors the chance that a condition that disrupted the first element will not do the same to its replacement.

robustness
Providing stable reliability despite changing conditions.

Reliability of Communication between Two Employees, with Redundant Phone Policy FIGURE **15.4**

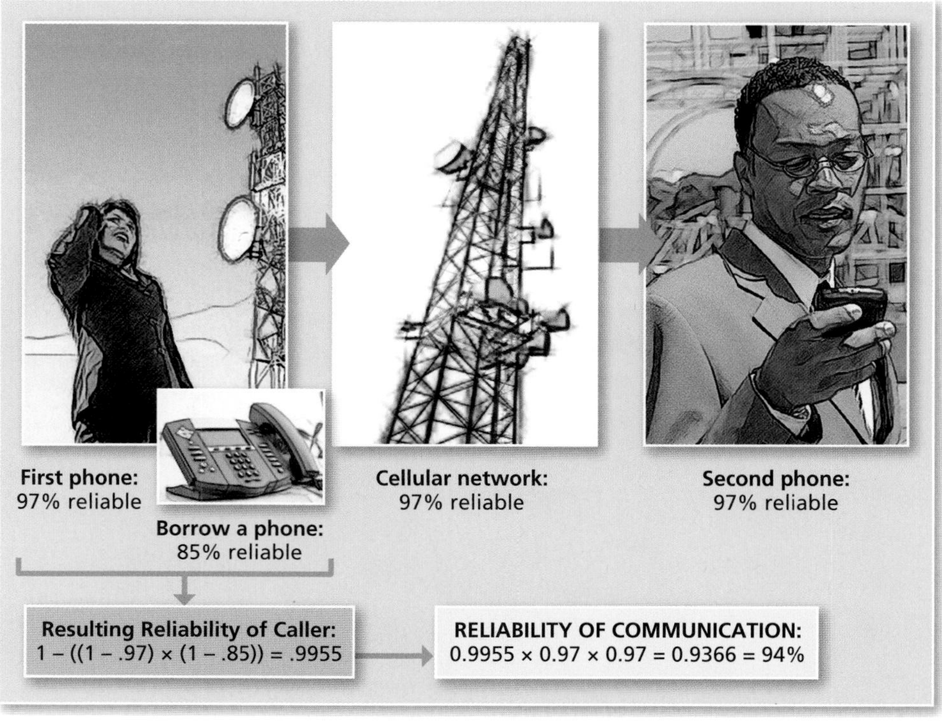

Regardless of whether redundancy takes the form of exact duplication, it is necessary to first identify the result of the redundancy before calculating the overall reliability of a complex system, as we demonstrate in Scenario 2.

Scenario 2

Reliability and Redundancy

The incident manager at warehouse 4 has learned that the leadership of RDRS will loan a partner agency some of warehouse 4's assets. Specifically, RDRS has decided to transfer half of warehouse 4's all-terrain vehicles (ATVs) to an overseas partner, to assist in a humanitarian relief operation. The partner agency is anxious to receive the ATVs because a cargo plane leaving Singapore Changi Airport (SIN) in 48 hours can transport these vehicles directly to the disaster site at no cost to the partner agency. RDRS headquarters has asked the warehouse 4 incident manager to determine the best method to ship the ATVs to Singapore, with the greatest chance of reaching that airport before the departure of the free cargo flight.

The incident manager understands the other agency's anxiety, because RDRS also receives free shipping from its corporate supporter Global Freightways, but rarely with a guarantee that any certain shipment will be carried on any certain flight. Instead, Global Freightways generously transports RDRS shipments on standby at no cost, meaning that RDRS's cargo is placed onboard only if there is room after all paid cargo is loaded. The incident manager knows from previous experience that Global Freightways flies nonstop from San Francisco (SFO) to Singapore (SIN), and phoned the Global Freightways dispatch center to learn that one flight does leave late enough to allow delivery of the ATV shipment to SFO and arrives early enough to make the partner agency's free connection. The freight agent confirmed that this is a popular flight within the cargo network, so the probability of the ATV shipment getting on board that one flight is about 70%.

Given this low probability, the freight agent had another suggestion: deliver the ATV shipment to Los Angeles (LAX) instead. From there, Global Freightways can load it on a flight to its hub in Anchorage, Alaska (ANC), after which it can transfer to either of two flights to SIN that will arrive before the partner agency's deadline. On this route, the chances of flying on standby out of LAX is 90%, the chance of making the first flight from ANC is only 50%, but the second flight, 90%. Although these chances mostly sound better, the incident manager is uncomfortable with the complexity of the LAX itinerary.

Which airport should the incident manager send the ATV shipment to? How much better is the chance of an on-time arrival in Singapore for this route versus its alternative?

Analysis

Here, each flight is a component of the overall route to Singapore (SIN), which is a system. Thus, the chance of the ATV shipment being loaded and transported on a certain flight is the reliability of that particular component of the system.

RDRS ATV SHIPPING DECISION DATA

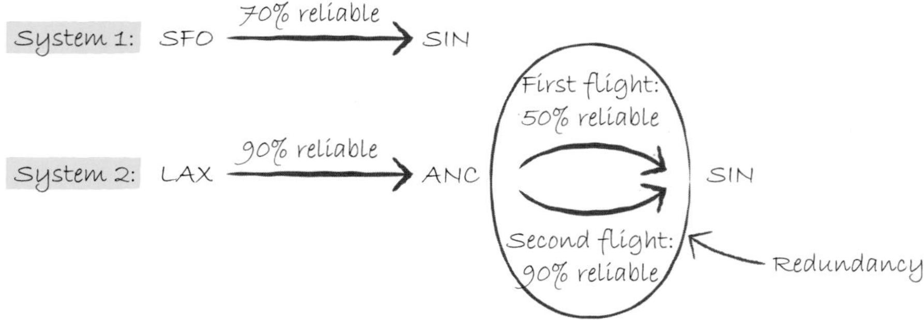

The reliability of system 1, the nonstop flight from SFO to SIN, is 70%. The incident manager is initially uncomfortable with system 2 because its overall reliability is not as readily apparent. To determine this reliability, we first determine the combined reliability of the redundant flights from ANC to SIN:

RELIABILITY OF ANC TO SIN SEGMENT OF SYSTEM 2:

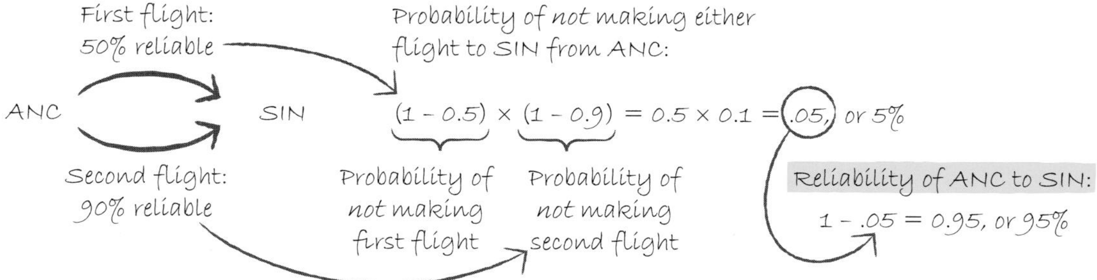

We now know that the combined availability of the two flights from ANC to SIN is 95%. From this, we can determine the overall reliability of the LAX to ANC to SIN routing. Travel from LAX to ANC and travel from ANC to SIN are two interdependent elements of that system, so we calculate their joint probability of success by multiplying their individual reliabilities:

RELIABILITY OF SYSTEM 2, LAX TO ANC TO SIN

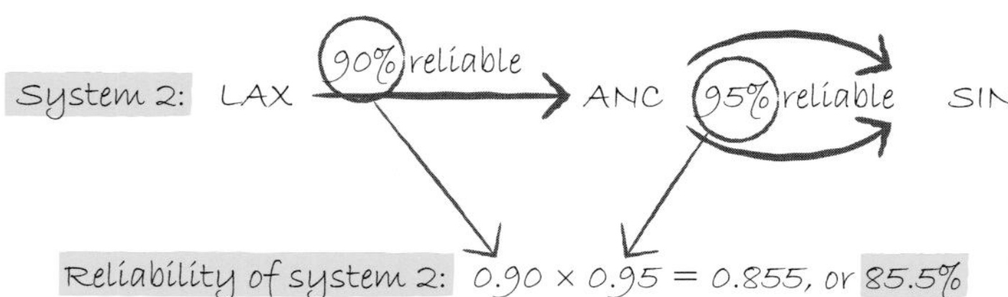

Insight The incident manager should send the ATV shipment to Los Angeles Airport, to await transport to Anchorage and then transfer to the next available flight to Singapore. Following this route, there is an 85.5% chance the ATVs will arrive in time for connecting with the partner agency's free flight, which is better than the 70% chance of the shipment being flown direct to Singapore if the incident manager sends it to San Francisco instead. ■

In the case of RDRS, the redundancy provided by multiple flights from Global's Anchorage hub is essentially free. This no-cost redundancy is similar to the benefits of contingency planning, which can create virtual redundancies to certain processes through advance planning. However, this strategy has its limits, and the reliability of true redundancy usually requires additional investment in a system, to purchase duplicate elements just in case. Although redundant elements enhance system reliability, they generally measure poorly in terms of efficiency and utilization of resources. Arguably, an additional vulnerability of modern operations management may be overuse of powerful optimization techniques focused on short-term cost savings, which minimize any redundancy in the resulting solutions. Systems formed from these optimized designs may be highly sophisticated and efficient, yet literally quite fragile, losing all capability upon disruption of any one part of their designs.

Redundancy from Green Technology

The photovoltaic panels in this Californian farmland generate electricity for nearby facilities. Use of this green technology is widely recognized for reducing carbon emissions and dependency on fossil fuels, but less so for its additional benefit of redundancy. When relatively small installations such as this are added to wider energy grids, the existing traditional supply becomes a parallel, redundant element and the result is a somewhat more robust and resilient system overall, as the solar site can provide power to this local area in the event of failure of the older system, and vice versa.

Strategic Risks in Tactical Decisions

triage
A priority rule creating sequences intended to yield the most value from distinctly limited resources.

yield management
Policies and practices to maximize the benefit of a perishable resource such as service capacity.

Once the strategic design of a system is established, the chance exists that some future incident will require more than the system's design can provide. Emergency systems such as hospital treatment centers must then make rapid tactical decisions concerning how to use what capacity is available, a prioritization scheme known as triage. Unlike these hospitals, some businesses knowingly design and manage their capacity in a manner that will create small disruptions, embracing these shortages as strategic risk. Such organizations deliberately follow plans that result in the occasional outage, a tactic known as yield management. The most striking examples of this behavior are tactical policies for managing highly perishable resources when demand is distinctly uncertain. These limited resources may be tangible goods for sale or limited capacity to provide intangible services.

overbooking
Commitment or sale of resource in excess of its actual availability.

Overbooking An organization whose valuable capacity is both fixed and reserved in advance can benefit from overbooking. Airlines, cruise lines, and hotels routinely sell tickets and accept reservations in excess of the number of people they can serve, overbooking their resources to maximize profitability. In each of these situations, the source of uncertainty is not the number of customers making reservations, but the actual consumption that will take place at the time of the service. Each organization is aware of a small chance that each customer with a ticket or reservation might not show up to claim capacity, and thus the organization overbooks to assure that its capacity is not wasted. In addition to travel and hospitality, industries such as shipping, Internet service, and telecommunications gain from employing overbooking policies. A decision to overcommit a resource and expose it to the possibility of failure is the result of calculating the expected value of that overcommitment, weighing combined benefits and costs with the probabilities of actual turnout levels, using the same conceptual tools discussed earlier in Scenario 1b.

newsvendor problem
Choosing a quantity to meet a single period of uncertain demand, weighing the costs of ordering too much and too little.

Single-Period Inventory Planning Similar to answering the overbooking question, some organizations must decide how much to stock of something valuable for some single period of usefulness, after which any unused amount will be less valuable. This case is often called the newsvendor problem, referring to one of its best-known applications. A newsvendor routinely decides how many issues of daily newspapers to procure for sale at a retail newsstand, such as those found in train stations, airports, and other busy commuter areas. As a decision maker, the newsvendor balances three issues critical to single-period inventory planning:

- **Uncertain demand.** The newsvendor's decision is made difficult because the number of commuters who will stop to buy a newspaper is unknown, although past experience gives the newsvendor some expectations.
- **Risk of too little.** If the newsvendor orders too little, the newspapers will sell out early and the newsstand will lose both further sales that day and possibly its reputation as a reliable source, reducing the likelihood that disappointed customers will stop at the newsstand in the future.
- **Risk of too much.** If the newsvendor orders too much, some newspapers will remain unsold at the end of the day. This day is the single period in single-period inventory planning, because these newspapers cannot be sold at retail price the following day, having effectively perished. Under these conditions, the newsvendor will mitigate this loss by seeking some salvage value, such as selling the unused papers for recycling.

Ultimately, the number of daily newspapers purchased for a newsstand is identified by what amount is the most valuable to the newsvendor, given what is known about the likelihood of various levels of demand. Note that this decision maker is often forced to tolerate one risk to minimize another, as the risks of too much and too little work against one another. This type of analysis is yet another form of expected value, as we see in Scenario 3.

Single-Period Inventory Planning

Scenario 3

The RDRS incident manager just activated the messaging alert systems for volunteers to start the load out of emergency shelter supplies from warehouse 4. One particular supply needed for load out is not stocked at warehouse 4: bottled water. RDRS sends bottled water with its emergency shelter equipment, to assure that arriving evacuees are well hydrated while staff work to secure a more permanent clean water supply. However, warehouse 4 does not stock bottled water because of its partnership with a local bottling company, which is willing to provide bottled water from its own 24-hour warehouse at the very low cost of $72 per pallet. If a pallet of bottled water is not used at the shelter site, RDRS brings it back with its equipment and returns it to the bottling company, who then refunds RDRS's purchase cost, less a $30 restocking fee.

How many pallets are used at a shelter site is the result of several factors, impossible to know in advance. Each pallet contains 60 cases of bottled water, and a shelter site normally consumes two pallets before other supplies are found. However, sometimes there is adequate tap water at the shelter location, another charitable organization is distributing water, and/or the number of people arriving at the site is lower than expected. The incident manager has seen various combinations of these factors result in only half the normal consumption of pallets, at about 25% of shelter setups. Rarely, but occasionally, there is no supply or assistance at the site, and three pallets are consumed before RDRS establishes another supply.

If RDRS does not bring enough bottled water, evacuees do not go thirsty. Instead, RDRS sends out volunteers from the shelter site to shop for bottled water at any place they can find it, including convenience stores, supermarkets, and even vending machines. This is a necessary but expensive endeavor, as RDRS estimates that a pallet's worth of bottled water secured this way costs an average of $800. Luckily, the incident manager estimates that the likelihood of three pallets being needed is only 5%.

The incident manager must send a truck to the local bottling company to pick up bottled water for this load out. How many pallets should the truck pick up?

Continues

Analysis

To determine the number of pallets the truck should pick up from the local bottling company is to determine the order quantity in a single-period inventory planning problem. First, we organize the relevant information:

RDRS BOTTLED WATER PROBLEM FOR LOAD OUT

Decision: 1, 2, or 3 pallets?

Future States of Nature

Consumption at Site	Outcomes (Pallets Consumed)	Probability
Low	1	.25, or 25%
Normal	2	.70, or 70%
High	3	.05, or 5%

Probability of normal = 1 - .25 - .05 = .7

Costs per Pallet

Source	Cost
Bottling company, consumed at shelter site	\$72
Bottling company, returned from site	\$30
Retail shopping near shelter site	\$800

To decide whether to order one, two, or three pallets we need to know the expected value of each option for comparison, or in this case the expected cost of each option. We evaluate each option separately, to determine its costs under the three future states of nature, beginning with an order size of one pallet.

RDRS EXPECTED VALUE OF 1 PALLET

	Consumption at Site		
	Low	Normal	High
Pallets consumed	1	2	3
Pallets arriving	1	1	1
Pallets bought retail	1 - 1 = 0	2 - 1 = 1	3 - 1 = 2
Pallets returned	0	0	0
Cost, bottling company, consumed at shelter site	\$72	\$72	\$72
Cost, bottling company, returned from site	\$0	\$0	\$0
Cost, retail shopping near shelter site	\$0	\$800	\$1,600
Total cost	\$72	\$872	\$1,672

Expected value (cost) of 1 pallet: (.25 × 72) + (.7 × 872) + (.05 × 1,672) = \$712

Thus, the expected cost of picking up one pallet of bottled water is \$712, which is not likely to be the favored option. However, we cannot confirm this until we complete the same analysis for the other two options:

RDRS EXPECTED VALUE OF 2 PALLETS

	Consumption at Site		
	Low	Normal	High
Pallets consumed	1	2	3
Pallets arriving	2	2	2
Pallets bought retail	0	2 − 2 = 0	3 − 2 = 1
Pallets returned	2 − 1 = 1	0	0
Cost, bottling company, consumed at shelter site	$72	$144	$144
Cost, bottling company, returned from site	$30	$0	$0
Cost, retail shopping near shelter site	$0	$0	$800
Total cost	$102	$144	$944

Expected value (cost) of 2 pallets: (.25 × 102) + (.7 × 144) + (.05 × 944) = $173.50

RDRS EXPECTED VALUE OF 3 PALLETS

	Consumption at Site		
	Low	Normal	High
Pallets consumed	1	2	3
Pallets arriving	3	3	3
Pallets bought retail	0	0	0
Pallets returned	3 − 1 = 2	3 − 2 = 1	0
Cost, bottling company, consumed at shelter site	$72	$144	$216
Cost, bottling company, returned from site	$60	$30	$0
Cost, retail shopping near shelter site	$0	$0	$0
Total cost	$132	$174	$216

Expected value (cost) of 3 pallets: (.25 × 132) + (.7 × 174) + (.05 × 216) = $165.60

Finally, we compare the expected values of the options to choose the best single-period order size.

SELECTING AN ORDER SIZE

Order Size	Expected Value (Cost)
1 pallet	$712
2 pallets	$173.50
3 pallets	$165.60

Note: Because these expected values represent the cost of each option, the *best* option is the one with the *lowest* expected value.

Insight The incident manager should instruct the truck's crew to pick up three pallets of water from the bottling company, because this option has the best expected value. Even though there is only a 5% chance that the third pallet will be used at the shelter site, the bottling company's low prices and the ease with which RDRS can return unused pallets makes it worthwhile to send this larger amount. ■

Trade Show Single-Period Inventory Planning

Trade shows are retailing events in which participating vendors move their inventory into a rented space within some larger public venue, such as the convention center here. Traveling trade show retailers face their own version of the so-called newsvendor problem, as they decide how much inventory to ship to a trade show location. Shipping too little results in stocking out and losing sales. Shipping too much, however, requires the vendor to decide whether to fund shipment of unsold merchandise back for sale elsewhere or dispose of it at this location. This problem often motivates the discounting of prices on unsold merchandise late in a tradeshow event.

OPERATING DESPITE DISRUPTION

Even the best risk management will not avoid all incidents, and good business continuity planning does not necessarily restore normalcy immediately. While industries such as emergency response routinely operate in disruptive environments, all organizations suffer at least the occasional major disruption, confronted with working through that incident. Successful operation despite disruption begins with the ability to organize on short notice and continues through to performance in real-time, all enhanced by practices familiar to industries that routinely handle disruptive incidents. The ultimate in such organizations are those that respond to the largest of all disruptions, the disaster, discussed at the end of this section.

Temporary Organization

One distinction between an emergency and a disaster is the number of organizations required for successful response. While a task made necessary by an emergency is usually handled by the resources of one organization, disasters are large enough to require the simultaneous contribution of multiple organizations. This cooperative effort creates one larger temporary organization, dedicated solely to the resolution of that incident. In planning for disruption, governments establish incident command systems, such as in the National Incident Management System (NIMS) of the United States, to speed the assembly of this larger organization at the onset of disasters. Incident command systems are templates for organizational structure into which arriving parties fit themselves as needed, so each might instantly understand its role in the greater temporary organization.

incident command system
A predetermined structure that organizes available parties into one temporary organization to resolve an incident.

However, emergency response is not the only industry that relies on the swift creation of temporary organizations. A growing number of project-based industries rely on successful temporary organization more than ever, including software development, building construction, film production, biotechnology, and consulting services. Furthermore, any business in the midst of a disruption may discover the need to temporarily reorganize, an internal version of the larger interorganizational problem. Regardless of the setting, industries skilled in swift and successful spontaneous organization employ these common practices:

- **Unity of command.** Unity of command refers to a pattern that assures each person receives instructions from one other person. This creates the chain of command that ultimately links every participant to a single person in charge and protects participants from receiving conflicting instructions. While unity of command is easy to recognize in military and emergency organizations, it is used in numerous other settings. Large, uncertain projects rely on the centrality of a good project manager, and individuals participating in an effective temporary organization can generally tell you who their one supervisor, coordinator, or go-to person is, indicating their link to the overall command structure.

- **Span of control.** Skillful assembly of a temporary organization limits the number of resources, including people, that each participant manages directly. This number is known as the span of control for that participant, commonly set between three and five and definitely no more than seven. These numbers represent a zone over which human decision making appears to be at its best, neither underutilized nor overloaded.
- **Common terminology.** Industries relying on unrehearsed coordination to solve novel problems train their participants in terminology, so that complex issues can be communicated effectively. In some cases, government agencies establish this shared language, such as the substantial glossary of terms within NIMS. In other cases, terms originate from standard industry usage or are advocated by professional organizations. Emergency medicine, film production, and software development are each an example of an industry known for its lingo, potentially puzzling to outsiders but understood by industry members.

Even if a business does not belong to a project-based industry, awareness of these practices can prove helpful in working against disruption. Organizations including restaurants, hospitals, and schools can all benefit from declaring one person in charge and temporarily assigning functions to specific people to allow them to focus when these organizations suddenly find themselves disrupted. Furthermore, unity of command should not be confused with centralized organizational policy, where an organization assigns all authority and decision making to the one person or group in charge. In contrast to that policy, most successful temporary organizations expect everyone to make decisions and solve problems at their particular location, while passing information on their activities back through the chain of command to keep the central coordinator informed of all developments.

centralized organizational policy Assigning decision making and authority to one individual or set of individuals within a larger organization.

One Temporary Organization from Three Available Groups

Two different fire/rescue organizations and one military unit have converged at the site of this building collapse, using an incident command system to temporarily merge their operations into one organized effort. Visible here is a bucket brigade, in which the combined group moves a large amount of material by continuously passing small amounts between members. This contingency practice is an effective process for shifting the location of goods, water, or debris when more efficient motorized equipment is either unavailable, or in the case of an unstable building, inadvisable.

Performance

real-time
The present point in time; now.

Performance is critical to any operation, but most important when operating in the presence of disruption. This is because the unexpected nature of disruption shifts decision making into real-time, when otherwise it would be conducted in advance. Regardless of how much effort is invested in contingency planning or how much of a system design is devoted to redundancy, an organization always faces the possibility of the truly unexpected and will then be forced to develop yet another solution in the moment. Industries such as emergency response, film production, medical intervention, and military operations all share reputations for their abilities to expect the unexpected and succeed despite unforeseen circumstances. Not surprisingly, their operations likewise share certain features closely associated with successful performance in real-time.

workaround
A temporary solution developed in response to an unexpected loss or obstacle.

Creativity and Bricolage The link between creativity and successful performance despite disruption occurs in many different settings, such as work practices shared by film making and police intervention. One of the most significant forms of potential crisis, disruptive innovation, is itself powered by creativity. One thread that runs through these settings is surprises, or unexpected factors that impede the understood direction of work. Successfully dealing with surprises is a key to navigating disruption, often by creating a workaround, or temporary solution to defeat the negative aspect of the surprise. Workarounds are often manual substitutes for technological systems that suddenly fail to perform, such as recording data with pencil and paper when the online entry system is down. However, workarounds differ from contingency plans in that a workaround is created on-the-spot, as opposed to developed in advance of the disruption.

bricolage
A creation from what happened to be available during its formation.

Creating workarounds in real-time requires improvisation, often by using available resources in new ways. Examples of managerial improvisation include flatbed truck trailers used as platforms, cargo boxes used as shelters, cat litter used to stop the spread of flammable liquids, and clear plastic food wrap used to control bleeding and ultimately save a life. Each of these solutions is an example of bricolage, a term borrowed from the creative arts. A bricolage is any creation developed from what happened to be at hand, and so bricolage challenges managers to rethink the potential of resources that happen to be available. This is the ultimate in thinking outside the box, an ability vital to operating despite disruption. The process of temporary organization is itself a conceptual form of bricolage, as a new organization forms from the personnel of multiple existing organizations that happen to be there.

Bricolage with Cargo Containers

Cargo containers are large steel boxes designed to transport goods by ship, rail, or roadway. However, the cargo containers in this picture have been pressed into use as temporary housing, to restore shelter after a major earthquake. These sturdy, stackable structures solve the problem of rapid, reliable shelter with some creative adaptation.

Sense-making and Situational Awareness Successful response to a disruption requires timely recognition of the disruption. History, however, is filled with counter-examples—stories of individuals and organizations *slow* to recognize the magnitude of an incident. For example, when Hurricane Katrina hit New Orleans in 2005 and when Hurricane Gustav hit Baton Rouge in 2008, the true scope of damage to each city was not grasped until several days after the damage occurred. In the confusion and ambiguity that follows widespread disruption, the cognitive process known as sense-making often becomes overwhelmed, leading us to incorrect assessments of the situation. Sense-making is a constant process in which people and organizations assign meaning to information they are receiving—they "make sense of it"—but normalization may interfere, causing us to not see what we don't want to see. Further, because people tend to favor plausible information when flooded with multiple reports on something uncertain, accurate information may be pushed aside, as what we consider plausible may in fact actually be inaccurate.

sense-making Assigning meaning to experience.

Sense-making creates situational awareness in an individual or organization, or fails to do so in a rapidly changing environment. Good situational awareness correctly recognizes potential future states of nature, the theoretical foundation of effective decision making for any type of operation. Sense-making and situational awareness are the most difficult to maintain, however, when the environment is turbulent and uncertain. Organizations which routinely operate under these conditions provide some interesting patterns of successful practice:

situational awareness An individual or organization's comprehension of the surrounding environment and its potential near-future states.

- *Work in groups.* Sense-making appears to be strengthened by groups, as a team of minds collaborating to make sense of something are often more successful than an individual's attempt to process the same complex and fluctuating information.
- *Have an open forum for group communication.* A team of minds engaged in sense-making must have a means of sharing observations and insights. This open forum can be a large common workspace such as in an air traffic control center, or a website where distant participants can post and read each other's messages. Radio communication often supports this role, as emergency, convention, and sporting event management all feature the use of personal radios tuned to a common frequency, so production teams can stay in constant contact to maintain their shared understanding of the current operation.
- *Cultivate multiple sources of information.* Under routine circumstances, an organization streamlines the information relevant to routine decision making, such as a computer screen that displays the exact on-hand inventory of some item at its nearest location. However, under rapidly changing conditions, precisely what needs to be known for optimal sense-making can be elusive, so groups under these conditions often refer to multiple sources. As an example, a typical emergency operations center monitors multiple radio frequencies to gather information from the field but also relies on heads-up information displays from multiple other sources, including local airport radar, online postings within social media sites, webcam networks, and television news.

It may not be possible to avoid all difficulties in sense-making and situational awareness when an organization experiences the unexpected. A retailer does not need the real-time sense-making abilities of emergency response or air traffic control to provide excellent customer service. However, if that same retailer suffers a major disruption, it could temporarily adopt some of these habits, such as appointing a team of people to spearhead the problem, declaring one large meeting room as mission control where they work until the disruption is resolved. Once routine operations are restored, the sense-making response team can disband and return to their individual offices as normal.

Airport Towers for Situational Awareness

Almost any airport, large or small, features at least one iconic control tower on its premises, such as pictured here. The employees at work in the top floors of this tower use sophisticated information systems to manage the surrounding aircraft traffic safely. However, their decision support technology could be housed anywhere, and thus is not the reason for the tower. Due to the extreme importance of sense-making and situational awareness in this industry, these employees work at the top of a tower to maintain a parallel source of relevant information gathered by looking out of its windows.

Problems with Performance Measurement Evaluating performance during disruption is notoriously difficult, and researchers continue to debate what performance measures are appropriate. Most organizations, including public organizations, are designed to operate under routine conditions, pursuing efficiency and optimization on behalf of their stakeholders. In this setting, performance measures are well known from a long history of use, such as gross profit, return on assets, and utilization. However, each organization was originally designed to be effective in its mission, or capable of meeting its purpose. Well-known performance measures clarify its efficiency—how well it puts the design to use. At the outset of a disruption, an organization's original effectiveness is impaired, and restoration of its effectiveness should become the first priority in decision making. For example, a company may not normally take employees away from full-time duties and dispatch them to drive to multiple sites to collect data, but if the company relies on this data and its computer information network is down, then this workaround may be the only appropriate action. Normally, the information network would be far more efficient at providing that data, but this is not relevant if the network is not available, and the sooner the company recognizes this change in relevancy, the better.

Another familiar and logical performance measure from routine operation is progress relative to plan, such as "we are 3 days behind schedule" or "we've exceeded our production target for this week." Although organizations should have plans for disruption, this type of measurement is far less helpful than in routine operations. Performance during disruption frequently blurs the distinction between planning and implementation, as decision makers are confronted with new, incomplete information. Crisis and disaster response are recognized as evolving processes, and organizations adapted to these environments engage in iterative planning, constantly revising the plan at short intervals, even as that plan is being acted upon. Thus, it is generally not practical, or even relevant, to assess progress against plan under these conditions, because multiple plans will have been generated and discarded before resolution is achieved. Furthermore, this revising and discarding of plans is a natural outcome of disruption, and should not be assumed inefficient.

iterative planning
Deliberately adjusting plans at short intervals, to reflect emerging information.

Finally, performance measures from routine operations can inhibit successful bricolage, as reflected in the French philosopher Voltaire's quote, "the perfect is the enemy of the good." Large, modern operations often emphasize optimization of their resources, using powerful mathematical tools to identify solutions that maximize a given objective

optimization
Identification of the best alternative.

Efficiency versus Effectiveness in Donkey Transport

Donkeys can easily carry 30% of their body weight long distances, and are particularly agile on steep and uneven terrain. Once a major mode of transportation and commerce, donkeys have long been replaced by more efficient internal combustion engine technology. However, some organizations maintain these valuable assets as an alternative logistical solution to very difficult conditions. Humanitarian relief, search-and-rescue, archeology, ecotourism, and natural resource management are all examples, and their modern-day operations may include donkeys, horses, dog teams, and even llamas, taking advantage of the unique effectiveness of each in certain environments.

such as profitability. Naïve use of optimization has already been noted for its role in driving redundancy out of modern operations, inadvertently making these networks more vulnerable to disruption. However, even if optimization is used wisely under routine conditions, it becomes a damaging mindset during disruption. Brilliant workarounds often use resources in roles for which their design is not optimal and may call upon older, less-efficient processes as temporary bridges to effectiveness. Furthermore, multiple workarounds often exist to meet an immediate objective, and first determining which one is distinctly optimal is often of little value when compared to routine conditions. Rather, decision makers should recognize when "it's all good," and choose one reasonable alternative promptly to restore effectiveness.

Disaster Logistics

When a government declares a disaster, it recognizes an unexpected incident with the highest magnitude of potential loss, signaling different organizations to drop their usual boundaries and meld together into a single cooperative response. That transformation is vital to the effectiveness of the disaster logistics that follow, managing the flow of resources to address the problem. Because disaster logistics requires multiple organizations to move resources on short notice and under imperfect conditions, it can be viewed as the ultimate challenge in supply chain management.

Disaster logistics has long been the domain of the NGO, or nonprofit, nongovernmental organization. Organizations such as the International Federation of Red Cross and Red Crescent Societies, Oxfam International, and the Salvation Army maintain capacity for response to emergencies and disasters, and are sometimes the first organization to make contact with disaster victims in remote areas. However, many commercial organizations have also been recognized for lending their resources and logistical expertise during times of disaster, a list that includes Walmart, United Parcel Service, and Coca-Cola. Whether a full-time or part-time member of the disaster logistics industry, understanding how any one of these organizations succeeds at this most challenging form of supply chain management begins with examining disaster itself.

NGO
A nongovernmental organization, understood to be a nonprofit organization as well.

Disaster Life Cycles At first glance, disaster logistics appears similar to commercial supply chain management, employing resources such as people, aircraft, warehouses, trucks, and inventory to conduct familiar activities such as purchasing, loading, transporting, stocking, and measuring. However, these similarities are somewhat misleading, in that the keys

FIGURE 15.5 Disaster Life Cycle versus Traditional Project Life Cycle

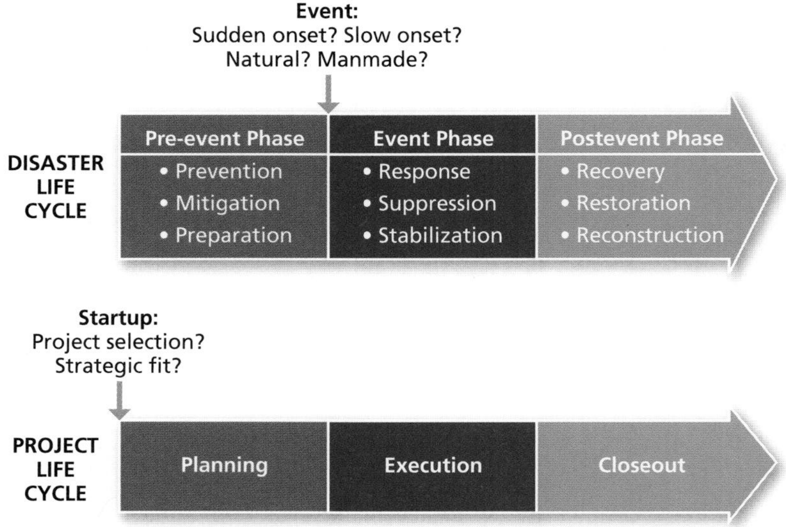

to success in modern supply chain management are not identical to those of successful disaster logistics. Despite shared resources and processes, disaster logistics more closely resembles a specialized form of project, progressing through a set of distinct phases. Figure 15.5 illustrates the kinship between disaster logistics and project management by comparing the so-called disaster life cycle with the traditional view of a project's life cycle.

Both project management in general and disaster logistics in particular begin with a planning phase, but commercial projects are *selected* whereas disasters *happen*. In traditional project work, then, more detail is known concerning what will be required, so activities can be arranged accordingly. However, while many disaster response organizations select a strategic focus for their activities, they often do not know where or when they will respond to the next disaster. Thus, the pre-event planning phase of a disaster consists of general preparation and risk management.

Actual project planning done prior to a disaster can also vary with the type of disaster:

- *Sudden versus slow onset disasters.* An earthquake is an example of a sudden onset disaster, one which strikes abruptly. Slow onset disasters, however, begin with a crisis period and unfold over time, such as famine following drought. Slow onset disasters allow more time for planning activities, and may even allow enough time to focus on efficiency as well as effectiveness in developing solutions for disaster relief.
- *Natural versus manmade disasters.* Disasters are also divided according to their causes. Natural disasters such as earthquakes and storms build up historical data that can be analyzed to loosely forecast the likelihood of these events in certain regions. While the individual incidents are random, the region's preparations can be focused on its particular vulnerabilities, such as hurricane and typhoon preparedness for coastal cities. In contrast, manmade disasters such as industrial accidents and acts of terrorism are not as easy to anticipate broadly, but human involvement in these causes suggests that they are stronger candidates for prevention efforts.

Both commercial projects and disaster logistics launch into action at some point in their life cycle. Projects such as construction and software upgrades can choose this timing, whereas disaster relief must activate when a disaster dictates the need. A traditional project such as building construction is also likely to follow its original plan more closely than disaster response, as the uncertainties of the disaster cause its original plans to be revised as the event phase progresses. Once the direct work of response is completed, ending the progress of harm, a large-scale disaster is also likely to require considerably more attention and energy to its postevent phase than a traditional project requires in its corresponding closeout. Closeout of a large commercial project involves wrap-up activities such as closing contracts and gathering feedback, but ending the progression of harm during the middle phase of a disaster life cycle only sets the stage for repairing the harm already inflicted, a recovery phase that could be thought of as a second distinct project by itself.

Safety Stock, Staging, and the Last-Mile Problem Disaster logistics also depend heavily on some inventory management concepts less common to commercial supply chains, and sometimes considered detrimental to their success. Safety stock, for example, is a necessary evil from a commercial perspective, because inventory held as safety stock protects the supply chain from shortages, but otherwise only hides problems and adds expense. However, since safety stock provides a buffer against unexpected changes in supply or demand, virtually anything waiting in a warehouse within a disaster logistics network could be argued as safety stock by definition. Where safety stock may be suspected as waste in a commercial operation, its availability is central to a successful disaster response.

safety stock Inventory held to protect against uncertain supply or demand.

Related to the concept of safety stock is the concept of staging, an activity common to emergency response but rare in commercial operations. Inventory and other assets can be staged by moving them into a forward position ahead of any request for them. As an example, multiple ambulances may be transferred from their routine locations to stage near a large event or incident, where they wait for further instructions. Note that the exact need for these ambulances is not known at the time of staging, and some or all of the ambulances may not, in fact, be required, being released later to return to their routines. Although staging is a key to effective response under extreme uncertainty, it seldom appears efficient, as staging often results in what looks like idleness and wasted effort from the perspective of a commercial operation.

staging Retrieving or positioning inventory or other resources before they are required.

Finally, all supply chain networks must solve their individual last-mile problems, although commercial supply chains rarely confront this issue more than once. The last-mile problem of a supply chain is the question of what transportation to assign to its end, bringing inventory to the exact location of the consumer. As an example, fresh fruit may

last-mile problem (or last-kilometer problem) The challenge of completing delivery of a good or a service, especially if the destination is remote or disrupted by disaster.

The Last-Mile Problem after an Earthquake

Some large-scale incidents damage ground transportation networks, interfering with last-mile delivery of resources even after debris is cleared away. One extremely important task early in the event phase of a disaster is rapid assessment of which routes are still open and which routes, such as this valley road, are no longer available to ground logistics. Global positioning systems are extremely valuable at this stage, as responders now have an efficient means of documenting and communicating these obstacles as they are found. Prior to GPS, this work was complicated by the fact that disasters often destroy street signs as well, reducing an observer's ability to determine and report exact locations.

travel by air freight and then truck to a supermarket's supply depot, where the shipment is subdivided and reloaded onto local delivery trucks destined for retail stores. The last-mile problem is solved for this supply chain as these trucks leave the smaller shipments at each store and personnel transfer the fruit to display racks, ready to be retrieved by the consumer. In contrast, disaster logisticians may have to solve their last-mile problems repeatedly, because disasters occur at unscheduled locations and often destroy the local transportation infrastructure. A shipment of disaster relief may proceed swiftly via aircraft and truck, only to be brought to a stop near its destination by a collapsed bridge. If available, helicopters are often highly effective at solving the last-mile problem through disrupted terrain, although other past solutions have included mule teams, snow mobiles, bicycles, and large numbers of volunteers on foot, each carrying a small amount of an otherwise stalled shipment. Because transportation across the last mile of a disaster supply chain is generally far less efficient than the thousands of miles of transportation system preceding it, valuable disaster relief often accumulates at the ports of entry into a large disaster area, as it can be shipped to the last mile much faster than it can be shipped across it.

Although modern operations are more vulnerable to increasing frequency of disaster, it is important to remember that, just as the nature of disaster has evolved, so has society's capacity to answer these challenges. Some formerly frequent and devastating incidents such as polio outbreaks and theater fires are now relatively rare. In some cases, an advance in science or technology moved an external risk such as polio into the preventable category, allowing its exclusion from modern society by the proaction of a vaccination program. However, in cases like theater fire, that type of disaster is now rare because that type of operation has been deliberately strengthened against it (more clearly marked exits, overhead sprinkler systems, etc.). Increasing frequency of disruption can be met with increased understanding of how best to operate despite disruption, and use of that knowledge to build ever more resilient systems.

SUMMARY

Unexpected incidents and the disruptions they cause are an inevitable part of operations management. Traditional decision theory provides tools for informed decision making in the face of this uncertainty, modeling the future as several possible outcomes that can be logically combined at the present time to estimate expected value. However, this approach is naturally limited by its dependence on knowing what is uncertain, and excludes the possibility of the completely unexpected. This concept of the known unknown is the foundation of business analysis, although unknown unknowns including emergencies, disruptive innovation, and disasters are just as likely to pose external risks to an organization. High interconnectivity and other features of modern systems are also more likely to propagate these disruptions when they do strike, making risk management more important than ever.

Despite their uncertain nature, disruptions can be planned for in advance of incidents. Business continuity plans propose procedures to use when struck by disruption, to assure the organization continues operating despite the unexpected incident. Organizations can increase the reliability and resiliency of their systems by introducing redundancy, although this may appear unattractive from a cost-optimization perspective. In certain cases, an organization's plans may even knowingly result in disruption, as these systems follow the tactics of yield management to maximize the benefits of a limited resource by tolerating the risk of shortage or excess. However, some disruption will occur that cannot be answered with preexisting plans, and successful operation despite this disruption often depends on an ability to organize quickly, use available resources in new ways, and maintain good situational awareness despite confusing information. Organizations engaged in disaster logistics meet all these challenges, answering the ultimate challenge in supply chain management.

Key Terms

Black Swan
bricolage
business continuity plan
centralized organizational policy
chance event
confirmation bias
contingency plan
crisis
disruptive innovation
expected value
framing
future states of nature
groupthink
incident
incident command system
iterative planning
known unknown
last-mile problem
newsvendor problem
NGO
normalization
optimization
outcome bias
overbooking
proaction
probabilistic
propagate
redundancy
reliability
resilience
risk
real-time
robustness
safety stock
sense-making
situational awareness
staging
triage
unknown unknown
workaround
yield management

Discussion Questions

1. Why is a "Black Swan crisis" technically impossible?
2. If an event is unforeseeable, how can a good contingency plan help?
3. In disaster planning, which is more important, mitigation or response? Why?
4. How do robustness and redundancy relate to biomimicry, the copying of design principles from natural systems?
5. How does Voltaire's quote, "the perfect is the enemy of the good," relate to the well-known problem, "paralysis of analysis"?

PROBLEMS

Minute Answer

Short answers appear in Appendix A. Go to **NoteShaper.com** for full video tutorials on each question.

1. If an organization deliberately tolerates a possibility of loss, is this possibility a strategic or an external risk?
2. Consider three organizations, one operating during an emergency, one during a crisis, and one during a disaster. By definition of the three terms, which organization has the best potential to stop any loss before it happens?
3. If a company considers 10 different future states of nature to be equally likely, and each of the 10 has a different value, how can that company calculate the expected value?
4. Is disruptive innovation more likely to create an emergency or a crisis?
5. A manager assumes an unlikely request in an order must be the result of some unusual customer. Is this an example of outcome bias or normalization?

6. Someone complains about a supplier who makes mistakes and a manager shrugs and says, "At least they're consistent." Did the manager just comment on the reliability or the robustness of the supplier's performance?
7. Does increasing system complexity without increasing redundancy then increase or decrease system reliability?
8. Does increasing redundancy increase or decrease reliability?
9. Does increasing redundancy increase or decrease overall utilization of the system?
10. Which requires improvisation—business impact analysis or bricolage?
11. Is the newsvendor problem an example of overbooking or yield management?
12. If a group of people stop the discussion of an important decision for fear of an argument between two members, the outcome of that decision is in danger of suffering from what?

Quick Start

13. There is a 60% chance of sales of 1 million, a 30% chance of sales of 2 million, and a 10% chance of sales of 3 million. What is the expected value of sales?
14. A chance event can result in three future states of nature, the first two states having a probability of 20% each. What is the probability of the third future state of nature?
15. An operation consists of two steps, the first of which has a reliability of 97% and the second a reliability of 99%. What is the reliability of the operation?
16. An operation consists of two steps, the first of which has a reliability of 97% and the second a reliability of 99%. What is the probability that the operation will fail?
17. A component has a reliability of 98% and is backed up by a redundant component with the same probability. What is their combined reliability?
18. A processer has a 10% probability of freezing, at which point an identical backup processor is activated. What is the probability they both freeze?

Ramp Up

19. There is a 60% chance of a loss of $100, a 30% chance of sales of $100, and a 10% chance of sales of $200. What is the expected value of sales?
20. An ambulance generally transports between one and eight patients a day. If the ambulance crew reports no particular pattern within that range, what is the expected value of the daily number of transports for this ambulance?

Full Scenarios

21. The Arms Hotel has 56 rooms. A rented room represents $150 in profit, while turning away a customer who made a reservation (but the Arms Hotel did not have a room available) costs $100. However many reservations the Arms Hotel accepts, there is a 50% chance that exactly that number of customers will show up to claim their reservations, and a 50% chance that one less than the total number of reservations will show up.
    a. What are the two future states of nature the Arms Hotel faces?
    b. What is the expected value of the policy of accepting exactly 56 reservations?
    c. What is the expected value of the policy of accepting exactly 57 reservations?
    d. The Arms Hotel already has 56 reservations for tomorrow, and a customer has just called who wants to book a room for tomorrow. Should the Arms Hotel tell this customer yes or no?

22. Damon Telecom is designing a new workhorse satellite to eventually replace all the orbital satellites it manages in its telecommunication network. The design of this satellite consists of five interdependent subsystems, as indicated here:

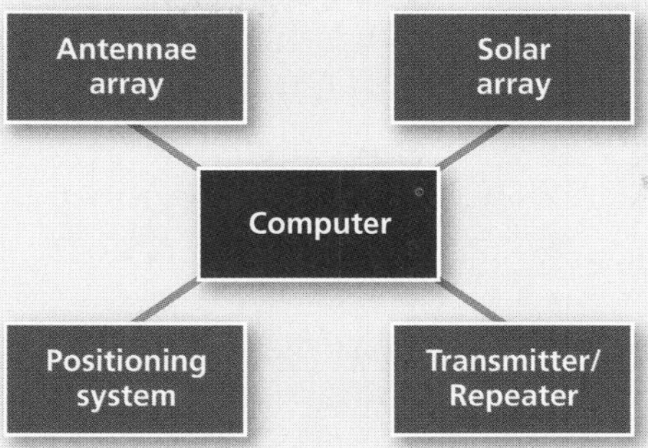

The satellites Damon currently has in place use subsystems that are 99% reliable over a 10-year period, but Damon Telecom is annoyed to have already lost use of two of these older satellites. Some managers argue that the new generation of satellites should feature two computers and two solar arrays, duplicating the two subsystems known to have been lost in Damon's failed satellites. A few argue that the antennae array and transmitter/repeater subsystems represent obsolete satellite design that invites problems: both these systems should be redesigned as one integrated system built by one contractor.

a. What is the 10-year reliability of Damon Telecom's current satellite design?
b. If a redundant computer were added, how reliable would the computer subsystem be?
c. If the computer and solar array subsystems were duplicated as proposed, what would be the 10-year reliability of the satellite then?
d. If no redundant elements were added, but the antennae array and transmitter/repeater were successfully redesigned into a single subsystem with a 10-year reliability of 99%, what would be the resulting reliability of the satellite?

CASE STUDY: CONVEX PRODUCTIONS, REVISITED

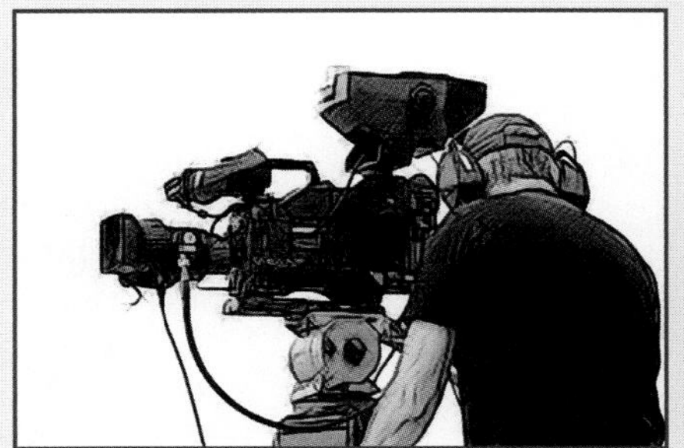

Recall from Chapter 1 that Convex Productions produces full-length motion pictures for distribution worldwide. Convex has just purchased the rights to a movie script entitled *Native Sun*, which it intends to develop as its next project. *Native Sun* is the story of an orphaned human raised by an alien race, visiting Earth on business and becoming entangled in intrigue here. Its simultaneous classification as science fiction/fantasy and action/adventure is expected to draw a broad audience, although the big-budget nature of *Native Sun* poses several risks. Nonetheless, Convex Productions is close to closing a deal with its longtime funding partner, Malomar Pictures, who will hopefully green light the film in a few days. Upon receiving the green light, Convex can begin spending Malomar's money on the *Native Sun* project.

Convex Productions has agreed to purchase completion insurance for the project, guaranteeing the return of Malomar's investment if *Native Sun* suffers some catastrophic setback during filming, such as the death of a leading actor. However, Malomar remains concerned about *Native Sun* as an investment. The completion insurance policy protects against disruptions preventing the movie from being released, but does not guarantee its timely release into the marketplace. For the best yield on its substantial investment, Malomar wants assurance that *Native Sun* will be released in time for the summer block buster season, beginning in late May. If *Native Sun* were green-lighted in the next few days, Convex Productions then would have only 38 to 42 weeks to release the movie when Malomar feels it would maximize box office profits and only 46 weeks to benefit from any momentum in the summer movie season at all. To accomplish this, Convex must complete three phases of work between green light and movie release, as illustrated here:

Native Sun Project, from Green Light to Release

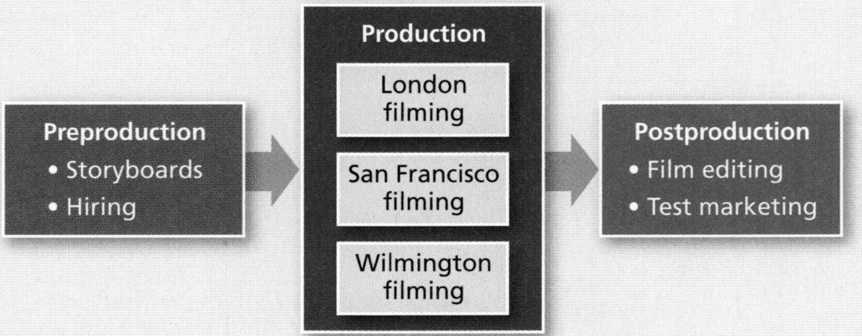

Some aspects of the *Native Sun* project are easy to anticipate: preproduction should take 6 weeks from green light, and postproduction should require 16 weeks of work after filming, including several sneak previews in which the film is test marketed with small audiences and then reedited, based on their feedback. Actual movie production, however, is subject to some uncertainty. *Native Sun* will be filmed in three different locations, and Convex estimates that this work would normally take about 6 weeks at each location. However, unexpected events occur during filming and propagate quickly in this type of project, such as a permit to close streets expiring before filming there finishes, delayed because one actor was sick with the flu. As a result, Convex's production experts agree that when it rains, it pours in film production, and disruption of any amount in 6 weeks' worth of work generally means it will take about 10 weeks to complete all that work instead.

Happily, filming in London is not likely to be disrupted, because filming there is done on constructed sets in the closed, controlled environment of Lamplight Studios. Here the only real risk to a 6-week completion time is the possibility of flu or similar, so Convex estimates only a 5% chance of disruption and delay there. However, filming in Wilmington, North Carolina, and San Francisco, California, are both done on location, meaning primarily outdoors, and thus both rely on favorable weather. Wilmington will provide rural backdrops, while San Francisco is needed for its iconic city landscape. Thus, filming in San Francisco is further complicated by the city permitting process, allowing Convex to briefly interfere with the flow of city traffic at key locations on certain dates. As a result, Convex estimates a 10% chance of disruption and delay in Wilmington, while double that probability for the work on location in San Francisco.

The original estimates of 6 or 10 weeks at each location reflect Convex Productions' preferred style of scheduling, in which its cast and crew work at one location until all work there is finished, and then move to the next location. Convex could protect itself against the possibility of disruption with an alternate schedule that holds each of the three locations open for 18 weeks, flying personnel between the three throughout that period. This allows filming to work around disruptions by shifting activity elsewhere, guaranteeing that all production work will be finished in about 18 weeks. This alternate schedule is not preferred by Convex because it often doubles the direct expense of filming, while cast and crew dislike it for being complicated and tiring. To hurry the completion of *Native Sun*, Convex also has the option of skipping the test marketing/reediting phase of postproduction. In this option, *Native Sun* is edited once, based on the director's best estimate of what the audience most wants to see, and then sent straight to market without any sneak previews to check the director's assumptions. This cuts time required for postproduction in half, but increases the risk of *Native Sun* not being as popular and profitable as if improved by the test-marketing process. Malomar Pictures would be most upset by this shortcut, as its conversations with Convex Productions so far have been based on the commonsense assumption that a movie and investment this large would be finished through test marketing, to maximize the potential return on the investment.

In addition to Malomar's desire for a summer release, Convex Productions has its own reasons to worry about prompt completion of the film. For every week that passes, *Native Sun* is exposed to the danger of being twinned by a rival production company, who rushes a similar story into production for release at the same time or earlier, pilfering Convex's marketing efforts. Even now there is a rumor that a notorious low-budget movie producer has hired a writer to develop a script with the working title *Wayward Home*. This industry rumor describes *Wayward Home* as "an action story about a guy raised by aliens who visits Earth for the first time." If this rumor is true, then *Native Sun* must arrive in theaters as early in the summer as possible, to claim the interested movie audience and defeat the appearance of *Wayward Home*.

Questions

1. Describe each and all of the distinct risks discussed in the *Native Sun* project. What type of risk does each represent?
2. Assume that *Native Sun* receives the green light from Malomar Pictures. If Convex Productions uses its preferred type of production scheduling, and test markets *Native Sun* according to Malomar's expectations, what is the expected value of the time until *Native Sun*'s release? What is the chance that *Native Sun* arrives in the market in time for the summer blockbuster season?
3. Using your work to question 2, describe the benefit of the alternative production schedule, in which Convex keeps all three locations open for 18 weeks.
4. Now state your recommendations to Convex Productions on how to proceed from the green light on *Native Sun*, assuming that signal occurs in the next few days. What risks are you choosing to minimize, and at what cost, if any? What risks do your recommendations tolerate or even create, if any?

BIBLIOGRAPHY

Anderson, D., D. Sweeney, and T. Williams. 2005. *An Introduction to Management Science: Quantitative Approaches to Decision Making*, 11th ed. Cincinnati, OH: South-Western/Thomson Learning.

APICS. 2011. *APICS 2011 Supply Chain Risk: Challenges and Practices.* Chicago: APICS, The Association for Operations Management.

Austin, R., and L. Devin. 2003. *Artful Making: What Managers Need to Know About How Artists Work.* Upper Saddle River, NJ: FT Prentice Hall.

Bakker, R. 2010. "Taking Stock of Temporary Organizational Forms: A Systematic Review and Research Agenda." *International Journal of Management Reviews* 12: 466–86.

Bechky, B., and G. Okhuysen. 2011. "Expecting the Unexpected? How SWAT Officers and Film Crews Handle Surprises." *Academy of Management Journal* 54(2): 239–61.

Boin, A. 2009. "The New World of Crises and Crisis Management: Implications for Policy Making and Research." *Review of Policy Research* 26(4): 367–77.

Brody, B., and M. Schmittlein. 2012. "Business Continuity 101." *Risk Management*, January/February: 14–15.

Buchanan, L., and A. O'Connell. 2006. "A Brief History of Decision Making." *Harvard Business Review*, January: 33–41.

Haddow, G., J. Bullock, and C. Damon. 2008. *Introduction to Emergency Management*. Oxford, UK: Elsevier Inc.

Jones, V. 2011. "How to Avoid Disaster: RIM's Crucial Role in Business Continuity Planning." *Information Management*, November/December: 36–40.

Jongejan, R., S. Jonkman, and J. Vrijling. 2012. "The Safety Chain: A Delusive Concept." *Safety Science* 50: 1299–303.

Kaplan, R., and A. Mikes. 2012. "Managing Risks: A New Framework." *Harvard Business Review*, June: 48–60.

Kingsolver, B., S. Hopp, and C. Kingsolver. 2007. *Animal, Vegetable, Miracle.* New York: HarperCollins.

Kovács, G., and K. Spens. 2009. "Identifying Challenges in Humanitarian Logistics." *International Journal of Physical Distribution & Logistics Management* 29(6): 506–28.

Taleb, N. 2010. *The Black Swan: The Impact of the Highly Improbable.* New York: Random House.

Taleb, N., D. Goldstein, and M. Spitznagel. 2009. "The Six Mistakes Executives Make in Risk Management." *Harvard Business Review*, October.

Tinsley, C., R. Dillon, and P. Madsen. 2011. "How to Avoid Catastrophe." *Harvard Business Review*, April: 90–97.

Thatcher, J. 2012. "The Broken Chain: Uncovering the Sources of Supply Disruptions." *APICS Magazine* 22(3): 10–11.

APPENDIX A: ANSWERS

Chapter 1: Introduction to Operations Management

Minute Answer

1) truck, fuel, cargo; 2) inputs and outputs; 3) tactical decision making; 4) higher; 5) principles governing conduct delineating good from bad; 6) planning horizon; 7) the best alternative; 8) inventory; 9) incident; 10) nongovernmental organization; 11) lower; 12) production.

Quick Start

13) tactical; 14) strategic; 15) implementation; 16) implementation; 17) strategic.

Ramp Up

18) negotiating lease—point A; drilling for oil—point C; refining fuel—point D; transporting fuel—point B; 19) barn-raiser—point A; cake mix—point B; repair of electrical grid—point C; maintenance of ATMs—point D; hosting and promotion of musical group—point E.

Chapter 2: Providing Goods and Services

Minute Answer

1) the future; 2) make-to-stock; 3) less capital investment; 4) maturity; 5) it will decrease; 6) rapid growth; 7) higher; 8) goal alignment; 9) maturity; 10) competitive advantage; 11) order qualifier; 12) total productivity measure.

Quick Start

13) the first plant; 14) 1.5 engines per employee day; 15) 19.23 visitors per officer labor-hour; 16) 41.875 meals per part-time labor-hour; 17) 0.000536 miles of road per dollar.

Ramp Up

18) The plant was more productive per day during the 4-day week; 19) The 4-person crew was more productive by 0.208 miles of lane per person-hour; 20) 140% of labor expense.

Scenarios

21) a. 17 utility poles per hour; b. Labor productivity will drop by 5.89 poles per hour, or –35%; c. 0.447 (poles per \$ spent) for current and 0.303 (poles per \$ spent) for Northlands.

22) a. Bronson is most productive using this measure; b. Archer is the most productive now by 0.000039 miles of road per \$, or 1%; c. Bronson has the higher productivity by 0.000075 miles of road per \$, or 2.4%; d. It differs because Bronson is more labor productive, so advantage will shift to Bronson as labor becomes more costly relative to materials and equipment.

Chapter 3: Product Quality and Development

Minute Answer

1) quality as conformance; 2) quality as conformance; 3) service; 4) strong negative correlation; 5) linear; 6) histogram; 7) fishbone diagram; 8) quality circle; 9) cradle-to-cradle; 10) delayed differentiation; 11) assignable variation; 12) quality function deployment.

Quick Start

13) value feature B; 14) value feature A; 15) technical spec 3.

Ramp Up

16) negatively correlated, $r = -0.7176$.

Scenarios

17) a. Broken gearing mechanism requiring frequent repair and mechanical failure of turnstile;
b. Fishbone diagram; c. First Improvement 2, then Improvement 1.

18) a. I only; b. II only; c. I and III;
d. ● = Strong positive correlation
○ = Some positive correlation
⊠ = Strong negative correlation
× = Some negative correlation

	Relative Importance (out of 100)	Thickness of shell	Depth of nap	Density of nap	% Nylon in nap	% Latex in shell
Easy to see	30		⊠			
Doesn't bounce funny	30	●		○		⊠
Stays bouncy	30	●		○	○	⊠
Stays clean	10		⊠			

Chapter 4: Forecasting

Minute Answer

1) less; 2) more; 3) negative; 4) shorter-term; 5) past relevant data; 6) seasonal; 7) 0.2; 8) simple exponential smoothing; 9) Delphi method; 10) ME; 11) the actual observation from that period; 12) coefficient of determination.

Quick Start

13) 3; 14) MAD 5, MSE 29.67; 15) 1.8; 16) 3.0; 17) MAPE 4.7%; 18) 42.8; 19) 265, 15.9%; 20) −125, −6.3%.

Ramp Up

21) 0.35; 22) 3125; 23) fourth month; third month; third month (again); 24) 0.60, 0.36.

Scenarios

25) a. 50; b. 65, 57.5; c. 78; d. 35 student appointments, appointments decline by 15 per week.
26) a. Monday, Saturday; b. 600 and 644, variation between days not consistent with usual seasonality; c. 545, 470.
27) a. 37550.12, 1120700.1; b. 24.9; c. 200.12, probably not, $x = 0$ outside of relevant range.
28) a. 451 rolls of insulation; b. 0.686 or 68.6%; c. −0.828; when air temperature goes down, insulation sales go up.
29) a. −8; b. −18.4%; c. ME −3.6, MSE 59.6, MAD 6.8, MAPE 17.30%, tracking signal −2.65; d. 40.3, −16%; e. 42.32.
30) a. 31.78; b. −4.20; c. 32.33.
31) a. July = 0.41, September = 2.25; b. May = 7 tons, October = 260 tons.
32) a. $y = 5399.2 + 29.722x$; b. $R^2 = 0.6264$ means that 62.64% of the data is explained by the model; c. A project 110 days long would cost $8668.62; d. Regression formula for Supply chain of $y = 1542 + 57.988x$ explains 96.55%, Marketing formula $y = 6928.1 + 18.348x$ explains 91.12%, compared to 62.64% in original model. Thus, a project 110 days long for Supply chain would be forecast at $7920.68 and for Marketing $8946.38.

Chapter 5: Capacity and Waiting

Minute Answer

1) work breaks, routine maintenance, bad weather; 2) optimal operating level; 3) diseconomies of scale; 4) distraction; 5) queuing theory; 6) balking; 7) the order in which arrivals will be served; 8) cost of system capacity; 9) it will get longer, increases; 10) reneging; 11) design capacity; 12) effective capacity; 13) capacity cushion.

Quick Start

14) 0.75 or 75%; 15) 0.82 or 82%; 16) 334 meter upgrades; 17) 500 Mercedes cars; 18) 0.625 or 62.5%; 19) 1 customer; 20) 1.67 customers in the system; 21) 0.1 hour or 6 minutes waiting in line; 22) 0.167 hour or 10 minutes in the system; 23) 0.375 or 37.5% of no customers in the system.

Ramp Up

24) 66,667 donuts; 25) 0.44 or 44%; 26) $70; 27) 691; 28) The booth is idle 90% of the time; 29) 3 minutes.

Scenarios

30) a. $300,000; b. 15 years; c. BE now 12.5 years.
31) a. 95% or 190 rafts; b. determinants of effective capacity; c. 0.5 or 50%; d. 5,000 rentals; e. 6,250 rentals; f. diseconomies of scale; g. $9.
32) a. the design capacity of the phone; b. a determinant of the effective capacity; c. 50%.
33) a. 1000 cars; b. $335.
34) a. 1.63; b. 7 minutes; c. 10 minutes; d. 70%; e. 7.2%.
35) a. 0.336 hour or 20.1 minutes; b. 0.833 or 83.3%; c. 4.17; d. 5; e. 0.52.
36) a. 12 minutes; b. 4.17; c. 30; d. 0.167 or 16.7%; e. 7.5 minutes improvement.
37) a. 66.67%; b. 16 minutes, 33.33%; c. 2 cars.
38)

a. Time	Check-points	b. Av length of line (L_q)	Prob. of waiting to be screened (λ/μ)
5am–6am	2	4.17 people	83.33%
6am–8am	6	3.34 people	80.56%
8am–4pm	4	2.25 people	75.00% (lowest)
4pm–7pm	6	3.34 people	80.56%
7pm–10pm	1	4.17 people	83.33%

Chapter 6: Process And Facility Selection

Minute Answer

1) fixed position layout; 2) traffic patterns; 3) little flexibility for customers, relatively prone to disruption, relatively higher capital investment requirement, relatively lower job satisfaction; 4) hybrid layout; 5) U; 6) 20 workstations; 7) 30 seconds; 8) make-to-stock; 9) assemble-to-order; 10) speed it up; 11) fixed position; 12) minimize traffic within facility.

Quick Start

13) 1.4 minutes; 14) 0.53 or 53%; 15) 9.6 seconds; 16) 0.67 minutes; 17) 320 units; 18) 4; 19) 0.819 or 81.9%; 20) 0.35 or 35%.

Ramp Up

21) 24; 22) 10 hours; 23) 100; 24) 2.

Scenarios

25) a. Company B; b. Company A; c. Company A; d. Company B.
26) a. 10 hours daily; b. 14 stations; c. 67%.
27) a. 50 seconds; b. 5 workstations; c. Station 5 has maximum idle time, Efficiency = 0.736 or 7.36%, Balance delay = 0.73 or 73%; d. It has one more station than the theoretical minimum.

28) a. Differences are order of completing tasks and idle time at stations, they are equally efficient; b. Most trouble adding 3 seconds to task C as task C time to complete currently equals the cycle time.
29) a. 20 cars per hour; b. Efficiency is 67%; c. 15 cars per hour.
30) a. main elevators; b. gift store, admin offices, food court; c. emergency room, admitting, food court.
31) a. 12 minutes.; b. 4 work stations; c. first work station; d. fourth work station.

Chapter 7: Project Management

Minute Answer

1) longest; 2) task A must be completed first; 3) zero; 4) beta distribution; 5) normal distribution; 6) critical path activities; 7) milestone; 8) PERT; 9) 7; 10) 2 days; 11) backward scheduling; 12) it will remain unchanged.

Quick Start

13) 5 days; 14) 7 days; 15) 8 days; 16) 6 days; 17) 7 days; 18) expected time 4.8 days, variance 1.36 days; 19) two paths; 20) 3 days.

Ramp Up

21) 18 days; 22) 5 days; 23) 0.7746 or 77%; 24) 0.0036 or 0.36%; 25) 49.5%; 26) 67%.

Scenarios

27) a. 10 days; b. B,E.
28) a. A,B,C; b. 5; c. A,D,J with completion time of 32 days; d. 12 days; e. 22 days.
29) a. A,E,H,I,J with a completion time of 17 days; b. 4 days; c. 0 days; d. decline.
30) a. Paths are: A–B–G–H–I, A–B–C–H–I, D–E–F–K–L, D–E–J–K–L; b. 19 days; c. D–E–J–K–L; d. 2 days; e. 10 days from now; f. 12 days from now.
31) a. B–D–H–I–J; b. 11 days; c. 2 days; d. crash D (1 day), E (1 day), G (1 day), and H (2 days), $700.
32) a. 9 hours; b. 2 hours; c. 72%.

Chapter 8: Location Planning and Logistics

Minute Answer

1) fixed costs; 2) not in my back yard; 3) variable costs; 4) intermodal containers; 5) buyer; 6) passenger airlines; 7) maritime shipping; 8) air freight; 9) averaged; 10) it is twice as important; 11) factor rating; 12) neither, they are equally preferable.

Quick Start

13) $X=1.7$, $Y=3.7$; 14) $X=0.71$, $Y=3.29$; 15) location B; 16) 8,000 units; 17) factor rating; 18) location A; 19) 50; 20) 45.

Ramp Up

21) Each factor should be assigned a weight of 1/5, or 20%; 22) $20,000; 23) 1/3 or 33%; 24) from 0 to ½, or 50%.

Scenarios

25) a. $X=0.2$, $Y=2.4$; b. $X=2$, $Y=0.3$; c) $X=-0.8$, $Y=4.1$.
26) a. I. false. II. false. III. true; b. location 1; c. 0.2 cost, 0.6 availability, 0.2 size; d. location 1.
27) a. 8.2; b. 5.33; c. the courtyard; d. yes—Murdock.
28) a. Hong Kong; b. 10,000 units; c. 1 unit to 3333 units.
29) a. location A; b. location B.

Chapter 9: Purchasing and Supply Chain Partnering

Minute Answer

1) downstream; 2) inbound; 3) X = annual expenditure, Y = risk/exposure; 4) high attractiveness of account and high $ value of business; 5) no; 6) sales agent; 7) tender; 8) apparent authority; 9) a purchase order; 10) boilerplate.

Quick Start

11) long-term partnering agreement; 12) The United Nations Convention on Contracts for International Sale of Goods apply automatically unless specifically excluded in contract.

Ramp Up

13) company B; 14) $11,332.

Scenarios

15) a. surgical supplies and pharmaceuticals; b. hay and grain; c. commercial-grade horse supplies, not including hay and grain.
16) a. daily janitorial services; b. upholstery and carpet cleaning, quarterly; c. soft drinks, popcorn and candy; d. toilet paper and liquid soap for public restrooms.
17) a. Dawson Commercial Cleaning Services; b. Fulton Maintenance and Facilities Service; c. 82.5; d. Fulton Maintenance and Facilities Service.

Chapter 10: Inventory Management

Minute Answer

1) increases; 2) increases; 3) increases; 4) decreases; 5) increases; 6) nothing; 7) doubles; 8) C class; 9) when; 10) increases; 11) stock keeping unit; 12) fixed cost.

Quick Start

13) 250 SKUs; 14) 45 boxes; 15) 49 boxes; 16) 26.5 weeks; 17) $19.60; 18) 50 musical greeting cards; 19) 5 units; 20) 25%.

Ramp Up

21) 85.6 gallons; 22) $1073.33; 23) 0.983 or 98.3%; 24) 12; 25) it will decrease.

Scenarios

26) a. $1,700; b. 120 units; c. 500 with 5% discount; d. 30.
27) a. $382.1; b. 191 bottles; c. 23.89 times per year; d. 75 bottles; e. order 1000 bottles at a time with discount.
28) a. 18.25 days; b. 2,920 slats, 18.25 days; c. 2,190 slats.
29) a. 461.6, 100 times per annum; b. EPQ = 764, TC = 314, savings = $147.6; c. 465 spaces.
30) a. safety stock of 20 units for all three SKUs; b. SKU 1 service level 78.81%, SKU 2 service level 97.72%, SKU 3 service level 77.04%.
31) a. 60 parts; b. 12 days; c. 6 days; d. 120 parts; e. 20 parts per day.

Chapter 11: Aggregate and Material Requirements Planning

Minute Answer

1) medium or intermediate term; 2) disaggregation; 3) chase demand strategy; 4) capacity cushion; 5) WIP; 6) raw materials; 7) level 0; 8) level 4; 9) the number of child items required to assemble one of the parent; 10) finite loading; 11) enterprise resource planning (ERP); 12) higher.

Quick Start

13) 5; 14) 8; 15) 47; 16) 54.5; 17) 300; 18) week 5; 19) item X; 20) a shortage of 500 units

Ramp Up

21) 37 units; 22) 132 units; 23) 49.5 units; 24) 40 A's week 2, 30 B's week 1, 30 C's week 1; 25) 2,000 units; 26) 136 units; 27) –25%.

Scenarios

28) a. 0; b. 50; c. $75.
29) a. 5,000 bows; b. month 3; c. $85,000.
30) a. 125 workers at end of July; b. 2,000,000 units; c. Aug 500,000 Sept 1, 500,000 Oct 2,000,000 Nov 1,000,000 Dec 500,000.
31) a. 5,000 units; b. 7,500 units; c. 15,000 units; d. $202,500.
32) a. part A: 200 week 3, 100 week 6, 100 week 8; part B: 50 week 1, 100 week 4, 100 week 6; part C: 150 week 1, 100 week 4, 100 week 6; part D: 100 week 3; b. all 0; c. only 100 As will be ordered in weeks 6 and 8, 50 Bs in week 6, 50 Cs in week 4 and 100 Cs in week 6, and no Ds will be ordered.
33) a. 3 levels; b. part A: 10 week 2, 20 week 3, 10 week 4, 10 week 5; part B: 20 week 2, 20 week 4; part C: 50 week 3; c. part C.
34) a. item F; b. items I and J; c. I,Y,Z,K,L,AA,BB,E,CC, DD,O,P,EE,FF, and R; d. level 3; e. 5 weeks.

Chapter 12: Lean Operations

Minute Answer Drill

1) implicit; 2) pull system; 3) reaction to signals; 4) inventory within the system; 5) waste, anything the customer will not pay for; 6) withdraw or use; 7) inventory; 8) waste; 9) explicit or push; 10) 1; 11) poka yoke; 12) increase.

Quick Start

13) 2; 14) 10; 15) 11; 16) 2 of part A and 8 of part B.

Ramp Up

17) uncertainties; 18) inventory, to expose uncertainties for fixing; 19) 3; 20) increase number of kanban cards; 21) reduce inventory of that part.

Scenarios

22) a. product A = 93.75 days, product B = 125 days, product C = 31.25 days; b. product A = 6, product B = 8, product C = 2; c. babababc babababc
23) a. 8; b. They should be reduced by half, or down to 4.

Chapter 13: Quality Control

Minute Answer

1) in control; 2) random variation; 3) The process is out of control; 4) type I error; 5) type II error; 6) less; 7) The process is capable of supporting the product's design specification; 8) decrease; 9) increases this risk, 10) decreases this probability; 11) narrower; 12) decrease.

Quick Start

13) 12.24; 14) 0.54; 15) 0.0894; 16) 1.25; 17) UCL 12.04, LCL 12.02; 18) UCL 0.0656, LCL 0.0144; 19) UCL 0.07, LCL 0; 20) UCL 52.7, LCL 17.3; 21) 5.2%.

Ramp Up

22) 2.75; 23) 1.53; 24) 0.2; 25) $\sigma = 0.0005$; 26) 2.34; 27) 0.062 or 6.2%.

Full Scenarios

28) a. UCL 501.2, LCL 498.8; b. 0.167, not capable of supporting those requirements.
29) a. UCL 351.37, LCL 350.66; b. UCL 1.49, LCL 0; c. While range is in control the sample mean shows the process is out of control.

30) a. mean 0.21, standard deviation 0.0576; b. UCL 0.3828, LCL 0.0372; c. UCL 20.2, LCL 0.8; They are similar if the limits on the *p*-chart are translated back into counts, based on the assumption of 50 candies.

Chapter 14: Scheduling

Minute Answer

1) makespan; 2) high; 3) backward scheduling; 4) work remaining to be done; 5) makespan; 6) average flowtime; 7) average tardiness; 8) zero; 9) work, in real time; 10) finite loading; 11) flowtime; 12) FCFS, first come, first served.

Quick Start

13) 2; 14) 0; 15) 5 weeks; 16) 7 days; 17) 2 weeks; 18) 6 weeks; 19) last; 20) first.

Ramp Up

21) tardiness = 0, job Beta is not late; 22) 1 week; 23) job B; 24) job C.

Scenarios

25) a. 2 hours; b. 6 hours; c. 11 hours.
26) a. 2 weeks; b. 6 weeks; c) 3.33 weeks.
27) a. 40 hours; b. E,D,C,B,A, 28 hours; c. E = 8 hours, D = 14 hours, C = 19 hours, B = 23 hours, A = 28 hours; d. No, 11 hours.
28) a. DL040, AA887, SW023, SA009; b. DL040 on day 5, AA887 on day 11, SW023 on day 14, SA009 on day 16; c. 16 days.
29) a. 7.5 hours; b. Y&W, 1.5 hours; c. Y,W&X, 1 hour; d. EDD has lower average tardiness but SPT has fewer late jobs and lower average flowtime.
30) a. SPT; b. SPT; c. EDD 5 hours, SPT 1 hour, CR 5 hours.

Chapter 15: Incident and Disruption Management

Minute Answer

1) strategic risk; 2) the one operating during a crisis, 3) average the ten values; 4) crisis; 5) normalization; 6) robustness; 7) decrease; 8) increase; 9) decrease, 10) bricolage; 11) yield management; 12) groupthink.

Quick Start

13) 1.5 million; 14) 60%; 15) 96.03%; 16) 3.97%, 17) 99.96%; 18) 1.00%.

Ramp Up

19) a loss of $10; 20) 4.5 patients.

Scenarios

21) a. all reservations showing up, one less than all showing up; b. $8325; c. $8350; d. yes.
22) a. 95.1%; b. 99.99%; c. 97.01%; d. 96.06%.

APPENDIX B: *z*-VALUES FROM INFINITY TO *z*

Areas under the Standardized Normal Curve, from Infinity to *z*

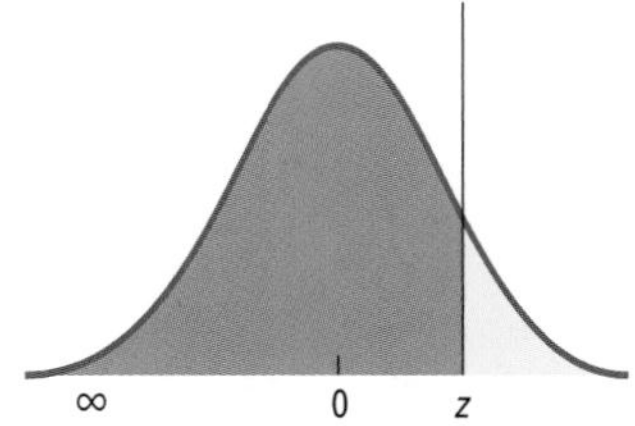

z	0.00	0.01	0.02	0.03	0.04	0.05	0.06	0.07	0.08	0.09
0.0	0.5	0.504	0.508	0.512	0.516	0.5199	0.5239	0.5279	0.5319	0.5359
0.1	0.5398	0.5438	0.5478	0.5517	0.5557	0.5596	0.5636	0.5675	0.5714	0.5753
0.2	0.5793	0.5832	0.5871	0.591	0.5948	0.5987	0.6026	0.6064	0.6103	0.6141
0.3	0.6179	0.6217	0.6255	0.6293	0.6331	0.6368	0.6406	0.6443	0.648	0.6517
0.4	0.6554	0.6591	0.6628	0.6664	0.67	0.6736	0.6772	0.6808	0.6844	0.6879
0.5	0.6915	0.695	0.6985	0.7019	0.7054	0.7088	0.7123	0.7157	0.719	0.7224
0.6	0.7257	0.7291	0.7324	0.7357	0.7389	0.7422	0.7454	0.7486	0.7517	0.7549
0.7	0.758	0.7611	0.7642	0.7673	0.7704	0.7734	0.7764	0.7794	0.7823	0.7852
0.8	0.7881	0.791	0.7939	0.7967	0.7995	0.8023	0.8051	0.8078	0.8106	0.8133
0.9	0.8159	0.8186	0.8212	0.8238	0.8264	0.8289	0.8315	0.834	0.8365	0.8389
1.0	0.8413	0.8438	0.8461	0.8485	0.8508	0.8531	0.8554	0.8577	0.8599	0.8621
1.1	0.8643	0.8665	0.8686	0.8708	0.8729	0.8749	0.877	0.879	0.881	0.883
1.2	0.8849	0.8869	0.8888	0.8907	0.8925	0.8944	0.8962	0.898	0.8997	0.9015
1.3	0.9032	0.9049	0.9066	0.9082	0.9099	0.9115	0.9131	0.9147	0.9162	0.9177
1.4	0.9192	0.9207	0.9222	0.9236	0.9251	0.9265	0.9279	0.9292	0.9306	0.9319
1.5	0.9332	0.9345	0.9357	0.937	0.9382	0.9394	0.9406	0.9418	0.9429	0.9441
1.6	0.9452	0.9463	0.9474	0.9484	0.9495	0.9505	0.9515	0.9525	0.9535	0.9545
1.7	0.9554	0.9564	0.9573	0.9582	0.9591	0.9599	0.9608	0.9616	0.9625	0.9633
1.8	0.9641	0.9649	0.9656	0.9664	0.9671	0.9678	0.9686	0.9693	0.9699	0.9706
1.9	0.9713	0.9719	0.9726	0.9732	0.9738	0.9744	0.975	0.9756	0.9761	0.9767
2.0	0.9772	0.9778	0.9783	0.9788	0.9793	0.9798	0.9803	0.9808	0.9812	0.9817
2.1	0.9821	0.9826	0.983	0.9834	0.9838	0.9842	0.9846	0.985	0.9854	0.9857
2.2	0.9861	0.9864	0.9868	0.9871	0.9875	0.9878	0.9881	0.9884	0.9887	0.989
2.3	0.9893	0.9896	0.9898	0.9901	0.9904	0.9906	0.9909	0.9911	0.9913	0.9916
2.4	0.9918	0.992	0.9922	0.9925	0.9927	0.9929	0.9931	0.9932	0.9934	0.9936
2.5	0.9938	0.994	0.9941	0.9943	0.9945	0.9946	0.9948	0.9949	0.9951	0.9952
2.6	0.9953	0.9955	0.9956	0.9957	0.9959	0.996	0.9961	0.9962	0.9963	0.9964
2.7	0.9965	0.9966	0.9967	0.9968	0.9969	0.997	0.9971	0.9972	0.9973	0.9974
2.8	0.9974	0.9975	0.9976	0.9977	0.9977	0.9978	0.9979	0.9979	0.998	0.9981
2.9	0.9981	0.9982	0.9982	0.9983	0.9984	0.9984	0.9985	0.9985	0.9986	0.9986
3.0	0.9987	0.9987	0.9987	0.9988	0.9988	0.9989	0.9989	0.9989	0.999	0.999

APPENDIX C: z-VALUES FROM ZERO TO z

Areas under the Standardized Normal Curve, from Zero to z

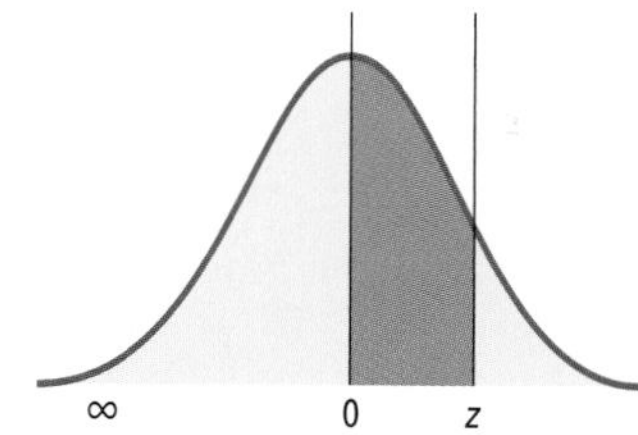

z	0.00	0.01	0.02	0.03	0.04	0.05	0.06	0.07	0.08	0.09
0.0	0	0.004	0.008	0.012	0.016	0.0199	0.0239	0.0279	0.0319	0.0359
0.1	0.0398	0.0438	0.0478	0.0517	0.0557	0.0596	0.0636	0.0675	0.0714	0.0753
0.2	0.0793	0.0832	0.0871	0.091	0.0948	0.0987	0.1026	0.1064	0.1103	0.1141
0.3	0.1179	0.1217	0.1255	0.1293	0.1331	0.1368	0.1406	0.1443	0.148	0.1517
0.4	0.1554	0.1591	0.1628	0.1664	0.17	0.1736	0.1772	0.1808	0.1844	0.1879
0.5	0.1915	0.195	0.1985	0.2019	0.2054	0.2088	0.2123	0.2157	0.219	0.2224
0.6	0.2257	0.2291	0.2324	0.2357	0.2389	0.2422	0.2454	0.2486	0.2517	0.2549
0.7	0.258	0.2611	0.2642	0.2673	0.2704	0.2734	0.2764	0.2794	0.2823	0.2852
0.8	0.2881	0.291	0.2939	0.2967	0.2995	0.3023	0.3051	0.3078	0.3106	0.3133
0.9	0.3159	0.3186	0.3212	0.3238	0.3264	0.3289	0.3315	0.334	0.3365	0.3389
1.0	0.3413	0.3438	0.3461	0.3485	0.3508	0.3531	0.3554	0.3577	0.3599	0.3621
1.1	0.3643	0.3665	0.3686	0.3708	0.3729	0.3749	0.377	0.379	0.381	0.383
1.2	0.3849	0.3869	0.3888	0.3907	0.3925	0.3944	0.3962	0.398	0.3997	0.4015
1.3	0.4032	0.4049	0.4066	0.4082	0.4099	0.4115	0.4131	0.4147	0.4162	0.4177
1.4	0.4192	0.4207	0.4222	0.4236	0.4251	0.4265	0.4279	0.4292	0.4306	0.4319
1.5	0.4332	0.4345	0.4357	0.437	0.4382	0.4394	0.4406	0.4418	0.4429	0.4441
1.6	0.4452	0.4463	0.4474	0.4484	0.4495	0.4505	0.4515	0.4525	0.4535	0.4545
1.7	0.4554	0.4564	0.4573	0.4582	0.4591	0.4599	0.4608	0.4616	0.4625	0.4633
1.8	0.4641	0.4649	0.4656	0.4664	0.4671	0.4678	0.4686	0.4693	0.4699	0.4706
1.9	0.4713	0.4719	0.4726	0.4732	0.4738	0.4744	0.475	0.4756	0.4761	0.4767
2.0	0.4772	0.4778	0.4783	0.4788	0.4793	0.4798	0.4803	0.4808	0.4812	0.4817
2.1	0.4821	0.4826	0.483	0.4834	0.4838	0.4842	0.4846	0.485	0.4854	0.4857
2.2	0.4861	0.4864	0.4868	0.4871	0.4875	0.4878	0.4881	0.4884	0.4887	0.489
2.3	0.4893	0.4896	0.4898	0.4901	0.4904	0.4906	0.4909	0.4911	0.4913	0.4916
2.4	0.4918	0.492	0.4922	0.4925	0.4927	0.4929	0.4931	0.4932	0.4934	0.4936
2.5	0.4938	0.494	0.4941	0.4943	0.4945	0.4946	0.4948	0.4949	0.4951	0.4952
2.6	0.4953	0.4955	0.4956	0.4957	0.4959	0.496	0.4961	0.4962	0.4963	0.4964
2.7	0.4965	0.4966	0.4967	0.4968	0.4969	0.497	0.4971	0.4972	0.4973	0.4974
2.8	0.4974	0.4975	0.4976	0.4977	0.4977	0.4978	0.4979	0.4979	0.498	0.4981
2.9	0.4981	0.4982	0.4982	0.4983	0.4984	0.4984	0.4985	0.4985	0.4986	0.4986
3.0	0.4987	0.4987	0.4987	0.4988	0.4988	0.4989	0.4989	0.4989	0.499	0.499

INDEX